The Geography of Presidential Elections
in the United States, 1868–2004

The Geography
of Presidential Elections
in the United States,
1868–2004

ALBERT J. MENENDEZ

McFarland & Company, Inc., Publishers

Jefferson, North Carolina, and London

LIBRARY OF CONGRESS CATALOGUING-IN-PUBLICATION DATA

Menendez, Albert J.
The geography of presidential elections in the
United States, 1868–2004 / Albert J. Menendez
p.   cm.
Includes bibliographical references and index.

ISBN 0-7864-2217-3 (illustrated case binding : 50# alkaline paper)

1. Presidents — United States — Election — History.
2. Party affiliation — United States — States.
3. Voting — United States — States — History.
4. Political culture — United States — Regional Disparities.   I. Title.
JK524.M48   2005   324.973'09 — dc22   2005004744

British Library cataloguing data are available

Cover illustration ©2005 Creatas

Manufactured in the United States of America

*McFarland & Company, Inc., Publishers
Box 611, Jefferson, North Carolina 28640
www.mcfarlandpub.com*

For Shirley

Contents

PART I.
STATE AND NATIONAL RESULTS

PART II.
COUNTY RESULTS

vii

Preface

The Geography of Presidential Elections in the United States, 1868–2004 depicts the long-standing and significant factors of regionalism and sectionalism in the quadrennial voting for the U.S. chief executive. Even after the Civil War restored the nation's wholeness, the first postwar election showed the persistence of regional voting patterns. These patterns became even more pronounced in the succeeding elections of the nineteenth century and beyond.

Other related factors — the rise of urbanism and the cultural and economic disparity between the new metropolitan areas and rural America, followed by the rise of suburbanization in the mid–twentieth century — will become apparent as each election's geographical contours are explored. Ethnic ancestry and religious affiliation are also important factors that frequently influence voting and shape regional patterns. Building a winning coalition depends on the right strategies, and each election has had its own internal dynamic.

In this book narrative sketches of the geographical contours of each presidential race are included along with tables of the electoral votes for each election and tables showing the states where the major candidates were able to secure their greatest percentages of the vote.

Concentrating on the geography of presidential voting since the Civil War will give readers another angle by which to in-terpret historical trends. If demography is destiny, so is geography to some extent. Changing population trends, migration patterns and cultural differences help to influence the geography of U.S. politics.

This book explores the ever-changing political destiny of the United States. The election narratives and the county data both reveal, for example, how the South has moved away from being a solidly Democratic South from the 1880s until World War II to, after a period of transition, a solidly Republican South since the 1980s. The 11 states of the Old Confederacy faithfully supported every losing Democratic candidate from Winfield Hancock in 1880 to Adlai Stevenson in the 1950s, but was the only region to oppose Democrat Bill Clinton twice in the 1990s. And Clinton was a native of the region.

By contrast, New England changed from being the most loyal outpost of the Grand Old Party from 1856 to the 1960s into a Democratic stronghold today. Similar pro–Democratic trends can be found in parts of the Midwest and the Pacific Coast. States that were once the most likely to support Republicans from Lincoln until Eisenhower are now among the least likely to back Republicans. (One can argue that the party of Lincoln has itself changed dramatically.)

I remember, as a 10-year-old child during the excitement of the first Eisenhower-

Stevenson election of 1952, being given a board game of American politics for Christmas. I was enchanted by that game and played it until the board disintegrated. As I recall, all the southern states were solidly Democratic, while most of the Northeast was staunchly Republican, making the game's outcome dependent on the handful of swing states in the middle of the country.

Today, such a game would have to be dramatically redrawn because of the geographical changes in U.S. politics during the last half century.

Part II includes a state-by-state compilation of the winning party for each county in the 35 elections during this time period.

Sources and Interpretations

There is no central source for collecting and publishing presidential election returns on a national basis. Thus, there is often a slight difference in tabulations. I have examined many different sets of returns and have generally used Congressional Quarterly's *Presidential Elections Since 1789* as a reliable source. For county data, *The World Almanac and Book of Facts* has maintained a high degree of reliability from the 1860s and remained my basic source until *America at the Polls* appeared. That volume, which covers the elections of 1920 to 1964, and its subsequent volume, *America at the Polls 2* (the 1968–1984 elections), and *America Votes* for 1988, 1992, 1996, and 2000 are, in my judgment, the most reliable. Two exceptions are 1924 and 1980, because the aforementioned volumes combined the "other" party votes in these two elections, making it appear that Bob La Follette carried a few more counties than he did. The La Follette vote by county was most accurately depicted in the 1925 *World Almanac*. The Anderson vote in 1980 is most accurately delineated in the 1981 *World Almanac*.

I have classified each county by the party whose candidate secured the highest number of votes in that county. Some previous compilers chose to combine all other parties into one category and claimed that an anonymous entity called "other" received the highest number of votes. The trouble with that reasoning is that people do not vote for "other" parties. In 1912, for example, they voted for Wilson the Democrat, Taft the Republican, Roosevelt the Progressive or Debs the Socialist (and in a few states for a Prohibitionist); whoever secured the highest number of votes is the winner in that county. It makes no sense to me to combine the Roosevelt and Debs votes and award a county to "other parties" if neither Roosevelt nor Debs came in first in the popular vote.

Occasionally, there has been a question of interpretation. For example, the Populist Party in 1896 — the remnants of the 1892 national Populist campaign — ran separate electors pledged to William Jennings Bryan, the Democratic presidential candidate, in a few states. This slate actually finished first in a few California counties. But since the Populist vote was counted as a Bryan vote in most states, I have classified these counties as "D" for Democrat. (The Populist slate supported Bryan but endorsed a different candidate for vice president than the regular Democratic ticket.)

But Populist slates in 1900, 1904 and 1908 did not endorse the Democrats and carried a few counties in Georgia and Texas. Those counties are classified as "Po" because theirs was a genuine independent third-party effort. In 1916 a handful of counties in Georgia and Louisiana were carried by an Independent Progressive slate backing former president Theodore Roosevelt, who had run on the Progressive Party ticket in 1912. This effort received no support from Roosevelt, who had returned to the Republican ranks and endorsed its nominee, Charles Evans Hughes.

In 1880, 12 Virginia counties* voted for Hancock on the "Readjusters" ticket rather than the "Regular Democratic" ticket, but they have been classified as Democratic counties since their votes were included with the Hancock vote by the Virginia canvassing authorities.

Then we have the strange situation in which "no returns" were received by the state canvassing boards, particularly in Texas in the early part of the 20th century. For some reason, counties that clearly existed and that had reported returns in previous presidential elections did not report any presidential votes. This happened in Texas in 17 counties in 1900, 6 counties in 1904, 15 counties in 1908 and 1 county in 1912 and 1916.

Texas also has made it impossible to know for certain which party carried about 12 counties in 1920 because the state canvassing board combined votes for the American Party, the Black and Tan Republicans, and the Socialists. Therefore, these counties have been listed as giving more votes to "other" parties than to the Democrats or the Republicans. *America at the Polls*; *The Presidential Vote, 1896–1932*; and the *Texas Almanac* all agree about the reporting of the 1920 vote.

---

*Bland, Buchanan, Dickenson, Greene, Highland, Lee, Page, Russell, Scott, Smyth, Tazewell, Wise.

Codes for
Party Designations

Codes for Major Party Designations

D. . . . . Democratic Party

R. . . . . Republican Party

Codes for Other Party Designations

A . . . . . American Independent Party (George Wallace, 1968)

BR. . . . Bolting Republican (1884, Georgia)

G. . . . . Greenback Party

IP . . . . Independent Progressive (1916)

NR . . . No returns received

O . . . . Others (1920 Texas). The state canvassing board combined the votes for the "American party," the Socialists, and the "Black and Tan Republicans." In 11 counties they outpolled the two major parties.

P . . . . Progressive Party (Robert La Follette, 1924; Theodore Roosevelt, 1912)

PE. . . . Ross Perot (1992, 1996)

PO . . . Populist Party (1892, 1900, 1904, 1908)

S . . . . . Socialist Party (1912)

SR. . . . States' Rights Party (Strom Thurmond, 1948). There were also States' Rights parties (often called unpledged electors) that carried counties in South Carolina, Mississippi, Louisiana, Tennessee, and Virginia in 1956 and in Mississippi and Louisiana in 1960. All are designated SR.

T. . . . . Indicates that the presidential vote in the county was tied between two candidates, so no party carried it.

TR . . . Texas Regulars. An independent slate calling itself the Texas Regulars carried one county in Texas in 1944.

UL . . . Union Labor (1888)

- . . . . A dash (-) in the election year indicates that the county did not yet exist. For example, La Paz County, Arizona, cast its first presidential vote in 1984.

PART I

STATE AND NATIONAL RESULTS

1868

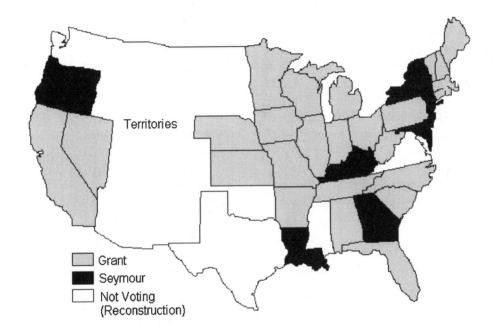

Territories

Grant
Seymour
Not Voting
(Reconstruction)

The first election after the Civil War resulted in a Republican victory led by the victorious Union Army general Ulysses S. Grant. Grant defeated New York governor Horatio Seymour, the Democratic nominee, by 52.7 percent to 47.3 percent. His electoral vote margin was much greater, 214 to 80, since he carried 26 states to Seymour's 8 states.

Most of the South had returned to the Union, but Mississippi, Texas and Virginia were still under Reconstruction and did not participate. In Florida the legislature cast the electoral vote. There was no popular vote counted in Florida.

The nation was strongly polarized, with Grant receiving almost 79 percent of the vote in Vermont, while Seymour received the support of almost 75 percent in Kentucky.

In the 7 southern states where popular votes were cast, Grant received 405,019 and Seymour, 430,856. Grant's popular vote percentage was 48.5 percent but his electoral vote advantage was 38–16 because he carried 5 of the states. (Including Florida, Grant won 41–16 in the South.) In the rest of the country Grant won 2,608,631 votes to Seymour's 2,277,888, or 53.4 percent. This was slightly lower than Lincoln's 55 percent in the same states in 1864. The one new state, Nebraska, voted for Grant, 64 percent to 36 percent.

In comparison with 1864, Seymour

carried the 3 states that had voted for Mc-Clellan: Delaware, Kentucky, and New Jersey. His strongest states were Kentucky, Louisiana and Maryland. Seymour also carried Maryland, Oregon, and his home state of New York, all of which had gone for Lincoln in 1864.

Grant held the Lincoln states, but his California vote dropped 8 percentage points, and he squeaked ahead in the Golden State with just 50.2 percent. He dropped 7 points in Delaware, 5 points in Kentucky, 10 points in Kansas, 13 points in Missouri, 9 points in West Virginia, and 23 points in Maryland (where Union troops occupied Baltimore and kept Democrats from voting in 1864). There was a clear Democratic trend in many states.

But Grant's vote exceeded Lincoln's by 1 point in Lincoln's home state of Illinois, by 3 points in Maine, 2 points in Michigan, 3 points in New Hampshire, 5 points in Rhode Island and 3 points in Vermont. Grant gained in the far reaches of the North, while losing support in the states that bordered the Confederacy.

Grant's top 10 states included 4 in New England, 4 in the Midwest, and Tennessee and West Virginia (both highly unusual for a Republican).

Seymour's top 10 included 3 in the border states (Maryland, Delaware, Kentucky), 2 in the North (New Jersey, New York), 3 in the South (Louisiana, Alabama, Georgia), and 2 in the far West (Oregon, California). The Seymour support was the most varied for a Democratic candidate and was undoubtedly affected by the Reconstruction in the South.

TOP 10 STATES, 1868

Grant	Percentage		Seymour	Percentage
1. Vermont	78.6		1. Kentucky	74.6
2. Massachusetts	69.8		2. Louisiana	70.7
3. Kansas	68.8		3. Maryland	67.2
4. Tennessee	68.4		4. Georgia	64.3
5. Rhode Island	66.7		5. Delaware	59.0
6. Nebraska	63.9		6. New Jersey	50.9
7. Maine	62.4		7. New York	50.6
8. Iowa	61.9		8. Oregon	50.4
9. Minnesota	60.8		9. California	49.8
10. West Virginia	58.8		10. Alabama	48.8

ELECTORAL VOTES, 1868

States[1]	Electoral Votes	Grant	Seymour	States[1]	Electoral Votes	Grant	Seymour
Alabama	8	8	–	Indiana	13	13	–
Arkansas	5	5	–	Iowa	8	8	–
California	5	5	–	Kansas	3	3	–
Connecticut	6	6	–	Kentucky	11	–	11
Delaware	3	–	3	Louisiana	7	–	7
Florida	3	3	–	Maine	7	7	–
Georgia	9	–	9	Maryland	7	–	7
Illinois	16	16	–	Massachusetts	12	12	–

States[1]	Electoral Votes	Grant	Seymour	States[1]	Electoral Votes	Grant	Seymour
Michigan	8	8	–	Oregon	3	–	3
Minnesota	4	4	–	Pennsylvania	26	26	–
Missouri	11	11	–	Rhode Island	4	4	–
Nebraska	3	3	–	South Carolina	6	6	–
Nevada	3	3	–	Tennessee	10	10	–
New Hampshire	5	5	–	Vermont	5	5	–
New Jersey	7	–	7	West Virginia	5	5	–
New York	33	–	33	Wisconsin	8	8	–
North Carolina	9	9	–				
Ohio	21	21	–	Totals	294	214	80

1. Mississippi, Texas, and Virginia were not yet readmitted to the Union and did not participate in the election.

—————— 1872 ——————

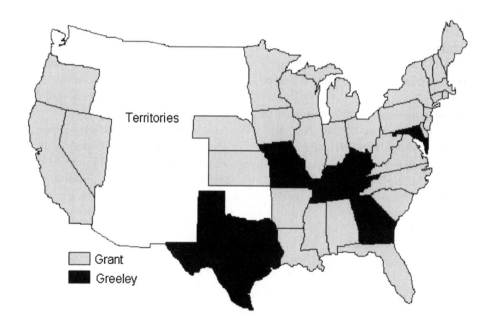

Territories

Grant
Greeley

President Grant sailed to reelection easily, winning about 56 percent of the vote and 286 electoral votes compared with New York newspaper editor Horace Greeley, the Democrat, who received about 44 percent of the vote. Greeley died before the electoral college met, and the non–Republican votes were scattered among several candidates. But Greeley carried Georgia, Kentucky, Maryland, Missouri, Tennessee and Texas, which altogether cast 66 electoral votes. Texas, Mississippi and Virginia had been readmitted to the Union, and Grant carried Mississippi and Virginia. Congress refused to accept the electoral votes of Arkansas and Louisiana because of "disruptive conditions during Reconstruction" (according to *Congressional Quarterly*), even though Grant supposedly won their 14 electoral votes. Grant carried 31 states and Greeley, 6. If all electoral votes had been counted, Grant would have received 300 and Greeley. 66.

A group of disgruntled Republicans, embarrassed by what they perceived to be corruption in the Grant administration, had endorsed Greeley on the Liberal Republican slate. However, Greeley was reviled as too liberal and too intellectual (by traditional Republicans), the same charges that would be leveled against George McGovern exactly 100 years later. But Greeley's 44 percent was certainly a respectable vote against an entrenched party and a war hero president (Greeley ran stronger in the popular vote than Al Smith, Adlai Stevenson [in 1956], George McGovern and Walter Mondale, who were also castigated as too liberal for the U.S. mainstream and who faced popular Republican incumbents or heirs apparent).

In comparison to 1868, Grant carried Delaware, Louisiana, New Jersey, New York and Oregon, which had all voted against him. But Missouri and Tennessee switched from Grant in 1868 to Greeley in 1872. Grant's percentage of the popular vote increased 10 points in Pennsylvania, 17 points in Maryland and 18 points in South Carolina. He dropped 7 points in West Virginia, barely holding the state.

The national vote increased 13 percent, and Grant's share of the popular vote increased 3 points: this was not a great landslide but a comfortable margin of victory. Grant's top 10 states included 4 in New England, Pennsylvania, Michigan, Nebraska and Kansas, as well as South Carolina and Mississippi.

Greeley did best in parts of the South (Texas, Georgia, Tennessee, Virginia, Arkansas), the border states (Missouri, Kentucky, Maryland, West Virginia), and Connecticut.

The vote soared in the South, where all 11 states had been restored to full participation. The total southern vote was up from 840,000 to nearly 1,420,000. Grant received 53.6 percent to Greeley's 46.4 percent — the region was only 2 percent less Republican than the nation. Grant gained 5 percentage points over his 1868 vote share in the South.

The border was the only region to go Democratic. Greeley outpolled Grant in the 5 border states by 358,853 to 318,171, or 53 percent to 47 percent. But even in the border states, Grant gained 6 percentage points.

Top 10 States, 1872

Grant	Percentage	Greeley	Percentage
1. Vermont	79.2	1. Texas	58.5
2. South Carolina	75.7	2. Missouri	55.5
3. Rhode Island	71.9	3. Georgia	55.0
4. Nebraska	70.7	4. Kentucky	52.3
5. Massachusetts	69.3	5. Tennessee	52.2
6. Maine	67.9	6. Maryland	50.3
7. Kansas	66.5	7. Virginia	49.5
8. Mississippi	63.5	8. Arkansas	47.8
9. Michigan	62.6	9. Connecticut	47.6
10. Pennsylvania	62.3	10. West Virginia	47.3

Electoral Votes, 1872

States	Electoral Votes	Grant	Hendricks[1]	Brown[1]	Jenkins[1]	Davis[1]
Alabama	10	10	-	-	-	-
Arkansas[2]	6	-	-	-	-	-
California	6	6	-	-	-	-
Connecticut	6	6	-	-	-	-
Delaware	3	3	-	-	-	-
Florida	4	4	-	-	-	-
Georgia[3]	11	-	-	6	2	-
Illinois	21	21	-	-	-	-
Indiana	15	15	-	-	-	-
Iowa	11	11	-	-	-	-
Kansas	5	5	-	-	-	-
Kentucky	12	-	8	4	-	-
Louisiana[2]	8	-	-	-	-	-
Maine	7	7	-	-	-	-
Maryland	8	-	8	-	-	-
Massachusetts	13	13	-	-	-	-
Michigan	11	11	-	-	-	-
Minnesota	5	5	-	-	-	-
Mississippi	8	8	-	-	-	-
Missouri	15	-	6	8	-	1
Nebraska	3	3	-	-	-	-
Nevada	3	3	-	-	-	-
New Hampshire	5	5	-	-	-	-
New Jersey	9	9	-	-	-	-
New York	35	35	-	-	-	-
North Carolina	10	10	-	-	-	-
Ohio	22	22	-	-	-	-
Oregon	3	3	-	-	-	-
Pennsylvania	29	29	-	-	-	-
Rhode Island	4	4	-	-	-	-
South Carolina	7	7	-	-	-	-
Tennessee	12	-	12	-	-	-
Texas	8	-	8	-	-	-
Vermont	5	5	-	-	-	-
Virginia	11	11	-	-	-	-
West Virginia	5	5	-	-	-	-
Wisconsin	10	10	-	-	-	-
Totals	366	286	42	18	2	1

1. For explanation of Democratic electoral votes, cast after Greeley's death, see pp. 11–12.
2. Congress refused to accept the electoral votes of Arkansas and Louisiana because of disruptive conditions during Reconstruction.
3. Three Georgia electoral votes cast for Greeley were not counted.

1876

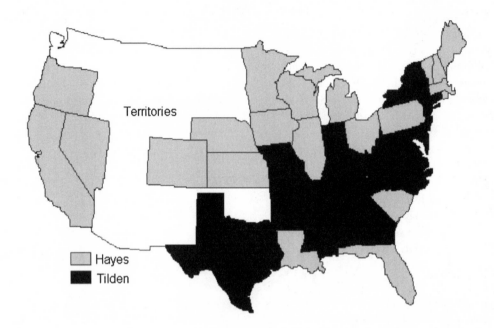

Territories

Hayes
Tilden

The 1876 election is one of the most written about because it was bitterly disputed at the time and because most historians do not believe that the outcome reflected the best of America's democratic traditions.

The election was close in the electoral college, even after most state returns were received. It was not close in the popular vote, with Democratic New York governor Samuel Tilden holding a 3-point lead over Republican Rutherford B. Hayes of Ohio. Tilden had won a clear majority of the popular vote and had carried the swing states of Indiana, New York, Connecticut and New Jersey in addition to the border states and most of the South. Hayes carried most of the North and Midwest.

But separate sets of election returns had been received from South Carolina, Louisiana, Florida, and in Oregon — where an unusual technicality threatened to disqualify one Republican elector.

Congress had adopted new rules (the

22nd Joint Rule) in 1865 that required that any objection to the electoral votes submitted by a state could only be counted by both the Senate and the House. Under this rule Congress had rejected the 1872 electoral vote from Louisiana and Arkansas and threw out 3 of the 11 electoral votes from Georgia. But the rule lapsed in 1876 because of bitter party divisions — the House was Democratic; the Senate, Republican. Congress now had no rules to govern a disputed election.

Of course, no one expected a disputed election. But when one occurred, Congress passed the Electoral Commission Law, establishing a 15-member commission that was to have final authority over disputed electoral votes, unless both houses of Congress agreed to overrule it. The commission was composed of 5 Senators, 5 House members and 5 Supreme Court justices.

In every instance the commission voted on party lines, 8 to 7 for the Republican electors in Louisiana, Florida and South

Carolina. In each case the Democratic House rejected the commission's vote, but the Republican Senate upheld it, and the decision stood.

Angry House Democrats threatened a filibuster, but the threat never materialized because Hayes and his supporters reached an agreement with Southerners, in which they promised to withdraw federal troops from the South and end Reconstruction.

A constitutional crisis was averted, and at 4:00 A.M. on March 2, 1877, the president of the Senate announced that Rutherford B. Hayes of the state of Ohio had been elected president with 185 electoral votes to his opponent's 184. Hayes arrived in the nation's capital late that same day and took the oath of office privately at the White House the next day on March 3, because March 4, Inauguration Day, fell on a Sunday. His formal inauguration took place on Monday, March 5, and a possible second Civil War was narrowly prevented.

Hayes carried 21 states and Tilden, 17. The strongest Hayes victories came in Vermont, Nebraska and Kansas. He carried 5 of the 6 New England states and most of the Midwest and Pennsylvania, though his Keystone State margin was only 2 percentage points. He carried his home state of Ohio by only 1 percentage point. He narrowly won California and Wisconsin. Hayes's top 10 states were 6 in the Midwest and West and 4 in New England.

Tilden outpolled Hayes by 51 percent to 48 percent. Tilden has remained the only presidential candidate to have won a majority of the popular vote while losing the presidency in the electoral college. More than a dozen presidents have received a minority of the total popular vote but an electoral vote majority. (Eighteen U.S. presidential elections have been decided this way, including those in 1992, 1996 and 2000.)

Tilden's greatest vote support came in Georgia and Texas, followed by Mississippi, Kentucky and Alabama. His margin was enormous in the border states. Tilden's vote exceeded 55 percent in the band of states from Delaware to Missouri. His top 10 states were all in the South (7) or the border region (3).

Indiana went Democratic for the first time since 1856, and Connecticut voted Democratic for the first time since 1852. Hayes was the first nominee of the Grand Old Party to lose Connecticut.

The new state of Colorado cast its 3 electoral votes for Hayes. Peter Cooper, of the Greenback Party, received 1 percent of the vote total (6 percent of the vote in Kansas).

The total national vote surged 30.1 percent, from 6.467 million to 8.413 million, one of the largest increases in U.S. presidential election history.

The pro–Tilden trend is exemplified in the county results. Tilden carried 57.8 percent of the counties and was the first Democrat since Buchanan in 1856 to carry more counties than his Republican opponent. Four years before, Greeley had only carried 38.3 percent of the counties.

Tilden swept the South 59.6 percent to 40.4 percent, winning a 353,000 vote majority. The southern vote increased 29.2 percent. Tilden's vote share was up 13 percentage points in the South — compared to 7 points nationally.

In the border states Tilden won 523,852 to 367,324, amassing 58.8 percent of the popular vote, a smaller gain of 6 points over Greeley's 1872 vote. The turnout was up 31.6 percent in the border states.

Hayes carried the North and West 2,926,963 to 2,671,211, or by 52.3 percent to 47.7 percent.

The North/South split was 11.7 percentage points, a difference that would increase in each succeeding election.

TOP 10 STATES, 1876

Hayes	Percentage	Tilden	Percentage
1. Vermont	68.4	1. Georgia	72.0
2. Nebraska	64.8	2. Texas	70.2
3. Kansas	63.1	3. Mississippi	68.1
4. Rhode Island	59.6	4. Kentucky	61.4
5. Minnesota	58.8	5. Alabama	60.0
6. Iowa	58.4	6. Arkansas	59.9
7. Massachusetts	57.8	7. Tennessee	59.8
8. Maine	56.6	8. Virginia	59.6
9. Nevada	52.7	9. Missouri	57.6
10. Michigan	52.4	10. West Virginia	56.8

ELECTORAL VOTES, 1876

States	Electoral Votes	Hayes	Tilden	States	Electoral Votes	Hayes	Tilden
Alabama	10	–	10	Missouri	15	–	15
Arkansas	6	–	6	Nebraska	3	3	–
California	6	6	–	Nevada	3	3	–
Colorado	3	3	–	New Hampshire	5	5	–
Connecticut	6	–	6	New Jersey	9	–	9
Delaware	3	–	3	New York	35	–	35
Florida[1]	4	4	–	North Carolina	10	–	10
Georgia	11	–	11	Ohio	22	22	–
Illinois	21	21	–	Oregon[1]	3	3	–
Indiana	15	–	15	Pennsylvania	29	29	–
Iowa	11	11	–	Rhode Island	4	4	–
Kansas	5	5	–	South Carolina[1]	7	7	–
Kentucky	12	–	12	Tennessee	12	–	12
Louisiana[1]	8	8	–	Texas	8	–	8
Maine	7	7	–	Vermont	5	5	–
Maryland	8	–	8	Virginia	11	–	11
Massachusetts	13	13	–	West Virginia	5	–	5
Michigan	11	11	–	Wisconsin	10	10	–
Minnesota	5	5	–				
Mississippi	8	–	8	Totals	369	185	184

1. For an explanation of disputed electoral votes of Florida, Louisiana, Oregon, and South Carolina, see pp. 14–15.

1880

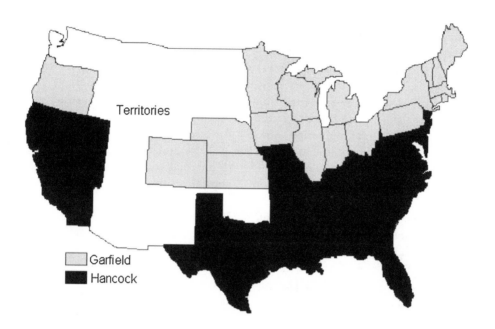

Territories

Garfield
Hancock

The Garfield-Hancock election was one of the closest in history. According to Congressional Quarterly's *Presidential Elections Since 1789*, Republican James Garfield received 4,446,158 votes to Democrat Winfield Hancock's 4,444,260, a difference of only 1,898 votes. The electoral vote margin was wide, though, with Garfield netting 214 votes and Hancock, 155. Both candidates carried 19 states, but Garfield won the 4 big ones: Illinois, New York, Ohio (his home state) and Pennsylvania (Hancock's home state), with a total of 107 electoral votes, exactly half his total. The rest of the country voted 155–107 for Hancock, but Republican dominance in the large population states carried the day.

The post–Civil War pattern prevailed. Garfield carried every New England state and all of the Northeast except New Jersey. He won the Midwest and the Plains states, and his mandate extended to Oregon.

Hancock added a new element to American politics: the solid South. For the first time since the Civil War, the Democrats won every one of the states of the Old Confederacy — a pattern that would prevail until 1920. The border states also supported Hancock, as did California, Nevada and New Jersey. Hancock's 95 southern electoral votes constituted a majority of his total, but it did not quite match Garfield's support in the "big four" states.

Of Hancock's top 10 states, 8 were in the South, with Texas leading the pack. Kentucky and Maryland from the border region were in ninth and tenth places respectively. One interesting historical tidbit is that Hancock lost his home county, Montgomery County, Pennsylvania, by 1 vote.

Garfield's strongest state was Vermont, where he took 70 percent of the vote. Nebraska was second, a bit of a geographical leap. Minnesota, Iowa, Wisconsin and Kansas were also strongly supportive of the Republican ticket, reflecting the popularity of Republican economic policies in the Northwest and the farm states. Rhode Island,

Michigan and New Hampshire were also in Garfield's top 10.

In some respects it was amazing that the Republicans won this election, since the bitterness of the 1876 election had not receded. But Hayes was not a particularly unpopular president, and he had never expressed any desire to seek a second term. So the Republicans nominated Garfield, an Ohio congressman and a lay preacher in the Disciples of Christ denomination, and hoped that voters would not link his candidacy to the controversy surrounding the 1876 race. It worked, but barely. The Republican vote remained about the same, while the Democratic vote fell off 3 percent.

The Republicans carried New York, Connecticut, and Indiana, which had gone Democratic in 1876, giving the GOP an additional 56 electoral votes. But the Democrats also bounced back, carrying 5 states that had gone for Hayes, including the disputed southern states of Florida, Louisiana, and South Carolina, and California and Nevada. These switches resulted in 27 new electoral votes for the Democrats and a net gain of 2 states. But their failure to win the big states resulted in their sixth straight presidential defeat.

The 1880 vote turnout increased 9.5 percent over 1876. A minor-party candidate, James B. Weaver, the standard bearer of the Greenback Party, received 3 percent of the total vote. His support reached 11.7 percent in Texas, 10 percent in Iowa, and nearly 10 percent in Kansas and Michigan. It was 9 percent in Missouri and 8 percent in West Virginia. The Greenback vote was an agrarian populist vote that reflected discontent among rural voters toward the economic policies of the major parties. It carried 19 counties.

Top 10 States, 1880

Garfield	Percentage	Hancock	Percentage
1. Vermont	70.0	1. Texas	66.8
2. Nebraska	62.9	2. South Carolina	65.5
3. Minnesota	62.3	3. Georgia	65.4
4. Rhode Island	62.2	4. Mississippi	64.7
5. Kansas	60.4	5. Louisiana	62.3
6. Massachusetts	58.5	6. Virginia	60.5
7. Iowa	56.9	7. Alabama	60.0
8. Wisconsin	54.0	8. Arkansas	56.1
9. Michigan	52.5	9. Kentucky	55.7
10. New Hampshire	51.9	10. Maryland	54.4

Electoral Votes, 1880

States	Electoral Votes	Garfield	Hancock	States	Electoral Votes	Garfield	Hancock
Alabama	10	–	10	Georgia	11	–	11
Arkansas	6	–	6	Illinois	21	21	–
California[1]	6	1	5	Indiana	15	15	–
Colorado	3	3	–	Iowa	11	11	–
Connecticut	6	6	–	Kansas	5	5	–
Delaware	3	–	3	Kentucky	12	–	12
Florida	4	–	4	Louisiana	8	–	8

States	Electoral Votes	Garfield	Hancock	States	Electoral Votes	Garfield	Hancock
Maine	7	7	–	Ohio	22	22	–
Maryland	8	–	8	Oregon	3	3	–
Massachusetts	13	13	–	Pennsylvania	29	29	–
Michigan	11	11	–	Rhode Island	4	4	–
Minnesota	5	5	–	South Carolina	7	–	7
Mississippi	8	–	8	Tennessee	12	–	12
Missouri	15	–	15	Texas	8	–	8
Nebraska	3	3	–	Vermont	5	5	–
Nevada	3	–	3	Virginia	11	–	11
New Hampshire	5	5	–	West Virginia	5	–	5
New Jersey	9	–	9	Wisconsin	10	10	–
New York	35	35	–				
North Carolina	10	–	10	Totals	369	214	155

1. California divided its electoral votes by congressional district.

1884

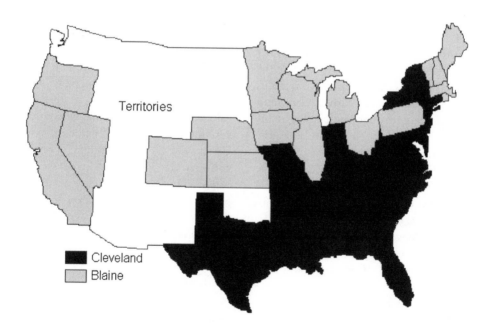

Territories

Cleveland
Blaine

The folklore surrounding this election has made it an election in which religion, sectionalism and other emotional social issues played a role. This stems from a late-in-the-campaign event in which an obscure Presbyterian minister, Reverend Samuel Burchard, addressed a pro–Republican gathering in New York City and called the Democrats the party "whose antecedents have been rum, Romanism and rebellion." The anti–Catholic slur became the focus of last-minute Democratic campaigning and may have lost the Republican candidate, Maine senator James G. Blaine, the election. Blaine was present at the gathering and was apparently too tired or embarrassed to respond to the remarks. But he did denounce them a few days later in New Haven, Connecticut, and later referred to Burchard as an "ass" in letters to colleagues.

Without a sophisticated election analysis, we will never know whether this remark cost the GOP the election. Religious membership data, precinct analysis and exit polling were then nonexistent or extremely primitive. But there were sharp Catholic/ Protestant differences in voting preferences in the North since the 1850s, and both parties tended to exploit them. The evidence suggests, ironically, that Blaine was *personally* less prejudiced in religious matters than other victorious Republicans of that era, including Grant, Garfield, Hayes and Harrison, but his name is synonymous with bigotry.

Suffice it to say that Blaine was the first Republican to lose the presidency since the first Republican candidate, John Fremont, ran in 1856. Democrat Grover Cleveland broke a 24-year drought and brought his party to power for the first time since the Civil War.

The election was extremely close in the popular vote. Cleveland received 4,874,621 (48.5%) votes to Blaine's 4,848,936 (48.3%), almost a repeat of the 1880 results.

Cleveland won the electoral college 219 to 182. He carried 20 states to Blaine's 18. Cleveland carried all 16 southern and border states, plus Indiana, New Jersey, Connecticut, and his home state of New York, where his victory margin was only 1,047 votes and may have resulted from the Burchard incident.

Cleveland gained the 36 New York votes, without which he would have lost. He also picked up Indiana and Connecticut, which had gone Republican 4 years before. California and Nevada, however, switched to Blaine. The Nevada result is perplexing, because the total presidential vote declined 30.3%. (Where did they all go?) The total national vote increased about 800,000, or 9.1%.

Cleveland's top 10 states included 7 in the South, especially South Carolina, where he won three-fourths of the vote, and the 3 border states of Delaware, Kentucky and Missouri. Blaine's included 6 in the Midwest and West (Minnesota, Kansas, Nebraska, Nevada, Colorado and Iowa) and 4 in the Northeast, including his home state of Maine, his birth state of Pennsylvania, and Vermont and Rhode Island.

In comparison with the 1880 election, Cleveland made strong gains in Iowa (14%), Nebraska (8%) and Delaware (5%). He also picked up 10 percentage points in South Carolina, though the Palmetto State's total vote declined 45.3%—the result, no doubt, of racial machinations.

Blaine gained 9 points in Nevada, where, as noted, the total vote declined sharply from the previous election. He also gained 9 points in Virginia, where the total vote increased 34.6%. (Blaine came within 2 points of carrying Virginia.) Presidential voting in the South in those days was characterized by large increases or decreases, depending on changing election laws. Blaine added 5 points to GOP strength in Louisiana (a heavily Catholic state) and 4 points in Maine.

The religious issue may not have had much of an impact on the vote, except in New York and Connecticut. Blaine still carried heavily Catholic Rhode Island and Massachusetts, though his margin declined from 25 points to 20 points in Rhode Island and from 19 points to 8 points in Massachusetts.

Top 10 States, 1884

Cleveland	Percentage		Blaine	Percentage
1. South Carolina	75.3		1. Vermont	66.5
2. Texas	69.5		2. Minnesota	58.8
3. Georgia	65.9		3. Kansas	58.1
4. Mississippi	64.3		4. Rhode Island	58.1
5. Alabama	60.4		5. Nebraska	57.3
6. Arkansas	57.8		6. Nevada	56.2
7. Louisiana	57.2		7. Maine	55.3
8. Delaware	56.6		8. Colorado	54.3
9. Kentucky	55.3		9. Pennsylvania	52.6
10. Missouri	53.5		10. Iowa	52.3

Electoral Votes, 1884

States	Electoral Votes	Cleveland	Blaine	States	Electoral Votes	Cleveland	Blaine-
Alabama	10	10	-	Missouri	16	16	-
Arkansas	7	7	-	Nebraska	5	-	5
California	8	-	8	Nevada	3	-	3
Colorado	3	-	3	New Hampshire	4	-	4
Connecticut	6	6	-	New Jersey	9	9	-
Delaware	3	3	-	New York	36	36	-
Florida	4	4	-	North Carolina	11	11	-
Georgia	12	12	-	Ohio	23	-	23
Illinois	22	-	22	Oregon	3	-	3
Indiana	15	15	-	Pennsylvania	30	-	30
Iowa	13	-	13	Rhode Island	4	-	4
Kansas	9	-	9	South Carolina	9	9	-
Kentucky	13	13	-	Tennessee	12	12	-
Louisiana	8	8	-	Texas	13	13	-
Maine	6	-	6	Vermont	4	-	4
Maryland	8	8	-	Virginia	12	12	-
Massachusetts	14	-	14	West Virginia	6	6	-
Michigan	13	-	13	Wisconsin	11	-	11
Minnesota	7	-	7				
Mississippi	9	9	-	Totals	401	219	182

1888

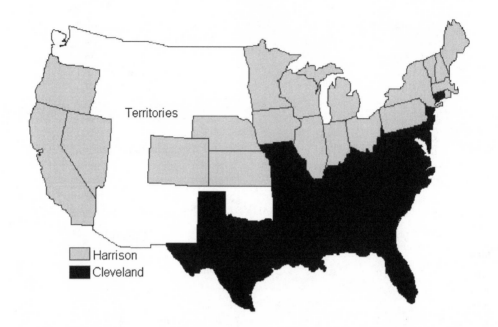

Territories

Harrison
Cleveland

The 1888 election is notable, if at all, because it was the last election before 2000 in which a candidate became president with an electoral vote majority, while losing the popular vote to his opponent.

Benjamin Harrison of Indiana, the Republican nominee, beat Democratic president Grover Cleveland by sweeping the North and West and by winning 233 electoral votes to Cleveland's 168 votes, mostly from the South and border states. Harrison carried 20 states to Cleveland's 18.

Harrison won every northern state except Connecticut and New Jersey. Cleveland carried all 16 southern and border states. It was a classic North vs. South division.

In comparison with 1884, Harrison carried Cleveland's home state of New York, then the largest state with a whopping 36 electoral votes. Indeed, Harrison carried the 4 largest states (Illinois, New York, Ohio and Pennsylvania) with their combined 111 electoral votes, almost half of his electoral college support. The only other state to

switch sides was Indiana. Harrison won both his home state and his opponent's home state, which was an unusual occurrence in a close election.

The national popular vote, however, moved slightly in a Democratic direction: Cleveland had edged Blaine by a 0.2 percentage point four years before but outpolled Harrison by a 0.8 percentage point, winning 5,534,488 votes to Harrison's 5,443,892, a margin of 90,596 votes.

But the minuscule shifts in Indiana (0.9 points) and in New York (0.6 points) made Harrison president. The total vote turnout increased 13%, or by 1.3 million votes.

Cleveland's top 10 states were in the South or in the border states (Delaware and Kentucky made the Democratic top 10). South Carolina, Mississippi and Louisiana were the big 3 Democratic states.

Harrison's top 10 states were in the Midwest–West–Old Northwest states of Nevada, Colorado, Kansas, Minnesota, Oregon and Nebraska, in addition to 4 New

England states, always including Vermont at the top of the list. Maine, Rhode Island and Massachusetts complete the list. Surprisingly, Pennsylvania missed the top 10 this time, coming in eleventh. Harrison won a majority of the total vote in 13 states; Cleveland in 12.

Many states were close in 1888. Cleveland carried Connecticut and West Virginia by just a few hundred votes. Four states were decided by less than 1 percentage point, including Harrison's win in Indiana, and Cleveland's squeaker in Virginia.

There were no major shifts in popular vote from 1884. Cleveland gained 9 points in Mississippi, 7 points in South Carolina and nearly 7 points in Alabama and Florida, none of which affected the outcome. He also gained almost 8 points in Michigan and 5 points in Rhode Island, but those states remained Republican. Harrison gained 5 points in Massachusetts and Vermont, merely adding to the Republican margins in Republican states. He gained about 3 points in Oregon, also padding the GOP margin. There was little crossover voting. Both parties rallied their base vote.

Minor parties took about 3% of the vote, the same as in 1884. The Prohibitionists received 2%, and topped 4% in Michigan, Minnesota, Nebraska and Wisconsin. A left-of-center splinter party called the Union Labor, took 11% in Kansas, 8% in Texas and 7% in Arkansas. They were on the ballot in 20 states. The Prohibition Party had become a national party, receiving votes in every state except South Carolina.

There were a couple of delightful oddities in this election. One is that Benjamin Harrison lost his home county of Marion, Indiana, and was the first Republican to lose there since John C. Fremont ran in 1856! This was not a rousing endorsement from the hometown folks in Indianapolis. But Harrison carried Cleveland's home county of Erie, New York (Buffalo). Nineteenth-century voters were apparently not sentimental about supporting the local lads. It should be noted that Erie County was then a Republican stronghold since supporting Lincoln in 1860 (but it voted for McClellan in 1864 as part of a quiet "peace protest" in the North that cost Lincoln 92 counties in 14 states that turned against him in the Civil War election).

Top 10 States, 1888

Harrison	Percentage		Cleveland	Percentage
1. Vermont	71.2		1. South Carolina	82.3
2. Maine	57.5		2. Mississippi	73.8
3. Nevada	57.5		3. Louisiana	73.4
4. Colorado	55.2		4. Georgia	70.3
5. Kansas	55.2		5. Alabama	67.0
6. Minnesota	54.2		6. Texas	65.5
7. Rhode Island	53.9		7. Florida	59.5
8. Oregon	53.8		8. Delaware	55.2
9. Nebraska	53.5		9. Arkansas	54.8
10. Massachusetts	53.4		10. Kentucky	53.3

Electoral Votes, 1888

States	Electoral Votes	Harrison	Cleveland	States	Electoral Votes	Harrison	Cleveland
Alabama	10	10	-	Missouri	16	-	16
Arkansas	7	-	7	Nebraska	5	5	-
California	8	8	-	Nevada	3	3	-
Colorado	3	3	-	New Hampshire	4	4	-
Connecticut	6	-	6	New Jersey	9	-	9
Delaware	3	-	3	New York	36	36	-
Florida	4	-	4	North Carolina	11	-	11
Georgia	12	-	12	Ohio	23	23	-
Illinois	22	22	-	Oregon	3	3	-
Indiana	15	15	-	Pennsylvania	30	30	-
Iowa	13	13	-	Rhode Island	4	4	-
Kansas	9	9	-	South Carolina	9	-	9
Kentucky	13	-	13	Tennessee	12	-	12
Louisiana	8	-	8	Texas	13	-	13
Maine	6	6	-	Vermont	4	4	-
Maryland	8	-	8	Virginia	12	-	12
Massachusetts	14	14	-	West Virginia	6	-	6
Michigan	13	13	-	Wisconsin	11	11	-
Minnesota	7	7	-				
Mississippi	9	-	9	Totals	401	233	168

1892

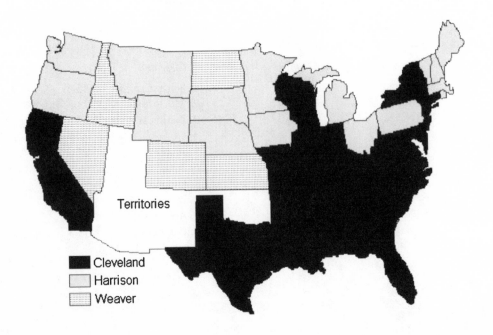

Territories

- ■ Cleveland
- ☐ Harrison
- ▨ Weaver

The 1892 election revealed some fissures beneath the once-solid surface of post–Civil War politics. For one thing, the strongest third party since 1860 mounted a challenge to the two major parties. The Populist, or People's Party, emerged as an economic protest party, primarily concentrated in the rural West but managing to get on the ballot in every state but Delaware and Louisiana. It was truly a national effort.

The Democrats ran former president Grover Cleveland for the third straight time, and the Republicans renominated President Benjamin Harrison. In some ways the election resembled the rematch of 1828, when John Quincy Adams and Andrew Jackson faced off again. And there was a "grudge" factor in both elections, since the Democrats outpolled their opponents in the popular vote in both 1824 and 1888, only to see an electoral vote majority for the GOP in 1888 and a House of Representatives decision in 1824, denying Jackson the presidency. (In 1840 there had been a rematch between Martin Van Buren and William Henry Harrison.) The Democrats — who also lost the disputed 1876 election — were determined to regain the presidency. They were successful.

Cleveland carried 23 states and won 277 electoral votes. He recaptured California by a margin of 124 votes, and returned New York, Illinois, Indiana (Harrison's home state), and Wisconsin to the Democratic column. The Wisconsin result was a major triumph since it was the first Democratic victory in the Badger State since 1852. He won the entire South and the border states (16 states in all) and won again in New Jersey and Connecticut.

Harrison won 16 states with 145 electoral votes. He carried all of New England except Connecticut, always loyal Pennsylvania, the Republican Great Lakes (Ohio, Michigan) and the Republican West (Minnesota, Iowa, Oregon and Nebraska).

His previous 233 electoral vote total

from four years before plummeted because of his loss of the 5 aforementioned states to Cleveland and 3 western states to General James Weaver, the Populist candidate (Colorado, Kansas and Nevada). Cleveland held all of the states he carried in 1888.

Harrison was successful in the new states that joined the Union, winning 4 out of 6 of them: South Dakota, Washington, Montana and Wyoming. Weaver won the other 2 new states of Idaho and North Dakota (by only 181 votes). An electoral peculiarity in North Dakota, however, resulted in 1 electoral vote for all 3 candidates. In the new states Harrison won 15 electoral votes, Weaver 4, and Cleveland 1.

While it was a truly national three-way campaign, there were some anomalies. Cleveland was not on the ballot in Colorado, Idaho, Kansas, North Dakota and Wyoming, because Democrats joined a "fusion" effort with Weaver as a strategic way to deny those states' electoral votes to Harrison. (It was successful in 4 of the 5 states.)

As noted, Weaver was not on the Delaware or Louisiana ballots, and President Harrison was not on the ballot in Florida (apparently, this was a result of disenfranchising the state's black voters, which lowered the total Florida vote from 65,000 in 1888 to 35,000 in 1892).

The popular vote shift was not great, unlike the electoral vote changes. Cleveland won by just under 1% in 1888 and by 3% in 1892. Losing in 1888 (in the electoral college), he received 48.6% of the vote. Winning in 1892 he won 46%. Harrison dropped from 47.8% to 43%. General Weaver received 8.5%, while the Prohibition candidate, John Bidwell, attracted 2%, mostly in Minnesota and Michigan.

Cleveland's best state was Florida, where he received 85% of the ballots cast, up from 60% the previous election when the Republicans were on the ballot. Eight other southern states were in his top 10, with the border state of Maryland coming in tenth. Cleveland received a majority of total votes cast in 14 states, including New Jersey and Connecticut, his strongest northern states.

Harrison received a majority of the vote in 7 states — 5 New England states (68.1% in Vermont), plus Pennsylvania and Wyoming. Iowa, South Dakota, Delaware and North Dakota were also areas of strength for the president.

Weaver received a majority in 4 states. Nevada was his best state where his insurgent candidacy garnered two-thirds of the vote. Other majorities came in Colorado, Idaho and Kansas. Nine of his top 10 states were in the West (including North Dakota, Wyoming, Nebraska, South Dakota and Oregon). One southern state, Alabama, placed ninth on his list. Weaver's 36.6% in Alabama came at the expense of the Republicans. Even Winston County, the pro–Union GOP county, voted for Weaver. The Harrison vote declined from 33% to 4% in Alabama.

Harrison's vote declined almost everywhere, except in Delaware and New Hampshire. In Delaware, there was an antitrend at work, since Harrison lost by only 1 point in 1892 compared to a 12-point loss in 1888.

Weaver carried 224 counties in the West and 51 in the South, the most impressive showing for a third-party candidate since the four-way race of 1860. He carried counties in 16 states, indicating a relatively strong national appeal — though he won nothing in the Northeast.

There were a large number of counties (419) changing sides in 1892. More of them involved switches to the Populist Party (216) than between the major parties (203).

Harrison lost three times as many of his 1888 counties (314) as did Cleveland (105). Harrison lost 165 counties to Cleveland, almost half of them (77) in the South, where racial voting patterns predominated. There were 29 Virginia counties that shifted to the Democrats, followed by 13 in North Carolina and 10 in Arkansas. Including the border states (18 counties), a clear majority of the counties switching to Cleveland were southern oriented.

Outside the South, Cleveland picked up 18 Harrison counties in Wisconsin, 9 in Ohio, 8 in Iowa, 8 in Indiana, and 6 in Illinois. Harrison lost 149 counties to Weaver, mostly in the West. Cleveland lost 67 counties to Weaver, some in the West and some in the South.

There were 38 counties that supported the losing candidates twice in a row, going for Cleveland in 1888 and for Harrison in 1892. These antitrend counties fit in no particular pattern, though 17 were in the South and 15 in the Midwest. The only cities that moved in this contrary direction were Omaha and Lansing.

Cleveland did better in the cities in 1892 than he had in 1888. In the North he carried such 1888 Harrison cities as Chicago, Gary, Evansville, Newark, Buffalo, Schenectady, Cleveland, Youngstown, Akron, Wilkes-Barre, Madison, Kenosha and Milwaukee. In the South he captured Little Rock, Natchez, Jacksonville (FL), Key West, Baton Rouge, Winston-Salem, Wilmington (NC), Raleigh, Chattanooga, Norfolk, Petersburg, Williamsburg and Winchester. He also won Annapolis and Frederick, MD.

Despite a major third-party effort, and the admission of 6 new states, the total national vote only increased 6%, going from 11.383 million to 12.056 million.

TOP 10 STATES, 1892

Cleveland	Percentage	Harrison	Percentage	Weaver	Percentage
1. Florida	85.0	1. Vermont	68.1	1. Nevada	66.7
2. South Carolina	77.6	2. Maine	54.0	2. Colorado	57.1
3. Louisiana	76.5	3. Massachusetts	51.9	3. Idaho	54.2
4. Mississippi	76.2	4. Pennsylvania	51.4	4. Kansas	50.3
5. Alabama	59.4	5. New Hampshire	51.1	5. North Dakota	49.0
6. Arkansas	59.3	6. Rhode Island	50.7	6. Wyoming	46.2
7. Georgia	58.0	7. Wyoming	50.6	7. Nebraska	41.5
8. Texas	57.7	8. Iowa	49.6	8. South Dakota	37.8
9. Virginia	56.2	9. South Dakota	49.5	9. Alabama	36.6
10. Maryland	53.4	10. Delaware	48.5	10. Oregon	34.3
		10. North Dakota	48.5		

ELECTORAL VOTES, 1892

States	Electoral Votes	Cleveland	Harrison	Weaver
Alabama	11	11	–	–
Arkansas	8	8	–	–
California[1]	9	8	1	–
Colorado	4	–	–	4
Connecticut	6	6	–	–
Delaware	3	3	–	–
Florida	4	4	–	–
Georgia	13	13	–	–
Idaho	3	–	–	3
Illinois	24	24	–	–
Indiana	15	15	–	–
Iowa	13	–	13	–
Kansas	10	–	–	10
Kentucky	13	13	–	–
Louisiana	8	8	–	–
Maine	6	–	6	–
Maryland	8	8	–	–
Massachusetts	15	–	15	–
Michigan[1]	14	5	9	–
Minnesota	9	–	9	–
Mississippi	9	9	–	–
Missouri	17	17	–	–
Montana	3	–	3	–
Nebraska	8	–	8	–
Nevada	3	–	–	3
New Hampshire	4	–	4	–
New Jersey	10	10	–	–
New York	36	36	–	–
North Carolina	11	11	–	–

States	Electoral Votes	Cleveland	Harrison	Weaver
North Dakota[1]	3	1	1	1
Ohio[1]	23	1	22	-
Oregon[1]	4	-	3	1
Pennsylvania	32	-	32	-
Rhode Island	4	-	4	-
South Carolina	9	9	-	-
South Dakota	4	-	4	-
Tennessee	12	12	-	-
Texas	15	15	-	-
Vermont	4	-	4-	-
Virginia	12	12	-	-
Washington	4	-	4	-
West Virginia	6	6	-	-
Wisconsin	12	12	-	-
Wyoming	3	-	3	-
Totals	444	277	145	22

1. These states split their votes along congressional district lines. In North Dakota a Populist elector voted for Cleveland.

1896

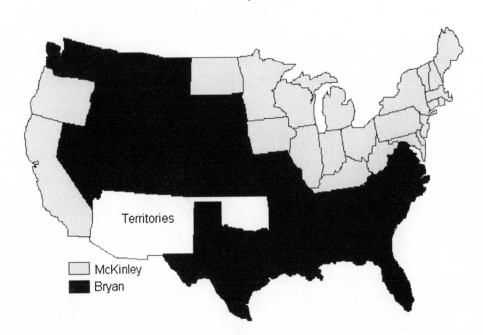

McKinley
Bryan

The 1896 election was one of the most dramatic, hard-fought contests in U.S. political history. The electorate was engaged, the media coverage extensive, and the turnout high (13.8 million compared to 12 million in 1892, an increase of 15%).

William McKinley won 51 percent to William J. Bryan's 47 percent and carried 23 states with 271 electoral votes. McKinley swept the North and Midwest and won a surprise victory in Kentucky, which had never voted for a Republican for president before. Bryan's electrifying "Cross of Gold" speech at the Democratic convention made him a hero in much of the rural West but it frightened eastern voters, who saw him as a dangerous demagogue and an economic radical who threatened their prosperity. McKinley carried all 67 counties in New England, and his popular vote exceeded most previous Republican candidates. The McKinley romp spread as far south as Maryland, where he amassed a 55% to 42% vote majority. Nine of his top 10 states were in the Northeast.

Bryan carried 11 southern states, plus Missouri, and 10 states in the West and the Plains, netting him 176 electoral votes. He carried 141 of the 154 counties in the mountain states. He was the first Democrat to win Kansas, Colorado, Idaho, Nebraska, Montana, South Dakota, Washington and Wyoming; he also carried Utah, which cast its first presidential vote.

Bryan's strongest states reflected his southern (Mississippi, South Carolina, Louisiana, Arkansas, Florida) and western (Colorado, Utah, Montana, Idaho) axis.

McKinley, whose vote reached 80.4% in Vermont, won his greatest victories in the 6 New England states, the 3 Middle Atlantic states (New York, New Jersey, Pennsylvania) and in Wisconsin. It is noteworthy that 4 of McKinley's strongest states (Connecticut, Wisconsin, New Jersey and New York) had

all gone for Democrat Grover Cleveland 4 years before. This underscores the Democratic defections in the North.

The election was polarized regionally. Nearly half of the states (22 of 45) went decisively for either McKinley or Bryan. McKinley carried 93% of the counties in the Northeast, while Bryan won 75% of the counties in the West. (The vote was close, however, in Wyoming, Oregon, Kentucky and North Dakota.)

Bryan carried the 4 states that had supported Weaver in 1892 and picked up the new state of Utah. He would have won the presidency had he not lost such a large segment of eastern and big-city Democrats, who feared that a combination of agrarian radicalism and religious fundamentalism would harm their lives.

The realignment of 1896, which revitalized the Republican Party, can be discerned in the large number of counties that switched sides between 1892 and 1896. Many entrenched Republican and Democratic counties moved toward the other party as a result of the issues and personalities of the 1896 campaign.

The supporters of the Populist Party of 1892, a farm-labor and economic discontent vote, flocked en masse to Bryan. Of the 275 counties* in 16 states that supported the Populists in 1892, 251 of them (91.3%) went for Bryan. Only 24 backed McKinley. In every state except North Dakota and Georgia (where about half the Populist counties went for McKinley), the Populist vote increased Democratic strength.

This Populist-Democratic connection was a major factor in Bryan's western victories and represented a major short-term realignment of a segment of the electorate. Four years before the Populist revolt, 68.3% of these counties had supported the Republican nominee Benjamin Harrison. Thus, in just 8 years, these counties shifted from 68%

---

*There were actually 276 counties, but one in Idaho was abolished before the 1896 election.

Republican to 9% Republican, with the Populists serving as a transition vehicle.

The key to the McKinley victory lies in metropolitan America. Even though most Americans resided in small towns and rural areas, and suburbs did not really exist, the city vote was becoming increasingly important.

McKinley won over 70% of the vote in a baker's dozen of large eastern counties, including 6 in Massachusetts (Bristol, Essex, Hampden, Middlesex, Norfolk and Worcester), 4 in Pennsylvania (Lancaster, Philadelphia, Allegheny and Chester), as well as Hartford, Connecticut; Camden, New Jersey; and St. Lawrence, New York. McKinley even carried Boston 60% to 35%. Nearly 60% supported the Republican candidate in St. Paul, Minnesota, and in President Grover Cleveland's hometown of Buffalo, New York. McKinley even carried the Democratic bastions of New York City and Jersey City. (Ironically, McKinley barely carried his hometown of Canton, Ohio, in Stark County.)

In the nation's 70 metropolitan counties, where at least 20,000 votes were cast, McKinley piled up a nearly 60% to 40% major party triumph. His margin over Bryan in the metropolitan counties was 737,991 votes, which offset Bryan's majority of 170,299 in the rest of the nation. Though urban America cast only 27.8% of the total vote, its decided preference for McKinley carried the day. In most of the other post–Civil War elections, the large population counties had been closely divided between the two parties, reflecting the national divisions. But 1896 opened a new era in Republican dominance in metropolitan areas that finally ended in 1932 (and in some areas in 1928).

The upheaval engendered by the 1896 vote affected a considerable number of counties. McKinley was the first Republican to carry 62 counties in 13 states, with 36 of them being in the South. While Bryan carried all 11 southern states, his victory margin was smaller than the margins of some previous Democrats. This was reflected in Georgia, where 15 counties bolted to the GOP, as did 10 in Texas and 9 in Virginia (mostly in the Shenandoah Valley and in the southwest mountains). One county in Alabama (Blount) and one in North Carolina (Buncombe, which includes Asheville), went Republican for the first time. Kentucky had 3 first-time GOP counties, including Jefferson (Louisville), where long-time Democratic voters gave McKinley a nearly 2–1 victory.

Perhaps the most surprising result was McKinley's victory in Springfield, Illinois (Sangamon County), which had never before supported the Republican presidential candidate, including Abraham Lincoln, who lost his home county twice. Peoria, Illinois, also voted Republican for the first time. Other first-timers included Hudson County, New Jersey (Jersey City); Bergen County, New Jersey; and Westchester County, New York, all Dutch-influenced prosperous counties just outside of New York City, where the GOP's cultural signals had been politically unappealing. McKinley also triumphed in Monmouth and Sussex Counties, New Jersey, and Rockland County, New York — all Democratic strongholds for many decades. Franklin County, Ohio, which includes Columbus, the state capital, went Republican for the first time, as did 3 Wisconsin counties with large German-ancestry populations (Kewaunee, Outagamie and Washington). In Texas, Galveston and Austin (Travis County) cast their first Republican vote, as did a few counties with Hispanic (Duval, Webb) and German (Lee, Guadalupe) populations. The McKinley campaign widened its net and brought in a new generation of voters, some of them no doubt rejecting the new Democratic Party and its standard-bearer.

Bryan also won many crossover votes, carrying 98 counties in 10 states that had never gone Democratic before. Most were in the relatively new states of Kansas (47), Nebraska (37) and Minnesota (6). A few counties in Oregon, Iowa, Nevada, Arkansas, Missouri, North Carolina and Virginia deserted their Republican leanings to support the "Great Commoner." In addition, about 24 counties (in Arkansas, Iowa, Missouri, Michigan, Minnesota, New Jersey, Ohio, Oregon, Pennsylvania and Virginia) voted Democratic for the first time since before the Civil War.

There was a religion-cultural factor in some of these swing counties that deserted their traditional party preference to support McKinley or Bryan. Many of the new McKinley counties were German Catholic (Elk, Pennsylvania, and Kewaunee, Wisconsin) or German Lutheran (Dodge, Wisconsin) or Dutch Reformed in their religious demography. The Bryan counties were often strongholds of evangelical, native-born Protestants.

In Missouri, for example, 7 Republican counties voted Democratic either for the first time ever or for the first time since 1856 (Dade, Dallas, Douglas, Jasper, Lawrence, Polk, Wright). Baptists and Methodists predominated, followed by Disciples of Christ and Presbyterians. These 4 groups composed 69% of the religious population in those counties, compared to 42% statewide. Only 6% were Catholics, compared to a 33% Catholic identification in Missouri as a whole.

In Michigan, 4 counties voting Democratic for the first time since before the Civil War (Branch, Calhoun, Eaton, Isabella) were fairly heavily Methodist, even though Catholics were by far the largest faith group in Michigan. In these pro-Bryan Michigan counties, Methodists, Baptists, Congregationalists and Presbyterians together outnumbered Catholics 43% to 29%, while statewide Catholics outnumbered these evangelical Protestants 47% to 18%.

TOP 10 STATES, 1896

McKinley	Percentage	Bryan	Percentage
1. Vermont	80.4	1. Mississippi	91.0
2. Massachusetts	69.5	2. South Carolina	85.3
3. New Hampshire	68.7	3. Colorado	84.9
4. Rhode Island	68.3	4. Washington	82.7
5. Maine	67.9	5. Nevada	81.2
6. Connecticut	63.2	6. Montana	79.9
7. Pennsylvania	61.0	7. Idaho	78.1
8. Wisconsin	59.9	8. Louisiana	76.4
9. New Jersey	59.7	9. Arkansas	73.7
10. New York	57.6	10. Florida	70.5

ELECTORAL VOTES, 1896

States	Electoral Votes	McKinley	Bryan	States	Electoral Votes	McKinley	Bryan
Alabama	11	–	11	California[1]	9	8	1
Arkansas	8	–	8	Colorado	4	–	4

States	Electoral Votes	McKinley	Bryan	States	Electoral Votes	McKinley	Bryan
Connecticut	6	6	–	North Carolina	11	–	11
Delaware	3	3	–	North Dakota	3	3	–
Florida	4	–	4	Ohio	23	23	–
Georgia	13	–	13	Oregon	4	4	–
Idaho	3	–	3	Pennsylvania	32	32	–
Illinois	24	24	–	Rhode Island	4	4	–
Indiana	15	15	–	South Carolina	9	–	9
Iowa	13	13	–	South Dakota	4	–	4
Kansas	10	–	10	Tennessee	12	–	12
Kentucky[1]	13	12	1	Texas	15	–	15
Louisiana	8	–	8	Utah	3	–	3
Maine	6	6	–	Vermont	4	4	–
Maryland	8	8	–	Virginia	12	–	12
Massachusetts	15	15	–	Washington	4	–	4
Michigan	14	14	–	West Virginia	6	6	–
Minnesota	9	9	–	Wisconsin	12	12	–
Missouri	17	–	17	Wyoming	3	–	3
Montana	3	–	3				
Nebraska	8	–	8	**Totals**	**447**	**271**	**176**
Nevada	3	–	3				
New Hampshire	4	4	–				
New Jersey	10	10	–				
New York	36	36	–				

1. These states split their electoral votes along congressional district lines.

1900

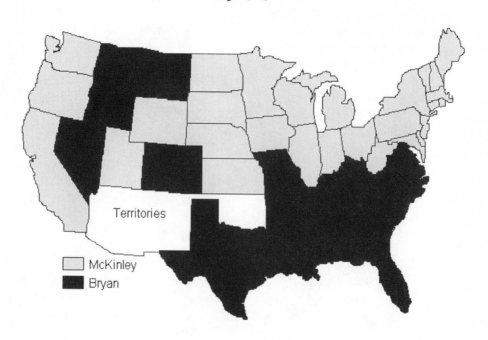

Territories

McKinley

Bryan

I. State and National Results (1900)

The rematch between President McKinley and Bryan was hard fought, though not as dramatic and exciting as their first meeting in 1896. The overall national vote (52% for McKinley, 46% for Bryan) represented only a 1-point gain for McKinley. His electoral vote margin was 292–155, a gain of 21 votes. Six states switched from Bryan to McKinley (Kansas, Nebraska, South Dakota, Utah, Washington, Wyoming) while 1 state (Kentucky) switched from McKinley to Bryan. The turnout of 13.9 million was only slightly higher (less than 1%) than in 1896.

A new set of issues influenced the course and direction of the campaign and the vote, primarily the Spanish-American War, which was popular in the West and much less so in the East. Beneath the surface of what appears to be a fairly predictable re-election with relatively little change was a considerable movement between the parties.

Amazingly, 328 counties switched from Bryan to McKinley. Fully 256 were in the prowar West, while 48 were in the South, 23 in the border states and only 1 in the East (Crawford County, Pennsylvania). At least 1 county in 29 of the 45 states switched to McKinley, including 45 in Kansas, 32 in Nebraska, 22 in South Dakota and 18 in Washington.

Moving in the opposite direction were 113 counties that switched from McKinley to Bryan. Most (81) were in the South, but 13 were in the West, 10 in the border states and 9 in the Northeast.

Both parties were moderately successful in raiding each other's bases. McKinley's rural strongholds, which ranged from Vermont to Cape Cod and the Massachusetts islands to eastern Kentucky and Tennessee, as well as some German and Scandinavian counties in the Midwest, gave the president 80%, down from 85% from 4 years before.

But it was in the eastern metropolitan counties where Bryan experienced a surge of new support. He gained 10 percentage points or more in 9 large eastern counties, topped by a 16.5% gain in Suffolk, Massachusetts (Boston). His other top gains were in Hartford, Connecticut; Queens, New York; and in 6 Massachusetts counties: Bristol, Essex, Hampden, Middlesex, Norfolk and Worcester. He carried few of these but his increased support was noteworthy. He also gained over 9% in Jefferson County, Kentucky (Louisville), enough to cause Kentucky to become the only state to switch to Bryan. Bryan's other major gains came in New Haven, New Orleans, Baltimore, and Providence. The pro–Bryan trend in urban America may have resulted from dissatisfaction with the Spanish-American War and the colonial policies of the McKinley administration in the Philippines, which came under U.S. control. One of the stated policies of the U.S. government, said McKinley, was to bring "Christianity to the natives." It apparently did not occur to him that the Philippines was the only Christian country in Asia, having been colonized by the Spanish and evangelized by Catholic missionaries 300 years before. Criticism of McKinley's policies was vocal in the Catholic press, and the pro–Bryan "swing" counties in urban America were 65% Catholic, according to the *1906 U.S. Census of Religious Bodies.*

McKinley still won most large population areas, with 75% in Philadelphia and 73% in Pittsburgh. He gained heavily in Salt Lake City and Denver and made modest gains in Minneapolis and San Francisco. McKinley's strongest metropolitan counties were in the East, despite declines in support, while Bryan carried Kansas City, Boston, New York City, Jersey City, Denver and the smaller Pennsylvania towns of Reading, York, Bethlehem and Easton.

Pro-Bryan swing counties were found in 19 states, including 22 in Texas and 21 in Georgia. (Several of these counties showed a dramatic decline in total votes due to the disenfranchisement of black voters.)

Some states had groups of counties moving in opposite directions. In North Carolina 18 counties switched to McKinley while 16 counties switched to Bryan. Similar patterns were found in Illinois, Indiana and Kentucky, indicating a considerable flux among the electorate.

Bryan's decline in the West reached near-collapse proportions in some states. In Colorado his vote fell from 85% to 56%. In Utah it declined from 83% to 48%.

McKinley carried 28 states, sweeping the North and Midwest and adding a number of western states. Bryan carried 17 states, basically the Old South plus Kentucky and Missouri in the border region and Montana, Nevada, Idaho and Colorado. McKinley's strongest states were in upper New England (Vermont, Maine, New Hampshire) and in the upper Midwest (North Dakota, Minnesota, Wisconsin, Michigan) as well as Pennsylvania, Rhode Island and Wyoming. Of Bryan's top 10 states 8 were in the South. The others were Nevada and Montana. McKinley also did very well in Iowa, Massachusetts and Connecticut.

McKinley was the first Republican to carry 32 counties in 12 states: 8 of them were in Alabama and 8 in North Carolina. Oregon contributed 4 converts to the GOP cause, while Georgia had 3 and Illinois, 2. One county bolted to the GOP in Arkansas, Texas, Delaware, Indiana, Ohio, Kentucky and Missouri. The South predominated, contributing 21 new counties to the Republicans, while 3 were in the border states, and 8 in the Midwest or West.

Bryan was the first Democrat to carry

3 North Carolina counties (Vance, Warren, Washington) and Waller County, Texas. Bryan also became the first Democrat to win 2 Georgia counties (Camden, McIntosh), 2 in North Carolina (Craven, Northampton) and 2 in Texas (Brazoria, Wharton) since Buchanan's 1856 victory.

Another factor in McKinley's reelection was his better showing in the "convert" counties of 1896. McKinley won back 62% of the Republican counties that defected to Bryan in 1896, and he still carried 55% of the Democratic counties that he had won in 1896. So, in the counties that broke dramatically with their heritage in 1896 — McKinley winning 62 and Bryan, 98 — in 1900 McKinley won 95 and Bryan won 65. The crossover/independent vote was leaning more Republican.

The 1900 results revealed that both parties were able to raid their opposition's base to some extent. The metropolitan vote went for McKinley 56% to 44%, a 4% gain for Bryan. The nonmetropolitan vote, however, switched from 51% to 49% for Bryan in 1896 to 52% to 48% for McKinley, a 3% McKinley gain. The metro area cast 29% of the total national vote, a small increase over 1896. The main geographic shift was West to East, with Bryan gaining in the McKinley strongholds of the East, while McKinley gained in Bryan's western strongholds.

McKinley's metropolitan margin dropped to 468,000 from 738,000, but he won nonmetropolitan America by 392,000, instead of losing it by 141,000. This enabled him to win reelection with a slightly higher national margin.

Top 10 States, 1900

McKinley	*Percentage*	*Bryan*	*Percentage*
1. Vermont	75.7	1. South Carolina	93.0
2. North Dakota	62.1	2. Mississippi	87.6
3. Maine	61.7	3. Louisiana	79.0
4. Pennsylvania	60.7	4. Florida	71.0

McKinley	Percentage	Bryan	Percentage
5. Minnesota	60.2	5. Georgia	66.9
6. Wisconsin	60.1	6. Arkansas	63.5
7. Rhode Island	59.7	7. Texas	63.4
8. New Hampshire	59.3	8. Nevada	62.2
9. Wyoming	58.8	9. Alabama	60.8
10. Michigan	58.1	10. Montana	58.4

Electoral Votes, 1900

States	Electoral Votes	McKinley	Bryan	States	Electoral Votes	McKinley	Bryan
Alabama	11	–	11	Nevada	3	–	3
Arkansas	8	–	8	New Hampshire	4	4	–
California	9	9	–	New Jersey	10	10	–
Colorado	4	–	4	New York	36	36	–
Connecticut	6	6	–	North Carolina	11	–	11
Delaware	3	3	–	North Dakota	3	3	–
Florida	4	–	4	Ohio	23	23	–
Georgia	13	–	13	Oregon	4	4	–
Idaho	3	–	3	Pennsylvania	32	32	–
Illinois	24	24	–	Rhode Island	4	4	–
Indiana	15	15	–	South Carolina	9	–	9
Iowa	13	13	–	South Dakota	4	4	–
Kansas	10	10	–	Tennessee	12	–	12
Kentucky	13	–	13	Texas	15	–	15
Louisiana	8	–	8	Utah	3	3	–
Maine	6	6	–	Vermont	4	4	–
Maryland	8	8	–	Virginia	12	–	12
Massachusetts	15	15	–	Washington	4	4	–
Michigan	14	14	–	West Virginia	6	6	–
Minnesota	9	9	–	Wisconsin	12	12	–
Mississippi	9	–	9	Wyoming	3	3	–
Missouri	17	–	17				
Montana	3	–	3	Totals	447	292	155
Nebraska	8	8	–				

1904

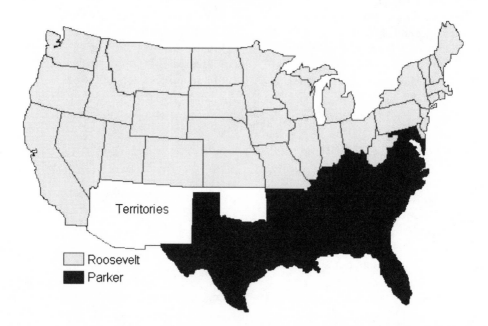

Roosevelt
Parker

The victory for Republican President Theodore Roosevelt, who succeeded to the nation's highest office after the assassination of William McKinley in September 1901, was the greatest since Grant's in 1872. Theodore Roosevelt won roughly 60% of the major-party vote to 40% for an obscure New York State judge, Alton B. Parker, the Democratic nominee. (The overall popular vote was 56.4% for Roosevelt, 37.6% for Parker, 3% for Socialist Eugene V. Debs, and 3% for other candidates.) The total vote declined 400,000 from 1900.

But Roosevelt, that "damned cowboy," according to Republican campaign strategist Mark Hanna, showed greater strength in the western states than in the traditional GOP bastions in the East and Midwest. Though Vermont remained his strongest state (78% support) as always, his next most impressive sources of voter support came from North Dakota (where he had lived briefly as a young man), Minnesota, South Dakota, Washington and Michigan. His top 10 states were rounded out by Pennsylvania,

Maine, Oregon and Wyoming (the West, again). Roosevelt clearly won the support of many who had backed Bryan in the two previous elections. Only 3 of Roosevelt's top 10 states were on McKinley's top 10 in 1896. This represented a major geographic shift in GOP strength and was undoubtedly due to Theodore Roosevelt's personality and policies, which were oriented toward conservation and trust-busting, both popular ideas in the West.

Roosevelt won 336 electoral votes to 140 for Parker, who carried only the South and Kentucky. (Maryland went for Roosevelt by 51 votes, but the peculiar electoral division in use at that time gave Parker 7 of Maryland's 8 electoral votes.)

Roosevelt carried every western state that had gone for Bryan twice (Colorado, Idaho, Missouri, Montana, Nevada) or once (Kansas, Nebraska, South Dakota, Utah, Washington, Wyoming). Theodore Roosevelt was the first Republican to carry Missouri since Grant in 1868.

Roosevelt was the first Republican

winner in 56 counties in 12 states: 26 of them in the Midwest and 21 in the West. Illinois contributed 16 counties that defected to the GOP for the first time, and there were 11 in Montana, 9 in Utah and 7 in Indiana, as well as 3 in Pennsylvania, 2 each in Ohio, Arkansas, and Georgia and 1 each in Iowa, Nevada, Tennessee and Virginia.

Supporting a Republican presidential candidate for the first time were such counties as York, Pennsylvania (a German Protestant area that had supported the Democrats since Jefferson and Jackson); and German Catholic Dubuque, Iowa. Another German county, Allen, Indiana (Fort Wayne), defected to Roosevelt, as did Northampton, Pennsylvania (the Easton-Bethlehem area).

In the entire North and West only 84 counties supported Parker, and most of those were in southern-leaning counties in Illinois (17), Indiana (18), and Ohio (17), where a combination of cultural factors and historical memories kept the Democrats afloat.

The nation's largest metropolitan areas favored Roosevelt by large margins. Parker could only carry Boston (Suffolk County), Jersey City (Hudson County), and most of New York City (New York, Queens and Richmond counties). Both Parker and Roosevelt were New Yorkers, and Parker was the Democratic nominee in a longtime Democratic city.

Parker carried a handful of traditional rural Democrats in Colorado, California, Iowa, Montana and Utah. He carried 5 rock-ribbed Democratic counties in rural Pennsylvania as well as Berks County, which included Reading and rural "Pennsylvania Dutch" voters. Three German counties in Wisconsin (Dodge, Ozaukee, Jefferson) and 3 Dutch counties in New Jersey (Sussex, Warren, Hunterdon) were all that remained of the many hundreds of northern and western counties that supported Grover Cleveland and William Jennings Bryan.

Parker's showing was not a complete disaster. His southern margins (over 90% in South Carolina and Mississippi) remained high and in many instances exceeded Bryan's 1900 vote percentage.

This election also brought forth an unusual countertrend: a conservative southern rural revolt that caused 88 counties in 12 southern and border states to switch from McKinley to Parker. The 1904 election was one of the few — very few — in U.S. history in which the Republican candidate was clearly more liberal or progressive than the Democrats, especially on civil rights. Consequently, 20 counties in Virginia, 18 in North Carolina, 12 in Alabama, 8 each in Texas and Arkansas, 7 in Maryland, 5 in Kentucky, 4 in Georgia, 2 each in South Carolina and West Virginia and 1 each in Louisiana and Tennessee moved against the national trend. Some of these counties also disenfranchised African-American voters in the process, making future Democratic victories secure. Seventeen of these counties had a an African-American population majority, but no voters from that population. (These pro–Parker counties stayed with the Democrats until 1928, when Hoover won a majority of them.)

The Socialist nominee, Eugene V. Debs, received 3% of the national vote, exceeding 9% in California and Montana.

Top 10 States, 1904

Roosevelt	Percentage		Parker	Percentage
1. Vermont	78.0		1. South Carolina	95.4
2. North Dakota	75.1		2. Mississippi	91.1
3. Minnesota	74.0		3. Louisiana	88.5
4. South Dakota	71.1		4. Alabama	73.4
5. Washington	70.0		5. Texas	71.5
6. Michigan	69.5		6. Florida	68.3
7. Pennsylvania	68.0		7. Georgia	63.7
8. Maine	67.4		8. Virginia	61.8
9. Oregon	67.3		9. North Carolina	59.7
10. Wyoming	66.9		10. Arkansas	55.4

Electoral Votes, 1904

States	Electoral Votes	Roosevelt	Parker	States	Electoral Votes	Roosevelt	Parker
Alabama	11	–	11	New Hampshire	4	4	–
Arkansas	9	–	9	New Jersey	12	12	–
California	10	10	–	New York	39	39	–
Colorado	5	5	–	North Carolina	12	–	12
Connecticut	7	7	–	North Dakota	4	4	–
Delaware	3	3	–	Ohio	23	23	–
Florida	5	–	5	Oregon	4	4	–
Georgia	13	–	13	Pennsylvania	34	34	–
Idaho	3	3	–	Rhode Island	4	4	–
Illinois	27	27	–	South Carolina	9	–	9
Indiana	15	15	–	South Dakota	4	4	–
Iowa	13	13	–	Tennessee	12	–	12
Kansas	10	10	–	Texas	18	–	18
Kentucky	13	–	13	Utah	3	3	–
Louisiana	9	–	9	Vermont	4	4	–
Maine	6	6	–	Virginia	12	–	12
Maryland[1]	8	1	7	Washington	5	5	–
Massachusetts	16	16	–	West Virginia	7	7	–
Michigan	14	14	–	Wisconsin	13	13	–
Minnesota	11	11	–	Wyoming	3	3	–
Mississippi	10	–	10				
Missouri	18	18	–	Totals	476	336	140
Montana	3	3	–				
Nebraska	8	8	–				
Nevada	3	3	–				

1. Maryland split its electoral votes by congressional district.

1908

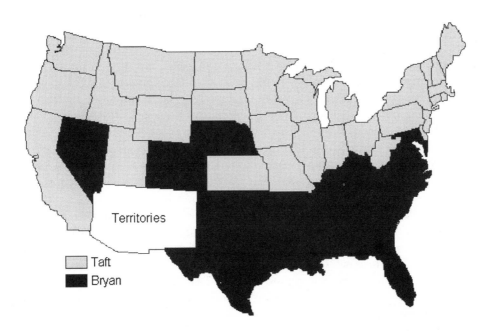

Territories

Taft
Bryan

In 1908 Republican William Howard Taft easily defeated the old Democratic warhorse William Jennings Bryan 52% to 43% and by 321 electoral votes to 162. It was Bryan's third presidential defeat, and it was his weakest showing. He lost by 4 percentage points in 1896, 6 points in 1900, and 9 points in 1908. Bryan's appeal had clearly diminished, and Taft led the Republicans to their fourth straight victory. (Bryan's progressively weaker electoral appeal stands in contrast to the only other three-time candidate, Kentucky senator Henry Clay, who drew a higher vote percentage in his later campaigns and narrowly lost his third try for the White House to James K. Polk in 1844.)

Bryan's decline is symbolized by his defeat in Missouri and Montana after carrying those states twice before. He managed to carry Colorado and Nevada for the third time, and he won his home state of Nebraska, which he lost in 1900. The South remained his only stronghold, and his vote topped 90% in South Carolina and Missis-

sippi. All of his 10 strongest states were in the South, though his 54% vote in Georgia and North Carolina was unimpressive. Bryan also carried the new state of Oklahoma. Bryan was the first Democrat to carry Kendall, Marion, and San Jacinto counties in Texas.

Taft's strongholds were in the Northeast and Midwest, returning to the McKinley pattern. All of the New England states except Massachusetts, plus Pennsylvania, Michigan, Minnesota and the Dakotas responded most enthusiastically to the Taft campaign. Taft carried every county in New England, and in Michigan, Washington, Oregon, Wyoming and North Dakota. Even in this relatively uneventful election, there were some noticeable voter changes in the counties. Taft was the first Republican to carry 17 counties, 12 of them in Georgia (Appling, Banks, Barton, Chatooga, Forsyth, Gordon, Murray, Screven, Walker, Webster, White and Whitfield). Most of the new GOP counties were in North Georgia. Five other counties joined the GOP ranks for the first time: Cullman, Alabama; Calhoun, Florida; Breathitt, Kentucky; Jackson, North Carolina; and Mingo, West Virginia.

In comparison with the two previous Bryan campaigns, a surprising number of counties changed sides. There were 161 counties in 26 states that deserted Bryan after supporting him twice before. Almost 63% of these counties (101) were in the West, while 41 were in the South, 18 in the border states and 1 in the Northeast (Sullivan County, Pennsylvania). There were 15 anti–Bryan counties in Kansas and Georgia, 14 in Missouri and 11 in California. These included the cities of Fresno and Bakersfield, California, and the counties around Denver, Colorado, which had been some of Bryan's most enthusiastic original supporters.

On the other hand, Bryan carried 69 counties in 15 states that had opposed him twice before. Almost half (33) were in the South, 23 in the Midwest and 13 in the border states. These included, ironically enough, Bryan's hometown of Lincoln, Nebraska (Lancaster County), and Omaha, Nebraska (Douglas County), which had resisted his political appeal twice before. Bryan also picked up Montgomery County, Ohio (Dayton); Hamilton County, Tennessee (Chattanooga); Fayette County, Kentucky (Lexington); and Vigo County, Indiana (Evansville), suggesting a somewhat greater appeal for the "Commoner" in urban areas, while his rural support declined.

There may have been a mild religious factor in the 1908 results since Taft's Unitarian religion was condemned by some Methodist and evangelical clergy. The 69 pro–Bryan counties were 80% Protestant, compared to 66% nationwide, according to the *1906 Census of U.S. Religious Bodies*. Methodists and Baptists constituted about 7% more of the population in the pro–Bryan counties than nationwide, but this is a minor factor compared to religious voting patterns in several other national elections.

Socialist candidate Eugene Debs siphoned off 2.8% of the national vote, doing particularly well in the West (California, Idaho, Montana, Nevada, Washington) and in Oklahoma and Florida.

TOP 10 STATES, 1908

Taft	*Percentage*	*Bryan*	*Percentage*
1. Vermont	75.1	1. South Carolina	93.8
2. Maine	63.0	2. Mississippi	90.1
3. Michigan	61.9	3. Louisiana	84.6
4. North Dakota	61.0	4. Texas	74.0
5. Rhode Island	60.8	5. Alabama	70.7
6. Connecticut	59.4	6. Florida	63.0
7. Minnesota	59.3	7. Virginia	60.5
8. New Hampshire	59.3	8. Arkansas	57.3
9. Pennsylvania	58.8	9. Georgia	54.6
10. South Dakota	58.8	10. North Carolina	54.2

Electoral Votes, 1908

States	Electoral Votes	Taft	Bryan	States	Electoral Votes	Taft	Bryan
Alabama	11	–	11	New Jersey	12	12	–
Arkansas	9	–	9	New York	39	39	–
California	10	10	–	North Carolina	12	–	12
Colorado	5	–	5	North Dakota	4	4	–
Connecticut	7	7	–	Ohio	23	23	–
Delaware	3	3	–	Oklahoma	7	–	7
Florida	5	–	5	Oregon	4	4	–
Georgia	13	–	13	Pennsylvania	34	34	–
Idaho	3	3	–	Rhode Island	4	4	–
Illinois	27	27	–	South Carolina	9	–	9
Indiana	15	15	–	South Dakota	4	4	–
Iowa	13	13	–	Tennessee	12	–	12
Kansas	10	10	–	Texas	18	–	18
Kentucky	13	–	13	Utah	3	3	–
Louisiana	9	–	9	Vermont	4	4	–
Maine	6	6	–	Virginia	12	–	12
Maryland[1]	8	2	6	Washington	5	5	–
Massachusetts	16	16	–	West Virginia	7	7	–
Michigan	14	14	–	Wisconsin	13	13	–
Minnesota	11	11	–	Wyoming	3	3	–
Mississippi	10	–	10				
Missouri	18	18	–	Totals	483	321	162
Montana	3	3	–				
Nebraska	8	–	8				
Nevada	3	–	3				
New Hampshire	4	4	–				

1. Maryland split its electoral votes by congressional district.

1912

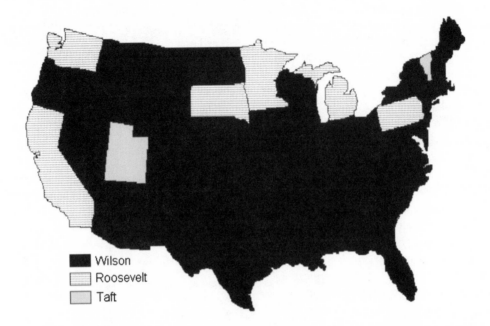

The election of 1912 was notable in several respects. It is often remembered as a warning signal for what an irresolvable intraparty split can render. The Republicans, still the majority party at that time — having held power for 44 of the previous 52 years — were torn apart by internal strife, handing the presidency to the Democrats.

The Democratic nominee, New Jersey governor Woodrow Wilson, carried 40 of the 48 states and won 435 electoral votes. He carried three-fourths of the nation's counties (2,204 out of 2,974, or 74.1%).

Coming in second was former president Theodore Roosevelt, who was denied the Republican nomination even though he outpolled President William Howard Taft in the Republican primaries. Roosevelt refused to accept the GOP convention's decision and ran on the Progressive Party ticket. Roosevelt carried 6 states (South Dakota, Pennsylvania, Michigan, Minnesota, California [by only 174 votes] and Washington) for 88 electoral votes. Roosevelt ran first in 487 counties. President Taft, the regular Re-

publican nominee, won only 2 states — Utah and Vermont — for 8 electoral votes and carried 279 counties, only 9% of the nation's total counties.

But the popular vote hardly reflected this landslide. Wilson won only 41.8% — less than Bryan received in all 3 of his losing campaigns. Roosevelt outpolled Taft 27.4% to 23.2%. The two Republicans together still received a slender majority of the popular vote, intimating that a united party would have won in 1912.

The Socialist nominee Eugene V. Debs ran a national campaign, drawing 6% of the vote and carrying 4 counties (Crawford, Kansas; Beltrami and Lake, Minnesota; and Burke, North Dakota).

Wilson won a majority of the popular vote in the 11 southern states only. His other 29 state victories were accomplished by a plurality.

In the new state of Arizona, Wilson's vote slightly exceeded the combined Roosevelt-Taft vote, but Debs ran ahead of Taft, reducing Wilson's vote to 44%. Wilson received 1% less of the national vote than had Bryan 4 years before. Wilson dropped 6 points in Nevada and 5 points in Colorado and Nebraska. His victory was due entirely to the Republican split. Only in New England and the South did he run slightly stronger than Bryan. (In Georgia his vote share increased 22 points.)

Of Wilson's 2,204 counties, he carried only 1,246 with a majority. The South was his only bastion of support. The Virginia-born Wilson carried 1,034 of the 1,082 southern counties, for a phenomenal total of 95.6%. Most were by majority vote.

Roosevelt won a majority in 296 counties and a plurality in 191. Taft could only amass a majority in 39 counties and a plurality in 240 counties. Both Roosevelt and Wilson had greater depth of support. Debs won his 4 counties with a plurality.

Wilson and Debs were on the ballot in all 48 states, Roosevelt on the ballot in all but Oklahoma, and Taft on the ballot in all except South Dakota and California (where he received some write-in votes).

Wilson's top 10 states were all in the South. His support ranged from 96% in South Carolina to 24% in Vermont and 27% in Michigan, the 2 states where he ran third. Roosevelt won a majority only in South Dakota, where he was in effect the Republican nominee. Six of his top 10 states were in the West or Midwest (California, Michigan, Minnesota, South Dakota, Washington and Illinois) while 4 (Maine, Pennsylvania, Vermont and New Jersey) were in the East. Theodore Roosevelt received less than 10% of the vote in Florida, Mississippi, South Carolina and Texas. Taft's strongest states were Utah, New Hampshire and Vermont, followed by Connecticut, Oklahoma, Rhode Island, New Mexico, Wyoming, Delaware and Wisconsin — a similar geographical pattern to the Roosevelt vote.

Eugene Debs ran stronger than any Socialist presidential candidate in history. His

vote exceeded 10% in 7 states: Nevada, Oklahoma, Montana, Arizona, Washington, California and Idaho. Filling out his top 10 were Oregon, Florida, and Ohio. Debs ran ahead of President Taft in Arizona, Nevada and Florida, and polled 900,000 votes out of 15 million cast.

The 1912 race was significant in several other respects. Arizona and New Mexico became the forty-seventh and forty-eighth states. Arizona had leaned Democratic during territorial days, and its vote reflected that. New Mexico leaned Republican and Taft only lost the Land of Enchantment by 7 percentage points to Wilson and it was in fact Taft's seventh strongest state. Taft was the victor in the Hispanic areas of Santa Fe and northern New Mexico, and received an amazing 77% of the vote in Valencia County.

Suffrage had been extended to women in California and Washington, which were both Roosevelt states. The total presidential vote, however, was only up 1% over 1908 and that was solely due to the increased vote in California and Washington. A campaign regarded by most historians as one of the most exciting in history apparently did not engage the electorate at the time. Turnout was down in Illinois, New York and Pennsylvania.

The big-city vote was not overwhelmingly for Wilson. He carried metropolitan America, but only by pluralities in most areas. Wilson won majorities in Jersey City and Kansas City but had to settle for modest pluralities elsewhere. He carried St. Paul, Minnesota, by only 5 votes over Roosevelt.

Roosevelt carried Chicago, Los Angeles, Pittsburgh, Oakland, Detroit, Duluth and Seattle.

Philadelphia, with its invincible Republican organization, remained loyal to Taft, as did Hartford, Albany, Salt Lake City and Syracuse. But Taft lost his hometown of Cincinnati to Wilson by 790 votes.

Debs received a formidable vote in several cities. In Milwaukee, he came second to

Wilson and received 28% of the presidential ballots. The Socialist candidate won 20% in Schenectady, New York, and his vote topped 10% in San Francisco, Los Angeles and Oakland.

The staunchest Republican counties preferred Roosevelt to Taft, a finding that strengthens the argument that the Republican bosses erred in renominating an unpopular president. The party bosses insisted on renominating Taft, though two-thirds of Republicans wanted someone else. It was a fateful decision, as the November balloting would later attest. Of the 514 counties in 34 states that supported every Republican nominee prior to 1912, Roosevelt carried 235 counties and Taft carried 113. Roosevelt dominated the GOP loyalists in Illinois, Iowa, Michigan, Minnesota, Pennsylvania, South Dakota and Tennessee. Taft was the favorite in New York, Wisconsin and Rhode Island.

In the dozen Republican primaries held in 1912, former president Theodore Roosevelt won 9 of them (California, Illinois, Maryland, Nebraska, New Jersey, Ohio, Oregon, Pennsylvania, South Dakota) and amassed 51.5% of the vote. President William Howard Taft won only Massachusetts and received 33.9% of the vote. Wisconsin senator Robert La Follette carried North Dakota and Wisconsin and received the support of 14.5% of GOP primary voters. (More than 2,250,000 Republican primary votes were cast.)

The division between the Republicans caused nearly one third (165 of 514) of the counties, or 32.1%, to go for Wilson for the first time since the Republican Party was founded. Wilson carried the majority of Republican counties in Indiana, Kansas, Nebraska, North Dakota, and Ohio. Many states were divided almost equally.

Roosevelt did poorly in his home state of New York, running third in the popular vote and failing to carry any of the 32 traditional GOP counties.

Because of the GOP split, there were a large number of first-time Democratic counties. Of the 165 longtime Republican counties that defected to Wilson, 110 voted Democratic for the first time for president. (Fifty-five had gone Democratic at least once before the Civil War, when the Whigs were the primary opposition.) Wilson was also a first-time Democratic winner in 40 counties in the new states of Arizona, New Mexico and Oklahoma.

The split in the Republican Party made it possible for Wilson to become the first Democrat to carry Iowa, Nebraska, New Hampshire, Ohio, and Rhode Island since 1852. Massachusetts, which had supported every Whig and Republican presidential candidate, bolted to Wilson. It had never supported a Democrat for the White House.

Oregon, which had not gone Democratic since 1868, went for Wilson. Wilson was also the first Democrat to carry North Dakota, which had first voted in 1892.

The election was close in many counties. Wilson edged out Roosevelt by 1 vote in Lincoln County, Colorado. Roosevelt beat Wilson by 1 vote in Clatsop County, Oregon. Taft beat Wilson by 1 vote in San Juan County, Utah.

The Debs vote was surprisingly widespread. Even in the rural South, Debs frequently ran second to Wilson, showing the weakness of the Republican Party at that time. In the Florida Panhandle, Debs was a strong second, receiving 24% in Calhoun County and 22% in Suwanee County. Debs topped 20% of the vote and ran second in 14 Texas counties and 6 Louisiana parishes, including Huey Long's Winn Parish, where the outspoken Socialist candidate drew 29% of the vote. In Oklahoma the Debs vote exceeded 20% in 30 counties. Impoverished and isolated rural voters responded more favorably to the Debs campaign than city dwellers.

The vote in 1912 was the apex for a Socialist presidential candidate. Debs's support exceeded 20% in 99 counties in 18 states (14 in the Midwest/West, 3 in the South, and 1 in the East). In Oklahoma the Debs vote topped 20% in 30 counties; it was the only state where Roosevelt was not on the ballot and where Debs may have received the entire protest vote of those who did not want Wilson or Taft. Texas (14), Washington (12), Minnesota (8), Nevada (7), Louisiana (6) and North Dakota (6) were the states with the largest number of strong Debs counties. Almost all the Debs strongholds were in rural America.

In addition to the 4 counties he carried, Debs ran second in 56 counties. His vote topped 30% in 11 counties.

Two other oddities in the 1912 race include the following:

• A small number of Bryan Democrats in the West defected to Roosevelt in 1912, apparently believing that he was more liberal than Wilson on issues that they cared about. (They also backed Roosevelt in 1904.) Yuma County, Colorado, and Lander County, Nevada were three-times loyal to Bryan but supported the Rough Rider in 1912. A large Debs vote was recorded in some of the Bryan counties also.

• In Oklahoma 4 counties (Dewey, Ellis, Grant, Pawnee) and 2 in Kentucky (Trigg, Caldwell) voted for Taft in 1912 after supporting Bryan against Taft in 1908. They moved in the opposite direction from the nation, failing to support Taft when he was an easy winner nationally but voting for him when he was ousted in the worst beating ever given an incumbent president.

Top 10 States, 1912

Wilson	%	Roosevelt	%	Taft	%	Debs	%
1. South Carolina	95.9	1. South Dakota	50.6	1. Utah	37.4	1. Nevada	16.5
2. Mississippi	88.9	2. California	41.8	2. New Hampshire	37.4	2. Oklahoma	16.4
3. Louisiana	76.8	3. Michigan	38.9	3. Vermont	37.1	3. Montana	13.5
4. Georgia	76.6	4. Minnesota	37.7	4. Connecticut	35.9	4. Arizona	13.4
5. Texas	72.7	5. Maine	37.4	5. Oklahoma	35.8	5. Washington	12.4
6. Alabama	69.9	6. Pennsylvania	36.5	6. Rhode Island	35.6	6. California	11.7
7. Florida	69.5	7. Vermont	35.2	7. New Mexico	35.2	7. Idaho	11.3
8. Virginia	65.9	8. Washington	35.2	8. Wyoming	34.4	8. Oregon	9.7
9. North Carolina	59.2	9. Illinois	33.7	9. Delaware	32.9	9. Florida	9.5
10. Arkansas	55.0	10. New Jersey	33.6	10. Wisconsin	32.7	10. Ohio	8.7

Electoral Votes, 1912

States	Electoral Votes	Wilson	Roosevelt	Taft	States	Electoral Votes	Wilson	Roosevelt	Taft
Alabama	12	12	–	–	Delaware	3	3	–	–
Arizona	3	3	–	–	Florida	6	6	–	–
Arkansas	9	9	–	–	Georgia	14	14	–	–
California[1]	13	2	11	–	Idaho	4	4	–	–
Colorado	6	6	–	–	Illinois	29	29	–	–
Connecticut	7	7	–	–	Indiana	15	15	–	–

States	Electoral Votes	Wilson	Roosevelt	Taft	States	Electoral Votes	Wilson	Roosevelt	Taft
Iowa	13	13	–	–	Oklahoma	10	10	–	–
Kansas	10	10	–	–	Oregon	5	5	–	–
Kentucky	13	13	–	–	Pennsylvania	38	–	38	–
Louisiana	10	10	–	–	Rhode Island	5	5	–	–
Maine	6	6	–	–	South Carolina	9	9	–	–
Maryland	8	8	–	–	South Dakota	5	–	5	–
Massachusetts	18	18	–	–	Tennessee	12	12	–	–
Michigan	15	–	15	–	Texas	20	20	–	–
Minnesota	12	–	12	–	Utah	4	–	–	4
Missouri	18	18	–	–	Vermont	4	–	–	4
Montana	4	4	–	–	Virginia	12	12	–	–
Nebraska	8	8	–	–	Washington	7	–	7	–
Nevada	3	3	–	–	West Virginia	8	8	–	–
New Hampshire	4	4	–	–	Wisconsin	13	13	–	–
New Jersey	14	14	–	–	Wyoming	3	3	–	–
New Mexico	3	3	–	–					
New York	45	45	–	–	Totals	531	435	88	8
North Carolina	12	12	–	–					
North Dakota	5	5	–	–					
Ohio	24	24	–	–					

1. California divided its electoral votes by congressional district.

1916

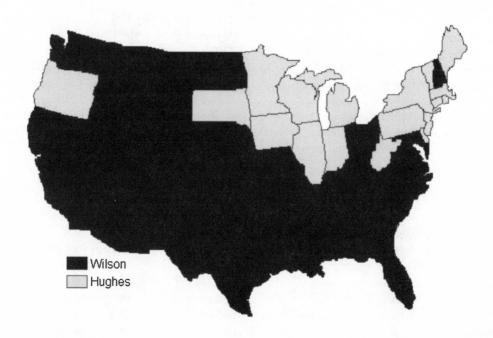

Wilson
Hughes

President Woodrow Wilson won re-election in one of the closest elections in the twentieth century, edging out his GOP opponent, Justice Charles Evans Hughes, by 277 electoral votes to 254. (He carried 30 states to 18 for Hughes.) Wilson won by only 3 percentage points (49% to 46%), and received just under half of the popular vote. It was the second time Wilson had won the presidency without a majority of the total popular vote.

Still, it was an impressive victory since the feuding GOP was reunited. The party's factional split had allowed Wilson to win 4 years before, but a reunified party thought it could re-take the White House. The election was dramatically close, and both candidates went to bed on election night thinking Hughes had won. Late returns from California, which went for Wilson by just 4,000 votes, put Wilson over the top.

Wilson's victory was achieved by welding a coalition between the South and the West, while Hughes won the East. In the entire West, Hughes carried only Oregon and South Dakota. In the Northeast, Wilson carried only New Hampshire by 56 votes.

Wilson was immensely popular in rural areas, which enabled him to carry 2,039 counties to 976 for Hughes. The South alone provided the Virginia-born and Georgia- and South Carolina–bred president the popular and electoral vote majority. He won all 126 electoral votes in the region and 74.1% of the major-party popular vote.

His southern popular-vote majority of 863,727 offset a 272,342-vote majority for Hughes in the rest of the country. (It was to be 60 years later that another southern Democrat, Jimmy Carter, won the presidency because of the South.) Wilson won almost 97% of the vote in South Carolina and 93% in Mississippi. His strongest states were all in the South, except for Colorado, which was his tenth strongest state.

Wilson, of course, carried fewer states than in 1912, since the reunited Republicans were able to return 13 states to their column (Connecticut, Delaware, Illinois, Indiana, Iowa, Maine, Massachusetts, New Jersey, New York, Oregon, Rhode Island, West Virginia and Wisconsin).

The total vote nationally increased by 3.5 million, most of it due to the enfranchisement of women in Illinois, Kansas and Montana. In Illinois the total vote was nearly 2.2 million, compared to 1.7 million in New York, which had not yet extended suffrage to women. The women's vote apparently helped Wilson carry Kansas and Montana, but Illinois was the fifth strongest state for Hughes, suggesting that the newly enfranchised females were not strongly favorable to either candidate.

Wilson was the first Democrat to carry Ohio, New Hampshire and California in a two-way race since the Civil War. One irony was Wilson's poor showing in his home state of New Jersey, where he had been governor and where he maintained his voting residence. (Wilson remains the only president to win reelection while losing his home state.) New Jersey was Hughes's second strongest state, just behind loyally Republican Vermont. Hughes ran stronger in Wilson's home state than he did in his home state of New York, though he carried both.

Wilson's triumph could not have been achieved without his receiving a segment of the Teddy Roosevelt vote in 1912. Wilson carried Washington and California, which had backed Roosevelt's insurgency campaign, and he carried several hundred of the counties that supported Roosevelt in 1912, particularly in the West. Surprisingly, Wilson also swept Utah with nearly 60% of the vote in 1 of the 2 states to support Taft in 1912. There was undoubtedly a crossover vote for Wilson in the West, perhaps related to the "peace" issue. (Kane County, Utah, for example, has only voted Democratic once in its 108-year history, and that was for Wilson in 1916.)

Wilson's immense appeal in 1916 is exemplified by his being the first Democrat to carry 70 counties in 16 states. Most of these counties backed Theodore Roosevelt 4 years before. All but 2 were in the West or Midwest. Wilson was also the first Democrat to carry Duluth, Minnesota.

Admittedly, 13 of these counties cast their first presidential vote, and 6 cast their second presidential vote, but Wilson's triumph in some of the older counties (Lorain, Ohio; and Sullivan, New Hampshire) was a major breakthrough for his party.

Justice Hughes did well in many of the nation's large metropolitan counties, carrying Philadelphia by more than 2–1. He was the first Republican to carry Ozaukee County, Wisconsin, a German-American bailiwick. Hughes ran ahead of the normal Republican vote in many midwestern German-American counties, where there was a growing wariness about Wilson's foreign policies. But Hughes was also the first Republican winner in Carteret and Clay counties, in North Carolina.

Hughes was the first Republican victor since Grant in 1868 in Boone County, West Virginia; Lewis County, Tennessee; and Montgomery County, Missouri.

Seven of the strongest states for Hughes were in the Northeast and 3 were in the Midwest (Iowa, Illinois and Michigan).

Hughes ran particularly well in the old pro–Union counties in eastern Tennessee and Kentucky, achieving 91.9% in Leslie County, Kentucky, and 90.4% in Sevier County, Tennessee. He also exceeded 80% in two German-American counties: Gasconade in Missouri and McPherson in South Dakota.

Hughes also carried several dozen counties that had supported William Jennings Bryan 3 times and Wilson in 1912, suggesting that there was a small undercurrent of anti–Wilson feeling in some areas.

The 1912–1916 county changes indicate the flux of the electorate. Wilson retained about a third (38 of 117) of the counties that had never supported a Democrat until Wilson in 1912. He did particularly well among the new Democrats in Nebraska, Wyoming and North Dakota, but almost all of the Wilson converts in Indiana, Iowa, Oregon, Tennessee and Wisconsin switched back to Hughes.

In the new states of Arizona, New Mexico and Oklahoma, the first-time Democrats were much more loyal, with 37 of the 40 Wilson counties going for him again.

Incidentally, the malapportionment of national politics can be seen in this election. The South, where blacks were counted as part of the population in order to apportion congressional representation and to determine electoral votes but were denied the vote in many areas, cast only 10% of the national popular vote but 23.7% of the electoral votes.

Swing voting was pronounced in 1916. Despite Roosevelt's endorsement of Hughes, a sizable chunk of Roosevelt's supporters voted for Wilson, causing 28.6% of Roosevelt's 1912 counties to support Wilson. The likeliest Wilson supporters among former Progressive voters tended to live in cities. In Illinois the only Wilson county of the 27 that backed Theodore Roosevelt was Peoria. In Iowa the counties containing Des Moines and Sioux City backed the president but the rural Roosevelt supporters went for Hughes. Wilson carried the counties containing Wichita, Kansas City (Kansas), Kalamazoo, Grand Rapids, Jackson (Michigan), Duluth, Lorain (Ohio) and the Washington cities of Seattle, Spokane and Tacoma.

Regionally, there was a western tilt to the Roosevelt/Wilson crossover vote. All 18 Roosevelt counties in Nebraska supported Wilson, as did a majority in Idaho, Kansas, Montana, Utah and Washington.

Wilson won a big chunk of the Progressive Republican vote. Despite Theodore Roosevelt's endorsement by Hughes, Wilson carried 59 of the 109 counties that supported TR in 1912 and would later support La Follette.

Southern and border state Roosevelt supporters, on the other hand, were traditional Republicans, and Hughes carried 49 of the 54 Roosevelt counties (including all 18 in Tennessee) in that region.

Roosevelt supporters in the North and Great Lakes went solidly for Hughes (55 of 60 Michigan counties went back to the GOP).

A surprising development came in the loyal Taft counties: 26% of them defected to Wilson. Again, there was a western orientation to this unexpected shift. Wilson carried the majority of Taft counties in Colorado (all of them Hispanic), Idaho, Montana, Nebraska, Oklahoma, Oregon, Utah and Wyoming. All 20 Taft counties in Utah switched to Wilson.

But in the South and the border region, 52 of 57 Republican counties stayed with Hughes. So did all GOP counties in Illinois, New York, Pennsylvania, Rhode Island and Vermont.

In comparison to the 1912 vote, Wilson gained 7 percentage points. His vote percentage increased in every state but Florida and North Carolina. His support surged 26 points in Utah, 21 in Montana and Washington, 20 in Idaho and 18 in Colorado and Wyoming.

The Hughes share (46%) was 4 points less than the combined Taft-Roosevelt vote in 1912. His vote declined in the western states where Wilson gained, but Hughes also dropped 10 points in Massachusetts, 14 points in Michigan, 11 points in Minnesota, and 10 points in Vermont. In only 5 states did Hughes gain: 4 points in his home state of New York, 4 points in California, 1 point in North Carolina and in Wisconsin, and less than 1% in New Jersey.

While Wilson ran stronger in the cities than most previous Democrats, he still lost 51.5% to 48.5% to Hughes in the nation's metropolitan centers. Hughes carried Philadelphia by a 103,000 margin, Chicago by 56,000, Pittsburgh by 25,000 and Los Angeles by 21,000. Wilson carried New York City by 45,000, Boston by 19,000, San Francisco by 15,000 and Cleveland by 20,000.

Hughes won by 168,000 votes in metropolitan America, but Wilson won by 748,000, or 53 percent to 47%, in nonmetropolitan America. This urban/rural gap had persisted since the Civil War, with the GOP running a bit stronger in the centers of commerce. It was finally to be disrupted and reversed by the Al Smith Revolution of 1928 and even more by the Roosevelt Revolution that followed.

Metropolitan America was also growing, slowly, and 31.3% of the national vote in 1916 came in these counties. That trend would accelerate in the coming decades.

The Socialist candidate Allan Benson took 3% of the national vote (more than Ralph Nader 84 years later) and received a phenomenal 15% in Oklahoma and 9% in Nevada. The Socialist vote declined by half, probably because many Debs supporters from 1912 opted for Wilson, because of the "peace" issue and because Wilson's New Freedom domestic programs included many planks on Socialist platforms: direct election of U.S. senators, income tax, improvement of working conditions for the laboring classes, child labor prohibitions and other progressive and ameliorative measures.

The Socialist vote fell by half in 1916, with a 3% vote for Allen L. Benson, the Socialist nominee, who drowned before the election. In the 20 strongest Debs counties in 1912, where he averaged 32% of the vote, the Benson vote declined to 20%, still an impressive figure for a minor-party candidate. In these counties Wilson's vote rose from 42% to 53%, while Hughes's 27% was about the same as the combined Taft-Roosevelt vote in 1912. Thus, in the counties where Debs received his highest level of support, about 60% of Socialist voters stayed with their party and 40% voted for Wilson.

Every election has its quirks. Three Georgia counties (Fannin, Gilmer and Pickens) and 2 parishes in Louisiana (Iberia and Lafourche) voted for an independent Progressive slate linked to former president Theodore Roosevelt, even though Roosevelt was not a candidate and had endorsed Hughes. What made the behavior even more bizarre is that 4 of the 5 counties (all except Pickens) had voted for Wilson, not Roosevelt, in 1912.

TOP 10 STATES, 1916

Wilson	Percentage	Hughes	Percentage
1. South Carolina	96.7	1. Vermont	62.4
2. Mississippi	93.3	2. New Jersey	54.4
3. Louisiana	85.9	3. Iowa	54.3
4. Georgia	80.0	4. Pennsylvania	54.2
5. Texas	77.0	5. Illinois	52.6
6. Alabama	76.0	6. Michigan	52.2
7. Florida	69.3	7. Rhode Island	51.1
8. Virginia	66.8	8. Maine	51.0
9. Arkansas	66.6	9. New York	50.9
10. Colorado	60.7	10. Massachusetts	50.5

ELECTORAL VOTES, 1916

States	Electoral Votes	Wilson	Hughes	States	Electoral Votes	Wilson	Hughes
Alabama	12	12	-	Mississippi	10	10	-
Arizona	3	3	-	Missouri	18	18	-
Arkansas	9	9	-	Montana	4	4	-
California	13	13	-	Nebraska	8	8	-
Colorado	6	6	-	Nevada	3	3	-
Connecticut	7	-	7	New Hampshire	4	4	-
Delaware	3	-	3	New Jersey	14	-	14
Florida	6	6	-	New Mexico	3	3	-
Georgia	14	14	-	New York	45	-	45
Idaho	4	4	-	North Carolina	12	12	-
Illinois	29	-	29	North Dakota	5	5	-
Indiana	15	-	15	Ohio	24	24	-
Iowa	13	-	13	Oklahoma	10	10	-
Kansas	10	10	-	Oregon	5	-	5
Kentucky	13	13	-	Pennsylvania	38	-	38
Louisiana	10	10	-	Rhode Island	5	-	5
Maine	6	-	6	South Carolina	9	9	-
Maryland	8	8	-	South Dakota	5	-	5
Massachusetts	18	-	18	Tennessee	12	12	-
Michigan	15	-	15	Texas	20	20	-
Minnesota	12	-	12	Utah	4	4	-

States	Electoral Votes	Wilson	Hughes	States	Electoral Votes	Wilson	Hughes
Vermont	4	–	4	Wyoming	3	3	–
Virginia	12	12	–				
Washington	7	7	–	Totals	531	277	254
West Virginia[1]	8	1	7				
Wisconsin	13	–	13				

1. West Virginia divided its electoral votes by congressional district.

1920

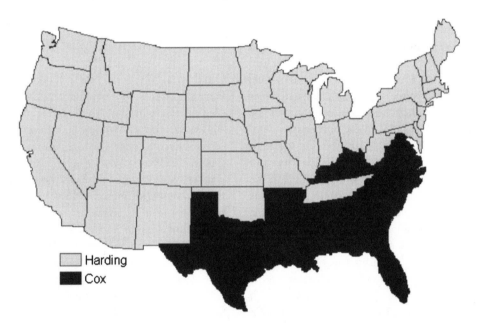

Harding
Cox

Republican senator Warren Harding of Ohio won a landslide in the first election in which women voted. The voters' disillusion with the aftermath of World War I, and a kind of exhaustion coupled with a right-wing backlash against immigration and religious minorities, fueled the Harding victory. But his triumph was so complete that he carried every non–southern state except Kentucky (which is culturally southern) and even cracked open the Solid South by carrying Tennessee. Tennessee had not gone Republican since 1868, and no southern state had voted Republican for president since 1876.

Harding carried 37 states with 404 electoral votes to Ohio Democratic governor James Cox's 11 states and 127 electoral votes. The popular vote was 60% to 34% (64% to 36% of the major party vote), the most one-sided election in history. The South stood alone, going for Cox 62% to 33%. His top 10 states were there.

Harding carried every northern and western state that had gone for Woodrow Wilson in 1916, fueled by a national 15 percentage point shift from Democrat to Republican, one of the highest levels of voter change from one election to the next in U.S. political history. The surge for Harding was especially pronounced in the upper Midwest, where 6 of his top 10 states were located, including North Dakota, which beat out Vermont for the most Republican state. (Michigan, Wisconsin, Iowa, Minnesota and Illinois were among Harding's strongest states.) Three New England states and New Jersey also made the Harding list.

Harding gained 32 percentage points in North Dakota, 25 points in Colorado, 25 points in Idaho, and 22 points in Wisconsin. He was the first Republican to carry Oklahoma.

There were 82 counties in 20 states that voted Republican for the first time in history, including 26 in Oklahoma, 13 in Illinois, 7 in Texas, 5 each in Indiana and Ohio, 4 in Tennessee, 3 each in Missouri and Pennsylvania, and 1 or 2 each in other states. (Of these counties, 33 were in the North and West, 31 in the border states and 18 in the South.) A number of German Catholic counties (Clinton, Illinois; and Mercer and Putnam in Ohio) bolted to the GOP, as did several German Protestant counties (Schoharie, New York; and Berks, Pennsylvania among them). Anger at U.S. involvement in World War I and the nativist aftermath caused the Democrats to lose counties that they had carried since the days of Andrew Jackson. (Palm Beach County, Florida; Behar County, Texas (San Antonio); and two Cajun parishes in southern Louisiana, Acadia and Vermilion, also defected to the Republicans.)

Two states resisted the Harding trend somewhat. North Carolina gave the GOP ticket only a 1.5% gain and Kentucky less than a 3% gain. In both states a handful of counties gave Cox a higher percentage of their votes than Wilson had received. Only two quirky counties in the entire nation switched from Hughes in 1916 to Cox in 1920: Polk, North Carolina; and Manistee, Michigan — the only Democratic county in Michigan.

Socialist Eugene Debs received almost a million votes, or 4% of the total in his last run for the White House. His strongest states were Wisconsin (11.5%), followed by Minnesota, New York, Nevada, California, Oklahoma, Oregon, North Dakota and Pennsylvania. Debs carried no counties, including the 4 he won in 1912. His banner county was Lake, Minnesota, where he received 31% of the presidential vote. His vote exceeded 20% in 3 Wisconsin counties (Milwaukee, Manitowoc and Marathon) and in Isanti County, Minnesota. His vote declined from 1912 in most states, except New York and Pennsylvania. He scored well in the Bronx (17%) and in Berks County, Pennsylvania (Reading), where he received 12%.

A Farmer-Labor candidate, Parley Christensen, took 1% nationally, and 19% in South Dakota and Washington, where many disgruntled farmers voted against the major parties.

TOP 10 STATES, 1920

Harding	Percentage	Cox	Percentage
1. North Dakota	77.8	1. South Carolina	96.1
2. Vermont	75.8	2. Mississippi	84.0
3. Michigan	72.8	3. Georgia	71.0
4. Wisconsin	71.1	4. Louisiana	69.2
5. Iowa	70.9	5. Alabama	66.7
6. Minnesota	70.6	6. Florida	62.1
7. Maine	68.9	7. Virginia	61.3
8. Massachusetts	68.5	8. Texas	59.2
9. Illinois	67.8	9. Arkansas	57.9
10. New Jersey	67.6	10. North Carolina	56.7

Electoral Votes, 1920

States	Electoral Votes	Harding	Cox	States	Electoral Votes	Harding	Cox
Alabama	12	–	12	Nevada	3	3	–
Arizona	3	3	–	New Hampshire	4	4	–
Arkansas	9	–	9	New Jersey	14	14	–
California	13	13	–	New Mexico	3	3	–
Colorado	6	6	–	New York	45	45	–
Connecticut	7	7	–	North Carolina	12	–	12
Delaware	3	3	–	North Dakota	5	5	–
Florida	6	–	6	Ohio	24	24	–
Georgia	14	–	14	Oklahoma	10	10	–
Idaho	4	4	–	Oregon	5	5	–
Illinois	29	29	–	Pennsylvania	38	38	–
Indiana	15	15	–	Rhode Island	5	5	–
Iowa	13	13	–	South Carolina	9	–	9
Kansas	10	10	–	South Dakota	5	5	–
Kentucky	13	–	13	Tennessee	12	12	–
Louisiana	10	–	10	Texas	20	–	20
Maine	6	6	–	Utah	4	4	–
Maryland	8	8	–	Vermont	4	4	–
Massachusetts	18	18	–	Virginia	12	–	12
Michigan	15	15	–	Washington	7	7	–
Minnesota	12	12	–	West Virginia	8	8	–
Mississippi	10	–	10	Wisconsin	13	13	–
Missouri	18	18	–	Wyoming	3	3	–
Montana	4	4	–				
Nebraska	8	8	–	Totals	531	404	127

1924

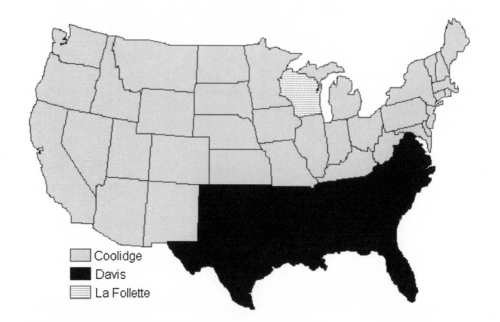

Coolidge
Davis
La Follette

The 1924 election was one of the more significant three-way battles in political history even though there was little doubt that President Calvin Coolidge would coast to reelection as he did 54% to 29% over Democrat John Davis. Davis was a compromise choice reached on the 103rd ballot of a bitterly contested Democratic convention that pitted rural versus urban America, with religious and cultural antagonisms coming to the fore. Neither the party's southern Prohibitionist and Bryanite wing nor its urban, progressive wing could agree on a candidate, so the party drafted a Wall Street lawyer from West Virginia who had served in Congress from 1911 to 1913. The failure of the Democratic convention to condemn the Ku Klux Klan, which had terrorized Catholic, Jewish, black and foreign-born Americans for a half decade and had captured state governments in many states, angered liberals and helped make possible the third-party candidacy of Wisconsin's legendary Progressive Republican Senator "Fighting Bob" La Follette.

Prosperity and the conservative temper of the times made Coolidge a shoo-in for reelection, though La Follette, who was on the ballot in every state except Louisiana, fought the president hard in the West.

Coolidge carried 35 states with 382 electoral votes to Davis's 12 states and 136 electoral votes. La Follette carried only Wisconsin and its 13 votes. Only a few states changed sides. Coolidge picked up Kentucky from the Democrats and Davis regained Oklahoma and Tennessee. Wisconsin switched from Harding to La Follette.

Davis was the weakest Democratic presidential candidate in history. The Democratic nominee carried no northern or western states and ran third in 12 of them.

The South moved against the national mood, going stronger for Davis (67% to 28%) than it had for Cox. Without the South and the border states, Davis would have had no electoral votes and a pitiful popular vote.

Because of the predictable outcome

and the choice of candidates, the voter turnout was low, barely 50% of the eligible electorate. But a surprising number of counties switched sides for an election with little drama or uncertainty.

La Follette's vote was Republican and midwestern, and all but 3 of the 223 counties he carried had gone for Harding in 1920. He carried counties in 15 western states, and all of his strongest states were in the West. A religious analysis based on the *1926 U.S. Census of Religious Bodies* shows that Catholics were 43.4% and Lutherans 33.7% of the population in the counties carried by the Wisconsin senator. Lutherans were the most overrepresented since they constituted only 9.6% of the national religious population at that time. La Follette carried 109 counties in 11 western states that had gone for Theodore Roosevelt in 1912, showing the Progressive Republican link between the two candidates. The Theodore Roosevelt/Robert La Follette counties were even more heavily Lutheran (42.0%), and 20% of the voters were of Norwegian ancestry (as was La Follette).

La Follette's strength was largely confined to rural and small-town areas. Outside of the Wisconsin cities he carried, he won only Sacramento and ran a close second to Coolidge in San Francisco and St. Paul. In the East he received a respectable vote in Cleveland and Pittsburgh.

There were 180 counties that switched from Harding to Davis: 86 in the South and 58 in the border states. There were 26 counties that switched from Cox to Coolidge, with 11 in the South and 6 in the border states. Thus, most of the major party interchanges came in the South.

As a taciturn New Englander, Coolidge's appeal was strongest in his native region, and all 6 New England states appear on his top 10, as well as Pennsylvania and New Jersey in the East. The La Follette vote kicked most of the 1920 Republican states off the Coolidge top 10, leaving only Michigan and Kansas there. Michigan was Coolidge's second-best state (after his birth state of Vermont).

Coolidge, despite a national decline of 6 percentage points, ran 3 points stronger than Harding in Maine and Michigan and 2 points in Vermont. But his vote plunged 34 points in Wisconsin and 30 points in volatile North Dakota.

Davis gained 14 points in Texas, picking up most of the 1920 third-party votes. He also recaptured Hudson County, New Jersey; made a modest gain in Boston; and made a strong gain in New York City, where he cut the Republican victory margin from 440,000 for Harding to 136,000 for Coolidge. (Davis was the only pro–League of Nations candidate, which may have helped him in some liberal Eastern cities. In the large metropolitan counties nationally, Coolidge won by 26 percentage points compared to Harding's 33-point edge.)

While Coolidge was one of the least charismatic presidential candidates, his candidacy was appealing in some areas. He was the first Republican candidate — not Lincoln or Teddy Roosevelt — to carry 16 counties in 5 states, 8 of them in Texas. He carried 3 in Kentucky, 3 in Ohio, and 1 in Indiana that had been Democratic since before the Civil War. He also carried Pinellas County, Florida.

Top 10 States, 1924

Coolidge	Percentage	Davis	Percentage	La Follette	Percentage
1. Vermont	78.2	1. South Carolina	96.6	1. Wisconsin	54.0
2. Michigan	75.4	2. Mississippi	89.4	2. North Dakota	45.2
3. Maine	72.0	3. Louisiana	76.4	3. Minnesota	41.3
4. Pennsylvania	65.3	4. Georgia	74.0	4. Montana	37.9
5. Massachusetts	62.3	5. Texas	73.6	5. South Dakota	37.0
6. New Jersey	62.2	6. Alabama	68.8	6. Idaho	36.5
7. Connecticut	61.5	7. Virginia	62.5	7. Nevada	36.3
8. Kansas	61.5	8. Arkansas	61.2	8. Washington	35.8
9. New Hampshire	59.8	9. North Carolina	59.0	9. California	33.1
10. Rhode Island	59.6	10. Florida	56.9	10. Wyoming	31.5

Electoral Votes, 1924

States	Electoral Votes	Coolidge	Davis	La Follette
Alabama	12	–	12	–
Arizona	3	3	–	–
Arkansas	9	–	9	–
California	13	13	–	–
Colorado	6	6	–	–
Connecticut	7	7	–	–
Delaware	3	3	–	–
Florida	6	–	6	–
Georgia	14	–	14	–
Idaho	4	4	–	–
Illinois	29	29	–	–
Indiana	15	15	–	–
Iowa	13	13	–	–
Kansas	10	10	–	–
Kentucky	13	13	–	–
Louisiana	10	–	10	–
Maine	6	6	–	–
Maryland	8	8	–	–
Massachusetts	18	18	–	–
Michigan	15	15	–	–
Minnesota	12	12	–	–
Mississippi	10	–	10	–
Missouri	18	18	–	–
Montana	4	4	–	–
Nebraska	8	8	–	–
Nevada	3	3	–	–
New Hampshire	4	4	–	–
New Jersey	14	14	–	–
New Mexico	3	3	–	–
New York	45	45	–	–

States	Electoral Votes	Coolidge	Davis	La Follette
North Carolina	12	-	12	-
North Dakota	5	5	-	-
Ohio	24	24	-	-
Oklahoma	10	-	10	-
Oregon	5	5	-	-
Pennsylvania	38	38	-	-
Rhode Island	5	5	-	-
South Carolina	9	-	9	-
South Dakota	5	5	-	-
Tennessee	12	-	12	-
Texas	20	-	20	-
Utah	4	4	-	-
Vermont	4	4	-	-
Virginia	12	-	12	-
Washington	7	7	-	-
West Virginia	8	8	-	-
Wisconsin	13	-	-	13
Wyoming	3	3	-	-
Totals	531	382	136	13

1928

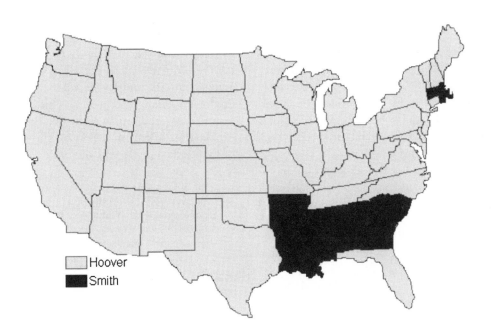

Hoover
Smith

The 1928 election is notable for many things. It was the first election in which a Roman Catholic, New York governor Alfred E. Smith, was nominated by a major party for the highest office in the land. His nomination brought forth some of the worst bigotry and hysteria in U.S. political history, causing a major disruption to traditional voting patterns, especially among southern Protestants and rural voters everywhere. Of course, the Prohibition issue, prosperity, and the cultural clash between urban and rural value systems affected the outcome of the vote. The Republican winner was Herbert Hoover, who had never held electoral office but had served in Republican cabinets during the 1920s.

A hard-fought, dramatic and exciting election brought 36.8 million voters to the polls, an increase of 7.7 million, or 26%, over 1924. Hoover carried 40 states and won an overwhelming 444 electoral votes. Smith carried 8 states with 87 electoral votes. The Hoover landslide was helped by the defection of 5 southern states (Florida, North Carolina, Tennessee, Texas and Virginia) to the Republican ticket. Hoover was the first Republican victor in history in Texas, the first since 1872 to win North Carolina and Virginia and the first since 1876 to carry Florida. The Hoover top 10 were a crazy quilt of geographic disparities: Maine and Vermont in upper New England; Kansas, Michigan, and Colorado in the interior; Washington and California on the coast; and Delaware, Pennsylvania and Ohio. No other GOP candidate had fashioned such an odd coalition. Only 3 of Hoover's top 10 states were on Harding's top 10 list, and 5 were on the Coolidge list. Smith's top 10 included 7 southern states, plus his unusual triumphs in Massachusetts and Rhode Island and his home state of New York, where he was narrowly defeated.

Only two states moved in the opposite direction: Massachusetts and Rhode Island, the nation's most heavily Catholic states.

The Smith victory in those two lower New England states was the second for a Democrat, and the first for a Democrat in a two-way race (Wilson won them in 1912). Smith still held on in Dixie, winning 64 electoral votes to Hoover's 62, and winning 51% to 49% of the popular vote. It was the worst Democratic showing in the South since Reconstruction. Smith's victories were concentrated in the Deep South states where Democratic loyalties were unshakable.

Smith's near-record low electoral vote count (only the 1872 Democratic total was lower) does not reflect some bright spots in his support. The New York governor received 41% of the vote compared to Hoover's 58%. This was an increase of 12 percentage points over the Davis vote in 1924 and 7 points better than Cox's 1920 vote. It did not compare to the Wilson and Bryan support levels because of rural defections, but the geographic base of the Smith vote led to the Roosevelt victories of the future. For one thing, Smith was the first Democrat to win a majority (51%) of the vote in the nation's dozen largest cities, an achievement that eluded Woodrow Wilson and Grover Cleveland (both were two-term Democratic presidents). Smith received the highest vote ever given to a Democrat among Catholic and Jewish voters, though the lowest among Protestants. This is why historian Alan Lichtman wrote that the best explanation among all factors for the shape of the 1928 vote was religious affiliation.

> Of all possible explanations for the distinctive political alignments of 1928, religion is the best. A bitter conflict between Catholics and Protestants emerged in the presidential election of 1928: religious considerations preoccupied the public, commanded the attention of political leaders, and sharply skewed the behavior of voters. Regardless of their ethnic background, their stand on prohibition, their economic status, and other politically salient attributes, Catholics and Protestants split far more decisively in 1928 than in either pre-

vious or subsequent elections. No other division of the electorate stands out so distinctively in that presidential year. This cleft between Catholics and Protestants was not confined to particular regions of the nation, to either city or country, to either church members or nominal Protestants. Both Protestants and Catholics responded to the religious tensions in 1928.*

Hundreds of counties switched parties between 1924 and 1928, particularly in the 6 states that defected from Davis to Hoover. Hoover carried 515 counties that had gone for Davis. Only 49 were outside the South. The northern defectors were 77% Protestant and 23% Catholic, according to the *1926 Census of U.S. Religious Bodies.* In the South the 466 Hoover/Davis counties were 95% Protestant. These 515 anti–Smith counties were distributed in 24 states.

Smith carried 71 counties that had supported Coolidge in 1924. In these counties nearly 54% of the religious population was Catholic. Included in the Coolidge-Smith swing counties were counties containing such cities as San Francisco, New Haven, Boston, New York, St. Paul, St. Louis, Albany, Providence and Scranton.

The vote in the counties carried by La Follette was largely shaped by religion. In the 179 counties that shifted from La Follette to Hoover, only 33.7% of the residents were Catholic. In the 44 counties that shifted from La Follette to Smith, 58.5% were Catholic. But the La Follette counties had always been Republican. Less than 10% of the vote went to Davis. Those who did not support La Follette were for Coolidge. An extrapolation of the data shows that 61% of La Follette supporters in these 223 counties voted for Smith. (While La Follette had

died in 1925, his family endorsed Smith.) Four years later voters in these counties would switch en masse to the Democrats.

Another proof of the connection between religion and the vote was the fact that 86% of voters in the 215 counties that gave 80% or more of their votes to Hoover were Protestants, far above the national Protestant percentage of the U.S. population. Hoover also carried 2,172 counties to Smith's 912.

In this extraordinary election, 809 counties voted for a party different from the one they had supported 4 years before. In that respect 1928 was a precursor for the great upheaval of 1932.

RELIGIOUS AFFILIATION AND THE 1928 SWING VOTE IN COUNTIES		
Candidates Supported	*% Protestant*	*% Catholic*
Hoover-Davis (North)	76.7	23.3
Hoover-Davis (South)	95.0	5.0
Coolidge-Smith	46.3	53.7
La Follette–Smith	41.5	58.5
La Follette–Hoover	66.3	33.7

The realignment (temporary as it proved to be) of 1928 caused 246 counties to cast their first Republican majority votes for president. These counties were located in 20 states. Of the 246 counties, 183 were in the South, 42 in the border states, and 21 in the North and West. Texas was the location for 107 of these counties, followed by 29 in Virginia, 21 in Kentucky, 19 in Florida, 13 in Oklahoma, 9 in Arkansas and 7 in New Mexico and North Carolina. In Pennsylvania three rock-ribbed Democratic rural counties — Columbia, Greene and Monroe — broke a century of loyalty to the party of Jefferson and Jackson and defected to Hoover. In the South, counties that in-

*Allan J. Lichtman *Prejudice and the Old Politics: The Presidential Election of 1928* (Chapel Hill: The University of North Carolina Press, 1979), p. 231.

cluded Birmingham, Tampa, Orlando, Durham, Charlotte, Nashville, Dallas, Fort Worth, Roanoke, Newport News, Norfolk and Richmond cast their first-ever Republican presidential majority votes.

There were 12 counties where Smith was the first-ever Democratic winner, including 5 in North Dakota and 3 in South Dakota. (Interestingly, 4 of these counties were German Lutheran farm counties.) Lackawanna, Pennsylvania (Scranton); Bristol, Rhode Island; Chittenden, Vermont; and Iron, Wisconsin were the others.

Smith was the first Democrat to carry Berkshire and Bristol Counties in Massachusetts since 1844. He was the first Dem-

ocratic standard bearer to carry Franklin County, New York, since 1856 and Clinton County, New York, since 1864. (Both are French ancestry areas.) Smith was also the first Democrat since Grover Cleveland in 1892 to carry Albany, New York (where he was well known and respected as governor); Elk and Luzerne counties in Pennsylvania (both with heavily Catholic populations); and Audubon and Plymouth counties in Iowa, where Danish and German voters predominated.

In states where the religious issue was most intense, voter turnout swelled, increasing almost 50% in Pennsylvania, where a million new voters showed up at the polls.

TOP 10 STATES, 1928

Hoover	Percentage	Smith	Percentage
1. Kansas	72.0	1. South Carolina	91.4
2. Michigan	70.4	2. Mississippi	82.2
3. Maine	68.6	3. Louisiana	76.3
4. Washington	67.1	4. Arkansas	60.3
5. Vermont	66.9	5. Georgia	56.0
6. Delaware	65.8	6. Alabama	51.3
7. Pennsylvania	65.2	7. Massachusetts	50.2
8. Ohio	64.9	8. Rhode Island	50.2
9. California	64.7	9. Texas	48.0
10. Colorado	64.7	10. New York	47.4

ELECTORAL VOTES, 1928

States	Electoral Votes	Hoover	Smith	States	Electoral Votes	Hoover	Smith
Alabama	12	–	12	Iowa	13	13	–
Arizona	3	3	–	Kansas	10	10	–
Arkansas	9	–	9	Kentucky	13	13	–
California	13	13	–	Louisiana	10	–	10
Colorado	6	6	–	Maine	6	6	–
Connecticut	7	7	–	Maryland	8	8	–
Delaware	3	3	–	Massachusetts	18	–	18
Florida	6	6	–	Michigan	15	15	–
Georgia	14	–	14	Minnesota	12	12	–
Idaho	4	4	–	Mississippi	10	–	10
Illinois	29	29	–	Missouri	18	18	–
Indiana	15	15	–	Montana	4	4	–

States	Electoral Votes	Hoover	Smith	States	Electoral Votes	Hoover	Smith
Nebraska	8	8	–	South Carolina	9	–	9
Nevada	3	3	–	South Dakota	5	5	–
New Hampshire	4	4	–	Tennessee	12	12	–
New Jersey	14	14	–	Texas	20	20	–
New Mexico	3	3	–	Utah	4	4	–
New York	45	45	–	Vermont	4	4	–
North Carolina	12	12	–	Virginia	12	12	–
North Dakota	5	5	–	Washington	7	7	–
Ohio	24	24	–	West Virginia	8	8	–
Oklahoma	10	10	–	Wisconsin	13	13	–
Oregon	5	5	–	Wyoming	3	3	–
Pennsylvania	38	38	–				
Rhode Island	5	–	5	Totals	531	444	87

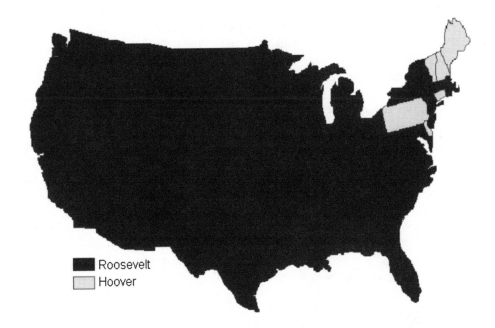

■ Roosevelt
☐ Hoover

New York governor Franklin D. Roosevelt (FDR) won the first of four historic landslides in this Depression year when he ousted GOP president Herbert Hoover by almost the same margin by which Hoover had been elected in 1928. FDR's major-party vote majority was 59% to 41%, the same as Hoover over Smith. This repre-sented an 18% national "swing" against the party in power, one of the highest voter swings in U.S. history. The New York governor who promised a "New Deal" for the American people carried 42 states and won 472 electoral votes. President Hoover carried 6 states and won 59 electoral votes. Hoover was reduced to the support of 4

New England states and tiny Delaware. He also carried Pennsylvania, the second-largest state at that time, which was still dominated by a legendary Republican political machine.

Roosevelt's strongest states were in the South, where a combination of historical memory and Depression misery gave him such an overwhelming dominance that 4 states (South Carolina, Mississippi, Louisiana and Georgia) recorded more than 90% of their ballots for the Roosevelt-Garner ticket.

But a major factor in the "Democratic sweep" was the revolt in farm states... the Midwest, Plains region and the Rocky Mountain region, where FDR carried almost all of the counties that had supported Hoover. (FDR carried all 109 counties that voted for both Theodore Roosevelt in 1912 and La Follette in 1924, shattering the Progressive Republican base.) Scores of counties went Democratic for the first time in history, including many in the Scandinavian farm belt that had not supported Bryan, Cleveland or Wilson. In Minnesota, for example, 35 counties went Democratic for the first time. Both Minnesota and Michigan voted Democratic for the first time since 1852. FDR broke through a hard core of traditional Republican support, becoming the first Democrat to carry 158 counties in 19 states. Of them, 149 were in the North and West and 9 in the border region. Minnesota (35 counties), Iowa (26), South Dakota (19), Wisconsin (18), and Michigan (10) were the states with the most counties voting Democratic for the first time. There were also 9 counties in North Dakota, 8 in New Mexico, 7 in Oklahoma, 6 in Washington, 5 in Illinois, 3 each in California and Indiana, 2 each in Kansas and Wyoming and 1 each in Kentucky, Missouri, Nebraska, Ohio and Pennsylvania. Longtime Republican bastions (including Orange County, California, and Allegheny County, Pennsylvania [Pittsburgh] fell to the man from Dutchess County, New York,

which, however, voted Republican as it always did. FDR was also the first Democrat since the Civil War to carry 56 counties in 15 states. He was the first Democrat to carry Genesee County in Michigan and Franklin County in Vermont since 1836.

FDR's gains in many states were astounding and unprecedented. His popular-vote percentage increased 40 points in Texas, 38 points in Oklahoma, 36 points in Georgia and 34 points in Florida. The anti-Smith Democrats returned to their party in droves.

New England was the only region where the vote did not change greatly from 1928, particularly in Massachusetts and Connecticut. And Hoover did manage to carry 15 of the nation's 106 largest cities, including Philadelphia, Hartford, and Des Moines. Hoover had little to cheer about. He managed to carry a few of the old-line cities and held FDR's popular vote gains to less than 10% in the 21 largest cities, where FDR's 59% was only a 6-point gain over Smith's 53%. Hoover carried 55 counties that had gone for Wilson in 1916, including the cities of Colorado Springs, Hartford, New Haven, Kalamazoo, Grand Rapids, Columbus, Lincoln, Youngstown and Canton. The most prosperous areas were far less anti-Hoover than rural and small-town America. But the president carried only 372 counties out of 3,093, the lowest number ever carried by a major-party candidate (except for Taft in the multiparty battle of 1912). Not one county shifted from Smith in 1928 to Hoover in 1932 (though Hoover gained 7 points in Elk County, Pennsylvania), while 1,791 counties switched from Hoover in 1928 to FDR in 1932.

The total vote increased from 36.8 million to 39.7 million, or about 8%. The increases were greatest in the western states (up 25% in California), but turnout declined in Pennsylvania by 300,000 (nearly 10%), and in Maryland, Virginia and Mississippi.

Norman Thomas, the Socialist candidate, received nearly 3% of the national vote (FDR had 57.4% and Hoover, 39.6% of all voters). Thomas did best in Washington, Oregon, Wisconsin and Montana. He was on the ballot in 46 states (all except, ironi-cally, the old Socialist strongholds of Oklahoma and Nevada). He received 20% of the vote in Berks County, Pennsylvania, where his running mate, labor leader James H. Mauerer, resided.

Top 10 States, 1932

Roosevelt	Percentage	Hoover	Percentage	Thomas	Percentage
1. South Carolina	98.0	1. Vermont	57.7	1. Wisconsin	4.8
2. Mississippi	96.0	2. Maine	55.8	2. Oregon	4.2
3. Louisiana	92.8	3. Pennsylvania	50.8	3. New York	3.8
4. Georgia	91.6	4. Delaware	50.6	4. Montana	3.6
5. Texas	88.2	5. New Hampshire	50.4	5. Connecticut	3.4
6. Arkansas	86.3	6. Connecticut	48.5	6. Pennsylvania	3.2
7. Alabama	84.8	7. New Jersey	47.6	7. Colorado	3.0
8. Florida	74.5	8. Ohio	47.0	8. Wyoming	2.9
9. Oklahoma	73.3	9. Massachusetts	46.6	9. California	2.9
10. North Carolina	69.9	10. West Virginia	44.5	10. Washington	2.8

Electoral Votes, 1932

States	Electoral Votes	Roosevelt	Hoover	States	Electoral Votes	Roosevelt	Hoover
Alabama	11	11	–	Missouri	15	15	–
Arizona	3	3	–	Montana	4	4	–
Arkansas	9	9	–	Nebraska	7	7	–
California	22	22	–	Nevada	3	3	–
Colorado	6	6	–	New Hampshire	4	–	4
Connecticut	8	–	8	New Jersey	16	16	–
Delaware	3	–	3	New Mexico	3	3	–
Florida	7	7	–	New York	47	47	–
Georgia	12	12	–	North Carolina	13	13	–
Idaho	4	4	–	North Dakota	4	4	–
Illinois	29	29	–	Ohio	26	26	–
Indiana	14	14	–	Oklahoma	11	11	–
Iowa	11	11	–	Oregon	5	5	–
Kansas	9	9	–	Pennsylvania	36	–	36
Kentucky	11	11	–	Rhode Island	4	4	–
Louisiana	10	10	–	South Carolina	8	8	–
Maine	5	–	5	South Dakota	4	4	–
Maryland	8	8	–	Tennessee	11	11	–
Massachusetts	17	17	–	Texas	23	23	–
Michigan	19	19	–	Utah	4	4	–
Minnesota	11	11	–	Vermont	3	–	3
Mississippi	9	9	–	Virginia	11	11	–

States	Electoral Votes	Roosevelt	Hoover	States	Electoral Votes	Roosevelt	Hoover
Washington	8	8	–	Wyoming	3	3	–
West Virginia	8	8	–				
Wisconsin	12	12	–	Totals	531	472	59

1936

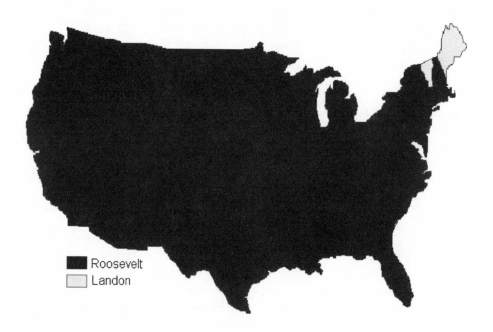

■ Roosevelt
□ Landon

President Roosevelt won one of the greatest landslides in election history, winning reelection to a second term. Receiving 61% of the votes compared to 37% for Kansas governor Alf Landon, FDR carried 46 states with 523 electoral votes to Landon's 2 states (Maine and Vermont) with 8 electoral votes. Roosevelt added nearly 5 million new votes to his totals, while Landon picked up 1 million. The total votes cast increased 15% over 1932. Roosevelt's triumph included victories in many of the Hoover counties in New Jersey and Michigan. In a sort of delayed reaction, Pennsylvania flocked to FDR's banner, giving him more than 1 million new votes and 57% support. Roosevelt's victory in Pennsylva-nia was the first for a Democrat since Pennsylvanian James Buchanan won there in 1856.

FDR's victory was very much an urban one. He carried 104 of the 106 largest cities and won 14 of the 15 that had gone for Hoover. Philadelphia went Democratic for the first time since 1856. Only Pasadena, California, a prosperous WASP enclave, opposed FDR every time he ran, and Syracuse, New York, was the only large city to switch from FDR to Landon.

But hidden in the landslide was a small countertrend. Landon carried 203 counties that had gone for Roosevelt, indicating some rural displeasure with the Roosevelt administration. Landon gained 8 percentage points in South Dakota, 5 points in Nebraska and 3 points each in Missouri and Iowa, with his gains concentrated in rural areas. Most of the counties that shifted to Landon were strongholds of the evangelical Protestant tradition — Methodists especially, but also populated by Baptists, Congregationalists, Presbyterians and Disciples of Christ, according to the *1936 U.S. Census of Religious Bodies*. The pro–Landon counties were 78% Protestant and disproportionately Methodist, especially in Iowa and Ohio. (Roosevelt favored the repeal of Prohibition, which Landon did not; this may have been a possible factor.)

But FDR won landslides among the Catholic, Jewish, and even African American communities. (African Americans switched to FDR, voting Democratic for the first time by a 2–1 margin, after having supported Hoover 2–1 in both 1932 and 1928.)

Roosevelt's top 10 states were mostly in the South, though Nevada came in tenth. (South Carolina gave FDR 98.6% of its vote.) Roosevelt gained 13 percentage points in Utah, 12 points in Pennsylvania, 10 points each in New Jersey and Montana and 9 points in Washington.

Landon's strongest states (such as they were) were the 3 upper New England states; Massachusetts, Delaware and Pennsylvania in the East; and four Midwestern states (Kansas, Iowa, South Dakota, Indiana).

Roosevelt continued to add to the Democratic breakthroughs. He was the first Democrat to carry 26 counties in 15 states: 5 of these counties were in Michigan, 4 in Ohio and 3 in Massachusetts. Included were some fairly large population counties: Riverside, California; Delaware, Indiana; Black Hawk, Iowa; Worcester, Massachusetts; and Monroe, New York. (The cities of Muncie, Indiana; Cedar Falls, Iowa; and Rochester, New York, were in these counties.) Newport, Rhode Island, a faithful Whig and Republican stronghold for a century, went for FDR, as did Anderson County, Tennessee,

in the eastern part of the state. (Anderson was the headquarters of the newly formed Tennessee Valley Authority and the site of Oak Ridge.) FDR carried 137 of the 158 counties that had defected to the Democrats for the first time in 1932, a strong indication that the Roosevelt realignment had held in the second election.

FDR completely dominated metropolitan America. Of the roughly 200 metropolitan counties, only 24 backed Landon. The Kansas governor carried the Philadelphia suburbs; Long Island; the Hudson River Valley of New York; some New York City, Chicago, and Boston suburbs; many upstate New York metro areas (Niagara, Broome, Chautauqua, Oneida and Rensselear counties); and the old faithful of Lancaster County, Pennsylvania.

Landon did well only in the prosperity belt of the suburban Northeast, where the *Literary Digest* had predicted a nationwide sweep for Landon. (That grotesque error, based on a flawed methodology of only surveying voters who had telephones, caused the eminent journal to go out of business.) Landon had the overwhelming support of newspapers and was endorsed by the two previous Democratic presidential nominees, John Davis and Al Smith, but his campaign failed to resonate with the American people in the pivotal 1936 election.

A third-party candidate, William Lemke of North Dakota, running on the extreme right-wing Union Party ticket, was initially expected to be a major player. He was backed by the influential radio priest, Father Charles Coughlin, and other apostles of discontent. But he received just 2% of the national vote and failed to be a factor anywhere. His vote, however, came from Roosevelt's 1932 coalition, not from Republicans. Lemke did manage to garner 13% in his home state, North Dakota, and 30% in Burke County, which was long sympathetic to minor-party candidates, having supported Socialist Eugene Debs in 1912.

Lemke also received more than 5% in Minnesota, Rhode Island, Wisconsin, Michigan, and Massachusetts (the last state was home to his running mate, Thomas O'Brien). Lemke's vote was concentrated in German Catholic and Scandinavian Lutheran areas.

TOP 10 STATES, 1936

Roosevelt	Percentage	Landon	Percentage	Lemke	Percentage
1. South Carolina	98.6	1. Vermont	56.4	1. North Dakota	13.4
2. Mississippi	97.0	2. Maine	55.5	2. Minnesota	6.6
3. Louisiana	88.8	3. New Hampshire	48.0	3. Massachusetts	6.4
4. Georgia	87.1	4. Kansas	46.0	4. Rhode Island	6.3
5. Texas	87.1	5. Delaware	44.9	5. Oregon	5.3
6. Alabama	86.4	6. Iowa	42.7	6. Wisconsin	4.8
7. Arkansas	81.8	7. South Dakota	42.5	7. Ohio	4.4
8. Florida	76.1	8. Indiana	41.9	8. Michigan	4.2
9. North Carolina	73.4	9. Massachusetts	41.8	9. Idaho	3.8
10. Nevada	72.8	10. Pennsylvania	40.8	10. South Dakota	3.5

ELECTORAL VOTES, 1936

States	Electoral Votes	Roosevelt	Landon	States	Electoral Votes	Roosevelt	Landon
Alabama	11	11	–	Nevada	3	3	–
Arizona	3	3	–	New Hampshire	4	4	–
Arkansas	9	9	–	New Jersey	16	16	–
California	22	22	–	New Mexico	3	3	–
Colorado	6	6	–	New York	47	47	–
Connecticut	8	8	–	North Carolina	13	13	–
Delaware	3	3	–	North Dakota	4	4	–
Florida	7	7	–	Ohio	26	26	–
Georgia	12	12	–	Oklahoma	11	11	–
Idaho	4	4	–	Oregon	5	5	–
Illinois	29	29	–	Pennsylvania	36	36	–
Indiana	14	14	–	Rhode Island	4	4	–
Iowa	11	11	–	South Carolina	8	8	–
Kansas	9	9	–	South Dakota	4	4	–
Kentucky	11	11	–	Tennessee	11	11	–
Louisiana	10	10	–	Texas	23	23	–
Maine	5	–	5	Utah	4	4	–
Maryland	8	8	–	Vermont	3	–	3
Massachusetts	17	17	–	Virginia	11	11	–
Michigan	19	19	–	Washington	8	8	–
Minnesota	11	11	–	West Virginia	8	8	–
Mississippi	9	9	–	Wisconsin	12	12	–
Missouri	15	15	–	Wyoming	3	3	–
Montana	4	4	–				
Nebraska	7	7	–	Totals	531	523	8

1940

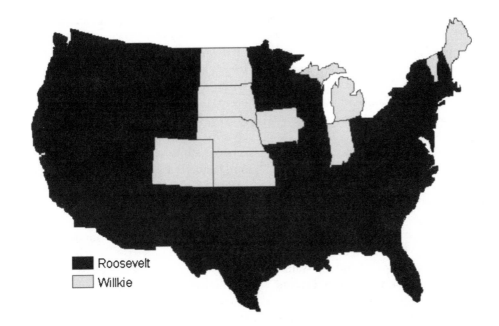

■ Roosevelt
□ Willkie

FDR's successful third-term bid was accomplished by a solid 55% to 45% popular vote margin and an electoral vote sweep of 449 to 82. FDR won 38 states, while 10 voted for Wendell Willkie, "the barefoot lawyer from Wall Street," whose partisans packed the Republican Convention in Philadelphia and may have swayed delegates into nominating a man who had never held public office.

Roosevelt repeated his southern, western, and big-state dominance. Willkie carried Michigan, his one large state victory, and Indiana, his home state, as well as Colorado, Iowa, Kansas, Nebraska, and the Dakotas, showing a breakthrough into the Midwest. Willkie carried Maine and Vermont as usual but failed to win Connecticut, New Hampshire, Delaware, and Pennsylvania — all Hoover states from 1932.

Ethnicity affected the 1940 vote more than in perhaps any election in the twentieth century. German-Americans were furious with FDR's foreign policy, which they saw as inevitably leading to another war with their ancestral homeland, and the majority of the 697 counties that switched to Willkie were predominantly German. For example, Willkie received 92% of the ballots cast in McIntosh County, North Dakota; 87% in Gillespie County, Texas; and 81% in Campbell County, South Dakota: three counties where voters were almost entirely of German ancestry.

But there was also a smaller, pro–Roosevelt trend among voters of English ancestry, who approved of the president's foreign policy of quiet support to the Allies. FDR ran ahead of his 1936 vote in the predominantly English-ancestry counties in Maine, Maryland, Kentucky, Virginia, Tennessee and North Carolina, and 13 counties switched from Landon to Roosevelt. (FDR gained 6% in Maine and nearly carried the state.) Franco-Americans in New England and Louisiana were also more pro–FDR in 1940 than in 1936, and Assumption Parish, Louisiana, shifted from Landon to Roosevelt.

Among the English-descent voters in Tennessee, FDR carried 3 counties (Mc-Minn, Morgan, and Roane) that he had lost in 1936. In White County, his vote rose from 58% to 77%.

The one exception that proves the rule is Wisconsin, the state with the highest population of German-Americans, which narrowly backed FDR because of his huge margin among voters of Scandinavian, English, and Polish descent.

FDR's strongest states were in the South, while Willkie's centers of strength were almost all in the Midwest and West (only Vermont and Maine in the East remained in Willkie's top 10). South Dakota was Willkie's number one state — a first for that state.

FDR won 55% to 45%, down from his 61% to 37% sweep over Landon. Willkie made his biggest gain in North Dakota, where he more than doubled Landon's percentage of the vote, increasing 29 percentage points. He gained 15 to 18 points in Nebraska, Oregon, South Dakota and Wisconsin, and 10 to 14 points in Colorado, Kansas, Michigan, Montana, Nevada, Ohio, and Washington. Roosevelt improved on his 1936 showing in Maine, Vermont, New Hampshire and North Carolina.

There were 3 unusual breakthrough counties. FDR was the first Democrat to carry Kennebec County, Maine, and Roane County, Tennessee, where support for the Allied cause in Europe may have been a major factor. Willkie was the first Republican to carry Franklin County, Indiana, by a 58% to 42% margin. Franklin County, however, was not his home county. Willkie grew up in Ellwood* in Madison County, which voted for Roosevelt. (Willkie carried FDR's home county of Dutchess in New York.)

FDR was also the first Democratic winner since 1836 in Essex County, Vermont; since 1856 in Morgan County, Tennessee; and since 1880 in Calvert County, Maryland.

Support for FDR was unshakable in the nation's 106 largest cities. He carried 97 of them, while only 9 went for Willkie, fewer than the number Hoover carried in 1932. Willkie edged FDR in German-oriented Cincinnati and in the cities of Fort Wayne, Indianapolis and Tulsa, which had gone for FDR twice. Willkie gained 20 percentage points in the oil city of Tulsa (where no Democrat has won since 1936). Willkie gained 18 points in Fort Wayne, Indiana's most heavily German-settled city.

Roosevelt carried most metropolitan counties, but Willkie made impressive gains of 19 points in Queens County, New York, where voters were mostly of German, Italian or Irish ancestry; nearly 19 points in heavily German Milwaukee; and 17 points in substantially Italian Staten Island (Richmond County, New York). But Willkie also gained in liberal San Francisco, St. Paul and St. Louis. His vote share increased 10 percentage points or more in 29 large counties in the North and West (including Spokane, Washington; and Portland, Oregon). (In the metro areas, FDR gained in Portland, Maine; and Manchester, New Hampshire.)

Willkie was successful in regaining many of the Republican counties that defected to FDR in 1932, carrying 100 of the 158 counties. But FDR did better in the 26 counties that voted Democratic for the first time in 1936. He carried 15 of them to Willkie's 11.

One of the ironies of the 1940 election is that Wendell Willkie, a firm internationalist and later author of the book *One World* (1944), received the overwhelming support of the nation's isolationist voters and "America Firsters" who saw no vital U.S. interest in the outcome of the war in Europe.

---

*Willkie kicked off his campaign before a gigantic crowd in Ellwood on August 17, 1940.

Top 10 States, 1940

Roosevelt	Percentage		Willkie	Percentage
1. Mississippi	95.7		1. South Dakota	57.4
2. South Carolina	95.6		2. Nebraska	57.2
3. Louisiana	85.9		3. Kansas	56.9
4. Alabama	85.2		4. North Dakota	55.1
5. Georgia	84.8		5. Vermont	54.8
6. Texas	80.9		6. Iowa	52.0
7. Arkansas	78.4		7. Maine	51.1
8. Florida	74.0		8. Colorado	50.9
9. North Carolina	74.0		9. Indiana	50.5
10. Virginia	68.1		10. Michigan	49.9

Electoral Votes, 1940

States	Electoral Votes	Roosevelt	Willkie	States	Electoral Votes	Roosevelt	Willkie
Alabama	11	11	–	Nevada	3	3	–
Arizona	3	3	–	New Hampshire	4	4	–
Arkansas	9	9	–	New Jersey	16	16	–
California	22	22	–	New Mexico	3	3	–
Colorado	6	–	6	New York	47	47	–
Connecticut	8	8	–	North Carolina	13	13	–
Delaware	3	3	–	North Dakota	4	–	4
Florida	7	7	–	Ohio	26	26	–
Georgia	12	12	–	Oklahoma	11	11	–
Idaho	4	4	–	Oregon	5	5	–
Illinois	29	29	–	Pennsylvania	36	36	–
Indiana	14	–	14	Rhode Island	4	4	–
Iowa	11	–	11	South Carolina	8	8	–
Kansas	9	–	9	South Dakota	4	–	4
Kentucky	11	11	–	Tennessee	11	11	–
Louisiana	10	10	–	Texas	23	23	–
Maine	5	–	5	Utah	4	4	–
Maryland	8	8	–	Vermont	3	–	3
Massachusetts	17	17	–	Virginia	11	11	–
Michigan	19	–	19	Washington	8	8	–
Minnesota	11	11	–	West Virginia	8	8	–
Mississippi	9	9	–	Wisconsin	12	12	–
Missouri	15	15	–	Wyoming	3	3	–
Montana	4	4	–				
Nebraska	7	–	7	Totals	531	449	82

1944

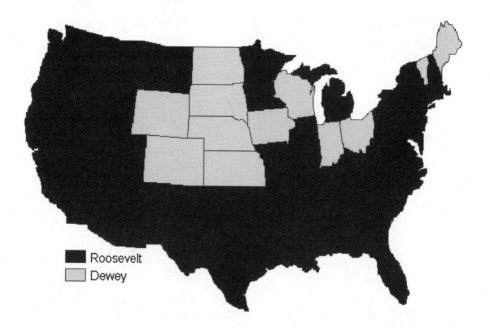

FDR's "Last Hurrah" campaign was unusual in a couple of respects. For one thing, the total vote went down, from 50 million to 48 million, for the first time in a presidential contest since 1904. This was probably due to the fact that this was a wartime election, with disruptions to civilian life. There was also less of a shift in voter preference (FDR won 54% to 46%, a decline of only 1 point), and fewer counties changed sides than in any twentieth-century election. Most people had decided whether they liked FDR or not after 12 years in office, and there was little desire to change presidents in the middle of World War II.

FDR won 36 states and 432 electoral votes, to 12 states and 99 electoral votes for his opponent, New York governor Thomas E. Dewey. Dewey captured three 1940 Roosevelt states: Wisconsin, Wyoming and Ohio, the latter being the home of his running mate, Governor John Bricker. But Michigan switched back to FDR from Willkie. Michigan was one of the few states

where the total vote increased (about 6%). Other states that experienced a voter increase were California, Connecticut, Georgia, Virginia, New Hampshire and Washington. Six other states had a very slight increase in their total votes.

In 35 states the total vote declined, and in 14 states it fell 10 points or more. Voter turnout plunged 21 percentage points in North Dakota, 20 points in South Dakota and over 15 points each in Alabama, Kansas, Missouri, Montana, New Mexico and West Virginia.

FDR's top 10 states were all in the South, while 8 of Dewey's top 10 were in the Midwest or the Plains. Kansas and Nebraska moved ahead of South Dakota as Dewey's strongest states. Wyoming, which had backed FDR 3 times, was Dewey's tenth-strongest state.

Two counties are noteworthy. Wells County, Indiana, voted Republican for the first time in its history. While rejecting Lincoln, Grant, and Teddy Roosevelt, it went for Thomas E. Dewey during FDR's last campaign. Kent County, Rhode Island, went Democratic for the first time in 108 years, when it had supported Martin van Buren in 1836.

While the national voter shift between 1940 and 1944 was small, Dewey gained 9 points in Arkansas, 7 points each in Maryland, North Carolina and Tennessee, 6 points in Virginia, 5 points each in Arizona, Louisiana, Montana, and Nevada, and 4 points each in Alabama, Florida and Wyoming—all southern and western states where an early hint of growing conservatism revealed itself.

FDR added 2 points to his 1940 showing in Rhode Island and 1 point in North Dakota.

In Texas, a group of disgruntled conservative Democrats calling themselves the Texas Regulars polled 12% of the presidential vote and carried 1 county.

Of the 106 largest cities, Roosevelt carried 96 and Dewey, 10. Dewey won Peoria, Illinois, and Wichita, Kansas, which had gone for FDR 3 times, but Roosevelt carried Berkeley, California; Allentown, Pennsylvania; and Syracuse, New York, which he had lost to Willkie in 1940.

Two bits of trivia add to the drama of the 1944 campaign:

• Dewey carried the hometowns of both President Roosevelt (Hyde Park, New York) and his running mate Harry Truman (Independence, Missouri).
• Two former presidential candidates, Alfred E. Smith and Wendell Willkie, both died in New York City during the 1944 campaign. Smith died on October 4 and Willkie died 4 days later.

TOP 10 STATES, 1944

Roosevelt	Percentage	Dewey	Percentage
1. Mississippi	93.6	1. Kansas	60.2
2. South Carolina	87.6	2. Nebraska	58.6
3. Georgia	81.7	3. South Dakota	58.3
4. Alabama	81.3	4. Vermont	57.1
5. Louisiana	80.6	5. North Dakota	53.8
6. Texas	71.4	6. Colorado	53.2
7. Florida	70.3	7. Indiana	52.4
8. Arkansas	70.0	8. Maine	52.4
9. North Carolina	66.7	9. Iowa	52.0
10. Virginia	62.4	10. Wyoming	51.2

ELECTORAL VOTES, 1944

States	Electoral Votes	Roosevelt	Dewey	States	Electoral Votes	Roosevelt	Dewey
Alabama	11	11	–	Florida	8	8	–
Arizona	4	4	–	Georgia	12	12	–
Arkansas	9	9	–	Idaho	4	4	–
California	25	25	–	Illinois	28	28	–
Colorado	6	–	6	Indiana	13	–	13
Connecticut	8	8	–	Iowa	10	–	10
Delaware	3	3	–	Kansas	8	–	8

States	Electoral Votes	Roosevelt	Dewey	States	Electoral Votes	Roosevelt	Dewey
Kentucky	11	11	–	Ohio	25	–	25
Louisiana	10	10	–	Oklahoma	10	10	–
Maine	5	–	5	Oregon	6	6	–
Maryland	8	8	–	Pennsylvania	35	35	–
Massachusetts	16	16	–	Rhode Island	4	4	–
Michigan	19	19	–	South Carolina	8	8	–
Minnesota	11	11	–	South Dakota	4	–	4
Mississippi	9	9	–	Tennessee	12	12	–
Missouri	15	15	–	Texas	23	23	–
Montana	4	4	–	Utah	4	4	–
Nebraska	6	–	6	Vermont	3	–	3
Nevada	3	3	–	Virginia	11	11	–
New Hampshire	4	4	–	Washington	8	8	–
New Jersey	16	16	–	West Virginia	8	8	–
New Mexico	4	4	–	Wisconsin	12	–	12
New York	47	47	–	Wyoming	3	–	3
North Carolina	14	14	–				
North Dakota	4	–	4	Totals	531	432	99

1948

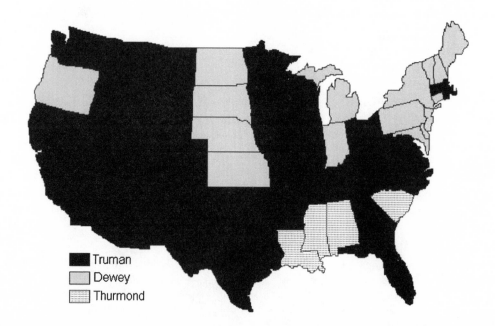

Truman
Dewey
Thurmond

President Harry Truman's come-from-behind victory, which eluded and surprised most pollsters and political prognosticators, is still being written about. Three books about the fabled 1948 campaign appeared during its fiftieth anniversary year alone.

Truman carried 28 states, with 303 electoral votes, to Dewey's 16 states and 189 electoral votes. South Carolina governor Strom Thurmond, running on the States' Rights ticket of opposition to civil rights, carried four Deep South states and 39 electoral votes (including one faithless Truman elector from Tennessee, where Thurmond ran third). Thurmond's campaign was solely regional, and his 2% national support was confined entirely to the South, where he received 22% of the votes and carried Alabama, Mississippi, Louisiana and South Carolina. The other minor-party candidate, former vice president Henry Wallace, also received 2% of the votes but carried no states or counties. Wallace was a true national candidate, however, being on the ballot in all states but Illinois, Nebraska and Oklahoma.

What makes the 1948 election so fascinating is that there was a great deal of change in the electorate that could be missed by merely looking at the popular and electoral college votes. Truman's margin (49.6% to 45.1%) over Governor Dewey, who made his second try for the White House, was not much different from FDR's 1944 victory. Most of Truman's small popular vote loss went to ex–Democrats on his right (Thurmond) or left (Wallace). But Dewey was unable to capitalize on the Democratic dissension, and his popular vote actually declined 1%.

But Dewey did nearly double his electoral votes, from 99 to 189, as a result of carrying his home state, New York, and the neighboring states of Pennsylvania, New Jersey, and Connecticut, for a net gain of 106 electoral votes. Dewey also carried 5 other 1944 Roosevelt states (Delaware, Maryland, Michigan, New Hampshire, and Oregon), for an additional 40 electoral votes. This could have brought him tantalizingly close to victory with 245 electoral votes if he had carried all of his 1944 states. (The election would have been thrown into

the House of Representatives: Truman 247, Dewey 245, Thurmond, 39.)

But this constitutional crisis was averted by a totally unexpected factor: Truman carried 5 states (Colorado, Iowa, Ohio, Wisconsin, and Wyoming) that had gone for Dewey in 1944, giving him 56 additional electoral votes and the presidency. Thus, 18 of the 48 states changed sides between 1944 and the first postwar presidential election of 1948.

Truman put together a most unusual coalition: the cities, the South, and a crossover vote from farmers and small-town dwellers in the West. Truman won 54% to 39% in the nation's largest cities, despite a strong 6% Henry Wallace vote (mostly in New York City, Los Angeles and San Francisco). Truman carried 85 of the nation's 106 largest cities, while Dewey carried 15 and Thurmond, 6. This city vote assured Truman's victory in a number of states, including Illinois and California. And he carried 7 of the 11 states of the Old Confederacy, winning 51% of the popular vote in the South to Dewey's 27% and Thurmond's 22%.

But his upset victory was really won mostly in the countryside. Truman carried 249 counties in 29 states that had gone for Dewey in 1944. Included in the Truman crossover counties were Middlesex County, Massachusetts; and Oneida County, New York, which had never voted for Roosevelt and had not gone Democratic since 1912.

Truman's strongest states suggested that his own "border state" persona (liberal on economic issues, moderate on social questions) was a powerful factor. Texas and Oklahoma were his best states, and he also did extremely well in the other border states of Missouri, Kentucky and West Virginia. The loyal Democratic South (Arkansas, Georgia, North Carolina) and increasingly liberal Minnesota and Rhode Island were the states that responded most enthusiastically to the man from Independence.

Dewey's only bright spot came in the Northeast, where he carried 9 of the 11 states, losing only heavily Catholic Massachusetts and Rhode Island. (The Henry Wallace vote also hurt Truman in New York, Connecticut and Maryland.) But Dewey swept 60% of the vote in the nation's burgeoning suburbs, a precursor to the Eisenhower sweep of the next decade. And Dewey carried about 24 counties in the resort areas of Florida, in the Piedmont section of North Carolina, and in the Shenandoah Valley of Virginia, which would all become increasingly Republican in the decades to come. He also captured some normally Democratic counties in California and Nevada. There were no major breakthrough counties, though Dewey was the first Republican since 1888 to carry Williamsburg, Virginia, and the first since 1896 to carry Austin County, Texas.

Dewey carried 81 counties in 19 states that had supported FDR in all 4 of his campaigns. This was the first indication of a chink in the New Deal armor. Of these New Deal counties that defected to Dewey, 19 were in Virginia, 17 in California, 11 in Florida, 5 each in North Carolina and Utah, 4 each in North Dakota and Oregon, 3 in Nevada, and others scattered in 11 states. Many of these counties have remained GOP strongholds 5 decades later. (Among the cities, Dewey carried Knoxville, Tennessee, and Omaha, Nebraska, which all had liked FDR 4 times.)

Six of Dewey's strongest states were in the East (3 in upper New England and the mid–Atlantic states of Pennsylvania, New Jersey and Delaware) while 4 were in the Plains (Nebraska, Kansas and the Dakotas).

In the metropolitan areas, Dewey increased his vote in many southern cities (he gained 28 points in Houston and 22 points in Fort Worth) and in the normally GOP suburbs of New York, Chicago, Philadelphia and Los Angeles. Dewey made striking gains, though not enough for victory, in

places as far apart as Camden, New Jersey; Wilmington, Delaware; Louisville, Kentucky; Toledo, Ohio; and Salt Lake City, Utah. He ran unusually well in liberal cities like San Francisco, Oakland, Portland (Oregon), Philadelphia, Sacramento, Seattle and Cleveland. The metro areas he carried were generally settled by high income earners and historically Republican.

Truman's metro areas were the traditional ethnic and blue-collar towns and suburbs that had embraced the New Deal and remained loyal to Truman's Fair Deal policies. Truman ran stronger than FDR in the Boston, Kansas City and St. Louis regions (in both the inner cities and the suburbs). He also improved on FDR's vote in Denver, St. Paul and Tulsa.

In terms of major party voting shifts, Truman ran ahead of FDR in 18 states, generally in the heartland of middle America from Montana to West Virginia. Dewey improved on his showing in 30 states, including the far West, the South and the East. Every coastline state showed an improvement in the Dewey vote except Massachusetts.

A large number of counties changed sides between 1944 and 1948. There were 623 counties, about 1 of 5 in the nation, that voted for a different party in 1948 from the one it had supported in 1944.

There were 265 counties in the South that shifted from Roosevelt to Thurmond, 249 counties (mostly in the North and West) that shifted from Dewey to Truman, 108 counties that switched from Roosevelt to Dewey, and 1 county that switched from a third party to Dewey.

The switching from party to party was so widespread that at least 1 county in all but 2 states (Connecticut and Arizona) changed sides. President Truman especially benefited from the 1944 Dewey counties that switched their allegiance to Truman. These pro–Truman counties were located in 29 states. Geographically, 172 of the counties were in the

North and West, 68 in the border states and 9 in the South. Of Truman's 249 crossover counties, 32 were in Minnesota, 32 in Missouri, 24 in Wisconsin, 21 in Indiana, 17 each in South Dakota and Colorado, 16 in Oklahoma, 14 in Iowa and 11 each in Kentucky and Ohio.

Dewey captured 108 counties in 27 states that had supported Roosevelt: 66 of them were in the North and West, 41 in the South, and one in the border state of Delaware. Virginia, with 19 counties and California with 18, had the largest number of pro–Dewey counties, followed by Florida (11), North Dakota (8), Utah (6) and North Carolina (5).

Thurmond carried 265 counties in 9 southern states. He carried every county in Mississippi, all but 1 in Alabama, and all but 2 in his home state of South Carolina. His support was regional, or perhaps it should be said, subregional, since his maximum strength was in the Deep South. He did not carry any counties in North Carolina or Texas. His vote was largely rural and small town but he did carry Birmingham, Memphis, Mobile, Montgomery, New Orleans, and Shreveport (all among the 106 largest cities at that time), and also the smaller cities of Augusta, Columbia, Charleston and Greenville.

While Thurmond's vote was unquestionably a Democratic vote — his party was often called the Dixiecrats or the States' Rights Democrats — it should be noted that in parts of the rural South some of the protest votes that went for Dewey in 1944 went to Thurmond in 1948. In Winn Parish, Louisiana (ancestral home of Huey Long), Dewey's vote declined from 39% to 11%. In Effingham County, Georgia, Dewey's vote declined from 46% to 12%.

Henry Wallace polled 500,000 votes in New York (8% of the state total) and 200,000 votes (5%) in California. The former vice president drew nearly 4% in North Dakota and Washington and 3% in Mon-

tana and Oregon. His national vote was 2.4%, the same as Thurmond's.

Wallace did best in a few big cities, receiving 13.5% in New York City, 8% each in Los Angeles and Berkeley in California, 6% in San Francisco, 5% each in Oakland, California; Paterson, New Jersey; and Yonkers, New York; and 4% in Albany, New York and Seattle and Tacoma in Washington.

In the nation's counties, Wallace's top 3 showings were The Bronx, Kings (Brooklyn), and New York (Manhattan) counties, New York, followed by Williams County, North Dakota, where he received almost 14% of the vote.

Wallace's protest vote exceeded 10% in these counties: Musselshell, Montana; Mountrail, North Dakota; McCone, Montana; and Sullivan, New York. Most of these were hardscrabble rural areas, though Sullivan is a resort area in the Catskill Mountains and the most Jewish rural county in the United States.

Wallace's vote topped 6% in 34 counties: 10 of them were in North Dakota; 5 each in Montana and New York; 3 each in Idaho, Michigan, and Wisconsin; 2 in Michigan; and 1 each in Arizona, California and Washington.

In his book *The Future of American Politics*, pollster and analyst Samuel Lubell discovered that Wallace had carried a few precincts in African-American neighborhoods in the Bronx, Jewish precincts in Los Angeles, and Latino precincts in the Ybor City section of Tampa.

While Wallace's national vote fizzled (he was getting 8% in national polls earlier in the campaign), his was the last protest on the far left of the U.S. political spectrum until Ralph Nader arrived on the scene five decades later.

Despite the excitement of the four-way race in 1948, the total vote increased less than 2%. Only about 800,000 more people voted in 1948 than in 1944, and in terms of the turnout of eligible voting-age population, there was probably an overall decline.

The vote did increase by 500,000, or 14% in California, and 20% in Florida, both areas of postwar migration. Arizona increased 30%; New Mexico, 23%; Louisiana, 19%; Nevada, 15%; Arkansas, 14%; and Utah, 11%. (Strom Thurmond's candidacy pushed the vote up 38% in South Carolina.)

But the vote declined in the big states of New York, Ohio, Pennsylvania, Illinois, Michigan and New Jersey. Even in Truman's home state of Missouri, the vote barely increased, and in his running mate Alben Barkley's home state of Kentucky the vote declined 5%.

TOP 10 STATES, 1948

Truman	Percentage	Dewey	Percentage
1. Texas	66.0	1. Vermont	61.5
2. Oklahoma	62.7	2. Maine	56.7
3. Arkansas	61.7	3. Nebraska	54.2
4. Georgia	60.8	4. Kansas	53.6
5. Missouri	58.1	5. New Hampshire	52.4
6. North Carolina	58.0	6. North Dakota	52.2
7. Rhode Island	57.6	7. South Dakota	51.8
8. West Virginia	57.3	8. Pennsylvania	50.9
9. Minnesota	57.2	9. New Jersey	50.3
10. Kentucky	56.7	10. Delaware	50.0

Wallace	Percentage	Thurmond	Percentage
1. New York	8.2	1. Mississippi	87.2
2. California	4.7	2. Alabama	79.7
3. North Dakota	3.8	3. South Carolina	72.0
4. Washington	3.5	4. Louisiana	49.1
5. Montana	3.3	5. Georgia	20.3
6. Oregon	2.9	6. Arkansas	16.5
7. Minnesota	2.3	7. Florida	15.5
8. Nevada	2.3	8. Tennessee	13.4
9. Idaho	2.3	9. Virginia	10.4
10. Michigan	2.2	10. Texas	9.1
10. New Jersey	2.2		

ELECTORAL VOTES, 1948

States	Electoral Votes	Truman	Dewey	Thurmond
Alabama	11	–	–	11
Arizona	4	4	–	–
Arkansas	9	9	–	–
California	25	25	–	–
Colorado	6	6	–	–

States	Electoral Votes	Truman	Dewey	Thurmond
Connecticut	8	-	8	-
Delaware	3	-	3	-
Florida	8	8	-	-
Georgia	12	12	-	-
Idaho	4	4	-	-
Illinois	28	28	-	-
Indiana	13	-	13	-
Iowa	10	10	-	-
Kansas	8	-	8	-
Kentucky	11	11	-	-
Louisiana	10	-	-	10
Maine	5	-	5	-
Maryland	8	-	8	-
Massachusetts	16	16	-	-
Michigan	19	-	19	-
Minnesota	11	11	-	-
Mississippi	9	-	-	9
Missouri	15	15	-	-
Montana	4	4	-	-
Nebraska	6	-	6	-
Nevada	3	3	-	-
New Hampshire	4	-	4	-
New Jersey	16	-	16	-
New Mexico	4	4	-	-
New York	47	-	47	-
North Carolina	14	14	-	-
North Dakota	4	-	4	-
Ohio	25	25	-	-
Oklahoma	10	10	-	-
Oregon	6	-	6	-
Pennsylvania	35	-	35	-
Rhode Island	4	4	-	-
South Carolina	8	-	-	8
South Dakota	4	-	4	-
Tennessee[1]	12	11	-	1
Texas	23	23	-	-
Utah	4	4	-	-
Vermont	3	-	3	-
Virginia	11	11	-	-
Washington	8	8	-	-
West Virginia	8	8	-	-
Wisconsin	12	12	-	-
Wyoming	3	3	-	-
Totals	531	303	189	39

1. One Truman elector in Tennessee voted for Thurmond.

1952

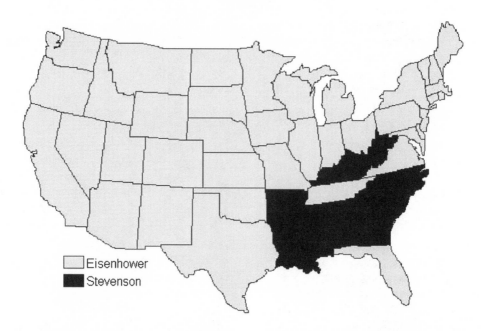

Eisenhower
Stevenson

General Dwight D. Eisenhower brought the GOP back to power after a 20-year period of Democratic rule. This election brought the New Deal–Fair Deal era to an end. Ike, as he was affectionately called, carried 39 states with 442 electoral votes, while his Democratic opponent, Governor Adlai Stevenson of Illinois, won 9 states with 89 electoral votes. Ike's popular vote win was 55% to 44%. His electoral vote was eerily similar to Hoover's 1928 victory, the last GOP triumph. The national vote increased from 49 million to more than 61 million, a 26% increase that showed how much this exciting election had engaged the voters.

Eisenhower swept the entire nation outside the South. He won 23 of Truman's 28 states, even winning in Texas and Oklahoma, where Truman had won his most impressive victories 4 years before, as well as the 16 Dewey states. Stevenson carried 5 of Truman's states and the 4 Thurmond states, including Alabama, the home of his running mate, Senator John Sparkman. Out-side the Old South, Stevenson carried only Kentucky and West Virginia.

Eisenhower's most impressive victory came, as usual, in Vermont, and also in North Dakota, Nebraska, South Dakota, Kansas and Maine, bringing together the historic bastions of upper New England and the Great Plains in a geographical pattern that resembled the Lincoln and McKinley coalitions. Eight of the GOP top 10 were in the West or Midwest. Stevenson's top 10 states, led by Georgia, were mostly southern or in the border region (West Virginia and Kentucky).

Eisenhower swept the suburbs, the rural North and West, and even broke the solid South by carrying Virginia, Tennessee, Texas and Florida — all "outer South" states where migration had begun to offset Democratic memories. Ike's strongest southern vote came in the prosperous metropolitan areas.

Adlai Stevenson, the one modern presidential candidate most beloved by liberal intellectuals, won 53% of the vote in the nation's largest cities but his strongest states were in the South. Perhaps the bright spot in the Stevenson campaign was Philadelphia, where he triumphed by a 161,000-vote margin compared to Truman's 7,000-vote victory. But he lost his home state of Illinois and was not able to withstand a Republican landslide fueled by a desire for change, an end to the Korean War, and fear of international communism.

There were small gains for Stevenson in several New York and Philadelphia suburbs and in upper-income and academic communities (the Survey Research Center at the University of Michigan estimates that 31% of "professional and business" people voted for Stevenson compared to 20% who supported Truman).

The movement toward Eisenhower encompassed the entire nation. While varying in its intensity, the pro–Eisenhower trend was almost universal. Only 1 county in the nation supported Dewey in 1948 and Stevenson in 1952: Dawson County, Georgia, a rural area north of Atlanta.

In the Deep South there was still a reluctance to break with the historic Democratic allegiance. A majority of the Thurmond counties (205 out of 265) went for Stevenson. But Eisenhower gained more percentage points than Stevenson in the Thurmond states of South Carolina and Louisiana. Only in Mississippi and Alabama, the two other Thurmond states, did Stevenson gain more percentage points over Truman than Eisenhower gained over Dewey. (A majority of Thurmond counties went for Eisenhower only in South Carolina and Florida.)

Eisenhower ran 10 percentage points ahead of Dewey's 1948 vote. He gained 29 percentage points in Texas, 19 in North Dakota, 18 in Idaho, 15 in Minnesota, 16 in Montana, 17 in Oklahoma, 17 in South Dakota, and 15 in Wyoming. The West was the region most responsive to the Eisenhower campaign.

The first Republican victory since 1928 was uniform in many respects. The total vote increased in every state, with a phenomenal rise from 101,000 to 341,000 in South Carolina. The vote doubled in Alabama and nearly doubled in Florida. Eisenhower ran ahead of the 1948 Republican vote percentage in all 48 states, so there was an undeniable national trend toward the Eisenhower-Nixon ticket.

The GOP ticket won some dramatic victories in rural areas: Ike received 93% in Plaquemines Parish, Louisiana, a rural fiefdom of political boss Leander Perez, a 1948 Thurmond backer. Eisenhower's vote reached 91% in McIntosh County, North Dakota; 90% in Campbell County, South Dakota; and 92% in Gillespie County, Texas — all three German-Lutheran farm communities. Eisenhower also carried 53 counties in 13 states that had never before supported a Republican candidate for president. Most (48) were in the South. Eisenhower won some impressive victories in the South, winning 2–1 in Charleston, South Carolina; in Shreveport, Louisiana; in Dallas, Texas; and better than 2–1 in St. Petersburg, Orlando, Fort Lauderdale and Palm Beach, Florida.

In 5 of the 8 states where Truman was a big winner in 1948 (especially in New Mexico, Missouri and Kentucky), the strongest 1948 Truman counties had a greater swing to Eisenhower than the statewide shift. In all the states, except West Virginia, the counties where Truman did best in 1948 shifted to Eisenhower in much greater numbers than did voters in the nation. The pro–Eisenhower swing in the Truman strongholds exceeded the national voter change in New Mexico, Oklahoma, Colorado, Minnesota, Missouri and Montana. It appears that many of President Truman's most enthusiastic supporters were bitterly disillusioned by 1952 and embraced the Republican candidate with open arms.

TOP 10 STATES, 1952

Eisenhower	Percentage	Stevenson	Percentage
1. Vermont	71.5	1. Georgia	69.7
2. North Dakota	71.0	2. Alabama	64.6
3. South Dakota	69.3	3. Mississippi	60.4
4. Nebraska	69.2	4. Arkansas	55.9
5. Kansas	68.8	5. North Carolina	53.9
6. Maine	66.0	6. Louisiana	52.9
7. Idaho	65.4	7. West Virginia	51.9
8. Iowa	63.8	8. South Carolina	50.7
9. Wyoming	62.7	9. Kentucky	49.9
10. Nevada	61.4	10. Tennessee	49.7

ELECTORAL VOTES, 1952

States	Electoral Votes	Eisenhower	Stevenson	States	Electoral Votes	Eisenhower	Stevenson
Alabama	11	–	11	Nevada	3	3	–
Arizona	4	4	–	New Hampshire	4	4	–
Arkansas	8	–	8	New Jersey	16	16	–
California	32	32	–	New Mexico	4	4	–
Colorado	6	6	–	New York	45	45	–
Connecticut	8	8	–	North Carolina	14	–	14
Delaware	3	3	–	North Dakota	4	4	–
Florida	10	10	–	Ohio	25	25	–
Georgia	12	–	12	Oklahoma	8	8	–
Idaho	4	4	–	Oregon	6	6	–
Illinois	27	27	–	Pennsylvania	32	32	–
Indiana	13	13	–	Rhode Island	4	4	–
Iowa	10	10	–	South Carolina	8	–	8
Kansas	8	8	–	South Dakota	4	4	–
Kentucky	10	–	10	Tennessee	11	11	–
Louisiana	10	–	10	Texas	24	24	–
Maine	5	5	–	Utah	4	4	–
Maryland	9	9	–	Vermont	3	3	–
Massachusetts	16	16	–	Virginia	12	12	–
Michigan	20	20	–	Washington	9	9	–
Minnesota	11	11	–	West Virginia	8	–	8
Mississippi	8	–	8	Wisconsin	12	12	–
Missouri	13	13	–	Wyoming	3	3	–
Montana	4	4	–				
Nebraska	6	6	–	Totals	531	442	89

1956

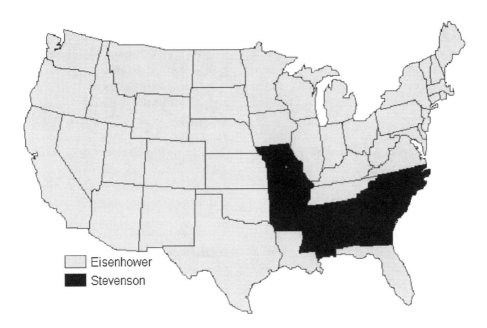

Eisenhower
Stevenson

In the first rematch of candidates since Bryan and McKinley faced off for a second time in 1900, President Eisenhower again confronted Adlai Stevenson. The president won a greater victory than in 1952, carrying 41 states with 457 electoral votes, to Stevenson's 7 states and 73 electoral votes. (One Alabama elector voted for an obscure judge, Walter B. Jones, rather than for Stevenson, who carried the state.) Eisenhower penetrated the South even further, carrying Louisiana, Kentucky and West Virginia, which had all supported Stevenson in 1952. The one bright spot for Stevenson was Missouri, which he carried after losing it 4 years before. Missouri was usually a barometer state. The last time it had supported a losing national candidate was in 1900, when the Show Me state went for William Jennings Bryan.

This time, 5 of Ike's top 10 states were in the East. Stevenson's strongest states were still in the south and border states, but Minnesota and Washington also appeared.

Eisenhower's share of the popular vote

was up only 2%. This would seem to indicate that this was a ho-hum election, especially since the national vote increased by less than 1% and was down in many states (9% in Oklahoma, 12% in South Carolina).

But there was actually a significant amount of candidate switching. Eisenhower carried 180 counties in 34 states that had gone for Stevenson in the previous election. He won Providence County, Rhode Island; Hudson County (Jersey City), New Jersey; and the blue-collar San Francisco suburb of Contra Costa County. The president gained many counties in the swing states that he won (Louisiana, Kentucky, West Virginia) and was the first Republican to ever carry New Orleans, and by a 59% to 41% sweep of the major party vote.

Eisenhower was the strongest GOP candidate since Coolidge in 1924 in the largest cities, where he won 49.9%, and became the first Republican to carry Chicago and Baltimore since 1928. Eisenhower carried Milwaukee, the first time a Republican did so since Harding in 1920. But Stevenson won New York City, Boston, Philadelphia, Pittsburgh, Cleveland, Detroit and St. Louis. Of the 180 pro–Eisenhower swing counties, 99 were in the South, 38 in the border states, and 43 in the North and West. The pro–Eisenhower counties were most common in Louisiana (29), Texas (23), Kentucky (23), and North Carolina (11).

Stevenson carried 114 counties in 23 states that had gone for Eisenhower in 1952. Most were in rural America, where voters were dissatisfied with the Eisenhower administration's farm and agricultural policies and had flocked to the Stevenson-Kefauver ticket. (Tennessee senator Estes Kefauver had a large following among farmers.) Stevenson did gain the blue-collar Detroit suburb of Macomb County, Michigan and also Clark County (Las Vegas), Nevada as well as some coastal counties in Oregon and Washington, but his major gains came in nonmetropolitan America. In most states, Eisenhower gained in metropolitan areas while Stevenson gained in nonmetropolitan areas. The pro–Stevenson swing votes were most numerous in the North and West (56) compared to 46 in the South and 12 in the border states. These pro–Stevenson swing counties were most numerous in Texas (28), Minnesota (12), South Dakota (11) and Washington (9).

In the Deep South, there were rumblings of discontent with both national parties because of the civil rights movement. So-called States' Rights parties carried 34 counties total in South Carolina, Louisiana, Mississippi, Tennessee, and Virginia. Most were in black-belt counties, where the majority of the population was African American but only whites voted. Twenty-six of the States Rights counties had gone for Eisenhower in 1952 and 8 for Stevenson. In those parts of the South where African Americans were allowed to vote, Eisenhower generally made gains, carrying Orleans Parish (New Orleans), Louisiana; Shelby County (Memphis) Tennessee; and Duval County (Jacksonville), Florida, as well as several rural counties where African Americans were enfranchised, for example, Charles City, Virginia; McIntosh, Georgia; and Macon, Alabama.

Eisenhower still gained in the South, and 76% of his county gains from Stevenson in 1952 were in the South and the border region. Only 51% of Stevenson's county gains from Eisenhower's 1952 vote were in the South and the border region.

This reelection brought even more new counties to the Republican standard than in 1952. There were 56 counties in 14 states that cast their first-ever Republican presidential vote. A number of counties included prominent southern cities, such as Mobile, Montgomery, Little Rock, Columbus (Georgia), Baton Rouge, New Orleans, Memphis, and Corpus Christi. Two of the oldest counties in Kentucky — Marion and Nelson — broke with more than 100 years of support for Democrats to back Ike, as did Hancock County on Mississippi's Gulf Coast. These victories show Ike's considerable appeal to Catholic voters in 1956. Nelson County, Kentucky, includes Bardstown, which was settled by English Catholics from Maryland and is the location of one of the oldest Roman Catholic cathedrals in the country. Hancock is the most French-oriented county in Mississippi.

Eisenhower carried 39 of the 53 counties that had never gone Republican for president until they supported him in 1952. They still liked Ike, although 7 went back to Stevenson and 7 South Carolina counties defected to the States' Rights slate.

The 1956 turnout increased mainly in the Sun Belt states (Nevada, Alabama, Arizona, Florida and Virginia), all of which experienced a 10% or more increase. In the large states only Michigan and California showed significant increases over 1952. Nevada and, surprisingly, Alabama had the largest percentage increases. Neighboring

Mississippi had the biggest decrease (13%) in turnout, followed by South Carolina (12%), Oklahoma (9%), North Dakota and Texas (both with 6%).

TOP 10 STATES, 1956

Eisenhower	Percentage	Stevenson	Percentage
1. Vermont	72.2	1. Georgia	66.4
2. Maine	70.9	2. Mississippi	58.2
3. New Hampshire	66.1	3. Alabama	56.5
4. Nebraska	65.5	4. Arkansas	52.5
5. Kansas	65.4	5. North Carolina	50.7
6. New Jersey	64.7	6. Missouri	50.1
7. Utah	64.6	7. Tennessee	48.6
8. Connecticut	63.7	8. Minnesota	46.1
9. North Dakota	61.9	9. West Virginia	45.9
10. Wisconsin	61.6	10. South Carolina	45.4
		10. Washington	45.4

ELECTORAL VOTES, 1956

States	Electoral Votes	Eisenhower	Stevenson	States	Electoral Votes	Eisenhower	Stevenson
Alabama[1]	11	–	10	New Hampshire	4	4	–
Arizona	4	4	–	New Jersey	16	16	–
Arkansas	8	–	8	New Mexico	4	4	–
California	32	32	–	New York	45	45	–
Colorado	6	6	–	North Carolina	14	–	14
Connecticut	8	8	–	North Dakota	4	4	–
Delaware	3	3	–	Ohio	25	25	–
Florida	10	10	–	Oklahoma	8	8	–
Georgia	12	–	12	Oregon	6	6	–
Idaho	4	4	–	Pennsylvania	32	32	–
Illinois	27	27	–	Rhode Island	4	4	–
Indiana	13	13	–	South Carolina	8	–	8
Iowa	10	10	–	South Dakota	4	4	–
Kansas	8	8	–	Tennessee	11	11	–
Kentucky	10	10	–	Texas	24	24	–
Louisiana	10	10	–	Utah	4	4	–
Maine	5	5	–	Vermont	3	3	–
Maryland	9	9	–	Virginia	12	12	–
Massachusetts	16	16	–	Washington	9	9	–
Michigan	20	20	–	West Virginia	8	8	–
Minnesota	11	11	–	Wisconsin	12	12	–
Mississippi	8	–	8	Wyoming	3	3	–
Missouri	13	–	13				
Montana	4	4	–	Totals	531	457	73
Nebraska	6	6	–				
Nevada	3	3	–				

1. One Stevenson elector voted for Alabama judge Walter B. Jones.

1960

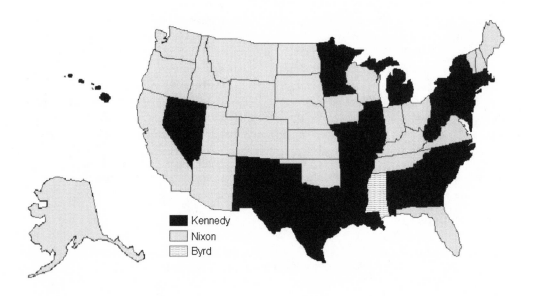

Kennedy
Nixon
Byrd

The 1960 election was the closest in popular vote in the twentieth century. Massachusetts senator John F. Kennedy (JFK) defeated Vice President Richard Nixon by 49.7% to 49.5% of the 68.3 million ballots cast. Kennedy carried 23 states with 303 electoral votes while Nixon carried 26 states with 219 electoral votes. Mississippi gave its 8 electors to a States' Rights ticket, calling itself "unpledged Democrats." These 8 Mississippians, joined by 6 from Alabama (under a complicated unpledged electors system that deprived Kennedy, who won 57% of the vote in the state, of 6 electors) and 1 Nixon elector from Oklahoma, voted for Virginia senator Harry Byrd. Two new states joined the Union — Alaska, which went for Nixon, and Hawaii, which backed Kennedy.

JFK put together his winning coalition by combining the Northeast (except upper New England), most of the South, and a few large states like Illinois and Michigan. Nixon carried the reliably Republican Midwest and far West and broke into the upper South border areas. Nixon's most impres-

sive victories came in Nebraska, Kansas and Oklahoma (where religious prejudice hurt JFK), while Kennedy's strongest states were Rhode Island, Georgia and Massachusetts.

JFK won 61% of the votes in the nation's 16 largest cities, an 11-point increase over the Stevenson vote in 1956. JFK's national gain was 8%. The big-city votes netted Kennedy a vote margin of 2,730,000, which was reflective of the polyglot, multicultural ethos of metropolitan America. The urban megalopolis was much more religiously and racially diverse than suburbia or the countryside in 1960.

As in 1928, religion was a major factor in the voting, since JFK was the second Catholic nominated by the Democrats for president. He had to overcome the unspoken stigma that no Catholic would ever be elected U.S. president, despite an explicit ban on religious tests for public office in Article Six of the U.S. Constitution.

The voting patterns and the country and state returns indicate how significant a factor religion was in 1960. While scholars disagree about the impact, an authoritative

University of Michigan Survey Research Center study found that JFK lost 1.5 million more votes than he gained because of anti–Catholic voting among Protestants, especially Protestant Democrats in the South and the rural North.

The percentage of the Catholic population in the states was closely correlated with the percentage gain in Kennedy support over Stevenson, but this did not guarantee a victory for JFK. He did win 9 of the 12 most heavily Catholic-populated states but still lost Wisconsin, New Hampshire and Vermont. Political party heritage and tradition played a major role since JFK also carried a number of southern states with tiny Catholic populations, such as Alabama, Georgia, Arkansas and the Carolinas. A sympathetic vote for JFK by coreligionists probably shifted New Jersey, Connecticut, Maryland and New Mexico into the Kennedy column, but antipathy toward his religious faith cost him Tennessee, Kentucky, Oklahoma, and possibly Florida, Ohio and Washington.

Kennedy carried 408 counties in 46 states that had supported Eisenhower. But despite the national gain for the Democratic ticket in what was forecast to be a Democratic year, 97 counties switched from Stevenson to Nixon. These antitrend counties were concentrated in Texas, Oklahoma, Missouri, and Kentucky but extended as far as Washington State. Furthermore, Kennedy ran weaker than Stevenson in 977 counties in 33 states — 1 out of 3 counties in the United States — even in many he carried. Most were in the South or the rural border states. An anti-Catholic belt stretched from northern Texas through Oklahoma and into southeastern Missouri, northeastern Arkansas, west-central Kentucky and west Tennessee.

In comparison with 1928, Kennedy lost 158 counties that had supported Smith. This might have resulted from an increasing incidence of anti–Catholicism, chang-

ing social or demographic trends, or a weakening of Democratic Party loyalties. Most were predominantly Baptist counties, but some included socially conservative Catholics of German ancestry, and a few of the Smith-Nixon counties were primarily German Lutheran.

Kennedy also failed to carry 28 counties that had supported all Democrats for president except Smith, another indication of anti–Catholicism. And there were 254 counties that had supported the 5 previous Democratic winners (FDR and Truman) but went for Nixon.

The persistence of anti–Catholic voting was centered in rural America. Kennedy ran well ahead of Stevenson and Smith in almost all northern and western cities and suburbs, and he did quite well in urban Florida and Texas.

In the anti–Kennedy backlash areas, there was a strong religious factor. In particular, Baptists were dominant in the anti-Kennedy swing counties throughout the South, the border states, and in Illinois and New Mexico. Lutherans composed the largest denomination in the anti–Kennedy counties in Pennsylvania, Wisconsin, Minnesota and the Dakotas while Methodists and Dutch Reformed Christians were strongest in the anti–Kennedy counties in Iowa and Indiana.

In the counties that went for Stevenson and Nixon, only 7.7% of the religious population was Catholic, compared to 57.6% that was Baptist, according to *Churches and Church Membership in the United States, 1971.* In the counties that went for Eisenhower and Kennedy, 65.3% of the religious population was Catholic.

JFK did well among independent and swing voters. Of the 294 counties that had switched to or against Eisenhower in 1956, Kennedy carried 188 of them, Nixon won 97, and the States' Rights splinter tickets in Dixie carried 9.

Kennedy also won back 36 of the 56

counties that had cast their first Republican presidential majorities for Eisenhower in 1956. Nixon held only 17 of them and 3 in Louisiana voted for a States' Rights party.

Nixon's geographic base was centered in the West and Midwest, with South Dakota, Iowa, Arizona, North Dakota, Indiana and Wyoming among his strongest states, in addition to Nebraska, Kansas and Oklahoma.

Kennedy's geographical coalition linked lower New England (Connecticut, Massachusetts, Rhode Island) to the mid–Atlantic (New York, Maryland, West Virginia) and to the Deep South (Georgia, Alabama, North Carolina, South Carolina). Only Nevada in the West stood out as a strong JFK state. Kennedy carried only Nevada and New Mexico in the entire West.

Geographically, the 1960 election was primarily a clash between East and West, with JFK winning in the northern and southern portions of the East while Nixon was strongest in the West and Midwest. The 8-point national gain for Kennedy was accomplished mostly in the East, though he also gained 10 points in Illinois and Wisconsin.

A major factor in 1960 was the difference in voting patterns between urban and rural areas, with the suburbs in the middle. The other story was the intense level of anti–Kennedy voting in rural America. While Kennedy ran ahead of Stevenson in popular-vote percentage in 42 of the 48 states that voted in both races, he lost ground in at least 1 county each in 33 states.

Even in states where Kennedy gained support overall, there was a backlash in rural areas. In Pennsylvania, where Kennedy gained 8 percentage points, he ran behind Stevenson in a dozen rural counties. A review of local township and precinct returns (available in Pennsylvania and a few other states) found that anti–Kennedy voting occurred in 65 of the 67 counties. Even in counties where Kennedy ran a point or two

ahead of the 1956 ticket (as in Berks), he ran behind in a majority of the precincts in the countryside. The same was true in Wisconsin, which also publishes detailed precinct data. In many towns in both states, JFK ran 10 to 20 points behind Stevenson. More than 100 towns in Pennsylvania and Wisconsin switched from Stevenson to Nixon.

An examination of several demographic factors reveals that religious affiliation is the best explanation for the anti–Kennedy backlash. There was a near absence of Catholics (under 10% generally) in the anti–Kennedy counties, and a disproportionately large percentage of Southern Baptists in the southern and border state anti–Kennedy counties, extending also into eastern New Mexico. (In Baptist Roosevelt County, Kennedy ran 16 points behind Stevenson.) In Pennsylvania, Colorado, and Iowa, Lutherans and Methodists predominated in the anti–Kennedy counties, while Lutherans were the most prominent in Minnesota, Wisconsin, South Dakota, Montana and Nebraska anti–Kennedy counties. German and Dutch ancestry were also linked to some extent with the voting patterns but were secondary to religion. In Douglas County, South Dakota, JFK dropped 11 points. The population there is a mixture of Dutch and German, and the Reformed Church and Lutherans are the dominant religions. Kennedy also ran exceptionally poorly in the Dutch counties of Michigan and Iowa. His worst Iowa decline came in Marion County, where the Dutch town of Pella is located.

But there were also declines in Kennedy's strength in some metro counties. The senator lost 7 percentage points in Nashville (Davidson County), Tennessee; and Atlanta (Fulton County), Georgia. He ran weaker than Stevenson in Oklahoma City; Greenville, South Carolina; Jackson, Mississippi; and Birmingham, Alabama. In smaller metropolitan areas he ran 7 to 10 points behind

Stevenson in Paducah, Kentucky; and Macon, Georgia; and a few points weaker in Pensacola and Lakeland, Florida; in Columbus, Georgia; Shreveport, Louisiana; and Chattanooga and Knoxville, Tennessee.

Outside the South, his support declined 4 points in York, Pennsylvania, and 1 point in Fresno, California.

The States' Rights Party cost the Democrats Mississippi, where they carried 54 counties, and it also placed first in 17 Louisiana counties. The 1960 States' Righters had been Democrats, since 51 of the 71 counties went for Stevenson in 1956, while 10 supported Eisenhower and 10 supported the 1956 States' Rights Party.

The majority of the counties that supported the 1956 States' Rights parties, however, went for Nixon in 1960 — as they had gone for Eisenhower in 1952. There were apparently two different strains of States' Rights voters in the rural South.

These 1956 States' Rights/1960 Nixon counties included Prince Edward, Virginia, which closed its public schools rather than integrate them; Fayette, Tennessee; and Caldwell, Louisiana.

In the counties in Louisiana and Mississippi that supported the States' Rights parties in *both* 1956 and 1960, Kennedy slipped into third place in 1960, suggesting that both anti–Catholicism and racism were factors influencing the electorate.

(In contrast, the counties that cast their first-ever Republican vote for Ike in 1952 supported Nixon. The break with the Democrats must have been more ideological and more permanent for these counties than for the 1956 Ike counties — which must have been more personality oriented.)

The excitement of the Kennedy-Nixon race brought nearly 7 million new voters to the polls, an 11% increase. Every state recorded a higher presidential vote in 1960 than in 1956, ranging from 1% in West Virginia to 37% in both Arizona and Florida. Other large increases of 20% or more came

in Louisiana, South Carolina, New Mexico and Mississippi. Increases were 15 percent to 20% in California, Maine, Minnesota, North Carolina and Texas. Small increases of 2 percent to 4% were recorded in Montana, Iowa, and South Dakota.

The states with the largest increase in turnout narrowly favored Kennedy 50.5 percent to 49.5% in major party vote, but this was only a 5.4% increase over Stevenson's 1956 vote, less than Kennedy's 8% national vote gain.

Nixon carried 15 counties in 3 states that had never gone Republican for president before 1960. Five were in Arkansas (Clay, Craighead, Fulton, Randolph, Sharp), 4 in Missouri (Dunklin, Oregon, Reynolds, Shannon), and 2 in Oklahoma (Atoka, Garvin). Also included were Houston County, Alabama; Caldwell Parish, Louisiana; Dyer County, Tennessee; and Moore County, Texas.

Kennedy ran 10 percentage points or more behind Stevenson's 1956 vote in all but 2 of these counties. There was an enormous anti–Kennedy vote in northeastern Arkansas and southeastern Missouri, undoubtedly related to the religious issue. Since Al Smith carried all of these counties in 1928, it can be reasonably assumed that anti–Catholicism increased as a salient political issue between 1928 and 1960 in this slice of rural America.

The religious configuration of these counties was 67% Baptist (mostly white Southern Baptists), 19% Methodist and only 4% Catholic. Almost 10% belonged to other evangelical Protestant churches. In 1926 the *U.S. Census of Religious Bodies* recorded that in these counties 40.5% of the religious population was Baptist, 29.5% was Methodist, 9% belonged to the Churches of Christ and 3.5% were Catholic. About 17.5% belonged to other Protestant denominations. The large percentage increase in Baptists may have been a crucial factor in the 1960 vote.

Nixon was also the first Republican since 1868 to carry Marion and Scott counties in Arkansas and Madison County in Tennessee. He was the first Republican since 1872 to carry Barnwell County, South Carolina, and the first since 1884 to carry Fayette County, Tennessee.

JFK did not have any breakthrough counties where longtime Republican voters switched to his side. He mainly revitalized the old New Deal Democratic coalition.

In a few counties his victory was quite a departure from the past. He was the first Democrat since 1836 to carry Norfolk County, Massachusetts, a growing and prosperous suburb south of Boston, and he was the first Democratic winner since 1912 in Niagara County, New York. One unusual victory came in Madison County, North Carolina, where JFK was the first Democratic victor since 1876. Local factors played a role in Madison, where a long-dominant Republican machine had been ousted in the late 1950s, and that may have spilled over into the 1960 presidential race.

Kennedy also carried 45 counties that had been mostly Republican since 1920. In these 45 pro–Kennedy GOP counties, Catholics outnumbered Protestants 71% to 29% in 1971 data, up from 60% to 40% in 1926 data. He was the first Democrat since 1932 to carry Charles County, Maryland; Franklin County, New York; and Socorro County, New Mexico, all rural Catholic strongholds.

Scholars may disagree about the final impact of religion on the 1960 vote but one preeminent analyst of elections, V.O. Key, Jr., concluded, "Of the appeals peculiar to the campaign, the religious issue evidently by far outweighed all others. For some people, it reinforced the pull of partisanship; for others, it ran counter to the tugs of party loyalty.... Probably the best guess is that Kennedy won in spite of rather than because of the fact that he was a Catholic."[*]

TOP 10 STATES, 1960

Kennedy	Percentage	Nixon	Percentage
1. Rhode Island	63.6	1. Nebraska	62.1
2. Georgia	62.5	2. Kansas	60.4
3. Massachusetts	60.2	3. Oklahoma	59.0
4. Alabama	56.8	4. Vermont	58.6
5. Connecticut	53.7	5. South Dakota	58.2
6. Maryland	53.6	6. Maine	57.0
7. West Virginia	52.7	7. Iowa	56.7
8. New York	52.5	8. Arizona	55.5
9. North Carolina	52.1	9. North Dakota	55.4
10. South Carolina	51.2	10. Wyoming	55.0
10. Nevada	51.2	10. Indiana	55.0

[*]Paul T. David, ed., *The Presidential Election and Transition 1960–61* (Washington, DC: Brookings Institution, 1961), pp. 174–175.

ELECTORAL VOTES, 1960

States	Electoral Votes	Kennedy	Nixon	Byrd	States	Electoral Votes	Kennedy	Nixon	Byrd
Alabama[1]	11	5	–	6	Nevada	3	3	–	–
Alaska	3	–	3	–	New Hampshire	4	–	4	–
Arizona	4	–	4	–	New Jersey	16	16	–	–
Arkansas	8	8	–	–	New Mexico	4	4	–	–
California	32	–	32	–	New York	45	45	–	–
Colorado	6	–	6	–	North Carolina	14	14	–	–
Connecticut	8	8	–	–	North Dakota	4	–	4	–
Delaware	3	3	–	–	Ohio	25	–	25	–
Florida	10	–	10	–	Oklahoma[1]	8	–	7	1
Georgia	12	12	–	–	Oregon	6	–	6	–
Hawaii	3	3	–	–	Pennsylvania	32	32	–	–
Idaho	4	–	4	–	Rhode Island	4	4	–	–
Illinois	27	27	–	–	South Carolina	8	8	–	–
Indiana	13	–	13	–	South Dakota	4	–	4	–
Iowa	10	–	10	–	Tennessee	11	–	11	–
Kansas	8	–	8	–	Texas	24	24	–	–
Kentucky	10	–	10	–	Utah	4	–	4	–
Louisiana	10	10	–	–	Vermont	3	–	3	–
Maine	5	–	5	–	Virginia	12	–	12	–
Maryland	9	9	–	–	Washington	9	–	9	–
Massachusetts	16	16	–	–	West Virginia	8	8	–	–
Michigan	20	20	–	–	Wisconsin	12	–	12	–
Minnesota	11	11	–	–	Wyoming	3	–	3	–
Mississippi	8	–	–	8					
Missouri	13	13	–	–	Totals	537	303	219	15
Montana	4	–	4	–					
Nebraska	6	–	6	–					

1. For an explanation of the split electoral votes, see the text.

1964

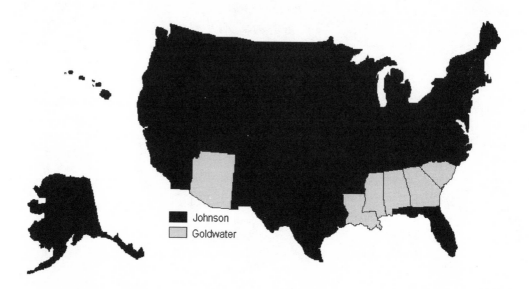

Johnson
Goldwater

President Lyndon Johnson (LBJ) won one of the great landslides in U.S. political history, carrying 44 states with 486 electoral votes to Arizona senator Barry Goldwater's 6 states and 52 electoral votes. LBJ carried every state that had supported Nixon in 1960 except Goldwater's home state of Arizona, but LBJ lost 4 Kennedy states in the Deep South to Goldwater.

The amount of party switching was enormous. For the first time in history a Democrat carried Vermont, and for the first time a Democrat carried every single county in Vermont and Maine. Maine went Democratic for the first time since 1912. Goldwater won only 1 county in New England — Carroll County, New Hampshire. Johnson also swept every county in New York and New Jersey. More than 1,000 counties switched from Nixon to Johnson, including a majority of the 1,858 counties Nixon had carried. Forty-six counties in 11 states voted Democratic for the first time in history, and 106 other counties voted Democratic for the first time since Wilson or earlier. Somerset County, Maine, and Saratoga County, New

York, went Democratic for the first time since 1836. Of the 46 first-ever Democratic counties, 10 were in New York, 8 in Vermont, 7 in Michigan, 5 in Ohio, 4 each in Massachusetts and Pennsylvania, 3 in Kansas, 2 in Kentucky, and 1 each in Illinois, Indiana and New Jersey. Some of the counties were almost synonymous with the Grand Old Party: Ocean, New Jersey, a center of Methodist beach resorts; Barnstable, Massachusetts (Cape Cod); Dukes, Massachusetts (Martha's Vineyard); Douglas, Kansas (Lawrence, and the University of Kansas); Chautauqua, New York, home of the self-improvement Summer Schools; Wabash, Indiana. Most of these counties were small town or rural, white and Protestant.

The one Goldwater bright spot was the Deep South, where Goldwater was the first Republican winner since Reconstruction. Goldwater was the first Republican to carry Georgia. He was the first Republican since 1872 to carry Alabama and Mississippi and the first Republican since 1876 to carry South Carolina.

There were 221 counties in 9 southern states that went Republican for the first time either in history or since the Reconstruction era. Mississippi, usually the most or second-most Democratic state in the nation, became the most Republican state. Most of Goldwater's strongest states were in the South or in the Rocky Mountain states of Arizona and Idaho. The Goldwater vote in the Deep South was a white segregationist vote, solely due to Goldwater's opposition to the 1964 Civil Rights Act. (Goldwater carried all 71 southern counties that had gone for States Rights fringe parties in 1960.) Since African Americans were deprived of the franchise in much of the rural South, the Goldwater candidacy was seen as a last-ditch attempt to save the old ways of white supremacy. But northern Republicans rebelled against such a shift in the party's traditional support for civil rights and defected to Johnson, who also ran as the inheritor, preserver and extender of the Kennedy tradition.

The "moderate" South also rejected Goldwater, as Tennessee, Virginia and Florida switched from Nixon to Johnson. And the "loyalist" South (North Carolina, Arkansas and Texas) stood firm for LBJ. But the South was the only real battleground in 1964, with LBJ winning 81–47 in the electoral college and 51% to 49% in popular votes. Outside the South the electoral vote margin for Johnson was 405 to 5. Nationally, he won 61% to 39%, an 11-point gain over Kennedy's 1960 vote. Johnson received 70% of the big-city vote.

For the first time in history, 5 of the Democratic candidate's top 10 states were in New England — the bastion of Republicanism since Fremont and Lincoln. Rhode Island, Hawaii and Massachusetts were the 3 strongest Johnson states. Michigan, which used to appear on Republican top 10, was Johnson's eighth-best state. Alaska and Vermont were there also, as were New York, Connecticut and West Virginia. Also, for the first time in history, no southern state appeared on a Democratic top 10.

Seven of Goldwater's strongest states were in the South, two were in the Mountain West, and one — Nebraska — was in the farm belt.

Goldwater was the first Republican to carry 113 counties in 9 southern states. Georgia had 46 of them and Mississippi had 33. Other states with first-ever Republican counties include Alabama (14), Florida (8), Louisiana (6), South Carolina (4) and Arkansas (2). In addition, 108 counties in the same states went Republican for the first time since Reconstruction or the McKinley era.

In the North and West, only 17 counties out of roughly 2,000 gave Goldwater a higher vote percentage than they had given Nixon in 1960. Only 5 counties switched from Kennedy to Goldwater outside the South: Camas and Custer, Idaho; Dorchester, Maryland; Osage, Missouri; and Emmons, North Dakota. Most of the pro-Goldwater counties were in the above states, in addition to Arizona, Nebraska and Nevada.

There were also 32 counties in 13 states (particularly in Idaho, Oklahoma, Arizona, Utah, Montana and New Mexico) that voted for Truman in 1948 and Goldwater in 1964. Several were farm counties, including Lincoln County, Washington. A vague kind of sagebrush populism characterized their voting patterns.

The 1964 election was a tale of two nations: the South versus the rest of the country. Goldwater ran ahead of his national vote percentage (38.5%) in every southern state except LBJ's Texas. (In 1960 Nixon exceeded his national percentage in only 3 southern states and Eisenhower in 1956 in no southern state.) But Goldwater was rejected almost everywhere else. He ran behind Nixon in 99% of the counties in the North and West.

The South was the only region to see

significant increases in the presidential vote. The turnout was up 55% in Georgia, 37% in Mississippi, 36% in South Carolina, and 35% in Virginia.

Nationally the vote rose only 2.6%. Vote turnout declined 10% in Maine.

Radical shifts in 1960–64 political behavior were common in 1964. In Miller County, Georgia, the Republican vote ballooned from 5% for Nixon to 86% for Goldwater. In Seminole County, Georgia,

the GOP vote increased from 5% to 75%. In Amite County, Mississippi, Republican support went up from 12% to 96%. On the other hand, the Democratic vote surged from 23% for Kennedy to 59% for Johnson in Orange County, Vermont. In Wayne County, New York, the Democrats went up from 31% to 64%. In Hancock County, Maine, the Democratic vote increased from 22% to 54%.

TOP 10 STATES, 1964

Johnson	Percentage	Goldwater	Percentage
1. Rhode Island	80.9	1. Mississippi	87.1
2. Hawaii	78.8	2. Alabama	69.5
3. Massachusetts	76.2	3. South Carolina	58.9
4. Maine	68.8	4. Louisiana	56.8
5. New York	68.6	5. Georgia	54.1
6. West Virginia	67.9	6. Arizona	50.4
7. Connecticut	67.8	7. Idaho	49.1
8. Michigan	66.7	8. Florida	48.9
9. Vermont	66.3	9. Nebraska	47.4
10. Alaska	65.9	10. Virginia	46.2

ELECTORAL VOTES, 1964

States	Electoral Votes	Johnson	Goldwater	States	Electoral Votes	Johnson	Goldwater
Alabama	10	–	10	Kentucky	9	9	–
Alaska	3	3	–	Louisiana	10	–	10
Arizona	5	–	5	Maine	4	4	–
Arkansas	6	6	–	Maryland	10	10	–
California	40	40	–	Massachusetts	14	14	–
Colorado	6	6	–	Michigan	21	21	–
Connecticut	8	8	–	Minnesota	10	10	–
Delaware	3	3	–	Mississippi	7	–	7
District of Columbia	3	3	–	Missouri	12	12	–
Florida	14	14	–	Montana	4	4	–
Georgia	12	–	12	Nebraska	5	5	–
Hawaii	4	4	–	Nevada	3	3	–
Idaho	4	4	–	New Hampshire	4	4	–
Illinois	26	26	–	New Jersey	17	17	–
Indiana	13	13	–	New Mexico	4	4	–
Iowa	9	9	–	New York	43	43	–
Kansas	7	7	–	North Carolina	13	13	–

States water	Electoral Votes	Johnson	Gold-water	States water	Electoral Votes	Johnson	Gold-water
North Dakota	4	4	–	Utah	4	4	–
Ohio	26	26	–	Vermont	3	3	–
Oklahoma	8	8	–	Virginia	12	12	–
Oregon	6	6	–	Washington	9	9	–
Pennsylvania	29	29	–	West Virginia	7	7	–
Rhode Island	4	4	–	Wisconsin	12	12	–
South Carolina	8	–	8	Wyoming	3	3	–
South Dakota	4	4	–				
Tennessee	11	11	–	Totals	538	486	52
Texas	25	25	–				

—— 1968 ——

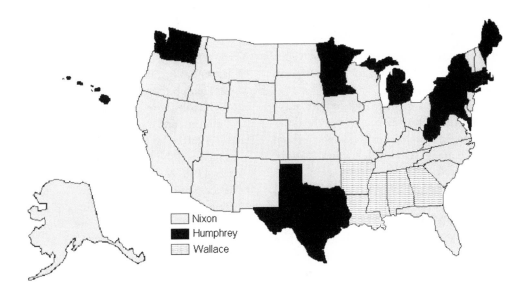

Nixon
Humphrey
Wallace

The 1968 election was one of the closest of the twentieth century in popular votes, with former vice president Richard Nixon edging out the incumbent vice president Hubert Humphrey 43.4% to 42.7%. Alabama governor George Wallace ran a national campaign that put him on all 50 state ballots, netting him 13.5% of the vote as a representative of the American Independent Party.

But Nixon put together a more convincing electoral vote margin, 301 to 191 for Humphrey, than the popular-vote tally would have predicted. Nixon won 32 states; Humphrey 13; and Wallace, 5. Nixon thus won back most of the states that had gone for Johnson in 1964 but won only 2 of Goldwater's 6 states — Arizona and South Carolina (where he got help from Senator Strom Thurmond). Four of Wallace's 5 states had gone for Goldwater, showing how much of a white backlash vote Goldwater had received. Only one state, Arkansas, switched from Johnson to Wallace. The

Arkansas result represented a massive rejection of the Democrats, since Humphrey ran third in a state that had backed every Democratic presidential candidate since 1876. Wallace garnered 46 electoral votes.

The vaunted "realignment" of 1964 proved illusory. Of the 152 Republican counties that defected to Johnson for the first time ever or since Reconstruction, all but 8 (7 of them in Democratic vice presidential candidate Edmund Muskie's home state of Maine) went back to the GOP for Nixon. (Of the 46 first-time Democratic counties in 1964, only one — Plymouth, Massachusetts — stayed with Humphrey.) Of the 221 southern Democratic counties that defected to Goldwater for the first time or since Reconstruction, just 3 voted for Nixon, while 210 went for Wallace and 8 for Humphrey (because of the Voting Rights Act of 1965, which enfranchised African Americans.)

A comparison with 1960 might prove more meaningful since Nixon was the GOP candidate in both elections. Nixon picked up 8 Kennedy states (Delaware, Illinois, Missouri, Nevada, New Jersey, New Mexico, North Carolina, and South Carolina) while Humphrey carried Maine and Washington, which had gone to Nixon. Nixon had a broader regional appeal in 1968 than in 1960.

Nixon carried states in every region, while Humphrey's support was limited mostly to the northeast, much like Dewey's support in 1948. Wallace's strength in the rural South was so intense that he carried 578 counties in 14 states, almost as many as Humphrey's 683. Nixon carried 1,849 counties, similar to his 1960 showing but more strategically located for electoral college purposes.

The 1968 election was very anti–Democratic; its nominee ran 18 percentage points weaker than the 1964 standard bearer and failed to carry 1,600 counties that had supported the 1964 nominee.

Humphrey's one bright spot was his 58% to 35% triumph over Nixon (with 7% for Wallace) in the nation's largest cities. This showing was slightly better than Kennedy's 1960 victory over the same opponent, but the total votes in the big cities declined from 11.7 million in 1964 (and 12 million in 1960) to only 10.6 million in 1968. Humphrey's share of the urban pie could have carried him to a narrow victory but the pie was smaller.

Nixon's strongest states were almost all in the West, with Nebraska, Idaho and Utah taking the top spots, along with the Dakotas, Wyoming, Arizona, Kansas and Iowa. Republican Vermont squeaked in at tenth place after having deserted the party in 1964.

In comparison to 1960, Nebraska was Nixon's strongest state both times. Only Oklahoma, his third-best state in 1960, and Maine, fell off the GOP top 10. Oklahoma's 1960 Nixon vote was fueled by anti–Catholicism, and a strong challenge by Wallace in 1968, who drew 20% in the Sooner State, reduced Nixon to only a plurality victory in 1968. Maine, of course, reversed itself because of its enormous affection for Ed Muskie, one of the few times in political history that a vice presidential nominee affected the outcome in his home state.

Humphrey's strongest states were 4 New England states, led by Rhode Island and Massachusetts in the top 2 positions. Hawaii was third and Maine was fourth. (Maine is also one of the few states to be on one party's top 10 in one election and on the other party's top 10 in the election immediately following.) Humphrey's home state of Minnesota and pro-labor Michigan and West Virginia were on the Humphrey top 10, along with New York and Pennsylvania. For the second straight election, no southern state appeared on the Democrats' top 10, probably because Humphrey carried only Texas by 1 percentage point and ran third in most of the region. Five of

Humphrey's top 10 states, including Connecticut, were on JFK's 1960 list.

Wallace's strongest states were all in the South, where he won a majority of the vote in Alabama and Mississippi; a plurality in Louisiana, Georgia and Arkansas; and ran second in Tennessee, South Carolina and North Carolina.

Wallace was a national candidate, receiving votes in all 50 states. But his approach to the issues and his style and demeanor resonated primarily in the South. His victory in 578 counties made him the strongest third-party candidate in modern history, though his electoral vote total was second to Roosevelt in 1912, and his popular vote fell below that of Roosevelt, La Follette and later, Perot.

Wallace drew most of his 1968 support from 1964 Goldwater voters. This was particularly true in Alabama, Mississippi, north Louisiana, the Panhandle counties west of the Suwanee River in Florida, south Georgia, eastern Arkansas, western Tennessee, and southside Virginia. But Wallace carried dozens of counties that supported Johnson in 1964. This was the pattern in Arkansas, middle Tennessee, eastern North Carolina, the South Carolina upcountry, northeastern Florida, and North Georgia. Outside the South, the Wallace counties in western Kentucky, eastern Oklahoma and southeast Missouri had gone for Johnson. Wallace showed a remarkable ability to draw from both parties in the rural South and border areas.

It was noteworthy that Wallace carried 195 counties that supported all 4 Democratic nominees from 1952 to 1964. He carried only 71 counties that had supported all 4 Republican nominees during that time frame. But Wallace did carry Caddo, Louisiana (Shreveport); Polk, Florida (Lakeland); and Hamilton, Tennessee (Chattanooga), which were presidential Republican bastions since Eisenhower. Wallace clearly won some voters who had been voting Republican in presidential elections. Still, his widest appeal came from traditional southern Democrats who defected to Goldwater in 1964, carrying 210 counties that fit that description.

Wallace's appeal in the North clearly followed historic southern migration patterns and the location of the Mason-Dixon line. Contrary to some early and inaccurate reporting, Wallace ran strongest, not in white ethnic neighborhoods of northern cities, but in the southern-leaning counties from southern New Jersey through the eastern shore of Maryland, to the southernmost counties of Pennsylvania, Ohio, Illinois and Indiana. (Wallace did receive fairly strong support [10 percent to 15%] in some working-class white neighborhoods in Baltimore, Philadelphia, Pittsburgh, Cleveland and Milwaukee, but his strongest non–Southern support came in Warren and Clermont counties in southwest Ohio and in isolated Esmeralda, Mineral and Nye counties in Nevada.) He also did well in Alexander County, Illinois, in the state's Deep South "Egypt" region and in the "Little Dixie" counties of eastern New Mexico, southeast Missouri and western Kentucky.

The handful of pro–Goldwater counties in the North and West voted 2–1 for Nixon over Humphrey and gave Wallace 16% support, a bit higher than his average national support.

In parts of the rural South, support for Wallace was nearly unanimous. The Alabama governor received 91.7% of the ballots cast in Geneva County, Alabama, and 91.2% in George County, Mississippi. His vote exceeded 82% in 20 counties in Alabama, Mississippi, Florida and Georgia.

One unusual sidelight to the 1968 election is that Nixon was the first Republican to ever carry 9 counties in 6 states: Callaway and Platte, Missouri; Union, North Carolina; Marshall, Oklahoma; Spartanburg and Dillon, South Carolina; Putnam, Tennessee; and Amherst and Craig, Virginia. The Republican breakthrough into the South and border South continued, though largely unnoticed, in 1968.

Nixon was also the first Republican since Reconstruction to carry 10 counties in 6 southern and border states, mostly in Missouri and West Virginia but including Arkansas, Georgia, North Carolina and South Carolina. He was the first Republican since 1888 to carry Wake County (Raleigh), North Carolina.

The impact of the 1965 Voting Rights Act can be seen in South Carolina, where Humphrey carried 11 counties that had not gone for a Democrat since FDR in 1944 (Allendale, Bamberg, Beaufort, Calhoun, Clarendon, Dorchester, Hampton, Jasper, Orangeburg, Sumter, Williamsburg). All (except Beaufort) are in the "black-belt" areas, where African Americans are a majority of the population.

Top 10 States, 1968

Nixon	*Percentage*	*Humphrey*	*Percentage*	*Wallace*	*Percentage*
1. Nebraska	59.8	1. Rhode Island	64.0	1. Alabama	65.9
2. Idaho	56.8	2. Massachusetts	63.0	2. Mississippi	63.5
3. Utah	56.5	3. Hawaii	59.8	3. Louisiana	48.3
4. North Dakota	55.9	4. Maine	55.3	4. Georgia	42.8
5. Wyoming	55.8	5. Minnesota	54.0	5. Arkansas	38.9
6. Arizona	54.8	6. New York	49.7	6. Tennessee	34.0
7. Kansas	54.8	7. West Virginia	49.6	7. South Carolina	32.3
8. South Dakota	53.3	8. Connecticut	49.5	8. North Carolina	31.3
9. Iowa	53.0	9. Michigan	49.2	9. Florida	28.5
10. Vermont	52.8	10. Pennsylvania	47.6	10. Virginia	23.6

Electoral Votes, 1968

States	*Electoral Votes*	*Nixon*	*Humphrey*	*Wallace*
Alabama	10	–	–	10
Alaska	3	3	–	–
Arizona	5	5	–	–
Arkansas	6	–	–	6
California	40	40	–	–
Colorado	6	6	–	–
Connecticut	8	–	8	–
Delaware	3	3	–	–
District of Columbia	3	–	3	–
Florida	14	14	–	–
Georgia	12	–	–	12
Hawaii	4	–	4	–
Idaho	4	4	–	–
Illinois	26	26	–	–
Indiana	13	13	–	–
Iowa	9	9	–	–
Kansas	7	7	–	–

States	Electoral Votes	Nixon	Humphrey	Wallace
Kentucky	9	9	–	–
Louisiana	10	–	–	10
Maine	4	–	4	–
Maryland	10	–	10	–
Massachusetts	14	–	14	–
Michigan	21	–	21	–
Minnesota	10	–	10	–
Mississippi	7	–	–	7
Missouri	12	12	–	–
Montana	4	4	–	–
Nebraska	5	5	–	–
Nevada	3	3	–	–
New Hampshire	4	4	–	–
New Jersey	17	17	–	–
New Mexico	4	4	–	–
New York	43	–	43	–
North Carolina[1]	13	12	–	1
North Dakota	4	4	–	–
Ohio	26	26	–	–
Oklahoma	8	8	–	–
Oregon	6	6	–	–
Pennsylvania	29	–	29	–
Rhode Island	4	–	4	–
South Carolina	8	8	–	–
South Dakota	4	4	–	–
Tennessee	11	11	–	–
Texas	25	–	25	–
Utah	4	4	–	–
Vermont	3	3	–	–
Virginia	12	12	–	–
Washington	9	–	9	–
West Virginia	7	–	7	–
Wisconsin	12	12	–	–
Wyoming	3	3	–	–
Totals	538	301	191	46

1. One North Carolina Nixon elector voted for Wallace.

1972

Nixon
McGovern

President Nixon won a landslide by 61% to 38% over South Dakota senator George McGovern. He carried 49 states with 520 electoral votes to 1 state (Massachusetts) and the District of Columbia with 17 electoral votes for McGovern. It was the second greatest electoral college rout in history up to that time.

Nixon added the Wallace vote, carrying 572 of the 578 counties that backed Wallace in 1968, to his base. (The only 6 Wallace counties supporting McGovern were Bullock, Lowndes and Wilcox in Alabama and Houston, Perry and Stewart in Tennessee.) But he also pummeled McGovern in Humphrey counties, carrying 575 of Humphrey's 683 counties.

A small countertrend caused 16 counties to switch from Nixon to McGovern (10 of them in South Dakota). McGovern carried Rusk County, Wisconsin and Stevens County, Minnesota, both of which had gone to Nixon in 1968. He ran ahead of Humphrey in a number of counties in Iowa, Minnesota and Wisconsin — an area that the *Washington Post* labeled the "morality belt."

Voters in this area said they were most concerned about public morality and honesty in elected officials.

Nixon's best state was Mississippi, showing his complete dominance of the white South and the relative lukewarmness of African Americans and Hispanic southerners to the McGovern/Shriver ticket. Of the South's 1,100 counties, McGovern carried just 26. Nationally, McGovern carried only 130 counties, the fewest ever carried by a major-party candidate. The South Dakotan had little support in rural America. His appeal remained in the cities, where, for example, he won by a 2 to 1 landslide in Boston and San Francisco. McGovern still won 51.3% in the nation's dozen largest cities, which was slightly better than Stevenson's 1956 vote.

Nixon's top 10 states were heavily southern. Only Nebraska and Wyoming were not southern or border states. Oklahoma was back on Nixon's top 10, in third place, as in 1960. The Southeast was well represented (Georgia, Alabama, Florida, the Carolinas), as was Arkansas, which had never appeared on a Republican top 10 before.

McGovern's sole victory came in Massachusetts, a state filled with college students and others who were strongly antiwar in their sentiments. Rhode Island was second. Kennedy, Johnson, Humphrey and McGovern all ran strongly in these 2 heavily Catholic states. Most of McGovern's other best states were in the West and Midwest, with former rival Hubert Humphrey's Minnesota giving McGovern a slightly higher vote than his home state of South Dakota. While it was a blow for McGovern to lose his home state, it is not that unusual. Stevenson, Landon, Smith, Davis, and Taft all lost their home states. So did Bryan and Wilson.

Oregon, Michigan, Wisconsin, California and New York were more favorable to McGovern than most states. Illinois and Iowa were tied for tenth place. Many of these states had routinely appeared on Republican top 10 decades ago. Their tilt since the 1960s has clearly been in a Democratic direction.

The overwhelming victory of President Nixon overshadowed a smaller antitrend that eventually had an impact on politics. It does not show up much in county data but can be identified in smaller voting unit data (from precincts, wards, election districts) and in exit polls. McGovern ran ahead of Humphrey among young professionals, college graduates and those without strong religious ties or identifications. McGovern's vote percentage exceeded Humphrey's in the Beacon Hill area of Boston, the Society Hill neighborhood in Philadelphia, some of the Lakefront wards in Chicago, and similar gentrified inner-city "bohemian" clusters throughout the country. The trends observed here came to fruition more than a decade later.

In college towns throughout the United States, where antiwar sentiments were most pronounced, McGovern ran well ahead of Humphrey. This is one area where the impact of the new 18- to 21-year-old vote was felt. McGovern carried State College, Pennsylvania, the home of Penn State University and a longtime Republican area that had gone for Nixon in 1968. A similar result came in the college towns of Edinboro, Pennsylvania, and Marlboro, Vermont. McGovern ran decidedly stronger than Humphrey in Iowa City and Ames in Iowa; in Hanover and Durham in New Hampshire; in Amherst, Massachusetts; and in Princeton, New Jersey. While hardly noticed in the postelection commentary, these results represent a long-term Democratic trend in academic communities nationwide.

In 1972 the desertion of the McGovern-Shriver ticket by southern Democrats reached titanic proportions. There were 120 counties in 13 southern and border states that went Republican for the first time. There were 37 such counties in Texas, 17 each in Arkansas and Tennessee, 14 in Kentucky and 12 in Georgia. Other states with first-time-ever Republican victories included Oklahoma (6), Florida (5), North Carolina (5), South Carolina (2), Virginia (2), Louisiana (1), Missouri (1) and West Virginia (1).

Nixon was the first Republican since Reconstruction to carry 73 counties in 12 southern and border states, most of them in Tennessee, Arkansas, and North Carolina. Nixon was the first Republican since Abraham Lincoln in 1864 to carry Howard and Randolph counties in Missouri and Fulton, Hickman and Marshall counties in Kentucky. Nixon was also the first Republican since the McKinley era to carry 42 counties in 8 southern states. These 226 counties were clearly anti–McGovern, since almost all of them went back to Jimmy Carter in 1976.

The voter turnout increased from 73.2 to 77.7 million, or about 6%. The enfranchisement of 18 to 21 year olds was expected to swell the electorate more than it actually did. The total vote was up 1.1 million in California, a solid 15% increase. California was an ideologically driven state, where both McGovern and Goldwater ran stronger than nationwide. Large liberal Democratic and conservative Republican bases were energized in California.

Florida's vote increased 18%, largely due to population gain, as was true in Arizona, where the total vote increased 28%, and in New Mexico, where turnout was up 18%. The vote also increased in Nevada, Montana, New Hampshire, Vermont, North Dakota, Oregon, Texas, Utah, Washington, and Wyoming. None of the big population states other than California experienced a large gain, except for Minnesota and Wisconsin, where turnout was up almost 10%.

Turnout declined in much of the South, and was down 20% in George Wallace's strongest counties.

John Schmitz, a congressman from southern California and a John Birch Society member, received 1 million votes (1.4%) on the American Party ticket, a remnant of the 1968 Wallace campaign. Schmitz's largest vote support came in Idaho, where he received 9.3% of the vote, and he ran second to Nixon in Fremont, Jefferson, Lemhi and Madison counties in the conservative Mormon southeastern part of the state. Schmitz amassed 5% of Oregon's vote, topping 10% in 5 counties. Schmitz won 6% in Utah and 11% in Utah County, home to Brigham Young University. Schmitz also received 4% in Washington State and in Louisiana.

The 1972 Nixon landslide had little effect on American politics. His party failed to win either house of Congress, and the Watergate scandal soon engulfed and ultimately destroyed his presidency in 1974.

Top 10 States, 1972

Nixon	Percentage	McGovern	Percentage
1. Mississippi	78.2	1. Massachusetts	54.2
2. Georgia	75.0	2. Rhode Island	46.8
3. Oklahoma	73.7	3. Minnesota	46.1
4. Alabama	72.4	4. South Dakota	45.5
5. Florida	71.9	5. Wisconsin	43.7
6. South Carolina	70.8	6. Oregon	42.3
7. Nebraska	70.5	7. Michigan	41.8
8. North Carolina	69.5	8. California	41.5
9. Wyoming	69.0	9. New York	41.2
10. Arkansas	68.9	10. Illinois	40.5
		10. Iowa	40.5

Electoral Votes, 1972

States	Electoral Votes	Nixon	McGovern	States	Electoral Votes	Nixon	McGovern
Alabama	9	9	–	Colorado	7	7	–
Alaska	3	3	–	Connecticut	8	8	–
Arizona	6	6	–	Delaware	3	3	–
Arkansas	6	6	–	District of Columbia	3	–	3
California	45	45	–	Florida	17	17	–

States	Electoral Votes	Nixon	McGovern	States	Electoral Votes	Nixon	McGovern
Georgia	12	12	–	North Carolina	13	13	–
Hawaii	4	4	–	North Dakota	3	3	–
Idaho	4	4	–	Ohio	25	25	–
Illinois	26	26	–	Oklahoma	8	8	–
Indiana	13	13	–	Oregon	6	6	–
Iowa	8	8	–	Pennsylvania	27	27	–
Kansas	7	7	–	Rhode Island	4	4	–
Kentucky	9	9	–	South Carolina	8	8	–
Louisiana	10	10	–	South Dakota	4	4	–
Maine	4	4	–	Tennessee	10	10	–
Maryland	10	10	–	Texas	26	26	–
Massachusetts	14	–	14	Utah	4	4	–
Michigan	21	21	–	Vermont	3	3	–
Minnesota	10	10	–	Virginia[1]	12	11	–
Mississippi	7	7	–	Washington	9	9	–
Missouri	12	12	–	West Virginia	6	6	–
Montana	4	4	–	Wisconsin	11	11	–
Nebraska	5	5	–	Wyoming	3	3	–
Nevada	3	3	–				
New Hampshire	4	4	–	Totals	538	520	17
New Jersey	17	17	–				
New Mexico	4	4	–				
New York	41	41	–				

1. One Virginia Nixon elector voted for the Libertarian Party candidate, John Hospers.

1976

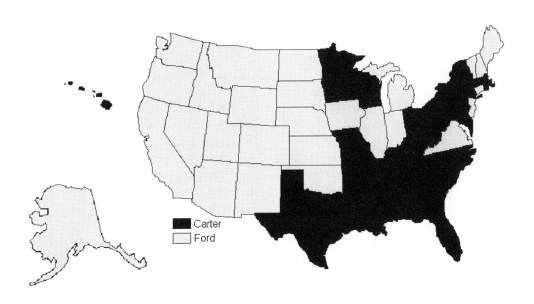

Carter

Ford

The 1976 election brought forth a number of new candidates and political strategies, finally pitting a little-known former governor of Georgia named Jimmy Carter against President Gerald Ford, a longtime Michigan congressman who became president after the resignation of Richard Nixon.

Both Carter and Ford fought a spirited primary campaign and their nominations were not completely sealed until the conventions (especially in Ford's case). Ford barely defeated former California governor Ronald Reagan for the GOP nomination, and Carter fought off a varied field of contenders. Carter won only 39% of the 16 million Democratic primary voters, while Ford beat Reagan 53% to 46% among the 10 million Republican primary voters.

In November, though, both parties rallied to their standard bearers and consolidated their base voters. Carter edged Ford 50% to 48% of all votes and won by 297 to 240 in the electoral college. (One Ford elector in Washington State voted for Reagan.) His major-party vote majority was 51% to 49%.

Carter was the first victor to owe his election solely to the South since Woodrow Wilson in 1916. Carter's electoral vote majority of 297 to 240 was fashioned from his victory in 10 of the 11 southern states (all but Virginia) plus most of the industrial Northeast and Midwest. Unlike Wilson, though, he won almost no states in the West (only reliably Democratic Hawaii, in a relative squeaker). Carter carried 23 states and Ford carried 27.

There was a clear religious factor in the 1976 voting as southern Baptists, who had played a key role in anti–Kennedy balloting in 1960, were resolutely pro–Carter in 1976. He carried all of the most heavily Baptist states except Oklahoma, where he lost by 1 percentage point.

He won 5 of the 6 border states plus Minnesota and Wisconsin. Carter carried Ohio, Wisconsin, and Tennessee, which had rejected both Kennedy and Humphrey in 1960 and 1968. But he lost Connecticut and Michigan, which had supported Kennedy and Humphrey, though the Michigan result was probably a reflection of home-state loyalty toward Ford.

Carter fashioned a Truman-like victory, winning cities and rural areas, while losing to Ford heavily in the nation's suburbs and small cities and towns. Ford swept the West, winning impressively in the Mormon states of Utah and Idaho, and he also carried upper New England.

Carter ran 13 percentage points ahead of McGovern, and he gained in every state, ranging from 42 points in Georgia to 1 point in Alaska. It was a true national voter shift. Carter ran 34 points ahead of McGovern in Arkansas, and more than 20 points ahead of McGovern in every southern state but Texas and Virginia. He also gained more than 20 points in Oklahoma and West Virginia.

But Carter's gains were much below the national average in a few states other than Alaska: He gained fewer than 6 points in Massachusetts, Michigan, Oregon, South Dakota and Wisconsin. In all 6 New England states, his gain was lower than the national average, but in all 17 southern and border states, he exceeded his national gain. The cultural clash between New England and the South — a mainstay of U.S. politics for over a century — was alive and well in 1976.

But Carter was able to transcend these differences, winning his greatest victories in Georgia, Arkansas, and West Virginia, while also retaining Massachusetts and Rhode Island among his top 10 states. (Seven were in the South, and 1, Minnesota, was in the Midwest.)

Ford's strongest states had a distinct western tilt, with 7 of the top 10 being in that region, anchored by Utah, Idaho and Wyoming. New Hampshire and Vermont were on the list, as were Colorado and Indiana. The Ford coalition resembled the Willkie-Dewey days of the 1940s. One key to the Carter sweep of Dixie was the shift of the 1968 Wallace vote to Georgia's governor. Carter carried 513 Wallace counties, while Ford carried only 65 of them. Ford did, however, carry some of the large population centers that backed Wallace. He carried the counties that included the cities of Shreveport, Baton Rouge, Jackson, Montgomery, Birmingham, Mobile and Pensacola.

Carter's solid victory in the counties carried by Wallace 8 years before was a major factor in his near-sweep of the region. There were, however, some differences within the Wallace counties. This was a reassertion of traditional political preferences that predated the Wallace and Carter candidacies. Of the Wallace counties that had backed all four Democrats from 1952 to 1964, Carter carried 98.5% of them. But of the Wallace counties that had preferred Republican presidential nominees, Carter carried only 61.5% of them. Some of the Wallace counties that supported Ford were large population centers such as Shreveport, Birmingham, Montgomery, Mobile, and Pensacola. But Carter was clearly the favorite among 1968 Wallace voters. And this did not affect his overwhelming support among African Americans.

Carter won 1,709 counties to Ford's 1,402. Amazingly, he carried 1,582 counties that had gone for Nixon in 1972 — more than half of them. He lost only 3 McGovern counties to Ford: Washtenaw, Michigan, home of Ford's alma mater, the University of Michigan; Clay, South Dakota, home to the University of South Dakota; and Pitkin, Colorado, home to the fashionable ski resort of Aspen.

Carter did surprisingly well in Republican rural areas, winning Loudon and Fentress counties, Tennessee and Crittenden county in Kentucky, which had not voted Democratic in a century. The Georgian carried 47 counties in 13 states that had not

gone Democratic either since the Roosevelt days or since 1952. All but 2 had large Baptist populations. (Baptists outnumbered Catholics 55% to 7% in these pro–Carter Republican counties.)

Carter also won many northern and western rural counties that had not supported Kennedy or Humphrey. These counties were 82% Protestant, with Methodists and Lutherans the dominant Protestant groups. In contrast, counties that supported Kennedy and Humphrey but not Carter were 69% Catholic. Catholics were also 65% of the population in the counties that supported all three Democrats in 1960, 1968 and 1976 but were only 37% in the counties that backed Nixon and Ford.

Carter made remarkable inroads into a small swing vote of Republican Protestants in small-town America. But as the election of 1980 demonstrated, it did not last.

While the 1976 election was the third closest race since 1960, it represented the fourth straight large shift in voter sentiment, since Carter ran 13 points ahead of McGovern in major-party vote percentage. The 1964–1976 cycle was one of the most volatile in U.S. political history.

The 1976 race also pitted the South and, to some extent, the East against the West. Carter, the first Deep South resident since Zachary Taylor to become president, carried every southern state except Virginia. His southern electoral votes carried him to the White House, the first time the South had effectively elected a president since Wilson in 1916. Carter held enough of the industrial East to overcome a Ford sweep of the West and Midwest. Carter's southern heritage also helped him win 5 of the 6 border states, losing only Oklahoma. (Carter won 15 of the 17 states that are considered the South or the border South by some cultural geographers.)

The 1976 turnout was only 4.9% above 1972, an increase of less than 4 million votes. However, the total vote surged in

Carter's native South (up 25% in Georgia, 23% in Tennessee, and 22% in Florida and Louisiana). The total vote declined by 600,000, or 9%, in New York and by 500,000, or 6%, in California. Enthusiasm waned in many of the nation's largest states. It was up 600,000 in Texas, however, and a more than 10% increase was experienced in Minnesota and Wisconsin, two civic-minded states where voter turnout is always high. The same was true in Maine (up 16%). Fast-growing Alaska had the largest turnout increase of nearly 30%.

Top 10 States, 1976

Carter	Percentage	Ford	Percentage
1. Georgia	66.7	1. Utah	62.4
2. Arkansas	65.0	2. Idaho	59.3
3. West Virginia	58.0	3. Wyoming	59.3
4. South Carolina	56.2	4. Nebraska	59.2
5. Massachusetts	56.1	5. Alaska	57.9
6. Tennessee	55.9	6. Arizona	56.4
7. Alabama	55.7	7. New Hampshire	54.7
8. Rhode Island	55.4	8. Vermont	54.4
9. North Carolina	55.2	9. Colorado	54.0
10. Minnesota	54.9	10. Indiana	53.3

Electoral Votes, 1976

States	Electoral Votes	Carter	Ford	States	Electoral Votes	Carter	Ford
Alabama	9	9	–	Massachusetts	14	14	–
Alaska	3	–	3	Michigan	21	–	21
Arizona	6	–	6	Minnesota	10	10	–
Arkansas	6	6	–	Mississippi	7	7	–
California	45	–	45	Missouri	12	12	–
Colorado	7	–	7	Montana	4	–	4
Connecticut	8	–	8	Nebraska	5	–	5
Delaware	3	3	–	Nevada	3	–	3
District of Columbia	3	3	–	New Hampshire	4	–	4
Florida	17	17	–	New Jersey	17	–	17
Georgia	12	12	–	New Mexico	4	–	4
Hawaii	4	4	–	New York	41	41	–
Idaho	4	–	4	North Carolina	13	13	–
Illinois	26	–	26	North Dakota	3	–	3
Indiana	13	–	13	Ohio	25	25	–
Iowa	8	–	8	Oklahoma	3	–	3
Kansas	7	–	7	Oregon	6	–	6
Kentucky	9	9	–	Pennsylvania	27	27	–
Louisiana	10	10	–	Rhode Island	4	4	–
Maine	4	–	4	South Carolina	8	8	–
Maryland	10	10	–	South Dakota	4	–	4

States	Electoral Votes	Carter	Ford
Tennessee	10	10	–
Texas	26	26	–
Utah	4	–	4
Vermont	3	–	3
Virginia	12	–	12
Washington[1]	9	–	8
West Virginia	6	6	–

States	Electoral Votes	Carter	Ford
Wisconsin	11	11	–
Wyoming	3	–	3
Totals	538	297	240

1. One Ford elector in Washington state voted for Ronald Reagan.

1980

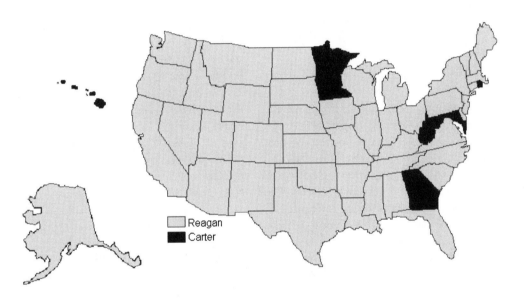

Reagan
Carter

Former California governor Ronald Reagan coasted to victory over President Jimmy Carter, carrying 44 states with 489 electoral votes to Carter's 6 states and 49 electoral votes. It was the worst defeat for an incumbent president since Hoover's 1932 defeat, and even Hoover had more electoral votes. Reagan's triumph encompassed the entire nation, with an especially delicious victory in every southern state but Georgia. Carter was reduced to an unusual half-dozen states including Rhode Island, Hawaii, Minnesota (home of his vice president, Walter Mondale), Maryland, West Virginia, and Georgia. Nine of Carter's top 10 states were in the South or border states. In this three-way election, 3 of the 6 states Carter carried were not on his top 10, and 7 of his top 10 states went in 1980 for Reagan.

A landslide of this magnitude usually means a popular-vote victory of 20 percentage points, but Reagan won by just under 10 points (51 percent to 41%). The lopsided electoral vote (91% for Reagan) was affected somewhat by Reagan's narrow (2% or less) victory in Alabama, Arkansas, Kentucky, Mississippi, North Carolina, South Carolina, Tennessee, and Massachusetts (itself an extraordinary result as it was the only state George McGovern carried). With just a slight tilt in the above-mentioned states, Carter would have received a more respectable 125 votes.

Reagan won a landslide in the West, beating Carter 73% to 21% in Utah, and he carried California by a bigger margin than Nixon's over McGovern. Even liberal New York went for the most conservative GOP candidate since Goldwater. Reagan carried 2,212 counties to Carter's 898. Reagan carried almost half of Carter's 1976 counties, compared to a tiny number (13) that switched from Ford to Carter. (Most of the Ford 1976/Carter 1980 counties were in New York and Mississippi, a highly incongruous pairing.)

All 10 of Reagan's strongest states were in the West, with Utah and Idaho at the head of the pack. The interior West and the farm belt were especially favorable to Reagan, a man of the West, who was born in Illinois and lived for many years in California. Reagan's most significant gains over Ford's vote came in the South and West. He ran weaker than Ford only in Vermont.

A third-party candidate, John Anderson, a maverick liberal Republican and a House representative from Illinois, received nearly 7% of the votes cast, mostly in New England, in prosperous suburbs on both coasts, and in Colorado's "granola belt" counties where young professionals and independents lived. But Anderson was not really a spoiler. He carried no states and no counties and did not even run second in a single county. (A few New England villages and a few college towns in Iowa were the only places where Anderson ran second.) If every Anderson vote had gone to Carter, the president would still have lost the election. (And, pointedly, on election night, Anderson expressed gratification that Carter had been defeated.) Six of Anderson's strongest states were in New England and 4 were in the far West.

Carter's GOP crossover voters in 1976

deserted him in droves. Of the 47 longtime Republican counties that went for Carter in 1976, only 13 remained loyal in 1980. And he managed to lose counties that had even voted for McGovern 8 years before.

Anderson's vote differed from almost all previous third-party movements. Protest movements from the 1880s to the present did best among the dispossessed, the discontented and the downtrodden. They won their largest support in the lower-income strata of society and generally in depressed rural areas or inner cities. But Anderson's vote was primarily from the middle to upper-middle class, centered around well-educated professionals. He drew best from self-styled independents and probably did a bit better among Republicans than Democrats. In New England his vote was strong in the old liberal Republican small towns, where he often ran second to Reagan.

Anderson had considerable drawing power in liberal college towns and he did especially well in Hanover, New Hampshire (Dartmouth College); Ames, Iowa (Iowa State University); and Iowa City, Iowa (University of Iowa). Anderson ran second to Carter in the precincts surrounding the two Iowa colleges, where he clearly cut into the Democratic vote.

Anderson ran strongly among Jewish voters (15% to 20%), especially in New York. But his vote, while probably Democratic in the Jewish community, did not hurt Carter as much as expected, because Reagan also won some Jewish Democratic crossover votes. Reagan actually led Carter 42% to 37% among New York Jewish voters with Anderson receiving over 21%, according to the ABC-TV exit poll. In Philadelphia, Reagan was the first Republican in memory to carry one of the two Jewish wards in the northeast sector of the city.

Anderson's vote was above average (12 percent to 15%) among Lutherans in the Midwest and among "Yankee" Protestants, who belonged to the mainline churches. He also did well in the liberal ski resorts of Colorado, securing 20% of the Aspen vote. He ran best among the well-to-do, the very well educated, and among secular voters who are not church members (17% from this group voted for Anderson, mainly at Carter's expense).

Five million more people voted in 1980 than in 1976, a 6% increase. Turnout increased in 45 states, and declined only in Massachusetts, New Jersey, New York, Pennsylvania, and West Virginia.

In round numbers the total vote was up 720,000 in California; 536,000 in Florida; 470,000 in Texas; 270,000 in Louisiana; 256,000 in Michigan; and over 150,000 in Alabama, North Carolina, Ohio,

Oregon, Virginia, Washington and Wisconsin. As can be seen, the West and the South recorded the greatest increases in voter turnout. The largest percentage increases were in Alaska (28%), Idaho (27%), and Nevada (23%).

Ed Clark, the Libertarian Party candidate, received 1% of the national vote. His most impressive showing came in Alaska, where he took 11.7% of the vote and ran ahead of John Anderson, who received 7%. Clark also ran ahead of his national vote in several other western states, including Colorado (2.2%), California (1.7%), Idaho (1.9%), Arizona (2.2%), Montana (2.7%), Nevada (1.8%), Oregon (2.2%), Washington (1.7%) and Wyoming (2.6%).

Top 10 States, 1980

Reagan	Percentage	Carter	Percentage	Anderson	Percentage
1. Utah	72.8	1. Georgia	55.8	1. Massachusetts	15.2
2. Idaho	66.5	2. West Virginia	49.8	2. Vermont	14.9
3. Nebraska	65.5	3. Tennessee	48.4	3. Rhode Island	14.4
4. North Dakota	64.2	4. Mississippi	48.1	4. New Hampshire	12.9
5. Wyoming	62.6	5. South Carolina	48.1	5. Connecticut	12.2
6. Nevada	62.5	6. Rhode Island	47.7	6. Colorado	11.0
7. Arizona	60.6	7. Kentucky	47.6	7. Hawaii	10.6
8. Oklahoma	60.5	8. Arkansas	47.5	8. Washington	10.6
9. South Dakota	60.5	9. Alabama	47.4	9. Maine	10.2
10. Kansas	57.9	10. North Carolina	47.2	10. Oregon	9.5

Electoral Votes, 1980

States	Electoral Votes	Reagan	Carter	States	Electoral Votes	Reagan	Carter
Alabama	9	9	–	Hawaii	4	–	4
Alaska	3	3	–	Idaho	4	4	–
Arizona	6	6	–	Illinois	26	26	–
Arkansas	6	6	–	Indiana	13	13	–
California	45	45	–	Iowa	8	8	–
Colorado	7	7	–	Kansas	7	7	–
Connecticut	8	8	–	Kentucky	9	9	–
Delaware	3	3	–	Louisiana	10	10	–
District of Columbia	3	–	3	Maine	4	4	–
Florida	17	17	–	Maryland	10	–	10
Georgia	12	–	12	Massachusetts	14	14	–

States	Electoral Votes	Reagan	Carter	States	Electoral Votes	Reagan	Carter
Michigan	21	21	–	Pennsylvania	27	27	–
Minnesota	10	–	10	Rhode Island	4	–	4
Mississippi	7	7	–	South Carolina	8	8	–
Missouri	12	12	–	South Dakota	4	4	–
Montana	4	4	–	Tennessee	10	10	–
Nebraska	5	5	–	Texas	26	26	–
Nevada	3	3	–	Utah	4	4	–
New Hampshire	4	4	–	Vermont	3	3	–
New Jersey	17	17	–	Virginia	12	12	–
New Mexico	4	4	–	Washington	9	9	–
New York	41	41	–	West Virginia	6	–	6
North Carolina	13	13	–	Wisconsin	11	11	–
North Dakota	3	3	–	Wyoming	3	3	–
Ohio	25	25	–				
Oklahoma	8	8	–	Totals	638	489	49
Oregon	6	6	–				

1984

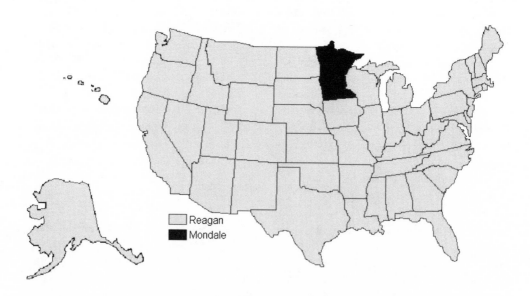

Reagan
Mondale

President Ronald Reagan was reelected in another one of the great landslides, carrying 49 states with 525 electoral votes, while his opponent, former vice president Walter Mondale, carried his home state of Minnesota and the District of Columbia for 13 electoral votes. The popular-vote majority fell a little below previous victories for Harding, FDR, LBJ and Nixon, but was still a hefty 59% to 41%. Reagan's 54,455,075 vote total was the highest ever recorded in a U.S. presidential election and was exceeded finally by John Kerry and George W. Bush's vote totals in the 2004 election.

Reagan carried 2,780 counties to Mondale's 332. Reagan's huge southern victory helped him carry more than 600 of Carter's counties from 1980. Reagan gained 19 percentage points in Georgia, 14 points in South Carolina, and over 10 points in much of the South and New England.

Mondale picked up 35 counties in 14 states that had gone for Reagan in 1980. Mondale made modest gains in the Dakotas, Iowa and California, and he won comfortably in the big cities. Metropolitan and suburban areas went for Reagan easily, and the president ran stronger in most metros in 1984 than in 1980. Three exceptions were the San Francisco, Pittsburgh and Washington, D.C., areas, where Mondale posted gains. Symbolic of the pro–Mondale trend in these regions were Marin and Santa Cruz counties in California and Arlington and Alexandria counties in Virginia — all high-income areas that switched from Reagan to Mondale.

The Anderson vote proved to be insignificant in 1984. Even though Anderson endorsed Mondale, and exit polls showed the Anderson vote going about 70% to 30% for Mondale over Reagan, Anderson's strongest counties showed no significant shift in Mondale's direction. There was more shifting between the major-party candidates according to exit polls (13% of voters switched from Reagan to Mondale; 18% switched from Carter to Reagan).

Reagan's victory was sweetened by the fact that he carried 52 counties that had gone for McGovern just 12 years earlier. Reagan was also the first Republican in history to carry Monroe County, Missouri, in the state's Little Dixie region, where Mark Twain was born in 1835. Monroe County had been rejecting Republican presidential candidates for nearly 130 years.

Native Americans switched their support from Reagan in 1980 to Mondale in 1984. Counties in Arizona, New Mexico and South Dakota exemplified this countertrend.

Nine of Reagan's top 10 states were in the West, with Utah, Idaho and Nebraska the top 3 again. North Dakota, in fourth place in 1980, fell off the list, as did South Dakota. New Hampshire and Alaska were new to the Reagan top 10.

Mondale's campaign resonated with a very different group of voters. Nine of his top 10 states were not on the Carter top 10 in 1980. Only West Virginia appeared on both lists. Five of Mondale's strongest states were in the Northeast (Massachusetts, New York, Pennsylvania, Rhode Island, Maryland). Minnesota, Iowa and Wisconsin were on the Mondale top 10. The appearance of Iowa shows the Hawkeye State's drift toward the Democrats during the 1980s. Hawaii reappeared for the first time since Humphrey's 1968 effort. Not a single southern state appeared on Mondale's top 10.

Turnout rose 6 million in Ronald Reagan's reelection bid, a 7% increase over 1980. Turnout was up in 43 states, down in only 7 (Idaho, Indiana, Michigan, Rhode Island, South Dakota, West Virginia and Wisconsin). Even New York, which had experienced declines in 1980 and 1976, registered an increase of 600,000 votes. In California, turnout jumped 900,000; in Florida, 500,000; and in Texas, 856,000. Increases of more than 150,000 votes were also recorded in Arizona, Georgia, Louisiana, New Jersey, North Carolina, Ohio, Pennsylvania and Virginia.

TOP 10 STATES, 1984

Reagan	Percentage	Mondale	Percentage
1. Utah	74.5	1. Minnesota	49.7
2. Idaho	72.4	2. Massachusetts	48.4
3. Nebraska	70.6	3. Rhode Island	48.0
4. Wyoming	70.5	4. Maryland	47.0
5. New Hampshire	68.6	5. Pennsylvania	46.0
6. Oklahoma	68.6	6. Iowa	45.9
7. Alaska	66.7	7. New York	45.8
8. Arizona	66.4	8. Wisconsin	45.0
9. Kansas	66.3	9. West Virginia	44.6
10. Nevada	65.8	10. Hawaii	43.8

ELECTORAL VOTES, 1984

States	Electoral Votes	Reagan	Mondale	States	Electoral Votes	Reagan	Mondale
Alabama	9	9	–	Nebraska	5	5	–
Alaska	3	3	–	Nevada	4	4	–
Arizona	7	7	–	New Hampshire	4	4	–
Arkansas	6	6	–	New Jersey	16	16	–
California	47	47	–	New Mexico	5	5	–
Colorado	8	8	–	New York	36	36	–
Connecticut	8	8	–	North Carolina	13	13	–
Delaware	3	3	–	North Dakota	3	3	–
District of Columbia	3	–	3	Ohio	23	23	–
Florida	21	21	–	Oklahoma	8	8	–
Georgia	12	12	–	Oregon	7	7	–
Hawaii	4	4	–	Pennsylvania	25	25	–
Idaho	4	4	–	Rhode Island	4	4	–
Illinois	24	24	–	South Carolina	8	8	–
Indiana	12	12	–	South Dakota	3	3	–
Iowa	8	8	–	Tennessee	11	11	–
Kansas	7	7	–	Texas	29	29	–
Kentucky	9	9	–	Utah	5	5	–
Louisiana	10	10	–	Vermont	3	3	–
Maine	4	4	–	Virginia	12	12	–
Maryland	10	10	–	Washington	10	10	–
Massachusetts	13	13	–	West Virginia	6	6	–
Michigan	20	20	–	Wisconsin	11	11	–
Minnesota	10	–	10	Wyoming	3	3	–
Mississippi	7	7	–				
Missouri	11	11	–	Totals	538	525	13
Montana	4	4	–				

1988

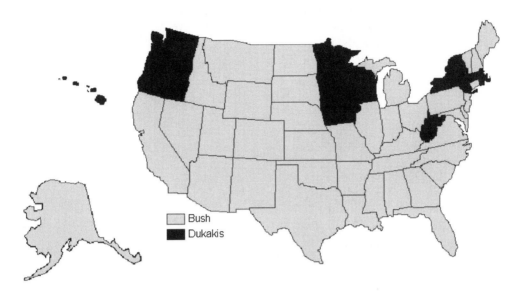

Bush
Dukakis

Vice President George Bush became the first sitting vice president to win the presidency since Martin Van Buren in 1836. The Bush victory was decisive: 40 states with 426 electoral votes to Massachusetts governor Michael Dukakis's 10 states and 111 electoral votes. (One West Virginia Dukakis elector insisted on voting for Dukakis's running mate, Texas senator Lloyd Bentsen.) The popular-vote tally was about 54% to 46%, pretty much in the range of the Reagan 1980 and Eisenhower 1952 margins. This was the first election since 1940 in which the incumbent party won its third election in a row.

For the second time in a row, a Republican carried all 11 southern states, and in 2 of them, Georgia and Tennessee, Bush's vote support equaled Reagan's. Bush even carried 7 counties that had gone to Mondale in Georgia, Tennessee and South Carolina. All were rural, though 1 (Bibb County, Georgia), included the small city of Macon.

Dukakis, however, carried 10 states, more than Carter in 1980 and Stevenson in 1952 and 1956. The Massachusetts governor captured New York and held a number of usually Democratic states (Massachusetts, Rhode Island, Hawaii, West Virginia, Minnesota). His 3 strongest states were an unusual trio: Rhode Island, Iowa and Hawaii, which have little in common. His most remarkable triumph was surely in Iowa, a Republican-leaning state historically, but the second strongest supporter of Dukakis. Iowa was undergoing harsh economic times and voted Democratic for the first time since 1964. Another surprise was Oregon, which had also eluded the Democrats since LBJ. Washington State, which had not gone Democratic since Humphrey in 1968, also backed Dukakis, as did marginal Wisconsin.

It is noteworthy that Dukakis carried 62 counties that had not backed a Democrat since LBJ in 1964. Most were in the upper Midwest and on the Pacific Coast; 2 Vermont counties (Addison and Windham) were included in the East. Interestingly, the pro–Dukakis counties were heavily Lutheran in religion; nearly 25% of residents in these counties belonged to Lutheran churches, four times the national average of 6% Lutheran.

Bush's top 3 states were Utah, New Hampshire and Idaho. Two were the most Mormon states but New Hampshire bordered Massachusetts. Four southern states (South Carolina, Florida, Mississippi, and Georgia) made the Bush list. So did Wyoming, Nebraska and Arizona. Bush's election was accomplished by maintaining the Reagan coalition. Still, Dukakis carried 493 Reagan counties and added 5 percentage points to the Democratic popular vote — even more in the West. His native East remained lukewarm, with 6 of the 9 northeastern states going for Bush. Two disappointments for Dukakis were Maryland and Pennsylvania, where he added only a few points in two of Mondale's strongest states and failed to carry either of them. Dukakis registered his largest gains over Mondale's vote in states where he had no chance of victory, such as North Dakota, South Dakota, Nebraska, Kansas, and Oklahoma.

The total votes cast declined 1 million from 1984; this was the first presidential election turnout decline since 1944. Declines were most severe in Illinois, Pennsylvania, New York, Michigan, Arkansas, Louisiana, Ohio, Oklahoma, Tennessee and West Virginia. Even Alaska recorded its first-ever decline in presidential vote turnout.

The percentage turnout of voting-age population was the lowest since 1924. Another indication of voter apathy was the fact that only 34% of newspapers endorsed either candidate, down from 55% in 1984. Even the normally pro–Democratic *Washington Post* refused to endorse, publishing a kind of "pox on both your houses" editorial.

But 1988 turnout was up 382,000 (or 4%) in California, and it increased 14% in Arizona, where the total vote was up 146,000. New Hampshire, Bush's second-strongest state, recorded a solid 16% increase in total vote, and fast-growing Nevada was up 22%.

Top 10 States, 1988

Bush	Percentage	Dukakis	Percentage
1. Utah	66.2	1. Rhode Island	55.6
2. New Hampshire	62.4	2. Iowa	54.7
3. Idaho	62.1	3. Hawaii	54.3
4. South Carolina	61.5	4. Massachusetts	53.2
5. Florida	60.9	5. Minnesota	52.9
6. Wyoming	60.5	6. West Virginia	52.2
7. Nebraska	60.2	7. New York	51.6
8. Arizona	60.0	8. Wisconsin	51.4
9. Mississippi	59.9	9. Oregon	51.3
10. Georgia	59.8	10. Washington	50.0
10. Indiana	59.8		

Electoral Votes, 1988

States	Electoral Votes	Bush	Dukakis	States	Electoral Votes	Bush	Dukakis
Alabama	9	9	–	Arkansas	6	6	–
Alaska	3	3	–	California	47	47	–
Arizona	7	7	–	Colorado	8	8	–

States	Electoral Votes	Bush	Dukakis	States	Electoral Votes	Bush	Dukakis
Connecticut	8	8	–	New Mexico	5	5	–
Delaware	3	3	–	New York	36	–	36
District of Columbia	3	–	3	North Carolina	13	13	–
Florida	21	21	–	North Dakota	3	3	–
Georgia	12	12	–	Ohio	23	23	–
Hawaii	4	–	4	Oklahoma	8	8	–
Idaho	4	4	–	Oregon	7	–	7
Illinois	24	24	–	Pennsylvania	25	25	–
Indiana	12	12	–	Rhode Island	4	–	4
Iowa	8	–	8	South Carolina	8	8	–
Kansas	7	7	–	South Dakota	3	3	–
Kentucky	9	9	–	Tennessee	11	11	–
Louisiana	10	10	–	Texas	29	29	–
Maine	4	4	–	Utah	5	5	–
Maryland	10	10	–	Vermont	3	3	–
Massachusetts	13	–	13	Virginia	12	12	–
Michigan	20	20	–	Washington	10	–	10
Minnesota	10	–	10	West Virginia[1]	6	–	5
Mississippi	7	7	–	Wisconsin	11	–	11
Missouri	11	11	–	Wyoming	3	3	–
Montana	4	4	–				
Nebraska	5	5	–				
Nevada	4	4	–	**Totals**	538	426	111
New Hampshire	4	4	–				
New Jersey	16	16	–				

1. One Dukakis elector voted for Dukakis's running mate, Lloyd Bentsen.

1992

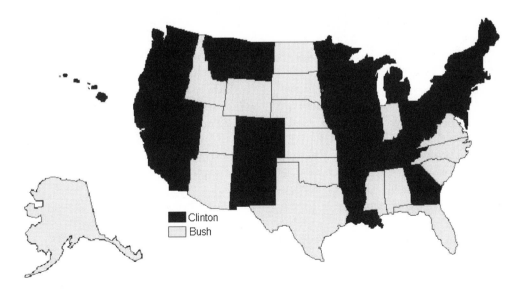

Clinton
Bush

An all-southern Democratic ticket (Arkansas governor Bill Clinton and Tennessee senator Al Gore) brought the Democrats their first victory since 1976. Clinton carried 32 states, 22 more than Dukakis in 1988, and received 370 electoral votes, while President Bush carried 18 states and garnered 168 electoral votes. Clinton won 43% to 37%, while a strong independent contender, Texas billionaire Ross Perot, received 19%.

Clinton won states in every region and was particularly successful in breaking into what had been the solid Republican West. He swept all 9 states in the Northeast (11 if you count Maryland and Delaware) and 4 of the 5 Pacific Coast states. He was the first Democrat since LBJ to carry Colorado, Illinois, Montana, Nevada, New Hampshire, New Jersey, New Mexico, and Vermont — which all cast a total of 64 electoral votes. Even New Hampshire, Bush's second-strongest state in 1988, fell into the Clinton corner. Clinton carried a majority of the states that Bush had carried in 1988.

Ironically, the Clinton-Gore ticket won only 4 of 11 southern states. Bush's 3 strongest states were Mississippi, South Carolina and Alabama. Clinton's Arkansas joined Maryland and New York as his most supportive states.

A comparison with the last Democratic victory in 1976 shows how much America had changed in just 16 years. Clinton carried 15 states that had gone for Ford while Bush carried 6 southern states that had supported Carter. Ten of the Clinton/Ford states were in the West or Midwest, and 5 were in the East. It is exceedingly rare that 21 of 50 states would change sides when the same party won in 1976 and 1992 by fairly similar popular-vote margins. Cultural and religious factors rivaled economic change in causing this realignment.

County changes are also reflective of the 1976 to 1992 shift. Clinton carried 304 counties that had supported Ford, and many were large, politically potent metropolitan areas, especially the eastern suburbs. Even more counties — 489 — switched from Carter to Bush. But they were almost all in the rural South, particularly in Texas and Georgia. (Only 23 counties outside the South went for Carter and Bush.) Consequently, Clinton was the first winner since JFK to carry a minority of counties, winning 1,517 to Bush's 1,580.

Ross Perot mounted the strongest independent candidacy since Teddy Roosevelt in 1912, winning nearly 1 out of 5 votes, or almost 20 million. But Perot's strength was broad rather than deep. He carried only 14 counties — far fewer than Wallace in 1968, Thurmond in 1948 or La Follette in 1924. The Perot counties were in Maine, Kansas, Texas, Colorado, Nevada and California. Perot ran second in 345 counties, many of them in rural areas of Idaho, Kansas, Nebraska and Utah.

Perot's strongest showing came in Maine, where his vote topped 30% and where he ran second to Clinton. All of his other strongest areas of strength were in the West, especially in Alaska, Utah (where he ran second to Bush), Idaho, Kansas, Nevada and Montana. And he received more than 20% of the vote in New England. All of the counties he carried were rural and often isolated. His strongest level of support came in nonmetro areas but he received over 25% of the vote in San Diego, Dallas, Phoenix, Salt Lake City, Anchorage, Reno and Buffalo.

Most of Perot's votes came from Independents and Republicans. Of the 1992 Perot voters who voted in 1988, 65% had gone for Bush and 35% for Dukakis (all 14 of the counties he carried had supported Bush). But Perot attracted 6 million new voters.

Clinton carried 718 counties that supported Bush in 1988. Bush carried 21 of the Dukakis counties, mostly in rural Iowa, the only state where Clinton ran weaker against Bush than Dukakis had.

Almost unnoticed by national columnists and political analysts was Clinton's extraordinary appeal to longtime Republican voters in a number of areas. Clinton carried 23 counties that had not gone for a Democrat since the FDR-Truman days or before. Three Illinois and Tennessee counties had never gone for a Democrat for president. Two Missouri counties (Hickory, Warren) last backed a Democrat when Stephen Douglas carried them in 1860! Union County, Tennessee, last went Democratic in 1868 and Johnson and Pope counties in Illinois last went Democratic with Stephen Douglas in 1860. Clinton's Republican breakthroughs were also found in Minnesota, South Dakota, Virginia, Washington, Wyoming, Arizona and Louisiana.

Only two southern states were on the Clinton top 10: the home states of Clinton and Gore. An eastern tilt to the Clinton strongholds was apparent, with 6 states in the Northeast (including Maryland and West Virginia, two border states that increasingly resemble the Northeast in presidential voting behavior). Amazingly, once-Republican Vermont made it to the Clinton top 10. So did Illinois, his fourth-strongest state, even though it had gone for every Republican from 1968 to 1988. Almost every county in New England went for Clinton.

President Bush's top 10 were more southern (6 states) than western (4 states), making his coalition more like that of Nixon in 1972 or Goldwater in 1964. Nine of Perot's top 10 states were in the West, including Wyoming, Oregon and Minnesota.

The three-way battle of 1992 brought almost 13 million more voters to the polls than in 1988, a 14% increase. This was the largest percentage increase and the largest popular-vote increase since 1952. Every single state had a higher vote count.

In round numbers the total vote increased by nearly 1,250,000 in California; 1,000,000 in Florida; 727,000 in Texas; 605,000 in Michigan; 546,000 in Illinois; 512,000 in Georgia; just under 500,000 in Illinois; and 440,000 in New York. Even in somewhat smaller states the vote soared: up 423,000 in Washington; 367,000 in Virginia; 478,000 in North Carolina; 346,000 in Tennessee; 315,000 in Arizona; and 300,000 in Missouri.

This was the first presidential election in which more than 100 million Americans voted.

There was a modest correlation between voter turnout increase and the Perot candidacy. Exit polls found that 6 million Perot voters had not voted in 1988, accounting for almost half of the new voters.

TOP 10 STATES, 1992

Clinton	Percentage	Bush	Percentage	Perot	Percentage
1. Arkansas	53.2	1. Mississippi	49.7	1. Maine	30.4
2. Maryland	49.8	2. South Carolina	48.0	2. Alaska	28.4
3. New York	49.7	3. Alabama	47.6	3. Utah	27.3
4. Illinois	48.6	4. Nebraska	46.6	4. Idaho	27.0
5. West Virginia	48.4	5. Virginia	45.0	5. Kansas	27.0
6. Hawaii	48.1	6. North Dakota	44.2	6. Nevada	26.2
7. Massachusetts	47.5	7. North Carolina	43.4	7. Montana	26.1
8. Tennessee	47.1	8. Utah	43.4	8. Wyoming	25.6
9. Rhode Island	47.0	9. Indiana	42.9	9. Oregon	24.2
10. Vermont	46.1	10. Georgia	42.9	10. Minnesota	24.0

Electoral Votes, 1992

States	Electoral Votes	Clinton	Bush	States	Electoral Votes	Clinton	Bush
Alabama	9	–	9	Nebraska	5	–	5
Alaska	3	–	3	Nevada	4	4	–
Arizona	8	–	8	New Hampshire	4	4	–
Arkansas	6	6	–	New Jersey	15	15	–
California	54	54	–	New Mexico	5	5	–
Colorado	8	8	–	New York	33	33	–
Connecticut	8	8	–	North Carolina	14	–	14
Delaware	3	3	–	North Dakota	3	–	3
District of Columbia	3	3	–	Ohio	21	21	–
Florida	25	–	25	Oklahoma	8	–	8
Georgia	13	13	–	Oregon	7	7	–
Hawaii	4	4	–	Pennsylvania	23	23	–
Idaho	4	–	4	Rhode Island	4	4	–
Illinois	22	22	–	South Carolina	8	–	8
Indiana	12	–	12	South Dakota	3	–	3
Iowa	7	7	–	Tennessee	11	11	–
Kansas	6	–	6	Texas	32	–	32
Kentucky	8	8	–	Utah	5	–	5
Louisiana	9	9	–	Vermont	3	3	–
Maine	4	4	–	Virginia	13	–	13
Maryland	10	10	–	Washington	11	11	–
Massachusetts	12	12	–	West Virginia	5	5	–
Michigan	18	18	–	Wisconsin	11	11	–
Minnesota	10	10	–	Wyoming	3	–	3
Mississippi	7	–	7				
Missouri	11	11	–	Totals	538	370	168
Montana	3	3	–				

1996

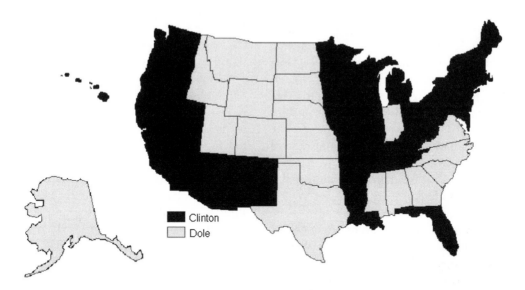

President Bill Clinton was easily re-elected, 49% to 41%, and with 379 electoral votes from 31 states, while his opponent, Kansas senator Bob Dole, received 159 electoral votes from 19 states. Ross Perot ran again but received only 8% of the votes, less than half of his remarkable 1992 support. For the second time in a row, the victorious candidate failed to win a majority of the popular vote and carried fewer counties (1,525) than his opponent (1,587).

Five states changed sides. Clinton won Florida and Arizona (where he was the first Democratic winner since Truman in 1948). Dole recaptured Montana, Colorado and Georgia from Clinton. In the three pro–Dole states, the Perot defectors and new migrants to the Atlanta and Denver suburbs caused the states to shift to the GOP column. Migration patterns probably influenced the pro–Clinton shift in Arizona and Florida, where he ran well ahead of the Democratic norm in such cities as Phoenix, Palm Beach and Fort Lauderdale.

While the national outcome changed little (Clinton's overall "gain" was only 1.4%), and the election resulted in 8 million

fewer ballots cast, there were significant changes at the county level. Clinton picked up 170 counties in 34 states that had gone for Bush in 1992. A number were large population "establishment suburbs" in the Northeast and Midwest, including Fairfield, Connecticut; Bergen, New Jersey; Suffolk, New York; Oakland, Michigan; and Lake, Illinois. These were generally prestigious, high-income areas. Clinton also carried Macomb County, Michigan, a middle-income, largely Catholic suburb of Detroit.

Clinton continued his appeal to small-town Republicans, winning Porter County, Indiana, which had not gone for a Democrat since 1852. Grundy County, Iowa and Waushara County, Wisconsin went Democratic for the first time since FDR in 1932. Even in the South, Clinton was the first Democrat since Stevenson in 1952 to carry Montgomery County, Alabama, and Richland Parish, Louisiana. He was the first Democrat since FDR in 1944 to carry Lincoln Parish in North Louisiana and Plaquemines Parish in the southeast part of the state. Clinton was the first Democrat since LBJ in 1964 to carry 25 upstate New York counties.

Bob Dole also showed an ability to cut into Democratic strength, carrying 168 counties in 31 states that had gone for Clinton. They were heavily rural, except for San Diego, Fresno, and Riverside in California; and Sangamon (Springfield), Illinois. Dole made inroads in the Democratic rural South, particularly in tobacco country. He was only the second Republican in history to carry Owen County, Kentucky. The largest number of pro–Dole counties were in Texas, California, Kentucky, Mississippi and Illinois. (Five Arkansas counties also switched to Dole.)

One factor overshadows many others: In 46 of the 50 states, Clinton either gained more or lost less in metropolitan than in nonmetropolitan counties. (Only in Iowa, Minnesota, Wisconsin and Alaska was this not true.) Dole gained in rural and small-town America, paving the way for even greater gains in the same areas by George W. Bush in 2000.

The Perot defectors helped Dole somewhat, particularly in the West. (The Perot vote collapsed most drastically in Colorado, Kansas and Texas.) In the Northeast, former Perot voters went more for Clinton. Dole carried 11 of the Perot counties, while Clinton won the 3 in Maine, which had larger populations than Perot's western counties.

Perot's vote remained relatively high in isolated areas in the Florida Panhandle, up-state New York, eastern Ohio and in the coal-mining counties from southeastern Illinois to West Virginia, where Perot's vote was often higher in 1996 than in 1992.

Thus, in an election often dismissed as insignificant, voters in 352 counties changed their minds in just 4 years and laid the groundwork for the bitter and divisive election of 2000.

In terms of gains or losses among the major parties, Clinton improved on his 1992 vote in 28 states, lost ground in 17 states, and remained essentially at the same level in 5 states (Pennsylvania, California, South Dakota, Alabama, and Arkansas). Clinton made large gains in New Jersey, Massachusetts, Rhode Island, Connecticut, New York, Maine, New Hampshire, and Hawaii. He made moderate gains in Vermont, Florida, and Louisiana.

Dole's only significant gain came in his home state of Kansas. Modest Dole gains were recorded in Montana, Wyoming, Colorado, North Carolina and Alaska. Dole's top 10 states were a blend of western and southern states.

Clinton's top 10 states were even more eastern (7 of them) than in 1992. Hawaii, Illinois, and Arkansas were the only non–Eastern states on Clinton's top 10. New Jersey (Republican from 1968 to 1988), Vermont and Connecticut were among Clinton's most avid supporters, something that would have been unthinkable for a Democrat in 1956.

Seven of Perot's top 10 states were in the West. West Virginia, Rhode Island, North Dakota and Oklahoma appeared among the strongest supporters of Perot in 1996, replacing Utah, Kansas, Oregon and Nevada.

The 1996 election saw the most dramatic decline in the presidential vote in modern times. Only 96 million voted, compared to 104 million in 1992. This decline of 8.2 million voters, or nearly 8%, was much larger than the declines of 1988 and 1944. Even though Ross Perot made a second bid for the White House, he received less than half of his 1992 vote, which appears to be a major factor in the overall decline. Clinton gained about 2.5 million votes; Dole picked up only 95,000; Perot lost 11.7 million and the vote for minor-party candidates increased by 900,000.

According to the Committee for the Study of the American Electorate, only 49% of the voting-age population turned out in 1996, one of the lowest figures ever recorded.

The vote declined 1.1 million in California, 740,000 in Illinois and by more than 400,000 in Michigan, New York, Ohio, Pennsylvania, and Texas. In percentage loss, the greatest 1996 declines were in Illinois, Connecticut, Rhode Island, North Dakota and Wisconsin — states with traditionally high voter turnouts. (Oklahoma also had a large drop in votes.)

Even the fastest-growing states (Arizona, Florida, Georgia, Nevada) had a lower presidential vote in 1996 than in 1992. Only Idaho and Wyoming recorded small vote increases.

The nation's capital, the District of Columbia, experienced a loss of 18.4% of its 1992 vote — the highest single percentage decline in the country.

Consumer advocate Ralph Nader was on the ballot in 21 states and in the District of Columbia and received less than 1% of the national vote. (He received write-in votes in 15 other states.) But he received a noticeable vote in Oregon, Washington, California, Maine, Colorado, New Mexico and Wisconsin. His strongest support was concentrated in coastal communities in Washington State, Oregon, California and Maine. His 2 strongest counties were Mendocino and Humboldt on the northern California coast. His vote exceeded 5% in college towns like Boulder, Colorado; Madison, Wisconsin (Dane County); Ithaca, New York (Tompkins County); and in the Santa Fe–Taos area of New Mexico. In LaPlata County, Colorado, a college/academic area, his vote was large enough to shift the county to Dole. In college towns in Vermont, Nader also made an impact. Nader's strongest vote share came from Oregon (3.6%), Alaska (3.1%), Washington (2.7%), Maine (2.5%), California (2.4%), New Mexico (2.4%), and Vermont (2.2%). In the District of Columbia, where he lives, Nader polled 2.6%.

TOP 10 STATES, 1996

Clinton	Percentage	Dole	Percentage	Perot	Percentage
1. Massachusetts	61.5	1. Utah	54.4	1. Maine	14.2
2. Rhode Island	59.7	2. Kansas	54.3	2. Montana	13.6
3. New York	59.5	3. Nebraska	53.7	3. Idaho	12.7
4. Hawaii	56.9	4. Idaho	52.2	4. Wyoming	12.3
5. Illinois	54.3	5. Alaska	50.8	5. North Dakota	12.2
6. Maryland	54.3	6. Alabama	50.1	6. Minnesota	11.8
7. Arkansas	53.7	7. South Carolina	49.8	7. West Virginia	11.3
8. New Jersey	53.7	8. Mississippi	49.2	8. Rhode Island	11.2
9. Vermont	53.4	9. Texas	48.8	9. Alaska	10.9
10. Connecticut	52.8	10. North Carolina	48.7	10. Oklahoma	10.8

ELECTORAL VOTES, 1996

States	Electoral Votes	Clinton	Dole	States	Electoral Votes	Clinton	Dole
Alabama	9	–	9	Connecticut	8	8	–
Alaska	3	–	3	Delaware	3	3	–
Arizona	8	8	–	District of Columbia	3	3	–
Arkansas	6	6	–	Florida	25	25	–
California	54	54	–	Georgia	13	–	13
Colorado	8	–	8	Hawaii	4	4	–

States	Electoral Votes	Clinton	Dole	States	Electoral Votes	Clinton	Dole
Idaho	4	–	4	North Carolina	14	–	14
Illinois	22	22	–	North Dakota	3	–	3
Indiana	12	–	12	Ohio	21	21	–
Iowa	7	7	–	Oklahoma	8	–	8
Kansas	6	–	6	Oregon	7	7	–
Kentucky	8	8	–	Pennsylvania	23	23	–
Louisiana	9	9	–	Rhode Island	4	4	–
Maine	4	4	–	South Carolina	8	–	8
Maryland	10	10	–	South Dakota	3	–	3
Massachusetts	12	12	–	Tennessee	11	11	–
Michigan	18	18	–	Texas	32	–	32
Minnesota	10	10	–	Utah	5	–	5
Mississippi	7	–	7	Vermont	3	3	–
Missouri	11	11	–	Virginia	13	–	13
Montana	3	–	3	Washington	11	11	–
Nebraska	5	–	5	West Virginia	5	5	–
Nevada	4	4	–	Wisconsin	11	11	–
New Hampshire	4	4	–	Wyoming	3	–	3
New Jersey	15	15	–				
New Mexico	5	5	–	Totals	538	379	159
New York	33	33	–				

2000

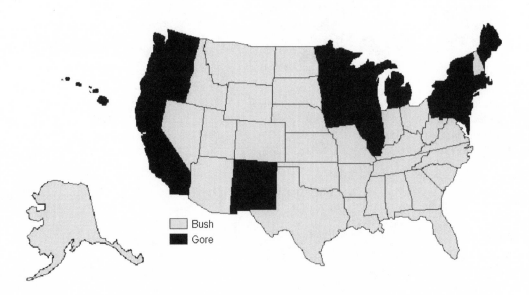

Bush
Gore

The 2000 election was the first since 1888 in which the losing candidate in the popular vote secured the presidency because of a slim 271–267 (one of Gore's District of Columbia electors cast a blank ballot in December, giving Gore 266) electoral vote majority. As in the disputed election of 1876, the outcome depended on contested votes in Florida. The final vote — Gore with 48.3%, Bush with 47.8%—was the closest since Kennedy-Nixon in 1960 and just ahead of the Nixon-Humphrey 1968 outcome. It was also the third election in a row in which no candidate secured a popular-vote majority. The last time that happened was in the 1880s.

Both candidates showed strong areas of support in an election that revealed a deeply divided electorate. Texas governor George W. Bush carried 30 states, sweeping the entire South, most of the border South and most of the West. Vice President Al Gore won the Northeast, a majority of states from Michigan to Minnesota, and the Pacific Coast, for a total of 20 states. All of Bush's top 10 states were in the West or Southwest, while 7 of Gore's top 10 were in the Northeast. Once-Republican Illinois and California remained Gore strongholds. Bush's strongest state was Wyoming, home of his running mate, former congressman Dick Cheney.

Bush won a Reagan-style landslide in rural areas and carried 2,439 counties (the so-called red America in the postelection maps) to Gore's 673 counties (blue America). In virtually every state, Bush's greatest gains over Dole's 1996 vote came in non-metropolitan counties. Bush carried more counties than Reagan in 1980, his father in 1988, or Eisenhower in 1952 and 1956. If there was ever a two-nation thesis (as Disraeli described Britain in the nineteenth century), this bizarre election confirmed it. Many of the counties Bush carried, though, had a small population. Gore, for example, carried Minnesota by winning the large metropolitan centers even though Bush carried a large majority of the state's counties. There were 854 counties that switched from Clinton in 1996 to Bush in 2000, compared to just 2 that switched from Dole in 1996 to Gore in 2000 (Charles County, Maryland, and Orange County, Florida).

Bush's southern triumph was due to white voters, especially Baptists. Bush weaved together traditional suburban and small-town southern Republicans — the remnants of the Wallace vote in 1968 (Bush won 66% to 32% in the 20 strongest Wallace counties)—and he won 87 of the 97 anti–Catholic swing counties of 1960. (Bush received 92% of the vote at the Bob Jones University precinct in Greenville, South Carolina, an indicator of this vote.)

Bush's appeal to nonmetropolitan and conservative Protestant voters netted him an upset victory in Al Gore's home state of Tennessee. Gore's loss of his home state was the first defeat for a candidate at home since George McGovern lost South Dakota in 1972. More important, it was the first defeat for a candidate who won the popular vote nationally but lost his home state since Woodrow Wilson lost New Jersey in 1916.

Bush won 11 states that had gone for Clinton in 1996, including Clinton's home state of Arkansas, and West Virginia, a state that in the past only supported Republicans in GOP landslide years. Louisiana, Clinton's strongest southern state outside of Tennessee and Arkansas, went for Bush. New Hampshire was the only northeastern state to back Bush, by 1%, due in part to the Nader vote, which also was higher in Florida than Bush's margin over Gore.

Bush was the first Republican in history to carry Morgan County, Kentucky; Wolfe County, Kentucky; and Greenlee County, Arizona. He was the first Republican since 1920 to carry Red Lake County, Minnesota, and the first since 1928 to carry Cottle County, Texas.

Gore, however, won a landslide in

the nation's 23 largest population counties, amassing 11,097,961 votes to Bush's 6,900,332 — a 59% to 37% sweep (Nader received 548,643). The urban-rural divide in 2000 was as great as it had been in 1936 and 1928. Gore carried the prestigious "establishment suburbs," with 55%, only 1 point below Clinton's 56% in 1996. And Gore ran ahead of Clinton in a number of eastern suburbs, including Fairfield County, Connecticut, and Montgomery County, Maryland, which Gore carried by 108,000 votes compared to Clinton's 81,000.

Gore also carried a number of once-Republican counties that had defected to Clinton, such as in the Philadelphia suburbs. Most were suburban or small metropolitan areas. He held Columbus, Ohio, and the major Detroit suburbs as well as coastal California and southern Florida. Gore had strong Catholic support, especially in the Northeast, where his 3 most impressive victories were recorded (Rhode Island, New York, Massachusetts).

Bush won 62% to 35% in the exurbs, or newly emergent suburbs on the outskirts of larger suburbs and cities. The exurbs remained a Republican-trending area in the 2002 congressional elections and are found mostly in the South and West. But Gore's disastrous showing in the rural heartland contributed to his electoral vote defeat. He carried fewer counties, despite winning by half a percentage point, than Barry Goldwater, who lost by 22 percentage points. Gore carried fewer counties than Humphrey or Dukakis.

A comparison of the 2000 election with the last Republican victory in 1988 shows how much the country had changed. Bush carried 347 counties that backed Dukakis, almost all of them in the rural South and Midwest. Only 1% were in the Northeast. Gore carried 206 counties that supported George H. W. Bush, a majority

of them in metropolitan centers and 31% of them in the Northeast.

White rural America became much more Republican between George H.W. Bush's 1988 victory and George W. Bush's 2000 victory; the large metro areas moved in the opposite direction and just as dramatically. While Gore crushed George W. Bush by 4,197,629 votes in 2000, Dukakis only defeated George H.W. Bush by 462,950. (Dukakis received 9,032,105 votes, or 51.3%, while Bush received 8,569,155, or 48.7%.) Gore's percentage-point victory margin in the "big counties" was 22.4% compared to Dukakis's 2.6% margin.*

The 2000 election attracted 105.4 million voters, the highest in U.S. history. It just surpassed the previous high of 104.4 million in 1992. About 9 million more people voted in 2000 than had done so in 1996, a 9.5% increase. Despite his defeat, Al Gore received the largest popular vote ever received by a Democrat.

The vote was up in all states except Kansas, Louisiana, and South Dakota. Booming Nevada had the highest percentage increase (31%), followed by Delaware (21%), South Carolina (20%), Wisconsin and Alaska (18%), Utah and North Carolina (16%), Colorado (15%), and Texas, New Hampshire and Vermont (14%). Other 10 percent to 13% increases were recorded in Florida, Georgia, Kentucky, Maryland, Minnesota, Mississippi, and Virginia. The states experiencing a considerable increase in turnout were found throughout the nation. While the Sun belt and far West have traditionally been leaders in turnout increases, Delaware, South Carolina, Kentucky, Maryland, Vermont and Mississippi showed unusually high interest in the 2000 election.

Ralph Nader, running on the Green Party ticket, made a national campaign effort in 2000 and secured a ballot position

*See *The Rhodes Cook Letter* (July 2001).

in 43 states. His national vote was just less than 3% (2.7 percent), and for a time Democrats feared that his candidacy would cost them Wisconsin, Minnesota, Iowa, Washington, Oregon and New Mexico. As it turned out, Gore held all of those states through a concentrated and intense Democratic campaign effort.

Nader's strongest states were conservative Alaska, where he polled 10%, and liberal Vermont, Massachusetts and Rhode Island. Nader ran strongest in the West, where 6 of his top 10 states were located, and in New England, where the other 4 were located.

The 2000 election shows that American politics is now sharply divided by ideology and resembles European confessional politics. Religious affiliation and involvement and marital status are sharper dividing points in politics than income or education, according to exit polls.

Voters who attend church weekly or more were twice as likely to support Bush than voters whose attendance at religious services is occasional, rare, or nonexistent. This attendance factor holds for all religious groups and has been growing as a political predictor for a decade. Bush also ran stronger among voters who were married with children while Gore ran best among single voters.

Income, education and gender are not as pronounced political differentiators. Republicans still do better as voters' incomes rise, but the difference in Republican support from the highest to the lowest income level has diminished since the 1950s. Women are still several percentage points more supportive of Democrats than men, but that difference began to surface as politically significant in 1980 and has not increased much. Education is an unusual factor. Democrats do best among voters with the highest and lowest levels of formal education (i.e., with two or more college degrees or without a high school degree), while Republicans do best with voters who have moderate levels of education (i.e., one college degree or a high school diploma). This has been true, according to exit polls, since the 1988 election.

These ideological factors affect region and geography, particularly in an age of "clustering," where voters seem to migrate to regions, or areas within regions, where they feel culturally at home, as it were.

The South, rural Midwest and the Rocky Mountains are unshakably Republican regions for the moment. The Democratic bastions are the Northeast, the Upper Great Lakes, and the Pacific Coast. The lifestyles and value systems of these regions, rooted to a large extent in religion and ethnicity, differ greatly from each other and seem likely to persist in the near future. The nation is as sharply divided culturally and politically as at any time since the Civil War, resulting in what many commentators call a 50–50 blue states/red states political draw. Culturally "moderate" states like Pennsylvania, Iowa, Ohio and Colorado may be the political battlegrounds of the future. But one cannot predict presidential elections with any degree of confidence in an age fraught with uncertainty and influenced by international events that no one can foresee.*

*For an excellent analysis of political trends on the eve of the 2004 election, see Stanley B. Greenberg, *The Two Americas* (New York: St. Martin's Press, 2004).

Top 10 States, 2000

Bush	Percentage	Gore	Percentage	Nader	Percentage
1. Wyoming	67.8	1. Rhode Island	61.0	1. Alaska	10.1
2. Idaho	67.2	2. New York	60.2	2. Vermont	6.9
3. Utah	66.8	3. Massachusetts	59.8	3. Massachusetts	6.4
4. Nebraska	62.2	4. Maryland	56.5	4. Rhode Island	6.1
5. North Dakota	60.7	5. New Jersey	56.1	5. Hawaii	5.9
6. Oklahoma	60.3	6. Connecticut	55.9	6. Montana	5.9
7. South Dakota	60.3	7. Hawaii	55.8	7. Maine	5.7
8. Texas	59.3	8. Delaware	55.0	8. Colorado	5.3
9. Alaska	58.6	9. Illinois	54.6	9. Minnesota	5.2
10. Montana	58.4	10. California	53.4	10. Oregon	5.0

Electoral Votes, 2000

States	Electoral Votes	Bush	Gore	States	Electoral Votes	Bush	Gore
Alabama	9	9	–	New Hampshire	4	4	–
Alaska	3	3	–	New Jersey	15	–	15
Arizona	8	8	–	New Mexico	5	–	5
Arkansas	6	6	–	New York	33	–	33
California	54	–	54	North Carolina	14	14	–
Colorado	8	8	–	North Dakota	3	3	–
Delaware	3	–	3	Ohio	21	21	–
District of Columbia[1]	3	–	2	Oklahoma	8	8	–
Florida	25	25	–	Oregon	7	–	7
Georgia	13	13	–	Pennsylvania	23	–	23
Hawaii	4	–	4	Rhode Island	4	–	4
Idaho	4	4	–	South Carolina	8	8	–
Illinois	22	–	22	South Dakota	3	3	–
Indiana	12	12	–	Tennessee	11	11	–
Iowa	7	–	7	Texas	32	32	–
Kansas	6	6	–	Utah	5	5	–
Kentucky	8	8	–	Vermont	3	–	3
Louisiana	9	9	–	Virginia	13	13	–
Maine	4	–	4	Washington	11	–	11
Maryland	10	–	10	West Virginia	5	5	–
Massachusetts	12	–	12	Wisconsin	11	–	11
Michigan	18	–	18	Wyoming	3	3	–
Minnesota	10	–	10				
Mississippi	7	7	–	Totals	538	271	266
Missouri	11	11	–				
Montana	3	3	–				
Nebraska	5	5	–				
Nevada	4	4	–				

1. One Gore elector in the District of Columbia cast a blank ballot as a protest for the district's denial of statehood.

2004

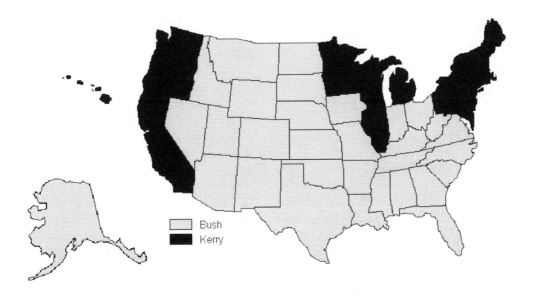

President George W. Bush received 62,040,287 votes to Senator John F. Kerry's 59,027,612 votes. The major party percentage was 51.2% for Bush and 48.8% for Kerry, a margin of 2.4%.

Other candidates received 1,225,944 votes, making the total vote percentage 50.73% for Bush, 48.27% for Kerry, and 1.00% for all others.

Bush received 286 electoral votes from 31 states while Kerry received 251 electoral votes from 19 states and the District of Columbia. (One Kerry elector in Minnesota voted for vice presidential candidate John Edwards for president.)

The total vote cast was a record in U.S. history, reaching 122,293,843 million. The increase in vote over the previous election, 16,897,216 million, was the highest in history, but the percentage increase, 16.0%, was lower than in 1952. (These are "final but unofficial returns" from all state election offices as of December 31, 2004. Most state returns are final, official and certified, but some are not.)

This was the first election since 1988 in which the winner received more than 50% of the popular votes.

Bush's reelection was the weakest in U.S. history. His 2.46% popular vote margin over Kerry was even lower than Wilson's 1916 reelection margin of 3.2%. His overall gain from 2000, adjusting for the Nader vote decline, was only 1.5%, about the same as Bill Clinton's 1996 reelection improvement over his 1992 vote. And Clinton won by a larger margin and received more electoral votes than Bush.

As a general rule, first-term presidents are reelected by a comfortable margin (Clinton in 1996), win by a landslide (Roosevelt 1936, Eisenhower 1956, Nixon 1972, Reagan 1984), or are defeated (Taft 1912, Hoover 1932, Carter 1980, George H.W. Bush 1992). Bush's electoral vote margin of 286–251 was also the second lowest for a first-term incumbent, narrowly edging out Wilson's 277–254 showing in 1916.

Bush was the fifth wartime president to be reelected (Lincoln 1864, Wilson 1916, FDR 1944, Nixon 1972).

As a result of the enormous turnout,

George W. Bush received the highest popular vote ever given a presidential candidate, and John Kerry received the highest vote ever given an unsuccessful candidate — and the second-highest popular vote ever.

Though Bush had a less than impressive victory in the popular and electoral votes, he did, however, achieve a party victory, since the Republicans gained seats in the Senate and the House, a feat not achieved by any reelected first-term incumbent president since FDR in 1936.

Bush also overcame a historical hurdle: He is the only president to be reelected who won the electoral vote but lost the popular vote in his first race. John Quincy Adams lost to Andrew Jackson in a rematch in 1828, and Benjamin Harrison was defeated in a rematch with Grover Cleveland in 1892. Rutherford B. Hayes, winner of the disputed 1876 election, did not seek reelection in 1880.

There were only three swing states in 2004. New Hampshire switched to Kerry, even though in 1988, the last time a Massachusetts Democrat headed the ticket, it was the second strongest Republican state. Iowa voted Republican for the first time since Reagan carried the state in 1984. In 1988 it was the second most Democratic state in the nation. After rejecting a Bush family member three times, it finally supported a Bush, albeit by less than 1%. New Mexico, the closest state in popular vote in 2000, went narrowly for Bush, perhaps reflecting the small gains Bush made among Hispanic voters in the nation's most Hispanic state. This shift of only three states from one candidate to the other was the fewest number ever recorded in any presidential election.

Six states have become barometers since they have supported the winner in all nine elections since 1972: Arkansas, Kentucky, Louisiana, Missouri, Ohio, and Tennessee. Collectively, they gave Bush 54.7% of the major party vote in 2004, and 52.9% in 2000.

Eleven states have become reliable Republican strongholds since supporting Richard Nixon in 1968. For 10 straight elections they have backed the GOP's candidate. They are: Alaska, Idaho, Indiana, Kansas, Nebraska, North Dakota, Oklahoma, South Dakota, Utah, Virginia and Wyoming. In 2004 these "Republican loyalists" gave Bush 62.0% of the major party vote, compared to 60.6% in 2000.

Generally speaking, the Red States were even more Red in 2004 than in 2000, but the Blue States were slightly less Blue. The top 10 Bush states in 2000 gave Bush 63.7% of the major party votes in 2004 compared to 62.8% in 2000. The top ten Gore states gave Gore 58.9% and Kerry 56.4%. Bush gained slightly more in Democratic, competitive, marginal and barometer states than in Republican ones in his second race for the White House.

On a county basis, this pattern is also true. In the counties where Bush's vote exceeded 70% in 2000, i.e., the reddest of the red, his 2004 major party vote was up 2%. In the bluest counties, where Gore's vote topped 70%, Bush gained 1.5%.

Metropolitan Areas

Dividing the nation into metropolitan and nonmetropolitan counties makes political sense since many of the divisions now rending the political fabric are defined by this broad categorization. Metropolitan America — the great cities and their close-in suburbs — remains Democratic and gives the Democrats the bulk of their vote. Nonmetropolitan America — rural areas, small towns, and the burgeoning exurbs — is the area of greatest Republican strength.

In metropolitan America, Senator Kerry outpolled President Bush by a margin of 6,252,535. In nonmetropolitan America, Bush defeated Kerry by 9,265,010. In terms of voter change from 2000 to 2004, Bush recorded small gains in the metropolitan counties (1.3%) and in the nonmetropolitan counties (1.7%). The vote increase was greater in the nonmetro areas (17.3%) than in metro areas (14.9%).

Within the same region, the 2004 results often moved in different and occasionally surprising directions. In the Kerry stronghold of New England, for example, the Democratic nominee gained in more Republican upper New England, carrying three of the four Bush counties in Vermont, three of the five in Maine, and one Bush county in New Hampshire. His only national pickup was New Hampshire, and his largest statewide gain was in Vermont. Bush gained modestly in more Democratic lower New England, even running ahead of his 2000 showing in Kerry's home state of Massachusetts and in Gore's strongest state, Rhode Island. The only New England county to switch from Gore to Bush was Litchfield County, Connecticut.

In Pennsylvania Bush gained several points in the western Democratic counties (Cambria, Fayette, Greene, Washington) while Kerry picked up a point or two in Republican Lancaster and Chester Counties.

The importance of the metropolitan vote to the Democrats cannot be ignored. Kerry carried eight states because of his overwhelming victory in one county within each state. He carried Washington in Seattle (King County), Oregon in Portland (Multnomah County), Minnesota in Minneapolis (Hennepin County), Illinois in Chicago (Cook County), Wisconsin in Milwaukee County, Michigan in Detroit (Wayne County), Pennsylvania in Philadelphia County, and Delaware in Wilmington (New Castle County).

Within metro America, the Democrats continued their overwhelming support in the nation's cities. Kerry received 83% in San Francisco, 82% in Seattle, 80% in Chicago, 81% in Philadelphia, 78% in Boston 82% in Baltimore, 82% in the Manhattan Borough of New York City, 81% in St. Louis, and 89% in Washington, D.C.

The Vote in Key Metropolitan Counties
Major Party Vote Percent

	% Bush 2000	% Gore 2000	% Bush 2004	% Kerry 2004	% Bush Gain or Loss
All Metros	42.8	57.2	44.1	55.9	+1.3
More than 500,000 votes	39.7	60.3	41.0	59.0	+1.3
200,000–500,000 votes	45.4	54.6	46.6	53.4	+1.2
Large Metros	*% Bush 2000*	*% Gore 2000*	*% Bush 2004*	*% Kerry 2004*	*% Bush Gain or Loss*
Democratic	29.1	70.9	30.5	69.5	+1.4
Republican	62.6	37.4	62.8	37.2	+0.2
Closely Divided	50.0	50.0	51.0	49.0	+1.0
Small Metros	*% Bush 2000*	*% Gore 2000*	*% Bush 2004*	*% Kerry 2004*	*% Bush Gain or Loss*
Democratic	30.7	69.3	31.9	68.1	+1.2
Republican	68.5	31.5	68.4	31.6	-0.1
Closely Divided	50.6	49.4	51.4	47.6	+0.8

Suburbia

America's suburbs remained almost evenly divided in 2004, with sharp differences between regions and types of suburbia. Twenty prestigious suburbs, which I have labeled the "establishment suburbs," were once the backbone of the moderate, internationalist wing of the Republican Party and provided the GOP with huge victory margins from 1940 through 1988, with the exception of 1964, when these voters rejected Barry Goldwater. But in 1992 Bill Clinton edged out President George H.W. Bush by 2 percentage points, inaugurating a new Democratic era. Clinton in 1996 and Gore in 2000 won easily, by 10- to 12-point margins in the major party vote. John Kerry racked up the fourth straight Democratic victory, by 54% to 46%, in these well-to-do suburbs, which stretch from Boston to Washington and include some around Detroit, Chicago and San Francisco. Bush made a 1% gain, but he was still weaker than his father's 1992 showing.

Another group of "old-line Republican" suburbs, primarily in the Midwest, West and South, gave Bush 61%, a gain of 1% over 2000. Sixteen suburban counties were very closely contested in 2000, going 51% to 49% for Gore in major party vote. In 2004 they could hardly have been any closer, with Kerry edging out Bush 50.2% to 49.8%. Bush's 1% gain was consistent throughout suburbia.

In a number of "Sun Belt exurbs," stretching from Maryland to Texas, Bush had greater success, winning 70% of the vote in 2004 compared to 69% in 2000. These include many fast-growing counties on the outskirts of the older suburbia. The 2004 total vote increased 29.9% over 2000 in the Sun Belt exurbs, compared to 17.9% in the closely divided suburbs, 12.8% in the old-line Republican suburbs and 12.3% in the establishment suburbs.

Another study of the exurbs, including some that are not in the Sun Belt states, reaches a similar conclusion. The *Los Angeles Times* analyzed the 100 counties that the Census Bureau identified as the fastest growing in population since the 2000 Census. These counties are found in 30 states. Ronald Brownstein and Richard Rainey wrote:

> The center of the Republican presidential coalition is moving toward the distant edges of suburbia.
>
> In this month's election, President Bush carried 97 of the nation's 100 fastest-growing counties, most of them "exurban" communities that are rapidly transforming farmland into subdivisions and shopping malls on the periphery of major metropolitan areas.
>
> Together, these fast-growing communities provided Bush a punishing 1.72 million vote advantage over Democrat John F. Kerry, according to a *Times* analysis of election results. That was almost half the president's total margin of victory.
>
> These growing areas, filled largely with younger families fleeing urban centers in search of affordable homes, are providing the GOP a foothold in blue Democratic-leaning states and solidifying the party's control over red Republican-leaning states.*

Bush received 63% of the vote in these 100 counties, and his margin of victory rose from 1.06 million votes in 2000 to 1.72 million. These counties have been leaning Republican for a long while, and 74 of them went for Bob Dole in 1996. But the Republican share of an ever-increasing segment of the national vote continues to rise. Georgia, Texas and Florida contain the highest number of high-growth counties (41 of the 100 are in these three Sun Belt states).

---

*Ronald Brownstein and Richard Rainey, "GOP Plants Flag on New Voting Frontier," *Los Angeles Times*, November 22, 2004.

Pro-Bush Swing Counties

Unbeknownst to most analysts, Bush showed unusual strength in his 2000 race in 108 counties in Arizona, Kentucky, Minnesota, Montana, Texas and West Virginia. He ran ahead of Reagan, Nixon, and Eisenhower in the landslide victories of 1984, 1972 and 1956. Many of the rural counties (and they were all far off the beaten path) supported Adlai Stevenson in 1956. Bush received 67.2% of the major party vote in these counties, where his personal appeal was surprising, considering that he ran much weaker nationwide than the three popular Republican presidents. In 2004 Bush's appeal had not waned in these counties, where he received 70% of the major party vote. He was stronger in the Texas and West Virginia pro–Bush counties but weaker in the pro–Bush counties in Montana.

The Nader Counties

Ralph Nader's vote exceeded 10% in two dozen counties in 2000, 10 of them in Colorado. Other states with at least 1 county in this category include California, Kansas, Massachusetts, Minnesota, Montana, New York, Texas, Utah, Vermont and Washington. The 2000 vote in these deep-green counties was 48% for Gore, 39% for Bush and nearly 12% for Nader. In 2004 the Nader vote shifted overwhelmingly to Kerry, giving the Massachusetts senator a 63% to 37% landslide. (Less than 1% went for Nader or the remnants of the Green Party.) The Democratic margin rose from 9 points to 26 points, and the total vote increased 11.1%.

The impact of the Nader vote can be seen in several counties, particularly in those with a large university. In Boulder County, Colorado, Kerry's margin was 52,638 compared to Gore's 19,110 margin. In Austin, Texas (Travis County), a Bush margin of 15,709 in 2000 became a Kerry romp by 49,155. In Douglas County, Kansas, Kerry won by 7,359 and Gore by 1,187. Nader's 2004 vote was negligible, only a fraction of his 2000 vote (only 461,243 votes compared to 2,882,738). Even with Nader's decline, his top two states remained the same as in 2000, Alaska (1.6%) and Vermont (1.4%).

Academia

There are several dozen counties throughout the United States where a university or college is the dominant employer and cultural influence and where a large share of the electorate are students, professors and administrators. In 40 university-oriented counties throughout the United States, Kerry ran stronger than Gore. Kerry's margin of victory was 404,000 votes compared to Gore's 169,000. Kerry beat Bush 58% to 41%, while Gore's margin was 50% to 42% with 7% for Nader. The total vote increased 17.8%, which was higher than the national percentage increase. These figures correlate with the exit polls, which showed a comfortable majority for Kerry among voters with more than one college degree and among voters younger than 30.

Top Ten States, 2004

Bush	Percentage		Kerry	Percentage
1. Utah	71.5		1. Massachusetts	61.9
2. Wyoming	68.9		2. Rhode Island	59.4
3. Idaho	68.4		3. Vermont	58.9
4. Nebraska	65.9		4. New York	58.4
5. Oklahoma	65.6		5. Maryland	55.9
6. North Dakota	62.9		6. Illinois	54.8
7. Alabama	62.5		7. California	54.3
8. Kansas	62.0		8. Connecticut	54.3
9. Alaska	61.1		9. Hawaii	54.0
10. Texas	61.1		10. Delaware	53.4

Eight of Bush's top 10 states were in the West or Great Plains states, including Oklahoma, Nebraska and Kansas. Utah replaced Wyoming as Bush's strongest state. The only southern states were Alabama and Texas. Bush ran stronger in Alabama than in any other southern state.

Eight of Bush's top 10 states in 2000 remained on the 2004 list. South Dakota and Montana fell off, being replaced by Alabama and Kansas.

Kerry's top states were also roughly similar to Gore's, though New Jersey (Gore's fifth highest) fell off because of the Bush gains in the New York City area. Vermont surged to third place and was the state where Kerry gained the most over Gore. Vermont had been Nader's second strongest state in 2000, which prevented the Green Mountain State from making Gore's top 10. Kerry's home state of Massachusetts was his best state, moving up from third place on Gore's list.

County Switches

There were only a few areas where voter sentiments changed much during Bush's first term. A panoramic view of the United States shows that Bush's most significant gains were recorded in rural central Oklahoma, northern Alabama, the south Jersey shore, southern Delaware, and the greater New York City area. Kerry's greatest gains came in northern New England and in rural Montana, Idaho, Colorado, Wyoming and South Dakota.

Bush carried 153 counties that had supported Gore while Kerry carried 64 counties that had supported Bush in 2000. Thus, about 7% of the nation's more than 3,000 counties changed sides, one of the lowest percentages in presidential election history.

Bush carried 18 of the 36 counties Gore had carried in Tennessee and all 9 Gore counties in Oklahoma. He carried 9 of the 13 Gore counties in Missouri and 9 of the 15 Gore counties in Kentucky. Bush also carried 7 of the 18 counties that supported Gore in Alabama, 11 of the 32 Gore counties in Arkansas and 9 of the 24 Gore counties in Illinois. To add insult to injury to the Democrats in the South and the Border South, more than half of the counties that switched from Gore in 2000 to Bush in 2004 were in the South (76 counties) or the Border South (31). As if the Democrats had not done poorly enough in the South and Border areas, they lost another 107 counties in 2004.

There were no historic breakthrough counties for Bush in 2004, as in 2000, but he did carry 40 counties that had not gone Republican for president since Nixon's 1972 landslide over McGovern. There was at least one pro–Bush swing county in 27 states.

Very few of the pro–Bush swing counties contained any cities. The few exceptions were St. Joseph County, Indiana (South Bend); Caddo Parish, Louisiana (Shreveport); Kanawha County, West Virginia (Charleston); and Pinellas County, Florida (St. Petersburg). Pinellas, a onetime Republican stronghold, went for Clinton and Gore three times but went back to Bush by only 226 votes out of more than 450,000 cast.

Of the 64 counties that shifted from Bush in 2000 to Kerry in 2004, 9 were in Minnesota, 7 in Colorado, 6 in Kentucky and 6 in Virginia. There was at least one pro–Kerry swing county in 24 states. Only 19 of the 64 (or 30%) were in the South or border states compared to 70% of the pro–Bush swing counties.

A few of the pro–Kerry swing counties included good-size cities, including Chatham, Georgia (Savannah); Marion, Indiana (Indianapolis); Guilford, North Carolina (Greensboro); Mecklenburg, North Carolina (Charlotte); Travis, Texas (Austin); and Stark, Ohio (Canton), President William McKinley's home county, which surely must have been a disappointment to Bush political adviser Karl Rove.

Kerry managed a few breakthrough counties that merit some notice. He was the first Democrat since FDR in 1936 to carry Alpine County, California, and the first since FDR in 1940 to carry neighboring Mono County. (Both are mountain counties bordering Nevada). Kerry was the first Democrat since Truman in 1948 to carry Albemarle County, Virginia, a fashionable suburb of Charlottesville that is home to such celebrities as John Grisham and Sissy Spacek, and the independent city of Danville. Four counties went Democratic for the first time since LBJ in 1964: San Juan, Colorado; Marion, Indiana; Fairfax, Virginia; and Fairfax City, Virginia.

Many of the pro–Kerry swing counties were ski resorts in Colorado and Wyoming, or university-oriented counties in Colorado, Indiana, Kansas, Montana, Texas, and Virginia (Williamsburg, home of the College of William and Mary, switched to Kerry).

Anti-Catholicism?

The fact of John Kerry's Catholicism did not become an issue per se, as it had been during the Kennedy and Smith campaigns of 1960 and 1928. Attacks on Kerry by conservative, right-wing and traditionalist Catholic organizations, and criticism of his position by Catholic bishops and even cardinals in Illinois and Pennsylvania, and virtual endorsement of Bush by bishops in Colorado, North Dakota and Nebraska added an element rarely seen in campaigns in the United States Evangelical and fundamentalist groups also mobilized especially intensely for the Bush campaign.

Given the large Bush gains in the states and counties that were most resistant to a Catholic nominee in 1960, it is difficult not to conclude that the kind of Protestantism that has shaped the culture in these areas had made voters so hostile to a Catholic — even 44 years after JFK barely won the presidency — that religious animosity still influences elections. Religion is often a subconscious or unconscious aspect of voting behavior that may elude precise definitions or exit polling.

Of the 97 anti–Kennedy "swing counties" in 1960, i.e., Democratic counties that voted for Nixon, 92 went for Bush over Kerry, compared to 87 that supported him over Gore.

Observers from as far away as the London-based *Economist* noted that Republicans were mounting an intense effort to register the Amish and Mennonites in Lancaster County, Pennsylvania, and Holmes County,

Ohio. Mennonites often vote but Amish rarely do. The last time they did so was in 1960, in a determined effort to defeat the Democratic candidate, who happened to be a Catholic. Why they ignored other liberal candidates (McGovern, Mondale, Dukasis, et al.) but mobilized to vote against Kerry again raises warning signals that religious animosity still persists in parts of rural America. It may be, of course, that Bush's personal identification with evangelical Christianity, his constant references to religious belief in his speeches, and the clear and unmistakable impact of his religious views on public policy caused the enormous effort mounted in evangelical, Pentecostal and fundamentalist churches. Perhaps any Democratic nominee would have been the target for this massive mobilization of a religious community.

In a postelection analysis, Evelyn Nieves wrote, "Republicans registered more than 300 new voters in each of three mostly Amish districts in Lancaster County, Pennsylvania. In Leacock Township, the GOP nearly doubled its voter rolls from 1,000 to 1,800, with all but a handful of the new voters being Amish or Mennonite."*

The extent to which anti–Catholicism affected the outcome of the vote will most likely remain in the realm of speculation. It may be that the political culture of the United States in 2004 is so different from 1960 that this historic prejudice played no significant role. It may be that we will never know until the Republicans happen to nominate a Catholic for the nation's highest office. That may be a long time in the future if the historical record is any guide. Since 1856 the Republicans have nominated 75 white Protestant men, most of English or Scots Irish ancestry, for president and vice president, compared to one obscure white Catholic male in 1964 for vice president (Rep. William Miller of New York).

This closed door policy could change, of course, but the party's cozy ties to the Religious Right make it unlikely. The Democrats don't have a terrific record on this score either, but they have nominated six Catholics for president or vice president (Smith in 1928, Kennedy in 1960, Muskie in 1968, Shriver in 1972, Ferraro in 1984, Kerry in 2004), one Greek Orthodox Christian for president (Dukakis, 1988) and one Jew for vice president (Lieberman, 2000).

As the United States becomes more religiously diverse, and since religious liberty and religious harmony are two of the attributes of U.S. society that are often cited as appealing to potential immigrants, it will be of some interest to see if more religious, racial or ethnic diversity might characterize the presidency in the future.

The South

The 2004 election is the second straight time that the South elected a Republican president. All 153 electoral votes from the 11 states of the Old Confederacy went for Bush, while he lost 252 to 133 in the rest of the country. More than half of Bush's electoral votes came from 11 states that once routinely gave all of their votes to the Democrats. In the popular vote, Bush amassed 19,942,893 to Kerry's 14,903,392 in the South, a victory margin of 5,039,501 votes. In the rest of the nation, Kerry won by 2,026,826 million popular votes.

It should be noted that the South was not a total washout for the Kerry-Edwards ticket. Kerry carried the counties including Atlanta, Nashville, Memphis, New Orleans, Jackson, Montgomery, Columbia, Richmond, Norfolk, Miami, Fort Lauderdale, and West Palm Beach.

He even carried the counties including Charlotte, Greensboro, Austin and Savannah, which had gone for Bush in 2000.

*Evelyn Nieves, "GOP's Soft Sell Swayed the Amish," *Washington Post*, December 30, 2004.

In a number of counties which he lost, Kerry ran stronger than Gore, including Raleigh, Charleston, Asheville, and Dallas, where he came within 10,000 votes of defeating Bush in a county that has gone Republican in 13 of the last 14 presidential elections. In Dallas, Bush's victory margin dropped from 47,000 to 10,000 votes.

Kerry won a record vote in Northern Virginia, which is hardly Southern anymore, and became the first Democrat since LBJ to carry Fairfax County.

The South remains the most distinctive region in terms of presidential politics. The states of the Old Confederacy have rarely been battlegrounds. They have tended toward either the Democrats from the post–Civil War days until the close of the New Deal or to the Republicans since the civil rights era and the migration of northerners to the region (reinforced by the resurgence of religious fundamentalism in politics).

All 11 Southern states voted for 8 Democratic winners (1888, 1892, 1912, 1916, 1932, 1936, 1940, 1944) and 4 Republican winners (1972, 1984, 1988, 2000). As loyal Democrats, every Southern state supported 7 Democratic losing candidates (1880, 1888, 1896, 1900, 1904, 1908, 1924).

Ten Southern states backed the losing Democrat in 1920. This tendency to go solidly for one party or the other is also demonstrated in 1976, when 10 Southern states supported the regional favorite, Democrat Jimmy Carter, and then in 1980 when 10 Southern states switched to Republican Ronald Reagan against Carter.

Only in the immediate post–Civil War era (1868–1876) and in the civil rights era (1948–1968) was the South divided in its presidential allegiance. (This was also true in 1928, and to a lesser extent in 1992 and 1996, when an all-southern Democratic ticket could only manage wins in four southern states).

There are some other notable aspects of the 2004 campaign. One was the unprecedented amounts of money spent by both parties and by independent groups supporting the party efforts. A national survey put the final amount at $2.22 billion.*

Also, unlike Presidents Reagan in 1984 and Eisenhower in 1956, who hardly even mentioned their opponents, Bush spent an unusually large part of his campaign criticizing Kerry rather than emphasizing his record as an incumbent seeking reelection. For his part, Kerry also attacked the Bush administration's policies on a range of issues.

Newspaper endorsements favored Kerry, according to *Editor & Publisher*, the newspaper industry's trade journal. By late October, 208 newspapers with a combined circulation of 20.8 million had endorsed Kerry compared to 188 newspapers with 14.5 million subscribers that endorsed Bush. At least 60 newspapers that had endorsed Bush in 2000 switched to Kerry in 2004, or remained neutral this time. Even President Bush's hometown paper in tiny Crawford, Texas, endorsed the Democratic nominee, as did the prestigious weekly *The Economist*, both of which endorsed Bush four years before. In some U.S. presidential campaigns, as much as 90% of newspapers endorsed the Republican nominee, including Landon in 1936 and Eisenhower in 1952.

A torrent of books appeared in 2004, on both sides of the partisan divide, though *Publishers Weekly* concluded, "The red side won the popular vote, but the blue state arguments prevailed in the publishing count."†

The Blue State/Red State paradigm has

---

*Thomas B. Edsall and James V. Grimaldi, "On November 2, GOP Got More Bang for its Billion, Analysis Shows," *Washington Post*, December 30, 2004.

†"Revenge of the Blue States," *Publishers Weekly* 251, December 6, 2004, pp. 36–37.

become inescapable as it reflects the changing political geography of the United States and is a pattern heavily influenced by demography. The regional patterns of the past, i.e., a Democratic South vs. a Republican North, are long gone, except perhaps in New England and the South, where political loyalties have been exchanged since the 1950s — New England, a Republican stronghold from the Civil War through the New Deal, is now a Democratic bastion, while the solid Democratic South has become the solid Republican South. But the reasons for that shift are demographic and cultural. The rest of the nation is deeply divided and has changed in response to similar demographic trends.

While the Republican Party, especially during the two campaigns of George W. Bush, has adopted an explicit "family values" strategy in its platforms and in the emphasis of the candidates' rhetoric, the voting patterns do not reflect this orientation. For example, Bush carried all 10 states with the highest levels of divorce (Tennessee, Nevada, Alabama, Arkansas, Oklahoma, Kentucky, etc.), according to data compiled by the Centers for Disease Control.* In 2003 new data show Arkansas, Mississippi and Kentucky had very high levels of divorce.† Bush carried all of the states with the highest levels of violent crime, high prison populations, executions, and all of the states which allow corporal punishment in public schools. He carried 17 of the 19 states which once banned interracial marriage (before a 1967 U.S. Supreme Court decision striking down these prohibitions). Bush carried all 10 states with the lowest levels of educational attainment, including West Virginia, Kentucky, Indiana, Oklahoma and six southern states.

Bush lost all but 1 of the 10 states with the highest levels of educational attainment (Colorado was the exception). Bush carried all 10 poorest states.

This socioeconomic or sociocultural pattern is replicated in the county-level election returns. Something major has transformed U.S. voting behavior in the last generation, and the geography of election behavior reflects these shifts far more than historical memory or traditional voting patterns would suggest.

Another factor to remember: There are Red sections in Blue States and Blue sections within Red States. There is no clear-cut pattern that explains the most recent divisions in presidential voting. It is a rare state in which every or nearly every county supports the same party. (Among the Red States there are Nebraska, Kansas, Idaho and Utah, and among the Blue States there are Vermont, Rhode Island, and Massachusetts.)

In Blue State Maryland, for example, the Democrats are generally victorious because of their overwhelming dominance in Baltimore and the Washington, D.C., suburbs (Montgomery and Prince Georges counties, which are among the best educated, wealthiest and most multi-cultural areas in the United States). But rural Maryland, including the Eastern Shore, the ex-urban counties of Carroll and Harford, and western Maryland, where Garrett County has never supported a Democrat for president, are Red State enclaves in a state generally seen as safely Blue. A similar pattern exists in Pennsylvania, a Blue State generally because of the Philadelphia and Pittsburgh subregions, while rural areas, especially the German-flavored Amish and Mennonite counties, are deep-dyed red in their unshakably Republican ways.

While the Red State/Blue State maps,

*See Blaine Harden, "Bible Belt Couples 'Put Asunder' More Despite New Efforts," *The New York Times*, May 21, 2001.

†Pam Belluck, "To Avoid Divorce, Move to Massachusetts." *The New* York Times, November 14, 2004.

especially those depicting the counties, are dramatic, they are distorted. They give the impression that this is a Republican country, because Bush carried nearly 80% of the counties. Remember, though, that he received only 53% of the electoral vote and 51% of the popular vote. Most Americans do not live in the wide-open spaces depicted on county maps. They live in large or medium-size metropolitan areas, which appear small on maps because a lot of people are jammed into them, and the population density is much greater in Democratic urban and suburban areas than in the Republican countryside.

But the real geography of U.S. presidential politics is rooted in and determined more by how individuals earn their living, their levels of education, and their practice of certain kinds of religious experiences than the historic, regional patterns of old. This phenomenon might best be described as cultural geography.

A seminal 2002 book, Richard Florida's *The Rise of the Creative Class*, advances the thesis that there is now "a large-scale re-sorting of people among cities and regions nationwide, with some regions becoming centers of the Creative Class, while others are composed of larger shares of Working Class and Service Class people…. This sorting is becoming more widespread and pronounced" (New York: Basic Books, p. 235).

Education, cultural diversity, and tolerance of divergent lifestyles are affected by this cultural and economic clustering, Florida argues. "Places that are home to large concentrations of the Creative Class also rank highly as centers of innovation and high-tech industry" (p. 243).

This geographical resettling along cultural and broad socioeconomic lines has long-range political implications and may prove unsettling to the cohesiveness of the United States. Says Florida, "Taken together, these findings suggest that a fast and disturbing change is afoot. The U.S. work-ing population is re-sorting itself geographically along class lines. This emerging geography defies categories like East Coast versus West Coast or Sunbelt versus Frost-belt.

"Significant concentrations of the Creative Class can be found in places like Omaha, Little Rock, Bloomington, Gainesville, Albany and Boise, as well as in more obvious high-tech centers like San Francisco, Austin and Seattle. The correlations between Creative Class and Working Class regions, and also between Creative Class and Service Class regions are consistently negative and significant, indicating that the different classes are sorting themselves into distinct regional centers. The new geography of class in America may well be giving use to a new form of segregation — different from racial segregation or the old schism between central city and suburb, and perhaps more threatening to national unity" (pp. 241–242).

It is therefore unsurprising that counties containing the highest percentage of creative class workers went for Gore by 56.4% to 37.7% for Bush and 4.8% for Nader. The service industry strongholds went for Bush 49.7% to 46.0% for Gore and 3.1% for Nader. Working-class areas supported Bush 57.7% to 39.7% for Gore and 1.6% for Nader. (About 1% in all three categories supported other minor party candidates).

In 2004 Kerry defeated Bush handily 61% to 39% in the major party vote in counties dominated by creative class voters, a gain of 1.7%. The service industry strongholds supported Bush 53% to 46%, a gain for the president of about 1.5%. Working-class areas gave Bush 59.6% and Kerry 40.4%, a gain of less than 1% for Bush. As Florida predicted, the gap between the working-class voters and the creative class voters continues to widen.

Turnout

As I have noted elsewhere, my use of the word "turnout" refers to the total vote cast in a given election compared to the total vote cast in the previous election. This is an actual, certifiable figure, not an estimate based on unreliable data. The term is often used to indicate the percentage of voters who voted as a percentage of "voting age population," i.e., adults over age 18. There are problems with this figure. For one thing, many states do not even require voter registration, and some allow voters to register on election day as they prepare to cast ballots. The over age 18 population is an estimate that differs from official U.S. Census data. People move frequently in the United States, and the voting age population reflects population mobility. Not all people over 18 are U.S. citizens and eligible to vote, and many Americans (2 million) are incarcerated and ineligible to vote. Some have been released from prison and cannot vote in some states, or are not automatically able to vote without filing petitions for restoration of voting rights. So the figure of "turnout" is only an estimate.

A *Washington Post* survey of state-by-state preliminary turnout figures claimed that turnout of voting age population increased in most states, but declined in California and New York. A *New York Times* survey said that turnout was high in South Dakota, Texas, Oklahoma, Ohio, Florida and Kentucky, all Bush states.

Nevada had the highest percentage increase in total vote in 2004, followed by Arizona, Florida, Georgia, and New Mexico. The other states on the top 10 were South Dakota, Colorado, Utah, North Carolina, and Oregon. Bush carried 9 of these 10 states.

In terms of actual vote numbers, Florida saw 1.646 million additional voters in 2004 than in 2000, and Texas and California both increased by 1 million. The total vote increased by more than 500,000 in Georgia, Illinois, Michigan, New York, Ohio and Pennsylvania.

TOP TEN STATES IN PERCENTAGE
INCREASE IN TOTAL VOTE 2000–2004

State	% Increase
1. Nevada	36.2
2. Arizona	31.5
3. Florida	27.6
4. Georgia	27.2
5. New Mexico	26.3
6. South Dakota	22.7
7. Colorado	22.3
8. Utah	20.4
9. North Carolina	20.3
10. Oregon	19.7

Party Registration

According to political analyst and *America Votes* editor Rhodes Cook, political party registration trends in the 27 states that require voters to declare a party affiliation favor Independents, while Democrats have declined, and Republicans have remained the same. In these states, the Democratic share of registrations has declined from 51% to 43% since 1987, while the proportion of voters who decline to identify with one of the two major parties has climbed from 16% to 24%. The Republican registration has remained at 33%. In round numbers, the "Independents" have picked up 11 million new voters, the Republicans 8 million, and the Democrats only 4.8 million.

Independents have gained almost everywhere, except Colorado and Kansas, where there has been a long-range Republican gain due in Colorado to the migration of white, middle class Protestant conservatives, and in Kansas to the resurgence of fundamentalist Protestantism, according to author Thomas Frank in his *What's the Mat-*

ter with Kansas? How Conservatives Won the Heart of America (New York: Metropolitan Books, 2004).

Independents have displaced Democrats as the largest group in registrations in Connecticut, Maine, Massachusetts, and Iowa, and Independents have moved ahead of Republicans in New Hampshire.

Republicans have moved ahead of Independents in Colorado and ahead of Democrats in Nevada. The number of registered Independents more than doubled in most of the southern and western states that maintain party registrations.

Since 1987 the Democratic percentage of registration declined 22% in Louisiana and North Carolina and more than 10% in Florida, Kentucky, Oklahoma, Maryland and Nevada. The Democrats maintained their percentage only in Delaware and New York. Republicans gained 5% to 10% in North Carolina, Louisiana, Kentucky, Oklahoma and Maryland, while losing ground in New York, Arizona and Connecticut.*

The surge of registrations over the summer and fall of 2004 seems to have resulted in a similar pattern, with new Independent registrations increasing by 700,000, Democrats by 800,000 and Republicans by 600,000. (The new registrations through September are 38% Democratic, 33% Independent and 29% Republican). The Republican share of the new voters is lower than during the early days of the Bush presidency.†

The presidential vote does not always correlate with party registration figures, since Bush easily won a number of southern and border states that have Democratic registration majorities. Exit polls showed that Bush did a bit better in holding the Republican vote than Kerry did among Democrats, as Bush won the support of 11% of Democrats while Kerry secured the backing of 8% of Republicans. A majority of self-designated Independents voted for Kerry, which is somewhat unusual since Independents have traditionally leaned Republican in close races.

Kerry also won among self-defined moderates (45% of voters in the exit polls), but Bush's victory came from the large turnout of those who call themselves conservatives (who were 34% of the electorate, up from 29% in 2000). The liberal 21% was unable to match the conservative vote for Bush.

Electoral Votes, 2004

States	Bush	Kerry	States	Bush	Kerry
Alabama	9	–	Idaho	4	–
Alaska	3	–	Illinois	–	21
Arizona	10	–	Indiana	11	–
Arkansas	6	–	Iowa	7	–
California	–	55	Kansas	6	–
Colorado	9	–	Kentucky	8	–
Connecticut	–	7	Louisiana	9	–
Delaware	–	3	Maine	–	4
District of Columbia	–	3	Maryland	–	10
Florida	27	–	Massachusetts	–	12
Georgia	15	–	Michigan	–	17
Hawaii	–	4	Minnesota	–	9[1]

*Rhodes Cook, "Moving On: More Voters are Steering Away from Party Labels," Washington Post, June 27, 2004.
†The Rhodes Cook Letter 5 (October 2004), pp. 10–11.

States	Bush	Kerry		States	Bush	Kerry
Mississippi	6	–		South Carolina	8	–
Missouri	11	–		South Dakota	3	–
Montana	3	–		Tennessee	11	–
Nebraska	5	–		Texas	34	–
Nevada	5	–		Utah	5	–
New Hampshire	–	4		Vermont	–	3
New Jersey	–	15		Virginia	13	–
New Mexico	5	–		Washington	–	11
New York	–	31		West Virginia	5	–
North Carolina	15	–		Wisconsin	–	10
North Dakota	3	–		Wyoming	3	–
Ohio	20	–				
Oklahoma	7	–		Totals	286	251[1]
Oregon	–	7				
Pennsylvania	–	21				
Rhode Island	–	4				

1. One Minnesota Kerry elector voted for John Edwards for president.

Here are a few additional tidbits of information about the 2004 election:

- Only 1% of voters opted for minor party candidates, the lowest showing for the also-rans since 1984, when only 0.6% voted for someone other than Reagan or Mondale. As usual, Alaska had the highest aggregate minor party percentage (3.4%). Oklahoma had no minor parties at all on the presidential ballot.
- Bush carried Jimmy Carter's home county (Sumter, Georgia) and George McGovern's home county (Davison, South Dakota). Bush won a landslide in Senator Zell Miller's home county (Towns, Georgia), where voters must not have been offended by the Democratic senator's vituperative comments about a fellow Democratic senator at the Republican National Convention.
- Kerry carried Vice President Cheney's home county (Teton, Wyoming) and Bush carried John Edwards' home county (Wake, North Carolina).
- The closest state in popular vote was New Mexico, for the second straight election. Bush carried the Land of Enchantment by 5,988 votes.

- The closest state in percentage, however, was Wisconsin, where Kerry edged Bush by 0.4%. Iowa was the second closest, giving Bush a margin of 0.7%. Perhaps these states, along with New Hampshire, Ohio, and Pennsylvania, should be colored purple, rather than red or blue, on the ubiquitous electoral maps.
- Of the nation's metropolitan counties, Bush made his greatest gain in Ocean County, New Jersey, where his major party voter support rose 10 percentage points.
- Another sign of the times: Florida and Texas recorded more popular votes than New York. Florida was second to California in total votes cast, followed by Texas in third and New York in fourth place.
- The closest county was Pope County, Minnesota, which went for Bush by 2 votes.
- Bush's strongest county was Ochiltree, Texas, where he received 92% of the votes. This Texas Panhandle county bordering Oklahoma was Bush's second-highest county in 2000 and Bob Dole's strongest county in 1996.
- Kerry's strongest county was Shannon,

South Dakota, where he received 84.6% of the votes in the county that contains the Pine Ridge Indian Reservation. Kerry carried all of the predominantly American Indian counties and townships in South Dakota, North Dakota, Wisconsin, Minnesota, Montana, Arizona, New Mexico and Maine.

The United States remains a deeply divided nation. The Republicans pulled ahead just enough in 2004 to retain an effective governing majority but did not achieve a mandate by any means.

The animosity and bitterness between the partisans of Bush and Kerry, and among party leaders and activists, reduce the chance of a consensus in the years ahead. A *Time* poll conducted two weeks before the election found that 70% of voters believed that the election of the man they opposed would have "a major negative impact on the country." Only 25% disagreed.*

Since 1868 the Republicans have won 21 presidential elections and the Democrats have been victorious 14 times. (Extending that record back to 1856 gives the GOP 23 victories and 15 losses). Thus, the younger Republicans have won 60% of the presidential races, while the older Democratic Party has won 40% of them. In that respect, at least, the 2004 election was not untypical.

*Nancy Gibbs, "The Morning After," *Time* 164, November 1, 2004, p. 32.

PART II

COUNTY RESULTS

Alabama

County	1868	1872	1876	1880	1884	1888	1892	1896	1900	1904	1908	1912
Autauga	R	R	D	D	D	D	D	D	D	D	D	D
Baldwin	D	R	D	D	D	D	D	D	D	D	D	D
Barbour	R	R	D	D	D	D	D	D	D	D	D	D
Bibb	D	D	D	D	D	D	PO	D	D	D	D	D
Blount	D	D	D	D	D	D	D	R	D	D	D	D
Bullock	R	R	D	R	D	D	D	D	D	D	D	D
Butler	D	D	D	D	D	D	PO	D	R	D	D	D
Calhoun	D	D	D	D	D	D	D	D	D	D	D	D
Chambers	D	D	D	D	D	D	D	D	D	D	D	D
Cherokee	D	D	D	D	D	D	D	D	R	D	D	P
Chilton	D	D	D	D	D	D	PO	D	R	D	R	D
Choctaw	D	D	D	D	D	D	PO	D	D	D	D	D
Clarke	D	D	D	D	D	D	D	D	D	D	D	D
Clay	D	D	D	D	D	D	D	D	R	D	D	D
Cleburne	R	D	D	D	D	D	D	D	D	D	R	D
Coffee	D	D	D	D	D	D	D	D	D	D	D	D
Colbert	D	D	D	D	R	R	D	R	D	D	D	D
Conecuh	D	R	D	D	D	D	PO	D	R	D	D	D
Coosa	D	D	D	D	D	D	PO	D	D	D	D	D
Covington	D	D	D	D	D	D	D	D	D	D	D	D
Crenshaw	D	D	D	D	D	D	D	D	D	D	D	D
Cullman	–	–	–	D	D	D	D	D	D	D	R	P
Dale	D	D	D	D	D	D	D	D	D	D	D	D
Dallas	R	R	R	D	D	D	D	D	D	D	D	D
De Kalb	R	R	D	D	D	D	D	D	D	D	D	D
Elmore	R	R	D	D	D	D	PO	D	D	D	D	D
Escambia	–	D	D	D	D	D	D	D	D	D	D	D
Etowah	D	D	D	D	D	D	D	D	D	D	D	D
Fayette	D	D	D	D	D	D	PO	D	R	D	D	D
Franklin	D	D	D	D	D	D	D	D	R	D	R	D
Geneva	–	D	D	D	D	D	D	D	D	D	D	D
Greene	R	R	R	R	R	D	D	D	D	D	D	D
Hale	R	R	R	D	R	D	D	D	D	D	D	D
Henry	D	D	D	D	D	D	D	D	D	D	D	D
Houston	D	D	D	D	D	D	D	NR	NR	D	D	D
Jackson	D	D	D	D	D	D	D	D	D	D	D	D
Jefferson	D	D	D	D	D	D	D	D	D	D	D	D
Lamar	D	D	D	D	D	D	D	D	D	D	D	D

143

County	1868	1872	1876	1880	1884	1888	1892	1896	1900	1904	1908	1912
Lauderdale	D	D	D	D	D	D	D	D	R	D	D	D
Lawrence	D	R	D	D	R	R	PO	R	D	D	D	D
Lee	D	R	D	D	D	D	D	D	D	D	D	D
Limestone	D	R	D	R	R	D	PO	D	R	D	D	D
Lowndes	R	R	R	R	D	D	D	D	D	D	D	D
Macon	R	R	D	D	D	D	PO	D	D	D	D	D
Madison	D	R	D	R	R	R	PO	D	D	D	D	D
Marengo	R	D	D	D	D	D	D	D	D	D	D	D
Marion	NR	R	D	D	D	D	D	D	D	D	D	D
Marshall	D	D	D	D	D	D	D	D	D	D	D	D
Mobile	D	D	D	D	D	D	D	D	D	D	D	D
Monroe	D	D	D	D	D	D	D	NR	D	D	D	D
Montgomery	R	R	R	R	R	D	D	D	D	D	D	D
Morgan	D	R	D	D	D	D	D	D	D	D	D	D
Perry	R	R	R	D	D	D	D	D	D	D	D	D
Pickens	D	D	D	D	D	D	D	D	D	D	D	D
Pike	D	D	D	D	D	D	D	D	D	D	D	D
Randolph	R	R	D	D	D	D	PO	D	D	D	D	D
Russell	R	R	D	D	D	D	D	D	D	D	D	D
St. Clair	R	D	D	D	D	D	PO	D	R	D	D	D
Shelby	D	D	D	D	D	D	D	D	R	D	R	P
Sumter	R	R	D	D	D	D	D	D	D	D	D	D
Talladega	R	R	D	R	R	R	D	D	D	D	D	D
Tallapoosa	D	D	D	D	D	D	D	D	D	D	D	D
Tuscaloosa	D	D	D	D	D	D	D	D	D	D	D	D
Walker	D	R	D	D	D	D	D	D	R	D	D	D
Washington	R	D	D	D	D	D	D	D	D	D	D	D
Wilcox	R	R	R	D	D	D	D	D	D	D	D	D
Winston	R	R	R	D	R	R	PO	R	D	R	R	P

County	1916	1920	1924	1928	1932	1936	1940	1944	1948	1952	1956	1960
Autauga	D	D	D	D	D	D	D	D	SR	D	D	D
Baldwin	D	D	D	R	D	D	D	D	SR	D	R	D
Barbour	D	D	D	D	D	D	D	D	SR	D	D	D
Bibb	D	D	D	D	D	D	D	D	SR	D	D	D
Blount	D	D	D	R	D	D	D	D	SR	D	D	D
Bullock	D	D	D	D	D	D	D	D	SR	D	D	D
Butler	D	D	D	D	D	D	D	D	SR	D	D	D
Calhoun	D	D	D	R	D	D	D	D	SR	D	D	D
Chambers	D	D	D	R	D	D	D	D	SR	D	D	D
Cherokee	D	D	D	R	D	D	D	D	SR	D	D	D
Chilton	R	R	R	R	D	D	D	D	SR	R	R	R
Choctaw	D	D	D	D	D	D	D	D	SR	D	D	D
Clarke	D	D	D	D	D	D	D	D	SR	D	D	D
Clay	D	D	D	R	D	D	D	D	SR	D	D	D
Cleburne	D	R	R	R	D	D	D	D	SR	D	D	D
Coffee	D	D	D	D	D	D	D	D	SR	D	D	D
Colbert	D	D	D	D	D	D	D	D	SR	D	D	D
Conecuh	D	D	D	R	D	D	D	D	SR	D	D	D

County	1916	1920	1924	1928	1932	1936	1940	1944	1948	1952	1956	1960
Coosa	D	D	D	R	D	D	D	D	SR	D	D	D
Covington	D	D	D	D	D	D	D	D	SR	D	D	D
Crenshaw	D	D	D	D	D	D	D	D	SR	D	D	D
Cullman	D	R	D	R	D	D	D	D	SR	D	D	D
Dale	D	D	D	D	D	D	D	D	SR	D	D	D
Dallas	D	D	D	D	D	D	D	D	SR	R	R	R
De Kalb	D	R	D	R	D	D	D	D	SR	D	D	D
Elmore	D	D	D	R	D	D	D	D	SR	D	D	D
Escambia	D	D	D	R	D	D	D	D	SR	D	D	D
Etowah	D	D	D	R	D	D	D	D	SR	D	D	D
Fayette	D	R	D	R	D	D	D	D	SR	D	D	D
Franklin	D	R	R	R	D	D	D	D	SR	D	R	R
Geneva	D	D	D	R	D	D	D	D	SR	D	D	D
Greene	D	D	D	D	D	D	D	D	SR	D	D	D
Hale	D	D	D	D	D	D	D	D	SR	D	D	D
Henry	D	D	D	D	D	D	D	D	SR	D	D	D
Houston	D	D	D	D	D	D	D	D	SR	D	D	R
Jackson	D	D	D	R	D	D	D	D	SR	D	D	D
Jefferson	D	D	D	R	D	D	D	D	SR	D	R	R
Lamar	D	D	D	D	D	D	D	D	SR	D	D	D
Lauderdale	D	D	D	D	D	D	D	D	SR	D	D	D
Lawrence	D	D	D	D	D	D	D	D	SR	D	D	D
Lee	D	D	D	D	D	D	D	D	SR	D	D	D
Limestone	D	D	D	D	D	D	D	D	SR	D	D	D
Lowndes	D	D	D	D	D	D	D	D	SR	D	D	D
Macon	D	D	D	D	D	D	D	D	SR	D	R	D
Madison	D	D	D	R	D	D	D	D	SR	D	D	D
Marengo	D	D	D	D	D	D	D	D	SR	D	D	D
Marion	D	D	D	D	D	D	D	D	SR	D	D	D
Marshall	D	D	D	R	D	D	D	D	SR	D	D	D
Mobile	D	D	D	D	D	D	D	D	SR	D	R	D
Monroe	D	D	D	D	D	D	D	D	SR	D	D	D
Montgomery	D	D	D	D	D	D	D	D	SR	D	R	R
Morgan	D	D	D	R	D	D	D	D	SR	D	D	D
Perry	D	D	D	D	D	D	D	D	SR	D	D	D
Pickens	D	D	D	D	D	D	D	D	SR	D	D	D
Pike	D	D	D	D	D	D	D	D	SR	D	D	D
Randolph	D	D	D	R	D	D	D	D	SR	D	D	D
Russell	D	D	D	D	D	D	D	D	SR	D	D	D
St. Clair	D	R	R	R	D	D	D	D	SR	D	R	D
Shelby	R	R	D	R	D	D	D	D	SR	D	R	D
Sumter	D	D	D	D	D	D	D	D	SR	D	D	D
Talladega	D	D	D	D	D	D	D	D	SR	D	D	D
Tallapoosa	D	D	D	D	D	D	D	D	SR	D	D	D
Tuscaloosa	D	D	D	D	D	D	D	D	SR	D	D	D
Walker	D	D	D	D	D	D	D	D	SR	D	D	D
Washington	D	D	D	D	D	D	D	D	SR	D	D	D
Wilcox	D	D	D	D	D	D	D	D	SR	D	D	D
Winston	R	R	R	R	D	R	R	R	R	R	R	R

County	1964	1968	1972	1976	1980	1984	1988	1992	1996	2000	2004
Autauga	R	A	R	D	R	R	R	R	R	R	R
Baldwin	R	A	R	R	R	R	R	R	R	R	R
Barbour	R	A	R	D	D	R	R	D	D	D	R
Bibb	R	A	R	D	D	R	R	R	R	R	R
Blount	R	A	R	D	R	R	R	R	R	R	R
Bullock	R	A	D	D	D	D	D	D	D	D	D
Butler	R	A	R	D	D	R	R	D	D	R	R
Calhoun	R	A	R	D	R	R	R	R	R	R	R
Chambers	R	A	R	D	D	R	R	D	D	R	R
Cherokee	D	A	R	D	D	R	D	D	D	R	R
Chilton	R	A	R	D	R	R	R	R	R	R	R
Choctaw	R	A	R	D	D	R	R	R	D	R	R
Clarke	R	A	R	D	D	R	R	R	D	R	R
Clay	R	A	R	D	D	R	R	R	R	R	R
Cleburne	R	A	R	D	R	R	R	R	R	R	R
Coffee	R	A	R	D	R	R	R	R	R	R	R
Colbert	D	A	R	D	D	D	D	D	D	D	R
Conecuh	R	A	R	D	D	R	R	D	D	D	R
Coosa	R	A	R	D	D	R	R	D	D	R	R
Covington	R	A	R	D	R	R	R	R	R	R	R
Crenshaw	R	A	R	D	D	R	R	D	D	R	R
Cullman	R	A	R	D	D	R	R	R	R	R	R
Dale	R	A	R	D	R	R	R	R	R	R	R
Dallas	R	A	R	D	D	D	D	D	D	D	D
De Kalb	R	A	R	D	R	R	R	R	R	R	R
Elmore	R	A	R	D	R	R	R	R	R	R	R
Escambia	R	A	R	D	R	R	R	R	R	R	R
Etowah	R	A	R	D	D	R	R	D	D	R	R
Fayette	R	A	R	D	D	R	R	D	D	R	R
Franklin	R	A	R	D	D	R	R	D	D	R	R
Geneva	R	A	R	D	R	R	R	R	R	R	R
Greene	R	D	D	D	D	D	D	D	D	D	D
Hale	R	A	R	D	D	D	D	D	D	D	D
Henry	R	A	R	D	R	R	R	R	R	R	R
Houston	R	A	R	R	R	R	R	R	R	R	R
Jackson	D	A	R	D	D	D	D	D	D	D	R
Jefferson	R	A	R	R	R	R	R	R	R	R	R
Lamar	R	A	R	D	D	R	R	R	R	R	R
Lauderdale	D	A	R	D	D	R	R	D	R	R	R
Lawrence	R	A	R	D	D	D	D	D	D	D	R
Lee	R	A	R	R	R	R	R	R	R	R	R
Limestone	D	A	R	D	D	R	R	R	R	R	R
Lowndes	R	A	D	D	D	D	D	D	D	D	D
Macon	D	D	D	D	D	D	D	D	D	D	D
Madison	R	A	R	D	R	R	R	R	R	R	R
Marengo	R	A	R	D	D	R	D	D	D	D	R
Marion	R	A	R	D	D	R	R	D	D	R	R
Marshall	R	A	R	D	D	R	R	R	R	R	R
Mobile	R	A	R	R	R	R	R	R	R	R	R

County	1964	1968	1972	1976	1980	1984	1988	1992	1996	2000	2004
Monroe	R	A	R	D	R	R	R	R	R	R	R
Montgomery	R	A	R	R	R	R	R	R	D	D	D
Morgan	R	A	R	D	D	R	R	R	R	R	R
Perry	R	A	R	D	D	D	D	D	D	D	D
Pickens	R	A	R	D	D	R	R	D	D	R	R
Pike	R	A	R	D	R	R	R	R	R	R	R
Randolph	R	A	R	D	D	R	R	R	R	R	R
Russell	R	A	R	D	D	D	D	D	D	D	D
St. Clair	R	A	R	D	R	R	R	R	R	R	R
Shelby	R	A	R	R	R	R	R	R	R	R	R
Sumter	R	D	D	D	D	D	D	D	D	D	D
Talladega	R	A	R	D	D	R	R	R	R	R	R
Tallapoosa	R	A	R	D	D	R	R	R	R	R	R
Tuscaloosa	R	A	R	D	R	R	R	R	R	R	R
Walker	R	A	R	D	D	R	D	D	D	R	R
Washington	R	A	R	D	D	R	R	D	D	R	R
Wilcox	R	A	D	D	D	D	D	D	D	D	D
Winston	R	A	R	D	R	R	R	R	R	R	R

—————— Alaska ——————

Population Center	1960	1964	1968	1972	1976	1980	1984	1988	1992	1996	2000	2004
Aleutians	D	D	R	R	R	R	R	R	R	R	R	R
Anchorage	R	D	R	R	R	R	R	R	R	R	R	R
Barrow	D	D	D	D	D	D	R	R	D	D	R	R
Fairbanks	D	D	R	R	R	R	R	R	R	R	R	R
Juneau	R	D	D	R	R	R	R	D	D	D	D	D
Ketchikan	R	D	R	R	R	R	R	R	R	R	R	R
Kodiak	D	D	R	R	R	R	R	R	R	R	R	R
Nome	R	D	D	R	R	D	R	R	R	D	R	R
Seward	D	D	D	R	R	R	R	R	R	R	R	R
Sitka	D	D	D	R	R	R	R	R	R	R	R	R

Alaska has no counties and is therefore excluded from most election studies. The major population centers, however, correspond to election district numbers, and their voting behavior can be traced back to 1960, when the state first voted in a presidential election.

—————— Arizona ——————

County	1912	1916	1920	1924	1928	1932	1936	1940	1944	1948	1952	1956
Apache	D	D	R	R	R	D	D	D	D	D	R	R
Cochise	D	D	R	R	R	D	D	D	D	D	R	R

County	1912	1916	1920	1924	1928	1932	1936	1940	1944	1948	1952	1956
Coconino	D	D	R	R	R	D	D	D	D	D	R	R
Gila	D	D	R	D	R	D	D	D	D	D	D	R
Graham	D	D	D	D	D	D	D	D	D	D	D	R
Greenlee	D	D	D	D	D	D	D	D	D	D	D	D
La Paz	–	–	–	–	–	–	–	–	–	–	–	–
Maricopa	D	D	R	R	R	D	D	D	D	D	R	R
Mohave	D	D	R	R	R	D	D	D	D	D	R	R
Navajo	D	D	R	R	R	D	D	D	D	D	R	R
Pima	D	R	R	R	R	D	D	D	D	D	R	R
Pinal	D	D	R	R	R	D	D	D	D	D	R	R
Santa Cruz	D	D	R	D	R	D	D	D	D	D	R	R
Yavapai	D	D	R	R	R	D	D	D	D	D	R	R
Yuma	D	D	R	R	R	D	D	D	D	D	R	D

County	1960	1964	1968	1972	1976	1980	1984	1988	1992	1996	2000	2004
Apache	R	D	R	R	D	R	R	D	D	D	D	D
Cochise	R	D	R	R	R	R	R	R	D	R	R	R
Coconino	R	R	R	R	R	R	R	R	D	D	D	D
Gila	D	D	D	R	D	R	R	R	D	D	R	R
Graham	R	D	R	R	R	R	R	R	R	R	R	R
Greenlee	D	D	D	D	D	D	D	D	D	D	R	R
La Paz	–	–	–	–	–	–	R	R	D	D	R	R
Maricopa	R	R	R	R	R	R	R	R	R	R	R	R
Mohave	R	D	R	R	R	R	R	R	R	R	R	R
Navajo	R	R	R	R	D	R	R	R	D	D	R	R
Pima	R	D	R	R	R	R	R	R	D	D	D	D
Pinal	D	D	D	R	D	R	R	R	D	D	R	R
Santa Cruz	D	D	R	R	R	R	R	R	D	D	D	D
Yavapai	R	R	R	R	R	R	R	R	R	R	R	R
Yuma	D	D	R	R	R	R	R	R	R	R	R	R

Arkansas

County	1868	1872	1876	1880	1884	1888	1892	1896	1900	1904	1908	1912
Arkansas	R	R	D	D	R	R	D	D	D	D	D	D
Ashley	NR	D	D	D	R	D	D	D	D	D	D	D
Baxter	–	–	D	D	D	D	D	D	D	D	D	D
Benton	R	D	D	D	D	D	D	D	D	D	D	D
Boone	–	D	D	D	D	D	D	D	D	D	D	D
Bradley	NR	D	D	D	D	D	D	D	D	D	D	D
Calhoun	D	D	D	D	D	D	D	D	D	D	D	D
Carroll	D	D	D	D	D	D	D	D	D	D	D	D
Chicot	R	R	R	R	R	R	R	D	R	D	R	D
Clark	D	R	D	D	D	D	D	D	D	R	D	D
Clay	–	–	D	D	D	D	D	D	D	D	D	D

County	1868	1872	1876	1880	1884	1888	1892	1896	1900	1904	1908	1912
Cleburne	–	–	–	–	D	D	D	D	D	D	D	D
Cleveland	–	–	D	D	D	D	D	D	D	D	D	D
Columbia	NR	D	D	D	D	D	D	D	D	D	D	D
Conway	R	D	D	R	R	D	D	D	D	D	D	D
Craighead	NR	D	D	D	D	D	D	D	D	D	D	D
Crawford	R	R	D	D	D	D	D	D	D	R	D	D
Crittenden	D	R	R	R	R	R	R	D	R	R	D	D
Cross	D	D	D	D	D	D	D	D	D	D	D	D
Dallas	D	D	D	D	D	D	D	D	D	D	D	D
Desha	R	R	R	R	R	R	D	D	D	D	D	D
Drew	D	D	D	D	R	D	D	D	D	D	D	D
Faulkner	–	–	D	D	D	D	D	D	D	D	D	D
Franklin	R	R	D	D	D	D	D	D	D	D	D	D
Fulton	NR	D	D	D	D	D	D	D	D	D	D	D
Garland	–	–	D	D	D	D	D	D	D	R	D	D
Grant	–	D	D	D	D	D	D	D	D	D	D	D
Greene	NR	NR	D	D	D	D	D	D	D	D	D	D
Hempstead	R	R	D	R	D	R	D	D	D	R	D	D
Hot Spring	NR	D	D	D	D	D	D	D	D	D	D	D
Howard	–	–	D	D	D	D	D	D	D	D	D	D
Independence	D	R	D	D	D	D	D	D	D	R	D	D
Izard	D	D	D	D	D	D	D	D	D	D	D	D
Jackson	D	R	D	G	D	D	D	D	D	D	D	D
Jefferson	R	R	R	R	R	R	D	D	R	D	D	D
Johnson	R	NR	D	D	D	D	D	D	D	D	D	D
Lafayette	NR	R	R	R	R	R	D	D	R	D	D	D
Lawrence	NR	D	D	D	D	D	D	D	D	D	D	D
Lee	–	–	R	R	D	R	D	D	D	D	D	D
Lincoln	–	R	R	R	R	R	R	D	D	D	D	D
Little River	D	R	R	R	R	R	D	D	D	D	D	D
Logan	–	R	D	D	D	D	D	D	D	D	D	D
Lonoke	–	–	D	D	D	D	D	D	D	D	D	D
Madison	R	D	D	D	D	D	D	D	D	R	R	D
Marion	R	D	D	D	D	D	D	D	D	D	D	D
Miller	–	–	D	D	D	D	D	D	D	D	D	D
Mississippi	NR	R	D	D	R	R	D	D	D	D	R	D
Monroe	R	R	R	R	R	R	D	D	D	D	R	D
Montgomery	R	D	D	D	D	D	D	D	D	R	D	D
Nevada	–	D	D	D	D	D	D	D	R	D	D	D
Newton	R	R	R	R	R	R	R	R	R	R	R	D
Ouachita	D	R	D	R	R	D	D	D	R	D	R	D
Perry	R	R	D	D	D	D	D	D	D	D	D	D
Phillips	R	R	R	R	R	R	D	D	D	D	D	D
Pike	R	R	D	D	D	D	D	D	D	R	R	D
Poinsett	D	NR	D	D	D	D	D	D	D	D	D	D
Polk	D	D	D	D	D	D	D	D	D	D	D	D
Pope	D	R	D	D	D	D	D	D	D	D	D	D
Prairie	D	D	D	D	D	D	D	D	D	R	D	D
Pulaski	R	R	R	R	R	R	D	D	D	D	D	D

County	1868	1872	1876	1880	1884	1888	1892	1896	1900	1904	1908	1912
Randolph	NR	D	D	D	D	D	D	D	D	D	D	D
St. Francis	D	D	D	D	D	R	R	D	R	D	R	D
Saline	D	D	D	D	D	D	D	D	D	D	D	D
Scott	R	NR	D	D	D	D	D	D	D	T	D	D
Searcy	R	R	R	R	R	R	R	R	R	R	R	D
Sebastian	R	R	D	D	D	D	D	D	D	D	D	D
Sevier	NR	D	D	D	D	D	D	D	D	D	D	D
Sharp	–	D	D	D	D	D	D	D	D	D	D	D
Stone	–	–	D	D	D	D	D	D	D	D	D	D
Union	D	R	D	D	D	D	D	D	D	D	D	D
Van Buren	D	D	D	D	D	D	D	D	D	D	D	D
Washington	R	D	D	D	D	D	D	D	D	D	D	D
White	D	D	D	D	D	D	D	D	D	D	D	D
Woodruff	–	R	D	R	D	D	D	D	D	D	D	D
Yell	R	D	D	D	D	D	D	D	D	D	D	D

County	1916	1920	1924	1928	1932	1936	1940	1944	1948	1952	1956	1960
Arkansas	D	R	D	D	D	D	D	D	D	R	R	D
Ashley	D	D	D	D	D	D	D	D	D	D	D	D
Baxter	D	D	D	D	D	D	D	D	D	D	R	R
Benton	D	D	D	R	D	D	D	R	D	R	R	R
Boone	D	D	D	D	D	D	D	D	D	R	R	R
Bradley	D	D	D	D	D	D	D	D	D	D	D	D
Calhoun	D	D	D	D	D	D	D	D	D	D	D	D
Carroll	D	D	D	R	D	D	D	D	D	R	R	R
Chicot	D	D	D	D	D	D	D	D	D	D	D	D
Clark	D	D	D	D	D	D	D	D	D	D	D	D
Clay	D	D	D	D	D	D	D	D	D	D	D	R
Cleburne	D	D	D	D	D	D	D	D	D	D	D	D
Cleveland	D	D	D	D	D	D	D	D	D	D	D	D
Columbia	D	D	D	D	D	D	D	D	D	D	D	D
Conway	D	D	D	D	D	D	D	D	D	D	D	D
Craighead	D	D	D	D	D	D	D	D	D	D	D	R
Crawford	D	D	D	D	D	D	D	D	D	R	R	R
Crittenden	D	D	D	D	D	D	D	D	SR	D	D	D
Cross	D	D	D	D	D	D	D	D	D	D	D	D
Dallas	D	D	D	D	D	D	D	D	D	D	D	D
Desha	D	D	D	D	D	D	D	D	D	D	D	D
Drew	D	D	D	D	D	D	D	D	D	D	D	D
Faulkner	D	D	D	D	D	D	D	D	D	D	D	D
Franklin	D	D	D	D	D	D	D	D	D	D	D	D
Fulton	D	D	D	D	D	D	D	D	D	D	D	R
Garland	D	D	D	D	D	D	D	D	D	R	R	R
Grant	D	D	D	D	D	D	D	D	D	D	D	D
Greene	D	D	D	D	D	D	D	D	D	D	D	D
Hempstead	D	D	D	D	D	D	D	D	D	D	D	D
Hot Spring	D	D	D	R	D	D	D	D	D	D	D	D
Howard	D	D	D	D	D	D	D	D	D	D	D	D

County	1916	1920	1924	1928	1932	1936	1940	1944	1948	1952	1956	1960
Independence	D	D	D	D	D	D	D	D	D	R	R	R
Izard	D	D	D	D	D	D	D	D	D	D	D	D
Jackson	D	D	D	D	D	D	D	D	D	D	D	D
Jefferson	D	D	D	D	D	D	D	D	D	D	D	D
Johnson	D	D	D	D	D	D	D	D	D	D	D	D
Lafayette	D	D	D	D	D	D	D	D	D	D	D	D
Lawrence	D	D	D	D	D	D	D	D	D	D	D	D
Lee	D	D	D	D	D	D	D	D	SR	D	D	D
Lincoln	D	R	D	D	D	D	D	D	D	D	D	D
Little River	D	D	D	D	D	D	D	D	D	D	D	D
Logan	D	R	D	D	D	D	D	D	D	D	D	D
Lonoke	D	D	D	D	D	D	D	D	D	D	D	D
Madison	D	R	D	R	D	D	D	R	R	R	R	R
Marion	D	D	D	D	D	D	D	D	D	D	D	R
Miller	D	D	D	D	D	D	D	D	D	D	D	D
Mississippi	D	D	D	D	D	D	D	D	D	D	D	D
Monroe	D	R	D	D	D	D	D	D	D	D	D	D
Montgomery	D	R	D	D	D	D	D	D	D	R	R	R
Nevada	D	R	D	D	D	D	D	D	D	D	D	D
Newton	R	R	R	R	D	R	R	R	R	R	R	R
Ouachita	D	D	D	D	D	D	D	D	D	D	D	D
Perry	D	D	D	D	D	D	D	D	D	D	D	D
Phillips	D	D	D	D	D	D	D	D	SR	D	D	D
Pike	D	R	D	D	D	D	D	D	D	D	D	R
Poinsett	D	D	D	D	D	D	D	D	D	D	D	D
Polk	D	D	D	R	D	D	D	D	D	R	R	R
Pope	D	D	D	D	D	D	D	D	D	D	D	D
Prairie	D	D	D	D	D	D	D	D	D	D	D	D
Pulaski	D	D	D	D	D	D	D	D	D	D	R	D
Randolph	D	D	D	D	D	D	D	D	D	D	D	R
St. Francis	D	D	D	D	D	D	D	D	D	D	D	D
Saline	D	D	D	D	D	D	D	D	D	D	D	D
Scott	D	D	D	D	D	D	D	D	D	D	D	R
Searcy	R	R	R	R	D	R	R	R	D	R	R	R
Sebastian	D	D	D	R	D	D	D	D	D	R	R	R
Sevier	D	D	D	D	D	D	D	D	D	D	D	D
Sharp	D	D	D	D	D	D	D	D	D	D	D	R
Stone	D	D	D	D	D	D	D	D	D	R	D	R
Union	D	D	D	D	D	D	D	D	D	D	D	R
Van Buren	D	R	D	D	D	D	D	D	D	D	D	D
Washington	D	D	D	R	D	D	D	D	D	R	R	R
White	D	D	D	D	D	D	D	D	D	D	D	D
Woodruff	D	D	D	D	D	D	D	D	D	D	D	D
Yell	D	D	D	D	D	D	D	D	D	D	D	D

County	1964	1968	1972	1976	1980	1984	1988	1992	1996	2000	2004
Arkansas	R	A	R	D	D	R	R	D	D	R	R
Ashley	R	A	R	D	D	R	D	D	D	D	R

County	1964	1968	1972	1976	1980	1984	1988	1992	1996	2000	2004
Baxter	R	R	R	R	R	R	R	D	R	R	R
Benton	R	R	R	R	R	R	R	R	R	R	R
Boone	D	R	R	D	R	R	R	D	R	R	R
Bradley	D	A	R	D	D	R	D	D	D	D	D
Calhoun	D	A	R	D	D	R	D	D	D	R	R
Carroll	R	R	R	D	R	R	R	D	R	R	R
Chicot	D	D	R	D	D	D	D	D	D	D	D
Clark	D	A	R	D	D	D	D	D	D	R	D
Clay	D	R	R	D	D	R	D	D	D	D	D
Cleburne	D	A	R	D	R	R	R	D	D	R	R
Cleveland	D	A	R	D	D	R	R	D	D	R	R
Columbia	R	A	R	D	R	R	R	D	D	R	R
Conway	D	D	R	D	D	R	D	D	D	R	R
Craighead	D	R	R	D	R	R	R	D	D	D	R
Crawford	D	A	R	D	R	R	R	R	R	R	R
Crittenden	D	A	R	D	D	R	R	D	D	D	D
Cross	D	A	R	D	D	R	R	D	D	D	R
Dallas	D	A	R	D	D	R	D	D	D	D	R
Desha	D	A	R	D	D	D	D	D	D	D	D
Drew	R	A	R	D	D	R	R	D	D	D	R
Faulkner	D	A	R	D	D	R	R	D	D	R	R
Franklin	D	A	R	D	R	R	R	D	D	R	R
Fulton	D	R	R	D	R	R	D	D	D	R	R
Garland	D	R	R	D	R	R	R	D	D	R	R
Grant	D	A	R	D	D	R	R	D	D	D	R
Greene	D	A	R	D	D	R	R	D	D	D	D
Hempstead	D	A	R	D	D	R	R	D	D	D	D
Hot Spring	D	A	R	D	D	D	D	D	D	D	D
Howard	R	A	R	D	D	R	R	D	D	R	R
Independence	D	R	R	D	D	R	R	D	D	R	R
Izard	D	A	R	D	D	R	R	D	D	D	R
Jackson	D	A	R	D	D	D	D	D	D	D	D
Jefferson	D	A	R	D	D	D	D	D	D	D	D
Johnson	D	D	R	D	D	R	R	D	D	R	R
Lafayette	D	A	R	D	D	R	D	D	D	D	D
Lawrence	D	A	R	D	D	R	D	D	D	D	D
Lee	D	D	R	D	D	D	D	D	D	D	D
Lincoln	D	A	R	D	D	D	D	D	D	R	D
Little River	D	A	R	D	D	R	D	D	D	D	D
Logan	D	R	R	D	R	R	R	D	D	R	R
Lonoke	D	A	R	D	R	R	R	D	D	R	R
Madison	D	R	R	D	R	R	R	D	D	R	R
Marion	D	R	R	D	R	R	R	D	D	R	R
Miller	D	A	R	D	R	R	R	D	D	R	R
Mississippi	D	A	R	D	D	R	R	D	D	D	D
Monroe	D	A	R	D	D	R	D	D	D	D	D
Montgomery	D	A	R	D	D	R	R	D	D	R	R
Nevada	D	A	R	D	D	R	D	D	D	D	R
Newton	D	R	R	D	R	R	R	D	R	R	R

County	1964	1968	1972	1976	1980	1984	1988	1992	1996	2000	2004
Ouachita	D	A	R	D	D	R	R	D	D	D	R
Perry	D	A	R	D	D	R	R	D	D	R	R
Phillips	D	D	R	D	D	D	D	D	D	D	D
Pike	D	A	R	D	D	R	R	D	D	R	R
Poinsett	D	A	R	D	D	R	D	D	D	D	D
Polk	D	R	R	D	R	R	R	D	R	R	R
Pope	D	R	R	D	R	R	R	R	D	R	R
Prairie	D	A	R	D	D	R	R	D	D	R	R
Pulaski	D	D	R	D	D	R	R	D	D	D	D
Randolph	D	A	R	D	D	R	D	D	D	D	D
St. Francis	D	A	R	D	D	R	D	D	D	D	D
Saline	D	A	R	D	D	R	R	D	D	R	R
Scott	D	A	R	D	D	R	R	D	D	R	R
Searcy	R	R	R	D	R	R	R	R	R	R	R
Sebastian	R	R	R	R	R	R	R	R	R	R	R
Sevier	D	A	R	D	D	R	R	D	D	R	R
Sharp	D	A	R	D	R	R	R	D	D	R	R
Stone	D	R	R	D	D	R	R	D	D	R	R
Union	R	A	R	D	R	R	R	D	D	R	R
Van Buren	D	R	R	D	R	R	R	D	D	R	R
Washington	D	R	R	D	R	R	R	D	D	R	R
White	D	A	R	D	D	R	R	D	D	R	R
Woodruff	D	A	R	D	D	D	D	D	D	D	D
Yell	D	A	R	D	D	R	R	D	D	R	R

California

County	1868	1872	1876	1880	1884	1888	1892	1896	1900	1904	1908	1912
Alameda	R	R	R	R	R	R	R	R	R	R	R	P
Alpine	R	R	R	R	R	R	R	D	R	R	R	P
Amador	D	R	D	D	D	D	D	D	R	R	R	D
Butte	R	R	R	D	R	D	R	D	R	R	R	D
Calaveras	R	R	D	R	R	R	R	R	R	R	R	D
Colusa	D	D	D	D	D	D	D	D	D	D	D	D
Contra Costa	R	R	R	R	R	R	R	R	R	R	R	P
Del Norte	D	R	D	D	R	D	D	R	R	R	R	P
El Dorado	D	R	D	D	D	D	D	D	D	R	D	D
Fresno	D	D	D	D	D	D	D	D	D	R	R	D
Glenn	–	–	–	–	–	–	D	D	D	R	D	D
Humboldt	R	R	R	R	R	R	R	R	R	R	R	P
Imperial	–	–	–	–	–	–	–	–	–	–	R	P
Inyo	R	R	D	R	R	R	R	D	D	R	D	D
Kern	D	D	D	D	D	D	D	D	D	R	R	D
Kings	–	–	–	–	–	–	–	D	R	R	R	D
Lake	D	D	D	D	D	D	D	D	D	R	D	D

County	1868	1872	1876	1880	1884	1888	1892	1896	1900	1904	1908	1912
Lassen	R	R	R	R	D	D	R	R	R	R	R	D
Los Angeles	D	R	D	R	R	R	R	R	R	R	R	P
Madera	–	–	–	–	–	–	–	D	R	R	R	D
Marin	R	R	R	R	R	R	R	R	R	R	R	D
Mariposa	D	D	D	D	D	D	D	D	D	D	D	D
Mendocino	D	D	D	D	D	D	D	R	R	R	R	D
Merced	D	D	D	D	D	D	D	D	D	R	R	D
Modoc	–	–	D	D	D	D	D	D	D	R	R	D
Mono	R	R	R	R	R	R	R	D	R	R	R	D
Monterey	D	R	R	R	R	R	R	D	R	R	R	D
Napa	R	R	R	R	R	R	R	R	R	R	R	D
Nevada	R	R	R	R	R	R	R	D	R	R	R	D
Orange	–	–	–	–	–	–	R	R	R	R	R	P
Placer	R	R	R	R	R	R	R	R	R	R	R	P
Plumas	R	R	R	R	R	R	R	R	R	R	R	P
Riverside	–	–	–	–	–	–	–	R	R	R	R	P
Sacramento	R	R	R	R	R	R	R	R	R	R	R	D
San Benito	–	–	D	D	D	D	D	D	D	R	R	D
San Bernardino	D	R	R	R	R	R	R	R	R	R	R	P
San Diego	D	R	R	R	R	R	R	R	R	R	R	D
San Francisco	D	R	R	D	R	D	D	R	R	R	R	D
San Joaquin	R	R	R	R	R	R	D	R	R	R	R	D
San Luis Obispo	R	R	D	R	R	R	R	D	D	R	R	P
San Mateo	R	R	R	R	R	R	R	R	R	R	R	D
Santa Barbara	R	R	R	R	R	R	R	R	R	R	R	P
Santa Clara	D	R	R	R	R	R	R	R	R	R	R	P
Santa Cruz	R	R	R	R	R	R	R	R	R	R	R	P
Shasta	R	R	D	D	R	R	R	D	D	R	R	D
Sierra	R	R	R	R	R	R	R	R	R	R	R	D
Siskiyou	D	R	D	D	D	D	D	D	R	R	R	D
Solano	R	R	R	R	R	R	R	R	R	R	R	D
Sonoma	D	R	D	D	R	D	D	R	R	R	R	D
Stanislaus	D	D	D	D	D	D	D	D	D	R	R	P
Sutter	R	R	D	R	R	R	R	R	R	R	R	D
Tehama	D	R	D	D	D	D	D	R	R	R	R	P
Trinity	R	R	D	R	R	T	R	R	R	R	R	D
Tulare	D	D	D	D	D	D	D	D	D	R	R	D
Tuolumne	D	R	D	D	R	D	D	D	D	R	R	D
Ventura	–	–	R	R	R	R	R	R	R	R	R	D
Yolo	D	R	D	D	D	D	D	D	D	R	R	D
Yuba	R	R	R	D	R	D	D	R	R	R	R	D

County	1916	1920	1924	1928	1932	1936	1940	1944	1948	1952	1956	1960
Alameda	R	R	R	R	D	D	D	D	D	R	R	D
Alpine	R	R	R	R	D	D	R	R	R	R	R	R
Amador	D	R	P	D	D	D	D	D	D	R	D	D
Butte	R	R	P	R	D	D	D	D	R	R	R	R

County	1916	1920	1924	1928	1932	1936	1940	1944	1948	1952	1956	1960
Calaveras	D	R	P	R	D	D	D	D	D	R	R	R
Colusa	D	R	R	R	D	D	D	D	D	R	R	R
Contra Costa	D	R	R	R	D	D	D	D	D	D	R	D
Del Norte	R	R	R	R	D	D	R	R	R	R	R	D
El Dorado	D	R	P	D	D	D	D	D	D	R	R	D
Fresno	D	R	R	R	D	D	D	D	D	D	D	D
Glenn	D	R	R	R	D	D	D	D	R	R	R	R
Humboldt	R	R	R	R	D	D	D	D	D	R	R	D
Imperial	D	R	R	R	D	D	D	R	R	R	R	R
Inyo	D	R	R	R	D	D	D	R	R	R	R	R
Kern	D	R	R	R	D	D	D	D	D	R	R	R
Kings	D	R	R	R	D	D	D	D	D	D	D	D
Lake	D	R	R	R	D	D	R	R	R	R	R	R
Lassen	D	R	P	R	D	D	D	D	D	D	D	D
Los Angeles	R	R	R	R	D	D	D	D	D	R	R	D
Madera	D	R	R	R	D	D	D	D	D	D	D	D
Marin	R	R	R	R	D	D	D	D	R	R	R	R
Mariposa	D	R	R	R	D	D	D	D	R	R	R	R
Mendocino	R	R	R	R	D	D	D	D	R	R	R	D
Merced	D	R	R	R	D	D	D	D	D	R	D	D
Modoc	D	R	R	R	D	D	D	D	D	R	R	R
Mono	D	R	R	R	D	D	D	R	R	R	R	R
Monterey	D	R	R	R	D	D	D	D	R	R	R	R
Napa	R	R	R	R	D	D	D	D	D	R	R	R
Nevada	D	R	P	R	D	D	D	D	R	R	R	R
Orange	R	R	R	R	D	D	R	R	R	R	R	R
Placer	D	R	P	D	D	D	D	D	D	R	D	D
Plumas	D	R	P	D	D	D	D	D	D	D	D	D
Riverside	R	R	R	R	R	D	R	R	R	R	R	R
Sacramento	D	R	P	R	D	D	D	D	D	D	D	D
San Benito	D	R	R	R	D	D	D	R	R	R	R	R
San Bernardino	R	R	R	R	D	D	D	D	R	R	R	R
San Diego	R	R	R	R	D	D	D	D	R	R	R	R
San Francisco	D	R	R	D	D	D	D	D	D	R	R	D
San Joaquin	D	R	R	R	D	D	D	D	R	R	R	R
San Luis Obispo	D	R	R	R	D	D	D	D	R	R	R	R
San Mateo	R	R	R	R	D	D	D	D	R	R	R	R
Santa Barbara	D	R	R	R	D	D	D	D	R	R	R	R
Santa Clara	R	R	R	R	D	D	D	D	R	R	R	R
Santa Cruz	D	R	R	R	D	D	R	R	R	R	R	R
Shasta	D	R	P	R	D	D	D	D	D	R	D	D
Sierra	D	R	P	R	D	D	D	D	D	R	R	D
Siskiyou	D	R	P	R	D	D	D	D	D	R	R	D
Solano	D	R	R	R	D	D	D	D	D	D	D	D
Sonoma	R	R	R	R	D	D	R	R	R	R	R	R
Stanislaus	D	R	R	R	D	D	D	D	R	R	D	D
Sutter	D	R	R	R	D	D	D	R	R	R	R	R
Tehama	D	R	R	R	D	D	D	D	R	R	R	R

County	1916	1920	1924	1928	1932	1936	1940	1944	1948	1952	1956	1960
Trinity	D	R	P	R	D	D	D	D	D	R	R	D
Tulare	D	R	R	R	D	D	D	D	D	R	R	R
Tuolumne	D	R	P	R	D	D	D	D	R	R	R	D
Ventura	R	R	R	R	D	D	D	D	D	R	R	D
Yolo	D	R	R	R	D	D	D	D	D	R	D	D
Yuba	D	R	R	R	D	D	D	D	D	R	R	R

County	1964	1968	1972	1976	1980	1984	1988	1992	1996	2000	2004
Alameda	D	D	D	D	D	D	D	D	D	D	D
Alpine	R	R	R	R	R	R	R	R	R	R	D
Amador	D	D	R	D	R	R	R	R	R	R	R
Butte	D	R	R	R	R	R	R	D	R	R	R
Calaveras	D	R	R	R	R	R	R	R	R	R	R
Colusa	D	R	R	R	R	R	R	R	R	R	R
Contra Costa	D	D	R	R	R	R	D	D	D	R	D
Del Norte	D	R	R	D	R	R	R	D	R	R	R
El Dorado	D	R	R	D	R	R	R	R	R	R	R
Fresno	D	D	R	D	R	R	R	D	R	R	R
Glenn	D	R	R	R	R	R	R	R	R	R	R
Humboldt	D	R	R	D	R	R	D	D	D	D	D
Imperial	D	R	R	R	R	R	R	D	D	D	D
Inyo	D	R	R	R	R	R	R	R	R	R	R
Kern	D	R	R	R	R	R	R	R	R	R	R
Kings	D	D	R	R	R	R	R	R	R	R	R
Lake	D	R	R	D	R	R	D	D	D	D	D
Lassen	D	D	R	D	R	R	R	R	R	R	R
Los Angeles	D	R	R	D	R	R	D	D	D	D	D
Madera	D	D	R	D	R	R	R	R	R	R	R
Marin	D	R	R	R	R	D	D	D	D	D	D
Mariposa	D	R	R	D	R	R	R	D	R	R	R
Mendocino	D	R	R	D	R	R	D	D	D	D	D
Merced	D	D	R	D	R	R	R	D	D	R	R
Modoc	D	R	R	R	R	R	R	R	R	R	R
Mono	R	R	R	R	R	R	R	R	R	R	D
Monterey	D	R	R	R	R	R	R	D	D	D	D
Napa	D	D	R	R	R	R	R	D	D	D	D
Nevada	D	R	R	R	R	R	R	R	R	R	R
Orange	R	R	R	R	R	R	R	R	R	R	R
Placer	D	D	R	D	R	R	R	R	R	R	R
Plumas	D	D	D	D	R	R	R	D	R	R	R
Riverside	D	R	R	R	R	R	R	D	R	R	R
Sacramento	D	D	R	D	R	R	R	D	D	D	D
San Benito	D	R	R	R	R	R	R	D	D	D	D
San Bernardino	D	R	R	R	R	R	R	D	D	R	R
San Diego	R	R	R	R	R	R	R	D	R	R	R
San Francisco	D	D	D	D	D	D	D	D	D	D	D
San Joaquin	D	R	R	R	R	R	R	D	D	R	R

County	1964	1968	1972	1976	1980	1984	1988	1992	1996	2000	2004
San Luis Obispo	D	R	R	R	R	R	R	D	R	R	R
San Mateo	D	D	R	R	R	R	D	D	D	D	D
Santa Barbara	D	R	R	R	R	R	R	D	D	D	D
Santa Clara	D	D	R	R	R	R	D	D	D	D	D
Santa Cruz	D	R	R	D	R	D	D	D	D	D	D
Shasta	D	D	D	D	R	R	R	R	R	R	R
Sierra	D	D	D	D	R	R	R	R	R	R	R
Siskiyou	D	R	R	R	R	R	R	D	R	R	R
Solano	D	D	R	D	R	R	D	D	D	D	D
Sonoma	D	R	R	R	R	R	D	D	D	D	D
Stanislaus	D	D	R	D	R	R	R	D	D	R	R
Sutter	R	R	R	R	R	R	R	R	R	R	R
Tehama	D	R	R	D	R	R	R	D	R	R	R
Trinity	D	D	R	D	R	R	R	PE	R	R	R
Tulare	D	R	R	R	R	R	R	R	R	R	R
Tuolumne	D	R	R	D	R	R	R	D	R	R	R
Ventura	D	R	R	R	R	R	R	D	D	R	R
Yolo	D	D	D	D	D	D	D	D	D	D	D
Yuba	D	R	R	D	R	R	R	R	R	R	R

Colorado

County	1880	1884	1888	1892	1896	1900	1904	1908	1912	1916	1920	1924
Adams	–	–	–	–	–	–	R	R	D	D	R	R
Alamosa	–	–	–	–	–	–	–	–	–	D	R	R
Arapahoe	R	R	R	PO	D	D	R	R	D	D	R	R
Archuleta	–	–	R	PO	D	R	R	D	D	D	R	R
Baca	–	–	–	PO	D	R	R	R	D	D	R	R
Bent	D	D	R	PO	D	R	R	R	D	D	R	R
Boulder	R	R	R	PO	D	D	R	D	D	D	R	R
Chaffee	D	R	R	PO	D	D	R	D	D	D	R	R
Cheyenne	–	–	–	R	D	R	R	R	D	D	R	R
Clear Creek	R	R	R	PO	D	D	R	D	D	D	R	R
Conejos	R	R	R	R	D	R	R	R	D	D	R	R
Costilla	D	R	R	R	D	R	R	R	R	D	R	R
Crowley	–	–	–	–	–	–	–	–	D	D	R	R
Custer	R	R	R	PO	D	D	D	D	D	D	R	R
Delta	–	R	R	PO	D	D	R	D	D	D	R	R
Denver	–	–	–	–	–	–	R	D	D	D	R	R
Dolores	–	R	R	PO	D	D	D	D	D	D	R	P
Douglas	R	R	R	R	D	D	R	R	D	D	R	R
Eagle	–	R	R	PO	D	D	R	D	D	D	R	R
Elbert	D	R	R	PO	D	D	R	R	D	D	R	R
El Paso	R	R	R	PO	D	R	R	R	D	D	R	R

County	1880	1884	1888	1892	1896	1900	1904	1908	1912	1916	1920	1924
Fremont	R	R	NR	PO	D	D	R	D	D	D	R	R
Garfield	–	R	R	PO	D	D	R	D	D	D	R	R
Gilpin	R	R	R	PO	D	D	R	D	D	D	R	R
Grand	R	R	R	PO	D	D	R	R	D	D	R	R
Gunnison	D	R	R	PO	D	D	R	D	D	D	R	R
Hinsdale	R	R	R	PO	D	D	R	D	D	D	R	R
Huerfano	D	D	R	R	D	R	R	R	R	D	R	R
Jackson	–	–	–	–	–	–	–	–	D	D	R	R
Jefferson	R	R	R	PO	D	D	R	R	D	D	R	R
Kiowa	–	–	–	R	D	R	R	R	D	D	R	R
Kit Carson	–	–	–	R	R	R	R	R	D	D	R	R
Lake	D	R	R	PO	D	D	R	D	D	D	R	R
La Plata	D	R	R	PO	D	D	R	D	D	D	R	D
Larimer	R	R	R	PO	D	D	R	R	D	D	R	R
Las Animas	D	D	D	PO	D	D	R	R	R	D	R	R
Lincoln	–	–	–	R	D	R	R	R	D	D	R	R
Logan	–	–	R	R	D	R	R	R	D	D	R	R
Mesa	–	R	R	PO	D	D	R	R	D	D	R	R
Mineral	–	–	–	–	D	D	D	D	D	D	R	R
Moffat	–	–	–	–	–	–	–	–	D	D	R	R
Montezuma	–	–	–	PO	D	D	D	D	D	D	R	D
Montrose	–	R	R	PO	D	D	R	D	D	D	R	R
Morgan	–	–	–	PO	D	R	R	R	D	D	R	R
Otero	–	–	–	PO	D	D	R	D	D	D	R	R
Ouray	R	R	R	PO	D	D	D	D	D	D	R	R
Park	R	R	R	PO	D	D	R	D	D	D	R	R
Phillips	–	–	–	R	D	R	R	R	D	D	R	R
Pitkin	–	R	R	PO	D	D	D	D	D	D	R	R
Prowers	–	–	–	PO	D	R	R	R	D	D	R	R
Pueblo	D	R	R	PO	D	R	R	D	D	D	R	R
Rio Blanco	–	–	–	PO	D	D	R	D	D	D	R	R
Rio Grande	R	R	R	PO	D	D	R	D	D	D	R	R
Routt	R	R	R	PO	D	D	R	D	D	D	R	R
Saguache	R	R	R	PO	D	D	R	D	D	D	R	R
San Juan	R	R	R	PO	D	D	D	D	D	D	R	R
San Miguel	–	R	R	PO	D	D	R	D	D	D	R	R
Sedgwick	–	–	–	PO	D	R	R	R	P	R	R	R
Summit	D	R	R	PO	D	D	D	D	D	D	R	R
Teller	–	–	–	–	–	D	R	D	D	D	R	R
Washington	–	–	R	R	R	R	R	R	D	D	R	R
Weld	R	R	R	PO	D	D	R	R	D	D	R	R
Yuma	–	–	–	PO	D	D	R	D	P	D	R	R

County	1928	1932	1936	1940	1944	1948	1952	1956	1960	1964	1968	1972
Adams	R	D	D	R	R	D	R	R	D	D	D	R
Alamosa	R	D	D	D	R	D	R	R	R	D	R	R
Arapahoe	R	D	D	R	R	D	R	R	R	D	R	R
Archuleta	R	D	D	R	R	D	R	R	D	D	R	R

County	1928	1932	1936	1940	1944	1948	1952	1956	1960	1964	1968	1972
Baca	R	D	D	R	R	D	R	R	R	D	R	R
Bent	R	D	D	R	R	D	R	R	R	D	R	R
Boulder	R	D	D	R	R	R	R	R	R	D	R	R
Chaffee	R	D	D	D	D	D	R	R	R	D	R	R
Cheyenne	R	D	D	R	R	R	R	R	R	D	R	R
Clear Creek	R	D	D	D	R	R	R	R	R	D	R	R
Conejos	D	D	D	D	D	D	R	R	D	D	D	R
Costilla	D	D	D	D	D	D	D	D	D	D	D	D
Crowley	R	D	D	R	R	R	R	R	R	D	R	R
Custer	R	D	D	R	R	R	R	R	R	D	R	R
Delta	R	D	D	R	R	D	R	R	R	D	R	R
Denver	R	D	D	D	D	D	R	R	D	D	D	R
Dolores	R	D	D	R	R	D	R	R	R	D	R	R
Douglas	R	D	D	R	R	R	R	R	R	D	R	R
Eagle	R	D	D	D	D	D	R	R	R	D	R	R
Elbert	R	D	R	R	R	R	R	R	R	R	R	R
El Paso	R	R	D	R	R	R	R	R	R	D	R	R
Fremont	R	D	D	R	R	R	R	R	R	D	R	R
Garfield	R	D	D	R	R	R	R	R	R	D	R	R
Gilpin	R	D	D	D	R	R	R	R	R	D	R	R
Grand	R	D	D	R	R	R	R	R	R	D	R	R
Gunnison	R	D	D	D	D	D	R	R	R	D	R	R
Hinsdale	R	D	D	R	R	R	R	R	R	R	R	R
Huerfano	D	D	D	D	D	D	D	D	D	D	D	R
Jackson	R	D	D	R	R	R	R	R	R	D	R	R
Jefferson	R	D	D	R	R	R	R	R	R	D	R	R
Kiowa	R	D	D	R	R	R	R	R	R	D	R	R
Kit Carson	R	D	R	R	R	R	R	R	R	D	R	R
Lake	R	D	D	D	D	D	D	R	D	D	D	R
La Plata	R	D	D	R	R	R	R	R	R	D	R	R
Larimer	R	R	D	R	R	R	R	R	R	D	D	R
Las Animas	D	D	D	D	D	D	D	R	D	D	D	R
Lincoln	R	D	D	R	R	R	R	R	R	D	R	R
Logan	R	D	D	R	R	R	R	R	R	D	R	R
Mesa	R	D	D	D	D	D	R	R	R	D	R	R
Mineral	D	D	D	D	R	D	R	R	D	D	D	R
Moffat	R	D	D	R	R	R	R	R	R	D	R	R
Montezuma	R	D	D	R	R	D	R	R	R	D	R	R
Montrose	R	D	D	R	R	D	R	R	R	D	R	R
Morgan	R	R	D	R	R	R	R	R	R	D	R	R
Otero	R	D	D	R	R	D	R	R	R	D	R	R
Ouray	R	D	D	D	R	R	R	R	R	D	R	R
Park	R	D	D	R	R	R	R	R	R	D	R	R
Phillips	R	D	D	R	R	R	R	R	R	D	R	R
Pitkin	R	D	D	D	R	D	R	R	R	D	R	D
Prowers	R	D	D	R	R	R	R	R	R	D	R	R
Pueblo	R	D	D	D	D	D	D	R	D	D	D	R
Rio Blanco	R	D	R	R	R	R	R	R	R	D	R	R
Rio Grande	R	D	D	R	R	R	R	R	R	D	R	R

County	1928	1932	1936	1940	1944	1948	1952	1956	1960	1964	1968	1972
Routt	R	D	D	D	D	D	R	R	R	D	R	R
Saguache	R	D	D	R	R	D	R	R	D	D	R	R
San Juan	D	D	D	R	R	D	R	R	D	D	R	R
San Miguel	R	D	D	D	D	D	R	R	D	D	R	R
Sedgwick	R	D	D	R	R	R	R	R	R	D	R	R
Summit	R	D	D	D	R	D	R	R	R	D	R	R
Teller	R	D	D	D	R	D	R	R	R	D	R	R
Washington	R	D	D	R	R	R	R	R	R	R	R	R
Weld	R	D	D	R	R	R	R	R	R	D	R	R
Yuma	R	D	D	R	R	R	R	R	R	D	R	R

County	1976	1980	1984	1988	1992	1996	2000	2004
Adams	D	R	R	D	D	D	D	D
Alamosa	R	R	R	R	D	D	R	R
Arapahoe	R	R	R	R	R	R	R	R
Archuleta	R	R	R	R	R	R	R	R
Baca	R	R	R	R	R	R	R	R
Bent	D	R	R	D	D	D	R	R
Boulder	R	R	R	D	D	D	D	D
Broomfield*	–	–	–	–	–	–	–	R
Chaffee	R	R	R	R	R	R	R	R
Cheyenne	D	R	R	R	R	R	R	R
Clear Creek	R	R	R	R	D	D	R	D
Conejos	D	R	R	D	D	D	R	D
Costilla	D	D	D	D	D	D	D	D
Crowley	R	R	R	R	R	R	R	R
Custer	R	R	R	R	R	R	R	R
Delta	R	R	R	R	R	R	R	R
Denver	D	R	D	D	D	D	D	D
Dolores	D	R	R	R	R	R	R	R
Douglas	R	R	R	R	R	R	R	R
Eagle	R	R	R	R	D	D	R	D
Elbert	R	R	R	R	R	R	R	R
El Paso	R	R	R	R	R	R	R	R
Fremont	R	R	R	R	R	R	R	R
Garfield	R	R	R	R	D	R	R	R
Gilpin	D	R	R	D	D	D	D	D
Grand	R	R	R	R	R	R	R	R
Gunnison	R	R	R	R	D	D	R	D
Hinsdale	R	R	R	R	R	R	R	R
Huerfano	D	D	D	D	D	D	D	R
Jackson	R	R	R	R	R	R	R	R
Jefferson	R	R	R	R	R	R	R	R
Kiowa	R	R	R	R	R	R	R	R
Kit Carson	R	R	R	R	R	R	R	R
Lake	R	R	R	D	D	D	D	D
La Plata	R	R	R	R	D	R	R	D
Larimer	R	R	R	R	D	R	R	R

County	1976	1980	1984	1988	1992	1996	2000	2004
Las Animas	D	D	D	D	D	D	D	D
Lincoln	R	R	R	R	R	R	R	R
Logan	R	R	R	R	R	R	R	R
Mesa	R	R	R	R	R	R	R	R
Mineral	R	R	R	R	D	D	R	R
Moffat	R	R	R	R	PE	R	R	R
Montezuma	R	R	R	R	R	R	R	R
Montrose	R	R	R	R	R	R	R	R
Morgan	R	R	R	R	R	R	R	R
Otero	R	R	R	R	D	D	R	R
Ouray	R	R	R	R	R	R	R	R
Park	R	R	R	R	R	R	R	R
Phillips	D	R	R	R	R	R	R	R
Pitkin	R	R	R	D	D	D	D	D
Prowers	D	R	R	R	R	R	R	R
Pueblo	D	D	D	D	D	D	D	D
Rio Blanco	R	R	R	R	R	R	R	R
Rio Grande	R	R	R	R	R	R	R	R
Routt	R	R	R	R	D	D	R	D
Saguache	R	R	R	D	D	D	D	D
San Juan	R	R	R	R	PE	R	R	D
San Miguel	D	R	R	D	D	D	D	D
Sedgwick	R	R	R	R	R	R	R	R
Summit	R	R	R	R	D	D	D	D
Teller	R	R	R	R	R	R	R	R
Washington	R	R	R	R	R	R	R	R
Weld	R	R	R	R	R	R	R	R
Yuma	R	R	R	R	R	R	R	R

*Note: Colorado created a new county, Broomfield, in 2001.

Connecticut

County	1868	1872	1876	1880	1884	1888	1892	1896	1900	1904	1908	1912
Fairfield	R	D	D	D	D	D	D	R	R	R	R	D
Hartford	R	R	D	R	D	R	R	R	R	R	R	R
Litchfield	R	R	D	R	D	R	R	R	R	R	R	R
Middlesex	R	R	R	R	R	R	R	R	R	R	R	D
New Haven	D	R	D	D	D	D	D	R	R	R	R	D
New London	R	R	R	R	R	R	D	R	R	R	R	D
Tolland	R	R	R	R	R	R	R	R	R	R	R	R
Windham	R	R	R	R	R	R	R	R	R	R	R	R

County	1916	1920	1924	1928	1932	1936	1940	1944	1948	1952	1956	1960
Fairfield	R	R	R	R	R	D	D	R	R	R	R	R
Hartford	D	R	R	R	R	D	D	D	D	R	R	D
Litchfield	R	R	R	R	R	R	R	R	R	R	R	R
Middlesex	R	R	R	R	R	D	R	R	R	R	R	D
New Haven	D	R	R	D	D	D	D	D	D	R	R	D
New London	D	R	R	R	R	D	D	D	D	R	R	D
Tolland	R	R	R	R	R	D	D	R	R	R	R	R
Windham	R	R	R	R	D	D	D	D	D	R	R	D

County	1964	1968	1972	1976	1980	1984	1988	1992	1996	2000	2004
Fairfield	D	R	R	R	R	R	R	R	D	D	D
Hartford	D	D	R	D	D	R	D	D	D	D	D
Litchfield	D	R	R	R	R	R	R	R	D	D	R
Middlesex	D	D	R	R	R	R	R	D	D	D	D
New Haven	D	D	R	R	R	R	R	D	D	D	D
New London	D	D	R	R	R	R	R	D	D	D	D
Tolland	D	D	R	R	R	R	R	D	D	D	D
Windham	D	D	R	D	R	R	R	D	D	D	D

——————— Delaware ———————

County	1868	1872	1876	1880	1884	1888	1892	1896	1900	1904	1908	1912
Kent	D	D	D	D	D	D	D	NR	R	R	R	D
New Castle	D	R	D	R	D	D	D	R	R	R	R	D
Sussex	D	R	D	D	D	R	D	R	R	R	R	D

County	1916	1920	1924	1928	1932	1936	1940	1944	1948	1952	1956	1960
Kent	D	D	D	R	D	D	D	D	R	R	R	D
New Castle	R	R	R	R	R	D	D	D	D	R	R	D
Sussex	R	R	R	R	D	D	D	R	R	R	R	R

County	1964	1968	1972	1976	1980	1984	1988	1992	1996	2000	2004
Kent	D	R	R	D	R	R	R	R	D	R	R
New Castle	D	R	R	D	R	R	R	D	D	D	D
Sussex	D	R	R	D	R	R	R	R	D	R	R

Florida

County	1872	1876	1880	1884	1888	1892	1896	1900	1904	1908	1912	1916
Alachua	R	R	R	R	D	D	D	D	D	D	D	D
Baker	D	R	D	D	D	D	D	D	D	D	D	D
Bay	–	–	–	–	–	–	–	–	–	–	–	D
Bradford	D	D	D	D	D	D	D	D	D	D	D	D
Brevard	NR	D	D	D	D	D	D	D	D	D	D	D
Broward	–	–	–	–	–	–	–	–	–	–	–	D
Calhoun	D	D	D	D	D	D	D	D	D	R	D	D
Charlotte	–	–	–	–	–	–	–	–	–	–	–	–
Citrus	–	–	–	–	D	D	D	D	D	D	D	D
Clay	D	NR	D	D	D	D	D	D	D	D	D	D
Collier	–	–	–	–	–	–	–	–	–	–	–	–
Columbia	R	D	D	D	D	D	D	D	D	D	D	D
Dade	R	R	NR	D	D	D	D	D	D	D	D	D
Desoto	–	–	–	–	D	D	D	D	D	D	D	D
Dixie	–	–	–	–	–	–	–	–	–	–	–	–
Duval	R	R	R	R	R	D	D	D	D	D	D	D
Escambia	R	R	D	D	D	D	D	D	D	D	D	D
Flagler	–	–	–	–	–	–	–	–	–	–	–	–
Franklin	D	D	D	D	D	D	D	D	D	D	D	D
Gadsden	R	R	D	D	D	D	D	D	D	D	D	D
Gilchrist	–	–	–	–	–	–	–	–	–	–	–	–
Glades	–	–	–	–	–	–	–	–	–	–	–	–
Gulf	–	–	–	–	–	–	–	–	–	–	–	–
Hamilton	D	D	D	D	D	D	D	D	D	D	D	D
Hardee	–	–	–	–	–	–	–	–	–	–	–	–
Hendry	–	–	–	–	–	–	–	–	–	–	–	–
Hernando	D	D	D	D	D	D	D	D	D	D	D	D
Highlands	–	–	–	–	–	–	–	–	–	–	–	–
Hillsborough	D	D	D	D	D	D	D	D	D	D	D	D
Holmes	D	D	D	D	D	D	D	D	D	D	D	D
Indian River	–	–	–	–	–	–	–	–	–	–	–	–
Jackson	R	D	D	D	D	D	D	D	D	D	D	D
Jefferson	R	R	R	R	R	D	D	D	D	D	D	D
Lafayette	D	D	D	D	D	D	D	D	D	D	D	D
Lake	–	–	–	–	D	D	D	D	D	D	D	D
Lee	–	–	–	–	D	D	D	D	D	D	D	D
Leon	R	R	R	R	D	D	D	D	D	D	D	D
Levy	D	D	D	D	D	D	D	D	D	D	D	D
Liberty	D	D	D	D	D	D	D	D	D	D	D	D
Madison	R	R	D	R	D	D	D	D	D	D	D	D
Manatee	D	D	D	D	D	D	D	D	D	D	D	D
Marion	R	R	R	R	D	D	D	D	D	D	D	D
Martin	–	–	–	–	–	–	–	–	–	–	–	–
Monroe	D	D	D	R	R	D	D	D	D	D	D	D
Nassau	R	R	R	R	D	D	D	D	D	D	D	D

County	1872	1876	1880	1884	1888	1892	1896	1900	1904	1908	1912	1916
Okaloosa	–	–	–	–	–	–	–	–	–	–	–	D
Okeechobee	–	–	–	–	–	–	–	–	–	–	–	–
Orange	D	D	D	D	D	D	D	D	D	D	D	D
Osceola	–	–	–	–	D	D	D	D	D	D	D	D
Palm Beach	–	–	–	–	–	–	–	–	–	–	D	D
Pasco	–	–	–	–	D	D	D	D	D	D	D	D
Pinellas	–	–	–	–	–	–	–	–	–	–	D	D
Polk	D	D	D	D	D	D	D	D	D	D	D	D
Putnam	D	D	R	R	R	D	D	D	D	D	D	D
St. Johns	D	D	D	D	D	D	D	D	D	D	D	D
St. Lucie	–	–	–	–	–	–	–	–	–	D	D	D
Santa Rosa	D	D	D	D	D	D	D	D	D	D	D	D
Sarasota	–	–	–	–	–	–	–	–	–	–	–	–
Seminole	–	–	–	–	–	–	–	–	–	–	–	D
Sumter	D	D	D	D	D	D	D	D	D	D	D	D
Suwannee	D	D	D	D	D	D	D	D	D	D	D	D
Taylor	D	D	D	D	D	D	D	D	D	D	D	D
Union	–	–	–	–	–	–	–	–	–	–	–	–
Volusia	D	D	D	D	R	D	D	D	D	D	D	D
Wakulla	D	D	D	D	D	D	D	D	D	D	D	D
Walton	D	D	D	D	D	D	D	D	D	D	D	D
Washington	D	D	D	D	D	D	D	D	D	D	D	D

County	1920	1924	1928	1932	1936	1940	1944	1948	1952	1956	1960	1964
Alachua	D	D	D	D	D	D	D	SR	R	R	R	D
Baker	D	D	R	D	D	D	D	D	D	D	D	D
Bay	D	D	D	D	D	D	D	D	D	D	D	R
Bradford	D	D	D	D	D	D	D	D	D	D	D	D
Brevard	D	D	R	D	D	D	D	D	R	R	R	D
Broward	R	D	R	D	D	D	D	R	R	R	R	R
Calhoun	D	D	D	D	D	D	D	D	D	D	D	R
Charlotte	D	D	R	D	D	D	D	R	R	R	R	D
Citrus	D	D	D	D	D	D	D	D	D	R	R	D
Clay	D	D	R	D	D	D	D	D	D	R	D	R
Collier	D	D	D	D	D	D	D	D	R	R	R	R
Columbia	D	D	D	D	D	D	D	D	D	D	D	R
Dade	D	D	R	D	D	D	D	D	R	R	D	D
Desoto	D	D	R	D	D	D	D	D	D	D	R	R
Dixie	D	D	R	D	D	D	D	D	D	D	D	D
Duval	D	D	R	D	D	D	D	D	D	R	D	R
Escambia	D	D	R	D	D	D	D	D	D	D	D	R
Flagler	D	D	R	D	D	D	D	SR	R	D	D	D
Franklin	D	D	D	D	D	D	D	D	D	D	D	R
Gadsden	D	D	D	D	D	D	D	D	D	D	D	R
Gilchrist	D	D	D	D	D	D	D	D	D	D	D	D
Glades	D	D	R	D	D	D	D	D	D	D	D	R
Gulf	D	D	D	D	D	D	D	D	D	D	D	R
Hamilton	D	D	D	D	D	D	D	D	D	D	D	D

County	1920	1924	1928	1932	1936	1940	1944	1948	1952	1956	1960	1964
Hardee	D	D	R	D	D	D	D	D	D	D	R	R
Hendry	D	D	R	D	D	D	D	D	D	R	D	R
Hernando	D	D	D	D	D	D	D	D	R	D	D	R
Highlands	D	D	R	D	D	D	D	D	R	R	R	R
Hillsborough	D	D	R	D	D	D	D	D	R	R	D	D
Holmes	D	D	R	D	D	D	D	D	D	D	D	R
Indian River	D	D	R	D	D	D	D	R	R	R	R	R
Jackson	D	D	D	D	D	D	D	D	D	D	D	R
Jefferson	D	D	D	D	D	D	D	D	D	D	D	R
Lafayette	D	D	D	D	D	D	D	D	D	D	D	R
Lake	D	D	R	D	D	D	D	R	R	R	R	R
Lee	D	D	R	D	D	D	D	R	R	R	R	R
Leon	D	D	D	D	D	D	D	D	D	D	D	R
Levy	D	D	D	D	D	D	D	D	D	D	D	D
Liberty	D	D	D	D	D	D	D	D	D	D	D	R
Madison	D	D	D	D	D	D	D	D	D	D	D	R
Manatee	D	D	R	D	D	D	D	R	R	R	R	R
Marion	D	D	R	D	D	D	D	D	R	R	D	R
Martin	D	D	R	D	D	D	D	R	R	R	R	R
Monroe	D	D	D	D	D	D	D	D	D	D	D	D
Nassau	D	D	R	D	D	D	D	D	D	D	D	R
Okaloosa	D	D	R	D	D	D	D	D	D	D	D	R
Okeechobee	D	D	R	D	D	D	D	D	D	D	D	R
Orange	D	D	R	D	D	D	D	R	R	R	R	R
Osceola	R	D	R	D	D	D	D	D	R	R	R	R
Palm Beach	R	R	R	D	D	D	D	R	R	R	R	R
Pasco	D	D	R	D	D	D	D	D	R	R	R	D
Pinellas	D	R	R	D	D	D	D	R	R	R	R	D
Polk	D	D	R	D	D	D	D	D	R	R	R	R
Putnam	D	D	R	D	D	D	D	D	R	R	D	R
St. Johns	D	D	D	D	D	D	D	SR	R	R	D	R
St. Lucie	D	D	R	D	D	D	D	D	R	R	R	D
Santa Rosa	D	D	R	D	D	D	D	D	D	D	D	R
Sarasota	D	D	R	D	D	D	D	R	R	R	R	R
Seminole	D	D	R	D	D	D	D	D	D	D	D	D
Sumter	D	D	R	D	D	D	D	D	D	D	D	R
Suwannee	D	D	D	D	D	D	D	D	D	D	D	R
Taylor	D	D	D	D	D	D	D	D	D	D	D	R
Union	D	D	D	D	D	D	D	D	D	D	D	D
Volusia	D	D	R	D	D	D	D	D	R	R	R	D
Wakulla	D	D	D	D	D	D	D	D	D	D	D	R
Walton	D	D	R	D	D	D	D	D	D	D	D	R
Washington	D	D	R	D	D	D	D	D	D	D	D	R

County	1968	1972	1976	1980	1984	1988	1992	1996	2000	2004
Alachua	D	R	D	D	R	R	D	D	D	D
Baker	A	R	D	D	R	R	R	R	R	R
Bay	A	R	D	R	R	R	R	R	R	R

County	1968	1972	1976	1980	1984	1988	1992	1996	2000	2004
Bradford	A	R	D	D	R	R	R	R	R	R
Brevard	R	R	D	R	R	R	R	R	R	R
Broward	R	R	D	R	R	R	D	D	D	D
Calhoun	A	R	D	D	R	R	R	D	R	R
Charlotte	R	R	R	R	R	R	R	R	R	R
Citrus	R	R	D	R	R	R	R	D	R	R
Clay	A	R	R	R	R	R	R	R	R	R
Collier	R	R	R	R	R	R	R	R	R	R
Columbia	A	R	D	D	R	R	R	R	R	R
Dade*	D	R	D	R	R	R	D	D	D	D
Desoto	A	R	D	R	R	R	R	R	R	R
Dixie	A	R	D	D	R	R	D	D	R	R
Duval	A	R	D	R	R	R	R	R	R	R
Escambia	A	R	R	R	R	R	R	R	R	R
Flagler	A	R	D	R	R	R	D	D	D	R
Franklin	A	R	D	D	R	R	R	D	R	R
Gadsden	A	R	D	D	D	D	D	D	D	D
Gilchrist	A	R	D	D	R	R	D	D	R	R
Glades	A	R	D	D	R	R	D	D	R	R
Gulf	A	R	D	D	R	R	R	D	R	R
Hamilton	A	R	D	D	R	R	D	D	R	R
Hardee	A	R	D	R	R	R	R	D	R	R
Hendry	A	R	D	R	R	R	R	R	R	R
Hernando	A	R	D	R	R	R	D	D	D	R
Highlands	R	R	R	R	R	R	R	R	R	R
Hillsborough	R	R	D	R	R	R	R	D	R	R
Holmes	A	R	D	R	R	R	R	R	R	R
Indian River	R	R	R	R	R	R	R	R	R	R
Jackson	A	R	D	D	R	R	R	R	R	R
Jefferson	A	R	D	D	R	R	D	D	D	D
Lafayette	A	R	D	D	R	R	R	R	R	R
Lake	R	R	R	R	R	R	R	R	R	R
Lee	R	R	R	R	R	R	R	R	R	R
Leon	A	R	D	D	R	R	D	D	D	D
Levy	A	R	D	D	R	R	D	D	R	R
Liberty	A	R	D	D	R	R	R	R	R	R
Madison	A	R	D	D	R	R	D	D	R	R
Manatee	R	R	R	R	R	R	R	R	R	R
Marion	A	R	D	R	R	R	R	R	R	R
Martin	R	R	R	R	R	R	R	R	R	R
Monroe	D	R	D	R	R	R	D	D	D	D
Nassau	A	R	D	R	R	R	R	R	R	R
Okaloosa	A	R	R	R	R	R	R	R	R	R
Okeechobee	A	R	D	D	R	R	D	D	R	R
Orange	R	R	R	R	R	R	R	R	D	D
Osceola	R	R	R	R	R	R	R	D	D	R
Palm Beach	R	R	R	R	R	R	D	D	D	D
Pasco	R	R	D	R	R	R	D	D	D	R
Pinellas	R	R	R	R	R	R	D	D	D	R

County	1968	1972	1976	1980	1984	1988	1992	1996	2000	2004
Polk	A	R	D	R	R	R	R	R	R	R
Putnam	A	R	D	D	R	R	D	D	R	R
St. Johns	A	R	D	R	R	R	R	R	R	R
St. Lucie	R	R	D	R	R	R	R	D	D	D
Santa Rosa	A	R	R	R	R	R	R	R	R	R
Sarasota	R	R	R	R	R	R	R	R	R	R
Seminole	R	R	R	R	R	R	R	R	R	R
Sumter	A	R	D	D	R	R	D	D	R	R
Suwannee	A	R	D	D	R	R	R	R	R	R
Taylor	A	R	D	D	R	R	R	D	R	R
Union	A	R	D	D	R	R	R	R	R	R
Volusia	R	R	D	R	R	R	D	D	D	D
Wakulla	A	R	D	D	R	R	R	D	R	R
Walton	A	R	D	R	R	R	R	R	R	R
Washington	A	R	D	R	R	R	R	R	R	R

*Dade County is now called Miami-Dade.

Georgia

County	1868	1872	1876	1880	1884	1888	1892	1896	1900	1904	1908	1912
Appling	D	D	D	D	D	D	D	D	D	D	R	D
Atkinson	–	–	–	–	–	–	–	–	–	–	–	–
Bacon	–	–	–	–	–	–	–	–	–	–	–	–
Baker	D	D	D	D	D	D	D	D	D	D	D	D
Baldwin	R	D	D	D	D	D	D	D	D	D	D	D
Banks	D	D	D	D	D	D	D	D	D	D	R	D
Barrow	–	–	–	–	–	–	–	–	–	–	–	–
Bartow	D	D	D	D	D	D	D	D	D	D	R	D
Ben Hill	–	–	–	–	–	–	–	–	–	–	R	D
Berrien	D	D	D	D	D	D	D	D	D	D	D	D
Bibb	R	D	D	D	D	D	D	D	D	D	D	D
Bleckley	–	–	–	–	–	–	–	–	–	–	–	–
Brantley	–	–	–	–	–	–	–	–	–	–	–	–
Brooks	D	D	D	D	D	D	D	D	D	D	D	D
Bryan	R	R	R	D	D	D	D	D	D	D	D	D
Bulloch	D	D	D	D	D	D	D	D	D	D	D	D
Burke	R	R	D	R	BR	D	D	D	D	D	D	D
Butts	D	R	D	D	D	D	D	D	D	D	D	D
Calhoun	D	R	D	R	D	D	D	D	D	D	D	D
Camden	R	R	R	R	R	R	R	R	D	D	R	D
Candler	–	–	–	–	–	–	–	–	–	–	–	–
Carroll	D	D	D	D	D	D	D	D	D	D	D	D
Catoosa	D	D	D	D	D	D	D	D	D	D	D	D
Charlton	D	R	D	D	D	D	D	–	D	D	D	D

County	1868	1872	1876	1880	1884	1888	1892	1896	1900	1904	1908	1912
Chatham	D	D	D	D	D	D	D	D	D	D	D	D
Chattahoochee	D	D	D	D	D	D	R	R	R	D	R	D
Chattooga	D	D	D	D	D	D	D	D	D	D	R	D
Cherokee	D	D	D	D	D	D	D	D	R	D	R	R
Clarke	D	R	D	D	D	D	D	D	D	D	D	D
Clay	D	R	D	D	D	D	D	R	D	D	D	D
Clayton	D	R	D	D	D	D	D	D	D	D	D	D
Clinch	D	D	D	D	D	D	D	D	D	D	D	D
Cobb	D	D	D	D	D	D	D	D	D	D	D	D
Coffee	D	D	D	D	D	D	D	R	R	D	D	D
Colquitt	D	T	D	D	D	D	D	D	D	D	D	D
Columbia	D	D	D	D	D	D	PO	R	D	D	PO	D
Cook	–	–	–	–	–	–	–	–	–	–	–	–
Coweta	D	R	D	D	D	D	D	D	D	D	D	D
Crawford	D	D	D	D	D	D	D	D	D	D	D	D
Crisp	–	–	–	–	–	–	–	–	–	–	D	D
Dade	D	D	D	D	D	D	D	D	D	D	D	D
Dawson	R	R	D	D	D	D	D	D	D	R	R	D
Decatur	D	R	R	D	R	D	D	D	D	D	D	D
De Kalb	D	D	D	D	D	D	D	D	D	D	D	D
Dodge	–	D	D	D	D	D	D	D	D	D	D	D
Dooly	D	D	D	D	D	D	D	D	D	D	D	D
Dougherty	D	R	D	R	D	D	D	D	D	D	D	D
Douglas	–	D	D	D	D	D	D	R	D	PO	PO	P
Early	D	D	D	D	D	D	D	D	D	D	D	D
Echols	D	D	D	D	D	D	D	D	D	D	D	D
Effingham	D	D	D	D	D	D	D	D	D	D	D	D
Elbert	D	D	D	D	D	D	D	R	D	D	D	D
Emanuel	D	D	D	D	D	D	D	D	D	D	D	D
Evans	–	–	–	–	–	–	–	–	–	–	–	–
Fannin	R	R	D	D	R	R	R	R	D	R	R	D
Fayette	D	R	D	D	D	D	D	D	D	D	D	D
Floyd	D	D	D	D	D	D	D	D	D	D	D	D
Forsyth	D	D	D	D	D	D	PO	D	D	D	R	D
Franklin	D	D	D	D	D	D	PO	D	D	D	D	D
Fulton	D	R	D	D	D	D	D	D	D	D	D	D
Gilmer	D	R	D	D	D	D	D	D	D	R	R	D
Glascock	D	D	D	D	D	D	PO	D	D	PO	PO	D
Glynn	R	R	R	R	R	D	D	D	D	D	D	D
Gordon	D	D	D	D	D	D	D	D	D	D	R	D
Grady	–	–	–	–	–	–	–	–	–	–	D	D
Greene	R	R	D	R	R	D	D	R	D	D	R	D
Gwinnett	D	D	D	D	D	D	D	D	D	D	D	D
Habersham	D	D	D	D	D	D	D	D	D	D	D	D
Hall	D	D	D	D	D	D	D	D	D	D	D	D
Hancock	D	D	D	D	D	D	D	D	D	D	D	D
Haralson	D	R	D	D	D	D	D	R	R	R	R	P
Harris	D	R	D	D	D	D	D	D	D	D	D	D
Hart	D	D	D	D	D	D	D	D	D	D	D	D

County	1868	1872	1876	1880	1884	1888	1892	1896	1900	1904	1908	1912
Heard	D	D	D	D	D	D	D	D	D	D	D	D
Henry	D	D	D	D	D	D	D	D	D	D	D	D
Houston	D	R	D	D	D	D	D	D	D	D	D	D
Irwin	D	D	D	D	D	D	D	D	D	D	D	D
Jackson	D	D	D	D	D	D	D	D	D	PO	D	D
Jasper	D	D	D	D	R	D	D	D	D	D	D	D
Jeff Davis	–	–	–	–	–	–	–	–	–	–	D	D
Jefferson	D	D	D	D	D	D	PO	D	D	R	D	D
Jenkins	–	–	–	–	–	–	–	–	–	–	D	D
Johnson	D	D	D	D	D	D	PO	R	R	PO	PO	D
Jones	D	D	D	R	D	D	D	D	D	D	D	D
Lamar	–	–	–	–	–	–	–	–	–	–	–	–
Lanier	–	–	–	–	–	–	–	–	–	–	–	–
Laurens	D	D	D	D	D	D	D	D	D	D	D	D
Lee	R	R	R	R	R	R	R	D	D	D	D	D
Liberty	D	R	R	R	R	R	R	R	R	R	R	D
Lincoln	D	D	D	D	D	D	PO	D	D	D	PO	D
Long	–	–	–	–	–	–	–	–	–	–	–	–
Lowndes	D	R	D	D	D	D	D	D	D	D	D	D
Lumpkin	D	D	D	D	D	D	D	R	D	D	D	D
McDuffie	–	D	D	D	D	D	PO	R	R	PO	PO	D
McIntosh	R	R	R	R	R	R	R	R	D	PO	R	D
Macon	D	R	D	R	D	D	D	D	D	D	D	D
Madison	D	D	D	D	D	D	D	D	D	D	D	D
Marion	D	D	D	D	D	D	D	R	D	D	D	D
Meriwether	D	R	D	D	D	D	D	D	D	D	D	D
Miller	D	D	D	D	D	D	D	D	D	D	D	D
Mitchell	D	R	D	R	D	D	D	D	D	D	D	D
Monroe	D	D	D	D	D	D	D	D	D	D	D	D
Montgomery	D	D	D	D	D	D	D	D	D	D	D	D
Morgan	R	R	D	R	D	D	D	R	D	D	D	D
Murray	D	D	D	D	D	D	D	D	D	D	R	D
Muscogee	D	D	D	D	D	D	D	D	D	D	D	D
Newton	D	R	D	D	D	D	D	D	D	D	D	D
Oconee	–	–	D	D	D	D	PO	R	D	PO	PO	D
Oglethorpe	D	D	D	D	D	D	D	D	D	D	D	D
Paulding	D	D	D	D	D	D	PO	D	R	PO	R	P
Peach	–	–	–	–	–	–	–	–	–	–	–	–
Pickens	R	R	D	R	R	R	R	R	R	R	R	P
Pierce	D	D	D	D	D	D	D	D	R	D	D	D
Pike	D	R	D	D	D	D	D	D	D	D	D	D
Polk	D	R	D	D	D	D	D	R	R	R	R	D
Pulaski	D	D	D	D	D	D	D	D	D	D	D	D
Putnam	R	R	D	D	D	D	D	D	D	D	D	D
Quitman	D	D	D	D	D	D	R	R	D	D	D	D
Rabun	D	D	D	D	D	D	D	D	D	D	D	D
Randolph	D	D	D	D	D	D	PO	D	D	D	D	D
Richmond	R	D	D	D	D	D	D	D	D	D	D	D
Rockdale	–	D	D	D	D	D	D	R	D	D	D	D

County	1868	1872	1876	1880	1884	1888	1892	1896	1900	1904	1908	1912
Schley	D	D	D	D	D	D	D	R	D	D	D	D
Screven	D	D	D	D	D	D	PO	D	D	D	R	D
Seminole	–	–	–	–	–	–	–	–	–	–	–	–
Spalding	D	R	D	R	D	D	D	D	D	D	D	D
Stephens	–	–	–	–	–	–	–	–	–	–	D	D
Stewart	D	D	D	D	D	D	D	D	D	D	D	D
Sumter	D	R	D	R	D	D	D	D	D	D	D	D
Talbot	D	D	D	D	R	D	D	D	D	D	D	D
Taliaferro	D	R	D	D	D	D	PO	R	D	D	D	D
Tattnall	D	D	D	D	D	D	D	R	D	D	D	D
Taylor	D	D	D	D	D	D	D	R	D	D	D	D
Telfair	D	D	D	D	D	D	D	D	D	D	D	D
Terrell	D	D	D	D	D	D	D	D	D	D	D	D
Thomas	R	R	D	D	D	D	D	R	D	D	D	D
Tift	–	–	–	–	–	–	–	–	–	–	D	D
Toombs	–	–	–	–	–	–	–	–	–	–	D	D
Towns	R	D	D	D	D	R	D	D	R	R	R	D
Treutlen	–	–	–	–	–	–	–	–	–	–	–	–
Troup	D	D	D	D	D	D	D	D	D	D	D	D
Turner	–	–	–	–	–	–	–	–	–	–	D	D
Twiggs	R	R	D	R	D	D	D	D	D	D	D	D
Union	D	D	D	D	D	D	D	D	D	R	R	D
Upson	D	D	D	D	D	D	D	D	D	D	D	D
Walker	D	D	D	D	D	D	D	D	D	D	R	D
Walton	D	D	D	D	D	D	D	D	D	D	D	D
Ware	D	D	D	D	D	D	D	D	D	D	D	D
Warren	D	D	D	D	D	D	PO	R	D	PO	PO	D
Washington	D	D	D	D	D	D	PO	R	D	D	D	D
Wayne	D	D	D	D	D	D	D	D	D	D	D	D
Webster	D	D	D	D	D	D	D	D	D	D	R	D
Wheeler	–	–	–	–	–	–	–	–	–	–	–	–
White	D	D	D	D	D	D	D	D	D	D	R	D
Whitfield	D	D	D	D	D	D	D	D	D	D	R	D
Wilcox	D	D	D	D	D	D	D	D	D	D	D	D
Wilkes	D	D	D	D	D	D	D	D	D	D	D	D
Wilkinson	D	D	D	D	D	D	D	D	D	D	D	D
Worth	D	D	D	D	D	D	D	D	D	R	D	D

County	1916	1920	1924	1928	1932	1936	1940	1944	1948	1952	1956	1960
Appling	D	D	D	R	D	D	D	D	D	D	D	D
Atkinson	–	D	D	D	D	D	D	D	D	D	D	D
Bacon	D	D	D	D	D	D	D	D	D	D	D	D
Baker	D	D	D	D	D	D	D	D	D	D	D	D
Baldwin	D	D	D	D	D	D	D	D	D	D	D	D
Banks	D	D	D	D	D	D	D	D	D	D	D	D
Barrow	D	D	D	R	D	D	D	D	D	D	D	D
Bartow	D	D	D	R	D	D	D	D	D	D	D	D
Ben Hill	D	D	D	D	D	D	D	D	D	D	D	D

County	1916	1920	1924	1928	1932	1936	1940	1944	1948	1952	1956	1960
Berrien	D	D	D	D	D	D	D	D	D	D	D	D
Bibb	D	D	D	D	D	D	D	D	D	D	D	D
Bleckley	D	D	D	D	D	D	D	D	D	D	D	D
Brantley	–	–	D	R	D	D	D	D	D	D	D	D
Brooks	D	D	D	D	D	D	D	D	D	D	D	D
Bryan	D	D	D	D	D	D	D	D	D	D	D	D
Bulloch	D	D	D	D	D	D	D	D	D	D	D	D
Burke	D	D	D	D	D	D	D	D	SR	D	D	D
Butts	D	D	D	D	D	D	D	D	D	D	D	D
Calhoun	D	D	D	D	D	D	D	D	D	D	D	D
Camden	D	D	D	D	D	D	D	D	D	D	D	D
Candler	D	D	D	D	D	D	D	D	D	D	D	D
Carroll	D	D	D	R	D	D	D	D	D	D	D	D
Catoosa	D	D	D	R	D	D	D	D	D	D	D	D
Charlton	D	D	D	D	D	D	D	D	D	D	D	D
Chatham	D	D	D	D	D	D	D	D	D	R	R	R
Chattahoochee	D	D	D	D	D	D	D	D	SR	D	D	D
Chattooga	D	R	D	R	D	D	D	D	D	D	D	D
Cherokee	D	D	D	R	D	D	D	D	D	D	D	D
Clarke	D	D	D	D	D	D	D	D	D	D	D	D
Clay	D	D	D	D	D	D	D	D	D	D	D	D
Clayton	D	D	D	R	D	D	D	D	D	D	D	D
Clinch	D	D	D	D	D	D	D	D	D	D	D	D
Cobb	D	D	D	R	D	D	D	D	D	D	D	D
Coffee	D	D	D	D	D	D	D	D	D	D	D	D
Colquitt	D	D	D	D	D	D	D	D	D	D	D	D
Columbia	D	D	D	D	D	D	D	D	SR	D	D	D
Cook	–	R	D	D	D	D	D	D	D	D	D	D
Coweta	D	D	D	D	D	D	D	D	D	D	D	D
Crawford	D	D	D	D	D	D	D	D	D	D	D	D
Crisp	D	D	D	D	D	D	D	D	D	D	D	D
Dade	D	D	D	D	D	D	D	D	D	D	D	D
Dawson	D	R	D	D	D	D	D	D	R	D	D	D
Decatur	D	D	D	R	D	D	D	D	D	D	D	D
De Kalb	D	D	D	R	D	D	D	D	D	D	D	D
Dodge	D	D	D	D	D	D	D	D	D	D	D	D
Dooly	D	D	D	D	D	D	D	D	D	D	D	D
Dougherty	D	D	D	D	D	D	D	D	D	D	D	D
Douglas	D	R	D	R	D	D	D	D	D	D	D	D
Early	D	D	D	D	D	D	D	D	D	D	D	D
Echols	D	–	D	D	D	D	D	D	D	D	D	D
Effingham	D	D	D	R	D	D	D	D	SR	R	R	R
Elbert	D	D	D	D	D	D	D	D	D	D	D	D
Emanuel	D	D	D	D	D	D	D	D	D	D	D	D
Evans	D	D	D	D	D	D	D	D	D	D	D	D
Fannin	IP	R	R	R	R	R	R	R	R	R	R	R
Fayette	D	D	D	D	D	D	D	D	D	D	D	D
Floyd	D	D	D	R	D	D	D	D	D	D	D	D
Forsyth	D	D	D	R	D	D	D	D	D	D	D	D

County	1916	1920	1924	1928	1932	1936	1940	1944	1948	1952	1956	1960
Franklin	D	D	D	R	D	D	D	D	D	D	D	D
Fulton	D	D	D	R	D	D	D	D	D	D	D	D
Gilmer	D	R	R	R	D	D	D	D	D	D	R	R
Glascock	IP	D	D	R	D	D	D	D	SR	D	D	D
Glynn	D	D	D	R	D	D	D	D	D	D	R	D
Gordon	D	R	D	R	D	D	D	D	D	D	D	D
Grady	D	D	D	D	D	D	D	D	D	D	D	D
Greene	D	D	D	D	D	D	D	D	D	D	D	D
Gwinnett	D	D	D	R	D	D	D	D	D	D	D	D
Habersham	D	R	D	R	D	D	D	D	D	D	D	D
Hall	D	D	D	R	D	D	D	D	D	D	D	D
Hancock	D	D	D	D	D	D	D	D	D	D	D	D
Haralson	D	R	R	R	D	D	D	D	D	D	D	D
Harris	D	D	D	D	D	D	D	D	D	D	D	D
Hart	D	D	D	D	D	D	D	D	D	D	D	D
Heard	D	D	D	D	D	D	D	D	D	D	D	D
Henry	D	D	D	D	D	D	D	D	D	D	D	D
Houston	D	D	D	D	D	D	D	D	D	D	D	D
Irwin	D	D	D	D	D	D	D	D	D	D	D	D
Jackson	D	D	D	D	D	D	D	D	D	D	D	D
Jasper	D	D	D	D	D	D	D	D	D	D	D	D
Jeff Davis	D	R	D	D	D	D	D	D	D	D	D	D
Jefferson	D	D	D	R	D	D	D	D	SR	D	D	D
Jenkins	D	D	D	D	D	D	D	D	D	D	D	D
Johnson	D	D	D	D	D	D	D	D	D	D	D	D
Jones	D	D	D	D	D	D	D	D	D	D	D	D
Lamar	–	–	D	D	D	D	D	D	D	D	D	D
Lanier	–	–	D	D	D	D	D	D	D	D	D	D
Laurens	D	D	D	D	D	D	D	D	D	D	D	D
Lee	D	D	D	D	D	D	D	D	SR	D	D	D
Liberty	D	D	D	R	D	D	D	D	D	D	R	D
Lincoln	D	D	D	D	D	D	D	D	SR	D	D	D
Long	–	–	D	R	D	D	D	D	D	D	D	D
Lowndes	D	D	D	D	D	D	D	D	D	D	D	D
Lumpkin	D	R	D	D	D	D	D	D	D	D	D	D
McDuffie	D	D	D	R	D	D	D	D	SR	D	D	D
McIntosh	D	D	D	R	D	D	D	D	D	D	R	D
Macon	D	D	D	D	D	D	D	D	D	D	D	D
Madison	D	D	D	R	D	D	D	D	D	D	D	D
Marion	D	D	D	D	D	D	D	D	D	D	D	D
Meriwether	D	D	D	D	D	D	D	D	D	D	D	D
Miller	D	D	D	D	D	D	D	D	D	D	D	D
Mitchell	D	D	D	D	D	D	D	D	D	D	D	D
Monroe	D	D	D	D	D	D	D	D	D	D	D	D
Montgomery	D	D	D	D	D	D	D	D	D	D	D	D
Morgan	D	D	D	D	D	D	D	D	D	D	D	D
Murray	D	R	D	R	D	D	D	D	D	D	D	D
Muscogee	D	D	D	D	D	D	D	D	D	D	R	R
Newton	D	D	D	D	D	D	D	D	D	D	D	D

County	1916	1920	1924	1928	1932	1936	1940	1944	1948	1952	1956	1960
Oconee	D	D	D	D	D	D	D	D	D	D	D	D
Oglethorpe	D	D	D	D	D	D	D	D	D	D	D	D
Paulding	IP	R	D	R	D	D	D	D	D	D	D	D
Peach	–	–	–	D	D	D	D	D	D	D	D	D
Pickens	D	R	R	R	D	D	D	R	R	R	R	R
Pierce	D	D	D	D	D	D	D	D	D	D	D	D
Pike	D	D	D	D	D	D	D	D	D	D	D	D
Polk	D	R	D	R	D	D	D	D	D	D	D	D
Pulaski	D	D	D	D	D	D	D	D	D	D	D	D
Putnam	D	D	D	D	D	D	D	D	D	D	D	D
Quitman	D	D	D	D	D	D	D	D	D	D	D	D
Rabun	D	D	D	D	D	D	D	D	D	D	D	D
Randolph	D	D	D	D	D	D	D	D	D	D	D	D
Richmond	D	D	D	R	D	D	D	D	SR	R	R	R
Rockdale	D	D	D	D	D	D	D	D	D	D	D	D
Schley	D	D	D	D	D	D	D	D	D	D	D	D
Screven	D	D	D	R	D	D	D	D	D	D	D	D
Seminole	–	–	D	D	D	D	D	D	D	D	D	D
Spalding	D	D	D	D	D	D	D	D	D	D	D	D
Stephens	D	D	D	D	D	D	D	D	D	D	D	D
Stewart	D	D	D	D	D	D	D	D	D	D	D	D
Sumter	D	D	D	D	D	D	D	D	D	D	D	D
Talbot	D	D	D	D	D	D	D	D	D	D	D	D
Taliaferro	D	D	D	D	D	D	D	D	D	D	D	D
Tattnall	D	D	D	R	D	D	D	D	D	D	D	D
Taylor	D	D	D	D	D	D	D	D	D	D	D	D
Telfair	D	D	D	D	D	D	D	D	D	D	D	D
Terrell	D	D	D	D	D	D	D	D	D	D	D	D
Thomas	D	D	D	D	D	D	D	D	D	D	D	D
Tift	D	D	D	D	D	D	D	D	D	D	D	D
Toombs	D	D	D	D	D	D	D	D	D	D	D	D
Towns	R	R	R	R	R	D	D	D	D	D	R	R
Treutlen	–	D	D	D	D	D	D	D	D	D	D	D
Troup	D	D	D	D	D	D	D	D	D	D	D	D
Turner	D	D	D	R	D	D	D	D	D	D	D	D
Twiggs	D	D	D	D	D	D	D	D	D	D	D	D
Union	D	R	D	R	D	D	D	D	D	D	D	R
Upson	D	D	D	D	D	D	D	D	D	D	D	D
Walker	D	D	D	R	D	D	D	D	D	D	D	D
Walton	D	D	D	D	D	D	D	D	D	D	D	D
Ware	D	D	D	D	D	D	D	D	D	D	D	D
Warren	D	D	D	R	D	D	D	D	D	D	D	D
Washington	D	D	D	D	D	D	D	D	D	D	D	D
Wayne	D	D	D	D	D	D	D	D	D	D	D	D
Webster	D	D	D	D	D	D	D	D	D	D	D	D
Wheeler	D	D	D	D	D	D	D	D	D	D	D	D
White	D	R	D	R	D	D	D	D	D	D	D	D
Whitfield	D	R	D	R	D	D	D	D	D	D	D	R
Wilcox	D	D	D	D	D	D	D	D	D	D	D	D

County	1916	1920	1924	1928	1932	1936	1940	1944	1948	1952	1956	1960
Wilkes	D	D	D	R	D	D	D	D	D	D	D	D
Wilkinson	D	D	D	D	D	D	D	D	D	D	D	D
Worth	D	D	D	D	D	D	D	D	D	D	D	D

County	1964	1968	1972	1976	1980	1984	1988	1992	1996	2000	2004
Appling	R	A	R	D	D	R	R	R	R	R	R
Atkinson	R	A	R	D	D	R	R	D	D	R	R
Bacon	R	A	R	D	D	R	R	D	R	R	R
Baker	R	A	R	D	D	D	D	D	D	D	D
Baldwin	R	A	R	D	D	R	R	D	D	R	R
Banks	D	A	R	D	D	R	R	R	R	R	R
Barrow	R	A	R	D	D	R	R	R	R	R	R
Bartow	D	A	R	D	D	R	R	R	R	R	R
Ben Hill	R	A	R	D	D	R	R	D	D	R	R
Berrien	R	A	R	D	D	R	R	D	D	R	R
Bibb	R	A	R	D	D	D	R	D	D	D	D
Bleckley	R	A	R	D	D	R	R	D	R	R	R
Brantley	R	A	R	D	D	R	R	D	R	R	R
Brooks	R	A	R	D	D	R	R	D	D	R	R
Bryan	R	A	R	D	D	R	R	R	R	R	R
Bulloch	R	A	R	D	D	R	R	R	R	R	R
Burke	R	A	R	D	D	R	R	D	D	D	R
Butts	D	A	R	D	D	R	R	D	D	R	R
Calhoun	R	A	R	D	D	D	D	D	D	D	D
Camden	R	A	R	D	D	R	R	R	R	R	R
Candler	R	A	R	D	D	R	R	D	R	R	R
Carroll	R	A	R	D	D	R	R	R	R	R	R
Catoosa	R	A	R	D	R	R	R	R	R	R	R
Charlton	R	A	R	D	D	R	R	R	R	R	R
Chatham	R	D	R	D	D	R	R	R	D	R	D
Chattahoochee	R	A	R	D	D	R	R	D	D	D	R
Chattooga	D	A	R	D	D	R	R	D	D	R	R
Cherokee	R	A	R	D	D	R	R	R	R	R	R
Clarke	D	R	R	D	D	R	D	D	D	D	D
Clay	R	A	R	D	D	D	D	D	D	D	D
Clayton	R	A	R	D	R	R	R	D	D	D	D
Clinch	R	A	R	D	D	R	R	R	D	R	R
Cobb	R	R	R	D	R	R	R	R	R	R	R
Coffee	R	A	R	D	D	R	R	R	R	R	R
Colquitt	R	A	R	D	D	R	R	R	R	R	R
Columbia	R	A	R	D	R	R	R	R	R	R	R
Cook	R	A	R	D	D	R	R	D	D	R	R
Coweta	D	A	R	D	D	R	R	R	R	R	R
Crawford	R	A	R	D	D	D	D	D	D	R	R
Crisp	R	A	R	D	D	R	D	D	R	R	R
Dade	R	A	R	D	R	R	R	R	R	R	R
Dawson	D	A	R	D	D	R	R	R	R	R	R
Decatur	R	A	R	D	D	R	R	D	D	R	R

County	1964	1968	1972	1976	1980	1984	1988	1992	1996	2000	2004
De Kalb	R	R	R	D	D	R	D	D	D	D	D
Dodge	R	A	R	D	D	R	R	D	D	R	R
Dooly	R	A	R	D	D	D	D	D	D	D	D
Dougherty	R	A	R	D	D	R	R	D	D	D	D
Douglas	R	A	R	D	R	R	R	R	R	R	R
Early	R	A	R	D	D	R	R	D	D	R	R
Echols	R	A	R	D	D	R	R	R	R	R	R
Effingham	R	A	R	D	D	R	R	R	R	R	R
Elbert	D	A	R	D	D	R	R	D	D	R	R
Emanuel	R	A	R	D	D	R	R	D	D	R	R
Evans	R	A	R	D	D	R	R	R	R	R	R
Fannin	R	R	R	D	R	R	R	R	R	R	R
Fayette	R	A	R	D	R	R	R	R	R	R	R
Floyd	R	A	R	D	D	R	R	R	R	R	R
Forsyth	D	A	R	D	D	R	R	R	R	R	R
Franklin	D	A	R	D	D	R	R	D	R	R	R
Fulton	D	D	R	D	D	D	D	D	D	D	D
Gilmer	R	R	R	D	D	R	R	R	R	R	R
Glascock	R	A	R	D	D	R	R	R	R	R	R
Glynn	R	A	R	D	D	R	R	R	R	R	R
Gordon	D	A	R	D	D	R	R	R	R	R	R
Grady	R	A	R	D	D	R	R	D	D	R	R
Greene	D	D	R	D	D	D	D	D	D	D	R
Gwinnett	R	A	R	D	R	R	R	R	R	R	R
Habersham	D	A	R	D	D	R	R	R	R	R	R
Hall	D	A	R	D	D	R	R	R	R	R	R
Hancock	D	D	R	D	D	D	D	D	D	D	D
Haralson	R	A	R	D	D	R	R	D	R	R	R
Harris	R	A	R	D	D	R	R	R	R	R	R
Hart	D	A	R	D	D	R	R	D	D	R	R
Heard	D	A	R	D	D	R	R	D	D	R	R
Henry	D	A	R	D	D	R	R	R	R	R	R
Houston	R	A	R	D	D	R	R	R	R	R	R
Irwin	R	A	R	D	D	R	R	D	D	R	R
Jackson	D	A	R	D	D	R	R	R	R	R	R
Jasper	R	A	R	D	D	R	R	D	D	R	R
Jeff Davis	R	A	R	D	D	R	R	D	R	R	R
Jefferson	R	A	R	D	D	R	R	D	D	D	D
Jenkins	R	A	R	D	D	R	R	D	D	R	R
Johnson	R	A	R	D	D	R	R	D	D	R	R
Jones	R	A	R	D	D	R	R	D	R	R	R
Lamar	R	A	R	D	D	R	R	D	D	R	R
Lanier	R	A	R	D	D	R	R	D	D	R	R
Laurens	R	A	R	D	D	R	R	D	R	R	R
Lee	R	A	R	D	R	R	R	R	R	R	R
Liberty	D	D	R	D	D	R	R	D	D	D	D
Lincoln	R	A	R	D	D	R	R	D	R	R	R
Long	D	A	R	D	D	R	R	D	D	R	R
Lowndes	R	A	R	D	R	R	R	R	R	R	R

County	1964	1968	1972	1976	1980	1984	1988	1992	1996	2000	2004
Lumpkin	D	A	R	D	D	R	R	D	R	R	R
McDuffie	R	A	R	D	D	R	R	R	R	R	R
McIntosh	D	D	R	D	D	D	D	D	D	D	R
Macon	R	A	R	D	D	D	D	D	D	D	D
Madison	D	A	R	D	D	R	R	R	R	R	R
Marion	R	A	R	D	D	D	D	D	D	R	R
Meriwether	D	A	R	D	D	R	R	D	D	D	R
Miller	R	A	R	D	D	R	R	D	D	R	R
Mitchell	R	A	R	D	D	D	R	D	D	D	R
Monroe	R	A	R	D	D	R	R	D	R	R	R
Montgomery	R	A	R	D	D	R	R	D	R	R	R
Morgan	D	A	R	D	D	R	R	D	R	R	R
Murray	D	A	R	D	D	R	R	R	R	R	R
Muscogee	R	R	R	D	D	R	R	D	D	D	D
Newton	D	A	R	D	D	R	R	D	R	R	R
Oconee	R	A	R	D	D	R	R	R	R	R	R
Oglethorpe	R	A	R	D	D	R	R	R	R	R	R
Paulding	D	A	R	D	D	R	R	R	R	R	R
Peach	R	A	R	D	D	D	D	D	D	D	R
Pickens	R	R	R	D	D	R	R	D	R	R	R
Pierce	R	A	R	D	D	R	R	R	R	R	R
Pike	R	A	R	D	D	R	R	R	R	R	R
Polk	D	A	R	D	D	R	R	D	R	R	R
Pulaski	R	A	R	D	D	R	D	D	D	R	R
Putnam	R	A	R	D	D	R	R	D	D	R	R
Quitman	R	A	R	D	D	D	D	D	D	D	D
Rabun	D	A	R	D	D	R	R	R	R	R	R
Randolph	R	A	R	D	D	R	D	D	D	D	D
Richmond	R	R	R	D	D	R	R	D	D	D	D
Rockdale	D	A	R	D	R	R	R	R	R	R	R
Schley	R	A	R	D	D	R	R	D	D	R	R
Screven	R	A	R	D	D	R	R	D	D	R	R
Seminole	R	A	R	D	D	R	R	D	D	R	R
Spalding	D	A	R	D	D	R	R	R	R	R	R
Stephens	D	A	R	D	D	R	R	R	R	R	R
Stewart	R	A	R	D	D	D	D	D	D	D	D
Sumter	R	A	R	D	D	R	R	D	D	R	R
Talbot	R	A	R	D	D	D	D	D	D	D	D
Taliaferro	D	D	R	D	D	D	D	D	D	D	D
Tattnall	R	A	R	D	D	R	R	R	R	R	R
Taylor	R	A	R	D	D	D	R	D	D	R	R
Telfair	R	A	R	D	D	D	R	D	D	D	R
Terrell	R	A	R	D	D	R	R	D	D	D	D
Thomas	R	A	R	D	D	R	R	R	R	R	R
Tift	R	A	R	D	D	R	R	R	R	R	R
Toombs	R	A	R	D	D	R	R	R	R	R	R
Towns	D	R	R	D	D	R	R	R	R	R	R
Treutlen	D	A	R	D	D	R	R	D	D	R	R
Troup	D	A	R	D	D	R	R	R	R	R	R

County	1964	1968	1972	1976	1980	1984	1988	1992	1996	2000	2004
Turner	R	A	R	D	D	R	R	D	D	R	R
Twiggs	R	A	R	D	D	D	D	D	D	D	D
Union	D	R	R	D	D	R	R	R	R	R	R
Upson	D	A	R	D	D	R	R	R	R	R	R
Walker	R	A	R	D	R	R	R	R	R	R	R
Walton	R	A	R	D	D	R	R	R	R	R	R
Ware	D	A	R	D	D	R	R	T	R	R	R
Warren	R	A	R	D	D	D	D	D	D	D	D
Washington	R	A	R	D	D	D	D	D	D	D	R
Wayne	R	A	R	D	D	R	R	R	R	R	R
Webster	R	A	R	D	D	D	D	D	D	D	D
Wheeler	D	A	R	D	D	R	R	D	D	R	R
White	D	A	R	D	D	R	R	R	R	R	R
Whitfield	D	R	R	D	D	R	R	R	R	R	R
Wilcox	R	A	R	D	D	R	R	D	D	R	R
Wilkes	R	A	R	D	D	R	R	D	D	R	R
Wilkinson	R	A	R	D	D	D	D	D	D	D	R
Worth	R	A	R	D	D	R	R	D	R	R	R

Hawaii

County	1960	1964	1968	1972	1976	1980	1984	1988	1992	1996	2000	2004
Hawaii	R	D	D	R	D	D	R	D	D	D	D	D
Honolulu	D	D	D	R	D	R	R	D	D	D	D	D
Kauai	R	D	D	R	D	D	R	D	D	D	D	D
Maui	R	D	D	R	D	D	R	D	D	D	D	D

Idaho

County	1892	1896	1900	1904	1908	1912	1916	1920	1924	1928	1932	1936
Ada	PO	D	R	R	R	P	R	R	R	R	D	D
Adams	–	–	–	–	–	R	R	R	R	R	D	D
Bannock	–	D	R	R	R	R	D	R	R	R	D	D
Bear Lake	PO	D	D	R	R	R	D	R	R	R	R	D
Benewah	–	–	–	–	–	–	D	R	R	R	D	D
Bingham	R	D	D	R	R	R	D	R	R	R	D	D
Blaine	–	D	D	R	D	D	D	R	R	R	D	D
Boise	PO	D	D	R	R	D	D	R	R	R	D	D
Bonner	–	–	–	–	R	P	D	R	P	R	D	D
Bonneville	–	–	–	–	–	R	D	R	R	R	D	D
Boundary	–	–	–	–	–	–	D	R	R	R	D	D

County	1892	1896	1900	1904	1908	1912	1916	1920	1924	1928	1932	1936
Butte	–	–	–	–	–	–	–	R	R	R	D	D
Camas	–	–	–	–	–	–	–	R	P	R	D	D
Canyon	–	D	R	R	R	P	D	R	R	R	D	D
Caribou	–	–	–	–	–	–	–	R	R	R	D	D
Cassia	PO	D	R	R	R	R	D	R	R	R	D	D
Clark	–	–	–	–	–	–	–	R	R	R	D	R
Clearwater	–	–	–	–	–	D	R	R	R	R	D	D
Custer	PO	D	D	R	D	D	D	R	R	R	D	D
Elmore	PO	D	D	R	R	D	D	R	P	R	D	D
Franklin	–	–	–	–	–	–	D	R	R	R	D	D
Fremont	–	D	R	R	R	R	D	R	R	D	D	D
Gem	–	–	–	–	–	–	D	R	P	R	D	D
Gooding	–	–	–	–	–	–	R	R	R	R	D	D
Idaho	PO	D	D	R	R	D	D	R	P	R	D	D
Jefferson	–	–	–	–	–	–	D	R	R	R	D	D
Jerome	–	–	–	–	–	–	–	R	R	R	D	D
Kootenai	PO	D	D	R	R	D	D	R	R	R	D	D
Latah	PO	D	R	R	R	P	D	R	R	R	D	D
Lemhi	R	D	D	R	R	D	D	R	R	R	D	D
Lewis	–	–	–	–	–	D	D	R	P	R	D	D
Lincoln	–	D	R	R	R	P	R	R	R	R	D	D
Madison	–	–	–	–	–	–	D	R	R	R	D	D
Minidoka	–	–	–	–	–	–	D	R	P	R	D	D
Nez Perce	PO	D	R	R	R	D	D	R	R	R	D	D
Oneida	R	D	R	R	R	R	D	R	R	R	D	D
Owyhee	PO	D	D	R	D	D	D	R	P	R	D	D
Payette	–	–	–	–	–	–	–	R	R	R	D	D
Power	–	–	–	–	–	–	D	R	R	R	D	D
Shoshone	PO	D	D	R	R	D	D	R	R	R	D	D
Teton	–	–	–	–	–	–	D	R	R	R	D	D
Twin Falls	–	–	–	–	R	D	D	R	R	R	D	D
Valley	–	–	–	–	–	–	–	R	P	R	D	D
Washington	PO	D	D	R	R	D	D	R	R	R	D	D

County	1940	1944	1948	1952	1956	1960	1964	1968	1972	1976	1980	1984
Ada	R	R	R	R	R	R	R	R	R	R	R	R
Adams	D	D	D	R	R	R	D	R	R	R	R	R
Bannock	D	D	D	R	R	D	D	R	R	R	R	R
Bear Lake	D	D	D	R	R	R	D	R	R	R	R	R
Benewah	D	D	D	R	R	D	D	D	R	D	R	R
Bingham	D	D	D	R	R	R	R	R	R	R	R	R
Blaine	D	D	D	R	R	R	D	R	R	R	R	R
Boise	D	D	D	R	R	R	D	R	R	R	R	R
Bonner	D	D	D	R	R	D	D	R	R	R	R	R
Bonneville	D	D	D	R	R	R	R	R	R	R	R	R
Boundary	D	R	D	R	R	D	D	R	R	R	R	R
Butte	D	R	D	R	R	D	D	R	R	R	R	R
Camas	D	D	D	R	R	D	R	R	R	R	R	R
Canyon	R	R	R	R	R	R	R	R	R	R	R	R

County	1940	1944	1948	1952	1956	1960	1964	1968	1972	1976	1980	1984
Caribou	D	D	D	R	R	R	D	R	R	R	R	R
Cassia	D	R	R	R	R	R	R	R	R	R	R	R
Clark	R	R	R	R	R	R	R	R	R	R	R	R
Clearwater	D	D	D	D	D	D	D	D	R	D	R	R
Custer	D	D	D	R	R	D	R	R	R	R	R	R
Elmore	D	D	D	R	R	D	D	R	R	R	R	R
Franklin	D	D	D	R	R	R	R	R	R	R	R	R
Fremont	D	D	D	R	R	R	D	R	R	R	R	R
Gem	D	D	D	R	R	R	D	R	R	R	R	R
Gooding	R	R	R	R	R	R	R	R	R	R	R	R
Idaho	D	D	D	R	R	D	D	R	R	R	R	R
Jefferson	D	D	D	R	R	R	R	R	R	R	R	R
Jerome	R	R	R	R	R	R	R	R	R	R	R	R
Kootenai	D	D	D	R	R	D	D	R	R	R	R	R
Latah	D	R	D	R	R	R	D	R	R	R	R	R
Lemhi	D	R	R	R	R	R	R	R	R	R	R	R
Lewis	D	D	D	D	D	D	D	D	R	D	R	R
Lincoln	R	R	R	R	R	R	R	R	R	R	R	R
Madison	D	D	D	R	R	R	R	R	R	R	R	R
Minidoka	D	R	D	R	R	R	R	R	R	R	R	R
Nez Perce	D	D	D	R	D	D	D	D	R	D	R	R
Oneida	D	D	D	R	R	R	R	R	R	R	R	R
Owyhee	D	R	R	R	R	R	R	R	R	R	R	R
Payette	R	R	R	R	R	R	R	R	R	R	R	R
Power	R	R	R	R	R	R	D	R	R	R	R	R
Shoshone	D	D	D	R	R	D	D	D	R	R	R	R
Teton	D	D	D	R	R	R	R	R	R	R	R	R
Twin Falls	R	R	R	R	R	R	R	R	R	R	R	R
Valley	D	R	R	R	R	R	D	R	R	R	R	R
Washington	D	R	R	R	R	R	D	R	R	R	R	R

County	1988	1992	1996	2000	2004
Ada	R	R	R	R	R
Adams	R	R	R	R	R
Bannock	R	R	R	R	R
Bear Lake	R	R	R	R	R
Benewah	R	D	R	R	R
Bingham	R	R	R	R	R
Blaine	R	D	D	D	D
Boise	R	R	R	R	R
Bonner	R	D	R	R	R
Bonneville	R	R	R	R	R
Boundary	R	R	R	R	R
Butte	R	R	R	R	R
Camas	R	R	R	R	R
Canyon	R	R	R	R	R
Caribou	R	R	R	R	R
Cassia	R	R	R	R	R
Clark	R	R	R	R	R

County	1988	1992	1996	2000	2004
Clearwater	D	D	R	R	R
Custer	R	R	R	R	R
Elmore	R	R	R	R	R
Franklin	R	R	R	R	R
Fremont	R	R	R	R	R
Gem	R	R	R	R	R
Gooding	R	R	R	R	R
Idaho	R	R	R	R	R
Jefferson	R	R	R	R	R
Jerome	R	R	R	R	R
Kootenai	R	R	R	R	R
Latah	D	D	D	R	R
Lemhi	R	R	R	R	R
Lewis	D	D	R	R	R
Lincoln	R	R	R	R	R
Madison	R	R	R	R	R
Minidoka	R	R	R	R	R
Nez Perce	D	D	D	R	R
Oneida	R	R	R	R	R
Owyhee	R	R	R	R	R
Payette	R	R	R	R	R
Power	R	R	R	R	R
Shoshone	D	D	D	R	R
Teton	R	R	R	R	R
Twin Falls	R	R	R	R	R
Valley	R	R	R	R	R
Washington	R	R	R	R	R

Illinois

County	1868	1872	1876	1880	1884	1888	1892	1896	1900	1904	1908	1912
Adams	D	D	D	D	D	D	D	R	D	R	D	D
Alexander	D	R	D	R	R	R	R	R	R	R	R	R
Bond	R	R	R	R	R	R	R	R	R	R	R	D
Boone	R	R	R	R	R	R	R	R	R	R	R	P
Brown	D	D	D	D	D	D	D	D	D	D	D	D
Bureau	R	R	R	R	R	R	R	R	R	R	R	P
Calhoun	D	D	D	D	D	D	D	D	D	D	D	D
Carroll	R	R	R	R	R	R	R	R	R	R	R	R
Cass	D	D	D	D	D	D	D	D	D	D	D	D
Champaign	R	R	R	R	R	R	R	R	R	R	R	P
Christian	D	D	D	D	D	D	D	D	D	R	D	D
Clark	D	T	D	D	D	D	D	D	D	R	R	D
Clay	R	R	D	D	R	R	R	D	R	R	R	D
Clinton	D	D	D	D	D	D	D	D	D	D	D	D

County	1868	1872	1876	1880	1884	1888	1892	1896	1900	1904	1908	1912
Coles	R	R	R	R	D	R	R	R	R	R	R	D
Cook	R	R	D	R	R	R	D	R	R	R	R	P
Crawford	D	R	D	D	D	D	D	D	R	R	R	D
Cumberland	D	D	D	D	D	D	D	D	D	R	D	D
De Kalb	R	R	R	R	R	R	R	R	R	R	R	P
De Witt	R	R	R	R	R	R	D	R	R	R	R	D
Douglas	R	R	R	R	R	R	R	R	R	R	R	D
Du Page	R	R	R	R	R	R	R	R	R	R	R	P
Edgar	D	R	D	D	D	D	R	R	D	R	R	D
Edwards	R	R	R	R	R	R	R	R	R	R	R	P
Effingham	D	D	D	D	D	D	D	D	D	D	D	D
Fayette	D	R	D	D	D	D	D	D	D	R	R	D
Ford	R	R	R	R	R	R	R	R	R	R	R	P
Franklin	D	D	D	D	D	D	D	D	D	R	R	D
Fulton	D	D	D	D	D	D	D	R	R	R	R	D
Gallatin	D	D	D	D	D	D	D	D	D	D	D	D
Greene	D	D	D	D	D	D	D	D	D	D	D	D
Grundy	R	R	R	R	R	R	R	R	R	R	R	R
Hamilton	D	D	D	D	D	D	D	D	D	D	D	D
Hancock	D	D	D	D	D	D	D	D	D	R	D	D
Hardin	D	D	D	D	D	D	D	D	D	R	R	R
Henderson	R	R	R	R	R	R	R	R	R	R	R	P
Henry	R	R	R	R	R	R	R	R	R	R	R	P
Iroquois	R	R	R	R	R	R	R	R	R	R	R	P
Jackson	D	R	D	D	R	D	R	R	R	R	R	D
Jasper	D	D	D	D	D	D	D	D	D	D	D	D
Jefferson	D	D	D	D	D	D	D	D	D	R	D	D
Jersey	D	D	D	D	D	D	D	D	D	D	D	D
Jo Daviess	R	R	R	R	R	R	D	R	R	R	R	D
Johnson	R	R	R	R	R	R	R	R	R	R	R	R
Kane	R	R	R	R	R	R	R	R	R	R	R	P
Kankakee	R	R	R	R	R	R	R	R	R	R	R	R
Kendall	R	R	R	R	R	R	R	R	R	R	R	P
Knox	R	R	R	R	R	R	R	R	R	R	R	P
Lake	R	R	R	R	R	R	R	R	R	R	R	P
La Salle	R	R	R	R	D	D	D	R	R	R	R	D
Lawrence	D	R	D	D	D	R	D	R	D	R	D	D
Lee	R	R	R	R	R	R	R	R	R	R	R	P
Livingston	R	R	R	R	R	R	R	R	R	R	R	D
Logan	R	R	R	R	D	D	D	R	D	R	D	D
McDonough	R	R	R	R	T	R	R	R	R	R	R	D
McHenry	R	R	R	R	R	R	R	R	R	R	R	P
McLean	R	R	R	R	R	R	R	R	R	R	R	D
Macon	R	R	R	R	R	R	R	R	R	R	R	D
Macoupin	D	D	D	D	D	D	D	D	D	R	D	D
Madison	R	R	D	R	D	R	D	R	R	R	R	D
Marion	D	D	D	D	D	D	D	D	D	R	D	D
Marshall	R	R	R	R	R	D	D	R	R	R	R	D
Mason	D	D	D	D	D	D	D	D	D	D	D	D

County	1868	1872	1876	1880	1884	1888	1892	1896	1900	1904	1908	1912
Massac	R	R	R	R	R	R	R	R	R	R	R	R
Menard	D	D	D	D	D	D	D	D	D	R	D	D
Mercer	R	R	R	R	R	R	R	R	R	R	R	P
Monroe	D	D	D	D	D	D	D	D	D	R	R	R
Montgomery	D	D	D	D	D	D	D	D	D	R	D	D
Morgan	D	R	D	D	D	D	D	R	R	R	R	D
Moultrie	D	D	D	D	D	D	D	D	D	R	R	D
Ogle	R	R	R	R	R	R	R	R	R	R	R	P
Peoria	D	D	D	D	D	D	D	R	R	R	R	P
Perry	R	R	R	R	R	D	D	D	R	R	D	D
Piatt	R	R	R	R	R	R	R	R	R	R	R	D
Pike	D	D	D	D	D	D	D	D	D	D	D	D
Pope	R	R	R	R	R	R	R	R	R	R	R	R
Pulaski	D	R	R	R	R	R	R	R	R	R	R	R
Putnam	R	R	R	R	R	R	R	R	R	R	R	P
Randolph	R	R	D	R	D	D	D	D	D	R	D	D
Richland	D	D	D	D	D	D	D	D	D	R	D	D
Rock Island	R	R	R	R	R	R	R	R	R	R	R	P
St. Clair	R	R	D	D	D	D	D	R	D	R	R	D
Saline	D	R	D	D	R	R	R	R	R	R	R	D
Sangamon	D	D	D	D	D	D	D	R	R	R	R	D
Schuyler	D	D	D	D	D	D	D	D	D	D	D	D
Scott	R	D	D	D	D	D	D	D	D	D	D	D
Shelby	D	D	D	D	D	D	D	D	D	R	D	D
Stark	R	R	R	R	R	R	R	R	R	R	R	P
Stephenson	R	R	R	R	R	R	D	R	R	R	R	D
Tazewell	D	R	D	D	D	D	D	D	D	R	D	D
Union	D	D	D	D	D	D	D	D	D	D	D	D
Vermilion	R	R	R	R	R	R	R	R	R	R	R	R
Wabash	D	D	D	D	D	D	D	D	D	D	D	D
Warren	R	R	R	R	R	R	R	R	R	R	R	P
Washington	R	R	R	R	R	R	R	R	R	R	R	D
Wayne	D	D	D	D	D	D	D	D	R	R	R	D
White	D	D	D	D	D	D	D	D	D	D	D	D
Whiteside	R	R	R	R	R	R	R	R	R	R	R	P
Will	R	R	R	R	R	R	R	R	R	R	R	P
Williamson	R	R	R	R	R	R	R	R	R	R	R	D
Winnebago	R	R	R	R	R	R	R	R	R	R	R	P
Woodford	D	D	D	D	D	D	D	T	D	R	R	D

County	1916	1920	1924	1928	1932	1936	1940	1944	1948	1952	1956	1960
Adams	D	R	R	R	D	D	R	R	D	R	R	R
Alexander	R	R	R	R	D	D	D	R	D	R	R	D
Bond	R	R	R	R	D	R	R	R	R	R	R	R
Boone	R	R	R	R	R	R	R	R	R	R	R	R
Brown	D	D	D	R	D	D	D	D	D	R	R	R
Bureau	R	R	R	R	D	R	R	R	R	R	R	R
Calhoun	D	R	R	R	D	D	R	R	R	R	R	R

County	1916	1920	1924	1928	1932	1936	1940	1944	1948	1952	1956	1960
Carroll	R	R	R	R	R	R	R	R	R	R	R	R
Cass	D	R	R	R	D	D	D	D	D	R	R	R
Champaign	R	R	R	R	D	D	R	R	R	R	R	R
Christian	D	R	R	R	D	D	D	D	D	R	R	D
Clark	D	R	R	R	D	D	R	R	R	R	R	R
Clay	R	R	R	R	D	D	R	R	R	R	R	R
Clinton	D	R	R	D	D	D	R	R	R	R	R	D
Coles	R	R	R	R	D	D	D	R	R	R	R	R
Cook	R	R	R	R	D	D	D	D	D	R	R	D
Crawford	D	R	R	R	D	D	R	R	R	R	R	R
Cumberland	D	R	R	R	D	D	R	R	R	R	R	R
De Kalb	R	R	R	R	R	R	R	R	R	R	R	R
De Witt	D	R	R	R	D	D	R	R	R	R	R	R
Douglas	R	R	R	R	D	D	R	R	R	R	R	R
Du Page	R	R	R	R	R	R	R	R	R	R	R	R
Edgar	D	R	R	R	D	D	R	R	R	R	R	R
Edwards	R	R	R	R	R	R	R	R	R	R	R	R
Effingham	D	R	D	D	D	D	D	R	D	R	R	R
Fayette	D	R	R	R	D	D	R	R	D	R	R	R
Ford	R	R	R	R	D	R	R	R	R	R	R	R
Franklin	D	R	R	D	D	D	D	D	D	D	R	R
Fulton	R	R	R	R	D	D	R	R	R	R	R	R
Gallatin	D	R	D	D	D	D	D	D	D	R	D	D
Greene	D	D	D	R	D	D	D	D	D	R	R	R
Grundy	R	R	R	R	D	R	R	R	R	R	R	R
Hamilton	D	R	D	R	D	D	R	R	R	R	R	R
Hancock	D	R	R	R	D	D	R	R	R	R	R	R
Hardin	R	R	R	R	D	R	R	R	R	R	R	R
Henderson	R	R	R	R	D	R	R	R	R	R	R	R
Henry	R	R	R	R	R	R	R	R	R	R	R	R
Iroquois	R	R	R	R	D	D	R	R	R	R	R	R
Jackson	R	R	R	R	D	R	R	R	R	R	R	R
Jasper	D	R	D	R	D	D	R	R	R	R	R	R
Jefferson	D	R	D	R	D	D	D	D	D	R	R	R
Jersey	D	R	D	R	D	D	R	R	D	R	R	R
Jo Daviess	R	R	R	R	D	R	R	R	R	R	R	R
Johnson	R	R	R	R	R	R	R	R	R	R	R	R
Kane	R	R	R	R	R	R	R	R	R	R	R	R
Kankakee	R	R	R	R	D	D	R	R	R	R	R	R
Kendall	R	R	R	R	R	R	R	R	R	R	R	R
Knox	R	R	R	R	D	R	R	R	R	R	R	R
Lake	R	R	R	R	R	R	R	R	R	R	R	R
La Salle	R	R	R	R	D	D	D	R	R	R	R	R
Lawrence	D	R	R	R	D	D	R	R	R	R	R	R
Lee	R	R	R	R	R	R	R	R	R	R	R	R
Livingston	R	R	R	R	D	R	R	R	R	R	R	R
Logan	R	R	R	R	D	D	R	R	R	R	R	R
McDonough	R	R	R	R	D	R	R	R	R	R	R	R
McHenry	R	R	R	R	R	R	R	R	R	R	R	R

County	1916	1920	1924	1928	1932	1936	1940	1944	1948	1952	1956	1960
McLean	R	R	R	R	D	D	R	R	R	R	R	R
Macon	R	R	R	R	D	D	D	D	D	R	R	R
Macoupin	D	R	R	D	D	D	D	D	D	D	D	D
Madison	R	R	R	R	D	D	D	D	D	D	D	D
Marion	D	R	R	R	D	D	D	D	D	R	R	R
Marshall	R	R	R	R	D	D	R	R	R	R	R	R
Mason	D	R	R	R	D	D	R	R	R	R	R	R
Massac	R	R	R	R	R	R	R	R	R	R	R	R
Menard	R	R	R	R	D	D	R	R	R	R	R	R
Mercer	R	R	R	R	R	R	R	R	R	R	R	R
Monroe	R	R	R	D	D	D	R	R	R	R	R	R
Montgomery	D	R	R	R	D	D	R	R	R	R	R	R
Morgan	R	R	R	R	D	D	R	R	R	R	R	R
Moultrie	D	R	R	R	D	D	D	R	R	R	R	R
Ogle	R	R	R	R	R	R	R	R	R	R	R	R
Peoria	D	R	R	R	D	D	D	R	R	R	R	R
Perry	R	R	R	D	D	D	R	R	R	R	R	R
Piatt	R	R	R	R	D	D	R	R	R	R	R	R
Pike	D	R	D	R	D	D	D	D	D	R	R	R
Pope	R	R	R	R	R	R	R	R	R	R	R	R
Pulaski	R	R	R	R	D	D	R	R	R	R	R	R
Putnam	R	R	R	R	D	D	R	R	R	R	R	R
Randolph	R	R	R	D	D	D	R	R	R	R	R	R
Richland	D	R	R	R	D	D	R	R	R	R	R	R
Rock Island	R	R	R	R	D	D	D	D	D	R	R	D
St. Clair	D	R	R	D	D	D	D	D	D	D	D	D
Saline	R	R	R	R	D	D	D	R	D	R	R	R
Sangamon	R	R	R	R	D	D	R	R	R	R	R	R
Schuyler	D	R	D	R	D	D	D	R	R	R	R	R
Scott	D	R	R	R	D	D	R	R	R	R	R	R
Shelby	D	R	R	R	D	D	D	R	D	R	R	R
Stark	R	R	R	R	D	R	R	R	R	R	R	R
Stephenson	R	R	R	R	D	D	R	R	R	R	R	R
Tazewell	D	R	R	R	D	D	D	R	D	R	R	R
Union	D	D	D	D	D	D	D	D	D	R	D	R
Vermilion	R	R	R	R	D	D	R	R	R	R	R	R
Wabash	D	R	R	D	D	D	D	R	R	R	R	R
Warren	R	R	R	R	D	R	R	R	R	R	R	R
Washington	R	R	R	R	D	R	R	R	R	R	R	R
Wayne	R	R	R	D	D	D	R	R	R	R	R	R
White	D	R	D	R	D	D	D	R	D	R	R	R
Whiteside	R	R	R	R	R	R	R	R	R	R	R	R
Will	R	R	R	R	D	D	R	R	R	R	R	R
Williamson	R	R	R	R	D	D	D	R	R	R	R	R
Winnebago	R	R	R	R	R	D	R	R	R	R	R	R
Woodford	R	R	R	R	D	D	R	R	R	R	R	R

County	1964	1968	1972	1976	1980	1984	1988	1992	1996	2000	2004
Adams	D	R	R	R	R	R	R	R	R	R	R
Alexander	D	D	R	D	D	D	D	D	D	D	D
Bond	D	R	R	R	R	R	R	D	D	R	R
Boone	R	R	R	R	R	R	R	R	R	R	R
Brown	D	R	R	D	R	R	R	D	R	R	R
Bureau	R	R	R	R	R	R	R	D	D	R	R
Calhoun	D	R	R	D	R	R	D	D	D	D	D
Carroll	R	R	R	R	R	R	R	R	R	R	R
Cass	D	R	R	D	R	R	D	D	D	R	R
Champaign	D	R	R	R	R	R	R	D	D	D	D
Christian	D	D	R	D	R	R	D	D	D	R	R
Clark	D	R	R	R	R	R	R	D	R	R	R
Clay	D	R	R	R	R	R	R	D	R	R	R
Clinton	D	R	R	R	R	R	R	D	D	R	R
Coles	D	R	R	R	R	R	R	D	D	R	R
Cook	D	D	R	D	D	D	D	D	D	D	D
Crawford	D	R	R	R	R	R	R	D	R	R	R
Cumberland	D	R	R	D	R	R	R	D	R	R	R
De Kalb	R	R	R	R	R	R	R	D	D	R	R
De Witt	D	R	R	R	R	R	R	R	R	R	R
Douglas	D	R	R	R	R	R	R	D	R	R	R
Du Page	R	R	R	R	R	R	R	R	R	R	R
Edgar	D	R	R	R	R	R	R	D	R	R	R
Edwards	R	R	R	R	R	R	R	R	R	R	R
Effingham	D	R	R	R	R	R	R	R	R	R	R
Fayette	D	R	R	D	R	R	R	D	D	R	R
Ford	R	R	R	R	R	R	R	R	R	R	R
Franklin	D	D	R	D	R	D	D	D	D	D	R
Fulton	D	D	R	R	R	R	D	D	D	D	D
Gallatin	D	D	R	D	R	D	D	D	D	D	R
Greene	D	R	R	D	R	R	R	D	D	R	R
Grundy	R	R	R	R	R	R	R	R	D	R	R
Hamilton	D	R	R	D	R	R	R	D	D	R	R
Hancock	D	R	R	R	R	R	D	D	D	R	R
Hardin	D	R	R	D	R	R	R	D	D	R	R
Henderson	D	R	R	R	R	R	D	D	D	D	D
Henry	D	R	R	R	R	R	D	D	D	D	R
Iroquois	R	R	R	R	R	R	R	R	R	R	R
Jackson	D	R	D	D	R	R	D	D	D	D	D
Jasper	D	R	R	R	R	R	R	D	R	R	R
Jefferson	D	R	R	D	R	R	D	D	D	R	R
Jersey	D	R	R	D	R	R	D	D	D	R	R
Jo Daviess	D	R	R	R	R	R	R	R	D	R	R
Johnson	R	R	R	R	R	R	R	D	R	R	R
Kane	R	R	R	R	R	R	R	R	R	R	R
Kankakee	D	R	R	R	R	R	R	D	D	R	R
Kendall	R	R	R	R	R	R	R	R	R	R	R
Knox	D	R	R	R	R	R	D	D	D	D	D
Lake	D	R	R	R	R	R	R	R	D	R	R

County	1964	1968	1972	1976	1980	1984	1988	1992	1996	2000	2004
La Salle	D	R	R	R	R	R	D	D	D	D	R
Lawrence	D	R	R	R	R	R	R	D	D	R	R
Lee	R	R	R	R	R	R	R	R	R	R	R
Livingston	R	R	R	R	R	R	R	R	R	R	R
Logan	D	R	R	R	R	R	R	R	R	R	R
McDonough	R	R	R	R	R	R	R	D	D	R	R
McHenry	R	R	R	R	R	R	R	R	R	R	R
McLean	D	R	R	R	R	R	R	R	R	R	R
Macon	D	D	R	D	R	R	D	D	D	D	R
Macoupin	D	D	R	D	R	R	D	D	D	D	R
Madison	D	D	R	D	R	R	D	D	D	D	D
Marion	D	R	R	D	R	R	R	D	D	R	R
Marshall	D	R	R	R	R	R	R	D	D	R	R
Mason	D	R	R	D	R	R	R	D	D	R	R
Massac	D	R	R	D	R	R	R	D	D	R	R
Menard	D	R	R	R	R	R	R	R	R	R	R
Mercer	D	R	R	R	R	R	D	D	D	D	D
Monroe	D	R	R	R	R	R	R	D	R	R	R
Montgomery	D	R	R	D	R	R	D	D	D	D	R
Morgan	D	R	R	R	R	R	R	R	R	R	R
Moultrie	D	R	R	D	R	R	R	D	D	R	R
Ogle	R	R	R	R	R	R	R	R	R	R	R
Peoria	D	R	R	R	R	R	R	D	D	D	D
Perry	D	R	R	D	R	R	D	D	D	D	R
Piatt	D	R	R	R	R	R	R	D	D	R	R
Pike	D	R	R	D	R	R	D	D	D	R	R
Pope	R	R	R	R	R	R	R	D	D	R	R
Pulaski	D	D	R	D	R	R	D	D	D	D	R
Putnam	D	R	R	R	R	R	D	D	D	D	D
Randolph	D	R	R	D	R	R	D	D	D	R	R
Richland	D	R	R	R	R	R	R	D	R	R	R
Rock Island	D	D	R	D	R	D	D	D	D	D	D
St. Clair	D	D	R	D	D	D	D	D	D	D	D
Saline	D	R	R	D	R	R	D	D	D	R	R
Sangamon	D	R	R	R	R	R	R	D	R	R	R
Schuyler	D	R	R	R	R	R	R	D	D	R	R
Scott	D	R	R	R	R	R	R	R	R	R	R
Shelby	D	R	R	D	R	R	R	D	D	R	R
Stark	R	R	R	R	R	R	R	R	R	R	R
Stephenson	D	R	R	R	R	R	R	R	R	R	R
Tazewell	D	R	R	R	R	R	R	D	R	R	R
Union	D	R	R	D	R	R	R	D	D	R	R
Vermilion	D	R	R	R	R	R	D	D	D	R	R
Wabash	D	R	R	R	R	R	R	R	R	R	R
Warren	R	R	R	R	R	R	R	D	D	R	R
Washington	R	R	R	R	R	R	R	R	R	R	R
Wayne	D	R	R	R	R	R	R	R	R	R	R
White	D	R	R	D	R	R	R	D	D	R	R
Whiteside	R	R	R	R	R	R	R	D	D	D	D

County	1964	1968	1972	1976	1980	1984	1988	1992	1996	2000	2004
Will	D	R	R	R	R	R	R	D	D	R	R
Williamson	D	R	R	D	R	R	D	D	D	R	R
Winnebago	D	R	R	R	R	R	R	D	D	R	R
Woodford	R	R	R	R	R	R	R	R	R	R	R

Indiana

County	1868	1872	1876	1880	1884	1888	1892	1896	1900	1904	1908	1912
Adams	D	D	D	D	D	D	D	D	D	D	D	D
Allen	D	D	D	D	D	D	D	D	D	R	D	D
Bartholomew	D	D	D	D	D	D	D	R	D	R	D	D
Benton	R	R	R	R	R	R	R	R	R	R	R	D
Blackford	D	D	D	D	D	D	D	D	D	R	D	D
Boone	R	R	R	R	D	R	R	D	D	R	D	D
Brown	D	D	D	D	D	D	D	D	D	D	D	D
Carroll	D	R	D	D	D	R	D	D	D	R	D	D
Cass	D	R	D	D	D	D	D	D	D	R	D	D
Clark	D	D	D	D	D	D	D	R	D	R	D	D
Clay	D	R	D	D	D	D	D	D	D	R	D	D
Clinton	R	R	D	D	D	R	R	D	R	R	D	D
Crawford	D	D	D	D	D	D	D	D	D	D	D	D
Daviess	D	R	D	D	D	R	R	D	D	R	R	D
Dearborn	D	D	D	D	D	D	D	D	D	D	D	D
Decatur	R	R	R	R	R	R	R	R	R	R	R	D
De Kalb	R	R	D	D	D	D	D	D	D	R	D	D
Delaware	R	R	R	R	R	R	R	R	R	R	R	D
Dubois	D	D	D	D	D	D	D	D	D	D	D	D
Elkhart	R	R	R	R	R	R	R	R	R	R	R	P
Fayette	R	R	R	R	R	R	R	R	R	R	R	D
Floyd	D	D	D	D	D	D	D	R	D	R	D	D
Fountain	D	R	R	D	D	R	R	D	R	R	R	D
Franklin	D	D	D	D	D	D	D	D	D	D	D	D
Fulton	D	R	D	D	D	D	D	D	D	R	R	D
Gibson	R	R	D	R	R	R	R	D	R	R	R	D
Grant	R	R	R	R	R	R	R	R	R	R	R	D
Greene	R	R	R	R	R	R	R	R	R	R	D	D
Hamilton	R	R	R	R	R	R	R	R	R	R	R	D
Hancock	D	D	D	D	D	D	D	D	D	D	D	D
Harrison	D	D	D	D	D	D	D	D	D	R	D	D
Hendricks	R	R	R	R	R	R	R	R	R	R	R	D
Henry	R	R	R	R	R	R	R	R	R	R	R	D
Howard	R	R	R	R	R	R	R	R	R	R	R	D
Huntington	R	R	D	D	D	R	D	R	R	R	R	D
Jackson	D	D	D	D	D	D	D	D	D	D	D	D
Jasper	R	R	R	R	R	R	R	R	R	R	R	D

County	1868	1872	1876	1880	1884	1888	1892	1896	1900	1904	1908	1912
Jay	R	R	D	R	R	R	R	D	R	R	D	D
Jefferson	R	R	R	R	R	R	R	R	R	R	R	D
Jennings	R	R	R	R	R	R	R	R	R	R	R	D
Johnson	D	D	D	D	D	D	D	D	D	D	D	D
Knox	D	D	D	D	D	D	D	D	D	R	D	D
Kosciusko	R	R	R	R	R	R	R	R	R	R	R	D
Lagrange	R	R	R	R	R	R	R	R	R	R	R	P
Lake	R	R	R	R	R	R	D	R	R	R	R	P
La Porte	R	R	D	D	D	D	D	R	R	R	R	D
Lawrence	R	R	R	R	R	R	R	R	R	R	R	D
Madison	D	D	D	D	D	D	D	R	R	R	D	D
Marion	R	R	R	R	R	D	D	R	R	R	R	D
Marshall	D	R	D	D	D	D	D	D	D	R	D	D
Martin	D	D	D	D	D	D	D	D	R	R	D	D
Miami	D	R	D	D	D	D	D	D	D	R	D	D
Monroe	R	R	R	R	R	R	R	R	R	R	R	D
Montgomery	D	R	D	R	R	R	D	R	R	R	D	D
Morgan	R	R	R	R	R	R	R	R	R	R	R	D
Newton	R	R	R	R	R	R	R	R	R	R	R	D
Noble	R	R	D	T	R	R	D	R	R	R	R	D
Ohio	R	R	R	R	R	R	R	R	R	R	D	D
Orange	D	D	D	D	D	R	R	R	R	R	R	D
Owen	D	D	D	D	D	D	D	D	D	D	D	D
Parke	R	R	R	R	R	R	R	R	R	R	R	D
Perry	D	R	D	D	D	D	D	R	D	D	D	D
Pike	R	R	D	D	D	R	R	D	D	R	D	D
Porter	R	R	R	R	R	R	R	R	R	R	R	R
Posey	D	D	D	D	D	D	D	D	D	D	D	D
Pulaski	D	R	D	D	D	D	D	D	D	R	D	D
Putnam	D	D	D	D	D	D	D	D	D	D	D	D
Randolph	R	R	R	R	R	R	R	R	R	R	R	P
Ripley	R	D	D	D	D	R	D	D	R	R	D	D
Rush	R	R	R	R	R	R	R	R	R	R	R	D
St. Joseph	R	R	R	R	D	D	D	R	R	R	R	D
Scott	D	D	D	D	D	D	D	D	D	D	D	D
Shelby	D	D	D	D	D	D	D	D	D	R	D	D
Spencer	R	R	D	D	D	R	D	R	R	R	R	D
Starke	D	D	D	D	D	D	D	R	R	R	R	D
Steuben	R	R	R	R	R	R	R	R	R	R	R	R
Sullivan	D	D	D	D	D	D	D	D	D	D	D	R
Switzerland	R	R	R	R	R	D	D	D	D	D	D	D
Tippecanoe	R	R	R	R	R	R	R	R	R	R	R	D
Tipton	D	D	D	D	D	D	D	D	D	R	D	D
Union	R	R	R	R	R	R	R	R	R	R	R	D
Vanderburgh	R	R	D	R	D	R	R	R	R	R	R	D
Vermillion	R	R	R	R	R	R	R	R	R	R	R	D
Vigo	R	R	D	R	R	R	D	R	R	R	D	D
Wabash	R	R	R	R	R	R	R	R	R	R	R	P
Warren	R	R	R	R	R	R	R	R	R	R	R	R

County	1868	1872	1876	1880	1884	1888	1892	1896	1900	1904	1908	1912
Warrick	D	D	D	D	D	D	D	D	D	R	R	D
Washington	D	D	D	D	D	D	D	D	D	D	D	D
Wayne	R	R	R	R	R	R	R	R	R	R	R	P
Wells	D	D	D	D	D	D	D	D	D	D	D	D
White	R	R	R	R	D	D	D	D	R	R	R	D
Whitley	D	D	D	D	D	D	D	D	D	R	D	D

County	1916	1920	1924	1928	1932	1936	1940	1944	1948	1952	1956	1960
Adams	D	R	D	D	D	D	R	R	R	R	R	R
Allen	R	R	R	R	D	D	R	R	R	R	R	R
Bartholomew	D	R	R	R	D	D	D	R	D	R	R	R
Benton	R	R	R	R	D	D	R	R	R	R	R	R
Blackford	D	R	R	R	D	D	D	D	D	R	R	R
Boone	D	R	R	R	D	D	R	R	R	R	R	R
Brown	D	D	D	D	D	D	D	D	D	R	R	R
Carroll	R	R	R	R	D	D	R	R	R	R	R	R
Cass	D	R	R	R	D	D	D	R	D	R	R	R
Clark	D	D	R	R	D	D	D	D	D	D	R	D
Clay	D	R	R	R	D	D	R	R	D	R	R	R
Clinton	D	R	R	R	D	D	R	R	D	R	R	R
Crawford	D	R	D	R	D	D	D	R	D	R	R	R
Daviess	R	R	R	R	D	D	R	R	R	R	R	R
Dearborn	D	R	R	R	D	D	D	R	D	R	R	R
Decatur	R	R	R	R	D	R	R	R	R	R	R	R
De Kalb	D	R	R	R	D	D	R	R	R	R	R	R
Delaware	R	R	R	R	R	D	D	D	D	R	R	R
Dubois	D	D	D	D	D	D	D	D	D	R	R	D
Elkhart	R	R	R	R	D	R	R	R	R	R	R	R
Fayette	R	R	R	R	D	D	R	R	D	R	R	R
Floyd	D	R	D	R	D	D	D	D	D	R	R	D
Fountain	R	R	R	R	D	D	R	R	R	R	R	R
Franklin	D	D	D	D	D	D	R	R	R	R	R	R
Fulton	R	R	R	R	D	R	R	R	R	R	R	R
Gibson	D	R	R	R	D	D	D	R	D	R	R	R
Grant	R	R	R	R	D	D	R	R	R	R	R	R
Greene	D	R	R	R	D	D	R	R	D	R	R	R
Hamilton	R	R	R	R	R	R	R	R	R	R	R	R
Hancock	D	D	D	R	D	D	D	R	D	R	R	R
Harrison	D	R	D	R	D	D	D	R	D	R	R	R
Hendricks	R	R	R	R	R	R	R	R	R	R	R	R
Henry	R	R	R	R	R	D	R	R	R	R	R	R
Howard	R	R	R	R	D	D	D	R	D	R	R	R
Huntington	D	R	R	R	D	D	R	R	R	R	R	R
Jackson	D	D	D	R	D	D	D	R	D	R	R	R
Jasper	R	R	R	R	D	R	R	R	R	R	R	R
Jay	R	R	R	R	D	D	D	R	R	R	R	R
Jefferson	R	R	R	R	D	R	R	R	R	R	R	R
Jennings	R	R	R	R	D	R	R	R	R	R	R	R

County	1916	1920	1924	1928	1932	1936	1940	1944	1948	1952	1956	1960
Johnson	D	D	R	R	D	D	R	R	D	R	R	R
Knox	D	R	D	R	D	D	D	D	D	R	R	R
Kosciusko	R	R	R	R	D	R	R	R	R	R	R	R
Lagrange	R	R	R	R	D	R	R	R	R	R	R	R
Lake	R	R	R	R	D	D	D	D	D	D	R	D
La Porte	R	R	R	R	D	D	R	R	R	R	R	R
Lawrence	R	R	R	R	R	R	R	R	R	R	R	R
Madison	D	R	R	R	D	D	D	D	D	R	R	R
Marion	R	R	R	R	D	D	R	R	R	R	R	R
Marshall	D	R	R	R	D	D	R	R	R	R	R	R
Martin	D	R	D	R	D	D	R	R	D	D	R	R
Miami	D	R	R	R	D	D	R	R	R	R	R	R
Monroe	R	R	R	R	D	D	R	R	R	R	R	R
Montgomery	R	R	R	R	D	D	R	R	R	R	R	R
Morgan	R	R	R	R	D	R	R	R	R	R	R	R
Newton	R	R	R	R	D	R	R	R	R	R	R	R
Noble	R	R	R	R	D	D	R	R	R	R	R	R
Ohio	D	R	D	R	D	D	D	R	D	R	R	R
Orange	R	R	R	R	D	R	R	R	R	R	R	R
Owen	D	R	D	R	D	D	R	R	R	R	R	R
Parke	R	R	R	R	D	D	R	R	R	R	R	R
Perry	D	R	D	D	D	D	R	R	D	R	R	D
Pike	D	R	R	R	D	D	R	R	R	R	R	R
Porter	R	R	R	R	R	R	R	R	R	R	R	R
Posey	D	R	R	R	D	D	D	R	D	R	R	R
Pulaski	R	R	R	R	D	D	R	R	R	R	R	R
Putnam	D	D	R	R	D	D	D	R	R	R	R	R
Randolph	R	R	R	R	R	R	R	R	R	R	R	R
Ripley	R	R	R	R	D	D	R	R	R	R	R	R
Rush	R	R	R	R	R	D	R	R	R	R	R	R
St. Joseph	D	R	R	R	D	D	D	D	D	R	R	D
Scott	D	D	D	R	D	D	D	D	D	R	R	R
Shelby	D	D	R	R	D	D	D	R	R	R	R	R
Spencer	R	R	D	R	D	D	R	R	D	R	R	R
Starke	R	R	R	R	D	D	R	R	R	R	R	R
Steuben	R	R	R	R	D	R	R	R	R	R	R	R
Sullivan	D	D	D	R	D	D	D	D	D	D	D	R
Switzerland	D	R	D	R	D	D	D	D	D	D	D	D
Tippecanoe	R	R	R	R	D	R	R	R	R	R	R	R
Tipton	D	R	R	R	D	D	R	R	R	R	R	R
Union	R	R	R	R	R	D	R	R	R	R	R	R
Vanderburgh	D	R	R	R	D	D	D	D	D	R	R	R
Vermillion	R	R	R	R	D	D	D	D	R	D	R	D
Vigo	D	R	R	R	D	D	D	D	D	D	R	D
Wabash	R	R	R	R	R	R	R	R	R	R	R	R
Warren	R	R	R	R	D	R	R	R	R	R	R	R
Warrick	R	R	R	R	D	D	R	R	D	R	R	R
Washington	D	D	D	R	D	D	D	R	D	R	R	R
Wayne	R	R	R	R	D	D	R	R	R	R	R	R

County	1916	1920	1924	1928	1932	1936	1940	1944	1948	1952	1956	1960
Wells	D	D	D	D	D	D	D	R	D	R	R	R
White	R	R	R	R	D	D	R	R	R	R	R	R
Whitley	D	R	R	R	D	D	R	R	R	R	R	R

County	1964	1968	1972	1976	1980	1984	1988	1992	1996	2000	2004
Adams	D	R	R	R	R	R	R	R	R	R	R
Allen	D	R	R	R	R	R	R	R	R	R	R
Bartholomew	D	R	R	R	R	R	R	R	R	R	R
Benton	D	R	R	R	R	R	R	R	R	R	R
Blackford	D	R	R	D	R	R	R	R	D	R	R
Boone	R	R	R	R	R	R	R	R	R	R	R
Brown	D	R	R	R	R	R	R	R	R	R	R
Carroll	D	R	R	R	R	R	R	R	R	R	R
Cass	D	R	R	R	R	R	R	R	R	R	R
Clark	D	D	R	D	R	R	R	D	D	R	R
Clay	D	R	R	R	R	R	R	R	R	R	R
Clinton	D	R	R	R	R	R	R	R	R	R	R
Crawford	D	R	R	D	R	R	R	D	D	R	R
Daviess	D	R	R	R	R	R	R	R	R	R	R
Dearborn	D	R	R	D	R	R	R	R	R	R	R
Decatur	D	R	R	R	R	R	R	R	R	R	R
De Kalb	D	R	R	R	R	R	R	R	R	R	R
Delaware	D	R	R	R	R	R	R	R	D	R	R
Dubois	D	D	R	D	R	R	R	R	R	R	R
Elkhart	D	R	R	R	R	R	R	R	R	R	R
Fayette	D	R	R	R	R	R	R	R	R	R	R
Floyd	D	D	R	D	R	R	R	D	D	R	R
Fountain	D	R	R	R	R	R	R	R	R	R	R
Franklin	D	R	R	R	R	R	R	R	R	R	R
Fulton	R	R	R	R	R	R	R	R	R	R	R
Gibson	D	R	R	D	R	R	R	D	D	R	R
Grant	D	R	R	R	R	R	R	R	R	R	R
Greene	D	R	R	D	R	R	R	D	R	R	R
Hamilton	R	R	R	R	R	R	R	R	R	R	R
Hancock	D	R	R	R	R	R	R	R	R	R	R
Harrison	D	R	R	D	R	R	R	D	R	R	R
Hendricks	R	R	R	R	R	R	R	R	R	R	R
Henry	D	R	R	R	R	R	R	R	R	R	R
Howard	D	R	R	R	R	R	R	R	R	R	R
Huntington	D	R	R	R	R	R	R	R	R	R	R
Jackson	D	R	R	R	R	R	R	R	R	R	R
Jasper	R	R	R	R	R	R	R	R	R	R	R
Jay	D	R	R	R	R	R	R	R	R	R	R
Jefferson	D	R	R	D	R	R	R	D	D	R	R
Jennings	D	R	R	R	R	R	R	R	R	R	R
Johnson	R	R	R	R	R	R	R	R	R	R	R
Knox	D	R	R	D	R	R	R	D	D	R	R
Kosciusko	R	R	R	R	R	R	R	R	R	R	R

County	1964	1968	1972	1976	1980	1984	1988	1992	1996	2000	2004
Lagrange	D	R	R	R	R	R	R	R	R	R	R
Lake	D	D	R	D	D	D	D	D	D	D	D
La Porte	D	R	R	R	R	R	R	D	D	R	D
Lawrence	D	R	R	R	R	R	R	R	R	R	R
Madison	D	R	R	R	R	R	R	R	D	R	R
Marion	D	R	R	R	R	R	R	R	R	R	D
Marshall	D	R	R	R	R	R	R	R	R	R	R
Martin	D	R	R	D	R	R	R	R	R	R	R
Miami	D	R	R	R	R	R	R	R	R	R	R
Monroe	D	R	R	R	R	R	R	D	D	R	D
Montgomery	D	R	R	R	R	R	R	R	R	R	R
Morgan	R	R	R	R	R	R	R	R	R	R	R
Newton	R	R	R	R	R	R	R	R	R	R	R
Noble	D	R	R	R	R	R	R	R	R	R	R
Ohio	D	R	R	D	R	R	R	R	R	R	R
Orange	D	R	R	R	R	R	R	R	R	R	R
Owen	D	R	R	D	R	R	R	R	R	R	R
Parke	D	R	R	R	R	R	R	R	R	R	R
Perry	D	D	R	D	D	R	D	D	D	D	R
Pike	D	R	R	D	D	R	R	D	D	R	R
Porter	R	R	R	R	R	R	R	R	D	R	R
Posey	D	R	R	D	R	R	R	D	D	R	R
Pulaski	D	R	R	R	R	R	R	R	R	R	R
Putnam	D	R	R	R	R	R	R	R	R	R	R
Randolph	D	R	R	R	R	R	R	R	R	R	R
Ripley	D	R	R	R	R	R	R	R	R	R	R
Rush	R	R	R	R	R	R	R	R	R	R	R
St. Joseph	D	D	R	R	R	R	R	D	D	D	R
Scott	D	D	R	D	D	R	R	D	D	D	R
Shelby	D	R	R	R	R	R	R	R	R	R	R
Spencer	D	R	R	D	R	R	R	D	D	R	R
Starke	D	R	R	D	R	R	R	D	D	R	R
Steuben	R	R	R	R	R	R	R	R	R	R	R
Sullivan	D	D	R	D	R	R	D	D	D	R	R
Switzerland	D	R	R	D	D	R	R	D	D	R	R
Tippecanoe	D	R	R	R	R	R	R	R	R	R	R
Tipton	D	R	R	R	R	R	R	R	R	R	R
Union	R	R	R	R	R	R	R	R	R	R	R
Vanderburgh	D	R	R	R	R	R	R	D	D	R	R
Vermillion	D	D	R	D	R	R	D	D	D	D	R
Vigo	D	R	R	D	R	R	R	D	D	R	R
Wabash	D	R	R	R	R	R	R	R	R	R	R
Warren	D	R	R	R	R	R	R	R	R	R	R
Warrick	D	R	R	D	R	R	R	D	D	R	R
Washington	D	R	R	D	R	R	R	D	R	R	R
Wayne	R	R	R	R	R	R	R	R	R	R	R
Wells	D	R	R	R	R	R	R	R	R	R	R
White	D	R	R	R	R	R	R	R	R	R	R
Whitley	D	R	R	R	R	R	R	R	R	R	R

Iowa

County	1868	1872	1876	1880	1884	1888	1892	1896	1900	1904	1908	1912
Adair	R	R	R	R	R	R	R	R	R	R	R	R
Adams	R	R	R	R	R	R	R	R	R	R	R	D
Allamakee	R	R	R	R	D	D	D	R	R	R	R	D
Appanoose	R	R	R	R	D	R	R	R	R	R	R	R
Audubon	T	R	R	R	R	R	D	R	R	R	R	P
Benton	R	R	R	R	R	R	D	R	R	R	R	D
Black Hawk	R	R	R	R	R	R	R	R	R	R	R	P
Boone	R	R	R	R	R	R	R	R	R	R	R	P
Bremer	R	R	R	R	R	D	D	R	R	R	D	D
Buchanan	R	R	R	R	R	R	R	R	R	R	R	D
Buena Vista	R	R	R	R	R	R	R	R	R	R	R	P
Butler	R	R	R	R	R	R	R	R	R	R	R	P
Calhoun	R	R	R	R	R	R	R	R	R	R	R	P
Carroll	R	R	R	R	D	D	D	D	D	R	D	D
Cass	R	R	R	R	R	R	R	R	R	R	R	R
Cedar	R	R	R	R	R	R	D	R	R	R	R	D
Cerro Gordo	R	R	R	R	R	R	R	R	R	R	R	P
Cherokee	R	R	R	R	R	R	R	R	R	R	R	P
Chickasaw	R	R	R	R	D	D	D	D	R	R	D	D
Clarke	R	R	R	R	R	R	R	R	R	R	R	D
Clay	R	R	R	R	R	R	R	R	R	R	R	P
Clayton	R	R	R	R	D	D	D	R	R	R	D	D
Clinton	R	R	R	R	D	D	D	R	R	R	R	D
Crawford	R	R	R	R	D	D	D	D	D	R	D	D
Dallas	R	R	R	R	R	R	R	R	R	R	R	R
Davis	R	R	D	G	D	D	D	D	D	R	D	D
Decatur	R	R	R	R	R	R	R	D	R	R	R	D
Delaware	R	R	R	R	R	R	R	R	R	R	R	D
Des Moines	R	R	R	R	D	D	D	R	R	R	R	D
Dickinson	R	R	R	R	R	R	R	R	R	R	R	P
Dubuque	D	D	D	D	D	D	D	D	D	R	D	D
Emmet	R	R	R	R	R	R	R	R	R	R	R	P
Fayette	R	R	R	R	R	R	R	R	R	R	R	D
Floyd	R	R	R	R	R	R	R	R	R	R	R	P
Franklin	R	R	R	R	R	R	R	R	R	R	R	P
Fremont	D	D	D	R	D	D	D	D	D	R	D	D
Greene	R	R	R	R	R	R	R	R	R	R	R	R
Grundy	R	R	R	R	R	R	R	R	R	R	R	P
Guthrie	R	R	R	R	R	R	R	R	R	R	R	D
Hamilton	R	R	R	R	R	R	R	R	R	R	R	P
Hancock	R	R	R	R	R	R	R	R	R	R	R	P
Hardin	R	R	R	R	R	R	R	R	R	R	R	P
Harrison	R	R	R	R	R	R	R	D	R	R	R	D
Henry	R	R	R	R	R	R	R	R	R	R	R	R
Howard	R	R	R	R	R	R	R	R	R	R	R	D

County	1868	1872	1876	1880	1884	1888	1892	1896	1900	1904	1908	1912
Humboldt	R	R	R	R	R	R	R	R	R	R	R	P
Ida	R	R	R	R	R	R	R	R	R	R	R	P
Iowa	R	R	R	R	D	D	D	R	R	R	R	D
Jackson	D	R	D	D	D	D	D	D	R	R	D	D
Jasper	R	R	R	R	R	R	R	R	R	R	R	D
Jefferson	R	R	R	R	R	R	R	R	R	R	R	R
Johnson	R	R	D	D	D	D	D	D	D	D	D	D
Jones	R	R	R	R	R	R	D	R	R	R	R	D
Keokuk	R	R	R	R	D	R	D	R	R	R	R	D
Kossuth	R	R	R	R	R	R	R	R	R	R	R	P
Lee	D	R	D	D	D	D	D	D	D	R	D	D
Linn	R	R	R	R	R	R	R	R	R	R	R	D
Louisa	R	R	R	R	R	R	R	R	R	R	R	R
Lucas	R	R	R	R	R	R	R	R	R	R	R	D
Lyon	–	R	R	R	R	R	D	R	R	R	R	P
Madison	R	R	R	R	R	R	R	R	R	R	R	R
Mahaska	R	R	R	R	R	R	R	R	R	R	R	D
Marion	R	R	R	R	D	R	D	D	T	R	D	D
Marshall	R	R	R	R	R	R	R	R	R	R	R	P
Mills	R	R	R	R	R	R	R	R	R	R	R	D
Mitchell	R	R	R	R	R	R	R	R	R	R	R	P
Monona	R	R	R	R	R	R	D	D	R	R	R	D
Monroe	R	R	R	R	R	R	D	D	R	R	R	P
Montgomery	R	R	R	R	R	R	R	R	R	R	R	P
Muscatine	R	R	R	R	D	D	D	R	R	R	R	P
O'Brien	R	R	R	R	R	R	R	R	R	R	R	P
Osceola	–	R	R	R	R	R	R	R	R	R	R	D
Page	R	R	R	R	R	R	R	R	R	R	R	P
Palo Alto	D	R	R	R	D	D	R	R	R	R	R	D
Plymouth	R	R	R	R	D	D	D	R	R	R	R	D
Pocahontas	R	R	R	R	R	R	R	R	R	R	R	P
Polk	R	R	R	R	R	R	R	R	R	R	R	P
Pottawat-tamie	R	R	R	R	D	D	D	R	R	R	R	D
Poweshiek	R	R	R	R	R	R	R	R	R	R	R	P
Ringgold	R	R	R	R	R	R	R	R	R	R	R	D
Sac	R	R	R	R	R	R	R	R	R	R	R	P
Scott	R	D	R	R	D	D	D	R	R	R	R	D
Shelby	R	R	R	R	R	D	D	D	R	R	R	D
Sioux	R	R	R	R	R	R	R	R	R	R	R	P
Story	R	R	R	R	R	R	R	R	R	R	R	P
Tama	R	R	R	R	R	D	D	R	R	R	R	D
Taylor	R	R	R	R	R	R	R	R	R	R	R	D
Union	R	R	R	R	R	R	R	D	R	R	R	D
Van Buren	R	R	R	R	R	R	R	R	R	R	R	D
Wapello	R	R	R	R	R	R	R	R	R	R	R	D
Warren	R	R	R	R	R	R	R	R	R	R	R	D
Washington	R	R	R	R	R	R	R	R	R	R	R	D
Wayne	R	R	R	R	D	R	R	D	R	R	R	D

County	1868	1872	1876	1880	1884	1888	1892	1896	1900	1904	1908	1912
Webster	R	R	R	R	R	R	R	R	R	R	R	D
Winnebago	R	R	R	R	R	R	R	R	R	R	R	P
Winneshiek	R	R	R	R	R	R	R	R	R	R	R	P
Woodbury	R	R	R	R	R	R	R	R	R	R	R	P
Worth	R	R	R	R	R	R	R	R	R	R	R	P
Wright	R	R	R	R	R	R	R	R	R	R	R	P

County	1916	1920	1924	1928	1932	1936	1940	1944	1948	1952	1956	1960
Adair	R	R	R	R	D	R	R	R	R	R	R	R
Adams	R	R	R	R	D	R	R	R	R	R	R	R
Allamakee	R	R	P	R	D	D	R	R	R	R	R	R
Appanoose	R	R	R	R	D	D	D	D	D	R	R	R
Audubon	R	R	R	D	D	D	D	D	D	R	R	R
Benton	R	R	R	R	D	D	D	D	D	R	R	R
Black Hawk	R	R	R	R	R	D	D	D	D	R	R	R
Boone	R	R	R	R	D	D	D	D	D	R	R	R
Bremer	R	R	R	R	D	D	R	R	R	R	R	R
Buchanan	R	R	R	R	D	D	R	R	R	R	R	R
Buena Vista	R	R	R	R	D	D	D	D	D	R	R	R
Butler	R	R	R	R	D	D	R	R	R	R	R	R
Calhoun	R	R	R	R	D	D	D	D	D	R	R	R
Carroll	R	R	R	D	D	D	D	R	D	R	R	D
Cass	R	R	R	R	D	R	R	R	R	R	R	R
Cedar	R	R	R	R	D	D	R	R	R	R	R	R
Cerro Gordo	R	R	R	R	D	D	D	D	D	R	R	R
Cherokee	D	R	R	R	D	D	R	R	D	R	R	R
Chickasaw	R	R	R	R	D	D	R	R	D	R	R	D
Clarke	R	R	R	R	D	D	R	R	R	R	R	R
Clay	R	R	R	R	D	D	D	D	D	R	R	R
Clayton	R	R	P	R	D	D	R	R	R	R	R	R
Clinton	R	R	R	R	D	D	R	R	R	R	R	R
Crawford	R	R	P	D	D	D	R	R	D	R	R	R
Dallas	R	R	R	R	D	D	D	R	R	R	R	R
Davis	D	R	R	R	D	D	D	D	D	R	R	R
Decatur	D	R	R	R	D	D	D	D	D	R	R	R
Delaware	R	R	R	R	D	R	R	R	R	R	R	R
Des Moines	R	R	R	R	D	D	R	R	D	R	R	R
Dickinson	R	R	R	R	D	D	D	D	D	R	R	R
Dubuque	D	R	P	D	D	D	R	D	D	R	R	D
Emmet	R	R	R	R	D	D	D	R	R	R	R	R
Fayette	R	R	R	R	D	D	R	R	R	R	R	R
Floyd	R	R	R	R	D	R	R	R	R	R	R	R
Franklin	R	R	R	R	D	D	R	R	R	R	R	R
Fremont	D	R	R	R	D	D	D	R	R	R	R	R
Greene	R	R	R	R	D	D	R	R	R	R	R	R
Grundy	R	R	R	R	D	D	R	R	R	R	R	R
Guthrie	R	R	R	R	D	R	R	R	R	R	R	R
Hamilton	R	R	R	R	D	D	D	D	D	R	R	R

County	1916	1920	1924	1928	1932	1936	1940	1944	1948	1952	1956	1960
Hancock	R	R	R	R	D	D	R	R	D	R	R	R
Hardin	R	R	R	R	D	D	R	R	R	R	R	R
Harrison	D	R	R	R	D	D	R	R	D	R	R	R
Henry	R	R	R	R	D	R	R	R	R	R	R	R
Howard	R	R	R	R	D	D	R	D	D	R	R	D
Humboldt	R	R	R	R	D	D	D	D	D	R	R	R
Ida	R	R	R	R	D	D	R	R	D	R	R	R
Iowa	R	R	R	R	D	D	R	R	R	R	R	R
Jackson	R	R	R	R	D	D	R	R	R	R	R	R
Jasper	D	R	R	R	D	D	D	D	D	R	R	R
Jefferson	R	R	R	R	D	R	R	R	R	R	R	R
Johnson	D	R	R	R	D	D	D	D	D	R	R	R
Jones	R	R	R	R	D	D	R	R	R	R	R	R
Keokuk	R	R	R	R	D	D	D	D	D	R	R	R
Kossuth	R	R	R	R	D	D	D	D	D	R	R	R
Lee	R	R	R	R	D	D	R	R	D	R	R	R
Linn	R	R	R	R	R	D	R	R	R	R	R	R
Louisa	R	R	R	R	D	D	R	R	R	R	R	R
Lucas	R	R	R	R	D	D	R	R	R	R	R	R
Lyon	R	R	P	R	D	D	R	R	R	R	R	R
Madison	R	R	R	R	D	R	R	R	R	R	R	R
Mahaska	D	R	R	R	D	D	R	R	D	R	R	R
Marion	D	R	R	R	D	D	D	D	D	R	R	R
Marshall	R	R	R	R	R	R	R	R	R	R	R	R
Mills	R	R	R	R	D	D	R	R	R	R	R	R
Mitchell	R	R	R	R	D	D	R	R	R	R	R	R
Monona	D	R	R	R	D	D	D	D	D	R	R	R
Monroe	R	R	R	R	D	D	D	D	D	R	R	R
Montgomery	R	R	R	R	D	R	R	R	R	R	R	R
Muscatine	R	R	R	R	D	D	R	R	R	R	R	R
O'Brien	R	R	R	R	D	D	R	R	R	R	R	R
Osceola	R	R	R	R	D	D	R	R	D	R	R	R
Page	R	R	R	R	D	R	R	R	R	R	R	R
Palo Alto	D	R	R	R	D	D	D	D	D	R	R	D
Plymouth	R	R	R	D	D	D	R	R	R	R	R	R
Pocahontas	R	R	P	R	D	D	D	D	D	R	R	R
Polk	R	R	R	R	R	D	D	D	D	R	R	R
Pottawat-tamie	D	R	R	R	D	D	R	R	R	R	R	R
Poweshiek	R	R	R	R	D	D	D	D	D	R	R	R
Ringgold	R	R	R	R	D	R	R	R	R	R	R	R
Sac	R	R	R	R	D	D	R	R	D	R	R	R
Scott	R	R	R	R	D	D	D	D	R	R	R	R
Shelby	D	R	R	D	D	D	R	R	D	R	R	R
Sioux	R	R	R	R	D	D	R	R	R	R	R	R
Story	R	R	R	R	R	D	R	R	R	R	R	R
Tama	R	R	R	R	D	D	D	D	D	R	R	R
Taylor	R	R	R	R	D	R	R	R	R	R	R	R
Union	R	R	R	R	D	R	R	R	R	R	R	R

County	1916	1920	1924	1928	1932	1936	1940	1944	1948	1952	1956	1960
Van Buren	R	R	R	R	D	R	R	R	R	R	R	R
Wapello	R	R	R	R	D	D	D	D	D	R	D	D
Warren	R	R	R	R	R	R	R	R	R	R	R	R
Washington	R	R	R	R	D	R	R	R	R	R	R	R
Wayne	R	R	R	R	D	D	R	R	D	R	R	R
Webster	R	R	R	R	D	D	D	D	D	R	R	R
Winnebago	R	R	P	R	D	D	R	R	R	R	R	R
Winneshiek	R	R	R	R	D	D	R	R	D	R	R	R
Woodbury	D	R	R	R	D	D	D	D	D	R	R	R
Worth	R	R	R	R	D	D	D	D	D	R	R	R
Wright	R	R	R	R	D	D	D	D	D	R	R	R

County	1964	1968	1972	1976	1980	1984	1988	1992	1996	2000	2004
Adair	D	R	R	R	R	R	D	R	D	R	R
Adams	D	R	R	D	R	R	D	D	D	R	R
Allamakee	R	R	R	R	R	R	R	R	D	R	R
Appanoose	D	R	R	D	R	R	D	D	D	R	R
Audubon	D	R	R	D	R	R	D	D	D	R	R
Benton	D	R	R	D	R	R	D	D	D	D	D
Black Hawk	D	R	R	R	R	R	D	D	D	D	D
Boone	D	R	R	D	R	D	D	D	D	D	D
Bremer	D	R	R	R	R	R	R	D	D	R	R
Buchanan	D	R	R	R	R	R	D	D	D	D	D
Buena Vista	D	R	R	R	R	R	D	R	R	R	R
Butler	R	R	R	R	R	R	R	R	D	R	R
Calhoun	D	R	R	R	R	R	D	R	D	R	R
Carroll	D	D	D	D	R	R	D	D	D	R	R
Cass	R	R	R	R	R	R	R	R	R	R	R
Cedar	D	R	R	R	R	R	D	D	D	D	R
Cerro Gordo	D	R	R	D	R	D	D	D	D	D	D
Cherokee	D	R	R	R	R	R	D	R	D	R	R
Chickasaw	D	R	R	D	R	R	D	D	D	D	D
Clarke	D	R	R	D	R	R	D	D	D	D	D
Clay	D	R	R	R	R	R	D	D	D	R	R
Clayton	D	R	R	R	R	R	D	D	D	D	D
Clinton	D	R	R	R	R	R	D	D	D	D	D
Crawford	D	R	R	D	R	R	D	D	D	R	R
Dallas	D	R	R	D	R	D	D	D	D	R	R
Davis	D	R	R	D	R	D	D	D	D	R	R
Decatur	D	R	R	D	R	R	D	D	D	R	R
Delaware	D	R	R	R	R	R	D	R	D	R	R
Des Moines	D	D	R	D	D	D	D	D	D	D	D
Dickinson	D	R	R	R	R	R	R	R	D	R	R
Dubuque	D	D	D	D	D	D	D	D	D	D	D
Emmet	D	R	R	R	R	R	D	D	D	R	R
Fayette	D	R	R	R	R	R	D	D	D	R	D
Floyd	D	R	R	D	R	R	D	D	D	D	D
Franklin	D	R	R	R	R	R	D	R	D	R	R

County	1964	1968	1972	1976	1980	1984	1988	1992	1996	2000	2004
Fremont	D	R	R	R	R	R	R	R	R	R	R
Greene	D	R	R	D	R	D	D	D	D	D	R
Grundy	D	R	R	R	R	R	R	R	R	R	R
Guthrie	D	R	R	D	R	R	D	D	D	R	R
Hamilton	D	R	R	D	R	R	D	D	D	R	R
Hancock	D	R	R	R	R	R	D	R	D	R	R
Hardin	D	R	R	R	R	R	D	D	D	R	R
Harrison	D	R	R	R	R	R	R	R	R	R	R
Henry	D	R	R	D	R	R	R	D	D	R	R
Howard	D	R	R	D	R	R	D	D	D	D	D
Humboldt	D	R	R	R	R	R	D	R	R	R	R
Ida	D	R	R	R	R	R	R	R	R	R	R
Iowa	D	R	R	R	R	R	D	R	D	R	R
Jackson	D	R	R	D	R	R	D	D	D	D	D
Jasper	D	R	R	D	R	R	D	D	D	R	D
Jefferson	D	R	R	R	R	R	R	R	D	R	D
Johnson	D	D	D	D	D	D	D	D	D	D	D
Jones	D	R	R	R	R	R	D	D	D	D	D
Keokuk	D	R	R	D	R	R	D	D	D	R	R
Kossuth	D	R	R	D	R	R	D	D	D	R	R
Lee	D	R	R	D	R	D	D	D	D	D	D
Linn	D	R	R	D	R	R	D	D	D	D	D
Louisa	D	R	R	R	R	R	D	D	D	D	R
Lucas	D	R	R	D	R	R	D	D	D	R	R
Lyon	R	R	R	R	R	R	R	R	R	R	R
Madison	D	R	R	D	R	R	D	D	D	R	R
Mahaska	D	R	R	R	R	R	R	R	R	R	R
Marion	D	R	R	D	R	R	D	R	R	R	R
Marshall	D	R	R	R	R	R	D	D	D	R	R
Mills	D	R	R	R	R	R	R	R	R	R	R
Mitchell	D	R	R	D	R	R	D	D	D	D	D
Monona	D	R	R	D	R	R	D	D	D	R	R
Monroe	D	D	R	D	R	D	D	D	D	R	R
Montgomery	D	R	R	R	R	R	R	R	R	R	R
Muscatine	D	R	R	R	R	R	D	D	D	D	D
O'Brien	R	R	R	R	R	R	R	R	R	R	R
Osceola	D	R	R	R	R	R	R	R	R	R	R
Page	R	R	R	R	R	R	R	R	R	R	R
Palo Alto	D	R	R	D	R	D	D	D	D	R	R
Plymouth	D	R	R	R	R	R	R	R	R	R	R
Pocahontas	D	R	R	D	R	R	D	D	D	R	R
Polk	D	D	R	D	R	D	D	D	D	D	D
Pottawat- tamie	D	R	R	R	R	R	R	R	R	R	R
Poweshiek	D	R	R	D	R	R	D	D	D	R	D
Ringgold	D	R	R	D	R	D	D	D	D	R	R
Sac	D	R	R	R	R	R	D	R	R	R	R
Scott	D	R	R	R	R	R	D	D	D	D	D
Shelby	D	R	R	R	R	R	R	R	R	R	R

County	1964	1968	1972	1976	1980	1984	1988	1992	1996	2000	2004
Sioux	R	R	R	R	R	R	R	R	R	R	R
Story	D	R	R	R	R	R	D	D	D	D	D
Tama	D	R	R	D	R	R	D	D	D	D	D
Taylor	D	R	R	R	R	R	D	D	D	R	R
Union	D	R	R	D	R	R	D	D	D	R	R
Van Buren	D	R	R	D	R	R	R	D	D	R	R
Wapello	D	D	R	D	D	D	D	D	D	D	D
Warren	D	R	R	D	R	R	D	D	D	R	R
Washington	D	R	R	R	R	R	D	R	D	R	R
Wayne	D	R	R	D	R	R	D	D	D	R	R
Webster	D	R	R	D	R	D	D	D	D	D	D
Winnebago	D	R	R	R	R	R	R	R	D	D	R
Winneshiek	D	R	R	R	R	R	D	D	D	R	D
Woodbury	D	R	R	D	R	R	D	R	D	R	R
Worth	D	R	R	D	R	D	D	D	D	D	D
Wright	D	R	R	D	R	R	D	D	D	R	R

Kansas

County	1868	1872	1876	1880	1884	1888	1892	1896	1900	1904	1908	1912
Allen	R	R	R	R	R	R	R	R	R	R	R	D
Anderson	R	R	R	R	R	R	R	D	R	R	R	D
Atchison	R	R	R	R	R	R	PO	R	R	R	R	D
Barber	–	–	D	R	R	R	PO	D	R	R	R	P
Barton	–	R	R	R	R	R	PO	D	D	R	D	D
Bourbon	R	R	R	R	R	R	PO	D	R	R	R	D
Brown	R	R	R	R	R	R	R	R	R	R	R	D
Butler	R	R	R	R	R	R	PO	D	R	R	R	P
Chase	R	R	R	R	R	R	PO	D	R	R	R	D
Chautauqua	–	R	R	R	R	R	R	R	R	R	R	R
Cherokee	–	D	R	R	R	R	PO	D	D	R	R	D
Cheyenne	–	–	–	–	–	R	R	R	R	R	R	P
Clark	–	–	–	–	–	R	PO	D	R	R	R	D
Clay	R	R	R	R	R	R	PO	D	R	R	R	D
Cloud	R	R	R	R	R	R	PO	D	R	R	R	D
Coffee	R	R	R	R	R	R	PO	D	R	R	R	D
Comanche	–	–	–	–	–	R	PO	D	R	R	R	P
Cowley	–	R	R	R	R	R	PO	D	R	R	R	P
Crawford	R	D	R	R	R	R	PO	D	D	R	R	S
Decatur	–	–	–	R	R	R	PO	D	D	R	D	D
Dickinson	R	R	R	R	R	R	PO	D	R	R	R	D
Doniphan	R	R	R	R	R	R	R	R	R	R	R	R
Douglas	R	R	R	R	R	R	R	R	R	R	R	P
Edwards	–	–	R	R	R	R	PO	D	R	R	R	D
Elk	–	R	R	R	R	R	PO	D	R	R	R	D

County	1868	1872	1876	1880	1884	1888	1892	1896	1900	1904	1908	1912
Ellis	D	R	R	R	D	D	PO	D	D	R	D	D
Ellsworth	R	D	R	R	R	R	R	R	R	R	R	D
Finney	–	–	–	–	R	R	R	R	R	R	R	P
Ford	–	–	D	R	R	R	R	D	R	R	R	D
Franklin	R	R	R	R	R	R	PO	D	R	R	R	D
Geary	R	R	R	R	R	R	PO	D	R	R	R	P
Gove	–	–	–	–	–	R	R	R	R	R	R	P
Graham	–	–	–	R	R	R	PO	D	D	R	R	D
Grant	–	–	–	–	–	R	R	D	R	R	R	P
Gray	–	–	–	–	–	R	R	R	R	R	R	D
Greeley	–	–	–	–	–	R	R	R	R	R	R	P
Greenwood	R	R	R	R	R	R	PO	D	R	R	R	D
Hamilton	–	–	–	–	–	R	R	D	D	R	R	D
Harper	–	–	–	R	R	R	PO	D	D	R	R	P
Harvey	–	R	R	R	R	R	R	R	R	R	R	P
Haskell	–	–	–	–	–	R	R	R	R	R	R	D
Hodgeman	–	–	–	R	R	R	R	R	R	R	R	P
Jackson	R	R	R	R	R	R	R	R	R	R	R	D
Jefferson	R	R	R	R	R	R	R	R	R	R	R	D
Jewell	–	R	R	R	R	R	PO	D	R	R	R	D
Johnson	R	R	R	R	R	R	R	D	R	R	R	D
Kearny	–	–	–	–	–	R	R	D	R	R	R	D
Kingman	–	–	R	R	R	R	PO	D	R	R	D	D
Kiowa	–	–	–	–	–	R	R	R	R	R	R	P
Labette	R	R	R	R	R	R	PO	D	D	R	R	D
Lane	–	–	–	–	–	R	R	R	R	R	R	D
Leavenworth	R	R	R	R	R	D	PO	D	R	R	R	D
Lincoln	–	R	R	R	R	R	PO	D	D	R	R	D
Linn	R	R	R	R	R	R	PO	D	R	R	R	D
Logan	–	–	–	–	–	R	R	R	R	R	R	P
Lyon	R	R	R	R	R	R	PO	D	R	R	R	D
McPherson	–	R	R	R	R	R	PO	D	R	R	R	P
Marion	R	R	R	R	R	R	R	R	R	R	R	D
Marshall	R	R	R	R	R	R	PO	R	R	R	R	D
Meade	–	–	–	–	–	R	R	R	R	R	R	P
Miami	R	R	R	R	R	R	PO	D	R	R	R	D
Mitchell	–	R	R	R	R	R	PO	D	R	R	R	D
Montgomery	–	R	R	R	R	R	PO	D	R	R	R	P
Morris	D	R	R	R	R	R	R	R	R	R	R	P
Morton	–	–	–	–	–	R	R	R	R	R	R	D
Nemaha	R	R	R	R	R	R	R	R	R	R	R	D
Neosho	R	R	R	R	R	R	PO	D	R	R	R	D
Ness	–	–	–	R	R	R	PO	D	D	R	R	P
Norton	–	R	R	R	R	R	PO	D	R	R	R	D
Osage	R	R	R	R	R	R	PO	D	R	R	R	D
Osborne	–	R	R	R	R	R	PO	D	R	R	R	D
Ottawa	R	R	R	R	R	R	PO	D	D	R	R	D
Pawnee	–	–	R	R	R	R	PO	D	D	R	R	D
Phillips	–	R	R	R	R	R	PO	D	R	R	R	D

County	1868	1872	1876	1880	1884	1888	1892	1896	1900	1904	1908	1912
Pottawato-mie	R	R	R	R	R	R	R	R	R	R	R	D
Pratt	–	–	–	R	R	R	PO	D	R	R	R	P
Rawlins	–	–	–	–	R	R	PO	D	D	R	D	D
Reno	–	R	R	R	R	R	R	R	R	R	R	D
Republic	R	R	R	R	R	R	R	R	R	R	R	D
Rice	–	R	R	R	R	R	PO	D	R	R	R	D
Riley	R	R	R	R	R	R	R	R	R	R	R	P
Rooks	–	–	R	R	R	R	PO	D	R	R	R	D
Rush	–	–	R	R	R	R	PO	D	D	R	D	D
Russell	–	R	R	R	R	R	R	R	R	R	R	P
Saline	R	R	R	R	R	R	PO	D	R	R	R	D
Scott	–	–	–	–	–	R	PO	D	D	R	R	D
Sedgwick	–	R	R	R	R	R	PO	D	R	R	R	P
Seward	–	–	–	–	–	R	R	R	R	R	R	D
Shawnee	R	R	R	R	R	R	R	R	R	R	R	D
Sheridan	–	–	–	R	R	R	PO	D	D	R	R	D
Sherman	–	–	–	–	–	R	PO	D	D	R	D	D
Smith	–	R	R	R	R	R	PO	D	D	R	R	D
Stafford	–	–	–	R	R	R	PO	D	D	R	R	D
Stanton	–	–	–	–	–	R	R	D	R	R	R	D
Stevens	–	–	–	–	–	R	PO	D	D	R	R	D
Sumner	–	R	R	R	R	R	PO	D	R	R	R	P
Thomas	–	–	–	–	–	R	PO	D	D	R	D	D
Trego	–	–	–	R	R	R	R	D	R	R	R	D
Wabaunsee	R	R	R	R	R	R	PO	R	R	R	R	D
Wallace	–	R	NR	NR	NR	R	PO	R	R	R	R	P
Washington	R	R	R	R	R	R	PO	R	R	R	R	D
Wichita	–	–	–	–	–	R	R	R	R	R	R	D
Wilson	R	R	R	R	R	R	R	D	R	R	R	P
Woodson	R	R	R	R	R	R	R	R	R	R	R	D
Wyandotte	D	R	R	R	R	R	R	D	R	R	D	P

County	1916	1920	1924	1928	1932	1936	1940	1944	1948	1952	1956	1960
Allen	R	R	R	R	R	R	R	R	R	R	R	R
Anderson	D	R	R	R	D	R	R	R	R	R	R	R
Atchison	D	R	R	R	D	D	R	R	R	R	R	R
Barber	D	R	R	R	D	D	R	R	R	R	R	R
Barton	D	R	R	R	D	D	R	R	R	R	R	R
Bourbon	D	R	R	R	D	D	R	R	R	R	R	R
Brown	R	R	R	R	R	R	R	R	R	R	R	R
Butler	D	R	R	R	D	D	R	R	R	R	R	R
Chase	D	R	R	R	D	D	R	R	R	R	R	R
Chautauqua	R	R	R	R	D	R	R	R	R	R	R	R
Cherokee	D	R	R	R	D	D	D	R	D	R	R	R
Cheyenne	D	R	R	R	D	D	R	R	R	R	R	R
Clark	D	R	R	R	D	D	D	R	R	R	R	R
Clay	R	R	R	R	D	R	R	R	R	R	R	R

County	1916	1920	1924	1928	1932	1936	1940	1944	1948	1952	1956	1960
Cloud	D	R	R	R	D	D	R	R	R	R	R	R
Coffee	D	R	R	R	D	R	R	R	R	R	R	R
Comanche	D	R	R	R	D	D	R	R	R	R	R	R
Cowley	D	R	R	R	D	D	R	R	R	R	R	R
Crawford	D	R	R	R	D	D	D	R	D	R	R	R
Decatur	D	R	R	R	D	D	R	R	R	R	R	R
Dickinson	D	R	R	R	D	R	R	R	R	R	R	R
Doniphan	R	R	R	R	R	R	R	R	R	R	R	R
Douglas	R	R	R	R	R	R	R	R	R	R	R	R
Edwards	D	R	R	R	D	D	R	R	R	R	R	R
Elk	D	R	R	R	D	R	R	R	R	R	R	R
Ellis	D	R	R	D	D	D	R	R	D	R	R	D
Ellsworth	R	R	R	D	D	R	R	R	R	R	R	R
Finney	D	R	R	R	D	D	R	R	R	R	R	R
Ford	D	R	R	R	D	D	R	R	D	R	R	R
Franklin	D	R	R	R	R	R	R	R	R	R	R	R
Geary	D	R	R	R	D	D	R	R	R	R	R	R
Gove	D	R	R	R	D	R	R	R	R	R	R	R
Graham	D	R	R	R	D	D	R	R	R	R	R	R
Grant	D	R	R	R	D	D	R	R	R	R	R	R
Gray	D	R	R	R	D	D	R	R	R	R	R	R
Greeley	R	R	R	R	D	R	R	R	R	R	R	R
Greenwood	R	R	R	R	D	D	R	R	R	R	R	R
Hamilton	D	R	R	R	D	D	R	R	R	R	R	R
Harper	D	R	R	R	D	D	R	R	R	R	R	R
Harvey	R	R	R	R	R	D	R	R	R	R	R	R
Haskell	D	R	R	R	D	D	R	R	R	R	R	R
Hodgeman	D	R	R	R	D	D	R	R	R	R	R	R
Jackson	R	R	R	R	D	R	R	R	R	R	R	R
Jefferson	R	R	R	R	D	R	R	R	R	R	R	R
Jewell	D	R	R	R	D	R	R	R	R	R	R	R
Johnson	D	R	R	R	R	R	R	R	R	R	R	R
Kearny	R	R	R	R	D	D	R	R	R	R	R	R
Kingman	D	R	R	R	D	D	R	R	R	R	R	R
Kiowa	D	R	R	R	R	D	R	R	R	R	R	R
Labette	D	R	R	R	D	D	R	R	R	R	R	R
Lane	D	R	R	R	D	D	R	R	R	R	R	R
Leavenworth	D	R	R	R	D	R	R	R	D	R	R	R
Lincoln	D	R	R	R	D	D	R	R	R	R	R	R
Linn	D	R	R	R	D	R	R	R	R	R	R	R
Logan	D	R	R	R	D	R	R	R	R	R	R	R
Lyon	D	R	R	R	D	D	R	R	R	R	R	R
McPherson	R	R	R	R	D	D	R	R	R	R	R	R
Marion	R	R	R	R	D	D	R	R	R	R	R	R
Marshall	R	R	R	R	D	R	R	R	R	R	R	R
Meade	D	R	R	R	R	D	R	R	R	R	R	R
Miami	D	R	R	R	D	R	R	R	D	R	R	R
Mitchell	D	R	R	R	D	D	R	R	R	R	R	R
Montgomery	D	R	R	R	R	R	R	R	R	R	R	R

County	1916	1920	1924	1928	1932	1936	1940	1944	1948	1952	1956	1960
Morris	D	R	R	R	R	D	R	R	R	R	R	R
Morton	D	R	R	R	D	D	R	R	R	R	R	R
Nemaha	R	R	R	R	D	D	R	R	R	R	R	R
Neosho	D	R	R	R	D	R	R	R	R	R	R	R
Ness	D	R	R	R	D	D	R	R	R	R	R	R
Norton	D	R	R	R	D	R	R	R	R	R	R	R
Osage	D	R	R	R	D	R	R	R	R	R	R	R
Osborne	D	R	R	R	R	R	R	R	R	R	R	R
Ottawa	D	R	R	R	D	D	R	R	R	R	R	R
Pawnee	D	R	R	R	D	D	R	R	R	R	R	R
Phillips	D	R	R	R	D	R	R	R	R	R	R	R
Pottawato-mie	R	R	R	R	D	R	R	R	R	R	R	R
Pratt	D	R	R	R	D	D	R	R	R	R	R	R
Rawlins	D	R	R	R	D	D	R	R	R	R	R	R
Reno	R	R	R	R	D	D	R	R	R	R	R	R
Republic	D	R	R	R	D	R	R	R	R	R	R	R
Rice	D	R	R	R	R	D	R	R	R	R	R	R
Riley	R	R	R	R	R	R	R	R	R	R	R	R
Rooks	D	R	R	R	D	R	R	R	R	R	R	R
Rush	D	R	R	R	D	D	R	R	R	R	R	R
Russell	R	R	R	R	D	D	R	R	R	R	R	R
Saline	D	R	R	R	D	D	R	R	R	R	R	R
Scott	D	R	R	R	D	D	R	R	R	R	R	R
Sedgwick	D	R	R	R	D	D	D	R	R	R	R	R
Seward	D	R	R	R	D	D	R	R	R	R	R	R
Shawnee	R	R	R	R	R	D	R	R	R	R	R	R
Sheridan	D	R	R	R	D	D	R	R	R	R	R	R
Sherman	D	R	R	R	D	D	R	R	R	R	R	R
Smith	D	R	R	R	D	R	R	R	R	R	R	R
Stafford	D	R	R	R	D	D	R	R	R	R	R	R
Stanton	R	R	R	R	D	D	R	R	R	R	R	R
Stevens	D	R	R	R	D	D	R	R	R	R	R	R
Sumner	D	R	R	R	D	D	R	R	R	R	R	R
Thomas	D	R	R	R	D	D	R	R	R	R	R	R
Trego	D	R	R	R	D	D	R	R	R	R	R	R
Wabaunsee	R	R	R	R	D	R	R	R	R	R	R	R
Wallace	D	R	R	R	D	R	R	R	R	R	R	R
Washington	R	R	R	R	D	R	R	R	R	R	R	R
Wichita	D	R	R	R	D	D	R	R	R	R	R	R
Wilson	D	R	R	R	D	R	R	R	R	R	R	R
Woodson	R	R	R	R	D	R	R	R	R	R	R	R
Wyandotte	D	R	R	R	D	D	D	D	D	D	D	D

County	1964	1968	1972	1976	1980	1984	1988	1992	1996	2000	2004
Allen	D	R	R	R	R	R	R	R	R	R	R
Anderson	D	R	R	D	R	R	R	PE	R	R	R
Atchison	D	R	R	D	R	R	R	D	D	R	R

County	1964	1968	1972	1976	1980	1984	1988	1992	1996	2000	2004
Barber	D	R	R	R	R	R	R	R	R	R	R
Barton	D	R	R	R	R	R	R	R	R	R	R
Bourbon	D	R	R	R	R	R	R	R	R	R	R
Brown	R	R	R	R	R	R	R	R	R	R	R
Butler	D	R	R	D	R	R	R	R	R	R	R
Chase	R	R	R	R	R	R	R	R	R	R	R
Chautauqua	R	R	R	R	R	R	R	R	R	R	R
Cherokee	D	R	R	D	R	R	R	D	R	R	R
Cheyenne	R	R	R	R	R	R	R	R	R	R	R
Clark	D	R	R	R	R	R	R	R	R	R	R
Clay	R	R	R	R	R	R	R	R	R	R	R
Cloud	D	R	R	D	R	R	R	R	R	R	R
Coffee	R	R	R	R	R	R	R	R	R	R	R
Comanche	D	R	R	R	R	R	R	R	R	R	R
Cowley	D	R	R	R	R	R	R	R	R	R	R
Crawford	D	R	R	D	R	R	D	D	D	R	R
Decatur	R	R	R	R	R	R	R	R	R	R	R
Dickinson	R	R	R	R	R	R	R	R	R	R	R
Doniphan	R	R	R	R	R	R	R	R	R	R	R
Douglas	D	R	R	R	R	R	R	D	D	D	D
Edwards	D	R	R	D	R	R	R	R	R	R	R
Elk	R	R	R	R	R	R	R	R	R	R	R
Ellis	D	R	R	D	R	R	D	D	R	R	R
Ellsworth	D	R	R	R	R	R	R	R	R	R	R
Finney	D	R	R	D	R	R	R	R	R	R	R
Ford	D	R	R	D	R	R	R	R	R	R	R
Franklin	D	R	R	R	R	R	R	R	R	R	R
Geary	D	R	R	R	R	R	R	R	R	R	R
Gove	D	R	R	R	R	R	R	R	R	R	R
Graham	R	R	R	R	R	R	R	R	R	R	R
Grant	D	R	R	R	R	R	R	R	R	R	R
Gray	D	R	R	D	R	R	R	R	R	R	R
Greeley	D	R	R	D	R	R	R	R	R	R	R
Greenwood	R	R	R	R	R	R	R	R	R	R	R
Hamilton	D	R	R	D	R	R	R	R	R	R	R
Harper	R	R	R	R	R	R	R	R	R	R	R
Harvey	D	R	R	R	R	R	R	R	R	R	R
Haskell	D	R	R	R	R	R	R	R	R	R	R
Hodgeman	D	R	R	D	R	R	R	R	R	R	R
Jackson	R	R	R	R	R	R	R	R	R	R	R
Jefferson	R	R	R	R	R	R	R	PE	R	R	R
Jewell	R	R	R	R	R	R	R	R	R	R	R
Johnson	R	R	R	R	R	R	R	R	R	R	R
Kearny	D	R	R	R	R	R	R	R	R	R	R
Kingman	D	R	R	D	R	R	R	R	R	R	R
Kiowa	R	R	R	R	R	R	R	R	R	R	R
Labette	D	R	R	D	R	R	R	D	R	R	R
Lane	D	R	R	R	R	R	R	R	R	R	R
Leavenworth	D	R	R	R	R	R	R	D	R	R	R

County	1964	1968	1972	1976	1980	1984	1988	1992	1996	2000	2004
Lincoln	R	R	R	R	R	R	R	R	R	R	R
Linn	R	R	R	R	R	R	R	R	R	R	R
Logan	D	R	R	R	R	R	R	R	R	R	R
Lyon	R	R	R	R	R	R	R	R	R	R	R
McPherson	D	R	R	R	R	R	R	R	R	R	R
Marion	R	R	R	R	R	R	R	R	R	R	R
Marshall	R	R	R	R	R	R	R	R	R	R	R
Meade	R	R	R	R	R	R	R	R	R	R	R
Miami	D	R	R	D	R	R	R	D	R	R	R
Mitchell	R	R	R	R	R	R	R	R	R	R	R
Montgomery	D	R	R	R	R	R	R	R	R	R	R
Morris	R	R	R	R	R	R	R	T	R	R	R
Morton	D	R	R	R	R	R	R	R	R	R	R
Nemaha	D	R	R	R	R	R	R	R	R	R	R
Neosho	D	R	R	R	R	R	R	R	R	R	R
Ness	D	R	R	D	R	R	R	R	R	R	R
Norton	R	R	R	R	R	R	R	R	R	R	R
Osage	D	R	R	R	R	R	R	R	R	R	R
Osborne	R	R	R	R	R	R	R	R	R	R	R
Ottawa	D	R	R	R	R	R	R	R	R	R	R
Pawnee	D	R	R	D	R	R	R	R	R	R	R
Phillips	R	R	R	R	R	R	R	R	R	R	R
Pottawato-mie	R	R	R	R	R	R	R	R	R	R	R
Pratt	D	R	R	R	R	R	R	R	R	R	R
Rawlins	R	R	R	R	R	R	R	R	R	R	R
Reno	D	R	R	D	R	R	R	R	R	R	R
Republic	R	R	R	R	R	R	R	R	R	R	R
Rice	D	R	R	D	R	R	R	R	R	R	R
Riley	R	R	R	R	R	R	R	R	R	R	R
Rooks	R	R	R	R	R	R	R	R	R	R	R
Rush	D	R	R	D	R	R	R	R	R	R	R
Russell	D	R	R	R	R	R	R	R	R	R	R
Saline	D	R	R	R	R	R	R	R	R	R	R
Scott	R	R	R	R	R	R	R	R	R	R	R
Sedgwick	D	R	R	R	R	R	R	R	R	R	R
Seward	R	R	R	R	R	R	R	R	R	R	R
Shawnee	D	R	R	R	R	R	R	D	R	R	R
Sheridan	D	R	R	R	R	R	R	R	R	R	R
Sherman	D	R	R	R	R	R	R	R	R	R	R
Smith	R	R	R	R	R	R	R	R	R	R	R
Stafford	D	R	R	D	R	R	R	R	R	R	R
Stanton	D	R	R	R	R	R	R	R	R	R	R
Stevens	D	R	R	R	R	R	R	R	R	R	R
Sumner	D	R	R	D	R	R	R	R	R	R	R
Thomas	D	R	R	R	R	R	R	R	R	R	R
Trego	D	R	R	R	R	R	R	R	R	R	R
Wabaunsee	R	R	R	R	R	R	R	PE	R	R	R
Wallace	R	R	R	R	R	R	R	R	R	R	R

County	1964	1968	1972	1976	1980	1984	1988	1992	1996	2000	2004
Washington	R	R	R	R	R	R	R	R	R	R	R
Wichita	D	R	R	D	R	R	R	R	R	R	R
Wilson	R	R	R	R	R	R	R	R	R	R	R
Woodson	R	R	R	R	R	R	R	R	R	R	R
Wyandotte	D	D	R	D	D	D	D	D	D	D	D

Kentucky

County	1868	1872	1876	1880	1884	1888	1892	1896	1900	1904	1908	1912
Adair	D	R	D	D	D	R	R	R	R	R	D	D
Allen	D	R	D	D	D	D	D	R	R	R	R	D
Anderson	D	D	D	D	D	D	D	D	D	D	D	D
Ballard	D	D	D	D	D	D	D	D	D	D	D	D
Barren	D	D	D	D	D	D	D	D	D	D	D	D
Bath	D	R	D	D	D	D	D	D	D	D	D	D
Bell	R	R	R	R	R	R	R	R	R	R	R	P
Boone	D	D	D	D	D	D	D	D	D	D	D	D
Bourbon	D	R	D	D	D	R	D	R	D	D	D	D
Boyd	D	R	D	R	R	R	D	R	R	R	R	D
Boyle	D	R	D	D	D	D	D	R	R	D	D	D
Bracken	D	D	D	D	D	D	D	D	D	D	D	D
Breathitt	D	D	D	D	D	D	D	D	D	D	R	D
Breckinridge	D	R	D	D	D	D	D	R	R	R	R	D
Bullitt	D	D	D	D	D	D	D	D	D	D	D	D
Butler	R	R	R	R	R	R	R	R	R	R	R	R
Caldwell	D	D	D	D	D	D	R	R	R	R	D	R
Calloway	D	D	D	D	D	D	D	D	D	D	D	D
Campbell	D	D	D	D	R	D	D	R	R	R	R	D
Carlisle	–	–	–	–	–	D	D	D	D	D	D	D
Carroll	D	D	D	D	D	D	D	D	D	D	D	D
Carter	R	R	D	R	R	R	R	R	R	R	R	D
Casey	D	D	D	D	D	R	R	R	R	R	R	D
Christian	D	R	R	R	R	R	R	R	R	R	R	R
Clark	D	R	D	D	D	D	D	D	D	D	D	D
Clay	R	R	R	R	R	R	R	R	R	R	R	R
Clinton	D	R	R	R	R	R	R	R	R	R	R	R
Crittenden	D	R	D	D	R	R	R	D	R	R	R	R
Cumberland	D	R	R	R	R	R	R	R	R	R	R	R
Daviess	D	D	D	D	D	D	D	D	D	D	D	D
Edmonson	D	R	D	D	D	R	R	R	R	R	R	D
Elliott	–	D	D	D	D	D	D	D	D	D	D	D
Estill	R	R	D	D	R	R	R	R	R	R	R	D
Fayette	D	R	R	R	R	D	D	R	R	D	D	D
Fleming	D	R	D	D	D	D	D	D	D	D	D	D
Floyd	D	D	D	D	D	D	D	D	D	D	D	D

County	1868	1872	1876	1880	1884	1888	1892	1896	1900	1904	1908	1912
Franklin	D	D	D	D	D	D	D	D	D	D	D	D
Fulton	D	D	D	D	D	D	D	D	D	D	D	D
Gallatin	D	D	D	D	D	D	D	D	D	D	D	D
Garrard	D	R	D	R	R	R	R	R	R	R	R	D
Grant	D	D	D	D	D	D	D	D	D	D	D	D
Graves	D	D	D	D	D	D	D	D	D	D	D	D
Grayson	D	R	D	D	D	R	D	D	R	R	R	D
Green	D	R	D	R	R	R	R	R	R	R	R	D
Greenup	R	R	D	R	R	R	R	R	R	R	R	D
Hancock	D	D	D	D	D	D	D	D	R	R	R	D
Hardin	D	D	D	D	D	D	D	D	D	D	D	D
Harlan	R	R	R	R	R	R	R	R	R	R	R	P
Harrison	D	D	D	D	D	D	D	D	D	D	D	D
Hart	D	R	D	D	D	D	D	R	R	R	R	D
Henderson	D	D	D	D	D	D	D	D	D	D	D	D
Henry	D	D	D	D	D	D	D	D	D	D	D	D
Hickman	D	D	D	D	D	D	D	D	D	D	D	D
Hopkins	D	D	D	D	D	D	D	D	D	D	D	D
Jackson	R	R	R	R	R	R	R	R	R	R	R	P
Jefferson	D	D	D	D	D	D	D	R	R	D	R	D
Jessamine	D	R	D	R	D	D	D	D	D	D	D	D
Johnson	R	R	R	R	R	R	R	R	R	R	R	P
Kenton	D	D	D	D	D	D	D	D	D	R	D	D
Knott	–	–	–	–	D	D	D	D	D	D	D	D
Knox	R	R	R	R	R	R	R	R	R	R	R	R
Larue	D	D	D	D	D	D	D	D	D	D	D	D
Laurel	R	R	R	R	R	R	R	R	R	R	R	D
Lawrence	D	D	D	D	D	R	D	R	R	R	R	D
Lee	–	R	R	R	R	R	R	R	R	R	R	D
Leslie	–	–	–	R	R	R	R	R	R	R	R	R
Letcher	D	R	NR	D	R	R	R	R	R	R	R	R
Lewis	R	R	D	R	R	R	R	R	R	R	R	R
Lincoln	D	D	D	D	D	D	D	R	R	D	D	D
Livingston	D	D	D	D	D	D	D	D	D	D	D	D
Logan	D	R	D	D	D	D	D	D	D	D	D	D
Lyon	D	R	D	D	D	D	D	D	D	D	D	D
McCracken	D	D	D	D	D	D	D	D	D	D	D	D
McCreary	–	–	–	–	–	–	–	–	–	–	–	P
McLean	D	D	D	D	D	D	D	D	D	D	D	D
Madison	D	R	D	D	D	D	D	R	R	D	R	D
Magoffin	R	R	D	R	R	R	R	R	R	R	R	R
Marion	D	D	D	D	D	D	D	D	D	D	D	D
Marshall	D	D	D	D	D	D	D	D	D	D	D	D
Martin	–	R	R	D	R	R	R	R	R	R	R	R
Mason	D	D	D	D	D	D	D	D	D	D	D	D
Meade	D	D	D	D	D	D	D	D	D	D	D	D
Menifee	–	D	D	D	D	D	D	D	D	D	D	D
Mercer	D	D	D	D	D	D	D	R	D	D	D	D
Metcalfe	D	R	D	R	R	R	R	R	R	R	R	D

County	1868	1872	1876	1880	1884	1888	1892	1896	1900	1904	1908	1912
Monroe	R	R	R	R	R	R	R	R	R	R	R	R
Montgomery	D	D	D	D	D	D	D	D	D	D	D	D
Morgan	D	D	D	D	D	D	D	D	D	D	D	D
Muhlenberg	D	R	D	D	D	R	R	R	R	R	R	D
Nelson	D	D	D	D	D	D	D	D	D	D	D	D
Nicholas	D	D	D	D	D	D	D	D	D	D	D	D
Ohio	D	R	D	D	D	R	D	D	R	R	R	D
Oldham	D	D	D	D	D	D	D	D	D	D	D	D
Owen	D	D	D	D	D	D	D	D	D	D	D	D
Owsley	R	R	R	R	R	R	R	R	R	R	R	R
Pendleton	D	D	D	D	D	D	D	D	D	D	D	D
Perry	R	R	R	R	D	R	R	R	R	R	R	R
Pike	D	D	D	D	D	R	D	R	R	R	R	R
Powell	D	D	D	D	D	D	D	D	D	D	D	D
Pulaski	R	R	R	R	R	R	R	R	R	R	R	D
Robertson	D	D	D	D	D	D	D	D	D	D	D	D
Rockcastle	D	D	D	D	R	R	R	R	R	R	R	R
Rowan	R	R	R	D	R	R	R	R	R	R	R	D
Russell	D	R	D	D	D	R	R	R	R	R	R	R
Scott	D	D	D	D	D	D	D	D	D	D	D	D
Shelby	D	D	D	D	D	D	D	D	D	D	D	D
Simpson	D	D	D	D	D	D	D	D	D	D	D	D
Spencer	D	D	D	D	D	D	D	D	D	D	D	D
Taylor	D	D	D	D	D	D	D	D	D	D	D	D
Todd	D	R	D	D	D	D	D	R	D	D	D	D
Trigg	D	D	D	D	D	R	D	D	D	D	D	R
Trimble	D	D	D	D	D	D	D	D	D	D	D	D
Union	D	D	D	D	D	D	D	D	D	D	D	D
Warren	D	R	D	D	D	D	D	D	D	D	D	D
Washington	D	R	D	D	D	R	D	R	D	D	D	D
Wayne	D	D	D	D	D	D	R	R	R	R	R	D
Webster	D	D	D	D	D	D	D	D	D	D	D	D
Whitley	R	R	R	R	R	R	R	R	R	R	R	P
Wolfe	D	D	D	D	D	D	D	D	D	D	D	D
Woodford	D	R	D	D	D	D	D	R	D	D	D	D

County	1916	1920	1924	1928	1932	1936	1940	1944	1948	1952	1956	1960
Adair	R	R	R	R	D	R	R	R	R	R	R	R
Allen	R	R	R	R	R	R	R	R	R	R	R	R
Anderson	D	D	D	R	D	D	D	D	D	D	D	D
Ballard	D	D	D	D	D	D	D	D	D	D	D	D
Barren	D	D	D	R	D	D	D	D	D	D	D	R
Bath	D	D	D	R	D	D	D	D	D	D	D	D
Bell	R	R	R	R	D	D	D	R	D	R	R	R
Boone	D	D	D	R	D	D	D	D	D	D	R	R
Bourbon	D	D	D	R	D	D	D	D	D	D	D	D
Boyd	R	R	R	R	D	D	D	D	D	R	R	R
Boyle	D	D	D	R	D	D	D	D	D	D	D	R

County	1916	1920	1924	1928	1932	1936	1940	1944	1948	1952	1956	1960
Bracken	D	D	R	R	D	D	D	D	D	D	R	R
Breathitt	D	D	D	D	D	D	D	D	D	D	D	D
Breckinridge	R	R	R	R	D	D	D	R	D	R	R	R
Bullitt	D	D	D	R	D	D	D	D	D	D	D	R
Butler	R	R	R	R	R	R	R	R	R	R	R	R
Caldwell	R	R	R	R	D	D	D	D	D	R	R	R
Calloway	D	D	D	D	D	D	D	D	D	D	D	D
Campbell	D	R	R	R	D	D	R	R	D	R	R	R
Carlisle	D	D	D	D	D	D	D	D	D	D	D	D
Carroll	D	D	D	D	D	D	D	D	D	D	D	D
Carter	R	R	R	R	D	R	R	R	R	R	R	R
Casey	R	R	R	R	R	R	R	R	R	R	R	R
Christian	R	R	R	R	D	D	D	D	D	D	D	D
Clark	D	D	D	R	D	D	D	D	D	D	D	R
Clay	R	R	R	R	R	R	R	R	R	R	R	R
Clinton	R	R	R	R	R	R	R	R	R	R	R	R
Crittenden	R	R	R	R	R	R	R	R	R	R	R	R
Cumberland	R	R	R	R	R	R	R	R	R	R	R	R
Daviess	D	D	D	R	D	D	D	D	D	R	R	R
Edmonson	R	R	R	R	R	R	R	R	R	R	R	R
Elliott	D	D	D	D	D	D	D	D	D	D	D	D
Estill	R	R	R	R	D	R	R	R	R	R	R	R
Fayette	D	D	R	R	D	D	D	D	D	R	R	R
Fleming	D	D	D	R	D	D	D	R	D	R	R	R
Floyd	D	D	D	D	D	D	D	D	D	D	D	D
Franklin	D	D	D	D	D	D	D	D	D	D	D	D
Fulton	D	D	D	D	D	D	D	D	D	D	D	D
Gallatin	D	D	D	R	D	D	D	D	D	D	D	D
Garrard	R	R	R	R	D	D	D	R	R	R	R	R
Grant	D	D	D	R	D	D	D	D	D	D	D	R
Graves	D	D	D	D	D	D	D	D	D	D	D	D
Grayson	R	R	R	R	D	R	R	R	R	R	R	R
Green	R	R	R	R	R	R	R	R	R	R	R	R
Greenup	R	R	R	R	D	D	D	D	D	D	R	R
Hancock	R	R	D	R	D	D	R	R	D	R	R	R
Hardin	D	D	D	R	D	D	D	D	D	D	R	R
Harlan	R	R	R	R	R	D	D	D	D	D	R	D
Harrison	D	D	D	D	D	D	D	D	D	D	D	D
Hart	D	R	D	R	D	D	D	D	D	D	R	R
Henderson	D	D	R	R	D	D	D	D	D	D	D	D
Henry	D	D	D	D	D	D	D	D	D	D	D	D
Hickman	D	D	D	D	D	D	D	D	D	D	D	D
Hopkins	D	D	D	D	D	D	D	D	D	D	D	D
Jackson	R	R	R	R	R	R	R	R	R	R	R	R
Jefferson	D	R	R	R	D	D	D	D	D	R	R	R
Jessamine	D	D	D	R	D	D	D	D	D	D	R	R
Johnson	R	R	R	R	R	R	R	R	R	R	R	R
Kenton	D	D	R	R	D	D	D	D	D	D	R	R
Knott	D	D	D	D	D	D	D	D	D	D	D	D

County	1916	1920	1924	1928	1932	1936	1940	1944	1948	1952	1956	1960
Knox	R	R	R	R	R	R	R	R	R	R	R	R
Larue	D	D	D	R	D	D	D	D	D	D	R	R
Laurel	R	R	R	R	R	R	R	R	R	R	R	R
Lawrence	R	R	R	R	D	D	D	R	D	R	R	R
Lee	R	R	D	R	D	R	R	R	R	R	R	R
Leslie	R	R	R	R	R	R	R	R	R	R	R	R
Letcher	R	R	R	R	D	D	D	D	D	D	R	R
Lewis	R	R	R	R	R	R	R	R	R	R	R	R
Lincoln	D	D	D	R	D	D	D	D	D	R	R	R
Livingston	D	D	D	R	D	D	D	D	D	D	D	R
Logan	D	D	D	R	D	D	D	D	D	D	D	D
Lyon	D	D	D	D	D	D	D	D	D	D	D	D
McCracken	D	D	D	R	D	D	D	D	D	D	D	D
McCreary	R	R	R	R	R	R	R	R	R	R	R	R
McLean	D	D	D	R	D	D	D	D	D	D	D	R
Madison	D	R	R	R	D	D	D	D	D	D	R	R
Magoffin	R	R	R	R	D	R	D	R	D	R	R	R
Marion	D	D	D	D	D	D	D	D	D	D	R	D
Marshall	D	D	D	D	D	D	D	D	D	D	D	D
Martin	R	R	R	R	R	R	R	R	R	R	R	R
Mason	D	D	D	R	D	D	D	D	D	D	R	R
Meade	D	D	D	D	D	D	D	D	D	D	D	D
Menifee	D	D	D	R	D	D	D	D	D	D	D	D
Mercer	D	D	D	R	D	D	D	D	D	D	R	R
Metcalfe	R	R	R	R	D	R	R	R	D	R	R	R
Monroe	R	R	R	R	R	R	R	R	R	R	R	R
Montgomery	D	D	D	R	D	D	D	D	D	D	D	D
Morgan	D	D	D	D	D	D	D	D	D	D	D	D
Muhlenberg	R	R	R	R	D	D	R	R	D	R	R	R
Nelson	D	D	D	D	D	D	D	D	D	D	R	D
Nicholas	D	D	D	R	D	D	D	D	D	D	D	D
Ohio	R	R	R	R	R	R	R	R	R	R	R	R
Oldham	D	D	D	R	D	D	D	D	D	D	R	R
Owen	D	D	D	D	D	D	D	D	D	D	D	D
Owsley	R	R	R	R	R	R	R	R	R	R	R	R
Pendleton	D	D	R	R	D	D	D	D	D	D	R	R
Perry	R	R	R	R	D	D	D	D	D	D	R	R
Pike	R	R	R	R	D	D	D	D	D	D	R	D
Powell	D	D	D	R	D	D	D	D	D	D	D	R
Pulaski	R	R	R	R	R	R	R	R	R	R	R	R
Robertson	D	D	D	R	D	D	D	D	D	D	D	D
Rockcastle	R	R	R	R	R	R	R	R	R	R	R	R
Rowan	R	R	R	R	D	D	D	D	D	D	R	R
Russell	R	R	R	R	R	R	R	R	R	R	R	R
Scott	D	D	D	R	D	D	D	D	D	D	D	D
Shelby	D	D	D	R	D	D	D	D	D	D	D	D
Simpson	D	D	D	D	D	D	D	D	D	D	D	D
Spencer	D	D	D	R	D	D	D	D	D	D	D	R
Taylor	D	R	R	R	D	R	R	R	D	R	R	R

County	1916	1920	1924	1928	1932	1936	1940	1944	1948	1952	1956	1960
Todd	D	D	D	R	D	D	D	D	D	D	D	D
Trigg	D	D	D	R	D	D	D	D	D	D	D	D
Trimble	D	D	D	D	D	D	D	D	D	D	D	D
Union	D	D	D	D	D	D	D	D	D	D	D	D
Warren	D	D	D	R	D	D	D	D	D	R	R	R
Washington	T	R	R	R	D	D	D	D	D	R	R	R
Wayne	R	R	R	R	D	R	R	R	R	R	R	R
Webster	D	D	D	D	D	D	D	D	D	D	D	D
Whitley	R	R	R	R	R	R	R	R	R	R	R	R
Wolfe	D	D	D	D	D	D	D	D	D	D	D	D
Woodford	D	D	D	R	D	D	D	D	D	D	R	R

County	1964	1968	1972	1976	1980	1984	1988	1992	1996	2000	2004
Adair	R	R	R	R	R	R	R	R	R	R	R
Allen	R	R	R	R	R	R	R	R	R	R	R
Anderson	D	R	R	D	D	R	R	R	R	R	R
Ballard	D	D	R	D	D	D	D	D	D	D	R
Barren	D	R	R	D	R	R	R	D	R	R	R
Bath	D	D	R	D	D	R	D	D	D	R	D
Bell	D	R	R	D	D	R	R	D	D	R	R
Boone	D	R	R	T	R	R	R	R	R	R	R
Bourbon	D	D	R	D	D	R	R	D	D	R	R
Boyd	D	R	R	D	D	R	D	D	D	D	R
Boyle	D	R	R	D	D	R	R	R	R	R	R
Bracken	D	R	R	D	D	R	R	D	R	R	D
Breathitt	D	D	D	D	D	D	D	D	D	D	R
Breckinridge	D	R	R	D	R	R	R	D	R	R	R
Bullitt	D	A	R	D	R	R	R	D	R	R	R
Butler	R	R	R	R	R	R	R	R	R	R	R
Caldwell	D	R	R	D	D	R	R	D	R	R	R
Calloway	D	D	R	D	D	R	R	D	R	R	R
Campbell	D	R	R	R	R	R	R	R	R	R	R
Carlisle	D	D	R	D	D	R	D	D	D	R	R
Carroll	D	D	D	D	D	R	D	D	D	R	R
Carter	D	R	R	D	R	R	D	D	D	R	D
Casey	R	R	R	R	R	R	R	R	R	R	R
Christian	D	A	R	D	R	R	R	R	R	R	R
Clark	D	R	R	D	D	R	R	D	D	R	R
Clay	R	R	R	R	R	R	R	R	R	R	R
Clinton	R	R	R	R	R	R	R	R	R	R	R
Crittenden	R	R	R	D	R	R	R	D	R	R	R
Cumberland	R	R	R	R	R	R	R	R	R	R	R
Daviess	D	R	R	D	D	R	R	D	R	R	R
Edmonson	R	R	R	R	R	R	R	R	R	R	R
Elliott	D	D	D	D	D	D	D	D	D	D	D
Estill	D	R	R	R	R	R	R	R	R	R	R
Fayette	D	R	R	R	R	R	R	R	D	R	R
Fleming	D	R	R	D	R	R	R	D	R	R	R

County	1964	1968	1972	1976	1980	1984	1988	1992	1996	2000	2004
Floyd	D	D	D	D	D	D	D	D	D	D	D
Franklin	D	D	R	D	D	R	R	D	D	D	R
Fulton	D	A	R	D	D	R	D	D	D	D	R
Gallatin	D	D	R	D	D	T	D	D	D	R	R
Garrard	D	R	R	R	R	R	R	R	R	R	R
Grant	D	R	R	D	D	R	R	R	R	R	R
Graves	D	D	R	D	D	R	D	D	D	R	R
Grayson	R	R	R	R	R	R	R	R	R	R	R
Green	D	R	R	R	R	R	R	R	R	R	R
Greenup	D	R	R	D	D	R	D	D	D	R	R
Hancock	D	R	R	D	D	R	R	D	D	R	R
Hardin	D	R	R	D	R	R	R	R	R	R	R
Harlan	D	D	R	D	D	D	D	D	D	D	R
Harrison	D	D	R	D	D	R	R	D	D	R	R
Hart	D	R	R	D	R	R	R	D	R	R	R
Henderson	D	D	R	D	D	R	D	D	D	D	R
Henry	D	D	R	D	D	R	D	D	D	R	R
Hickman	D	A	R	D	D	R	D	D	D	R	R
Hopkins	D	D	R	D	D	R	D	D	D	R	R
Jackson	R	R	R	R	R	R	R	R	R	R	R
Jefferson	D	R	R	R	R	R	R	D	D	D	D
Jessamine	R	R	R	R	R	R	R	R	R	R	R
Johnson	D	R	R	R	R	R	R	D	D	R	R
Kenton	D	R	R	R	R	R	R	R	R	R	R
Knott	D	D	D	D	D	D	D	D	D	D	D
Knox	D	R	R	R	R	R	R	R	R	R	R
Larue	D	R	R	D	D	R	R	D	R	R	R
Laurel	R	R	R	R	R	R	R	R	R	R	R
Lawrence	D	R	R	D	R	R	R	D	D	R	R
Lee	D	R	R	R	R	R	R	R	R	R	R
Leslie	R	R	R	R	R	R	R	R	R	R	R
Letcher	D	D	R	D	D	D	D	D	D	D	R
Lewis	R	R	R	R	R	R	R	R	R	R	R
Lincoln	D	R	R	D	R	R	R	R	R	R	R
Livingston	D	D	R	D	D	D	D	D	D	R	R
Logan	D	R	R	D	D	R	R	D	D	R	R
Lyon	D	D	R	D	D	D	D	D	D	R	R
McCracken	D	D	R	D	D	R	D	D	D	R	R
McCreary	R	R	R	R	R	R	R	R	R	R	R
McLean	D	D	R	D	D	R	D	D	D	R	R
Madison	D	R	R	D	R	R	R	R	R	R	R
Magoffin	D	R	R	D	D	D	D	D	D	R	D
Marion	D	D	R	D	D	R	D	D	D	R	R
Marshall	D	D	R	D	D	D	D	D	D	R	R
Martin	D	R	R	R	R	R	R	R	D	R	R
Mason	D	D	R	D	D	R	R	D	R	R	R
Meade	D	D	R	D	D	R	R	D	D	R	R
Menifee	D	D	D	D	D	D	D	D	D	R	D
Mercer	D	R	R	D	D	R	R	R	R	R	R

County	1964	1968	1972	1976	1980	1984	1988	1992	1996	2000	2004
Metcalfe	D	R	R	D	R	R	R	D	R	R	R
Monroe	R	R	R	R	R	R	R	R	R	R	R
Montgomery	D	R	R	D	D	R	R	D	D	R	R
Morgan	D	D	D	D	D	D	D	D	D	R	R
Muhlenberg	D	R	R	D	D	D	D	D	D	D	R
Nelson	D	D	R	D	D	R	R	D	D	R	R
Nicholas	D	D	R	D	D	R	R	D	D	R	R
Ohio	D	R	R	R	R	R	R	D	D	R	R
Oldham	D	R	R	R	R	R	R	R	R	R	R
Owen	D	D	R	D	D	R	D	D	R	R	R
Owsley	R	R	R	R	R	R	R	R	R	R	R
Pendleton	D	R	R	D	D	R	R	R	R	R	R
Perry	D	D	R	D	D	D	D	D	D	D	R
Pike	D	D	R	D	D	D	D	D	D	D	D
Powell	D	R	R	D	D	R	R	D	D	R	R
Pulaski	R	R	R	R	R	R	R	R	R	R	R
Robertson	D	R	R	D	D	R	D	D	R	R	R
Rockcastle	R	R	R	R	R	R	R	R	R	R	R
Rowan	D	R	R	D	D	R	R	D	D	R	D
Russell	R	R	R	R	R	R	R	R	R	R	R
Scott	D	D	R	D	D	R	R	R	R	R	R
Shelby	D	D	R	D	D	R	R	R	R	R	R
Simpson	D	D	R	D	D	R	R	D	D	R	R
Spencer	D	R	R	D	D	R	R	D	R	R	R
Taylor	D	R	R	D	R	R	R	R	R	R	R
Todd	D	A	R	D	D	R	R	D	R	R	R
Trigg	D	D	R	D	D	R	R	D	D	R	R
Trimble	D	D	R	D	D	R	D	D	D	R	R
Union	D	D	R	D	D	D	D	D	D	R	R
Warren	D	R	R	D	R	R	R	R	R	R	R
Washington	D	R	R	D	D	R	R	R	R	R	R
Wayne	D	R	R	R	R	R	R	R	R	R	R
Webster	D	D	R	D	D	D	D	D	D	R	R
Whitley	D	R	R	R	R	R	R	R	R	R	R
Wolfe	D	D	D	D	D	D	D	D	D	R	D
Woodford	D	R	R	D	D	R	R	R	R	R	R

Louisiana

County	1868	1872	1876	1880	1884	1888	1892	1896	1900	1904	1908	1912
Acadia	–	–	–	–	–	D	D	D	D	D	D	D
Allen	–	–	–	–	–	–	–	–	–	–	–	–
Ascension	R	R	R	R	R	D	D	D	D	D	D	D
Assumption	R	R	R	R	R	D	D	R	D	D	D	D
Avoyelles	D	R	R	D	D	D	D	D	D	D	D	D

County	1868	1872	1876	1880	1884	1888	1892	1896	1900	1904	1908	1912
Beauregard	–	–	–	–	–	–	–	–	–	–	–	–
Bienville	D	D	D	D	D	D	D	D	D	D	D	D
Bossier	D	R	R	D	D	D	D	D	D	D	D	D
Caddo	D	R	R	D	D	D	D	D	D	D	D	D
Calcasieu	D	D	D	D	D	D	D	D	D	D	D	D
Caldwell	D	D	D	D	D	D	D	D	D	D	D	D
Cameron	–	D	D	D	D	D	D	D	D	D	D	D
Catahoula	D	R	D	D	D	D	D	D	D	D	D	D
Claiborne	D	D	D	D	D	D	D	D	D	D	D	D
Concordia	R	R	R	D	R	D	D	D	D	D	D	D
De Soto	D	R	R	D	D	D	D	D	D	D	D	D
East Baton Rouge	D	R	R	D	R	R	D	D	D	D	D	D
East Carroll	R	R	NR	R	R	D	D	D	D	D	D	D
East Feliciana	D	R	NR	D	D	D	D	D	D	D	D	D
Evangeline	–	–	–	–	–	–	–	–	–	–	–	D
Franklin	D	D	D	D	D	D	D	D	D	D	D	D
Grant	–	R	NR	D	D	D	R	D	D	D	D	D
Iberia	–	R	R	R	D	D	D	D	D	D	D	D
Iberville	R	R	R	R	R	R	D	R	D	D	D	D
Jackson	D	R	D	D	D	D	D	D	D	D	D	D
Jefferson	D	R	R	R	R	R	D	D	D	D	D	D
Jefferson Davis	–	–	–	–	–	–	–	–	–	–	–	–
Lafayette	D	D	R	D	D	D	D	D	D	D	D	D
Lafourche	D	R	R	D	D	D	D	D	D	D	D	D
La Salle	–	–	–	–	–	–	–	–	–	–	–	D
Lincoln	–	–	D	R	D	D	R	D	D	D	D	D
Livingston	D	D	D	D	D	D	D	D	D	D	D	D
Madison	R	R	R	D	R	D	D	D	D	D	D	D
Morehouse	D	R	R	D	D	D	D	D	D	D	D	D
Natchitoches	R	R	R	D	D	D	D	D	D	D	D	D
Orleans	D	D	D	D	D	D	D	D	D	D	D	D
Ouachita	D	R	R	D	D	D	D	D	D	D	D	D
Plaquemines	R	R	R	R	R	R	R	D	D	D	D	D
Pointe Coupee	R	R	R	D	R	D	D	D	D	D	D	D
Rapides	R	R	R	D	D	D	D	D	D	D	D	D
Red River	–	R	R	D	D	D	D	D	D	D	D	D
Richland	–	D	D	D	D	D	D	D	D	D	D	D
Sabine	D	D	D	D	D	D	D	D	D	D	D	D
St. Bernard	D	R	R	D	R	D	D	D	D	D	D	D
St. Charles	R	R	R	R	R	R	R	R	D	D	D	D
St. Helena	D	D	D	D	D	D	D	D	NR	D	D	D
St. James	R	R	R	R	R	R	R	R	R	D	D	D
St. John the Baptist	D	R	R	R	R	R	R	R	D	D	D	D
St. Landry	D	D	D	D	D	D	D	D	D	D	D	D

County	1868	1872	1876	1880	1884	1888	1892	1896	1900	1904	1908	1912
St. Martin	D	R	R	R	R	D	D	D	D	D	D	D
St. Mary	D	R	R	R	R	D	D	D	D	D	D	D
St. Tammany	D	R	D	D	D	D	D	D	D	D	D	D
Tangipahoa	–	R	D	D	D	D	D	D	D	D	D	D
Tensas	R	R	R	D	D	D	D	D	D	D	D	D
Terrebonne	R	R	R	R	R	D	D	D	D	D	D	D
Union	D	R	D	D	D	D	D	D	D	D	D	D
Vermilion	D	D	D	D	D	D	D	D	D	D	D	D
Vernon	–	D	D	D	D	D	D	D	D	D	D	D
Washington	D	D	D	D	D	D	D	D	D	D	D	D
Webster	–	R	R	D	D	D	D	D	D	D	D	D
West Baton Rouge	R	R	R	R	D	D	D	R	D	D	D	D
West Carroll	R	R	R	D	D	D	D	D	D	D	D	D
West Feliciana	R	R	R	D	D	D	D	D	D	D	D	D
Winn	D	D	D	D	D	D	R	D	D	D	D	D

County	1916	1920	1924	1928	1932	1936	1940	1944	1948	1952	1956	1960
Acadia	D	R	D	D	D	D	D	D	SR	D	D	D
Allen	D	D	D	D	D	D	D	D	D	D	R	D
Ascension	D	D	D	D	D	D	D	D	SR	D	D	D
Assumption	D	R	R	D	D	R	D	D	SR	D	R	D
Avoyelles	D	D	D	D	D	D	D	D	SR	D	D	D
Beauregard	D	D	D	D	D	D	D	D	D	D	R	D
Bienville	D	D	D	D	D	D	D	D	SR	R	R	SR
Bossier	D	D	D	D	D	D	D	D	SR	R	R	R
Caddo	D	D	D	D	D	D	D	D	SR	R	R	R
Calcasieu	D	D	D	D	D	D	D	D	D	D	R	D
Caldwell	D	D	D	D	D	D	D	D	SR	D	SR	R
Cameron	D	D	D	D	D	D	D	D	D	D	D	D
Catahoula	D	D	D	D	D	D	D	D	SR	D	R	R
Claiborne	D	D	D	D	D	D	D	D	SR	R	R	SR
Concordia	D	D	D	D	D	D	D	D	SR	D	R	SR
De Soto	D	D	D	D	D	D	D	D	SR	R	R	SR
East Baton Rouge	D	D	D	D	D	D	D	D	D	D	R	D
East Carroll	D	D	D	D	D	D	D	D	SR	D	D	SR
East Feliciana	D	D	D	D	D	D	D	D	SR	D	D	SR
Evangeline	D	R	D	D	D	D	D	D	SR	D	D	D
Franklin	D	D	D	D	D	D	D	D	SR	D	D	SR
Grant	D	D	D	D	D	D	D	D	SR	D	R	SR
Iberia	IP	R	D	D	D	D	D	D	R	R	R	D
Iberville	D	R	D	D	D	D	D	D	D	D	D	D
Jackson	D	D	D	D	D	D	D	D	SR	D	R	R
Jefferson	D	D	D	D	D	D	D	D	SR	D	R	D

County	1916	1920	1924	1928	1932	1936	1940	1944	1948	1952	1956	1960
Jefferson												
Davis	D	R	D	D	D	D	D	D	D	D	R	D
Lafayette	D	R	D	D	D	D	D	D	SR	R	R	D
Lafourche	IP	R	D	D	D	D	D	D	SR	D	R	D
La Salle	D	D	D	D	D	D	D	D	SR	D	R	R
Lincoln	D	D	D	D	D	D	D	D	SR	R	R	R
Livingston	D	D	D	D	D	D	D	D	D	D	D	D
Madison	D	D	D	D	D	D	D	D	SR	R	SR	SR
Morehouse	D	D	D	D	D	D	D	D	SR	D	R	R
Natchitoches	D	D	D	D	D	D	D	D	SR	D	R	D
Orleans	D	D	D	D	D	D	D	D	SR	D	R	D
Ouachita	D	D	D	D	D	D	D	D	SR	D	R	R
Plaquemines	D	D	D	D	D	D	D	D	SR	R	R	SR
Pointe												
Coupee	D	D	D	D	D	D	D	D	SR	D	D	D
Rapides	D	D	D	D	D	D	D	D	SR	D	R	D
Red River	D	D	D	D	D	D	D	D	SR	D	D	SR
Richland	D	D	D	D	D	D	D	D	SR	D	SR	SR
Sabine	D	D	D	D	D	D	D	D	SR	D	R	R
St. Bernard	D	D	D	D	D	D	D	D	SR	R	R	SR
St. Charles	D	D	D	D	D	D	D	D	SR	D	R	D
St. Helena	D	D	D	D	D	D	D	D	SR	D	D	SR
St. James	D	R	D	D	D	D	D	D	D	D	R	D
St. John												
the Baptist	D	R	D	D	D	D	D	D	D	D	R	D
St. Landry	D	D	D	D	D	D	D	D	SR	R	R	D
St. Martin	D	R	D	D	D	D	D	D	SR	D	D	D
St. Mary	D	R	D	D	D	D	D	D	SR	R	R	D
St. Tam-												
many	D	D	D	D	D	D	D	D	SR	D	R	D
Tangipahoa	D	D	D	D	D	D	D	D	SR	D	R	D
Tensas	D	D	D	D	D	D	D	D	SR	R	R	R
Terrebonne	D	R	D	D	D	D	D	D	SR	D	R	D
Union	D	D	D	D	D	D	D	D	SR	D	R	R
Vermilion	D	R	D	D	D	D	D	D	SR	D	D	D
Vernon	NR	D	D	D	D	D	D	D	SR	D	R	D
Washington	D	D	D	D	D	D	D	D	SR	D	D	D
Webster	D	D	D	D	D	D	D	D	SR	D	R	SR
West Baton												
Rouge	D	D	D	D	D	D	D	D	D	D	D	D
West Carroll	D	D	D	D	D	D	D	D	SR	D	SR	SR
West												
Feliciana	D	D	D	D	D	D	D	D	SR	R	R	SR
Winn	D	D	D	D	D	D	D	D	SR	D	R	R

County	1964	1968	1972	1976	1980	1984	1988	1992	1996	2000	2004
Acadia	D	A	R	D	R	R	D	D	D	R	R
Allen	D	A	R	D	D	D	D	D	D	R	R

County	1964	1968	1972	1976	1980	1984	1988	1992	1996	2000	2004
Ascension	D	A	R	D	D	R	D	D	D	R	R
Assumption	D	A	R	D	D	R	D	D	D	D	D
Avoyelles	D	A	R	D	R	R	R	D	D	R	R
Beauregard	R	A	R	D	D	R	R	R	R	R	R
Bienville	R	A	R	D	D	R	D	D	D	D	R
Bossier	R	A	R	R	R	R	R	R	R	R	R
Caddo	R	A	R	R	R	R	R	D	D	D	R
Calcasieu	D	A	R	D	D	R	D	D	D	R	R
Caldwell	R	A	R	R	R	R	R	D	D	R	R
Cameron	D	A	R	D	D	R	D	D	D	R	R
Catahoula	R	A	R	D	R	R	R	D	D	R	R
Claiborne	R	A	R	R	R	R	R	D	D	R	R
Concordia	R	A	R	D	R	R	R	D	D	R	R
De Soto	R	A	R	D	D	R	D	D	D	R	R
East Baton Rouge	R	A	R	R	R	R	R	R	D	R	R
East Carroll	R	D	R	D	D	D	D	D	D	D	D
East Feliciana	R	A	R	D	D	R	D	D	D	R	R
Evangeline	D	A	R	D	R	R	D	D	D	R	R
Franklin	R	A	R	R	R	R	R	D	D	R	R
Grant	R	A	R	D	R	R	R	R	R	R	R
Iberia	R	A	R	R	R	R	R	D	D	R	R
Iberville	D	A	R	D	D	D	D	D	D	D	D
Jackson	R	A	R	D	R	R	R	D	D	R	R
Jefferson	R	A	R	R	R	R	R	R	R	R	R
Jefferson Davis	D	A	R	D	D	R	D	D	D	R	R
Lafayette	D	A	R	R	R	R	R	R	R	R	R
Lafourche	D	A	R	D	R	R	R	D	D	R	R
La Salle	R	A	R	R	R	R	R	R	R	R	R
Lincoln	R	A	R	R	R	R	R	R	D	R	R
Livingston	R	A	R	D	D	R	R	R	R	R	R
Madison	R	D	R	D	D	D	D	D	D	D	D
Morehouse	R	A	R	R	R	R	R	D	D	R	R
Natchitoches	R	A	R	D	D	R	R	D	D	R	R
Orleans	D	D	R	D	D	D	D	D	D	D	D
Ouachita	R	A	R	R	R	R	R	R	R	R	R
Plaquemines	R	A	R	R	R	R	R	R	D	R	R
Pointe Coupee	R	A	R	D	D	D	D	D	D	D	D
Rapides	R	A	R	D	R	R	R	R	D	R	R
Red River	R	A	R	D	D	R	R	D	D	R	R
Richland	R	A	R	R	R	R	R	R	D	R	R
Sabine	R	A	R	D	D	R	R	D	D	R	R
St. Bernard	R	A	R	D	R	R	R	R	D	R	R
St. Charles	D	A	R	D	D	R	R	R	D	R	R
St. Helena	R	A	R	D	D	D	D	D	D	D	D
St. James	D	D	R	D	D	D	D	D	D	D	D

County	1964	1968	1972	1976	1980	1984	1988	1992	1996	2000	2004
St. John the Baptist	D	A	R	D	D	R	D	D	D	D	D
St. Landry	D	A	R	D	D	R	D	D	D	D	R
St. Martin	D	A	R	D	D	R	D	D	D	R	R
St. Mary	D	A	R	D	D	R	R	D	D	R	R
St. Tammany	R	A	R	R	R	R	R	R	R	R	R
Tangipahoa	R	A	R	D	D	R	R	D	D	R	R
Tensas	R	A	R	D	D	R	R	D	D	D	D
Terrebonne	D	A	R	R	R	R	R	R	D	R	R
Union	R	A	R	R	R	R	R	R	R	R	R
Vermilion	D	A	R	D	R	R	D	D	D	R	R
Vernon	R	A	R	D	D	R	R	D	D	R	R
Washington	R	A	R	D	D	R	R	D	D	R	R
Webster	R	A	R	R	R	R	R	D	D	R	R
West Baton Rouge	D	A	R	D	D	D	D	D	D	D	R
West Carroll	R	A	R	D	R	R	R	R	R	R	R
West Feliciana	R	D	D	D	D	D	D	D	D	R	R
Winn	R	A	R	D	R	R	R	D	D	R	R

Maine

County	1868	1872	1876	1880	1884	1888	1892	1896	1900	1904	1908	1912
Androscoggin	R	R	R	R	R	R	R	R	R	R	R	D
Aroostook	R	R	R	D	R	R	R	R	R	R	R	P
Cumberland	R	R	R	R	R	R	R	R	R	R	R	D
Franklin	R	R	R	R	R	R	R	R	R	R	R	P
Hancock	R	R	R	R	R	R	R	R	R	R	R	D
Kennebec	R	R	R	R	R	R	R	R	R	R	R	P
Knox	R	R	R	D	R	R	R	R	D	R	R	D
Lincoln	R	R	R	D	R	R	R	R	R	R	R	D
Oxford	R	R	R	R	R	R	R	R	R	R	R	P
Penobscot	R	R	R	R	R	R	R	R	R	R	R	P
Piscataquis	R	R	R	R	R	R	R	R	R	R	R	P
Sagadahoc	R	R	R	R	R	R	R	R	R	R	R	D
Somerset	R	R	R	R	R	R	R	R	R	R	R	P
Waldo	R	R	R	D	R	R	R	R	R	R	R	D
Washington	R	R	R	R	R	R	R	R	R	R	R	D
York	R	R	R	R	R	R	R	R	R	R	R	D

County	1916	1920	1924	1928	1932	1936	1940	1944	1948	1952	1956	1960
Androscoggin	D	R	R	R	D	D	D	D	D	R	R	D
Aroostook	R	R	R	R	R	R	R	R	R	R	R	R
Cumberland	R	R	R	R	R	R	R	R	R	R	R	R
Franklin	R	R	R	R	R	R	R	R	R	R	R	R
Hancock	D	R	R	R	R	R	R	R	R	R	R	R
Kennebec	R	R	R	R	R	R	D	R	R	R	R	R
Knox	D	R	R	R	R	R	R	R	R	R	R	R
Lincoln	R	R	R	R	R	R	R	R	R	R	R	R
Oxford	R	R	R	R	R	R	R	R	R	R	R	R
Penobscot	R	R	R	R	R	R	R	R	R	R	R	R
Piscataquis	R	R	R	R	R	R	R	R	R	R	R	R
Sagadahoc	R	R	R	R	R	R	D	D	R	R	R	R
Somerset	R	R	R	R	R	R	R	R	R	R	R	R
Waldo	D	R	R	R	R	R	R	R	R	R	R	R
Washington	R	R	R	R	R	D	D	D	R	R	R	R
York	D	R	R	R	R	D	D	D	D	R	R	D

County	1964	1968	1972	1976	1980	1984	1988	1992	1996	2000	2004
Androscoggin	D	D	D	D	D	R	R	D	D	D	D
Aroostook	D	D	R	R	R	R	R	D	D	D	D
Cumberland	D	D	R	R	D	R	R	D	D	D	D
Franklin	D	D	R	R	R	R	R	D	D	D	D
Hancock	D	R	R	R	R	R	R	D	D	D	D
Kennebec	D	D	R	D	R	R	R	D	D	D	D
Knox	D	R	R	R	R	R	R	D	D	D	D
Lincoln	D	R	R	R	R	R	R	D	D	R	D
Oxford	D	D	R	R	R	R	R	D	D	D	D
Penobscot	D	D	R	R	R	R	R	D	D	R	D
Piscataquis	D	D	R	R	R	R	R	PE	D	R	R
Sagadahoc	D	D	R	R	R	R	R	D	D	D	D
Somerset	D	D	R	D	R	R	R	PE	D	D	D
Waldo	D	R	R	R	R	R	R	PE	D	R	D
Washington	D	D	R	R	R	R	R	D	D	R	R
York	D	D	R	D	R	R	R	D	D	D	D

Maryland

County	1868	1872	1876	1880	1884	1888	1892	1896	1900	1904	1908	1912
Allegany	D	R	D	R	R	R	R	R	R	R	R	D
Anne Arundel	D	R	D	D	D	R	D	R	R	D	D	D
Baltimore City	D	D	D	D	D	D	D	R	R	D	R	D
Baltimore County	D	D	D	D	D	D	D	R	R	D	D	D
Calvert	D	R	R	D	R	R	R	R	R	R	R	R
Caroline	D	R	D	D	D	R	D	R	R	D	D	D

County	1868	1872	1876	1880	1884	1888	1892	1896	1900	1904	1908	1912
Carroll	D	R	D	D	D	D	D	R	R	D	D	D
Cecil	D	R	D	D	D	D	D	R	D	D	D	D
Charles	D	R	D	R	R	R	R	R	R	R	R	R
Dorchester	D	R	D	R	R	R	R	R	R	R	D	D
Frederick	R	R	R	R	R	R	D	R	R	R	R	D
Garrett	–	–	R	R	R	R	R	R	R	R	R	P
Harford	D	R	D	D	D	D	D	R	D	D	D	D
Howard	D	R	D	D	D	D	D	R	D	D	D	D
Kent	D	R	D	D	D	D	D	R	R	D	D	D
Montgomery	D	D	D	D	D	D	D	D	D	D	D	D
Prince Georges	D	R	D	D	D	D	D	R	R	R	D	D
Queen Annes	D	D	D	D	D	D	D	D	D	D	D	D
St. Marys	D	R	R	R	R	R	R	R	R	D	R	R
Somerset	D	R	D	R	R	R	R	R	R	R	R	D
Talbot	D	R	D	D	D	R	R	R	R	R	D	D
Washington	D	R	D	R	R	R	D	R	R	R	R	D
Wicomico	D	D	D	D	D	D	D	D	D	D	D	D
Worcester	D	D	D	D	D	D	D	D	D	D	D	D

County	1916	1920	1924	1928	1932	1936	1940	1944	1948	1952	1956	1960
Allegany	R	R	R	R	R	D	D	R	D	R	R	R
Anne Arundel	D	R	D	R	D	D	D	R	R	R	R	R
Baltimore City	D	R	R	R	D	D	D	D	D	D	R	D
Baltimore County	D	R	D	R	D	D	D	R	R	R	R	R
Calvert	R	R	R	R	R	R	D	R	R	R	R	D
Caroline	D	D	D	R	D	D	D	R	R	R	R	R
Carroll	D	R	R	R	D	R	R	R	R	R	R	R
Cecil	D	D	R	R	D	D	D	D	D	R	R	R
Charles	R	R	R	R	D	R	R	R	R	R	R	D
Dorchester	D	R	R	R	D	D	D	D	D	R	R	D
Frederick	D	R	R	R	D	D	D	R	R	R	R	R
Garrett	R	R	R	R	R	R	R	R	R	R	R	R
Harford	D	R	D	R	D	D	R	R	R	R	R	R
Howard	D	R	D	R	D	D	D	R	R	R	R	R
Kent	D	D	D	R	D	D	D	D	D	R	R	R
Montgomery	D	D	D	R	D	D	D	R	R	R	R	D
Prince Georges	D	R	R	R	D	D	D	D	D	R	R	D
Queen Annes	D	D	D	D	D	D	D	D	D	R	R	D
St. Marys	D	R	D	D	D	D	D	R	D	R	R	D
Somerset	R	R	R	R	D	R	D	R	R	R	R	R
Talbot	D	D	D	R	D	D	R	R	R	R	R	R
Washington	D	R	R	R	D	D	D	R	R	R	R	R
Wicomico	D	D	D	R	D	D	D	D	D	R	R	R
Worcester	D	D	D	R	D	D	D	R	R	R	R	R

County	1964	1968	1972	1976	1980	1984	1988	1992	1996	2000	2004
Allegany	D	R	R	D	R	R	R	R	R	R	R
Anne Arundel	D	R	R	R	R	R	R	R	R	R	R
Baltimore City	D	D	D	D	D	D	D	D	D	D	D
Baltimore County	D	R	R	R	R	R	R	R	D	D	D
Calvert	D	D	R	D	R	R	R	R	R	R	R
Caroline	D	R	R	R	R	R	R	R	R	R	R
Carroll	D	R	R	R	R	R	R	R	R	R	R
Cecil	D	R	R	D	R	R	R	R	R	R	R
Charles	D	R	R	D	R	R	R	R	R	R	D
Dorchester	R	R	R	R	R	R	R	R	R	D	R
Frederick	D	R	R	R	R	R	R	R	R	R	R
Garrett	R	R	R	R	R	R	R	R	R	R	R
Harford	D	R	R	R	R	R	R	R	R	R	R
Howard	D	R	R	R	R	R	R	R	D	D	D
Kent	D	R	R	D	D	R	R	R	R	D	R
Montgomery	D	D	R	D	R	R	D	D	D	D	D
Prince Georges	D	R	R	D	D	D	D	D	D	D	D
Queen Annes	D	R	R	R	R	R	R	R	R	R	R
St. Marys	D	R	R	D	R	R	R	R	R	R	R
Somerset	D	R	R	D	D	R	R	R	D	D	R
Talbot	D	R	R	R	R	R	R	R	R	R	R
Washington	D	R	R	R	R	R	R	R	R	R	R
Wicomico	D	R	R	R	R	R	R	R	R	R	R
Worcester	D	R	R	R	R	R	R	R	R	R	R

—— Massachusetts ——

County	1868	1872	1876	1880	1884	1888	1892	1896	1900	1904	1908	1912
Barnstable	R	R	R	R	R	R	R	R	R	R	R	P
Berkshire	R	R	R	R	R	R	R	R	R	R	R	R
Bristol	R	R	R	R	R	R	R	R	R	R	R	R
Dukes	R	R	R	R	R	R	R	R	R	R	R	P
Essex	R	R	R	R	R	R	R	R	R	R	R	R
Franklin	R	R	R	R	R	R	R	R	R	R	R	R
Hampden	R	R	R	R	R	R	R	R	R	R	R	D
Hampshire	R	R	R	R	R	R	R	R	R	R	R	D
Middlesex	R	R	R	R	R	R	R	R	R	R	R	D
Nantucket	R	R	R	R	R	R	R	R	R	R	R	D
Norfolk	R	R	R	R	R	R	R	R	R	R	R	P
Plymouth	R	R	R	R	R	R	R	R	R	R	R	P
Suffolk	R	R	D	D	D	D	D	R	D	D	R	D
Worcester	R	R	R	R	R	R	R	R	R	R	R	R

County	1916	1920	1924	1928	1932	1936	1940	1944	1948	1952	1956	1960
Barnstable	R	R	R	R	R	R	R	R	R	R	R	R
Berkshire	R	R	R	D	D	D	D	D	D	R	R	D
Bristol	R	R	R	D	D	D	D	D	D	R	R	D
Dukes	R	R	R	R	R	R	R	R	R	R	R	R
Essex	R	R	R	R	R	D	D	D	D	R	R	D
Franklin	R	R	R	R	R	R	R	R	R	R	R	R
Hampden	R	R	R	D	D	D	D	D	D	R	R	D
Hampshire	R	R	R	R	R	D	D	D	D	R	R	D
Middlesex	R	R	R	R	R	R	R	R	D	R	R	D
Nantucket	D	R	R	R	R	R	R	R	R	R	R	R
Norfolk	R	R	R	R	R	R	R	R	R	R	R	D
Plymouth	R	R	R	R	R	R	R	R	R	R	R	R
Suffolk	D	R	R	D	D	D	D	D	D	D	D	D
Worcester	R	R	R	R	R	D	D	D	D	R	R	D

County	1964	1968	1972	1976	1980	1984	1988	1992	1996	2000	2004
Barnstable	D	R	R	R	R	R	R	D	D	D	D
Berkshire	D	D	D	D	D	R	D	D	D	D	D
Bristol	D	D	D	D	D	D	D	D	D	D	D
Dukes	D	R	R	D	D	D	D	D	D	D	D
Essex	D	D	D	D	R	R	D	D	D	D	D
Franklin	D	R	R	D	R	R	D	D	D	D	D
Hampden	D	D	D	D	D	R	D	D	D	D	D
Hampshire	D	D	D	D	D	D	D	D	D	D	D
Middlesex	D	D	D	D	D	D	D	D	D	D	D
Nantucket	D	R	R	R	R	R	D	D	D	D	D
Norfolk	D	D	D	D	R	R	D	D	D	D	D
Plymouth	D	D	R	D	R	R	R	D	D	D	D
Suffolk	D	D	D	D	D	D	D	D	D	D	D
Worcester	D	D	D	D	R	R	R	D	D	D	D

Michigan

County	1868	1872	1876	1880	1884	1888	1892	1896	1900	1904	1908	1912
Alcona	–	R	D	R	R	R	R	R	R	R	R	P
Alger	–	–	–	–	–	R	R	R	R	R	R	P
Allegan	R	R	R	R	R	R	R	R	R	R	R	P
Alpena	R	R	D	R	D	D	D	R	R	R	R	P
Antrim	R	R	R	R	R	R	R	R	R	R	R	P
Arenac	–	–	–	–	D	UL	PO	D	R	R	R	P
Baraga	–	–	D	D	R	D	D	R	R	R	R	P
Barry	R	R	R	R	D	R	R	R	R	R	R	P
Bay	R	R	D	R	D	D	D	D	R	R	R	P
Benzie	–	R	R	R	R	R	R	R	R	R	R	P
Berrien	R	R	R	R	D	R	R	R	R	R	R	P

County	1868	1872	1876	1880	1884	1888	1892	1896	1900	1904	1908	1912
Branch	R	R	R	R	R	R	R	D	R	R	R	D
Calhoun	R	R	R	R	R	R	R	D	R	R	R	P
Cass	R	R	R	R	R	R	R	R	R	R	R	D
Charlevoix	–	R	R	R	R	R	R	R	R	R	R	R
Cheboygan	D	R	D	R	D	D	D	D	R	R	R	P
Chippewa	–	R	D	R	R	R	R	R	R	R	R	P
Clare	–	R	R	R	D	D	D	R	R	R	R	P
Clinton	R	R	R	R	D	R	R	R	R	R	R	P
Crawford	–	–	–	R	R	D	D	T	R	R	R	R
Delta	D	R	R	R	R	R	R	R	R	R	R	P
Dickinson	–	–	–	–	–	–	R	R	R	R	R	R
Eaton	R	R	R	R	R	R	R	D	R	R	R	D
Emmet	D	D	D	R	D	D	D	R	R	R	R	P
Genesee	R	R	R	R	R	R	R	R	R	R	R	P
Gladwin	–	–	D	D	R	R	R	R	R	R	R	R
Gogebic	–	–	–	–	–	R	R	R	R	R	R	P
Grand Traverse	R	R	R	R	R	R	R	R	R	R	R	P
Gratiot	R	R	R	R	D	R	R	D	R	R	R	P
Hillsdale	R	R	R	R	R	R	R	R	R	R	R	P
Houghton	D	R	R	R	R	R	D	D	R	R	R	P
Huron	R	R	R	R	D	D	D	R	R	R	R	P
Ingham	R	R	R	R	D	D	R	D	R	R	R	P
Ionia	R	R	R	R	D	R	R	D	R	R	R	D
Iosco	R	R	R	R	R	D	R	R	R	R	R	P
Iron	–	–	–	–	–	R	R	R	R	R	R	R
Isabella	R	R	R	R	R	R	R	D	R	R	R	P
Jackson	R	R	D	R	D	R	R	D	R	R	R	P
Kalamazoo	R	R	R	R	R	R	R	R	R	R	R	P
Kalkaska	–	R	R	R	R	R	R	R	R	R	R	P
Kent	R	R	R	R	D	R	R	R	R	R	R	P
Keweenaw	D	R	R	R	R	R	R	R	R	R	R	P
Lake	–	R	R	R	R	R	R	R	R	R	R	P
Lapeer	R	R	R	R	R	R	R	R	R	R	R	P
Leelanau	R	R	R	R	R	R	R	R	R	R	R	P
Lenawee	R	R	R	R	R	R	R	R	R	R	R	D
Livingston	D	R	D	R	D	D	R	D	R	R	R	D
Luce	–	–	–	–	–	R	R	R	R	R	R	P
Mackinac	D	D	D	D	D	D	D	R	R	R	R	D
Macomb	R	R	D	D	D	D	D	R	R	R	R	D
Manistee	R	R	R	R	D	D	D	R	R	R	R	D
Marquette	R	R	R	R	R	R	R	R	R	R	R	P
Mason	R	R	R	R	R	R	R	R	R	R	R	P
Mecosta	R	R	R	R	R	R	R	R	R	R	R	P
Menominee	R	R	R	R	R	R	R	R	R	R	R	P
Midland	R	R	R	R	R	R	R	R	R	R	R	P
Missaukee	–	R	R	R	R	R	R	R	R	R	R	P
Monroe	D	R	D	D	D	D	D	D	R	R	R	D
Montcalm	R	R	R	R	R	R	R	R	R	R	R	P
Montmorency	–	–	–	–	D	D	D	R	R	R	R	R

County	1868	1872	1876	1880	1884	1888	1892	1896	1900	1904	1908	1912
Muskegon	R	R	R	R	R	R	R	R	R	R	R	P
Newaygo	R	R	R	R	D	R	R	R	R	R	R	P
Oakland	R	R	D	R	D	D	D	R	R	R	R	R
Oceana	R	R	R	R	R	R	R	R	R	R	R	P
Ogemaw	–	–	R	R	R	R	R	R	R	R	R	P
Ontonagon	D	R	D	R	R	D	D	R	R	R	R	R
Osceola	–	R	R	R	R	R	R	R	R	R	R	P
Oscoda	–	–	–	–	R	D	R	R	R	R	R	P
Otsego	–	–	R	R	R	R	R	R	R	R	R	R
Ottawa	R	R	R	R	R	R	R	R	R	R	R	P
Presque Isle	–	R	D	R	R	D	D	R	R	R	R	P
Roscommon	–	–	D	D	D	R	D	R	R	R	R	P
Saginaw	R	R	D	D	D	D	D	D	R	R	R	D
St. Clair	R	R	R	R	D	R	R	R	R	R	R	P
St. Joseph	R	R	R	R	D	R	R	D	D	R	R	P
Sanilac	R	R	R	R	R	R	R	R	R	R	R	P
Schoolcraft	–	R	R	R	R	R	D	R	R	R	R	R
Shiawassee	R	R	R	R	D	R	R	R	R	R	R	P
Tuscola	R	R	R	R	R	R	R	R	R	R	R	P
Van Buren	R	R	R	R	R	R	R	R	R	R	R	P
Washtenaw	D	R	D	D	D	D	D	R	R	R	R	D
Wayne	D	R	D	R	D	D	D	R	R	R	R	P
Wexford	–	R	R	R	R	R	R	R	R	R	R	P

County	1916	1920	1924	1928	1932	1936	1940	1944	1948	1952	1956	1960
Alcona	R	R	R	R	D	R	R	R	R	R	R	R
Alger	R	R	R	R	D	D	D	D	D	R	D	D
Allegan	R	R	R	R	R	R	R	R	R	R	R	R
Alpena	R	R	R	R	D	R	R	R	R	R	R	R
Antrim	R	R	R	R	R	R	R	R	R	R	R	R
Arenac	D	R	R	R	D	D	R	R	R	R	R	R
Baraga	R	R	R	R	D	D	R	D	R	R	R	D
Barry	R	R	R	R	R	R	R	R	R	R	R	R
Bay	R	R	R	R	D	D	D	D	D	R	R	D
Benzie	R	R	R	R	R	R	R	R	R	R	R	R
Berrien	R	R	R	R	D	D	R	R	R	R	R	R
Branch	R	R	R	R	D	R	R	R	R	R	R	R
Calhoun	D	R	R	R	D	D	R	R	R	R	R	R
Cass	D	R	R	R	D	D	R	R	R	R	R	R
Charlevoix	R	R	R	R	R	R	R	R	R	R	R	R
Cheboygan	R	R	R	R	D	D	R	R	R	R	R	R
Chippewa	R	R	R	R	R	D	R	R	R	R	R	R
Clare	R	R	R	R	D	R	R	R	R	R	R	R
Clinton	R	R	R	R	D	R	R	R	R	R	R	R
Crawford	D	R	R	R	D	D	R	R	R	R	R	R
Delta	R	R	R	R	D	D	D	D	D	R	R	D
Dickinson	R	R	R	R	D	D	D	D	D	R	R	D
Eaton	R	R	R	R	D	D	R	R	R	R	R	R
Emmet	R	R	R	R	D	D	R	R	R	R	R	R

County	1916	1920	1924	1928	1932	1936	1940	1944	1948	1952	1956	1960
Genesee	R	R	R	R	D	D	D	D	D	R	R	R
Gladwin	R	R	R	R	D	R	R	R	R	R	R	R
Gogebic	R	R	R	R	D	D	D	D	D	D	R	D
Grand Traverse	R	R	R	R	D	D	R	R	R	R	R	R
Gratiot	R	R	R	R	D	D	R	R	R	R	R	R
Hillsdale	R	R	R	R	R	R	R	R	R	R	R	R
Houghton	R	R	R	R	R	D	R	D	R	R	R	D
Huron	R	R	R	R	D	R	R	R	R	R	R	R
Ingham	R	R	R	R	D	D	R	R	R	R	R	R
Ionia	R	R	R	R	D	D	R	R	R	R	R	R
Iosco	R	R	R	R	R	R	R	R	R	R	R	R
Iron	R	R	R	R	R	D	D	D	D	D	R	D
Isabella	R	R	R	R	D	R	R	R	R	R	R	R
Jackson	D	R	R	R	D	D	R	R	R	R	R	R
Kalamazoo	D	R	R	R	R	D	R	R	R	R	R	R
Kalkaska	R	R	R	R	R	D	R	R	R	R	R	R
Kent	D	R	R	R	R	D	R	R	R	R	R	R
Keweenaw	R	R	R	R	R	R	R	D	R	R	R	R
Lake	R	R	R	R	D	D	R	R	R	R	R	R
Lapeer	R	R	R	R	R	R	R	R	R	R	R	R
Leelanau	R	R	R	R	D	R	R	R	R	R	R	R
Lenawee	R	R	R	R	R	R	R	R	R	R	R	R
Livingston	R	R	R	R	D	R	R	R	R	R	R	R
Luce	R	R	R	R	R	D	R	R	R	R	R	R
Mackinac	R	R	R	R	D	D	R	R	R	R	R	R
Macomb	R	R	R	R	D	D	D	D	D	R	D	D
Manistee	R	D	R	R	D	D	R	R	R	R	R	R
Marquette	R	R	R	R	R	D	D	D	D	R	R	D
Mason	R	R	R	R	D	D	R	R	R	R	R	R
Mecosta	R	R	R	R	R	R	R	R	R	R	R	R
Menominee	R	R	R	R	D	D	D	R	D	R	R	D
Midland	R	R	R	R	R	R	R	R	R	R	R	R
Missaukee	R	R	R	R	R	R	R	R	R	R	R	R
Monroe	D	R	R	R	D	D	R	R	R	R	R	D
Montcalm	R	R	R	R	D	R	R	R	R	R	R	R
Montmorency	R	R	R	R	D	D	R	R	R	R	R	R
Muskegon	R	R	R	R	D	D	D	D	D	R	R	R
Newaygo	R	R	R	R	R	R	R	R	R	R	R	R
Oakland	R	R	R	R	D	D	R	R	R	R	R	R
Oceana	R	R	R	R	D	D	R	R	R	R	R	R
Ogemaw	R	R	R	R	D	D	R	R	R	R	R	R
Ontonagon	R	R	R	R	D	D	D	D	R	R	R	R
Osceola	R	R	R	R	R	R	R	R	R	R	R	R
Oscoda	R	R	R	R	R	D	R	R	R	R	R	R
Otsego	R	R	R	R	D	D	R	R	R	R	R	R
Ottawa	R	R	R	R	R	R	R	R	R	R	R	R
Presque Isle	R	R	R	R	D	D	D	R	R	R	R	R
Roscommon	R	R	R	R	D	R	R	R	R	R	R	R
Saginaw	R	R	R	R	D	D	R	R	R	R	R	R

County	1916	1920	1924	1928	1932	1936	1940	1944	1948	1952	1956	1960
St. Clair	R	R	R	R	R	R	R	R	R	R	R	R
St. Joseph	D	R	R	R	D	R	R	R	R	R	R	R
Sanilac	R	R	R	R	R	R	R	R	R	R	R	R
Schoolcraft	R	R	R	R	R	D	D	D	R	R	R	R
Shiawassee	R	R	R	R	D	D	R	R	R	R	R	R
Tuscola	R	R	R	R	R	R	R	R	R	R	R	R
Van Buren	R	R	R	R	D	R	R	R	R	R	R	R
Washtenaw	R	R	R	R	R	R	R	R	R	R	R	R
Wayne	R	R	R	R	D	D	D	D	D	D	D	D
Wexford	R	R	R	R	R	D	R	R	R	R	R	R

County	1964	1968	1972	1976	1980	1984	1988	1992	1996	2000	2004
Alcona	D	R	R	R	R	R	R	D	D	R	R
Alger	D	D	R	D	D	R	D	D	D	R	D
Allegan	D	R	R	R	R	R	R	R	R	R	R
Alpena	D	R	R	R	R	R	R	D	D	D	R
Antrim	D	R	R	R	R	R	R	R	R	R	R
Arenac	D	R	R	D	R	R	D	D	D	D	D
Baraga	D	D	R	R	R	R	D	D	D	R	R
Barry	D	R	R	R	R	R	R	R	R	R	R
Bay	D	D	R	D	R	R	D	D	D	D	D
Benzie	D	R	R	R	R	R	R	D	D	R	R
Berrien	D	R	R	R	R	R	R	R	R	R	R
Branch	D	R	R	R	R	R	R	R	D	R	R
Calhoun	D	R	R	R	R	R	R	D	D	D	R
Cass	D	R	R	R	R	R	R	D	D	R	R
Charlevoix	D	R	R	R	R	R	R	D	R	R	R
Cheboygan	D	R	R	R	R	R	R	D	D	R	R
Chippewa	D	R	R	R	R	R	R	R	D	R	R
Clare	D	R	R	R	R	R	R	D	D	D	R
Clinton	D	R	R	R	R	R	R	R	R	R	R
Crawford	D	R	R	R	R	R	R	D	D	R	R
Delta	D	D	D	D	D	R	D	D	D	R	R
Dickinson	D	D	R	D	R	R	R	D	D	R	R
Eaton	D	R	R	R	R	R	R	R	R	R	R
Emmet	D	R	R	R	R	R	R	R	R	R	R
Genesee	D	D	R	D	D	R	D	D	D	D	D
Gladwin	D	R	R	R	R	R	R	D	D	R	R
Gogebic	D	D	R	D	D	D	D	D	D	D	D
Grand Traverse	D	R	R	R	R	R	R	R	R	R	R
Gratiot	D	R	R	R	R	R	R	R	D	R	R
Hillsdale	D	R	R	R	R	R	R	R	R	R	R
Houghton	D	D	R	R	R	R	R	D	D	R	R
Huron	D	R	R	R	R	R	R	R	D	R	R
Ingham	D	R	R	R	R	R	R	D	D	D	D
Ionia	D	R	R	R	R	R	R	R	R	R	R
Iosco	D	R	R	R	R	R	R	D	D	D	R
Iron	D	D	R	D	D	D	D	D	D	D	R
Isabella	D	R	R	R	R	R	R	D	D	D	D

County	1964	1968	1972	1976	1980	1984	1988	1992	1996	2000	2004
Jackson	D	R	R	R	R	R	R	R	R	R	R
Kalamazoo	D	R	R	R	R	R	R	D	D	D	D
Kalkaska	D	R	R	R	R	R	R	D	D	R	R
Kent	D	R	R	R	R	R	R	R	R	R	R
Keweenaw	D	D	R	D	R	D	D	D	D	R	R
Lake	D	D	D	D	D	R	D	D	D	D	D
Lapeer	D	R	R	R	R	R	R	R	D	R	R
Leelanau	D	R	R	R	R	R	R	R	R	R	R
Lenawee	D	R	R	R	R	R	R	D	D	R	R
Livingston	D	R	R	R	R	R	R	R	R	R	R
Luce	D	R	R	R	R	R	R	D	D	R	R
Mackinac	D	R	R	R	R	R	R	D	D	R	R
Macomb	D	D	R	R	R	R	R	R	D	D	R
Manistee	D	R	R	R	R	R	R	D	D	D	R
Marquette	D	D	R	R	D	R	D	D	D	D	D
Mason	D	R	R	R	R	R	R	R	D	R	R
Mecosta	D	R	R	R	R	R	R	D	D	R	R
Menominee	D	D	R	R	R	R	R	D	D	R	R
Midland	D	R	R	R	R	R	R	R	R	R	R
Missaukee	R	R	R	R	R	R	R	R	R	R	R
Monroe	D	D	R	D	R	R	R	D	D	D	R
Montcalm	D	R	R	R	R	R	R	D	D	R	R
Montmorency	D	R	R	R	R	R	R	D	D	R	R
Muskegon	D	R	R	R	R	R	R	D	D	D	D
Newaygo	D	R	R	R	R	R	R	R	R	R	R
Oakland	D	R	R	R	R	R	R	R	D	D	D
Oceana	D	R	R	R	R	R	R	R	D	R	R
Ogemaw	D	R	R	D	R	R	R	D	D	D	R
Ontonagon	D	D	R	D	R	R	D	D	D	R	R
Osceola	D	R	R	R	R	R	R	R	D	R	R
Oscoda	D	R	R	R	R	R	R	R	D	R	R
Otsego	D	R	R	R	R	R	R	R	R	R	R
Ottawa	R	R	R	R	R	R	R	R	R	R	R
Presque Isle	D	R	R	R	R	R	R	D	D	R	R
Roscommon	D	R	R	R	R	R	R	D	D	D	R
Saginaw	D	R	R	R	R	R	D	D	D	D	D
St. Clair	D	R	R	R	R	R	R	R	D	R	R
St. Joseph	D	R	R	R	R	R	R	R	R	R	R
Sanilac	R	R	R	R	R	R	R	R	R	R	R
Schoolcraft	D	D	R	D	R	R	D	D	D	R	R
Shiawassee	D	R	R	R	R	R	R	D	D	R	R
Tuscola	D	R	R	R	R	R	R	D	D	R	R
Van Buren	D	R	R	R	R	R	R	D	D	R	R
Washtenaw	D	R	D	R	D	R	D	D	D	D	D
Wayne	D	D	D	D	D	D	D	D	D	D	D
Wexford	D	R	R	R	R	R	R	D	D	R	R

Minnesota

County	1868	1872	1876	1880	1884	1888	1892	1896	1900	1904	1908	1912
Aitkin	–	R	R	R	R	R	R	R	R	R	R	P
Anoka	R	R	R	R	R	R	R	R	R	R	R	P
Becker	–	R	R	R	R	R	R	R	R	R	R	P
Beltrami	–	–	–	–	R	NR	R	D	R	R	R	S
Benton	R	R	D	D	D	D	PO	D	R	R	R	P
Big Stone	–	R	R	R	R	R	R	R	R	R	R	D
Blue Earth	R	R	R	R	R	R	R	R	R	R	R	D
Brown	R	R	R	R	D	D	D	R	R	R	D	D
Carlton	R	R	R	D	R	R	R	R	R	R	R	P
Carver	D	D	D	R	D	D	D	R	R	R	R	D
Cass	NR	R	R	R	R	R	R	R	R	R	R	P
Chippewa	–	R	R	R	R	R	R	R	R	R	R	P
Chisago	R	R	R	R	R	R	R	R	R	R	R	P
Clay	–	R	R	R	R	R	R	D	R	R	R	P
Clearwater	–	–	–	–	–	–	–	–	–	R	R	P
Cook	–	–	–	–	R	D	R	D	R	R	R	P
Cottonwood	–	R	R	R	R	R	R	R	R	R	R	P
Crow Wing	–	R	R	R	R	R	R	R	R	R	R	P
Dakota	D	D	D	D	D	D	D	D	R	R	R	D
Dodge	R	R	R	R	R	R	R	R	R	R	R	P
Douglas	R	R	R	R	R	R	R	R	R	R	R	P
Faribault	R	R	R	R	R	R	R	R	R	R	R	P
Fillmore	R	R	R	R	R	R	R	R	R	R	R	P
Freeborn	R	R	R	R	R	R	R	R	R	R	R	P
Goodhue	R	R	R	R	R	R	R	R	R	R	R	P
Grant	R	R	R	R	R	R	R	R	R	R	R	P
Hennepin	R	R	R	R	R	R	R	R	R	R	R	D
Houston	R	R	R	R	R	R	R	R	R	R	R	P
Hubbard	–	–	–	–	R	D	R	R	R	R	R	P
Isanti	R	NR	R	R	R	R	R	R	R	R	R	P
Itasca	–	–	–	–	–	D	D	R	R	R	R	P
Jackson	R	R	R	R	R	R	R	R	R	R	R	P
Kanabec	R	R	R	R	R	R	R	R	R	R	R	P
Kandiyohi	R	R	R	R	R	R	R	R	R	R	R	P
Kittson	–	R	R	R	R	R	PO	D	R	R	R	P
Koochiching	–	–	–	–	–	–	–	–	–	–	R	D
Lac Qui Parle	–	R	R	R	R	R	R	R	R	R	R	P
Lake	R	R	R	R	R	R	R	R	R	R	R	S
Lake of the Woods	–	–	–	–	–	–	–	–	–	–	–	–
Le Sueur	D	D	D	D	D	D	D	R	R	R	R	D
Lincoln	–	–	R	R	R	R	D	D	R	R	R	P
Lyon	–	–	R	R	R	R	R	R	R	R	R	P
McLeod	R	R	D	R	D	D	D	D	R	R	R	D
Mahnomen	–	–	–	–	–	–	–	–	–	–	R	D
Marshall	–	–	–	R	R	R	PO	D	R	R	R	P

County	1868	1872	1876	1880	1884	1888	1892	1896	1900	1904	1908	1912
Martin	R	R	R	R	R	R	R	R	R	R	R	P
Meeker	R	R	R	R	R	R	R	R	R	R	R	P
Mille Lacs	R	R	R	R	R	R	R	R	R	R	R	P
Morrison	D	D	D	D	D	D	D	R	R	R	R	D
Mower	R	R	R	R	R	R	R	R	R	R	R	P
Murray	–	R	R	R	R	R	R	R	R	R	R	P
Nicollet	R	R	R	R	R	R	R	R	R	R	R	D
Nobles	–	R	R	R	R	R	R	R	R	R	R	P
Norman	–	–	–	–	R	R	R	R	R	R	R	P
Olmsted	R	R	R	R	R	R	R	R	R	R	R	D
Otter Tail	R	R	R	R	R	R	R	D	R	R	R	P
Pennington	–	–	–	–	–	–	–	–	–	–	–	P
Pine	R	R	D	D	R	R	R	R	R	R	R	P
Pipestone	–	–	–	R	R	R	R	D	R	R	R	P
Polk	–	R	R	R	R	R	PO	D	R	R	R	P
Pope	R	R	R	R	R	R	R	R	R	R	R	P
Ramsey	D	D	D	D	R	D	D	R	R	R	R	D
Red Lake	–	–	–	–	–	–	–	–	D	R	R	D
Redwood	R	R	R	R	R	R	R	R	R	R	R	P
Renville	R	R	R	R	R	R	R	R	R	R	R	P
Rice	R	R	R	R	R	R	R	R	R	R	R	P
Rock	–	R	R	R	R	R	R	R	R	R	R	P
Roseau	–	–	–	–	–	–	–	D	R	R	R	P
St. Louis	R	R	R	R	R	R	R	R	R	R	R	P
Scott	D	D	D	D	D	D	D	D	D	R	D	D
Sherburne	R	R	R	R	R	R	R	R	R	R	R	P
Sibley	D	D	D	D	D	D	D	R	R	R	R	P
Stearns	D	D	D	D	D	D	D	D	D	R	D	D
Steele	R	R	R	R	R	R	R	R	R	R	R	D
Stevens	–	R	R	R	R	R	R	R	R	R	R	D
Swift	–	R	R	R	R	R	R	R	R	R	R	P
Todd	R	R	R	R	R	R	R	R	R	R	R	P
Traverse	–	–	–	–	R	R	R	D	R	R	R	D
Wabasha	R	R	R	R	D	D	D	R	R	R	R	D
Wadena	–	–	R	R	R	R	R	R	R	R	R	P
Waseca	R	R	R	R	R	R	R	R	R	R	R	D
Washington	R	R	R	R	R	R	R	R	R	R	R	P
Watonwan	R	R	R	R	R	R	R	R	R	R	R	P
Wilkin	–	R	R	R	R	R	R	D	R	R	R	D
Winona	R	R	D	R	D	D	D	R	D	R	D	D
Wright	R	R	R	R	R	R	R	R	R	R	R	P
Yellow Medicine	–	R	R	R	R	R	R	R	R	R	R	P

County	1916	1920	1924	1928	1932	1936	1940	1944	1948	1952	1956	1960
Aitkin	R	R	R	R	D	D	R	D	D	R	R	R
Anoka	R	R	R	R	D	D	D	D	D	D	D	D
Becker	R	R	P	R	D	D	D	D	D	R	D	D
Beltrami	D	R	P	R	D	D	D	D	D	R	R	D

County	1916	1920	1924	1928	1932	1936	1940	1944	1948	1952	1956	1960
Benton	R	R	P	D	D	D	R	R	D	R	R	D
Big Stone	D	R	R	D	D	D	D	D	D	R	D	D
Blue Earth	R	R	R	R	D	D	R	R	R	R	R	R
Brown	R	R	P	D	D	D	R	R	R	R	R	R
Carlton	D	R	R	R	D	D	D	D	D	D	D	D
Carver	R	R	P	R	D	R	R	R	R	R	R	R
Cass	D	R	R	R	D	D	D	D	D	R	R	R
Chippewa	R	R	P	R	D	D	D	D	D	R	R	R
Chisago	R	R	R	R	D	D	R	R	D	R	R	R
Clay	D	R	P	R	D	D	D	D	D	R	R	R
Clearwater	D	R	P	R	D	D	D	D	D	D	D	D
Cook	D	R	R	R	D	D	D	D	D	R	R	R
Cottonwood	R	R	R	R	D	D	R	R	D	R	R	R
Crow Wing	R	R	R	R	D	D	D	D	D	R	R	R
Dakota	D	R	P	D	D	D	D	D	D	D	R	D
Dodge	R	R	R	R	D	D	R	R	D	R	R	R
Douglas	R	R	P	R	D	D	R	R	D	R	R	R
Faribault	R	R	R	R	D	D	R	R	D	R	R	R
Fillmore	R	R	R	R	D	R	R	R	R	R	R	R
Freeborn	R	R	R	R	D	D	D	D	D	R	R	R
Goodhue	R	R	R	R	D	D	R	R	D	R	R	R
Grant	R	R	R	R	D	D	R	D	D	R	D	D
Hennepin	D	R	R	R	D	D	D	D	D	R	R	R
Houston	R	R	R	R	D	D	R	R	R	R	R	R
Hubbard	D	R	R	R	D	D	R	R	R	R	R	R
Isanti	R	R	P	R	D	D	D	D	D	R	D	R
Itasca	D	R	R	R	D	D	D	D	D	D	D	D
Jackson	R	R	R	R	D	D	D	D	D	R	R	D
Kanabec	R	R	P	R	D	D	R	R	D	R	R	R
Kandiyohi	D	R	P	R	D	D	D	D	D	R	D	R
Kittson	D	R	P	R	D	D	D	D	D	D	D	D
Koochiching	D	R	P	R	D	D	D	D	D	D	D	D
Lac Qui Parle	R	R	R	R	D	D	R	R	D	R	R	D
Lake	D	R	P	R	R	D	D	D	D	D	D	D
Lake of the Woods	–	R	P	R	D	D	D	D	D	D	D	D
Le Sueur	D	R	P	D	D	D	R	R	D	R	R	D
Lincoln	D	R	R	D	D	D	D	D	D	R	D	D
Lyon	D	R	R	R	D	D	D	D	D	R	R	D
McLeod	R	R	P	R	D	D	R	R	R	R	R	R
Mahnomen	D	R	P	D	D	D	D	D	D	D	D	D
Marshall	D	R	P	R	D	D	D	D	D	R	D	D
Martin	D	R	R	R	D	D	R	R	D	R	R	R
Meeker	R	R	P	R	D	D	R	R	D	R	R	R
Mille Lacs	R	R	R	R	D	D	D	D	D	R	R	R
Morrison	R	R	P	D	D	D	R	R	D	R	R	D
Mower	R	R	R	R	D	D	D	D	D	R	R	R
Murray	D	R	P	R	D	D	D	R	D	R	R	R
Nicollet	R	R	R	R	D	D	R	R	D	R	R	R

County	1916	1920	1924	1928	1932	1936	1940	1944	1948	1952	1956	1960
Nobles	R	R	P	R	D	D	R	R	D	R	R	R
Norman	D	R	P	R	D	D	D	D	D	R	D	D
Olmsted	R	R	R	R	D	D	R	R	D	R	R	R
Otter Tail	R	R	R	R	D	R	R	R	R	R	R	R
Pennington	D	R	P	D	D	D	D	D	D	D	D	D
Pine	R	R	P	R	D	D	D	D	D	R	D	D
Pipestone	R	R	R	R	D	D	R	R	D	R	R	R
Polk	D	R	P	R	D	D	D	D	D	R	D	D
Pope	R	R	P	R	D	D	D	D	D	R	R	R
Ramsey	D	R	R	D	D	D	D	D	D	D	D	D
Red Lake	D	R	P	D	D	D	D	D	D	D	D	D
Redwood	R	R	R	R	D	D	R	R	D	R	R	R
Renville	R	R	P	R	D	D	R	R	D	R	R	R
Rice	R	R	R	R	D	D	R	R	R	R	R	R
Rock	R	R	R	R	D	D	R	R	D	R	R	R
Roseau	D	R	P	R	D	D	D	D	D	D	D	D
St. Louis	D	R	R	R	D	D	D	D	D	D	D	D
Scott	D	R	P	D	D	D	R	R	D	R	R	D
Sherburne	R	R	R	R	D	D	R	R	D	R	R	R
Sibley	R	R	P	R	D	D	R	R	R	R	R	R
Stearns	R	R	P	D	D	D	R	R	D	R	R	D
Steele	R	R	R	R	D	D	R	R	R	R	R	R
Stevens	R	R	R	R	D	D	R	R	D	R	R	R
Swift	R	R	P	R	D	D	D	D	D	R	D	D
Todd	D	R	R	R	D	D	R	R	D	R	R	R
Traverse	D	R	P	D	D	D	D	D	D	R	D	D
Wabasha	R	R	R	R	D	D	R	R	D	R	R	R
Wadena	R	R	R	R	D	D	R	R	D	R	R	R
Waseca	R	R	P	R	D	D	R	R	R	R	R	R
Washington	R	R	R	R	D	D	R	R	D	R	R	D
Watonwan	R	R	R	R	D	D	R	R	D	R	R	R
Wilkin	D	R	R	R	D	D	D	R	D	R	R	R
Winona	R	R	P	R	D	D	R	R	D	R	R	R
Wright	R	R	R	R	D	D	R	R	R	R	R	R
Yellow Medicine	R	R	P	R	D	D	R	R	D	R	R	R

County	1964	1968	1972	1976	1980	1984	1988	1992	1996	2000	2004
Aitkin	D	D	R	D	D	D	D	D	D	D	R
Anoka	D	D	R	D	D	D	D	D	D	R	R
Becker	D	D	R	D	R	R	R	R	D	R	R
Beltrami	D	D	R	D	D	D	D	D	D	R	D
Benton	D	D	R	D	R	R	R	D	D	R	R
Big Stone	D	D	D	D	R	D	D	D	D	D	D
Blue Earth	D	R	R	D	R	R	D	D	D	R	D
Brown	D	R	R	R	R	R	R	R	R	R	R
Carlton	D	D	D	D	D	D	D	D	D	D	D
Carver	R	R	R	R	R	R	R	R	R	R	R
Cass	D	R	R	D	R	R	R	D	D	R	R

County	1964	1968	1972	1976	1980	1984	1988	1992	1996	2000	2004
Chippewa	D	D	R	D	R	R	D	D	D	R	D
Chisago	D	D	R	D	D	D	D	D	D	R	R
Clay	D	D	R	D	R	R	D	D	D	R	R
Clearwater	D	D	R	D	D	R	D	D	D	R	R
Cook	D	R	R	R	R	R	D	D	D	R	D
Cottonwood	D	R	R	R	R	R	R	R	D	R	R
Crow Wing	D	D	R	D	R	R	R	R	D	R	R
Dakota	D	D	R	D	D	R	D	D	D	R	R
Dodge	D	R	R	R	R	R	R	R	D	R	R
Douglas	D	R	R	D	R	R	R	R	R	R	R
Faribault	D	R	R	R	R	R	R	R	R	R	R
Fillmore	D	R	R	R	R	R	R	D	D	D	D
Freeborn	D	D	R	D	R	D	D	D	D	D	D
Goodhue	D	R	R	R	R	R	R	D	D	R	R
Grant	D	D	D	D	R	R	D	D	D	R	R
Hennepin	D	D	R	D	D	D	D	D	D	D	D
Houston	D	R	R	R	R	R	R	R	D	R	R
Hubbard	D	R	R	D	R	R	R	D	D	R	R
Isanti	D	D	R	D	D	R	D	D	D	R	R
Itasca	D	D	D	D	D	D	D	D	D	D	D
Jackson	D	D	R	D	R	D	D	D	D	R	R
Kanabec	D	D	R	D	D	R	D	D	D	R	R
Kandiyohi	D	D	D	,	D	R	R	D	D	D	R	R
Kittson	D	D	R	D	R	R	D	D	D	R	D
Koochiching	D	D	R	D	D	D	D	D	D	R	D
Lac Qui Parle	D	D	D	D	R	R	D	D	D	D	D
Lake	D	D	D	D	D	D	D	D	D	D	D
Lake of the Woods	D	D	R	D	R	R	R	D	D	R	R
Le Sueur	D	D	R	D	R	R	R	D	D	R	R
Lincoln	D	D	D	D	R	R	D	D	D	D	R
Lyon	D	D	R	D	R	R	R	R	D	R	R
McLeod	D	R	R	R	R	R	R	R	D	R	R
Mahnomen	D	D	D	D	R	R	D	D	D	R	D
Marshall	D	D	R	D	R	R	D	D	D	R	R
Martin	R	R	R	R	R	R	R	R	R	R	R
Meeker	D	D	R	D	R	R	R	D	D	R	R
Mille Lacs	D	D	R	D	D	R	D	D	D	R	R
Morrison	D	D	D	D	D	R	R	D	D	R	R
Mower	D	D	D	D	D	D	D	D	D	D	D
Murray	D	R	R	D	R	R	D	D	D	R	R
Nicollet	D	R	R	R	R	R	R	D	D	R	D
Nobles	D	D	D	D	R	R	D	D	D	R	R
Norman	D	D	R	D	D	D	D	D	D	R	D
Olmsted	D	R	R	R	R	R	R	R	R	R	R
Otter Tail	R	R	R	R	R	R	R	R	R	R	R
Pennington	D	D	R	D	R	R	D	D	D	R	R
Pine	D	D	R	D	D	D	D	D	D	D	D
Pipestone	D	R	R	D	R	R	R	R	D	R	R

County	1964	1968	1972	1976	1980	1984	1988	1992	1996	2000	2004
Polk	D	D	R	D	R	R	D	D	D	R	R
Pope	D	D	D	D	R	R	D	D	D	R	R
Ramsey	D	D	D	D	D	D	D	D	D	D	D
Red Lake	D	D	D	D	D	D	D	D	D	R	R
Redwood	D	R	R	R	R	R	R	R	R	R	R
Renville	D	R	R	D	R	R	D	D	D	R	R
Rice	D	D	R	D	D	D	D	D	D	D	D
Rock	D	R	R	R	R	R	R	R	R	R	R
Roseau	D	D	R	D	R	R	R	R	R	R	R
St. Louis	D	D	D	D	D	D	D	D	D	D	D
Scott	D	D	R	D	D	R	R	D	D	R	R
Sherburne	D	D	R	D	D	R	R	D	D	R	R
Sibley	R	R	R	R	R	R	R	D	D	R	R
Stearns	D	D	D	D	R	R	R	R	D	R	R
Steele	D	R	R	R	R	R	R	R	D	R	R
Stevens	D	R	D	D	R	R	D	D	D	R	R
Swift	D	D	D	D	D	D	D	D	D	D	D
Todd	D	R	R	D	R	R	R	D	D	R	R
Traverse	D	D	D	D	R	R	D	D	D	R	R
Wabasha	D	R	R	R	R	R	R	D	D	R	R
Wadena	D	R	R	D	R	R	R	R	R	R	R
Waseca	D	R	R	R	R	R	R	D	D	R	R
Washington	D	D	R	D	D	R	D	D	D	R	R
Watonwan	D	R	R	R	R	R	R	D	D	R	R
Wilkin	D	R	R	D	R	R	R	R	R	R	R
Winona	D	D	R	D	R	R	R	D	D	D	D
Wright	D	D	R	D	D	R	R	D	D	R	R
Yellow Medicine	D	D	R	D	R	R	D	D	D	R	R

Mississippi

County	1872	1876	1880	1884	1888	1892	1896	1900	1904	1908	1912	1916
Adams	R	R	D	R	R	D	D	D	D	D	D	D
Alcorn	D	D	D	D	D	D	D	D	D	D	D	D
Amite	R	D	D	D	D	D	D	D	D	D	D	D
Attala	R	D	D	R	D	D	D	D	D	D	D	D
Benton	D	D	D	D	D	D	D	D	D	D	D	D
Bolivar	R	R	R	R	R	D	D	D	D	D	NR	NR
Calhoun	D	D	D	D	D	D	D	D	D	D	D	D
Carroll	R	D	D	D	D	D	D	D	D	D	D	D
Chickasaw	R	D	D	D	D	PO	D	D	D	D	D	D
Choctaw	D	D	D	D	D	D	D	D	D	D	D	D
Claiborne	R	D	D	D	D	D	D	D	D	D	D	D
Clarke	R	D	D	D	D	D	D	D	D	D	D	D

County	1872	1876	1880	1884	1888	1892	1896	1900	1904	1908	1912	1916
Clay	R	D	D	D	D	D	D	D	D	D	D	D
Coahoma	R	R	R	R	R	D	D	D	D	D	D	D
Copiah	R	D	D	D	D	D	D	D	D	D	D	D
Covington	D	D	D	D	D	D	D	D	D	D	D	D
De Soto	R	D	D	D	D	D	D	D	D	D	D	D
Forrest	–	–	–	–	–	–	–	–	–	D	D	D
Franklin	D	D	D	D	D	D	D	D	D	D	D	D
George	–	–	–	–	–	–	–	–	–	–	D	D
Greene	D	D	D	D	D	D	D	D	D	D	D	D
Grenada	R	D	D	R	D	D	D	D	D	D	D	D
Hancock	R	D	D	D	D	D	D	D	D	D	D	D
Harrison	D	D	D	D	D	D	D	D	D	D	D	D
Hinds	R	D	D	D	D	D	D	D	D	D	D	D
Holmes	R	D	D	D	D	D	D	D	D	D	D	D
Humphreys	–	–	–	–	–	–	–	–	–	–	–	–
Issaquena	R	R	R	R	R	D	D	D	D	D	D	D
Itawamba	D	D	D	D	D	D	D	D	D	D	D	D
Jackson	D	D	D	D	D	D	D	D	D	D	D	D
Jasper	D	D	D	D	D	D	D	D	D	D	D	D
Jefferson	R	D	D	D	D	D	D	D	D	D	D	D
Jefferson Davis	–	–	–	–	–	–	–	–	–	D	D	D
Jones	D	D	D	D	D	D	D	D	D	D	D	D
Kemper	R	D	D	D	D	D	D	D	D	D	D	D
Lafayette	R	D	D	D	D	D	D	D	D	D	D	D
Lamar	–	–	–	–	–	–	–	–	D	D	D	D
Lauderdale	R	D	D	D	D	D	D	D	D	D	D	D
Lawrence	R	D	D	D	D	D	D	D	D	D	D	D
Leake	D	D	D	D	D	D	D	D	D	D	D	D
Lee	D	D	D	D	D	D	D	D	D	D	D	D
Leflore	R	D	D	D	D	D	D	D	D	D	D	D
Lincoln	R	D	R	D	D	D	D	D	D	D	D	D
Lowndes	R	D	D	D	D	D	D	D	D	D	D	D
Madison	R	D	D	D	D	D	D	D	D	D	D	D
Marion	R	D	D	D	D	D	D	D	D	D	D	D
Marshall	R	D	D	D	D	D	D	D	D	D	D	D
Monroe	R	D	D	D	D	D	D	D	D	D	D	D
Montgomery	R	D	D	D	D	D	D	D	D	D	D	D
Neshoba	D	D	D	D	D	D	D	D	D	D	D	D
Newton	D	D	D	D	D	D	D	D	D	D	D	D
Noxubee	R	D	D	D	D	D	D	D	D	D	D	D
Oktibbeha	R	D	D	D	D	D	D	D	D	D	D	D
Panola	R	D	R	R	D	D	D	D	D	D	D	D
Pearl River	–	–	–	–	–	D	D	D	D	D	D	D
Perry	D	D	D	D	D	D	D	D	D	D	D	D
Pike	R	D	D	D	D	D	D	D	D	D	D	D
Pontotoc	D	D	D	D	D	D	D	D	D	D	D	D
Prentiss	D	D	D	D	D	D	D	D	D	D	D	D
Quitman	–	–	D	D	R	D	D	D	D	D	D	D
Rankin	R	D	D	D	D	D	D	D	D	D	D	D

County	1872	1876	1880	1884	1888	1892	1896	1900	1904	1908	1912	1916
Scott	D	D	D	D	D	D	D	D	D	D	D	D
Sharkey	–	D	D	R	R	D	D	D	D	D	D	D
Simpson	D	D	D	D	D	D	D	D	D	D	D	D
Smith	D	D	D	D	D	D	D	D	D	D	D	D
Stone	–	–	–	–	–	–	–	–	–	–	–	D
Sunflower	R	D	D	D	D	D	D	D	D	D	D	D
Tallahatchie	R	D	D	D	D	D	D	D	D	D	D	D
Tate	–	D	D	D	D	D	D	D	D	D	D	D
Tippah	D	D	D	D	D	D	D	D	D	D	D	D
Tishomingo	D	D	D	D	D	D	D	D	D	D	D	D
Tunica	R	R	R	R	R	D	D	D	D	D	D	D
Union	D	D	D	D	D	D	D	D	D	D	D	D
Walthall	–	–	–	–	–	–	–	–	–	–	–	D
Warren	R	D	D	D	D	D	D	D	D	D	D	D
Washington	R	D	R	R	D	D	D	D	D	D	D	D
Wayne	R	D	D	D	D	D	D	D	D	D	D	D
Webster	–	D	D	D	D	D	D	D	D	D	D	D
Wilkinson	R	R	D	D	D	D	D	D	D	D	D	D
Winston	D	D	D	D	D	D	D	D	D	D	D	D
Yalobusha	D	D	G	D	D	D	D	D	D	D	D	D
Yazoo	R	D	D	D	D	D	D	D	D	D	D	D

County	1920	1924	1928	1932	1936	1940	1944	1948	1952	1956	1960	1964
Adams	D	D	D	D	D	D	D	SR	R	R	SR	R
Alcorn	D	D	D	D	D	D	D	SR	D	D	D	R
Amite	D	D	D	D	D	D	D	SR	D	D	SR	R
Attala	D	D	D	D	D	D	D	SR	D	D	D	R
Benton	D	D	D	D	D	D	D	SR	D	D	D	R
Bolivar	D	D	D	D	D	D	D	SR	R	SR	SR	R
Calhoun	D	D	D	D	D	D	D	SR	D	D	SR	R
Carroll	D	D	D	D	D	D	D	SR	D	D	SR	R
Chickasaw	D	D	D	D	D	D	D	SR	D	D	SR	R
Choctaw	D	D	D	D	D	D	D	SR	D	D	D	R
Claiborne	D	D	D	D	D	D	D	SR	R	D	SR	R
Clarke	D	D	D	D	D	D	D	SR	D	D	SR	R
Clay	D	D	D	D	D	D	D	SR	D	D	SR	R
Coahoma	D	D	D	D	D	D	D	SR	D	D	D	R
Copiah	D	D	D	D	D	D	D	SR	D	D	SR	R
Covington	D	D	D	D	D	D	D	SR	D	D	SR	R
De Soto	D	D	D	D	D	D	D	SR	D	D	D	R
Forrest	D	D	D	D	D	D	D	SR	R	R	R	R
Franklin	D	D	D	D	D	D	D	SR	D	D	SR	R
George	D	D	R	D	D	D	D	SR	D	D	SR	R
Greene	D	D	D	D	D	D	D	SR	D	D	SR	R
Grenada	D	D	D	D	D	D	D	SR	D	D	SR	R
Hancock	D	D	D	D	D	D	D	SR	D	R	D	R
Harrison	D	D	D	D	D	D	D	SR	D	D	D	R
Hinds	D	D	D	D	D	D	D	SR	R	D	SR	R
Holmes	D	D	D	D	D	D	D	SR	D	SR	SR	R

County	1920	1924	1928	1932	1936	1940	1944	1948	1952	1956	1960	1964
Humphreys	D	D	D	D	D	D	D	SR	D	SR	SR	R
Issaquena	D	D	D	D	D	D	D	SR	D	D	SR	R
Itawamba	D	D	D	D	D	D	D	SR	D	D	D	R
Jackson	D	D	D	D	D	D	D	SR	D	D	D	R
Jasper	D	D	D	D	D	D	D	SR	D	D	D	R
Jefferson	D	D	D	D	D	D	D	SR	R	D	SR	R
Jefferson Davis	D	D	D	D	D	D	D	SR	D	D	SR	R
Jones	D	D	D	D	D	D	D	SR	D	D	D	R
Kemper	D	D	D	D	D	D	D	SR	D	D	D	R
Lafayette	D	D	D	D	D	D	D	SR	D	D	D	R
Lamar	D	D	D	D	D	D	D	SR	D	D	SR	R
Lauderdale	D	D	D	D	D	D	D	SR	D	D	SR	R
Lawrence	D	D	D	D	D	D	D	SR	D	D	SR	R
Leake	D	D	D	D	D	D	D	SR	D	D	SR	R
Lee	D	D	D	D	D	D	D	SR	D	D	D	R
Leflore	D	D	D	D	D	D	D	SR	R	D	SR	R
Lincoln	D	D	D	D	D	D	D	SR	D	D	SR	R
Lowndes	D	D	D	D	D	D	D	SR	R	D	R	R
Madison	D	D	D	D	D	D	D	SR	R	SR	SR	R
Marion	D	D	D	D	D	D	D	SR	D	D	SR	R
Marshall	D	D	D	D	D	D	D	SR	D	D	SR	R
Monroe	D	D	D	D	D	D	D	SR	D	D	D	R
Montgomery	D	D	D	D	D	D	D	SR	D	D	SR	R
Neshoba	D	D	D	D	D	D	D	SR	D	D	D	R
Newton	D	D	D	D	D	D	D	SR	D	D	SR	R
Noxubee	D	D	D	D	D	D	D	SR	R	D	SR	R
Oktibbeha	D	D	D	D	D	D	D	SR	D	D	SR	R
Panola	D	D	D	D	D	D	D	SR	D	D	SR	R
Pearl River	D	D	R	D	D	D	D	SR	D	D	SR	R
Perry	D	D	D	D	D	D	D	SR	D	D	SR	R
Pike	D	D	D	D	D	D	D	SR	R	D	SR	R
Pontotoc	D	D	D	D	D	D	D	SR	D	D	D	R
Prentiss	D	D	D	D	D	D	D	SR	D	D	D	R
Quitman	D	D	D	D	D	D	D	SR	D	D	SR	R
Rankin	D	D	D	D	D	D	D	SR	D	D	SR	R
Scott	D	D	D	D	D	D	D	SR	D	D	SR	R
Sharkey	D	D	D	D	D	D	D	SR	R	SR	SR	R
Simpson	D	D	D	D	D	D	D	SR	D	D	SR	R
Smith	D	D	D	D	D	D	D	SR	D	D	D	R
Stone	D	D	R	D	D	D	D	SR	D	D	SR	R
Sunflower	D	D	D	D	D	D	D	SR	D	D	SR	R
Tallahatchie	D	D	D	D	D	D	D	SR	D	D	SR	R
Tate	D	D	D	D	D	D	D	SR	D	D	SR	R
Tippah	D	D	D	D	D	D	D	SR	D	D	D	R
Tishomingo	D	D	D	D	D	D	D	SR	D	D	D	R
Tunica	D	D	D	D	D	D	D	SR	D	D	R	R
Union	D	D	D	D	D	D	D	SR	D	D	D	R
Walthall	D	D	D	D	D	D	D	SR	D	D	SR	R
Warren	D	D	D	D	D	D	D	SR	R	R	D	R

County	1920	1924	1928	1932	1936	1940	1944	1948	1952	1956	1960	1964
Washington	D	D	D	D	D	D	D	SR	R	D	D	R
Wayne	D	D	D	D	D	D	D	SR	D	D	SR	R
Webster	D	D	D	D	D	D	D	SR	D	D	SR	R
Wilkinson	D	D	D	D	D	D	D	SR	R	SR	SR	R
Winston	D	D	D	D	D	D	D	SR	D	D	SR	R
Yalobusha	D	D	D	D	D	D	D	SR	D	D	SR	R
Yazoo	D	D	D	D	D	D	D	SR	D	SR	SR	R

County	1968	1972	1976	1980	1984	1988	1992	1996	2000	2004
Adams	A	R	D	R	R	R	D	D	D	D
Alcorn	A	R	D	D	R	R	D	D	R	R
Amite	A	R	D	D	R	R	D	D	R	R
Attala	A	R	D	D	R	R	R	R	R	R
Benton	A	R	D	D	R	D	D	D	D	D
Bolivar	A	R	D	D	D	D	D	D	D	D
Calhoun	A	R	D	D	R	R	R	R	R	R
Carroll	A	R	D	R	R	R	R	R	R	R
Chickasaw	A	R	D	D	R	R	D	D	R	R
Choctaw	A	R	R	R	R	R	R	R	R	R
Claiborne	D	D	D	D	D	D	D	D	D	D
Clarke	A	R	R	T	R	R	R	R	R	R
Clay	A	R	D	D	R	D	D	D	D	D
Coahoma	D	R	D	D	D	D	D	D	D	D
Copiah	A	R	D	D	R	R	R	D	R	R
Covington	A	R	D	R	R	R	R	R	R	R
De Soto	A	R	D	R	R	R	R	R	R	R
Forrest	A	R	R	R	R	R	R	R	R	R
Franklin	A	R	R	D	R	R	R	R	R	R
George	A	R	D	R	R	R	R	R	R	R
Greene	A	R	D	R	R	R	R	R	R	R
Grenada	A	R	R	D	R	R	R	R	R	R
Hancock	A	R	D	R	R	R	R	R	R	R
Harrison	A	R	R	R	R	R	R	R	R	R
Hinds	A	R	R	R	R	R	R	D	D	D
Holmes	D	D	D	D	D	D	D	D	D	D
Humphreys	A	R	D	D	D	D	D	D	D	D
Issaquena	A	R	D	D	R	D	D	D	D	D
Itawamba	A	R	D	D	R	R	R	R	R	R
Jackson	A	R	R	R	R	R	R	R	R	R
Jasper	A	R	D	D	R	R	D	D	R	D
Jefferson	D	D	D	D	D	D	D	D	D	D
Jefferson Davis	A	R	D	D	R	D	D	D	D	D
Jones	A	R	R	R	R	R	R	R	R	R
Kemper	A	R	D	D	R	R	D	D	D	D
Lafayette	A	R	D	D	R	R	R	R	R	R
Lamar	A	R	R	R	R	R	R	R	R	R
Lauderdale	A	R	R	R	R	R	R	R	R	R
Lawrence	A	R	D	R	R	R	R	D	R	R
Leake	A	R	D	D	R	R	R	R	R	R

County	1968	1972	1976	1980	1984	1988	1992	1996	2000	2004
Lee	A	R	D	D	R	R	R	R	R	R
Leflore	A	R	D	D	R	R	D	D	D	D
Lincoln	A	R	R	R	R	R	R	R	R	R
Lowndes	A	R	R	R	R	R	R	R	R	R
Madison	D	R	D	D	R	R	R	R	R	R
Marion	A	R	R	D	R	R	R	R	R	R
Marshall	D	R	D	D	D	D	D	D	D	D
Monroe	A	R	D	D	R	R	R	R	R	R
Montgomery	A	R	D	D	R	R	R	D	R	R
Neshoba	A	R	D	R	R	R	R	R	R	R
Newton	A	R	R	R	R	R	R	R	R	R
Noxubee	A	R	D	D	D	D	D	D	D	D
Oktibbeha	A	R	R	R	R	R	R	R	R	R
Panola	A	R	D	D	R	R	D	D	D	R
Pearl River	A	R	D	R	R	R	R	R	R	R
Perry	A	R	D	R	R	R	R	R	R	R
Pike	A	R	D	D	R	R	D	D	R	R
Pontotoc	A	R	D	D	R	R	R	R	R	R
Prentiss	A	R	D	D	R	R	R	R	R	R
Quitman	A	R	D	D	D	D	D	D	D	D
Rankin	A	R	R	R	R	R	R	R	R	R
Scott	A	R	R	R	R	R	R	R	R	R
Sharkey	A	R	D	D	D	D	D	D	D	D
Simpson	A	R	R	R	R	R	R	R	R	R
Smith	A	R	R	R	R	R	R	R	R	R
Stone	A	R	D	R	R	R	R	R	R	R
Sunflower	A	R	D	D	R	D	D	D	D	D
Tallahatchie	A	R	D	D	R	D	D	D	D	D
Tate	A	R	D	D	R	R	R	R	R	R
Tippah	A	R	D	D	R	R	R	R	R	R
Tishomingo	A	R	D	D	R	R	D	R	R	R
Tunica	D	R	D	D	D	D	D	D	D	D
Union	A	R	D	D	R	R	R	R	R	R
Walthall	A	R	D	D	R	R	R	D	R	R
Warren	A	R	R	R	R	R	R	R	R	R
Washington	A	R	D	D	R	R	D	D	D	D
Wayne	A	R	D	R	R	R	R	R	R	R
Webster	A	R	D	R	R	R	R	R	R	R
Wilkinson	D	R	D	D	D	D	D	D	D	D
Winston	A	R	D	D	R	R	R	R	R	R
Yalobusha	A	R	D	D	R	R	D	D	D	R
Yazoo	A	R	R	D	R	R	R	D	R	R

Missouri

County	1868	1872	1876	1880	1884	1888	1892	1896	1900	1904	1908	1912
Adair	R	R	R	R	R	R	R	R	R	R	R	D
Andrew	R	R	R	R	R	R	R	R	R	R	R	D
Atchison	R	R	R	D	R	R	D	D	D	R	R	D
Audrain	R	D	D	D	D	D	D	D	D	D	D	D
Barry	R	D	D	D	R	D	R	D	D	R	R	D
Barton	R	R	D	D	D	D	D	D	D	R	D	D
Bates	R	D	D	D	D	D	D	D	D	D	D	D
Benton	R	R	R	R	R	R	R	R	R	R	R	D
Bollinger	R	D	D	D	D	D	D	D	D	R	R	D
Boone	R	D	D	D	D	D	D	D	D	D	D	D
Buchanan	R	D	D	D	D	D	D	D	D	R	R	D
Butler	NR	D	D	D	D	D	D	D	R	R	R	D
Caldwell	R	R	R	R	R	R	R	R	D	R	R	D
Callaway	D	D	D	D	D	D	D	D	D	D	D	D
Camden	R	R	R	R	R	R	R	R	R	R	R	R
Cape Girardeau	R	D	D	D	D	R	R	R	R	R	R	D
Carroll	R	D	D	D	D	R	D	D	D	R	R	D
Carter	D	D	D	D	D	D	D	D	D	D	D	D
Cass	D	D	D	D	D	D	D	D	D	D	D	D
Cedar	R	R	R	R	D	D	R	D	R	R	R	D
Chariton	D	D	D	D	D	D	D	D	D	D	D	D
Christian	R	R	R	R	R	R	R	R	R	R	R	R
Clark	R	R	D	D	D	D	D	D	D	R	R	D
Clay	D	D	D	D	D	D	D	D	D	D	D	D
Clinton	D	D	D	D	D	D	D	D	D	D	D	D
Cole	R	D	D	D	D	D	D	D	D	D	D	D
Cooper	R	D	D	D	D	D	D	D	D	R	R	D
Crawford	D	D	D	D	D	R	R	R	R	R	R	R
Dade	R	R	R	R	R	R	R	D	R	R	R	D
Dallas	R	R	R	R	R	R	R	D	R	R	R	R
Daviess	R	R	D	D	R	D	D	D	D	R	R	D
De Kalb	R	R	R	D	R	R	D	D	D	R	R	D
Dent	R	D	D	D	D	D	D	D	D	D	D	D
Douglas	R	NR	R	G	R	R	R	D	R	R	R	P
Dunklin	NR	D	D	D	D	D	D	D	D	D	D	D
Franklin	R	R	D	R	R	R	R	R	R	R	R	R
Gasconade	R	R	R	R	R	R	R	R	R	R	R	R
Gentry	R	D	D	D	D	D	D	D	D	D	D	D
Greene	R	R	R	R	R	R	R	D	R	R	R	D
Grundy	R	R	R	R	R	R	R	R	R	R	R	P
Harrison	R	R	R	R	R	R	R	R	R	R	R	R
Henry	R	D	D	D	D	D	D	D	D	D	D	D
Hickory	R	R	R	R	R	R	R	R	R	R	R	R
Holt	R	R	R	R	R	R	R	R	R	R	R	R
Howard	D	D	D	D	D	D	D	D	D	D	D	D
Howell	R	R	D	D	D	D	D	D	R	R	R	D

County	1868	1872	1876	1880	1884	1888	1892	1896	1900	1904	1908	1912
Iron	R	D	D	D	D	D	D	D	D	D	D	D
Jackson	D	D	D	D	D	D	D	D	D	R	D	D
Jasper	R	R	R	R	R	R	R	D	D	R	R	D
Jefferson	D	D	D	D	D	D	D	R	D	R	R	D
Johnson	R	D	D	D	D	D	D	D	D	D	D	D
Knox	R	D	D	D	D	D	D	D	D	D	D	D
Laclede	R	D	D	D	R	R	R	D	D	R	R	D
Lafayette	R	D	D	D	D	D	D	D	D	D	D	D
Lawrence	R	R	R	R	R	R	R	D	R	R	R	D
Lewis	R	D	D	D	D	D	D	D	D	D	D	D
Lincoln	R	D	D	D	D	D	D	D	D	D	D	D
Linn	R	R	D	D	R	D	D	D	D	R	D	D
Livingston	R	D	D	D	R	D	D	D	D	R	R	D
McDonald	R	D	D	D	D	D	D	D	D	D	R	D
Macon	R	D	D	D	D	D	D	D	D	R	D	D
Madison	R	D	D	D	D	D	D	D	D	R	D	D
Maries	D	D	D	D	D	D	D	D	D	D	D	D
Marion	R	D	D	D	D	D	D	D	D	D	D	D
Mercer	R	R	R	R	R	R	R	R	R	R	R	P
Miller	R	R	R	R	R	R	R	R	R	R	R	R
Mississippi	D	D	D	D	D	D	D	D	D	D	D	D
Moniteau	R	D	D	D	R	R	D	D	D	D	D	D
Monroe	D	D	D	D	D	D	D	D	D	D	D	D
Montgomery	R	D	D	D	D	D	D	D	D	D	D	D
Morgan	R	D	D	D	D	D	D	D	R	R	R	R
New Madrid	D	D	D	D	D	D	D	D	D	D	D	D
Newton	R	R	D	D	D	D	D	D	D	R	D	D
Nodaway	R	R	D	D	R	R	D	D	D	R	D	D
Oregon	D	D	D	D	D	D	D	D	D	D	D	D
Osage	D	R	D	D	R	R	R	R	R	R	R	D
Ozark	R	R	R	R	R	R	R	R	R	R	R	P
Pemiscot	D	D	D	D	D	D	D	D	D	D	D	D
Perry	R	R	D	D	D	D	D	R	R	R	R	R
Pettis	R	D	D	D	D	R	D	D	R	R	R	D
Phelps	R	D	D	D	D	D	D	D	D	D	D	D
Pike	D	D	D	D	D	D	D	D	D	D	D	D
Platte	D	D	D	D	D	D	D	D	D	D	D	D
Polk	R	R	R	R	R	R	R	D	R	R	R	D
Pulaski	R	D	D	D	D	D	D	D	D	D	D	D
Putnam	R	NR	R	R	R	R	R	R	R	R	R	R
Ralls	R	D	D	D	D	D	D	D	D	D	D	D
Randolph	D	D	D	D	D	D	D	D	D	D	D	D
Ray	R	D	D	D	D	D	D	D	D	D	D	D
Reynolds	D	D	D	D	D	D	D	D	D	D	D	D
Ripley	D	D	D	D	D	D	D	D	D	D	D	D
St. Charles	R	D	D	R	R	R	R	R	R	R	R	R
St. Clair	R	D	D	G	D	D	D	D	D	R	D	D
St. Francois	D	D	D	D	D	D	D	D	D	R	R	D
St. Louis City	–	–	–	D	D	R	R	R	R	R	R	D

County	1868	1872	1876	1880	1884	1888	1892	1896	1900	1904	1908	1912
St. Louis County	R	D	D	R	R	R	R	R	R	R	R	R
Ste. Genevieve	D	D	D	D	D	D	D	D	D	D	D	D
Saline	R	D	D	D	D	D	D	D	D	D	D	D
Schuyler	R	R	D	D	D	D	D	D	D	D	D	D
Scotland	R	D	D	D	D	D	D	D	D	D	D	D
Scott	R	D	D	D	D	D	D	D	D	D	D	D
Shannon	D	D	D	D	D	D	D	D	D	D	D	D
Shelby	R	D	D	D	D	D	D	D	D	D	D	D
Stoddard	R	D	D	D	D	D	D	D	D	D	D	D
Stone	R	R	R	R	R	R	R	R	R	R	R	R
Sullivan	R	R	R	D	R	R	R	D	D	R	R	D
Taney	R	R	R	R	R	R	R	R	R	R	R	R
Texas	R	D	D	D	D	D	D	D	D	D	D	D
Vernon	D	D	D	D	D	D	D	D	D	D	D	D
Warren	R	R	R	R	R	R	R	R	R	R	R	R
Washington	D	D	D	D	D	D	D	R	R	R	R	D
Wayne	–	D	D	D	D	D	D	D	D	R	D	D
Webster	R	D	D	D	R	R	R	D	R	R	R	D
Worth	R	R	D	D	R	D	D	D	D	R	D	D
Wright	R	R	R	R	R	R	R	D	R	R	R	D

County	1916	1920	1924	1928	1932	1936	1940	1944	1948	1952	1956	1960
Adair	R	R	R	R	D	D	R	R	D	R	R	R
Andrew	R	R	R	R	D	R	R	R	R	R	R	R
Atchison	D	R	R	R	D	D	R	R	D	R	R	R
Audrain	D	D	D	D	D	D	D	D	D	D	D	D
Barry	D	R	R	R	D	R	R	R	R	R	R	R
Barton	D	R	R	R	D	D	R	R	D	R	R	R
Bates	D	R	D	R	D	D	R	R	D	R	R	R
Benton	R	R	R	R	D	R	R	R	R	R	R	R
Bollinger	R	R	R	R	D	R	R	R	R	R	R	R
Boone	D	D	D	D	D	D	D	D	D	D	D	D
Buchanan	D	R	R	R	D	D	D	D	D	R	R	R
Butler	R	R	R	R	D	R	R	R	D	R	R	R
Caldwell	R	R	R	R	D	R	R	R	R	R	R	R
Callaway	D	D	D	D	D	D	D	D	D	D	D	D
Camden	R	R	R	R	D	R	R	R	R	R	R	R
Cape Girardeau	R	R	R	R	D	D	R	R	D	R	R	R
Carroll	R	R	R	R	D	R	R	R	R	R	R	R
Carter	D	R	D	R	D	D	D	D	D	D	D	R
Cass	D	D	D	R	D	D	D	R	D	R	R	R
Cedar	R	R	R	R	D	R	R	R	R	R	R	R
Chariton	D	D	D	D	D	D	D	D	D	R	D	D
Christian	R	R	R	R	D	R	R	R	R	R	R	R
Clark	R	R	R	R	D	D	R	R	D	R	R	R
Clay	D	D	D	R	D	D	D	D	D	R	D	R
Clinton	D	D	D	R	D	D	D	D	D	R	R	R
Cole	D	R	R	R	D	D	D	R	D	R	R	R

County	1916	1920	1924	1928	1932	1936	1940	1944	1948	1952	1956	1960
Cooper	R	R	R	R	D	D	R	R	R	R	R	R
Crawford	R	R	R	R	D	R	R	R	R	R	R	R
Dade	R	R	R	R	D	R	R	R	R	R	R	R
Dallas	R	R	R	R	D	R	R	R	R	R	R	R
Daviess	D	R	R	R	D	D	R	R	D	R	R	R
De Kalb	D	R	R	R	D	R	R	R	R	R	R	R
Dent	D	R	D	R	D	D	D	D	D	R	D	R
Douglas	R	R	R	R	R	R	R	R	R	R	R	R
Dunklin	D	D	D	D	D	D	D	D	D	D	D	R
Franklin	R	R	R	R	D	R	R	R	D	R	R	R
Gasconade	R	R	R	R	R	R	R	R	R	R	R	R
Gentry	D	R	R	R	D	D	D	D	D	R	R	R
Greene	R	R	R	R	D	D	D	R	D	R	R	R
Grundy	R	R	D	R	D	R	R	R	R	R	R	R
Harrison	R	R	R	R	D	R	R	R	R	R	R	R
Henry	D	D	D	R	D	D	R	R	D	R	R	R
Hickory	R	R	R	R	R	R	R	R	R	R	R	R
Holt	R	R	R	R	D	R	R	R	R	R	R	R
Howard	D	D	D	D	D	D	D	D	D	D	D	D
Howell	R	R	R	R	D	R	R	R	R	R	R	R
Iron	D	D	D	R	D	D	D	D	D	D	D	R
Jackson	D	R	R	R	D	D	D	D	D	D	D	D
Jasper	D	R	R	R	D	D	R	R	D	R	R	R
Jefferson	R	R	R	R	D	D	D	D	D	D	D	D
Johnson	D	R	D	R	D	D	R	R	R	R	R	R
Knox	D	R	D	R	D	D	D	R	D	R	R	R
Laclede	R	R	R	R	D	R	R	R	R	R	R	R
Lafayette	D	R	R	R	D	R	R	R	R	R	R	R
Lawrence	R	R	R	R	D	R	R	R	R	R	R	R
Lewis	D	D	D	D	D	D	D	D	D	D	D	D
Lincoln	D	D	D	D	D	D	D	D	D	D	D	D
Linn	D	R	D	R	D	D	D	D	D	R	D	R
Livingston	D	R	R	R	D	D	R	R	D	R	R	R
McDonald	D	R	R	R	D	D	R	R	R	R	R	R
Macon	D	R	D	R	D	D	D	R	D	R	R	R
Madison	D	R	D	R	D	D	R	R	D	R	R	R
Maries	D	D	D	D	D	D	D	D	D	D	D	D
Marion	D	D	D	R	D	D	D	D	D	D	D	D
Mercer	R	R	R	R	D	R	R	R	R	R	R	R
Miller	R	R	R	R	D	R	R	R	R	R	R	R
Mississippi	D	D	D	D	D	D	D	D	D	D	D	D
Moniteau	R	R	R	R	D	R	R	R	D	R	R	R
Monroe	D	D	D	D	D	D	D	D	D	D	D	D
Montgomery	D	R	R	R	D	R	R	R	R	R	R	R
Morgan	R	R	R	R	D	R	R	R	R	R	R	R
New Madrid	D	R	D	R	D	D	D	D	D	D	D	D
Newton	D	R	R	R	D	D	R	R	R	R	R	R
Nodaway	D	R	R	R	D	D	R	R	D	R	R	R
Oregon	D	D	D	D	D	D	D	D	D	D	D	R

County	1916	1920	1924	1928	1932	1936	1940	1944	1948	1952	1956	1960
Osage	R	R	R	D	D	D	R	R	D	R	R	D
Ozark	R	R	R	R	R	R	R	R	R	R	R	R
Pemiscot	D	R	D	R	D	D	D	D	D	D	D	D
Perry	R	R	R	R	D	R	R	R	R	R	R	R
Pettis	D	R	R	R	D	D	R	R	D	R	R	R
Phelps	D	R	D	R	D	D	D	D	D	D	R	R
Pike	D	D	D	R	D	D	D	D	D	D	D	D
Platte	D	D	D	D	D	D	D	D	D	D	D	D
Polk	R	R	R	R	D	R	R	R	R	R	R	R
Pulaski	D	D	D	R	D	D	D	D	D	D	D	R
Putnam	R	R	R	R	R	R	R	R	R	R	R	R
Ralls	D	D	D	D	D	D	D	D	D	D	D	D
Randolph	D	D	D	D	D	D	D	D	D	D	D	D
Ray	D	D	D	D	D	D	D	D	D	D	D	D
Reynolds	D	D	D	D	D	D	D	D	D	D	D	R
Ripley	D	R	D	R	D	D	D	D	R	R	R	R
St. Charles	R	R	R	R	D	D	R	R	D	R	R	D
St. Clair	D	R	R	R	D	R	R	R	R	R	R	R
St. Francois	D	R	R	R	D	D	R	R	D	R	R	R
St. Louis City	R	R	R	D	D	D	D	D	D	D	D	D
St. Louis County	R	R	R	R	D	D	R	R	R	R	R	D
Ste. Genevieve	D	R	R	D	D	D	R	R	D	R	R	D
Saline	D	D	D	R	D	D	D	D	D	R	R	R
Schuyler	D	R	D	R	D	D	D	D	D	D	D	R
Scotland	D	R	D	R	D	D	D	D	D	R	D	R
Scott	D	R	D	D	D	D	D	D	D	D	D	D
Shannon	D	D	D	D	D	D	D	D	D	D	D	R
Shelby	D	D	D	D	D	D	D	D	D	D	D	D
Stoddard	D	R	D	R	D	D	D	D	D	D	D	R
Stone	R	R	R	R	D	R	R	R	R	R	R	R
Sullivan	D	R	R	R	D	R	R	R	D	R	R	R
Taney	R	R	R	R	R	R	R	R	R	R	R	R
Texas	D	R	D	R	D	D	R	D	D	R	D	R
Vernon	D	D	D	R	D	D	D	R	D	R	R	R
Warren	R	R	R	R	R	R	R	R	R	R	R	R
Washington	R	R	R	R	D	D	R	R	D	R	R	R
Wayne	D	R	D	R	D	D	D	R	D	D	R	R
Webster	R	R	R	R	D	R	R	R	R	R	R	R
Worth	D	R	R	R	D	D	R	R	D	R	D	R
Wright	R	R	R	R	D	R	R	R	R	R	R	R

County	1964	1968	1972	1976	1980	1984	1988	1992	1996	2000	2004
Adair	D	R	R	R	R	R	R	D	R	R	R
Andrew	D	R	R	R	R	R	R	D	R	R	R
Atchison	D	R	R	R	R	R	R	D	R	R	R
Audrain	D	R	R	D	R	R	D	D	D	R	R
Barry	D	R	R	R	R	R	R	R	R	R	R
Barton	D	R	R	R	R	R	R	R	R	R	R

County	1964	1968	1972	1976	1980	1984	1988	1992	1996	2000	2004
Bates	D	R	R	D	R	R	R	D	D	R	R
Benton	R	R	R	R	R	R	R	D	D	R	R
Bollinger	D	R	R	D	R	R	R	R	R	R	R
Boone	D	R	R	D	D	R	D	D	D	D	R
Buchanan	D	R	R	D	D	R	D	D	D	D	R
Butler	D	R	R	D	R	R	R	D	R	R	R
Caldwell	D	R	R	D	R	R	R	D	D	R	R
Callaway	D	R	R	R	R	R	R	D	D	R	R
Camden	R	R	R	R	R	R	R	R	R	R	R
Cape Girardeau	D	R	R	R	R	R	R	R	R	R	R
Carroll	D	R	R	D	R	R	R	D	D	R	R
Carter	D	R	R	D	R	R	R	D	R	R	R
Cass	D	R	R	D	R	R	R	R	R	R	R
Cedar	R	R	R	R	R	R	R	R	R	R	R
Chariton	D	R	R	D	R	R	D	D	D	R	R
Christian	R	R	R	R	R	R	R	R	R	R	R
Clark	D	R	R	D	R	R	D	D	D	R	R
Clay	D	R	R	D	R	R	R	D	D	D	R
Clinton	D	R	R	D	R	R	D	D	D	R	R
Cole	R	R	R	R	R	R	R	R	R	R	R
Cooper	D	R	R	R	R	R	R	R	R	R	R
Crawford	D	R	R	D	R	R	R	D	D	R	R
Dade	R	R	R	R	R	R	R	R	R	R	R
Dallas	R	R	R	D	R	R	R	D	R	R	R
Daviess	D	R	R	D	R	R	R	D	D	R	R
De Kalb	D	R	R	D	R	R	D	D	D	R	R
Dent	D	R	R	D	R	R	R	D	R	R	R
Douglas	R	R	R	R	R	R	R	R	R	R	R
Dunklin	D	D	R	D	D	R	D	D	D	R	R
Franklin	D	R	R	R	R	R	R	D	D	R	R
Gasconade	R	R	R	R	R	R	R	R	R	R	R
Gentry	D	R	R	D	R	R	D	D	D	R	R
Greene	D	R	R	R	R	R	R	R	R	R	R
Grundy	D	R	R	R	R	R	R	D	D	R	R
Harrison	D	R	R	R	R	R	R	D	R	R	R
Henry	D	R	R	D	R	R	R	D	D	R	R
Hickory	R	R	R	R	R	R	R	D	D	R	R
Holt	D	R	R	R	R	R	R	R	R	R	R
Howard	D	D	R	D	D	R	D	D	D	R	R
Howell	D	R	R	D	R	R	R	R	R	R	R
Iron	D	D	R	D	D	R	D	D	D	R	R
Jackson	D	D	R	D	D	D	D	D	D	D	D
Jasper	D	R	R	R	R	R	R	R	R	R	R
Jefferson	D	D	R	D	R	R	R	D	D	D	R
Johnson	D	R	R	D	R	R	R	D	R	R	R
Knox	D	R	R	D	R	R	D	D	D	R	R
Laclede	D	R	R	D	R	R	R	R	R	R	R
Lafayette	D	R	R	R	R	R	R	D	D	R	R
Lawrence	D	R	R	R	R	R	R	R	R	R	R

County	1964	1968	1972	1976	1980	1984	1988	1992	1996	2000	2004
Lewis	D	D	R	D	R	R	D	D	D	R	R
Lincoln	D	R	R	D	R	R	R	D	D	R	R
Linn	D	D	R	D	R	R	D	D	D	R	R
Livingston	D	R	R	D	R	R	R	D	D	R	R
McDonald	D	R	R	D	R	R	R	R	R	R	R
Macon	D	R	R	D	R	R	R	D	D	R	R
Madison	D	R	R	D	R	R	R	D	D	R	R
Maries	D	R	R	D	R	R	R	D	R	R	R
Marion	D	D	R	D	R	R	D	D	D	R	R
Mercer	D	R	R	D	R	R	D	D	D	R	R
Miller	R	R	R	R	R	R	R	R	R	R	R
Mississippi	D	D	R	D	D	D	D	D	D	D	R
Moniteau	R	R	R	R	R	R	R	R	R	R	R
Monroe	D	D	D	D	D	R	D	D	D	R	R
Montgomery	D	R	R	R	R	R	R	D	D	R	R
Morgan	R	R	R	R	R	R	R	D	R	R	R
New Madrid	D	D	R	D	D	R	D	D	D	D	R
Newton	D	R	R	R	R	R	R	R	R	R	R
Nodaway	D	R	R	D	R	R	D	D	D	R	R
Oregon	D	D	R	D	D	D	D	D	D	R	R
Osage	R	R	R	R	R	R	R	R	R	R	R
Ozark	R	R	R	R	R	R	R	R	R	R	R
Pemiscot	D	A	R	D	D	R	D	D	D	D	R
Perry	D	R	R	R	R	R	R	R	R	R	R
Pettis	D	R	R	D	R	R	R	R	R	R	R
Phelps	D	R	R	D	R	R	R	D	R	R	R
Pike	D	D	R	D	R	R	D	D	D	R	R
Platte	D	R	R	D	R	R	R	D	R	R	R
Polk	D	R	R	R	R	R	R	R	R	R	R
Pulaski	D	R	R	D	R	R	R	D	R	R	R
Putnam	R	R	R	R	R	R	R	R	R	R	R
Ralls	D	D	R	D	D	R	D	D	D	R	R
Randolph	D	D	R	D	R	R	D	D	D	R	R
Ray	D	D	R	D	D	R	D	D	D	D	R
Reynolds	D	D	R	D	D	D	D	D	D	R	R
Ripley	D	R	R	D	R	R	R	D	D	R	R
St. Charles	D	R	R	R	R	R	R	R	R	R	R
St. Clair	D	R	R	D	R	R	R	D	D	R	R
St. Francois	D	R	R	D	R	R	D	D	D	R	R
St. Louis City	D	D	D	D	D	D	D	D	D	D	D
St. Louis County	D	R	R	R	R	R	R	D	D	D	D
Ste. Genevieve	D	D	R	D	D	R	D	D	D	D	D
Saline	D	R	R	D	R	R	D	D	D	D	R
Schuyler	D	R	R	D	R	R	R	D	D	R	R
Scotland	D	R	R	D	R	R	R	D	D	R	R
Scott	D	D	R	D	R	R	R	D	D	R	R
Shannon	D	D	R	D	D	R	D	D	D	R	R
Shelby	D	D	R	D	R	R	D	D	D	R	R

County	1964	1968	1972	1976	1980	1984	1988	1992	1996	2000	2004
Stoddard	D	R	R	D	R	R	R	D	R	R	R
Stone	R	R	R	R	R	R	R	R	R	R	R
Sullivan	D	R	R	D	R	R	R	D	D	R	R
Taney	R	R	R	R	R	R	R	R	R	R	R
Texas	D	R	R	D	R	R	R	D	R	R	R
Vernon	D	R	R	D	R	R	R	D	D	R	R
Warren	R	R	R	R	R	R	R	D	R	R	R
Washington	D	R	R	D	R	R	D	D	D	D	R
Wayne	D	R	R	D	R	R	R	D	D	R	R
Webster	D	R	R	D	R	R	R	R	R	R	R
Worth	D	R	R	D	R	R	D	D	D	R	R
Wright	R	R	R	R	R	R	R	R	R	R	R

Montana

County	1892	1896	1900	1904	1908	1912	1916	1920	1924	1928	1932	1936
Beaverhead	R	D	D	R	R	D	D	R	R	R	D	D
Big Horn	–	–	–	–	–	–	D	R	R	R	D	D
Blaine	–	–	–	–	–	P	D	R	R	R	D	D
Broadwater	–	–	D	D	D	D	D	R	R	R	D	D
Carbon	–	D	R	R	R	D	D	R	R	R	D	D
Carter	–	–	–	–	–	–	–	R	R	R	D	D
Cascade	R	D	D	R	R	D	D	R	R	R	D	D
Chouteau	R	D	R	R	R	R	D	R	R	R	D	D
Custer	R	R	R	R	R	P	D	R	P	R	D	D
Daniels	–	–	–	–	–	–	–	R	P	R	D	D
Dawson	R	R	R	R	R	P	D	R	R	R	D	D
Deer Lodge	D	D	D	R	D	D	D	R	R	D	D	D
Fallon	–	–	–	–	–	–	D	R	R	R	D	D
Fergus	R	D	R	R	R	D	D	R	P	R	D	D
Flathead	–	D	D	R	R	P	D	R	R	R	D	D
Gallatin	D	D	D	R	R	D	D	R	R	R	D	D
Garfield	–	–	–	–	–	–	–	R	R	R	D	D
Glacier	–	–	–	–	–	–	–	R	R	D	D	D
Golden Valley	–	–	–	–	–	–	–	R	P	R	D	D
Granite	–	D	D	R	D	D	D	R	R	R	D	D
Hill	–	–	–	–	–	D	D	R	P	R	D	D
Jefferson	R	D	D	R	D	D	D	R	T	R	D	D
Judith Basin	–	–	–	–	–	–	–	R	R	R	D	D
Lake	–	–	–	–	–	–	–	R	P	R	D	D
Lewis and Clark	D	D	D	R	D	D	D	R	R	R	D	D
Liberty	–	–	–	–	–	–	–	R	P	R	D	D
Lincoln	–	–	–	–	–	D	D	R	P	R	D	D
McCone	–	–	–	–	–	–	–	R	P	R	D	D
Madison	R	D	D	R	D	D	D	R	R	R	D	D

County	1892	1896	1900	1904	1908	1912	1916	1920	1924	1928	1932	1936
Meagher	R	D	R	R	R	D	D	R	R	R	D	D
Mineral	–	–	–	–	–	–	D	D	P	R	D	D
Missoula	D	D	D	R	R	P	D	R	P	R	D	D
Musselshell	–	–	–	–	–	R	D	R	P	R	D	D
Park	R	D	R	R	R	D	D	R	R	R	D	D
Petroleum	–	–	–	–	–	–	–	R	R	R	D	D
Phillips	–	–	–	–	–	–	D	R	R	R	D	D
Pondera	–	–	–	–	–	–	–	R	P	R	D	D
Powder River	–	–	–	–	–	–	–	R	R	R	D	D
Powell	–	–	–	R	R	D	D	R	R	R	D	D
Prairie	–	–	–	–	–	–	D	R	R	R	D	D
Ravalli	–	D	D	R	R	P	D	R	P	R	D	D
Richland	–	–	–	–	–	–	D	R	R	R	D	D
Roosevelt	–	–	–	–	–	–	–	R	R	R	D	D
Rosebud	–	–	–	R	R	R	D	R	R	R	D	D
Sanders	–	–	–	–	R	D	D	R	P	R	D	D
Sheridan	–	–	–	–	–	–	D	R	P	R	D	D
Silver Bow	R	D	D	D	D	D	D	R	R	D	D	D
Stillwater	–	–	–	–	–	–	D	R	R	R	D	D
Sweet Grass	–	D	R	R	R	P	R	R	R	R	R	D
Teton	–	D	R	R	R	D	D	R	R	R	D	D
Toole	–	–	–	–	–	–	D	R	R	R	D	D
Treasure	–	–	–	–	–	–	–	R	R	R	D	D
Valley	–	D	R	R	R	P	D	R	R	R	D	D
Wheatland	–	–	–	–	–	–	–	R	R	R	D	D
Wibaux	–	–	–	–	–	–	D	R	R	R	D	D
Yellowstone	R	D	R	R	R	P	D	R	R	R	D	D

County	1940	1944	1948	1952	1956	1960	1964	1968	1972	1976	1980	1984
Beaverhead	R	R	R	R	R	R	R	R	R	R	R	R
Big Horn	D	R	R	R	R	R	D	R	R	D	R	D
Blaine	D	D	D	R	R	D	D	R	R	D	R	R
Broadwater	D	R	R	R	R	R	R	R	R	R	R	R
Carbon	D	R	D	R	R	R	D	R	R	R	R	R
Carter	D	D	D	R	R	R	R	R	R	R	R	R
Cascade	D	D	D	R	R	D	D	D	R	R	R	R
Chouteau	D	D	D	R	D	D	D	R	R	R	R	R
Custer	D	D	D	R	R	R	D	R	R	R	R	R
Daniels	D	D	D	R	R	D	D	R	R	R	R	R
Dawson	D	R	R	R	R	R	D	R	R	R	R	R
Deer Lodge	D	D	D	D	D	D	D	D	D	D	D	D
Fallon	R	R	R	R	R	R	R	R	R	R	R	R
Fergus	D	D	D	R	R	R	D	R	R	R	R	R
Flathead	D	R	D	R	R	R	D	R	R	R	R	R
Gallatin	D	D	R	R	R	R	R	R	R	R	R	R
Garfield	D	R	R	R	R	R	R	R	R	R	R	R
Glacier	D	D	D	R	R	D	D	D	R	R	R	R
Golden Valley	R	R	R	R	R	R	D	R	R	R	R	R
Granite	D	R	R	R	R	R	D	R	R	R	R	R

County	1940	1944	1948	1952	1956	1960	1964	1968	1972	1976	1980	1984
Hill	D	D	D	R	R	D	D	D	R	D	R	R
Jefferson	D	D	D	R	R	R	D	D	R	R	R	R
Judith Basin	D	D	D	R	D	D	D	R	R	R	R	R
Lake	R	R	R	R	R	R	D	R	R	R	R	R
Lewis and Clark	D	D	R	R	R	R	D	R	R	R	R	R
Liberty	D	D	D	R	R	R	D	R	R	R	R	R
Lincoln	D	D	D	D	R	D	D	D	R	D	R	R
McCone	D	D	D	R	D	D	D	R	R	D	R	R
Madison	D	R	R	R	R	R	R	R	R	R	R	R
Meagher	D	R	R	R	R	R	R	R	R	R	R	R
Mineral	D	D	D	R	R	D	D	D	R	D	R	R
Missoula	D	D	D	R	R	R	D	R	R	R	R	R
Musselshell	D	D	D	R	R	R	D	R	R	R	R	R
Park	D	R	R	R	R	R	D	R	R	R	R	R
Petroleum	D	R	D	R	R	R	D	R	R	R	R	R
Phillips	D	D	D	R	R	R	D	R	R	R	R	R
Pondera	D	D	D	R	R	D	D	R	R	R	R	R
Powder River	R	R	R	R	R	R	R	R	R	R	R	R
Powell	D	D	D	R	R	D	D	R	R	R	R	R
Prairie	R	R	D	R	R	R	R	R	R	R	R	R
Ravalli	D	R	R	R	R	R	D	R	R	R	R	R
Richland	D	D	D	R	R	R	D	R	R	R	R	R
Roosevelt	D	D	D	R	D	D	D	R	R	D	R	R
Rosebud	D	R	R	R	R	R	D	R	R	R	R	R
Sanders	D	D	D	R	R	R	D	R	R	R	R	R
Sheridan	D	D	D	D	D	D	D	D	R	D	R	R
Silver Bow	D	D	D	D	R	D	D	D	D	D	D	D
Stillwater	R	R	R	R	R	R	R	R	R	R	R	R
Sweet Grass	R	R	R	R	R	R	R	R	R	R	R	R
Teton	D	D	D	R	R	D	D	R	R	R	R	R
Toole	D	D	D	R	R	D	D	R	R	R	R	R
Treasure	D	R	D	R	R	R	D	R	R	R	R	R
Valley	D	D	D	R	D	D	D	R	R	R	R	R
Wheatland	D	R	R	R	R	R	D	R	R	R	R	R
Wibaux	D	R	D	R	R	D	D	R	R	D	R	R
Yellowstone	D	R	R	R	R	R	D	R	R	R	R	R

County	1988	1992	1996	2000	2004
Beaverhead	R	R	R	R	R
Big Horn	D	D	D	D	D
Blaine	D	D	D	R	R
Broadwater	R	R	R	R	R
Carbon	R	R	R	R	R
Carter	R	R	R	R	R
Cascade	R	D	D	R	R
Chouteau	R	R	R	R	R
Custer	R	R	R	R	R
Daniels	R	R	R	R	R

County	1988	1992	1996	2000	2004
Dawson	R	D	D	R	R
Deer Lodge	D	D	D	D	D
Fallon	R	R	R	R	R
Fergus	R	R	R	R	R
Flathead	R	R	R	R	R
Gallatin	R	R	R	R	R
Garfield	R	R	R	R	R
Glacier	D	D	D	D	D
Golden Valley	R	R	R	R	R
Granite	R	R	R	R	R
Hill	D	D	D	R	R
Jefferson	R	R	R	R	R
Judith Basin	R	R	R	R	R
Lake	R	D	R	R	R
Lewis and Clark	D	D	R	R	R
Liberty	R	R	R	R	R
Lincoln	D	R	R	R	R
McCone	R	R	R	R	R
Madison	R	R	R	R	R
Meagher	R	R	R	R	R
Mineral	D	D	D	R	R
Missoula	D	D	D	R	D
Musselshell	R	R	R	R	R
Park	R	R	R	R	R
Petroleum	R	R	R	R	R
Phillips	R	R	R	R	R
Pondera	R	R	R	R	R
Powder River	R	R	R	R	R
Powell	R	R	R	R	R
Prairie	R	R	R	R	R
Ravalli	R	R	R	R	R
Richland	R	R	R	R	R
Roosevelt	D	D	D	D	D
Rosebud	R	D	D	R	R
Sanders	D	D	R	R	R
Sheridan	R	D	D	R	R
Silver Bow	D	D	D	D	D
Stillwater	R	R	R	R	R
Sweet Grass	R	R	R	R	R
Teton	R	R	R	R	R
Toole	R	R	R	R	R
Treasure	R	R	R	R	R
Valley	R	D	R	R	R
Wheatland	R	R	R	R	R
Wibaux	R	R	R	R	R
Yellowstone	R	R	R	R	R

Nebraska

County	1868	1872	1876	1880	1884	1888	1892	1896	1900	1904	1908	1912
Adams	–	R	R	R	R	R	R	D	D	R	D	D
Antelope	–	R	R	R	R	R	PO	D	D	R	R	D
Arthur	–	–	–	–	–	–	–	–	–	–	–	–
Banner	–	–	–	–	–	–	R	R	R	R	R	P
Blaine	–	–	–	–	–	R	PO	R	R	R	R	D
Boone	–	R	R	R	R	R	PO	D	R	R	D	D
Box Butte	–	–	–	–	–	R	PO	D	R	R	D	D
Boyd	–	–	–	–	–	–	R	D	D	R	R	P
Brown	–	–	–	–	R	R	R	R	R	R	R	D
Buffalo	–	R	R	R	R	R	PO	D	D	R	R	D
Burt	R	R	R	R	R	R	R	R	R	R	R	D
Butler	R	R	R	R	D	D	PO	D	D	R	D	D
Cass	R	R	R	R	R	R	R	R	R	R	R	D
Cedar	R	D	D	D	D	D	PO	D	D	R	D	D
Chase	–	–	–	–	–	R	PO	D	R	R	R	P
Cherry	–	–	–	–	R	R	R	D	R	R	R	D
Cheyenne	–	D	D	D	R	R	R	D	R	R	R	D
Clay	–	R	R	R	R	R	R	D	R	R	D	D
Colfax	–	R	R	R	D	D	PO	D	D	R	D	D
Cuming	R	D	D	R	D	D	PO	D	D	R	D	D
Custer	–	–	–	R	R	R	PO	D	D	R	D	D
Dakota	R	R	NR	D	R	D	PO	D	D	R	R	D
Dawes	–	–	–	–	–	R	PO	D	R	R	R	P
Dawson	–	R	R	R	R	R	R	D	D	R	D	D
Deuel	–	–	–	–	–	–	R	R	R	R	R	P
Dixon	R	R	R	R	R	R	R	D	R	R	R	P
Dodge	R	R	R	R	D	D	R	R	R	R	D	D
Douglas	R	R	R	R	R	D	R	R	R	R	D	D
Dundy	–	–	–	–	R	R	PO	D	R	R	R	P
Fillmore	–	R	R	R	R	R	R	D	R	R	D	D
Franklin	–	R	R	R	R	R	PO	D	D	R	D	D
Frontier	–	R	NR	R	R	R	PO	D	R	R	R	D
Furnas	–	–	R	R	R	R	PO	D	R	R	D	D
Gage	R	R	R	R	R	R	R	R	R	R	R	D
Garden	–	–	–	–	–	–	–	–	–	–	–	P
Garfield	–	–	–	–	R	R	PO	D	R	R	R	P
Gosper	–	–	R	R	R	R	PO	D	D	R	D	D
Grant	–	–	–	–	–	D	PO	D	R	R	D	D
Greeley	–	–	R	R	D	D	PO	D	D	R	D	D
Hall	R	R	R	R	R	R	R	R	R	R	R	D
Hamilton	–	R	R	R	R	R	PO	D	R	R	D	D
Harlan	–	R	R	R	R	R	PO	D	D	R	D	D
Hayes	–	–	–	–	–	R	R	R	R	R	R	P
Hitchcock	–	–	R	R	R	R	PO	D	D	R	R	D
Holt	–	–	R	R	R	R	PO	D	D	R	D	D
Hooker	–	–	–	–	–	–	PO	D	D	R	R	D

County	1868	1872	1876	1880	1884	1888	1892	1896	1900	1904	1908	1912
Howard	–	R	R	R	R	D	PO	D	D	R	D	D
Jefferson	R	R	R	R	R	R	R	R	R	R	R	D
Johnson	R	R	R	R	R	R	R	R	R	R	R	D
Kearney	–	R	R	R	R	R	PO	D	D	R	D	D
Keith	–	–	D	D	D	R	PO	D	R	R	R	D
Keya Paha	–	–	–	–	–	R	PO	D	R	R	R	R
Kimball	–	–	–	–	–	–	R	R	R	R	R	P
Knox	R	R	R	R	R	R	R	D	D	R	D	D
Lancaster	R	R	R	R	R	R	R	R	R	R	D	D
Lincoln	D	R	R	R	R	R	PO	D	R	R	R	D
Logan	–	–	–	–	–	R	R	D	R	R	D	D
Loup	–	–	–	–	R	R	R	D	R	R	R	P
McPherson	–	–	–	–	–	–	R	D	R	R	R	P
Madison	D	NR	R	R	R	R	R	R	R	R	R	D
Merrick	R	R	R	R	R	R	R	D	R	R	R	D
Morrill	–	–	–	–	–	–	–	–	–	–	–	P
Nance	–	–	–	R	R	R	PO	D	R	R	R	D
Nemaha	R	R	R	R	R	R	PO	D	R	R	D	D
Nuckolls	–	R	R	R	R	R	PO	D	D	R	D	D
Otoe	R	R	R	R	R	D	R	R	R	R	D	D
Pawnee	R	R	R	R	R	R	R	R	R	R	R	D
Perkins	–	–	–	–	–	R	PO	D	D	R	D	D
Phelps	–	–	R	R	R	R	PO	D	R	R	R	P
Pierce	–	–	D	D	R	D	PO	D	R	R	D	D
Platte	R	R	D	R	D	D	PO	D	D	R	D	D
Polk	–	R	R	R	R	R	PO	D	D	R	D	D
Red Willow	–	–	R	R	R	R	PO	D	R	R	D	D
Richardson	R	R	R	R	R	R	R	D	D	R	D	D
Rock	–	–	–	–	–	–	R	R	R	R	R	P
Saline	–	R	R	R	R	R	R	R	R	R	D	D
Sarpy	D	R	D	D	R	D	R	D	D	R	D	D
Saunders	R	R	R	R	R	R	PO	D	D	R	D	D
Scotts Bluff	–	–	–	–	–	–	R	D	R	R	R	P
Seward	R	R	R	R	R	R	R	D	R	R	D	D
Sheridan	–	–	–	–	–	R	PO	D	D	R	D	D
Sherman	–	–	R	R	R	R	PO	D	D	R	D	D
Sioux	–	–	–	–	–	D	PO	D	D	R	R	P
Stanton	D	NR	R	R	D	D	PO	D	R	R	D	D
Thayer	–	R	R	R	R	R	R	R	R	R	R	D
Thomas	–	–	–	–	–	R	D	D	D	R	D	D
Thurston	–	–	–	–	–	–	R	D	R	R	R	D
Valley	–	–	R	R	R	R	PO	D	D	R	D	D
Washington	R	R	R	R	R	R	R	R	R	R	R	D
Wayne	–	R	R	R	R	R	R	D	R	R	R	D
Webster	–	R	R	R	R	R	PO	D	R	R	R	D
Wheeler	–	–	–	–	R	R	PO	D	D	R	D	D
York	–	R	R	R	R	R	R	R	R	R	R	D

County	1916	1920	1924	1928	1932	1936	1940	1944	1948	1952	1956	1960
Adams	D	R	R	R	D	D	R	R	R	R	R	R
Antelope	D	R	R	R	D	R	R	R	R	R	R	R
Arthur	D	R	P	R	D	R	R	R	R	R	R	R
Banner	D	R	R	R	D	D	R	R	R	R	R	R
Blaine	D	R	R	R	D	D	R	R	R	R	R	R
Boone	D	R	R	R	D	D	R	R	R	R	R	R
Box Butte	D	R	R	R	D	D	R	R	R	R	R	R
Boyd	D	R	P	R	D	D	R	R	R	R	R	R
Brown	D	R	R	R	D	R	R	R	R	R	R	R
Buffalo	D	R	R	R	D	D	R	R	R	R	R	R
Burt	R	R	R	R	D	D	R	R	R	R	R	R
Butler	D	R	R	D	D	D	D	D	D	R	R	D
Cass	D	R	R	R	D	D	R	R	R	R	R	R
Cedar	R	R	R	D	D	D	R	R	R	R	R	R
Chase	D	R	R	R	D	D	R	R	R	R	R	R
Cherry	D	R	R	R	D	D	R	R	R	R	R	R
Cheyenne	D	R	R	R	D	D	R	R	R	R	R	R
Clay	D	R	R	R	D	D	R	R	R	R	R	R
Colfax	D	R	R	D	D	D	R	R	R	R	R	R
Cuming	R	R	P	R	D	D	R	R	R	R	R	R
Custer	D	R	R	R	D	D	R	R	R	R	R	R
Dakota	D	R	R	D	D	D	D	D	D	R	R	R
Dawes	D	R	P	R	D	D	R	R	R	R	R	R
Dawson	D	R	R	R	D	D	R	R	R	R	R	R
Deuel	D	R	R	R	D	D	R	R	R	R	R	R
Dixon	D	R	R	R	D	D	R	R	R	R	R	R
Dodge	D	R	R	R	D	D	R	R	R	R	R	R
Douglas	D	R	R	R	D	D	D	D	D	R	R	R
Dundy	D	R	R	R	D	D	R	R	R	R	R	R
Fillmore	D	R	R	R	D	D	R	R	R	R	R	R
Franklin	D	R	R	R	D	D	R	R	R	R	R	R
Frontier	D	R	R	R	D	D	R	R	R	R	R	R
Furnas	D	R	R	R	D	R	R	R	R	R	R	R
Gage	D	R	R	R	D	D	R	R	R	R	R	R
Garden	D	R	R	R	D	R	R	R	R	R	R	R
Garfield	D	R	R	R	D	R	R	R	R	R	R	R
Gosper	D	R	P	R	D	D	R	R	R	R	R	R
Grant	D	R	R	R	D	D	R	R	R	R	R	R
Greeley	D	R	R	D	D	D	R	D	D	R	R	D
Hall	R	R	R	R	D	D	R	R	R	R	R	R
Hamilton	D	R	R	R	D	R	R	R	R	R	R	R
Harlan	D	R	R	R	D	D	R	R	R	R	R	R
Hayes	D	R	R	R	D	D	R	R	R	R	R	R
Hitchcock	D	R	R	R	D	D	R	R	R	R	R	R
Holt	D	R	R	R	D	D	R	R	R	R	R	R
Hooker	D	R	R	R	D	R	R	R	R	R	R	R
Howard	D	R	R	D	D	D	D	D	D	R	R	R
Jefferson	D	R	R	R	D	D	R	R	R	R	R	R
Johnson	R	R	R	R	D	D	R	R	R	R	R	R

County	1916	1920	1924	1928	1932	1936	1940	1944	1948	1952	1956	1960
Kearney	D	R	R	R	D	D	R	R	R	R	R	R
Keith	D	R	R	R	D	D	R	R	R	R	R	R
Keya Paha	D	R	R	R	R	R	R	R	R	R	R	R
Kimball	D	R	R	R	D	D	R	R	R	R	R	R
Knox	D	R	R	R	D	D	R	R	R	R	R	R
Lancaster	D	R	R	R	R	D	R	R	R	R	R	R
Lincoln	D	R	R	R	D	D	R	R	R	R	R	R
Logan	D	R	R	R	D	D	R	R	R	R	R	R
Loup	D	R	R	R	D	R	R	R	R	R	R	R
McPherson	D	R	R	R	D	R	R	R	R	R	R	R
Madison	R	R	R	R	D	D	R	R	R	R	R	R
Merrick	D	R	R	R	D	D	R	R	R	R	R	R
Morrill	D	R	R	R	D	D	R	R	R	R	R	R
Nance	D	R	R	R	D	D	R	R	R	R	R	R
Nemaha	D	R	R	R	D	D	R	R	R	R	R	R
Nuckolls	D	R	R	R	D	D	R	R	R	R	R	R
Otoe	D	R	R	R	D	D	R	R	R	R	R	R
Pawnee	R	R	R	R	D	D	R	R	R	R	R	R
Perkins	D	R	R	R	D	D	R	R	R	R	R	R
Phelps	D	R	R	R	D	D	R	R	R	R	R	R
Pierce	R	R	R	R	D	D	R	R	R	R	R	R
Platte	D	R	P	D	D	D	R	R	R	R	R	R
Polk	D	R	R	R	D	D	R	R	R	R	R	R
Red Willow	D	R	R	R	D	D	R	R	R	R	R	R
Richardson	D	R	R	R	D	D	R	R	R	R	R	R
Rock	D	R	R	R	D	R	R	R	R	R	R	R
Saline	D	R	R	D	D	D	D	D	D	R	D	D
Sarpy	D	R	R	R	D	D	D	D	D	R	R	R
Saunders	D	R	R	R	D	D	R	R	D	R	R	R
Scotts Bluff	D	R	R	R	D	D	R	R	R	R	R	R
Seward	R	R	R	R	D	D	R	R	R	R	R	R
Sheridan	D	R	R	R	D	D	R	R	R	R	R	R
Sherman	D	R	R	D	D	D	D	D	D	R	R	D
Sioux	D	R	P	R	D	D	R	R	R	R	R	R
Stanton	D	R	R	D	D	D	R	R	R	R	R	R
Thayer	R	R	R	R	D	D	R	R	R	R	R	R
Thomas	D	R	D	R	D	D	R	R	R	R	R	R
Thurston	D	R	R	D	D	D	D	D	D	R	R	R
Valley	D	R	R	R	D	R	R	R	R	R	R	R
Washington	D	R	R	R	D	D	R	R	R	R	R	R
Wayne	R	R	R	R	D	D	R	R	R	R	R	R
Webster	D	R	R	R	D	D	R	R	R	R	R	R
Wheeler	D	R	P	R	D	D	R	R	D	R	R	R
York	D	R	R	R	D	R	R	R	R	R	R	R

County	1964	1968	1972	1976	1980	1984	1988	1992	1996	2000	2004
Adams	D	R	R	R	R	R	R	R	R	R	R
Antelope	R	R	R	R	R	R	R	R	R	R	R
Arthur	R	R	R	R	R	R	R	R	R	R	R

County	1964	1968	1972	1976	1980	1984	1988	1992	1996	2000	2004
Banner	R	R	R	R	R	R	R	R	R	R	R
Blaine	R	R	R	R	R	R	R	R	R	R	R
Boone	D	R	R	R	R	R	R	R	R	R	R
Box Butte	R	R	R	R	R	R	R	R	R	R	R
Boyd	R	R	R	R	R	R	R	R	R	R	R
Brown	R	R	R	R	R	R	R	R	R	R	R
Buffalo	D	R	R	R	R	R	R	R	R	R	R
Burt	R	R	R	R	R	R	R	R	R	R	R
Butler	D	R	R	D	R	R	R	R	R	R	R
Cass	D	R	R	R	R	R	R	R	R	R	R
Cedar	D	R	R	R	R	R	R	R	R	R	R
Chase	R	R	R	R	R	R	R	R	R	R	R
Cherry	R	R	R	R	R	R	R	R	R	R	R
Cheyenne	R	R	R	R	R	R	R	R	R	R	R
Clay	D	R	R	R	R	R	R	R	R	R	R
Colfax	D	R	R	R	R	R	R	R	R	R	R
Cuming	R	R	R	R	R	R	R	R	R	R	R
Custer	R	R	R	R	R	R	R	R	R	R	R
Dakota	D	R	R	R	R	R	D	R	D	R	R
Dawes	R	R	R	R	R	R	R	R	R	R	R
Dawson	R	R	R	R	R	R	R	R	R	R	R
Deuel	R	R	R	R	R	R	R	R	R	R	R
Dixon	D	R	R	R	R	R	R	R	R	R	R
Dodge	R	R	R	R	R	R	R	R	R	R	R
Douglas	D	R	R	R	R	R	R	R	R	R	R
Dundy	R	R	R	R	R	R	R	R	R	R	R
Fillmore	D	R	R	R	R	R	R	R	R	R	R
Franklin	D	R	R	R	R	R	R	R	R	R	R
Frontier	R	R	R	R	R	R	R	R	R	R	R
Furnas	R	R	R	R	R	R	R	R	R	R	R
Gage	D	R	R	R	R	R	R	R	R	R	R
Garden	R	R	R	R	R	R	R	R	R	R	R
Garfield	R	R	R	R	R	R	R	R	R	R	R
Gosper	R	R	R	R	R	R	R	R	R	R	R
Grant	R	R	R	R	R	R	R	R	R	R	R
Greeley	D	R	R	D	R	R	R	R	R	R	R
Hall	D	R	R	R	R	R	R	R	R	R	R
Hamilton	R	R	R	R	R	R	R	R	R	R	R
Harlan	R	R	R	R	R	R	R	R	R	R	R
Hayes	R	R	R	R	R	R	R	R	R	R	R
Hitchcock	R	R	R	R	R	R	R	R	R	R	R
Holt	R	R	R	R	R	R	R	R	R	R	R
Hooker	R	R	R	R	R	R	R	R	R	R	R
Howard	D	R	R	R	R	R	R	R	R	R	R
Jefferson	D	R	R	R	R	R	R	R	R	R	R
Johnson	D	R	R	R	R	R	R	R	R	R	R
Kearney	D	R	R	R	R	R	R	R	R	R	R
Keith	R	R	R	R	R	R	R	R	R	R	R
Keya Paha	R	R	R	R	R	R	R	R	R	R	R

County	1964	1968	1972	1976	1980	1984	1988	1992	1996	2000	2004
Kimball	R	R	R	R	R	R	R	R	R	R	R
Knox	R	R	R	R	R	R	R	R	R	R	R
Lancaster	D	R	R	R	R	R	R	R	R	R	R
Lincoln	D	R	R	R	R	R	R	R	R	R	R
Logan	D	R	R	R	R	R	R	R	R	R	R
Loup	R	R	R	R	R	R	R	R	R	R	R
McPherson	R	R	R	R	R	R	R	R	R	R	R
Madison	R	R	R	R	R	R	R	R	R	R	R
Merrick	R	R	R	R	R	R	R	R	R	R	R
Morrill	R	R	R	R	R	R	R	R	R	R	R
Nance	D	R	R	R	R	R	R	R	R	R	R
Nemaha	D	R	R	R	R	R	R	R	R	R	R
Nuckolls	D	R	R	R	R	R	R	R	R	R	R
Otoe	R	R	R	R	R	R	R	R	R	R	R
Pawnee	R	R	R	R	R	R	R	R	R	R	R
Perkins	R	R	R	R	R	R	R	R	R	R	R
Phelps	R	R	R	R	R	R	R	R	R	R	R
Pierce	R	R	R	R	R	R	R	R	R	R	R
Platte	D	R	R	R	R	R	R	R	R	R	R
Polk	D	R	R	R	R	R	R	R	R	R	R
Red Willow	R	R	R	R	R	R	R	R	R	R	R
Richardson	D	R	R	R	R	R	R	R	R	R	R
Rock	R	R	R	R	R	R	R	R	R	R	R
Saline	D	D	R	D	R	R	D	D	D	R	R
Sarpy	D	R	R	R	R	R	R	R	R	R	R
Saunders	D	R	R	R	R	R	R	R	R	R	R
Scotts Bluff	R	R	R	R	R	R	R	R	R	R	R
Seward	D	R	R	R	R	R	R	R	R	R	R
Sheridan	R	R	R	R	R	R	R	R	R	R	R
Sherman	D	R	R	D	R	R	R	R	R	R	R
Sioux	R	R	R	R	R	R	R	R	R	R	R
Stanton	R	R	R	R	R	R	R	R	R	R	R
Thayer	D	R	R	R	R	R	R	R	R	R	R
Thomas	R	R	R	R	R	R	R	R	R	R	R
Thurston	D	R	R	R	R	R	D	R	D	R	D
Valley	R	R	R	R	R	R	R	R	R	R	R
Washington	D	R	R	R	R	R	R	R	R	R	R
Wayne	R	R	R	R	R	R	R	R	R	R	R
Webster	R	R	R	R	R	R	R	R	R	R	R
Wheeler	D	R	R	R	R	R	R	R	R	R	R
York	R	R	R	R	R	R	R	R	R	R	R

Nevada

County	1868	1872	1876	1880	1884	1888	1892	1896	1900	1904	1908	1912
Carson City*	R	R	R	R	R	R	R	D	D	R	R	D
Churchill	T	D	D	D	R	D	PO	D	D	R	R	D
Clark	–	–	–	–	–	–	–	–	–	–	–	D
Douglas	R	R	R	D	R	R	R	D	D	R	R	P
Elko	–	R	D	D	R	R	PO	D	D	R	D	D
Esmeralda	R	R	D	D	R	R	PO	D	D	R	D	D
Eureka	–	–	R	R	R	R	PO	D	D	R	R	D
Humboldt	R	R	D	D	D	D	PO	D	D	R	D	D
Lander	R	R	D	D	R	R	PO	D	D	R	D	P
Lincoln	D	D	D	D	D	D	PO	D	D	R	D	D
Lyon	R	R	R	R	R	R	PO	D	D	R	R	D
Mineral	–	–	–	–	–	–	–	–	–	–	–	D
Nye	T	R	D	D	R	R	PO	D	D	R	D	D
Pershing	–	–	–	–	–	–	–	–	–	–	–	–
Storey	R	R	R	D	R	R	PO	D	D	R	R	D
Washoe	R	R	R	D	R	R	PO	D	D	R	R	D
White Pine	–	R	T	D	R	R	PO	D	D	R	R	D

County	1916	1920	1924	1928	1932	1936	1940	1944	1948	1952	1956	1960
Carson City*	D	R	D	R	D	D	D	R	R	R	R	R
Churchill	D	R	R	R	D	D	D	R	R	R	R	R
Clark	D	D	P	R	D	D	D	D	D	R	D	D
Douglas	R	R	R	R	D	D	R	R	R	R	R	R
Elko	D	R	P	R	D	D	D	D	D	R	R	D
Esmeralda	D	R	R	D	D	D	D	D	D	R	R	D
Eureka	D	R	R	D	D	D	D	R	R	R	R	R
Humboldt	D	R	P	R	D	D	D	D	D	R	R	D
Lander	D	R	R	R	D	D	D	R	R	R	R	R
Lincoln	D	R	P	R	D	D	D	D	D	D	R	D
Lyon	D	R	R	R	D	D	D	R	R	R	R	R
Mineral	D	R	P	D	D	D	D	D	D	D	R	D
Nye	D	R	P	D	D	D	D	D	R	R	R	D
Pershing	–	R	P	R	D	D	D	R	R	R	R	D
Storey	D	R	R	D	D	D	D	D	R	R	R	R
Washoe	D	R	R	R	D	D	D	R	R	R	R	R
White Pine	D	R	R	R	D	D	D	D	D	R	R	D

County	1964	1968	1972	1976	1984	1984	1988	1992	1996	2000	2004
Carson City*	R	R	R	R	R	R	R	R	R	R	R
Churchill	R	R	R	R	R	R	R	R	R	R	R
Clark	D	D	R	D	R	R	R	D	D	D	D
Douglas	R	R	R	R	R	R	R	R	R	R	R
Elko	D	R	R	R	R	R	R	R	R	R	R
Esmeralda	D	R	R	D	R	R	R	R	R	R	R
Eureka	D	R	R	R	R	R	R	R	R	R	R

County	1964	1968	1972	1976	1984	1984	1988	1992	1996	2000	2004
Humboldt	D	R	R	R	R	R	R	R	R	R	R
Lander	D	R	R	R	R	R	R	R	R	R	R
Lincoln	D	R	R	R	R	R	R	R	R	R	R
Lyon	R	R	R	R	R	R	R	R	R	R	R
Mineral	D	D	R	D	R	R	R	R	D	R	R
Nye	D	R	R	D	R	R	R	R	R	R	R
Pershing	D	R	R	R	R	R	R	R	R	R	R
Storey	D	R	R	D	R	R	R	PE	R	R	R
Washoe	D	R	R	R	R	R	R	R	R	R	R
White Pine	D	D	R	D	R	R	R	D	R	R	R

*Carson City was Ormsby County prior to 1972.

New Hampshire

County	1868	1872	1876	1880	1884	1888	1892	1896	1900	1904	1908	1912
Belknap	R	D	D	D	D	R	R	R	R	R	R	D
Carroll	D	R	D	D	D	D	D	R	R	R	R	D
Cheshire	R	R	R	R	R	R	R	R	R	R	R	R
Coos	D	D	D	D	D	D	D	R	R	R	R	D
Grafton	R	D	D	D	R	R	R	R	R	R	R	D
Hillsborough	R	R	R	R	R	R	R	R	R	R	R	D
Merrimack	R	R	D	R	R	D	R	R	R	R	R	D
Rockingham	R	R	R	R	R	D	R	R	R	R	R	D
Strafford	R	R	R	R	R	R	R	R	R	R	R	D
Sullivan	R	R	R	R	R	R	R	R	R	R	R	R

County	1916	1920	1924	1928	1932	1936	1940	1944	1948	1952	1956	1960
Belknap	R	R	R	R	R	R	R	R	R	R	R	R
Carroll	R	R	R	R	R	R	R	R	R	R	R	R
Cheshire	R	R	R	R	R	R	R	R	R	R	R	R
Coos	D	R	R	R	D	D	D	D	D	R	R	D
Grafton	R	R	R	R	R	R	R	R	R	R	R	R
Hillsborough	D	R	R	D	D	D	D	D	D	D	R	D
Merrimack	R	R	R	R	R	R	R	R	R	R	R	R
Rockingham	R	R	R	R	R	R	R	R	R	R	R	R
Strafford	D	R	R	R	D	D	D	D	D	R	R	D
Sullivan	D	R	R	R	R	R	D	D	R	R	R	R

County	1964	1968	1972	1976	1980	1984	1988	1992	1996	2000	2004
Belknap	D	R	R	R	R	R	R	R	R	R	R
Carroll	R	R	R	R	R	R	R	R	R	R	R
Cheshire	D	R	R	R	R	R	R	D	D	D	D
Coos	D	D	R	D	R	R	R	D	D	R	D

County	1964	1968	1972	1976	1980	1984	1988	1992	1996	2000	2004
Grafton	D	R	R	R	R	R	R	D	D	D	D
Hillsborough	D	D	R	R	R	R	R	R	D	R	R
Merrimack	D	R	R	R	R	R	R	D	D	D	D
Rockingham	D	R	R	R	R	R	R	R	D	R	R
Strafford	D	D	R	R	R	R	R	D	D	D	D
Sullivan	D	R	R	R	R	R	R	D	D	R	D

New Jersey

County	1868	1872	1876	1880	1884	1888	1892	1896	1900	1904	1908	1912
Atlantic	R	R	R	R	R	R	R	R	R	R	R	D
Bergen	D	D	D	D	D	D	D	R	R	R	R	D
Burlington	R	R	D	R	R	R	R	R	R	R	R	D
Camden	R	R	R	R	R	R	R	R	R	R	R	D
Cape May	R	R	R	R	R	R	R	R	R	R	R	D
Cumberland	R	R	R	R	R	R	R	R	R	R	R	P
Essex	R	R	R	R	R	R	D	R	R	R	R	P
Gloucester	R	R	R	R	R	R	R	R	R	R	R	D
Hudson	D	D	D	D	D	D	D	R	D	D	R	D
Hunterdon	R	R	R	R	R	R	R	D	D	D	D	D
Mercer	D	R	R	R	R	R	R	R	R	R	R	D
Middlesex	D	R	D	D	D	D	D	R	R	R	R	D
Monmouth	D	D	D	D	D	D	D	R	R	R	R	D
Morris	R	R	R	R	R	R	D	R	R	R	R	D
Ocean	R	R	R	R	R	R	R	R	R	R	R	P
Passaic	R	R	R	R	R	R	R	R	R	R	R	P
Salem	R	R	R	R	R	R	D	R	R	R	R	D
Somerset	D	R	D	R	D	D	D	R	R	R	R	D
Sussex	D	D	D	D	D	D	D	R	D	D	D	D
Union	D	R	D	D	D	D	D	R	R	R	R	D
Warren	D	D	D	D	D	D	D	D	D	D	D	D

County	1916	1920	1924	1928	1932	1936	1940	1944	1948	1952	1956	1960
Atlantic	R	R	R	R	R	D	D	D	R	R	R	R
Bergen	R	R	R	R	R	D	R	R	R	R	R	R
Burlington	R	R	R	R	R	D	D	D	R	R	R	R
Camden	R	R	R	R	R	D	D	D	D	D	R	D
Cape May	R	R	R	R	R	D	R	R	R	R	R	R
Cumberland	R	R	R	R	R	D	D	D	R	R	R	D
Essex	R	R	R	R	R	D	D	R	R	R	R	D
Gloucester	R	R	R	R	R	D	R	R	R	R	R	R
Hudson	D	R	D	D	D	D	D	D	D	D	R	D
Hunterdon	D	R	R	R	R	D	R	R	R	R	R	R
Mercer	R	R	R	R	R	D	D	D	D	D	R	D
Middlesex	R	R	R	R	D	D	D	D	D	R	R	D

County	1916	1920	1924	1928	1932	1936	1940	1944	1948	1952	1956	1960
Monmouth	R	R	R	R	R	R	R	R	R	R	R	R
Morris	R	R	R	R	R	R	R	R	R	R	R	R
Ocean	R	R	R	R	R	R	R	R	R	R	R	R
Passaic	R	R	R	R	D	D	D	D	D	R	R	D
Salem	R	R	R	R	R	D	D	D	D	R	R	R
Somerset	R	R	R	R	R	D	R	R	R	R	R	R
Sussex	D	R	R	R	R	R	R	R	R	R	R	R
Union	R	R	R	R	R	D	R	R	R	R	R	R
Warren	D	R	R	R	D	D	D	R	R	R	R	R

County	1964	1968	1972	1976	1980	1984	1988	1992	1996	2000	2004
Atlantic	D	D	R	D	R	R	R	D	D	D	D
Bergen	D	R	R	R	R	R	R	R	D	D	D
Burlington	D	R	R	D	R	R	R	D	D	D	D
Camden	D	D	R	D	R	R	R	D	D	D	D
Cape May	D	R	R	R	R	R	R	R	D	R	R
Cumberland	D	D	R	D	R	R	R	D	D	D	D
Essex	D	D	R	D	D	D	D	D	D	D	D
Gloucester	D	R	R	D	R	R	R	D	D	D	D
Hudson	D	D	R	D	D	R	D	D	D	D	D
Hunterdon	D	R	R	R	R	R	R	R	R	R	R
Mercer	D	D	R	D	D	R	D	D	D	D	D
Middlesex	D	D	R	D	R	R	R	D	D	D	D
Monmouth	D	R	R	R	R	R	R	R	D	D	R
Morris	D	R	R	R	R	R	R	R	R	R	R
Ocean	D	R	R	R	R	R	R	R	D	R	R
Passaic	D	R	R	R	R	R	R	R	D	D	D
Salem	D	R	R	D	R	R	R	R	D	D	R
Somerset	D	R	R	R	R	R	R	R	R	R	R
Sussex	D	R	R	R	R	R	R	R	R	R	R
Union	D	R	R	R	R	R	R	D	D	D	D
Warren	D	R	R	R	R	R	R	R	R	R	R

New Mexico

County	1912	1916	1920	1924	1928	1932	1936	1940	1944	1948	1952	1956
Bernalillo	P	R	R	R	R	D	D	D	D	D	R	R
Catron	–	–	R	R	R	D	D	D	R	D	R	R
Chaves	D	D	D	D	R	D	D	D	D	D	R	R
Cibola	–	–	–	–	–	–	–	–	–	–	–	–
Colfax	D	D	R	R	R	D	D	D	D	D	R	R
Curry	D	D	D	D	R	D	D	D	D	D	R	R
De Baca	–	–	D	D	D	D	D	D	D	D	R	R
Dona Ana	R	R	R	R	R	D	D	D	D	D	R	R
Eddy	D	D	D	D	R	D	D	D	D	D	D	D

County	1912	1916	1920	1924	1928	1932	1936	1940	1944	1948	1952	1956
Grant	D	D	R	D	R	D	D	D	D	D	D	D
Guadalupe	D	D	R	R	R	D	D	D	R	R	R	R
Harding	–	–	R	R	R	D	D	D	R	D	R	R
Hidalgo	–	–	D	D	R	D	D	D	D	D	R	R
Lea	–	–	D	D	R	D	D	D	D	D	D	D
Lincoln	D	R	R	R	R	D	D	R	R	R	R	R
Los Alamos	–	–	–	–	–	–	–	–	–	–	D	R
Luna	D	D	D	R	R	D	D	D	D	D	R	R
McKinley	R	R	R	R	R	D	D	D	D	D	D	R
Mora	R	R	R	R	R	D	D	R	R	R	R	R
Otero	D	D	R	D	R	D	D	D	D	D	R	R
Quay	D	D	D	D	R	D	D	D	D	D	R	R
Rio Arriba	R	R	R	R	R	D	D	D	D	D	R	R
Roosevelt	D	D	D	D	R	D	D	D	D	D	R	R
Sandoval	P	D	R	R	R	D	D	D	R	D	R	R
San Juan	D	D	R	R	R	D	D	R	R	R	R	R
San Miguel	R	R	R	R	R	R	D	D	D	D	R	R
Santa Fe	R	R	R	R	R	D	D	D	R	R	R	R
Sierra	D	D	R	R	R	D	D	D	R	D	R	R
Socorro	D	R	R	R	R	D	R	R	R	R	R	R
Taos	R	R	R	R	R	D	D	D	R	D	D	R
Torrance	R	R	R	R	R	D	D	R	R	R	R	R
Union	D	D	R	D	R	D	D	D	R	D	R	R
Valencia	R	R	R	R	R	R	D	R	R	R	R	R

County	1960	1964	1968	1972	1976	1980	1984	1988	1992	1996	2000	2004
Bernalillo	R	D	R	R	R	R	R	R	D	D	D	D
Catron	R	D	R	R	R	R	R	R	R	R	R	R
Chaves	R	D	R	R	R	R	R	R	R	R	R	R
Cibola	–	–	–	–	–	–	R	D	D	D	D	D
Colfax	D	D	D	R	D	R	R	D	D	D	D	R
Curry	R	D	R	R	R	R	R	R	R	R	R	R
De Baca	R	D	R	R	D	R	R	R	D	D	R	R
Dona Ana	D	D	R	R	R	R	R	R	R	D	D	D
Eddy	D	D	R	R	D	R	R	R	D	D	R	R
Grant	D	D	D	R	D	R	D	D	D	D	D	D
Guadalupe	D	D	R	R	D	R	R	D	D	D	D	D
Harding	R	R	R	R	R	R	R	R	R	R	R	R
Hidalgo	D	D	D	R	D	R	R	R	D	D	R	R
Lea	D	D	R	R	R	R	R	R	R	R	R	R
Lincoln	R	R	R	R	R	R	R	R	R	R	R	R
Los Alamos	D	D	R	R	R	R	R	R	R	R	R	R
Luna	D	D	R	R	R	R	R	R	D	D	R	R
McKinley	D	D	D	R	D	R	D	D	D	D	D	D
Mora	D	D	R	R	D	D	D	D	D	D	D	D
Otero	D	D	R	R	R	R	R	R	R	R	R	R
Quay	R	D	R	R	D	R	R	R	R	R	R	R
Rio Arriba	D	D	D	D	D	D	D	D	D	D	D	D
Roosevelt	R	D	R	R	R	R	R	R	R	R	R	R

County	1960	1964	1968	1972	1976	1980	1984	1988	1992	1996	2000	2004
Sandoval	D	D	D	R	D	R	R	R	D	D	R	R
San Juan	R	D	R	R	R	R	R	R	R	R	R	R
San Miguel	D	D	D	D	D	D	D	D	D	D	D	D
Santa Fe	D	D	D	R	D	D	D	D	D	D	D	D
Sierra	R	D	R	R	R	R	R	R	D	D	R	R
Socorro	D	D	R	R	D	R	R	R	D	D	D	D
Taos	D	D	R	R	D	D	D	D	D	D	D	D
Torrance	R	D	R	R	D	R	R	R	R	R	R	R
Union	R	R	R	R	R	R	R	R	R	R	R	R
Valencia	D	D	R	R	D	R	R	R	D	D	R	R

New York

County	1868	1872	1876	1880	1884	1888	1892	1896	1900	1904	1908	1912
Albany	D	R	D	D	D	D	D	R	R	R	R	R
Allegany	R	R	R	R	R	R	R	R	R	R	R	R
Bronx	–	–	–	–	–	–	–	–	–	–	–	–
Broome	R	R	R	R	R	R	R	R	R	R	R	R
Cattaraugus	R	R	R	R	R	R	R	R	R	R	R	D
Cayuga	R	R	R	R	R	R	R	R	R	R	R	R
Chautauqua	R	R	R	R	R	R	R	R	R	R	R	R
Chemung	R	R	D	D	R	D	R	R	R	R	R	D
Chenango	R	R	R	R	R	R	R	R	R	R	R	R
Clinton	R	R	R	R	R	R	R	R	R	R	R	R
Columbia	D	D	D	R	R	R	D	R	R	R	R	D
Cortland	R	R	R	R	R	R	R	R	R	R	R	R
Delaware	R	R	R	R	R	R	R	R	R	R	R	R
Dutchess	R	D	R	R	R	R	R	R	R	R	R	R
Erie	R	R	R	R	R	R	D	R	R	R	R	D
Essex	R	R	R	R	R	R	R	R	R	R	R	R
Franklin	R	R	R	R	R	R	R	R	R	R	R	R
Fulton	R	R	R	R	R	R	R	R	R	R	R	R
Genesee	R	R	R	R	R	R	R	R	R	R	R	D
Greene	D	D	D	D	R	D	R	R	R	R	R	D
Hamilton	D	D	D	D	D	NR	D	NR	R	R	R	D
Herkimer	R	R	R	R	R	R	R	R	R	R	R	D
Jefferson	R	R	R	R	R	R	R	R	R	R	R	R
Kings	D	D	D	D	D	D	D	R	R	R	R	D
Lewis	R	R	D	R	R	R	R	R	R	R	R	D
Livingston	R	R	R	R	R	R	R	R	R	R	R	R
Madison	R	R	R	R	R	R	R	R	R	R	R	R
Monroe	R	R	R	R	R	R	R	R	R	R	R	D
Montgomery	R	R	D	R	R	R	R	R	R	R	R	R
Nassau	–	–	–	–	–	–	–	R	R	R	R	R
New York	D	D	D	D	D	D	D	R	D	D	D	D
Niagara	R	R	D	R	D	R	D	R	R	R	R	D

County	1868	1872	1876	1880	1884	1888	1892	1896	1900	1904	1908	1912
Oneida	R	R	R	R	D	R	R	R	R	R	R	D
Onondaga	R	R	R	R	R	R	R	R	R	R	R	R
Ontario	R	R	R	R	R	R	R	R	R	R	R	R
Orange	R	R	D	R	R	R	R	R	R	R	R	R
Orleans	R	R	R	R	R	R	R	R	R	R	R	R
Oswego	R	R	R	R	R	R	R	R	R	R	R	R
Otsego	R	D	D	D	D	R	R	R	R	R	R	D
Putnam	D	R	R	R	R	R	R	R	R	R	R	D
Queens	D	R	D	D	D	D	D	R	D	D	D	D
Rensselaer	R	R	D	R	R	R	D	R	R	R	R	D
Richmond	D	R	D	D	D	D	D	R	D	D	D	D
Rockland	D	D	D	D	D	D	D	R	R	R	R	D
St. Lawrence	R	R	R	R	R	R	R	R	R	R	R	R
Saratoga	R	R	R	R	R	R	R	R	R	R	R	R
Schenectady	R	R	D	R	R	R	D	R	R	R	R	D
Schoharie	D	D	D	D	D	D	D	D	D	D	D	D
Schuyer	R	R	R	R	R	R	R	R	R	R	R	R
Seneca	D	R	D	D	D	D	D	R	R	R	R	D
Steuben	R	R	R	R	R	R	R	R	R	R	R	D
Suffolk	R	R	D	R	D	R	R	R	R	R	R	D
Sullivan	D	R	D	D	D	R	R	R	R	R	R	D
Tioga	R	R	R	R	R	R	R	R	R	R	R	R
Tompkins	R	R	R	R	R	R	R	R	R	R	R	D
Ulster	D	R	D	R	R	R	D	R	R	R	R	D
Warrren	R	R	R	R	R	R	R	R	R	R	R	R
Washington	R	R	R	R	R	R	R	R	R	R	R	R
Wayne	R	R	R	R	R	R	R	R	R	R	R	R
Westchester	D	D	D	D	D	D	D	R	R	R	R	D
Wyoming	R	R	R	R	R	R	R	R	R	R	R	R
Yates	R	R	R	R	R	R	R	R	R	R	R	R

County	1916	1920	1924	1928	1932	1936	1940	1944	1948	1952	1956	1960
Albany	R	R	R	D	D	D	D	D	D	R	R	D
Allegany	R	R	R	R	R	R	R	R	R	R	R	R
Bronx	D	R	R	D	D	D	D	D	D	D	D	D
Broome	R	R	R	R	R	R	R	R	R	R	R	R
Cattaraugus	R	R	R	R	R	R	R	R	R	R	R	R
Cayuga	R	R	R	R	R	R	R	R	R	R	R	R
Chautauqua	R	R	R	R	R	R	R	R	R	R	R	R
Chemung	D	R	R	R	R	R	R	R	R	R	R	R
Chenango	R	R	R	R	R	R	R	R	R	R	R	R
Clinton	R	R	R	D	D	D	D	D	R	R	R	D
Columbia	R	R	R	R	R	R	R	R	R	R	R	R
Cortland	R	R	R	R	R	R	R	R	R	R	R	R
Delaware	R	R	R	R	R	R	R	R	R	R	R	R
Dutchess	R	R	R	R	R	R	R	R	R	R	R	R
Erie	R	R	R	R	R	D	D	D	D	R	R	D
Essex	R	R	R	R	R	R	R	R	R	R	R	R
Franklin	R	R	R	D	D	R	R	R	R	R	R	D

County	1916	1920	1924	1928	1932	1936	1940	1944	1948	1952	1956	1960
Fulton	R	R	R	R	R	R	R	R	R	R	R	R
Genesee	R	R	R	R	R	R	R	R	R	R	R	R
Greene	D	R	R	R	R	R	R	R	R	R	R	R
Hamilton	D	R	R	R	R	R	R	R	R	R	R	R
Herkimer	R	R	R	R	R	R	R	R	R	R	R	R
Jefferson	R	R	R	R	R	R	R	R	R	R	R	R
Kings	D	R	R	D	D	D	D	D	D	D	D	D
Lewis	R	R	R	R	R	R	R	R	R	R	R	R
Livingston	R	R	R	R	R	R	R	R	R	R	R	R
Madison	R	R	R	R	R	R	R	R	R	R	R	R
Monroe	R	R	R	R	R	D	D	D	D	R	R	R
Montgomery	R	R	R	R	R	D	R	R	R	R	R	D
Nassau	R	R	R	R	R	R	R	R	R	R	R	R
New York	D	R	R	D	D	D	D	D	D	D	D	D
Niagara	R	R	R	R	R	R	R	R	R	R	R	D
Oneida	R	R	R	R	R	R	R	R	D	R	R	D
Onondaga	R	R	R	R	R	R	R	R	R	R	R	R
Ontario	R	R	R	R	R	R	R	R	R	R	R	R
Orange	R	R	R	R	R	R	R	R	R	R	R	R
Orleans	R	R	R	R	R	R	R	R	R	R	R	R
Oswego	R	R	R	R	R	R	R	R	R	R	R	R
Otsego	D	R	R	R	R	R	R	R	R	R	R	R
Putnam	R	R	R	R	R	R	R	R	R	R	R	R
Queens	R	R	R	D	D	D	R	R	R	R	R	D
Rensselaer	R	R	R	D	D	R	R	R	R	R	R	R
Richmond	D	R	R	D	D	D	R	R	R	R	R	R
Rockland	R	R	R	R	R	R	R	R	R	R	R	R
St. Lawrence	R	R	R	R	R	R	R	R	R	R	R	R
Saratoga	R	R	R	R	R	R	R	R	R	R	R	R
Schenectady	R	R	R	R	R	D	R	R	R	R	R	R
Schoharie	D	R	R	R	R	R	R	R	R	R	R	R
Schuyer	R	R	R	R	R	R	R	R	R	R	R	R
Seneca	R	R	R	R	R	R	R	R	R	R	R	R
Steuben	R	R	R	R	R	R	R	R	R	R	R	R
Suffolk	R	R	R	R	R	R	R	R	R	R	R	R
Sullivan	R	R	R	R	D	D	R	R	R	R	R	R
Tioga	R	R	R	R	R	R	R	R	R	R	R	R
Tompkins	R	R	R	R	R	R	R	R	R	R	R	R
Ulster	R	R	R	R	R	R	R	R	R	R	R	R
Warrren	R	R	R	R	R	R	R	R	R	R	R	R
Washington	R	R	R	R	R	R	R	R	R	R	R	R
Wayne	R	R	R	R	R	R	R	R	R	R	R	R
Westchester	R	R	R	R	R	R	R	R	R	R	R	R
Wyoming	R	R	R	R	R	R	R	R	R	R	R	R
Yates	R	R	R	R	R	R	R	R	R	R	R	R

County	1964	1968	1972	1976	1980	1984	1988	1992	1996	2000	2004
Albany	D	D	R	D	D	D	D	D	D	D	D
Allegany	D	R	R	R	R	R	R	R	R	R	R

County	1964	1968	1972	1976	1980	1984	1988	1992	1996	2000	2004
Bronx	D	D	D	D	D	D	D	D	D	D	D
Broome	D	R	R	R	R	R	D	D	D	D	D
Cattaraugus	D	R	R	R	R	R	R	R	D	R	R
Cayuga	D	R	R	R	R	R	R	D	D	D	R
Chautauqua	D	R	R	R	R	R	R	D	D	R	R
Chemung	D	R	R	R	R	R	R	R	D	R	R
Chenango	D	R	R	R	R	R	R	R	D	R	R
Clinton	D	R	R	R	R	R	R	R	D	D	D
Columbia	D	R	R	R	R	R	R	R	D	D	D
Cortland	D	R	R	R	R	R	R	D	D	R	R
Delaware	D	R	R	R	R	R	R	R	D	R	R
Dutchess	D	R	R	R	R	R	R	R	D	R	R
Erie	D	D	R	D	D	D	D	D	D	D	D
Essex	D	R	R	R	R	R	R	R	D	R	R
Franklin	D	R	R	R	R	R	R	D	D	D	D
Fulton	D	R	R	R	R	R	R	R	D	R	R
Genesee	D	R	R	R	R	R	R	R	R	R	R
Greene	D	R	R	R	R	R	R	R	R	R	R
Hamilton	D	R	R	R	R	R	R	R	R	R	R
Herkimer	D	R	R	R	R	R	R	R	D	R	R
Jefferson	D	R	R	R	R	R	R	R	D	R	R
Kings	D	D	D	D	D	D	D	D	D	D	D
Lewis	D	R	R	R	R	R	R	R	D	R	R
Livingston	D	R	R	R	R	R	R	R	R	R	R
Madison	D	R	R	R	R	R	R	R	D	R	R
Monroe	D	R	R	R	D	R	R	D	D	D	D
Montgomery	D	R	R	R	R	R	D	D	D	D	R
Nassau	D	R	R	R	R	R	R	D	D	D	D
New York	D	D	D	D	D	D	D	D	D	D	D
Niagara	D	D	R	R	D	R	D	D	D	D	D
Oneida	D	R	R	R	R	R	R	R	D	R	R
Onondaga	D	R	R	R	R	R	R	D	D	D	D
Ontario	D	R	R	R	R	R	R	R	D	R	R
Orange	D	R	R	R	R	R	R	R	D	R	R
Orleans	D	R	R	R	R	R	R	R	R	R	R
Oswego	D	R	R	R	R	R	R	R	D	R	R
Otsego	D	R	R	R	R	R	R	D	D	R	R
Putnam	D	R	R	R	R	R	R	R	R	R	R
Queens	D	D	R	D	D	D	D	D	D	D	D
Rensselaer	D	R	R	R	R	R	R	D	D	D	D
Richmond	D	R	R	R	R	R	R	R	D	D	R
Rockland	D	R	R	R	R	R	R	D	D	D	R
St. Lawrence	D	R	R	R	R	R	R	D	D	D	D
Saratoga	D	R	R	R	R	R	R	R	D	R	R
Schenectady	D	D	R	R	R	R	D	D	D	D	D
Schoharie	D	R	R	R	R	R	R	R	D	R	R
Schuyer	D	R	R	R	R	R	R	R	D	R	R
Seneca	D	R	R	R	R	R	R	D	D	D	R
Steuben	D	R	R	R	R	R	R	R	R	R	R

County	1964	1968	1972	1976	1980	1984	1988	1992	1996	2000	2004
Suffolk	D	R	R	R	R	R	R	R	D	D	D
Sullivan	D	R	R	D	R	R	R	D	D	D	R
Tioga	D	R	R	R	R	R	R	R	R	R	R
Tompkins	D	R	R	R	R	D	D	D	D	D	D
Ulster	D	R	R	R	R	R	R	D	D	D	D
Warrren	D	R	R	R	R	R	R	R	D	R	R
Washington	D	R	R	R	R	R	R	R	D	R	R
Wayne	D	R	R	R	R	R	R	R	R	R	R
Westchester	D	R	R	R	R	R	R	D	D	D	D
Wyoming	D	R	R	R	R	R	R	R	R	R	R
Yates	D	R	R	R	R	R	R	R	D	R	R

North Carolina

County	1868	1872	1876	1880	1884	1888	1892	1896	1900	1904	1908	1912
Alamance	R	R	R	D	D	D	D	D	R	D	R	D
Alexander	D	D	D	D	D	D	D	D	R	R	R	D
Alleghany	D	D	D	D	D	D	D	D	D	D	D	D
Anson	D	R	D	D	D	D	D	D	D	D	D	D
Ashe	D	R	D	D	D	R	R	R	R	R	R	D
Avery	–	–	–	–	–	–	–	–	–	–	–	P
Beaufort	R	R	D	D	D	D	D	D	D	D	D	D
Bertie	R	R	R	R	R	D	D	R	D	D	D	D
Bladen	R	R	D	R	R	D	D	D	R	D	D	D
Brunswick	R	R	R	R	R	D	D	D	R	D	R	D
Buncombe	D	D	D	D	D	D	D	R	R	D	R	D
Burke	R	R	D	D	D	D	D	D	D	D	R	D
Cabarrus	D	D	D	D	D	D	D	D	D	D	R	D
Caldwell	D	D	D	D	D	D	D	D	R	R	R	D
Camden	R	R	D	D	D	R	R	R	R	D	D	D
Carteret	D	D	D	D	D	D	D	D	D	D	D	D
Caswell	R	R	R	R	R	R	R	R	D	D	D	D
Catawba	D	D	D	D	D	D	D	D	D	D	R	D
Chatham	R	R	D	D	D	D	PO	D	R	D	D	D
Cherokee	R	R	D	D	R	R	T	R	R	R	R	D
Chowan	R	R	R	R	R	R	R	R	R	D	D	D
Clay	D	D	D	D	D	D	D	D	D	D	D	P
Cleveland	D	R	D	D	D	D	D	D	D	D	D	D
Columbus	D	R	D	D	D	D	D	D	D	D	D	D
Craven	R	R	R	R	R	R	R	R	D	D	D	D
Cumberland	D	R	D	R	D	D	D	D	R	D	D	D
Currituck	D	NR	D	D	D	D	D	D	D	D	D	D
Dare	–	R	D	D	R	R	R	R	D	D	D	D
Davidson	R	R	D	R	R	R	D	R	R	R	R	D
Davie	D	R	D	D	R	R	R	D	R	R	R	D
Duplin	D	D	D	D	D	D	D	D	D	D	D	D

County	1868	1872	1876	1880	1884	1888	1892	1896	1900	1904	1908	1912
Durham	–	–	–	–	D	D	D	D	D	D	D	D
Edgecombe	R	R	R	R	R	R	D	R	D	D	D	D
Forsyth	R	R	R	R	D	R	D	R	R	D	R	D
Franklin	R	R	R	D	D	D	D	D	D	D	D	D
Gaston	R	D	D	R	D	D	D	D	D	D	D	D
Gates	D	D	D	D	D	D	D	D	D	D	D	D
Graham	NR	D	NR	NR	D	D	D	D	R	R	R	D
Granville	R	R	R	R	D	R	R	D	D	D	D	D
Greene	R	R	R	R	R	R	D	D	D	D	D	D
Guilford	R	R	D	D	D	R	D	D	D	D	D	D
Halifax	R	R	R	R	R	R	D	R	D	D	D	D
Harnett	D	R	D	D	D	D	D	D	D	D	D	D
Haywood	D	D	D	D	D	D	D	D	D	D	D	D
Henderson	R	R	D	R	R	R	R	R	R	R	R	D
Hertford	R	R	R	R	R	D	R	R	D	D	D	D
Hoke	–	–	–	–	–	–	–	–	–	–	–	D
Hyde	D	D	D	D	D	D	D	D	D	D	D	D
Iredell	D	D	D	D	D	D	D	D	D	D	D	D
Jackson	D	D	D	D	D	D	D	D	D	D	R	D
Johnston	D	R	D	D	D	D	D	D	D	D	R	D
Jones	R	R	R	R	D	D	D	D	D	D	D	D
Lee	–	–	–	–	–	–	–	–	–	–	D	D
Lenoir	R	R	R	R	D	D	D	D	D	D	D	D
Lincoln	D	D	D	D	D	D	D	D	R	D	D	D
McDowell	R	R	D	D	D	D	D	D	R	R	R	D
Macon	D	D	D	D	D	D	D	D	R	R	R	D
Madison	R	R	D	R	R	R	R	R	R	R	R	P
Martin	D	R	D	D	D	D	D	D	D	D	D	D
Mecklenburg	D	D	D	D	D	D	D	D	D	D	D	D
Mitchell	R	R	D	R	R	R	R	R	R	R	R	P
Montgomery	R	R	R	R	R	R	D	R	D	D	R	D
Moore	R	R	D	D	D	D	D	D	R	D	D	D
Nash	D	R	D	D	D	D	PO	D	D	D	D	D
New Hanover	R	R	R	R	R	R	D	R	D	D	D	D
Northampton	R	R	R	R	R	R	R	R	D	D	D	D
Onslow	D	D	D	D	D	D	D	D	D	D	D	D
Orange	D	D	D	D	D	D	D	D	R	D	R	D
Pamlico	–	R	D	D	D	D	D	D	R	D	D	D
Pasquotank	R	R	R	R	R	R	R	R	R	D	D	D
Pender	–	–	R	R	R	R	R	D	D	D	D	D
Perquimans	R	R	R	R	R	R	R	R	R	D	D	D
Person	D	D	D	D	D	D	R	D	D	D	R	D
Pitt	R	R	D	D	D	D	D	D	D	D	D	D
Polk	R	R	D	R	R	D	R	R	D	D	D	D
Randolph	R	R	D	D	D	R	D	R	R	D	R	D
Richmond	R	R	R	D	D	R	D	R	D	D	D	D
Robeson	D	R	D	D	D	D	D	D	D	D	D	D
Rockingham	D	D	D	D	D	D	R	D	D	D	R	D
Rowan	D	R	D	D	D	D	D	D	D	D	D	D

County	1868	1872	1876	1880	1884	1888	1892	1896	1900	1904	1908	1912
Rutherford	R	R	D	D	D	D	D	D	D	D	D	D
Sampson	D	R	D	D	D	D	PO	D	R	R	R	P
Scotland	–	–	–	–	–	–	–	–	D	D	D	D
Stanly	D	D	D	D	D	D	D	D	D	R	R	D
Stokes	R	D	D	D	D	D	R	R	R	R	R	R
Surry	R	R	D	D	R	D	D	R	R	R	R	R
Swain	–	D	D	D	D	D	D	D	R	R	R	P
Transylvania	D	D	D	D	D	R	D	R	R	D	R	D
Tyrrell	D	R	D	D	D	D	R	R	D	R	R	D
Union	D	D	D	D	D	D	D	D	D	D	D	D
Vance	–	–	–	–	R	R	R	R	D	D	D	D
Wake	R	R	R	R	D	R	D	D	D	D	D	D
Warren	R	R	R	R	R	R	R	R	D	D	D	D
Washington	R	R	R	R	R	R	R	R	D	D	R	D
Watauga	D	D	D	D	D	R	R	R	R	R	R	D
Wayne	D	R	D	D	D	D	D	D	D	D	D	D
Wilkes	R	R	R	R	R	R	R	R	R	R	R	P
Wilson	D	D	D	D	D	D	D	D	D	D	D	D
Yadkin	R	R	R	R	R	R	R	R	R	R	R	R
Yancey	D	D	D	D	D	D	D	D	R	D	D	D

County	1916	1920	1924	1928	1932	1936	1940	1944	1948	1952	1956	1960
Alamance	D	D	D	R	D	D	D	D	D	D	R	R
Alexander	R	R	R	R	D	D	D	R	R	R	R	R
Alleghany	D	D	D	D	D	D	D	D	D	D	R	D
Anson	D	D	D	D	D	D	D	D	D	D	D	D
Ashe	R	R	D	R	D	D	D	R	D	R	R	R
Avery	R	R	R	R	R	R	R	R	R	R	R	R
Beaufort	D	D	D	D	D	D	D	D	D	D	D	D
Bertie	D	D	D	D	D	D	D	D	D	D	D	D
Bladen	D	D	D	R	D	D	D	D	D	D	D	D
Brunswick	R	R	R	R	D	D	D	D	D	R	R	D
Buncombe	D	D	D	R	D	D	D	D	D	R	R	R
Burke	D	R	D	R	D	D	D	D	R	R	R	R
Cabarrus	R	R	D	R	D	D	D	D	D	R	R	R
Caldwell	D	R	D	R	D	D	D	D	D	R	R	R
Camden	D	D	D	D	D	D	D	D	D	D	D	D
Carteret	R	R	D	R	D	D	D	D	D	D	D	D
Caswell	D	D	D	D	D	D	PO	D	D	D	D	D
Catawba	R	R	R	R	D	D	D	D	R	R	R	R
Chatham	D	D	D	R	D	D	D	D	D	D	D	D
Cherokee	T	R	R	R	D	D	D	R	D	D	R	R
Chowan	D	D	D	D	D	D	D	D	D	D	D	D
Clay	R	R	R	R	D	D	D	R	D	R	R	R
Cleveland	D	D	D	D	D	D	D	D	D	D	D	D
Columbus	D	D	D	R	D	D	D	D	D	D	D	D
Craven	D	D	D	D	D	D	D	D	D	D	D	D
Cumberland	D	D	D	R	D	D	D	D	D	D	D	D
Currituck	D	D	D	D	D	D	D	D	D	D	D	D

County	1916	1920	1924	1928	1932	1936	1940	1944	1948	1952	1956	1960
Dare	D	D	D	D	D	D	D	D	D	D	R	D
Davidson	R	R	D	R	D	D	D	D	R	R	R	R
Davie	R	R	R	R	R	R	D	R	R	R	R	R
Duplin	D	D	D	R	D	D	D	D	D	D	D	D
Durham	D	D	D	R	D	D	D	D	D	D	D	D
Edgecombe	D	D	D	D	D	D	D	D	D	D	D	D
Forsyth	D	D	D	R	D	D	D	D	D	R	R	R
Franklin	D	D	D	D	D	D	D	D	D	D	D	D
Gaston	D	D	D	R	D	D	D	D	D	R	R	R
Gates	D	D	D	D	D	D	D	D	D	D	D	D
Graham	D	R	R	R	D	D	D	D	D	D	R	R
Granville	D	D	D	D	D	D	D	D	D	D	D	D
Greene	D	D	D	D	D	D	D	D	D	D	D	D
Guilford	D	D	D	R	D	D	D	D	D	R	R	R
Halifax	D	D	D	D	D	D	D	D	D	D	D	D
Harnett	D	D	D	R	D	D	D	D	D	D	D	D
Haywood	D	D	D	R	D	D	D	D	D	D	D	R
Henderson	R	R	R	R	D	D	D	D	R	R	R	R
Hertford	D	D	D	D	D	D	D	D	D	D	D	D
Hoke	D	D	D	D	D	D	D	D	D	D	D	D
Hyde	D	D	D	R	D	D	D	D	D	D	D	D
Iredell	D	D	D	R	D	D	D	D	D	R	R	R
Jackson	D	D	D	R	D	D	D	D	D	D	D	R
Johnston	D	D	R	R	D	D	D	D	D	D	D	D
Jones	D	D	D	R	D	D	D	D	D	D	D	D
Lee	D	D	D	D	D	D	D	D	D	D	D	D
Lenoir	D	D	D	D	D	D	D	D	D	D	D	D
Lincoln	D	D	D	R	D	D	D	D	R	R	R	R
McDowell	D	D	D	D	D	D	D	D	D	D	R	R
Macon	D	D	D	R	D	D	D	D	D	D	R	R
Madison	R	R	R	R	R	R	R	R	R	R	R	D
Martin	D	D	D	D	D	D	D	D	D	D	D	D
Mecklenburg	D	D	D	R	D	D	D	D	D	R	R	R
Mitchell	R	R	R	R	R	R	R	R	R	R	R	R
Montgomery	D	D	D	R	D	D	D	D	D	R	R	R
Moore	D	D	D	R	D	D	D	D	D	R	R	R
Nash	D	D	D	D	D	D	D	D	D	D	D	D
New Hanover	D	D	D	R	D	D	D	D	D	D	D	D
Northampton	D	D	D	D	D	D	D	D	D	D	D	D
Onslow	D	D	D	R	D	D	D	D	D	D	D	D
Orange	D	D	D	R	D	D	D	D	D	D	D	D
Pamlico	D	D	D	R	D	D	D	D	D	D	D	D
Pasquotank	D	D	D	D	D	D	D	D	D	D	D	D
Pender	D	D	D	R	D	D	D	D	D	D	D	D
Perquimans	D	D	D	D	D	D	D	D	D	D	D	D
Person	D	D	D	D	D	D	D	D	D	D	D	D
Pitt	D	D	D	D	D	D	D	D	D	D	D	D
Polk	R	D	D	R	D	D	D	D	D	D	R	R
Randolph	R	R	R	R	D	D	D	R	R	R	R	R

County	1916	1920	1924	1928	1932	1936	1940	1944	1948	1952	1956	1960
Richmond	D	D	D	D	D	D	D	D	D	D	D	D
Robeson	D	D	D	D	D	D	D	D	D	D	D	D
Rockingham	D	D	D	R	D	D	D	D	D	D	R	D
Rowan	D	D	D	R	D	D	D	D	D	R	R	R
Rutherford	D	D	D	R	D	D	D	D	D	R	R	R
Sampson	R	R	R	R	D	D	R	R	D	D	D	D
Scotland	D	D	D	D	D	D	D	D	D	D	D	D
Stanly	D	R	D	R	D	D	D	R	R	R	R	R
Stokes	R	R	R	R	D	D	D	D	D	D	R	R
Surry	R	R	R	R	D	D	D	D	D	D	R	R
Swain	R	R	R	R	D	D	D	D	D	D	R	D
Transylvania	R	R	R	R	D	D	D	D	D	R	R	R
Tyrrell	D	D	D	R	D	D	D	D	D	D	D	D
Union	D	D	D	D	D	D	D	D	D	D	D	D
Vance	D	D	D	D	D	D	D	D	D	D	D	D
Wake	D	D	D	D	D	D	D	D	D	D	D	D
Warren	D	D	D	D	D	D	D	D	D	D	D	D
Washington	D	D	D	R	D	D	D	D	D	D	D	D
Watauga	R	R	R	R	D	D	R	R	R	R	R	R
Wayne	D	D	D	R	D	D	D	D	D	D	D	D
Wilkes	R	R	R	R	R	R	R	R	R	R	R	R
Wilson	D	D	D	D	D	D	D	D	D	D	D	D
Yadkin	R	R	R	R	R	R	R	R	R	R	R	R
Yancey	D	R	D	R	D	D	D	D	D	D	D	D

County	1964	1968	1972	1976	1980	1984	1988	1992	1996	2000	2004
Alamance	D	A	R	D	R	R	R	R	R	R	R
Alexander	R	R	R	R	R	R	R	R	R	R	R
Alleghany	D	R	R	D	D	R	R	D	R	R	R
Anson	D	A	R	D	D	D	D	D	D	D	D
Ashe	D	R	R	R	R	R	R	R	R	R	R
Avery	R	R	R	R	R	R	R	R	R	R	R
Beaufort	D	A	R	D	R	R	R	R	R	R	R
Bertie	D	D	R	D	D	D	D	D	D	D	D
Bladen	D	A	R	D	D	D	D	D	D	D	R
Brunswick	D	A	R	D	D	R	R	D	R	R	R
Buncombe	D	R	R	D	R	R	R	D	D	R	R
Burke	D	R	R	D	R	R	R	R	R	R	R
Cabarrus	R	R	R	R	R	R	R	R	R	R	R
Caldwell	D	R	R	D	R	R	R	R	R	R	R
Camden	D	A	R	D	D	R	R	D	D	R	R
Carteret	D	R	R	D	R	R	R	R	R	R	R
Caswell	D	A	R	D	D	D	D	D	D	R	R
Catawba	R	R	R	R	R	R	R	R	R	R	R
Chatham	D	R	R	D	D	R	D	D	D	D	D
Cherokee	D	R	R	D	R	R	R	R	R	R	R
Chowan	D	A	R	D	D	R	R	D	D	D	R
Clay	D	R	R	D	R	R	R	R	R	R	R
Cleveland	D	A	R	D	D	R	R	R	R	R	R

County	1964	1968	1972	1976	1980	1984	1988	1992	1996	2000	2004
Columbus	D	A	R	D	D	R	D	D	D	D	R
Craven	D	A	R	D	R	R	R	R	R	R	R
Cumberland	D	D	R	D	D	R	R	D	D	D	R
Currituck	D	A	R	D	D	R	R	R	R	R	R
Dare	D	R	R	D	R	R	R	R	R	R	R
Davidson	R	R	R	R	R	R	R	R	R	R	R
Davie	R	R	R	R	R	R	R	R	R	R	R
Duplin	D	A	R	D	D	R	D	D	D	R	R
Durham	D	D	R	D	D	D	D	D	D	D	D
Edgecombe	D	A	R	D	D	D	D	D	D	D	D
Forsyth	D	R	R	D	R	R	R	R	R	R	R
Franklin	D	A	R	D	D	R	R	D	D	R	R
Gaston	D	R	R	D	R	R	R	R	R	R	R
Gates	D	A	R	D	D	D	D	D	D	D	D
Graham	D	R	R	D	R	R	R	R	R	R	R
Granville	D	A	R	D	D	R	D	D	D	D	R
Greene	D	A	R	D	D	R	D	D	R	R	R
Guilford	D	R	R	D	R	R	R	D	D	R	D
Halifax	D	A	R	D	D	D	D	D	D	D	D
Harnett	D	A	R	D	D	R	R	R	R	R	R
Haywood	D	R	R	D	D	R	D	D	D	R	R
Henderson	R	R	R	R	R	R	R	R	R	R	R
Hertford	D	D	R	D	D	D	D	D	D	D	D
Hoke	D	D	R	D	D	D	D	D	D	D	D
Hyde	D	A	R	D	D	R	D	D	D	R	R
Iredell	R	R	R	D	R	R	R	R	R	R	R
Jackson	D	R	R	D	D	R	R	D	D	R	R
Johnston	D	A	R	D	R	R	R	R	R	R	R
Jones	D	A	R	D	D	R	D	D	D	R	R
Lee	D	A	R	D	D	R	R	R	R	R	R
Lenoir	D	A	R	R	R	R	R	R	R	R	R
Lincoln	D	R	R	D	R	R	R	R	R	R	R
McDowell	D	R	R	D	R	R	R	R	R	R	R
Macon	D	R	R	D	R	R	R	R	R	R	R
Madison	D	R	R	D	D	R	R	D	D	R	R
Martin	D	A	R	D	D	R	D	D	D	D	R
Mecklenburg	D	R	R	D	R	R	R	R	D	R	D
Mitchell	R	R	R	R	R	R	R	R	R	R	R
Montgomery	D	R	R	D	D	R	R	D	D	R	R
Moore	D	R	R	R	R	R	R	R	R	R	R
Nash	D	A	R	D	R	R	R	R	R	R	R
New Hanover	D	R	R	D	R	R	R	R	R	R	R
Northampton	D	D	D	D	D	D	D	D	D	D	D
Onslow	D	A	R	D	R	R	R	R	R	R	R
Orange	D	D	D	D	D	D	D	D	D	D	D
Pamlico	D	A	R	D	D	R	R	D	R	R	R
Pasquotank	D	A	R	D	D	R	R	D	D	D	D
Pender	D	A	R	D	D	R	R	D	R	R	R
Perquimans	D	A	R	D	D	R	R	D	D	R	R

County	1964	1968	1972	1976	1980	1984	1988	1992	1996	2000	2004
Person	D	A	R	D	D	R	R	R	R	R	R
Pitt	D	A	R	D	R	R	R	D	R	R	R
Polk	D	R	R	D	R	R	R	R	R	R	R
Randolph	R	R	R	R	R	R	R	R	R	R	R
Richmond	D	A	R	D	D	D	D	D	D	D	D
Robeson	D	D	R	D	D	D	D	D	D	D	D
Rockingham	D	A	R	D	D	R	R	D	R	R	R
Rowan	D	R	R	D	R	R	R	R	R	R	R
Rutherford	D	R	R	D	R	R	R	R	R	R	R
Sampson	D	R	R	D	D	R	R	D	R	R	R
Scotland	D	D	R	D	D	R	D	D	D	D	D
Stanly	R	R	R	D	R	R	R	R	R	R	R
Stokes	D	R	R	D	R	R	R	R	R	R	R
Surry	D	R	R	D	R	R	R	R	R	R	R
Swain	D	R	R	D	D	R	D	D	D	R	R
Transylvania	D	R	R	D	R	R	R	R	R	R	R
Tyrrell	D	D	R	D	D	D	D	D	D	D	R
Union	D	R	R	D	D	R	R	R	R	R	R
Vance	D	A	R	D	D	R	D	D	D	D	D
Wake	D	R	R	R	R	R	R	D	R	R	R
Warren	D	A	R	D	D	D	D	D	D	D	D
Washington	D	D	R	D	D	D	D	D	D	D	D
Watauga	D	R	R	R	R	R	R	D	R	R	R
Wayne	D	A	R	R	R	R	R	R	R	R	R
Wilkes	R	R	R	R	R	R	R	R	R	R	R
Wilson	D	A	R	D	R	R	R	D	R	R	R
Yadkin	R	R	R	R	R	R	R	R	R	R	R
Yancey	D	R	R	D	D	R	R	D	R	R	R

North Dakota

County	1892	1896	1900	1904	1908	1912	1916	1920	1924	1928	1932	1936
Adams	–	–	–	–	R	P	D	R	P	R	D	D
Barnes	PO	R	R	R	R	D	D	R	R	R	D	D
Benson	R	R	R	R	R	P	R	R	P	R	D	D
Billings	R	R	R	R	R	R	R	R	R	R	D	D
Bottineau	PO	D	R	R	R	D	D	R	P	R	D	D
Bowman	–	–	–	–	R	P	D	R	P	R	D	D
Burke	–	–	–	–	–	S	D	R	P	R	D	D
Burleigh	R	R	R	R	R	R	D	R	R	R	D	D
Cass	R	R	R	R	R	D	D	R	R	R	D	D
Cavalier	PO	D	R	R	R	D	R	R	R	R	D	D
Dickey	PO	R	R	R	R	D	R	R	P	R	D	D
Divide	–	–	–	–	–	P	D	R	P	R	D	D
Dunn	–	–	–	–	R	P	D	R	P	D	D	D
Eddy	R	R	R	R	R	D	D	R	P	D	D	D

County	1892	1896	1900	1904	1908	1912	1916	1920	1924	1928	1932	1936
Emmons	R	R	R	R	R	D	R	R	P	D	D	D
Foster	R	R	R	R	R	D	D	R	R	D	D	D
Golden Valley	–	–	–	–	–	–	D	R	R	R	D	D
Grand Forks	R	R	R	R	R	D	D	R	R	R	D	D
Grant	–	–	–	–	–	–	–	R	P	R	D	D
Griggs	PO	D	R	R	R	D	D	R	P	R	D	D
Hettinger	–	–	–	–	R	R	R	R	P	R	D	D
Kidder	R	R	R	R	R	R	D	R	P	R	D	D
La Moure	PO	R	R	R	R	D	R	R	P	R	D	D
Logan	R	R	R	R	R	R	R	R	P	D	D	D
McHenry	R	R	R	R	R	D	D	R	P	R	D	D
McIntosh	R	R	R	R	R	P	R	R	P	D	D	D
McKenzie	–	–	–	–	R	D	D	R	P	D	D	D
McLean	R	R	R	R	R	D	D	R	P	D	D	D
Mercer	PO	R	R	R	R	P	R	R	P	D	D	D
Morton	R	R	R	R	R	P	R	R	P	D	D	D
Mountrail	–	–	–	–	–	R	D	R	P	R	D	D
Nelson	PO	R	R	R	R	D	R	R	R	R	D	D
Oliver	PO	R	R	R	R	P	R	R	P	R	D	D
Pembina	PO	D	R	R	R	D	R	R	R	R	D	D
Pierce	R	R	R	R	R	D	D	R	R	D	D	D
Ramsey	R	R	R	R	R	D	D	R	R	R	D	D
Ransom	R	R	R	R	R	P	D	R	P	R	D	D
Renville	–	–	–	–	–	D	D	R	P	R	D	D
Richland	PO	R	R	R	R	D	R	R	R	R	D	D
Rolette	R	D	R	R	R	D	D	R	P	D	D	D
Sargent	PO	D	R	R	R	D	R	R	P	D	D	D
Sheridan	–	–	–	–	–	P	R	R	P	R	D	D
Sioux	–	–	–	–	–	–	R	R	R	D	D	D
Slope	–	–	–	–	–	–	D	R	P	R	D	D
Stark	R	R	R	R	R	D	R	R	R	D	D	D
Steele	R	R	R	R	R	P	R	R	R	R	D	D
Stutsman	R	R	R	R	R	D	D	R	R	R	D	D
Towner	PO	D	R	R	R	D	D	R	R	R	D	D
Traill	R	R	R	R	R	P	R	R	R	R	D	D
Walsh	PO	D	R	R	R	D	D	R	R	D	D	D
Ward	R	R	R	R	R	D	D	R	R	R	D	D
Wells	R	R	R	R	R	P	R	R	P	R	D	D
Williams	PO	R	R	R	R	D	D	R	P	R	D	D

County	1940	1944	1948	1952	1956	1960	1964	1968	1972	1976	1980	1984
Adams	R	R	R	R	R	R	D	R	R	D	R	R
Barnes	R	R	R	R	R	R	D	R	R	R	R	R
Benson	D	D	D	R	R	R	D	D	R	D	R	R
Billings	R	R	R	R	R	D	D	R	R	R	R	R
Bottineau	R	R	R	R	R	R	D	R	R	R	R	R
Bowman	R	R	R	R	R	R	D	R	R	R	R	R
Burke	R	R	R	R	R	R	D	R	R	R	R	R
Burleigh	R	R	R	R	R	R	D	R	R	R	R	R

County	1940	1944	1948	1952	1956	1960	1964	1968	1972	1976	1980	1984
Cass	R	R	R	R	R	R	D	R	R	R	R	R
Cavalier	R	R	R	R	R	R	D	R	R	D	R	R
Dickey	R	R	R	R	R	R	D	R	R	D	R	R
Divide	D	D	R	R	R	R	D	R	R	R	R	R
Dunn	R	R	R	R	R	R	D	R	R	D	R	R
Eddy	D	D	R	R	R	R	D	R	R	D	R	R
Emmons	R	R	R	R	R	D	R	R	R	D	R	R
Foster	D	D	D	R	R	R	D	R	R	D	R	R
Golden Valley	R	R	R	R	R	R	R	R	R	R	R	R
Grand Forks	D	D	D	R	R	R	D	R	R	R	R	R
Grant	R	R	R	R	R	R	R	R	R	R	R	R
Griggs	D	D	D	R	R	D	D	R	R	D	R	R
Hettinger	R	R	R	R	R	R	D	R	R	R	R	R
Kidder	R	R	R	R	R	R	R	R	R	R	R	R
La Moure	R	R	R	R	R	R	D	R	R	R	R	R
Logan	R	R	R	R	R	R	R	R	R	R	R	R
McHenry	R	R	R	R	R	R	D	R	R	R	R	R
McIntosh	R	R	R	R	R	R	R	R	R	R	R	R
McKenzie	D	D	R	R	R	R	D	R	R	R	R	R
McLean	R	R	R	R	R	R	D	R	R	D	R	R
Mercer	R	R	R	R	R	R	R	R	R	R	R	R
Morton	R	R	R	R	R	D	D	R	R	D	R	R
Mountrail	D	D	D	R	D	D	D	D	R	D	R	R
Nelson	D	D	R	R	R	R	D	R	R	D	R	R
Oliver	R	R	R	R	R	R	D	R	R	R	R	R
Pembina	D	D	D	R	R	R	D	R	R	R	R	R
Pierce	R	R	R	R	R	D	D	R	R	D	R	R
Ramsey	R	R	R	R	R	R	D	R	R	R	R	R
Ransom	R	R	R	R	R	R	D	R	R	D	R	R
Renville	D	D	D	R	R	D	D	D	R	D	R	R
Richland	R	R	R	R	R	R	D	R	R	R	R	R
Rolette	D	D	D	R	D	D	D	D	D	D	D	D
Sargent	R	R	R	R	R	D	D	R	R	D	R	R
Sheridan	R	R	R	R	R	R	R	R	R	R	R	R
Sioux	R	R	R	R	R	D	D	D	R	D	R	D
Slope	R	R	R	R	R	R	D	R	R	R	R	R
Stark	R	R	R	R	R	D	D	R	R	R	R	R
Steele	D	D	D	R	R	R	D	D	R	D	R	R
Stutsman	R	R	R	R	R	R	D	R	R	R	R	R
Towner	R	R	R	R	R	R	D	R	R	D	R	R
Traill	R	R	R	R	R	R	D	R	R	R	R	R
Walsh	D	D	D	R	R	R	D	R	R	D	R	R
Ward	R	R	R	R	R	R	D	R	R	R	R	R
Wells	R	R	R	R	R	R	D	R	R	R	R	R
Williams	D	D	D	R	R	D	D	R	R	R	R	R

County	1988	1992	1996	2000	2004	County	1988	1992	1996	2000	2004
Adams	R	R	R	R	R	Benson	D	D	D	R	D
Barnes	R	R	R	R	R	Billings	R	R	R	R	R

County	1988	1992	1996	2000	2004	County	1988	1992	1996	2000	2004
Bottineau	R	R	R	R	R	Morton	R	R	R	R	R
Bowman	R	R	R	R	R	Mountrail	D	D	D	R	R
Burke	R	R	R	R	R	Nelson	D	R	D	R	R
Burleigh	R	R	R	R	R	Oliver	R	R	R	R	R
Cass	R	R	R	R	R	Pembina	R	R	R	R	R
Cavalier	R	R	R	R	R	Pierce	R	R	R	R	R
Dickey	R	R	R	R	R	Ramsey	R	R	D	R	R
Divide	D	D	D	R	R	Ransom	D	D	D	R	R
Dunn	R	R	R	R	R	Renville	R	R	R	R	R
Eddy	R	R	D	R	R	Richland	R	R	R	R	R
Emmons	R	R	R	R	R	Rolette	D	D	D	D	D
Foster	R	R	R	R	R	Sargent	D	D	D	R	R
Golden Valley	R	R	R	R	R	Sheridan	R	R	R	R	R
Grand Forks	R	R	R	R	R	Sioux	D	D	D	D	D
Grant	R	R	R	R	R	Slope	R	R	R	R	R
Griggs	R	R	R	R	R	Stark	R	R	R	R	R
Hettinger	R	R	R	R	R	Steele	D	D	D	R	D
Kidder	R	R	R	R	R	Stutsman	R	R	R	R	R
La Moure	R	R	R	R	R	Towner	D	D	D	R	R
Logan	R	R	R	R	R	Traill	R	R	D	R	R
McHenry	R	R	R	R	R	Walsh	R	R	R	R	R
McIntosh	R	R	R	R	R	Ward	R	R	R	R	R
McKenzie	R	R	R	R	R	Wells	R	R	R	R	R
McLean	R	R	R	R	R	Williams	R	R	R	R	R
Mercer	R	R	R	R	R						

Ohio

County	1868	1872	1876	1880	1884	1888	1892	1896	1900	1904	1908	1912
Adams	D	D	D	D	D	D	R	R	R	R	R	D
Allen	D	D	D	D	D	D	D	D	D	R	D	D
Ashland	D	D	D	D	D	D	D	D	D	D	D	D
Ashtabula	R	R	R	R	R	R	R	R	R	R	R	P
Athens	R	R	R	R	R	R	R	R	R	R	R	R
Auglaize	D	D	D	D	D	D	D	D	D	D	D	D
Belmont	R	R	D	R	R	R	R	R	R	R	R	D
Brown	D	D	D	D	D	D	D	D	D	D	D	D
Butler	D	D	D	D	D	D	D	D	D	D	D	D
Carroll	R	R	R	R	R	R	R	R	R	R	R	D
Champaign	R	R	R	R	R	R	R	R	R	R	R	D
Clark	R	R	R	R	R	R	R	R	R	R	R	R
Clermont	D	D	D	D	D	D	D	D	D	R	D	D
Clinton	R	R	R	R	R	R	R	R	R	R	R	R
Columbiana	R	R	R	R	R	R	R	R	R	R	R	D
Coshocton	D	D	D	D	D	D	D	D	D	R	D	D

County	1868	1872	1876	1880	1884	1888	1892	1896	1900	1904	1908	1912
Crawford	D	D	D	D	D	D	D	D	D	D	D	D
Cuyahoga	R	R	R	R	R	R	D	R	R	R	R	D
Darke	D	R	D	D	D	D	D	D	D	R	D	D
Defiance	D	D	D	D	D	D	D	D	D	D	D	D
Delaware	R	R	R	R	R	R	R	R	R	R	R	D
Erie	R	R	R	R	D	D	D	R	R	R	R	D
Fairfield	D	D	D	D	D	D	D	D	D	D	D	D
Fayette	R	R	R	R	R	R	R	R	R	R	R	D
Franklin	D	D	D	D	D	D	D	R	R	R	R	D
Fulton	R	R	R	R	R	R	R	R	R	R	R	P
Gallia	R	R	R	R	R	R	R	R	R	R	R	P
Geauga	R	R	R	R	R	R	R	R	R	R	R	P
Greene	R	R	R	R	R	R	R	R	R	R	R	R
Guernsey	R	R	R	R	R	R	R	R	R	R	R	R
Hamilton	R	D	D	R	R	R	R	R	R	R	R	D
Hancock	D	D	D	D	D	R	D	R	R	R	D	D
Hardin	R	R	R	R	R	R	R	R	R	R	R	D
Harrison	R	R	R	R	R	R	R	R	R	R	R	R
Henry	D	D	D	D	D	D	D	D	D	D	D	D
Highland	R	R	R	R	R	R	R	R	R	R	R	D
Hocking	D	D	D	D	D	D	D	D	R	R	D	D
Holmes	D	D	D	D	D	D	D	D	D	D	D	D
Huron	R	R	R	R	R	R	R	R	R	R	R	D
Jackson	R	R	R	R	R	R	R	R	R	R	R	D
Jefferson	R	R	R	R	R	R	R	R	R	R	R	R
Knox	R	R	D	D	R	R	D	D	R	R	R	D
Lake	R	R	R	R	R	R	R	R	R	R	R	P
Lawrence	R	R	R	R	R	R	R	R	R	R	R	R
Licking	D	D	D	D	D	D	D	D	D	R	D	D
Logan	R	R	R	R	R	R	R	R	R	R	R	D
Lorain	R	R	R	R	R	R	R	R	R	R	R	P
Lucas	R	R	R	R	R	R	R	R	R	R	R	D
Madison	R	R	R	R	R	R	R	R	R	R	R	R
Mahoning	R	R	R	R	R	R	D	R	R	R	R	D
Marion	D	D	D	D	D	D	D	D	D	R	D	D
Medina	R	R	R	R	R	R	R	R	R	R	R	P
Meigs	R	R	R	R	R	R	R	R	R	R	R	R
Mercer	D	D	D	D	D	D	D	D	D	D	D	D
Miami	R	R	R	R	R	R	R	R	R	R	R	D
Monroe	D	D	D	D	D	D	D	D	D	D	D	D
Montgomery	R	D	D	D	R	D	D	R	R	R	D	D
Morgan	R	R	R	R	R	R	R	R	R	R	R	D
Morrow	R	R	R	R	R	R	R	D	R	R	R	D
Muskingum	R	R	D	R	R	R	D	R	R	R	R	D
Noble	R	R	R	R	R	R	R	R	R	R	R	D
Ottawa	D	D	D	D	D	D	D	D	D	D	D	D
Paulding	R	R	R	R	R	R	D	D	R	R	R	D
Perry	D	D	D	D	R	R	D	D	R	R	R	D
Pickaway	D	D	D	D	D	D	D	D	D	D	D	D

County	1868	1872	1876	1880	1884	1888	1892	1896	1900	1904	1908	1912
Pike	D	D	D	D	D	D	D	R	R	D	D	D
Portage	R	R	R	R	R	R	R	R	R	R	R	D
Preble	R	R	R	R	R	R	R	R	R	R	R	D
Putnam	D	D	D	D	D	D	D	D	D	D	D	D
Richland	D	D	D	D	D	D	D	D	D	R	D	D
Ross	D	D	D	R	R	R	R	R	R	R	R	D
Sandusky	D	D	D	D	D	D	D	D	D	R	D	D
Scioto	R	R	R	R	R	R	R	R	R	R	R	R
Seneca	D	D	D	D	D	D	D	D	D	R	D	D
Shelby	D	D	D	D	D	D	D	D	D	D	D	D
Stark	R	R	D	R	R	D	D	R	R	R	R	D
Summit	R	R	R	R	R	R	D	R	R	R	R	D
Trumbull	R	R	R	R	R	R	R	R	R	R	R	P
Tuscarawas	D	D	D	D	D	D	D	D	D	R	D	D
Union	R	R	R	R	R	R	R	R	R	R	R	D
Van Wert	R	R	D	R	R	R	D	D	R	R	R	D
Vinton	D	D	D	D	D	D	D	R	R	R	R	D
Warren	R	R	R	R	R	R	R	R	R	R	R	R
Washington	R	R	D	R	R	R	R	R	R	R	D	D
Wayne	D	R	D	D	D	D	D	D	D	R	D	D
Williams	R	R	R	R	R	R	R	D	R	R	R	D
Wood	R	R	R	R	R	R	R	R	R	R	R	D
Wyandot	D	D	D	D	D	D	D	D	D	D	D	D

County	1916	1920	1924	1928	1932	1936	1940	1944	1948	1952	1956	1960
Adams	D	R	R	R	D	R	R	R	R	R	R	R
Allen	D	R	R	R	D	D	R	R	R	R	R	R
Ashland	D	R	R	R	D	D	R	R	R	R	R	R
Ashtabula	R	R	R	R	R	D	R	R	R	R	R	R
Athens	R	R	R	R	R	D	D	R	R	R	R	R
Auglaize	D	R	R	R	D	D	R	R	R	R	R	R
Belmont	D	R	R	R	D	D	D	D	D	D	R	D
Brown	D	D	D	R	D	D	D	R	D	R	R	R
Butler	D	D	R	R	D	D	D	D	D	R	R	R
Carroll	R	R	R	R	R	R	R	R	R	R	R	R
Champaign	R	R	R	R	D	R	R	R	R	R	R	R
Clark	D	R	R	R	D	D	D	D	R	R	R	R
Clermont	D	R	R	R	D	D	R	R	R	R	R	R
Clinton	R	R	R	R	R	R	R	R	R	R	R	R
Columbiana	R	R	R	R	D	D	D	R	R	R	R	R
Coshocton	D	R	R	R	D	D	R	R	R	R	R	R
Crawford	D	D	R	R	D	D	R	R	R	R	R	R
Cuyahoga	D	R	R	R	D	D	D	D	D	R	R	D
Darke	D	R	R	R	D	D	R	R	R	R	R	R
Defiance	D	R	R	R	D	D	R	R	R	R	R	R
Delaware	D	R	R	R	R	R	R	R	R	R	R	R
Erie	D	R	R	R	D	D	R	R	R	R	R	R
Fairfield	D	D	R	R	D	D	D	R	R	R	R	R
Fayette	R	R	R	R	D	D	R	R	R	R	R	R

County	1916	1920	1924	1928	1932	1936	1940	1944	1948	1952	1956	1960
Franklin	D	R	R	R	R	D	D	R	R	R	R	R
Fulton	R	R	R	R	D	R	R	R	R	R	R	R
Gallia	R	R	R	R	R	R	R	R	R	R	R	R
Geauga	R	R	R	R	R	R	R	R	R	R	R	R
Greene	R	R	R	R	R	D	R	R	R	R	R	R
Guernsey	D	R	R	R	D	D	R	R	R	R	R	R
Hamilton	R	R	R	R	D	D	R	R	R	R	R	R
Hancock	D	R	R	R	D	D	R	R	R	R	R	R
Hardin	D	R	R	R	D	D	R	R	R	R	R	R
Harrison	R	R	R	R	R	D	R	R	R	R	R	R
Henry	D	R	R	R	D	D	R	R	R	R	R	R
Highland	D	R	R	R	D	D	R	R	R	R	R	R
Hocking	D	R	R	R	D	D	D	R	D	R	R	R
Holmes	D	D	D	R	D	D	D	R	R	R	R	R
Huron	D	R	R	R	D	D	R	R	R	R	R	R
Jackson	R	R	R	R	R	R	R	R	R	R	R	R
Jefferson	R	R	R	R	D	D	D	D	D	D	R	D
Knox	D	R	R	R	R	D	R	R	R	R	R	R
Lake	R	R	R	R	R	D	R	R	R	R	R	D
Lawrence	R	R	R	R	R	D	D	R	D	R	R	R
Licking	D	R	R	R	D	D	D	R	R	R	R	R
Logan	R	R	R	R	R	R	R	R	R	R	R	R
Lorain	D	R	R	R	R	D	D	D	R	R	R	D
Lucas	D	R	R	R	D	D	D	R	D	R	R	D
Madison	R	R	R	R	D	D	R	R	R	R	R	R
Mahoning	D	R	R	R	R	D	D	D	D	D	R	D
Marion	D	R	R	R	D	D	R	R	R	R	R	R
Medina	D	R	R	R	R	D	R	R	R	R	R	R
Meigs	R	R	R	R	R	R	R	R	R	R	R	R
Mercer	D	R	D	D	D	D	R	R	D	R	R	R
Miami	R	R	R	R	R	D	R	R	R	R	R	R
Monroe	D	D	D	R	D	D	R	R	D	R	R	R
Montgomery	D	R	R	R	D	D	D	D	D	R	R	R
Morgan	R	R	R	R	R	R	R	R	R	R	R	R
Morrow	D	R	R	R	D	R	R	R	R	R	R	R
Muskingum	R	R	R	R	R	D	R	R	R	R	R	R
Noble	R	R	R	R	D	R	R	R	R	R	R	R
Ottawa	D	R	R	R	D	D	R	R	D	R	R	R
Paulding	R	R	R	R	D	D	R	R	R	R	R	R
Perry	R	R	R	R	R	D	R	R	R	R	R	R
Pickaway	D	D	D	R	D	D	D	R	D	R	R	R
Pike	D	R	D	R	D	D	D	D	D	D	D	D
Portage	D	R	R	R	D	D	D	D	D	R	R	R
Preble	D	R	R	R	D	D	R	R	R	R	R	R
Putnam	D	R	D	D	D	D	R	R	D	R	R	R
Richland	D	R	R	R	D	D	D	R	R	R	R	R
Ross	D	R	R	R	D	D	D	R	R	R	R	R
Sandusky	D	R	R	R	D	D	R	R	R	R	R	R
Scioto	R	R	R	R	R	D	D	R	D	R	R	R

County	1916	1920	1924	1928	1932	1936	1940	1944	1948	1952	1956	1960
Seneca	D	R	R	R	D	R	R	R	R	R	R	R
Shelby	D	D	D	R	D	D	R	R	D	R	R	R
Stark	D	R	R	R	R	D	D	D	R	R	R	R
Summit	D	R	R	R	D	D	D	D	D	D	R	D
Trumbull	R	R	R	R	R	D	D	D	D	D	R	D
Tuscarawas	D	R	R	R	D	D	D	D	D	R	R	R
Union	R	R	R	R	D	R	R	R	R	R	R	R
Van Wert	R	R	R	R	D	D	R	R	R	R	R	R
Vinton	D	R	R	R	R	R	R	R	R	R	R	R
Warren	R	R	R	R	R	R	R	R	R	R	R	R
Washington	D	R	R	R	D	R	R	R	R	R	R	R
Wayne	D	R	R	R	D	D	R	R	R	R	R	R
Williams	D	R	R	R	D	R	R	R	R	R	R	R
Wood	D	R	R	R	D	R	R	R	R	R	R	R
Wyandot	D	R	R	R	D	D	R	R	R	R	R	R

County	1964	1968	1972	1976	1980	1984	1988	1992	1996	2000	2004
Adams	D	R	R	D	R	R	R	R	R	R	R
Allen	R	R	R	R	R	R	R	R	R	R	R
Ashland	D	R	R	R	R	R	R	R	R	R	R
Ashtabula	D	R	R	D	R	R	D	D	D	D	D
Athens	D	R	D	D	D	R	D	D	D	D	D
Auglaize	D	R	R	R	R	R	R	R	R	R	R
Belmont	D	D	R	D	D	D	D	D	D	D	D
Brown	D	R	R	D	R	R	R	R	R	R	R
Butler	D	R	R	R	R	R	R	R	R	R	R
Carroll	D	R	R	R	R	R	R	D	D	R	R
Champaign	D	R	R	R	R	R	R	R	R	R	R
Clark	D	D	R	R	R	R	R	D	D	D	R
Clermont	D	R	R	R	R	R	R	R	R	R	R
Clinton	D	R	R	R	R	R	R	R	R	R	R
Columbiana	D	R	R	D	R	R	D	D	D	R	R
Coshocton	D	R	R	R	R	R	R	D	R	R	R
Crawford	D	R	R	R	R	R	R	R	R	R	R
Cuyahoga	D	D	R	D	D	D	D	D	D	D	D
Darke	D	R	R	R	R	R	R	R	R	R	R
Defiance	D	R	R	R	R	R	R	R	R	R	R
Delaware	R	R	R	R	R	R	R	R	R	R	R
Erie	D	R	R	R	R	R	R	D	D	D	D
Fairfield	D	R	R	R	R	R	R	R	R	R	R
Fayette	D	R	R	R	R	R	R	R	R	R	R
Franklin	D	R	R	R	R	R	R	R	D	D	D
Fulton	R	R	R	R	R	R	R	R	R	R	R
Gallia	D	R	R	R	R	R	R	R	D	R	R
Geauga	D	R	R	R	R	R	R	R	R	R	R
Greene	D	R	R	R	R	R	R	R	R	R	R
Guernsey	D	R	R	R	R	R	R	D	D	R	R
Hamilton	D	R	R	R	R	R	R	R	R	R	R
Hancock	R	R	R	R	R	R	R	R	R	R	R

County	1964	1968	1972	1976	1980	1984	1988	1992	1996	2000	2004
Hardin	D	R	R	R	R	R	R	R	R	R	R
Harrison	D	D	R	D	R	R	D	D	D	R	R
Henry	D	R	R	R	R	R	R	R	R	R	R
Highland	D	R	R	R	R	R	R	R	R	R	R
Hocking	D	R	R	D	R	R	R	D	D	R	R
Holmes	D	R	R	R	R	R	R	R	R	R	R
Huron	D	R	R	R	R	R	R	R	D	R	R
Jackson	D	R	R	D	R	R	R	R	D	R	R
Jefferson	D	D	R	D	D	D	D	D	D	D	D
Knox	D	R	R	R	R	R	R	R	R	R	R
Lake	D	R	R	D	R	R	R	R	D	R	R
Lawrence	D	R	R	D	R	R	R	D	D	R	R
Licking	D	R	R	R	R	R	R	R	R	R	R
Logan	D	R	R	R	R	R	R	R	R	R	R
Lorain	D	D	R	D	R	R	D	D	D	D	D
Lucas	D	D	D	D	R	R	D	D	D	D	D
Madison	D	R	R	R	R	R	R	R	R	R	R
Mahoning	D	D	R	D	D	D	D	D	D	D	D
Marion	D	R	R	R	R	R	R	R	R	R	R
Medina	D	R	R	R	R	R	R	R	R	R	R
Meigs	D	R	R	D	R	R	R	D	D	R	R
Mercer	D	D	R	R	R	R	R	R	R	R	R
Miami	D	R	R	R	R	R	R	R	R	R	R
Monroe	D	D	R	D	D	D	D	D	D	D	D
Montgomery	D	D	R	D	D	R	R	D	D	D	D
Morgan	D	R	R	R	R	R	R	R	R	R	R
Morrow	D	R	R	R	R	R	R	R	R	R	R
Muskingum	D	R	R	R	R	R	R	R	R	R	R
Noble	D	R	R	R	R	R	R	R	D	R	R
Ottawa	D	R	R	D	R	R	R	D	D	R	R
Paulding	D	R	R	R	R	R	R	R	R	R	R
Perry	D	R	R	D	R	R	R	D	D	R	R
Pickaway	D	R	R	R	R	R	R	R	R	R	R
Pike	D	D	R	D	D	R	R	D	D	R	R
Portage	D	D	R	D	R	R	R	D	D	D	D
Preble	D	R	R	R	R	R	R	R	R	R	R
Putnam	D	R	R	R	R	R	R	R	R	R	R
Richland	D	R	R	R	R	R	R	R	R	R	R
Ross	D	R	R	R	R	R	R	R	D	R	R
Sandusky	D	R	R	R	R	R	R	R	D	R	R
Scioto	D	R	R	D	R	R	R	D	D	R	R
Seneca	D	R	R	R	R	R	R	R	D	R	R
Shelby	D	R	R	R	R	R	R	R	R	R	R
Stark	D	R	R	R	R	R	R	D	D	R	D
Summit	D	D	R	D	D	R	D	D	D	D	D
Trumbull	D	D	R	D	D	D	D	D	D	D	D
Tuscarawas	D	D	R	D	R	R	R	D	D	R	R
Union	R	R	R	R	R	R	R	R	R	R	R
Van Wert	D	R	R	R	R	R	R	R	R	R	R

County	1964	1968	1972	1976	1980	1984	1988	1992	1996	2000	2004
Vinton	D	R	R	D	R	R	R	D	D	R	R
Warren	D	R	R	R	R	R	R	R	R	R	R
Washington	D	R	R	R	R	R	R	R	R	R	R
Wayne	D	R	R	R	R	R	R	R	R	R	R
Williams	D	R	R	R	R	R	R	R	R	R	R
Wood	D	R	R	R	R	R	R	D	D	R	R
Wyandot	D	R	R	R	R	R	R	R	R	R	R

Oklahoma

County	1908	1912	1916	1920	1924	1928	1932	1936	1940	1944	1948	1952
Adair	D	D	D	R	R	R	D	D	R	R	D	R
Alfalfa	R	R	D	R	R	R	D	D	R	R	R	R
Atoka	D	D	D	D	D	D	D	D	D	D	D	D
Beaver	R	R	D	R	R	R	D	D	R	R	D	R
Beckham	D	D	D	D	D	R	D	D	D	D	D	R
Blaine	R	R	R	R	R	R	D	D	R	R	R	R
Bryan	D	D	D	D	D	D	D	D	D	D	D	D
Caddo	D	D	D	R	R	R	D	D	D	D	D	R
Canadian	D	D	D	R	R	R	D	D	D	D	D	D
Carter	D	D	D	D	R	D	D	D	D	D	D	D
Cherokee	R	D	D	R	R	R	D	D	R	D	D	R
Choctaw	D	D	D	D	D	D	D	D	D	D	D	D
Cimarron	D	D	D	R	D	R	D	D	D	R	D	R
Cleveland	D	D	D	D	D	R	D	D	D	D	D	R
Coal	D	D	D	D	D	D	D	D	D	D	D	D
Comanche	D	D	D	R	D	R	D	D	D	D	D	D
Cotton	–	D	D	D	D	R	D	D	D	D	D	D
Craig	D	D	D	R	D	R	D	D	D	D	D	R
Creek	R	R	D	R	R	R	D	D	D	D	D	R
Custer	D	D	D	R	D	R	D	D	D	D	D	R
Delaware	D	D	D	R	D	R	D	D	D	R	D	R
Dewey	D	R	D	R	R	R	D	D	D	R	D	R
Ellis	D	R	R	R	R	R	D	D	R	R	R	R
Garfield	R	R	R	R	R	R	D	D	R	R	R	R
Garvin	D	D	D	D	D	D	D	D	D	D	D	D
Grady	R	D	D	D	D	R	D	D	D	D	D	D
Grant	D	R	D	R	R	R	D	D	R	R	R	R
Greer	D	D	D	D	D	R	D	D	D	D	D	D
Harmon	–	D	D	D	D	R	D	D	D	D	D	D
Harper	R	R	D	R	R	R	D	D	R	R	D	R
Haskell	D	D	D	R	D	R	D	D	D	D	D	D
Hughes	D	D	D	D	D	R	D	D	D	D	D	D
Jackson	D	D	D	D	D	R	D	D	D	D	D	D
Jefferson	D	D	D	D	D	R	D	D	D	D	D	D

County	1908	1912	1916	1920	1924	1928	1932	1936	1940	1944	1948	1952
Johnston	D	D	D	D	D	D	D	D	D	D	D	D
Kay	R	R	R	R	R	R	D	D	D	R	D	R
Kingfisher	R	R	R	R	R	R	D	D	R	R	R	R
Kiowa	D	D	D	R	D	R	D	D	D	D	D	R
Latimer	D	D	D	R	D	D	D	D	D	D	D	D
Le Flore	D	D	D	R	D	R	D	D	D	D	D	D
Lincoln	R	R	R	R	R	R	D	D	R	R	D	R
Logan	R	R	R	R	R	R	D	D	R	R	D	R
Love	D	D	D	D	D	D	D	D	D	D	D	D
McClain	D	D	D	D	D	R	D	D	D	D	D	D
McCurtain	D	D	D	D	D	D	D	D	D	D	D	D
McIntosh	R	D	D	D	D	R	D	D	D	D	D	D
Major	R	R	R	R	R	R	D	R	R	R	R	R
Marshall	D	D	D	D	D	D	D	D	D	D	D	D
Mayes	D	D	D	R	R	R	D	D	D	D	D	R
Murray	D	D	D	D	D	R	D	D	D	D	D	D
Muskogee	R	D	D	D	D	R	D	D	D	D	D	D
Noble	R	R	D	R	R	R	D	D	R	R	D	R
Nowata	R	R	D	R	R	R	D	D	D	R	D	R
Okfuskee	R	D	D	R	D	R	D	D	D	D	D	D
Oklahoma	R	D	D	D	D	R	D	D	D	D	D	R
Okmulgee	R	D	D	R	R	R	D	D	D	D	D	D
Osage	D	D	D	R	D	R	D	D	D	D	D	R
Ottawa	D	D	D	R	R	R	D	D	D	D	D	R
Pawnee	D	R	D	R	R	R	D	D	R	R	D	R
Payne	R	R	D	R	R	R	D	D	D	R	D	R
Pittsburg	D	D	D	R	D	D	D	D	D	D	D	D
Pontotoc	D	D	D	D	D	R	D	D	D	D	D	D
Pottawatomie	D	D	D	R	D	R	D	D	D	D	D	R
Pushmataha	D	D	D	R	D	R	D	D	D	D	D	D
Roger Mills	D	D	D	R	D	R	D	D	D	D	D	R
Rogers	D	D	D	R	D	R	D	D	R	R	D	R
Seminole	R	D	D	R	D	R	D	D	D	D	D	D
Sequoyah	R	D	D	R	D	R	D	D	D	D	D	D
Stephens	D	D	D	D	D	R	D	D	D	D	D	D
Texas	D	D	D	R	D	R	D	D	D	D	D	R
Tillman	D	D	D	D	D	R	D	D	D	D	D	D
Tulsa	D	D	D	R	R	R	D	D	R	R	R	R
Wagoner	R	D	D	R	D	R	D	D	R	R	D	R
Washington	R	D	D	R	R	R	D	D	R	R	R	R
Washita	D	D	D	D	D	R	D	D	D	D	D	R
Woods	R	R	D	R	R	R	D	D	D	R	D	R
Woodward	R	R	D	R	R	R	D	D	R	R	R	R

County	1956	1960	1964	1968	1972	1976	1980	1984	1988	1992	1996	2000
Adair	R	R	D	R	R	R	R	R	R	R	R	R
Alfalfa	R	R	R	R	R	R	R	R	R	R	R	R
Atoka	D	R	D	A	R	D	D	R	D	D	D	R
Beaver	R	R	R	R	R	R	R	R	R	R	R	R

County	1956	1960	1964	1968	1972	1976	1980	1984	1988	1992	1996	2000
Beckham	D	R	D	R	R	D	R	R	R	D	R	R
Blaine	R	R	R	R	R	R	R	R	R	R	R	R
Bryan	D	D	D	D	R	D	D	R	D	D	D	R
Caddo	D	R	D	R	R	D	R	R	D	D	D	R
Canadian	R	R	D	R	R	R	R	R	R	R	R	R
Carter	D	D	D	D	R	D	R	R	R	D	D	R
Cherokee	R	R	D	R	R	D	R	R	D	D	D	D
Choctaw	D	D	D	D	R	D	D	R	D	D	D	D
Cimarron	R	R	R	R	R	D	R	R	R	R	R	R
Cleveland	R	R	D	R	R	R	R	R	R	R	R	R
Coal	D	D	D	D	R	D	D	D	D	D	D	D
Comanche	D	R	D	R	R	R	R	R	R	R	R	R
Cotton	D	D	D	D	R	D	R	R	D	D	D	R
Craig	R	R	D	R	R	D	R	R	D	D	D	R
Creek	R	R	D	R	R	D	R	R	R	R	R	R
Custer	R	R	D	R	R	R	R	R	R	R	R	R
Delaware	R	R	D	R	R	D	R	R	R	D	R	R
Dewey	R	R	D	R	R	D	R	R	R	R	R	R
Ellis	R	R	R	R	R	R	R	R	R	R	R	R
Garfield	R	R	R	R	R	R	R	R	R	R	R	R
Garvin	D	R	D	D	R	D	R	R	D	D	D	R
Grady	D	R	D	D	R	D	R	R	R	R	R	R
Grant	R	R	D	R	R	D	R	R	R	R	R	R
Greer	D	R	D	D	R	D	R	R	D	D	D	R
Harmon	D	D	D	D	R	D	D	R	D	D	D	R
Harper	R	R	R	R	R	R	R	R	R	R	R	R
Haskell	D	R	D	D	R	D	D	D	D	D	D	D
Hughes	D	R	D	D	R	D	D	D	D	D	D	D
Jackson	D	D	D	D	R	D	R	R	R	R	R	R
Jefferson	D	D	D	D	R	D	D	R	D	D	D	R
Johnston	D	D	D	D	R	D	D	R	D	D	D	R
Kay	R	R	R	R	R	R	R	R	R	R	R	R
Kingfisher	R	R	R	R	R	R	R	R	R	R	R	R
Kiowa	D	R	D	R	R	D	R	R	D	D	D	R
Latimer	D	D	D	D	R	D	D	R	D	D	D	D
Le Flore	D	R	D	D	R	D	R	R	R	D	D	R
Lincoln	R	R	D	R	R	D	R	R	R	R	R	R
Logan	R	R	D	R	R	D	R	R	R	R	R	R
Love	D	D	D	D	R	D	D	R	D	D	D	R
McClain	D	R	D	R	R	D	R	R	R	R	R	R
McCurtain	D	D	D	D	R	D	D	R	D	D	D	R
McIntosh	D	R	D	D	R	D	D	R	D	D	D	D
Major	R	R	R	R	R	R	R	R	R	R	R	R
Marshall	D	D	D	R	R	D	D	R	D	D	D	R
Mayes	R	R	D	R	R	D	R	R	D	D	D	R
Murray	D	D	D	D	R	D	R	R	D	D	D	R
Muskogee	R	R	D	D	R	D	D	R	D	D	D	D
Noble	R	R	D	R	R	R	R	R	R	R	R	R
Nowata	R	R	D	R	R	D	R	R	D	D	D	R

County	1956	1960	1964	1968	1972	1976	1980	1984	1988	1992	1996	2000
Okfuskee	D	R	D	D	R	D	D	R	D	D	D	R
Oklahoma	R	R	D	R	R	R	R	R	R	R	R	R
Okmulgee	D	D	D	D	R	D	D	R	D	D	D	D
Osage	R	R	D	R	R	D	R	R	D	D	D	R
Ottawa	R	R	D	R	R	D	R	R	D	D	D	D
Pawnee	R	R	D	R	R	R	R	R	R	R	D	R
Payne	R	R	D	R	R	R	R	R	R	R	R	R
Pittsburg	D	D	D	D	R	D	D	R	D	D	D	R
Pontotoc	D	R	D	D	R	D	R	R	R	D	D	R
Pottawatomie	D	R	D	R	R	D	R	R	R	R	R	R
Pushmataha	D	R	D	A	R	D	D	R	D	D	D	R
Roger Mills	D	R	D	R	R	D	R	R	R	R	R	R
Rogers	R	R	D	R	R	D	R	R	R	R	R	R
Seminole	D	R	D	D	R	D	R	R	D	D	D	R
Sequoyah	D	R	D	R	R	D	R	R	R	D	D	R
Stephens	D	R	D	R	R	D	R	R	R	D	R	R
Texas	R	R	R	R	R	R	R	R	R	R	R	R
Tillman	D	D	D	D	R	D	R	R	D	D	D	R
Tulsa	R	R	R	R	R	R	R	R	R	R	R	R
Wagoner	R	R	D	R	R	D	R	R	R	R	R	R
Washington	R	R	R	R	R	R	R	R	R	R	R	R
Washita	D	R	D	R	R	D	R	R	R	D	R	R
Woods	R	R	R	R	R	R	R	R	R	R	R	R
Woodward	R	R	R	R	R	R	R	R	R	R	R	R

County	2004		County	2004		County	2004
Adair	R		Garfield	R		Major	R
Alfalfa	R		Garvin	R		Marshall	R
Atoka	R		Grady	R		Mayes	R
Beaver	R		Grant	R		Murray	R
Beckham	R		Greer	R		Muskogee	R
Blaine	R		Harmon	R		Noble	R
Bryan	R		Harper	R		Nowata	R
Caddo	R		Haskell	R		Okfuskee	R
Canadian	R		Hughes	R		Oklahoma	R
Carter	R		Jackson	R		Okmulgee	R
Cherokee	R		Jefferson	R		Osage	R
Choctaw	R		Johnston	R		Ottawa	R
Cimarron	R		Kay	R		Pawnee	R
Cleveland	R		Kingfisher	R		Payne	R
Coal	R		Kiowa	R		Pittsburg	R
Comanche	R		Latimer	R		Pontotoc	R
Cotton	R		Le Flore	R		Pottawatomie	R
Craig	R		Lincoln	R		Pushmataha	R
Creek	R		Logan	R		Roger Mills	R
Custer	R		Love	R		Rogers	R
Delaware	R		McClain	R		Seminole	R
Dewey	R		McCurtain	R		Sequoyah	R
Ellis	R		McIntosh	R		Stephen	R

County	2004		County	2004		County	2004
Texas	R		Wagoner	R		Woods	R
Tillman	R		Washington	R		Woodward	R
Tulsa	R		Washita	R			

Oregon

County	1868	1872	1876	1880	1884	1888	1892	1896	1900	1904	1908	1912
Baker	D	D	D	D	D	R	R	D	D	R	R	D
Benton	D	R	R	R	R	R	R	R	R	R	R	D
Clackamas	R	R	R	R	R	R	R	R	R	R	R	D
Clatsop	R	R	R	R	R	R	R	R	R	R	R	P
Columbia	D	R	D	R	R	R	R	R	R	R	R	P
Coos	R	R	R	R	R	R	PO	D	R	R	R	D
Crook	–	–	–	–	D	D	D	R	R	R	R	D
Curry	R	R	R	R	R	R	R	D	R	R	R	D
Deschutes	–	–	–	–	–	–	–	–	–	–	–	–
Douglas	R	R	R	R	R	R	R	D	R	R	R	D
Gilliam	–	–	–	–	–	R	R	R	R	R	R	R
Grant	D	R	R	R	D	R	R	D	R	R	R	R
Harney	–	–	–	–	–	–	D	D	D	R	R	D
Hood River	–	–	–	–	–	–	–	–	–	–	R	D
Jackson	D	D	D	D	D	D	PO	D	R	R	R	D
Jefferson	–	–	–	–	–	–	–	–	–	–	–	–
Josephine	D	R	D	D	D	R	PO	D	R	R	R	P
Klamath	–	–	–	–	D	D	PO	D	R	R	R	D
Lake	–	–	D	D	D	D	PO	D	R	R	R	D
Lane	D	R	R	D	R	R	R	D	R	R	R	D
Lincoln	–	–	–	–	–	–	–	R	R	R	R	R
Linn	D	R	D	D	D	D	PO	D	D	R	R	D
Malheur	–	–	–	–	–	–	–	D	D	R	R	D
Marion	R	R	R	R	R	R	R	R	R	R	R	D
Morrow	–	–	–	–	–	R	R	R	R	R	R	R
Multnomah	R	R	R	R	R	R	R	R	R	R	R	D
Polk	R	R	R	R	R	R	R	D	R	R	R	D
Sherman	–	–	–	–	–	–	R	R	R	R	R	R
Tillamook	R	R	R	R	R	R	R	R	R	R	R	R
Umatilla	D	D	D	D	D	D	PO	D	R	R	R	D
Union	D	R	D	D	D	R	PO	D	D	R	R	D
Wallowa	–	–	–	–	–	R	PO	D	R	R	R	D
Wasco	D	R	D	D	R	R	R	R	R	R	R	D
Washington	R	R	R	R	R	R	R	R	R	R	R	P
Wheeler	–	–	–	–	–	–	–	R	R	R	R	R
Yamhill	R	R	R	R	R	R	R	R	R	R	R	D

County	1916	1920	1924	1928	1932	1936	1940	1944	1948	1952	1956	1960
Baker	D	R	R	R	D	D	D	D	D	R	R	D
Benton	R	R	R	R	R	D	R	R	R	R	R	R
Clackamas	R	R	R	R	D	D	D	D	R	R	R	R
Clatsop	R	R	R	R	D	D	D	D	D	R	R	D
Columbia	R	R	R	R	D	D	D	D	D	D	D	D
Coos	D	R	R	R	D	D	D	D	R	R	D	D
Crook	D	R	R	R	D	D	D	D	D	R	R	D
Curry	R	R	R	R	D	D	D	R	R	R	R	D
Deschutes	–	R	R	R	D	D	D	D	D	R	R	R
Douglas	R	R	R	R	D	D	R	R	R	R	R	D
Gilliam	D	R	R	R	D	D	D	D	R	R	R	R
Grant	D	R	R	R	D	D	D	D	D	R	R	R
Harney	D	R	R	R	D	D	D	D	D	R	R	R
Hood River	R	R	R	R	D	D	D	R	R	R	R	R
Jackson	D	R	R	R	D	D	R	R	R	R	R	R
Jefferson	D	R	R	R	D	D	D	R	R	R	R	R
Josephine	R	R	R	R	D	D	R	R	R	R	R	R
Klamath	D	R	R	R	D	D	D	D	D	R	R	R
Lake	D	R	R	R	D	D	D	D	D	R	R	R
Lane	R	R	R	R	D	D	D	R	R	R	R	R
Lincoln	R	R	R	R	D	D	D	D	D	R	R	D
Linn	D	R	R	R	D	D	R	R	R	R	R	R
Malheur	D	R	R	R	D	D	D	R	R	R	R	R
Marion	R	R	R	R	D	D	R	R	R	R	R	R
Morrow	D	R	R	R	D	D	D	D	D	R	R	D
Multnomah	R	R	R	R	D	D	D	D	D	R	R	R
Polk	R	R	R	R	D	D	R	R	R	R	R	R
Sherman	D	R	R	R	D	D	D	D	R	R	R	R
Tillamook	R	R	R	R	D	D	D	D	D	R	R	D
Umatilla	D	R	R	R	D	D	R	R	D	R	R	R
Union	D	R	R	R	D	D	D	D	D	R	D	D
Wallowa	D	R	R	R	D	D	D	D	D	R	D	D
Wasco	D	R	R	R	D	D	D	R	R	R	R	D
Washington	R	R	R	R	D	D	D	R	R	R	R	R
Wheeler	R	R	R	R	D	D	R	R	R	R	R	R
Yamhill	R	R	R	R	D	D	D	R	R	R	R	R

County	1964	1968	1972	1976	1980	1984	1988	1992	1996	2000	2004
Baker	D	R	R	R	R	R	R	R	R	R	R
Benton	D	R	R	R	R	R	D	D	D	D	D
Clackamas	D	R	R	R	R	R	D	D	R	R	
Clatsop	D	D	D	D	D	D	D	D	D	D	D
Columbia	D	D	D	D	D	D	D	D	D	D	D
Coos	D	D	D	D	R	R	D	D	D	R	R
Crook	D	R	R	D	R	R	R	R	R	R	R
Curry	D	R	R	D	R	R	R	D	R	R	R
Deschutes	D	R	R	D	R	R	R	D	R	R	R
Douglas	D	R	R	R	R	R	R	R	R	R	R
Gilliam	D	R	R	R	R	R	R	R	D	R	R

County	1964	1968	1972	1976	1980	1984	1988	1992	1996	2000	2004
Grant	D	R	R	R	R	R	R	R	R	R	R
Harney	D	R	R	R	R	R	R	R	R	R	R
Hood River	D	R	R	R	R	R	D	D	D	D	D
Jackson	D	R	R	R	R	R	R	D	R	R	R
Jefferson	D	R	R	R	R	R	R	D	R	R	R
Josephine	R	R	R	R	R	R	R	R	R	R	R
Klamath	D	R	R	R	R	R	R	R	R	R	R
Lake	D	R	R	R	R	R	R	R	R	R	R
Lane	D	R	R	D	R	D	D	D	D	D	D
Lincoln	D	R	R	D	R	R	D	D	D	D	D
Linn	D	R	R	D	R	R	R	R	R	R	R
Malheur	R	R	R	R	R	R	R	R	R	R	R
Marion	D	R	R	R	R	R	R	R	D	R	R
Morrow	D	R	R	D	R	R	R	R	D	R	R
Multnomah	D	D	D	D	D	D	D	D	D	D	D
Polk	D	R	R	R	R	R	R	R	R	R	R
Sherman	D	R	R	R	R	R	R	R	R	R	R
Tillamook	D	D	R	D	D	R	D	D	D	R	R
Umatilla	D	R	R	R	R	R	R	R	R	R	R
Union	D	R	R	R	R	R	R	R	R	R	R
Wallowa	D	R	R	R	R	R	R	R	R	R	R
Wasco	D	D	R	D	R	R	D	D	D	R	R
Washington	D	R	R	R	R	R	R	D	D	D	D
Wheeler	D	R	R	D	R	R	R	R	R	R	R
Yamhill	D	R	R	R	R	R	R	R	R	R	R

Pennsylvania

County	1868	1872	1876	1880	1884	1888	1892	1896	1900	1904	1908	1912
Adams	D	R	D	D	D	D	D	R	D	R	D	D
Allegheny	R	R	R	R	R	R	R	R	R	R	R	P
Armstrong	R	R	R	R	R	R	R	R	R	R	R	P
Beaver	R	R	R	R	R	R	R	R	R	R	R	P
Bedford	D	R	D	D	R	R	R	R	R	R	R	P
Berks	D	D	D	D	D	D	D	D	D	D	D	D
Blair	R	R	R	R	R	R	R	R	R	R	R	P
Bradford	R	R	R	R	R	R	R	R	R	R	R	P
Bucks	D	R	D	D	D	D	D	R	R	R	R	D
Butler	R	R	R	R	R	R	R	R	R	R	R	P
Cambria	D	R	D	D	D	D	D	R	R	R	R	P
Cameron	R	R	R	R	R	R	R	R	R	R	R	P
Carbon	D	R	D	D	D	D	D	R	R	R	R	D
Centre	D	R	D	D	D	D	D	R	R	R	R	D
Chester	R	R	R	R	R	R	R	R	R	R	R	D
Clarion	D	R	D	D	D	D	D	D	D	R	D	D

County	1868	1872	1876	1880	1884	1888	1892	1896	1900	1904	1908	1912
Clearfield	D	D	D	D	D	D	D	R	R	R	R	P
Clinton	D	R	D	D	D	D	D	R	R	R	R	D
Columbia	D	D	D	D	D	D	D	D	D	D	D	D
Crawford	R	R	R	R	R	R	R	D	R	R	R	P
Cumberland	D	R	D	D	D	D	D	R	R	R	R	D
Dauphin	R	R	R	R	R	R	R	R	R	R	R	P
Delaware	R	R	R	R	R	R	R	R	R	R	R	R
Elk	D	D	D	D	D	D	D	R	R	R	R	P
Erie	R	R	R	R	R	R	R	R	R	R	R	D
Fayette	D	R	D	D	D	R	D	R	R	R	R	D
Forest	R	R	R	R	R	R	R	R	R	R	R	P
Franklin	R	R	R	R	R	R	R	R	R	R	R	D
Fulton	D	D	D	D	D	D	D	D	D	D	D	D
Greene	D	D	D	D	D	D	D	D	D	D	D	D
Huntingdon	R	R	R	R	R	R	R	R	R	R	R	P
Indiana	R	R	R	R	R	R	R	R	R	R	R	P
Jefferson	R	R	D	R	R	R	R	R	R	R	R	P
Juniata	D	R	D	D	D	D	D	R	R	R	R	P
Lackawanna	–	–	–	R	R	R	R	R	R	R	R	P
Lancaster	R	R	R	R	R	R	R	R	R	R	R	P
Lawrence	R	R	R	R	R	R	R	R	R	R	R	P
Lebanon	R	R	R	R	R	R	R	R	R	R	R	P
Lehigh	D	D	D	D	D	D	D	R	D	R	R	D
Luzerne	D	R	R	D	D	R	D	R	R	R	R	P
Lycoming	D	R	D	D	D	D	D	R	R	R	R	D
McKean	R	R	R	R	R	R	R	R	R	R	R	P
Mercer	R	R	R	R	R	R	R	R	R	R	R	P
Mifflin	R	R	D	R	D	R	R	R	R	R	R	P
Monroe	D	D	D	D	D	D	D	D	D	D	D	D
Montgomery	D	R	D	R	R	R	D	R	R	R	R	D
Montour	D	R	D	D	D	D	D	D	D	R	D	D
Northampton	D	D	D	D	D	D	D	D	D	R	D	D
Northumber-land	D	R	D	D	D	R	D	R	R	R	R	P
Perry	R	R	D	R	R	R	R	R	R	R	R	D
Philadelphia	R	R	R	R	R	R	R	R	R	R	R	R
Pike	D	D	D	D	D	D	D	D	D	D	D	D
Potter	R	R	R	R	R	R	R	R	R	R	R	P
Schuylkill	D	R	D	D	R	D	D	R	R	R	R	P
Snyder	R	R	R	R	R	R	R	R	R	R	R	P
Somerset	R	R	R	R	R	R	R	R	R	R	R	D
Sullivan	D	D	D	D	D	D	D	D	R	R	R	D
Susquehanna	R	R	R	R	R	R	R	R	R	R	R	D
Tioga	R	R	R	R	R	R	R	R	R	R	R	P
Union	R	R	R	R	R	R	R	R	R	R	R	P
Venango	R	R	R	R	R	R	R	R	R	R	R	P
Warren	R	R	R	R	R	R	R	R	R	R	R	P
Washington	R	R	R	R	R	R	R	R	R	R	R	P
Wayne	D	R	D	D	D	D	D	R	R	R	R	P

County	1868	1872	1876	1880	1884	1888	1892	1896	1900	1904	1908	1912
Westmoreland	D	R	D	D	D	R	R	R	R	R	R	P
Wyoming	D	R	D	D	D	R	R	R	R	R	R	D
York	D	D	D	D	D	D	D	D	D	R	D	D

County	1916	1920	1924	1928	1932	1936	1940	1944	1948	1952	1956	1960
Adams	D	R	R	R	D	D	R	R	R	R	R	R
Allegheny	R	R	R	R	D	D	D	D	D	D	R	D
Armstrong	R	R	R	R	R	D	R	R	R	R	R	R
Beaver	R	R	R	R	D	D	D	D	D	D	R	D
Bedford	R	R	R	R	R	R	R	R	R	R	R	R
Berks	D	R	R	R	D	D	D	D	D	R	R	R
Blair	R	R	R	R	R	D	R	R	R	R	R	R
Bradford	R	R	R	R	R	R	R	R	R	R	R	R
Bucks	R	R	R	R	R	D	R	R	R	R	R	R
Butler	R	R	R	R	R	R	R	R	R	R	R	R
Cambria	R	R	R	R	D	D	D	D	D	D	R	D
Cameron	R	R	R	R	R	R	R	R	R	R	R	R
Carbon	R	R	R	R	R	D	D	D	R	R	R	R
Centre	R	R	R	R	R	D	R	R	R	R	R	R
Chester	R	R	R	R	R	R	R	R	R	R	R	R
Clarion	D	R	R	R	D	R	R	R	R	R	R	R
Clearfield	D	R	R	R	D	D	D	R	R	R	R	R
Clinton	D	R	R	R	R	D	D	R	R	R	R	R
Columbia	D	D	D	R	D	D	D	D	R	R	R	R
Crawford	D	R	R	R	R	R	R	R	R	R	R	R
Cumberland	D	R	R	R	R	D	D	R	R	R	R	R
Dauphin	R	R	R	R	R	D	R	R	R	R	R	R
Delaware	R	R	R	R	R	R	R	R	R	R	R	R
Elk	R	R	R	D	D	D	R	D	D	R	R	D
Erie	D	R	R	R	D	D	R	R	R	R	R	D
Fayette	D	R	R	R	D	D	D	D	D	D	D	D
Forest	R	R	R	R	R	R	R	R	R	R	R	R
Franklin	R	R	R	R	R	D	R	R	R	R	R	R
Fulton	D	R	D	R	D	D	R	R	R	R	R	R
Greene	D	D	D	R	D	D	D	D	D	D	D	D
Huntingdon	R	R	R	R	R	R	R	R	R	R	R	R
Indiana	R	R	R	R	R	R	R	R	R	R	R	R
Jefferson	R	R	R	R	R	R	R	R	R	R	R	R
Juniata	R	R	R	R	D	D	D	R	R	R	R	R
Lackawanna	R	R	R	D	D	D	D	D	D	D	R	D
Lancaster	R	R	R	R	R	R	R	R	R	R	R	R
Lawrence	R	R	R	R	R	D	R	R	R	R	R	D
Lebanon	R	R	R	R	R	D	R	R	R	R	R	R
Lehigh	D	R	R	R	D	D	D	R	R	R	R	R
Luzerne	R	R	R	D	D	D	D	D	R	R	R	D
Lycoming	D	R	R	R	R	D	R	R	R	R	R	R
McKean	R	R	R	R	R	R	R	R	R	R	R	R
Mercer	D	R	R	R	R	D	R	R	R	R	R	R
Mifflin	R	R	R	R	R	D	D	R	R	R	R	R

County	1916	1920	1924	1928	1932	1936	1940	1944	1948	1952	1956	1960
Monroe	D	D	D	R	D	D	D	R	R	R	R	R
Montgomery	R	R	R	R	R	R	R	R	R	R	R	R
Montour	D	R	R	R	D	D	D	R	R	R	R	R
Northampton	D	R	R	R	D	D	D	D	D	R	R	D
Northumber-land	D	R	R	R	D	D	D	R	R	R	R	R
Perry	R	R	R	R	R	D	R	R	R	R	R	R
Philadelphia	R	R	R	R	R	D	D	D	D	D	D	D
Pike	D	R	R	R	D	D	R	R	R	R	R	R
Potter	R	R	R	R	R	R	R	R	R	R	R	R
Schuylkill	R	R	R	R	D	D	D	R	R	R	R	D
Snyder	R	R	R	R	R	R	R	R	R	R	R	R
Somerset	R	R	R	R	R	R	R	R	R	R	R	R
Sullivan	D	R	R	R	D	R	R	R	R	R	R	R
Susquehanna	R	R	R	R	R	R	R	R	R	R	R	R
Tioga	R	R	R	R	R	R	R	R	R	R	R	R
Union	R	R	R	R	R	R	R	R	R	R	R	R
Venango	D	R	R	R	R	R	R	R	R	R	R	R
Warren	R	R	R	R	R	R	R	R	R	R	R	R
Washington	R	R	R	R	D	D	D	D	D	D	D	D
Wayne	R	R	R	R	R	R	R	R	R	R	R	R
Westmoreland	R	R	R	R	D	D	D	D	D	D	D	D
Wyoming	R	R	R	R	R	R	R	R	R	R	R	R
York	D	R	R	R	D	D	D	D	D	R	R	R

County	1964	1968	1972	1976	1980	1984	1988	1992	1996	2000	2004
Adams	D	R	R	R	R	R	R	R	R	R	R
Allegheny	D	D	R	D	D	D	D	D	D	D	D
Armstrong	D	R	R	D	R	D	D	D	D	R	R
Beaver	D	D	R	D	D	D	D	D	D	D	D
Bedford	D	R	R	R	R	R	R	R	R	R	R
Berks	R	D	R	R	R	R	R	R	R	R	R
Blair	R	D	R	R	R	R	R	R	R	R	R
Bradford	D	R	R	R	R	R	R	R	R	R	R
Bucks	D	R	R	R	R	R	R	D	D	D	D
Butler	D	R	R	R	R	R	R	R	R	R	R
Cambria	D	D	R	D	D	D	D	D	D	D	R
Cameron	D	R	R	R	R	R	R	R	R	R	R
Carbon	D	D	R	D	R	R	R	D	D	D	R
Centre	D	R	R	R	R	R	R	D	D	R	R
Chester	D	R	R	R	R	R	R	R	R	R	R
Clarion	D	R	R	R	R	R	R	R	R	R	R
Clearfield	D	R	R	D	R	R	R	D	R	R	R
Clinton	D	R	R	D	R	R	D	D	D	R	R
Columbia	D	R	R	D	R	R	R	R	D	R	R
Crawford	D	R	R	R	R	R	R	R	R	R	R
Cumberland	D	R	R	R	R	R	R	R	R	R	R
Dauphin	D	R	R	R	R	R	R	R	R	R	R
Delaware	D	R	R	R	R	R	R	D	D	D	D

County	1964	1968	1972	1976	1980	1984	1988	1992	1996	2000	2004
Elk	D	D	R	D	R	R	R	D	D	R	R
Erie	D	D	R	D	R	R	D	D	D	D	D
Fayette	D	D	R	D	D	D	D	D	D	D	D
Forest	D	R	R	R	R	R	R	D	D	R	R
Franklin	D	R	R	R	R	R	R	R	R	R	R
Fulton	D	R	R	R	R	R	R	R	R	R	R
Greene	D	D	R	D	D	D	D	D	D	D	R
Huntingdon	D	R	R	R	R	R	R	R	R	R	R
Indiana	D	R	R	R	R	R	D	D	D	R	R
Jefferson	D	R	R	R	R	R	R	R	R	R	R
Juniata	D	R	R	R	R	R	R	R	R	R	R
Lackawanna	D	D	R	D	D	R	D	D	D	D	D
Lancaster	D	R	R	R	R	R	R	R	R	R	R
Lawrence	D	D	R	D	D	D	D	D	D	D	R
Lebanon	R	R	R	R	R	R	R	R	R	R	R
Lehigh	D	R	R	R	R	R	R	D	D	D	D
Luzerne	D	D	R	D	R	R	R	D	D	D	D
Lycoming	D	R	R	R	R	R	R	R	R	R	R
McKean	D	R	R	R	R	R	R	R	R	R	R
Mercer	D	R	R	D	R	D	D	D	D	D	R
Mifflin	D	R	R	R	R	R	R	R	R	R	R
Monroe	D	R	R	R	R	R	R	R	R	R	R
Montgomery	D	R	R	R	R	R	R	D	D	D	D
Montour	D	R	R	R	R	R	R	R	R	R	R
Northampton	D	D	R	D	R	R	R	D	D	D	D
Northumber-land	D	R	R	R	R	R	R	R	R	R	R
Perry	D	R	R	R	R	R	R	R	R	R	R
Philadelphia	D	D	D	D	D	D	D	D	D	D	D
Pike	D	R	R	R	R	R	R	R	R	R	R
Potter	D	R	R	R	R	R	R	R	R	R	R
Schuylkill	D	R	R	D	R	R	R	R	D	R	R
Snyder	R	R	R	R	R	R	R	R	R	R	R
Somerset	D	R	R	R	R	R	R	R	R	R	R
Sullivan	D	R	R	R	R	R	R	R	R	R	R
Susquehanna	D	R	R	R	R	R	R	R	R	R	R
Tioga	D	R	R	R	R	R	R	R	R	R	R
Union	R	R	R	R	R	R	R	R	R	R	R
Venango	D	R	R	R	R	R	R	R	R	R	R
Warren	D	R	R	R	R	R	R	D	D	R	R
Washington	D	D	R	D	D	D	D	D	D	D	D
Wayne	R	R	R	R	R	R	R	R	R	R	R
Westmoreland	D	D	R	D	D	D	D	D	D	R	R
Wyoming	D	R	R	R	R	R	R	R	R	R	R
York	D	R	R	R	R	R	R	R	R	R	R

Rhode Island

County	1868	1872	1876	1880	1884	1888	1892	1896	1900	1904	1908	1912
Bristol	R	R	R	R	R	R	R	R	R	R	R	R
Kent	R	R	R	R	R	R	R	R	R	R	R	R
Newport	R	R	R	R	R	R	R	R	R	R	R	R
Providence	R	R	R	R	R	R	R	R	R	R	R	D
Washington	R	R	R	R	R	R	R	R	R	R	R	R

County	1916	1920	1924	1928	1932	1936	1940	1944	1948	1952	1956	1960
Bristol	R	R	R	D	D	D	D	D	D	R	R	D
Kent	R	R	R	R	R	R	R	D	R	R	R	D
Newport	R	R	R	R	R	D	D	D	R	R	R	D
Providence	R	R	R	D	D	D	D	D	D	D	R	D
Washington	R	R	R	R	R	R	R	R	R	R	R	R

County	1964	1968	1972	1976	1980	1984	1988	1992	1996	2000	2004
Bristol	D	D	R	D	D	R	D	D	D	D	D
Kent	D	D	R	D	D	R	D	D	D	D	D
Newport	D	D	R	D	R	R	D	D	D	D	D
Providence	D	D	R	D	D	D	D	D	D	D	D
Washington	D	D	R	D	R	R	D	D	D	D	D

South Carolina

County	1868	1872	1876	1880	1884	1888	1892	1896	1900	1904	1908	1912
Abbeville	D	R	D	D	D	D	D	D	D	D	D	D
Aiken	–	R	D	D	D	D	D	D	D	D	D	D
Allendale	–	–	–	–	–	–	–	–	–	–	–	–
Anderson	D	R	D	D	D	D	D	D	D	D	D	D
Bamberg	–	–	–	–	–	–	–	–	D	D	D	D
Barnwell	R	R	D	D	D	D	D	D	D	D	D	D
Beaufort	R	R	R	R	R	R	R	R	R	D	D	D
Berkeley	–	–	–	–	R	D	R	D	D	D	D	D
Calhoun	–	–	–	–	–	–	–	–	–	–	D	D
Charleston	R	R	R	D	D	D	D	D	D	D	D	D
Cherokee	–	–	–	–	–	–	–	–	D	D	D	D
Chester	R	R	R	D	D	D	D	D	D	D	D	D
Chesterfield	D	R	D	D	D	D	D	D	D	D	D	D
Clarendon	R	R	R	D	D	D	D	D	D	D	D	D
Colleton	R	R	R	R	D	D	D	D	D	D	D	D
Darlington	R	R	R	D	D	D	D	D	D	D	D	D
Dillon	–	–	–	–	–	–	–	–	–	–	–	D
Dorchester	–	–	–	–	–	–	–	–	D	D	D	D

County	1868	1872	1876	1880	1884	1888	1892	1896	1900	1904	1908	1912
Edgefield	–	R	D	D	D	D	D	D	D	D	D	D
Fairfield	R	R	R	D	D	D	D	D	D	D	D	D
Florence	–	–	–	–	–	–	D	D	D	D	D	D
Georgetown	R	R	R	R	R	D	R	R	R	D	D	D
Greenville	–	–	–	–	D	D	D	D	D	D	D	D
Greenwood	–	–	–	–	–	–	–	–	D	D	D	D
Hampton	–	–	–	–	–	–	–	D	D	D	D	D
Horry	D	R	D	D	D	D	NR	D	D	D	D	D
Jasper	–	–	–	–	–	–	–	–	–	–	–	D
Kershaw	R	R	R	D	D	D	D	D	D	D	D	D
Lancaster	D	R	D	D	D	D	D	D	D	D	D	D
Laurens	D	R	D	D	D	D	D	D	D	D	D	D
Lee	D	R	D	D	D	D	D	–	–	D	D	D
Lexington	D	R	D	D	D	D	D	D	D	D	D	D
McCormick	D	R	D	D	D	D	D	–	–	–	–	–
Marion	R	R	D	D	D	D	D	D	D	D	D	D
Marlboro	–	–	–	–	–	–	–	D	D	D	D	D
Newberry	D	R	R	D	D	D	D	D	D	D	D	D
Oconee	D	R	D	D	D	D	D	D	D	D	D	D
Orangeburg	R	R	R	D	D	D	D	D	D	D	D	D
Pickens	D	R	D	D	D	D	D	D	D	D	D	D
Richland	R	R	R	D	D	D	D	D	D	D	D	D
Saluda	–	–	–	–	–	–	–	D	D	D	D	D
Spartanburg	D	D	D	D	D	D	D	D	D	D	D	D
Sumter	R	R	R	D	D	D	D	D	D	D	D	D
Union	D	D	D	D	D	D	D	D	D	D	D	D
Williamsburg	R	R	R	D	D	D	D	D	D	D	D	D
York	D	R	D	D	D	D	D	D	D	D	D	D

County	1916	1920	1924	1928	1932	1936	1940	1944	1948	1952	1956	1960
Abbeville	D	D	D	D	D	D	D	D	SR	D	D	D
Aiken	D	D	D	D	D	D	D	D	SR	D	R	R
Allendale	–	D	D	D	D	D	D	D	SR	R	SR	R
Anderson	D	D	D	D	D	D	D	D	D	D	D	D
Bamberg	D	D	D	D	D	D	D	D	SR	R	SR	R
Barnwell	D	D	D	D	D	D	D	D	SR	D	D	R
Beaufort	D	D	D	D	D	D	D	D	SR	R	R	R
Berkeley	D	D	D	D	D	D	D	D	SR	R	SR	D
Calhoun	D	D	D	D	D	D	D	D	SR	R	SR	R
Charleston	D	D	D	D	D	D	D	D	SR	R	SR	R
Cherokee	D	D	D	D	D	D	D	D	SR	D	D	D
Chester	D	D	D	D	D	D	D	D	SR	D	D	D
Chesterfield	D	D	D	D	D	D	D	D	SR	D	D	D
Clarendon	D	D	D	D	D	D	D	D	SR	R	SR	R
Colleton	D	D	D	D	D	D	D	D	SR	R	SR	R
Darlington	D	D	D	D	D	D	D	D	SR	D	D	D
Dillon	D	D	D	D	D	D	D	D	SR	D	D	D
Dorchester	D	D	D	D	D	D	D	D	SR	R	SR	R
Edgefield	D	D	D	D	D	D	D	D	SR	R	SR	R

County	1916	1920	1924	1928	1932	1936	1940	1944	1948	1952	1956	1960
Fairfield	D	D	D	D	D	D	D	D	SR	R	SR	D
Florence	D	D	D	D	D	D	D	D	SR	D	SR	D
Georgetown	D	D	D	D	D	D	D	D	SR	R	SR	D
Greenville	D	D	D	D	D	D	D	D	SR	R	D	R
Greenwood	D	D	D	D	D	D	D	D	SR	D	D	D
Hampton	D	D	D	D	D	D	D	D	SR	R	SR	D
Horry	D	D	D	D	D	D	D	D	SR	D	D	D
Jasper	D	D	D	D	D	D	D	D	SR	R	SR	R
Kershaw	D	D	D	D	D	D	D	D	SR	R	SR	R
Lancaster	D	D	D	D	D	D	D	D	SR	D	D	D
Laurens	D	D	D	D	D	D	D	D	SR	D	D	D
Lee	D	D	D	D	D	D	D	D	SR	R	SR	D
Lexington	D	D	D	D	D	D	D	D	SR	R	SR	R
McCormick	D	D	D	D	D	D	D	D	SR	D	D	D
Marion	D	D	D	D	D	D	D	D	SR	R	D	D
Marlboro	D	D	D	D	D	D	D	D	SR	D	D	D
Newberry	D	D	D	D	D	D	D	D	SR	R	D	D
Oconee	D	D	D	D	D	D	D	D	SR	D	D	D
Orangeburg	D	D	D	D	D	D	D	D	SR	R	SR	R
Pickens	D	D	D	D	D	D	D	D	SR	R	D	R
Richland	D	D	D	D	D	D	D	D	SR	R	SR	R
Saluda	D	D	D	D	D	D	D	D	SR	D	D	D
Spartanburg	D	D	D	D	D	D	D	D	D	D	D	D
Sumter	D	D	D	D	D	D	D	D	SR	R	SR	R
Union	D	D	D	D	D	D	D	D	SR	D	D	D
Williamsburg	D	D	D	D	D	D	D	D	SR	R	SR	R
York	D	D	D	D	D	D	D	D	SR	D	D	D

County	1964	1968	1972	1976	1980	1984	1988	1992	1996	2000	2004
Abbeville	D	A	R	D	D	R	R	D	D	R	R
Aiken	R	R	R	R	R	R	R	R	R	R	R
Allendale	R	D	R	D	D	D	D	D	D	D	D
Anderson	D	A	R	D	D	R	R	R	R	R	R
Bamberg	R	D	R	D	D	R	D	D	D	D	D
Barnwell	R	A	R	D	D	R	R	R	R	R	R
Beaufort	R	D	R	D	R	R	R	R	R	R	R
Berkeley	R	D	R	D	R	R	R	R	R	R	R
Calhoun	R	D	R	D	D	R	R	D	D	R	R
Charleston	R	R	R	D	R	R	R	R	R	R	R
Cherokee	D	A	R	D	D	R	R	R	R	R	R
Chester	D	D	R	D	D	R	R	D	D	D	R
Chesterfield	D	A	R	D	D	R	R	D	D	R	R
Clarendon	R	D	R	D	D	D	D	D	D	D	D
Colleton	R	R	R	D	D	R	R	R	R	R	R
Darlington	R	A	R	D	D	R	R	D	D	R	R
Dillon	D	R	R	D	D	R	R	D	D	D	D
Dorchester	R	D	R	D	R	R	R	R	R	R	R
Edgefield	R	R	R	D	D	D	R	D	R	R	R
Fairfield	D	D	R	D	D	D	D	D	D	D	D

County	1964	1968	1972	1976	1980	1984	1988	1992	1996	2000	2004
Florence	R	R	R	D	R	R	R	R	R	R	R
Georgetown	R	D	R	D	D	R	R	D	D	R	R
Greenville	R	R	R	R	R	R	R	R	R	R	R
Greenwood	R	A	R	D	D	R	R	R	R	R	R
Hampton	R	D	R	D	D	D	D	D	D	D	D
Horry	R	A	R	D	R	R	R	R	R	R	R
Jasper	R	D	R	D	D	D	D	D	D	D	D
Kershaw	R	R	R	D	R	R	R	R	R	R	R
Lancaster	D	A	R	D	D	R	R	D	D	R	R
Laurens	R	R	R	D	D	R	R	R	R	R	R
Lee	R	D	R	D	D	D	D	D	D	D	D
Lexington	R	R	R	R	R	R	R	R	R	R	R
McCormick	R	D	R	D	D	D	D	D	D	D	D
Marion	R	D	R	D	D	D	D	D	D	D	D
Marlboro	D	D	R	D	D	D	D	D	D	D	D
Newberry	R	R	R	D	R	R	R	R	R	R	R
Oconee	D	A	R	D	D	R	R	R	R	R	R
Orangeburg	R	D	R	D	D	D	D	D	D	D	D
Pickens	R	R	R	D	R	R	R	R	R	R	R
Richland	R	R	R	R	R	R	R	R	D	D	D
Saluda	R	D	R	D	D	R	R	R	R	R	R
Spartanburg	D	R	R	D	R	R	R	R	R	R	R
Sumter	R	D	R	D	R	R	R	R	D	R	D
Union	D	A	R	D	D	R	R	R	D	R	R
Williamsburg	R	D	R	D	D	D	D	D	D	D	D
York	D	R	R	D	D	R	R	R	R	R	R

———————— South Dakota ————————

County	1892	1896	1900	1904	1908	1912	1916	1920	1924	1928	1932	1936
Aurora	R	D	R	R	D	D	D	R	P	R	D	D
Beadle	R	R	R	R	R	P	D	R	R	R	D	D
Bennett	–	–	–	–	–	D	D	R	R	R	D	D
Bonhomme	R	R	R	R	R	P	D	R	R	R	D	D
Brookings	R	D	R	R	R	P	R	R	R	R	D	R
Brown	PO	D	R	R	R	D	D	R	R	R	D	D
Brule	R	D	D	R	D	D	D	R	P	D	D	D
Buffalo	R	D	D	R	R	D	D	R	R	R	D	D
Butte	PO	D	R	R	R	P	D	R	R	R	D	R
Campbell	R	R	R	R	R	P	R	R	R	R	D	R
Charles Mix	R	R	R	R	R	P	D	R	P	R	D	D
Clark	R	D	R	R	R	P	R	R	R	R	D	D
Clay	R	R	R	R	R	P	D	R	P	R	D	D
Codington	R	R	R	R	R	P	R	R	P	R	D	D
Corson	–	–	–	–	–	P	D	R	R	R	D	D

County	1892	1896	1900	1904	1908	1912	1916	1920	1924	1928	1932	1936
Custer	R	D	R	R	R	D	D	R	R	R	D	D
Davison	PO	D	R	R	R	P	R	R	R	R	D	D
Day	PO	D	R	R	R	P	R	R	R	R	D	D
Deuel	R	R	R	R	R	P	R	R	R	R	D	R
Dewey	–	–	–	–	–	P	D	R	R	R	D	D
Douglas	R	R	R	R	R	P	R	R	R	R	D	D
Edmunds	R	D	R	R	R	D	R	R	P	R	D	D
Fall River	R	D	R	R	R	P	D	R	R	R	D	D
Faulk	R	R	R	R	R	D	R	R	R	R	D	D
Grant	P0	R	R	R	R	P	R	R	P	R	D	D
Gregory	–	–	R	R	R	P	R	R	R	R	D	D
Haakon	–	–	–	–	–	–	D	R	R	R	D	D
Hamlin	R	R	R	R	R	P	R	R	R	R	D	R
Hand	PO	D	D	R	R	D	D	R	R	R	D	D
Hanson	PO	D	T	R	R	P	R	R	P	R	D	D
Harding	–	–	–	–	–	P	D	R	R	R	D	D
Hughes	R	R	R	R	R	D	R	R	R	R	D	D
Hutchinson	R	R	R	R	R	P	R	R	P	R	D	R
Hyde	R	R	R	R	R	P	R	R	R	R	D	R
Jackson	–	–	–	–	–	–	R	R	R	R	D	D
Jerauld	R	D	R	R	R	P	R	R	R	R	D	D
Jones	–	–	–	–	–	–	–	R	R	R	D	D
Kingsbury	R	D	R	R	R	P	R	R	R	R	D	R
Lake	PO	D	R	R	R	P	R	R	P	R	D	R
Lawrence	R	D	R	R	R	D	D	R	R	R	R	R
Lincoln	R	R	R	R	R	P	R	R	P	R	D	R
Lyman	–	R	R	R	R	P	D	R	R	R	D	D
McCook	PO	D	D	R	R	P	R	R	R	R	D	D
McPherson	R	R	R	R	R	P	R	R	P	D	D	R
Marshall	PO	D	R	R	R	P	D	R	R	R	D	D
Meade	PO	D	D	R	R	P	D	R	R	R	D	D
Mellette	–	–	–	–	–	D	D	R	R	R	D	D
Miner	R	D	D	R	R	P	R	R	P	R	D	D
Minnehaha	R	D	R	R	R	P	R	R	R	R	D	D
Moody	R	D	R	R	R	P	R	R	P	R	D	D
Pennington	R	D	R	R	R	D	D	R	R	R	D	D
Perkins	–	–	–	–	–	P	D	R	R	R	D	D
Potter	R	D	D	R	R	P	R	R	R	R	D	D
Roberts	R	R	R	R	R	P	R	R	P	R	D	D
Sanborn	R	R	R	R	R	P	D	R	R	R	D	D
Shannon	–	–	–	–	–	–	–	–	R	D	D	R
Spink	R	R	R	R	R	P	R	R	R	R	D	D
Stanley	R	D	R	R	R	D	D	R	R	R	D	D
Sully	R	R	R	R	R	P	R	R	R	R	D	R
Todd	–	–	–	–	–	–	–	–	R	D	D	D
Tripp	–	–	–	–	–	P	D	R	R	R	D	D
Turner	R	R	R	R	R	P	R	R	P	R	D	R
Union	PO	D	R	R	R	P	D	R	R	R	D	D
Walworth	PO	D	R	R	R	P	R	R	P	R	D	D

County	1892	1896	1900	1904	1908	1912	1916	1920	1924	1928	1932	1936
Yankton	R	R	R	R	R	P	D	R	P	R	D	D
Ziebach	–	–	–	–	–	P	R	R	R	R	D	D

County	1940	1944	1948	1952	1956	1960	1964	1968	1972	1976	1980	1984
Aurora	R	R	D	R	D	D	D	D	D	D	R	R
Beadle	D	D	D	R	R	R	D	D	R	D	R	R
Bennett	R	D	D	R	R	R	D	R	R	R	R	R
Bonhomme	R	R	R	R	R	R	D	R	D	D	R	R
Brookings	R	R	R	R	R	R	D	R	R	R	R	R
Brown	D	D	D	R	R	R	D	D	D	D	R	R
Brule	D	D	D	R	D	D	D	D	D	D	R	R
Buffalo	R	R	D	R	D	D	D	D	D	D	R	R
Butte	R	R	R	R	R	R	D	R	R	R	R	R
Campbell	R	R	R	R	R	R	R	R	R	R	R	R
Charles Mix	D	D	D	R	D	D	D	D	D	D	R	R
Clark	R	R	R	R	R	R	D	R	R	R	R	R
Clay	R	R	R	R	R	R	D	R	D	R	R	R
Codington	R	R	D	R	R	R	D	D	R	D	R	R
Corson	R	R	T	R	R	R	D	R	R	D	R	R
Custer	R	R	R	R	R	R	D	R	R	R	R	R
Davison	D	D	D	R	R	D	D	R	D	D	R	R
Day	D	R	D	R	D	D	D	D	D	D	R	R
Deuel	R	R	R	R	R	R	D	R	R	D	R	R
Dewey	R	R	R	R	R	R	D	R	D	R	R	R
Douglas	R	R	R	R	R	R	R	R	R	R	R	R
Edmunds	R	R	R	R	R	R	D	R	D	D	R	R
Fall River	R	R	R	R	R	R	R	R	R	R	R	R
Faulk	R	R	R	R	R	R	D	R	R	D	R	R
Grant	R	R	D	R	R	R	D	R	R	D	R	R
Gregory	R	R	D	R	R	R	D	R	R	D	R	R
Haakon	R	R	R	R	R	R	R	R	R	R	R	R
Hamlin	R	R	R	R	R	R	D	R	R	R	R	R
Hand	R	R	R	R	R	R	D	R	R	R	R	R
Hanson	R	R	R	R	D	D	D	R	D	D	R	R
Harding	R	R	R	R	R	R	R	R	R	R	R	R
Hughes	R	R	R	R	R	R	R	R	R	R	R	R
Hutchinson	R	R	R	R	R	R	R	R	R	R	R	R
Hyde	R	R	R	R	R	R	D	R	R	R	R	R
Jackson	R	R	R	R	R	R	D	R	R	R	R	R
Jerauld	R	R	R	R	R	R	D	R	R	D	R	R
Jones	R	R	R	R	R	R	D	R	R	R	R	R
Kingsbury	R	R	R	R	R	R	R	R	R	R	R	R
Lake	R	R	R	R	R	R	D	R	R	D	R	R
Lawrence	R	R	R	R	R	R	R	R	R	R	R	R
Lincoln	R	R	R	R	R	R	D	R	R	R	R	R
Lyman	R	R	R	R	R	R	D	R	R	R	R	R
McCook	R	R	R	R	R	R	D	R	D	D	R	R
McPherson	R	R	R	R	R	R	R	R	R	R	R	R
Marshall	R	R	D	R	R	R	D	D	D	D	R	R

County	1940	1944	1948	1952	1956	1960	1964	1968	1972	1976	1980	1984
Meade	R	R	R	R	R	R	D	R	R	R	R	R
Mellette	R	R	T	R	R	R	D	R	R	R	R	R
Miner	R	R	D	R	D	R	D	D	D	D	R	R
Minnehaha	R	R	R	R	R	R	D	R	R	R	R	R
Moody	R	R	R	R	R	R	D	R	D	D	R	R
Pennington	R	R	R	R	R	R	D	R	R	R	R	R
Perkins	R	R	R	R	R	R	R	R	R	R	R	R
Potter	R	R	R	R	R	R	D	R	R	R	R	R
Roberts	D	D	D	R	D	D	D	D	D	D	R	R
Sanborn	R	R	D	R	R	R	D	R	D	D	R	R
Shannon	R	R	D	R	D	D	D	D	D	D	D	D
Spink	D	R	D	R	D	R	D	D	R	D	R	R
Stanley	R	R	R	R	R	D	D	R	R	R	R	R
Sully	R	R	R	R	R	R	R	R	R	R	R	R
Todd	R	R	D	R	D	R	D	D	D	D	D	D
Tripp	R	R	D	R	R	R	D	R	R	R	R	R
Turner	R	R	R	R	R	R	R	R	R	R	R	R
Union	R	R	D	R	R	R	D	R	D	D	D	R
Walworth	R	R	R	R	R	R	D	R	R	R	R	R
Yankton	R	R	D	R	R	R	D	R	R	R	R	R
Ziebach	R	D	D	R	R	R	D	R	R	D	R	R

County	1988	1992	1996	2000	2004	County	1988	1992	1996	2000	2004
Aurora	D	D	R	R	R	Haakon	R	R	R	R	R
Beadle	R	D	D	R	R	Hamlin	R	R	R	R	R
Bennett	R	R	R	R	R	Hand	R	R	R	R	R
Bonhomme	R	D	D	R	R	Hanson	R	D	R	R	R
Brookings	R	R	R	R	R	Harding	R	R	R	R	R
Brown	D	D	D	R	R	Hughes	R	R	R	R	R
Brule	D	D	D	R	R	Hutchinson	R	R	R	R	R
Buffalo	D	D	D	D	D	Hyde	R	R	R	R	R
Butte	R	R	R	R	R	Jackson	R	R	R	R	R
Campbell	R	R	R	R	R	Jerauld	R	D	D	R	R
Charles Mix	D	D	D	R	R	Jones	R	R	R	R	R
Clark	R	R	R	R	R	Kingsbury	R	D	D	R	R
Clay	D	D	D	D	D	Lake	R	D	D	R	R
Codington	R	R	R	R	R	Lawrence	R	R	R	R	R
Corson	D	R	D	R	D	Lincoln	R	R	R	R	R
Custer	R	R	R	R	R	Lyman	R	R	R	R	R
Davison	R	D	R	R	R	McCook	R	R	R	R	R
Day	D	D	D	R	D	McPherson	R	R	R	R	R
Deuel	R	D	D	R	R	Marshall	D	D	D	R	R
Dewey	D	D	D	D	D	Meade	R	R	R	R	R
Douglas	R	R	R	R	R	Mellette	R	R	R	R	R
Edmunds	R	R	R	R	R	Miner	D	D	D	R	R
Fall River	R	R	R	R	R	Minnehaha	D	D	D	R	R
Faulk	R	R	R	R	R	Moody	D	D	D	R	R
Grant	R	R	D	R	R	Pennington	R	R	R	R	R
Gregory	R	R	R	R	R	Perkins	R	R	R	R	R

County	1988	1992	1996	2000	2004	County	1988	1992	1996	2000	2004
Potter	R	R	R	R	R	Todd	D	D	D	D	D
Roberts	D	D	D	R	D	Tripp	R	R	R	R	R
Sanborn	R	D	D	R	R	Turner	R	R	R	R	R
Shannon	D	D	D	D	D	Union	R	D	D	R	R
Spink	D	D	R	R	R	Walworth	R	R	R	R	R
Stanley	R	R	R	R	R	Yankton	R	R	R	R	R
Sully	R	R	R	R	R	Ziebach	D	R	D	R	D

Tennessee

County	1868	1872	1876	1880	1884	1888	1892	1896	1900	1904	1908	1912
Anderson	R	R	R	R	R	R	R	R	R	R	R	P
Bedford	R	D	D	D	D	D	D	D	D	D	D	D
Benton	R	D	D	D	D	D	D	D	D	D	D	D
Bledsoe	R	R	D	R	R	R	R	R	R	R	R	D
Blount	R	R	R	R	R	R	R	R	R	R	R	P
Bradley	R	R	R	R	R	R	R	R	R	R	R	D
Campbell	R	R	R	R	R	R	R	R	R	R	R	P
Cannon	R	D	D	D	D	D	D	D	D	D	D	D
Carroll	R	R	R	R	R	R	R	R	R	R	R	D
Carter	R	R	R	R	R	R	R	R	R	R	R	P
Cheatham	D	D	D	D	D	D	D	D	D	D	D	D
Chester	–	–	–	–	–	–	D	D	D	D	D	D
Claiborne	R	R	R	R	R	R	R	R	R	R	R	P
Clay	–	D	D	D	D	D	D	D	D	D	D	D
Cocke	R	R	R	R	R	R	R	R	R	R	R	R
Coffee	D	D	D	D	D	D	D	D	D	D	D	D
Crockett	–	–	–	–	D	D	D	D	D	D	D	D
Cumberland	R	R	R	R	R	R	R	R	R	R	R	D
Davidson	R	D	D	D	D	D	D	D	D	D	D	D
Decatur	R	D	D	D	D	D	D	D	R	R	D	D
De Kalb	R	D	D	D	D	D	D	R	D	R	R	D
Dickson	R	D	D	D	D	D	D	D	D	D	D	D
Dyer	D	D	D	D	D	D	D	D	D	D	D	D
Fayette	R	R	R	R	R	D	D	D	D	D	D	D
Fentress	R	R	R	R	R	R	R	R	R	R	R	R
Franklin	D	D	D	D	D	D	D	D	D	D	D	D
Gibson	–	D	D	D	D	D	D	D	D	D	D	D
Giles	D	R	D	D	D	D	D	D	D	D	D	D
Grainger	R	R	R	R	R	R	R	R	R	R	R	P
Greene	R	R	R	R	R	R	R	R	R	D	R	D
Grundy	R	D	D	D	D	D	D	D	D	D	D	D
Hamblen	–	R	R	R	R	R	R	R	R	R	R	D
Hamilton	R	R	R	R	R	R	D	R	R	R	D	D
Hancock	R	R	R	R	R	R	R	R	R	R	R	P

County	1868	1872	1876	1880	1884	1888	1892	1896	1900	1904	1908	1912
Hardeman	D	D	D	D	D	D	D	D	D	D	D	D
Hardin	R	R	R	R	R	R	R	R	R	R	R	R
Hawkins	R	R	R	R	R	R	R	R	R	R	R	D
Haywood	R	R	R	R	R	D	D	D	D	D	D	D
Henderson	R	D	D	R	R	R	R	R	R	R	R	P
Henry	R	D	D	D	D	D	D	D	D	D	D	D
Hickman	D	D	D	D	D	D	D	D	D	D	D	D
Houston	–	D	D	D	D	D	D	D	D	D	D	D
Humphreys	D	D	D	D	D	D	D	D	D	D	D	D
Jackson	D	D	D	D	D	D	D	D	D	D	D	D
Jefferson	R	R	R	R	R	R	R	R	R	R	R	P
Johnson	R	R	R	R	R	R	R	R	R	R	R	P
Knox	R	R	R	R	R	R	R	R	D	R	R	D
Lake	–	D	D	D	D	D	D	D	D	D	D	D
Lauderdale	D	D	D	D	D	D	D	D	D	D	D	D
Lawrence	D	D	D	D	D	D	D	D	D	R	R	D
Lewis	R	D	D	D	D	D	D	D	D	D	D	D
Lincoln	D	D	D	D	D	D	D	D	D	D	D	D
Loudon	–	R	R	R	R	R	R	R	R	R	R	D
McMinn	R	R	R	R	R	R	R	R	R	R	R	D
McNairy	R	D	D	D	D	D	R	R	R	R	R	D
Macon	R	R	D	D	R	R	R	R	R	R	R	R
Madison	R	D	D	D	D	D	D	D	D	D	D	D
Marion	R	R	R	R	R	R	R	R	R	R	R	D
Marshall	D	D	D	D	D	D	D	D	D	D	D	D
Maury	R	R	D	D	D	D	D	D	D	D	D	D
Meigs	R	D	D	D	D	D	D	D	D	D	D	D
Monroe	R	D	D	D	D	D	D	R	R	R	R	D
Montgomery	R	D	D	D	D	D	D	R	D	D	D	D
Moore	–	–	–	–	D	D	D	D	D	D	D	D
Morgan	R	R	R	R	R	R	R	R	R	R	R	P
Obion	D	D	D	D	D	D	D	D	D	D	D	D
Overton	R	D	D	D	D	D	D	D	D	D	D	D
Perry	R	D	D	D	D	D	D	D	D	D	D	D
Pickett	–	–	–	–	R	R	R	R	R	R	R	D
Polk	R	D	D	D	D	D	R	R	R	R	R	D
Putnam	–	D	D	D	D	D	D	D	D	D	D	D
Rhea	R	D	D	D	D	R	R	R	R	R	R	D
Roane	R	R	R	R	R	R	R	R	R	R	R	P
Robertson	D	D	D	D	D	D	D	D	D	D	D	D
Rutherford	R	D	D	D	D	D	D	D	D	D	D	D
Scott	R	R	R	R	R	R	R	R	R	R	R	P
Sequatchie	R	D	D	D	D	D	D	D	D	D	D	D
Sevier	R	R	R	R	R	R	R	R	R	R	R	P
Shelby	R	R	D	R	R	D	D	D	D	D	D	D
Smith	R	D	D	D	D	D	D	D	D	D	D	D
Stewart	D	D	D	D	D	D	D	D	D	D	D	D
Sullivan	R	D	D	D	D	D	D	D	D	D	D	D
Sumner	R	D	D	D	D	D	D	D	D	D	D	D

County	1868	1872	1876	1880	1884	1888	1892	1896	1900	1904	1908	1912
Tipton	D	D	D	D	D	D	D	D	D	D	D	D
Trousdale	–	D	D	D	D	D	D	D	D	D	D	D
Unicoi	–	–	–	–	R	R	R	R	R	R	R	P
Union	R	R	R	R	R	R	R	R	R	R	R	P
Van Buren	R	D	D	D	D	D	D	D	D	D	D	D
Warren	R	D	D	D	D	D	D	D	D	D	D	D
Washington	R	R	R	R	R	R	R	R	R	R	R	P
Wayne	R	R	D	R	R	R	R	R	R	R	R	R
Weakley	R	D	D	D	D	D	D	D	D	D	D	D
White	R	D	D	D	D	D	D	D	D	D	D	D
Williamson	D	D	D	D	D	D	D	D	D	D	D	D
Wilson	D	D	D	D	D	D	D	D	D	D	D	D

County	1916	1920	1924	1928	1932	1936	1940	1944	1948	1952	1956	1960
Anderson	R	R	R	R	R	D	D	D	D	R	R	R
Bedford	D	D	D	D	D	D	D	D	D	D	D	D
Benton	D	D	D	D	D	D	D	D	D	D	D	D
Bledsoe	R	R	R	R	D	D	D	R	R	R	R	R
Blount	R	R	R	R	R	R	R	R	R	R	R	R
Bradley	R	R	R	R	R	R	R	R	R	R	R	R
Campbell	R	R	R	R	R	R	R	R	R	R	R	R
Cannon	D	D	D	D	D	D	D	D	D	D	D	D
Carroll	R	R	R	R	D	D	D	R	D	R	R	R
Carter	R	R	R	R	R	R	R	R	R	R	R	R
Cheatham	D	D	D	D	D	D	D	D	D	D	D	D
Chester	D	D	D	D	D	D	D	D	D	R	D	R
Claiborne	R	R	R	R	D	D	R	R	R	R	R	R
Clay	D	R	D	D	D	D	D	D	D	D	D	R
Cocke	R	R	R	R	R	R	R	R	R	R	R	R
Coffee	D	D	D	D	D	D	D	D	D	D	D	D
Crockett	D	R	D	D	D	D	D	D	D	D	D	R
Cumberland	R	R	R	R	D	D	R	R	R	R	R	R
Davidson	D	D	D	R	D	D	D	D	D	D	D	D
Decatur	R	R	D	D	D	D	D	D	D	D	D	R
De Kalb	D	R	D	R	D	D	D	D	D	D	D	D
Dickson	D	D	D	D	D	D	D	D	D	D	D	D
Dyer	D	D	D	D	D	D	D	D	D	D	D	R
Fayette	D	D	D	D	D	D	D	D	SR	D	SR	R
Fentress	R	R	R	R	R	R	R	R	R	R	R	R
Franklin	D	D	D	D	D	D	D	D	D	D	D	D
Gibson	D	D	D	D	D	D	D	D	D	D	D	D
Giles	D	D	D	D	D	D	D	D	D	D	D	D
Grainger	R	R	R	R	R	R	R	R	R	R	R	R
Greene	R	R	R	R	D	D	R	R	R	R	R	R
Grundy	D	D	D	D	D	D	D	D	D	D	D	D
Hamblen	R	R	R	R	D	D	D	R	R	R	R	R
Hamilton	D	R	R	R	D	D	D	D	D	R	R	R
Hancock	R	R	R	R	R	R	R	R	R	R	R	R
Hardeman	D	D	D	D	D	D	D	D	D	D	D	D

County	1916	1920	1924	1928	1932	1936	1940	1944	1948	1952	1956	1960
Hardin	R	R	R	R	R	D	R	R	R	R	R	R
Hawkins	R	R	R	R	R	R	R	R	R	R	R	R
Haywood	D	D	D	D	D	D	D	D	D	D	D	D
Henderson	R	R	R	R	R	R	R	R	R	R	R	R
Henry	D	D	D	D	D	D	D	D	D	D	D	D
Hickman	D	R	D	D	D	D	D	D	D	D	D	D
Houston	D	D	D	R	D	D	D	D	D	D	D	D
Humphreys	D	D	D	D	D	D	D	D	D	D	D	D
Jackson	D	R	D	D	D	D	D	D	D	D	D	D
Jefferson	R	R	R	R	R	R	R	R	R	R	R	R
Johnson	R	R	R	R	R	R	R	R	R	R	R	R
Knox	R	R	R	R	D	D	D	R	R	R	R	R
Lake	D	D	D	D	D	D	D	D	D	D	D	D
Lauderdale	D	D	D	D	D	D	D	D	D	D	D	D
Lawrence	R	R	R	R	D	D	D	D	D	R	R	R
Lewis	R	R	D	D	D	D	D	D	D	D	D	D
Lincoln	D	D	D	D	D	D	D	D	D	D	D	D
Loudon	R	R	R	R	R	R	R	R	R	R	R	R
McMinn	R	R	R	R	R	R	D	D	R	R	R	R
McNairy	R	R	R	R	D	D	R	R	R	R	R	R
Macon	R	R	R	R	R	R	R	R	R	R	R	R
Madison	D	D	D	D	D	D	D	D	D	D	D	R
Marion	R	R	R	R	D	D	D	D	D	D	R	D
Marshall	D	D	D	D	D	D	D	D	D	D	D	D
Maury	D	D	D	D	D	D	D	D	D	D	D	D
Meigs	R	R	R	R	D	D	D	D	D	R	R	R
Monroe	R	R	R	R	D	D	D	R	R	R	R	R
Montgomery	D	D	D	D	D	D	D	D	D	D	D	D
Moore	D	D	D	D	D	D	D	D	D	D	D	D
Morgan	R	R	R	R	R	D	D	R	R	R	R	R
Obion	D	D	D	D	D	D	D	D	D	D	D	D
Overton	D	R	D	R	D	D	D	D	D	D	D	D
Perry	D	R	D	D	D	D	D	D	D	D	D	D
Pickett	R	R	R	R	D	R	R	R	R	R	R	R
Polk	R	R	R	R	D	D	D	D	R	R	R	R
Putnam	D	D	D	D	D	D	D	D	D	D	D	D
Rhea	R	R	D	R	D	D	D	R	R	R	R	R
Roane	R	R	R	R	R	R	D	R	R	R	R	R
Robertson	D	D	D	D	D	D	D	D	D	D	D	D
Rutherford	D	D	D	D	D	D	D	D	D	D	D	D
Scott	R	R	R	R	R	R	R	R	R	R	R	R
Sequatchie	D	D	D	D	D	D	D	D	D	D	D	D
Sevier	R	R	R	R	R	R	R	R	R	R	R	R
Shelby	D	D	D	D	D	D	D	D	SR	D	R	R
Smith	D	D	D	D	D	D	D	D	D	D	D	D
Stewart	D	D	D	D	D	D	D	D	D	D	D	D
Sullivan	D	D	D	R	D	D	D	D	D	R	R	R
Sumner	D	D	D	D	D	D	D	D	D	D	D	D
Tipton	D	D	D	D	D	D	D	D	D	D	D	D

County	1916	1920	1924	1928	1932	1936	1940	1944	1948	1952	1956	1960
Trousdale	D	D	D	D	D	D	D	D	D	D	D	D
Unicoi	R	R	R	R	R	R	R	R	R	R	R	R
Union	R	R	R	R	R	R	R	R	R	R	R	R
Van Buren	D	D	D	D	D	D	D	D	D	D	D	D
Warren	D	D	D	D	D	D	D	D	D	D	D	D
Washington	R	R	R	R	R	R	R	R	R	R	R	R
Wayne	R	R	R	R	R	R	R	R	R	R	R	R
Weakley	D	D	D	D	D	D	D	D	D	D	D	D
White	D	D	D	D	D	D	D	D	D	D	D	D
Williamson	D	D	D	D	D	D	D	D	D	D	D	D
Wilson	D	D	D	D	D	D	D	D	D	D	D	D

County	1964	1968	1972	1976	1980	1984	1988	1992	1996	2000	2004
Anderson	D	R	R	D	R	R	R	D	D	R	R
Bedford	D	A	R	D	D	R	R	D	D	D	R
Benton	D	D	A	R	D	D	D	D	D	D	D
Bledsoe	R	R	R	D	R	R	R	D	R	R	R
Blount	R	R	R	R	R	R	R	R	R	R	R
Bradley	R	R	R	R	R	R	R	R	R	R	R
Campbell	D	R	R	D	R	R	R	D	D	D	R
Cannon	D	A	R	D	D	D	D	D	D	D	R
Carroll	R	R	R	D	R	R	R	D	D	R	R
Carter	R	R	R	R	R	R	R	R	R	R	R
Cheatham	D	A	R	D	D	R	R	D	D	R	R
Chester	R	A	R	D	R	R	R	R	R	R	R
Claiborne	R	R	R	D	R	R	R	D	R	R	R
Clay	D	R	R	D	D	R	R	D	D	D	D
Cocke	R	R	R	R	R	R	R	R	R	R	R
Coffee	D	A	R	D	D	R	R	D	D	R	R
Crockett	R	A	R	D	D	R	R	D	D	D	R
Cumberland	D	R	R	D	R	R	R	R	R	R	R
Davidson	D	A	R	D	D	R	R	D	D	D	D
Decatur	D	A	R	D	D	R	R	D	D	D	R
De Kalb	D	R	R	D	D	D	D	D	D	D	R
Dickson	D	A	R	D	D	R	R	D	D	D	R
Dyer	D	A	R	D	D	R	R	D	D	R	R
Fayette	R	A	R	D	D	R	R	D	D	R	R
Fentress	R	R	R	D	R	R	R	D	D	R	R
Franklin	D	A	R	D	D	D	D	D	D	D	R
Gibson	D	A	R	D	D	R	R	D	D	D	R
Giles	D	A	R	D	D	R	D	D	D	D	R
Grainger	R	R	R	R	R	R	R	R	R	R	R
Greene	R	R	R	R	R	R	R	R	R	R	R
Grundy	D	A	R	D	D	D	D	D	D	D	D
Hamblen	R	R	R	D	R	R	R	R	R	R	R
Hamilton	R	A	R	R	R	R	R	R	R	R	R
Hancock	R	R	R	R	R	R	R	R	R	R	R
Hardeman	D	A	R	D	D	D	R	D	D	D	D
Hardin	R	R	R	D	R	R	R	D	R	R	R

County	1964	1968	1972	1976	1980	1984	1988	1992	1996	2000	2004
Hawkins	R	R	R	R	R	R	R	R	R	R	R
Haywood	R	A	R	D	D	D	D	D	D	D	D
Henderson	R	R	R	R	R	R	R	R	R	R	R
Henry	D	A	R	D	D	D	D	D	D	D	R
Hickman	D	A	R	D	D	D	D	D	D	D	R
Houston	D	A	D	D	D	D	D	D	D	D	D
Humphreys	D	A	R	D	D	D	D	D	D	D	D
Jackson	D	D	D	D	D	D	D	D	D	D	D
Jefferson	R	R	R	R	R	R	R	R	R	R	R
Johnson	R	R	R	R	R	R	R	R	R	R	R
Knox	R	R	R	R	R	R	R	R	R	R	R
Lake	D	A	R	D	D	D	D	D	D	D	D
Lauderdale	D	A	R	D	D	R	R	D	D	D	D
Lawrence	D	R	R	D	R	R	R	D	D	R	R
Lewis	D	D	D	D	D	R	D	D	D	D	R
Lincoln	D	A	R	D	D	D	R	D	R	R	R
Loudon	R	R	R	D	R	R	R	R	R	R	R
McMinn	R	R	R	D	R	R	R	R	R	R	R
McNairy	R	R	R	D	R	R	R	D	D	R	R
Macon	R	R	R	R	R	R	R	D	R	R	R
Madison	R	A	R	D	R	R	R	R	R	R	R
Marion	D	A	R	D	D	R	R	D	D	D	R
Marshall	D	A	R	D	D	R	R	D	D	D	R
Maury	D	A	R	D	D	R	R	D	D	R	R
Meigs	D	R	R	D	R	R	R	D	D	R	R
Monroe	R	R	R	D	R	R	R	R	R	R	R
Montgomery	D	A	R	D	D	R	R	D	D	R	R
Moore	D	A	R	D	D	R	R	D	D	R	R
Morgan	D	R	R	D	R	R	R	D	D	R	R
Obion	D	A	R	D	D	R	R	D	D	R	R
Overton	D	D	R	D	D	D	D	D	D	D	D
Perry	D	A	D	D	D	D	D	D	D	D	D
Pickett	R	R	R	R	R	R	R	D	R	R	R
Polk	D	R	R	D	D	R	R	D	D	R	R
Putnam	D	R	R	D	D	R	R	D	D	R	R
Rhea	R	R	R	D	R	R	R	R	R	R	R
Roane	D	R	R	D	R	R	R	D	D	R	R
Robertson	D	A	R	D	D	D	D	D	D	D	R
Rutherford	D	A	R	D	D	R	R	D	R	R	R
Scott	R	R	R	R	R	R	R	R	R	R	R
Sequatchie	D	A	R	D	R	R	R	D	D	R	R
Sevier	R	R	R	R	R	R	R	R	R	R	R
Shelby	D	D	R	D	D	R	R	D	D	D	D
Smith	D	A	R	D	D	D	D	D	D	D	D
Stewart	D	A	D	D	D	D	D	D	D	D	D
Sullivan	R	R	R	D	R	R	R	R	R	R	R
Sumner	D	A	R	D	D	R	R	D	R	R	R
Tipton	D	A	R	D	D	R	R	R	R	R	R
Trousdale	D	D	R	D	D	D	D	D	D	D	D

County	1964	1968	1972	1976	1980	1984	1988	1992	1996	2000	2004
Unicoi	R	R	R	R	R	R	R	R	R	R	R
Union	R	R	R	R	R	R	R	D	D	R	R
Van Buren	D	A	R	D	D	D	D	D	D	D	D
Warren	D	A	R	D	D	D	D	D	D	D	R
Washington	R	R	R	R	R	R	R	R	R	R	R
Wayne	R	R	R	R	R	R	R	R	R	R	R
Weakley	D	A	R	D	D	R	R	D	D	R	R
White	D	A	R	D	D	D	R	D	D	D	R
Williamson	D	A	R	D	R	R	R	R	R	R	R
Wilson	D	A	R	D	D	R	R	D	R	R	R

Texas

County	1872	1876	1880	1884	1888	1892	1896	1900	1904	1908	1912	1916
Anderson	D	D	D	D	D	D	D	D	D	D	D	D
Andrews	–	–	–	–	–	–	–	–	–	–	D	D
Angelina	D	D	D	D	D	D	D	D	D	D	D	D
Aransas	D	D	D	D	D	D	D	D	D	D	D	D
Archer	–	–	D	D	D	D	–	D	D	D	D	D
Armstrong	–	–	–	–	–	D	D	D	D	D	D	D
Atascosa	D	D	D	D	D	PO	D	D	D	D	D	D
Austin	D	D	R	R	D	D	R	D	D	D	D	D
Bailey	–	–	–	–	–	–	–	–	–	–	–	–
Bandera	D	D	D	D	D	PO	D	D	D	D	D	D
Bastrop	D	D	D	D	D	D	R	D	D	D	D	D
Baylor	–	–	D	D	D	D	D	D	D	D	D	D
Bee	D	D	D	D	D	D	D	D	D	D	D	D
Bell	D	D	D	D	D	D	D	D	D	D	D	D
Bexar	D	D	D	D	D	D	D	D	D	D	D	D
Blanco	D	D	G	D	D	D	D	D	D	D	D	D
Borden	–	–	–	–	–	D	D	D	D	D	D	D
Bosque	D	D	D	D	D	D	D	D	D	D	D	D
Bowie	D	D	D	D	D	D	D	NR	D	D	D	D
Brazoria	R	R	R	R	R	R	R	D	D	D	D	D
Brazos	D	D	D	D	R	D	R	D	NR	D	D	D
Brewster	–	–	–	–	D	D	D	D	D	D	D	D
Briscoe	–	–	–	–	–	D	D	D	NR	D	D	D
Brooks	–	–	–	–	–	–	–	–	–	–	D	D
Brown	D	D	D	D	D	D	D	D	NR	D	D	D
Burleson	D	D	D	D	D	D	D	D	D	D	D	D
Burnet	D	D	D	D	D	D	D	D	D	D	D	D
Caldwell	D	D	D	D	D	D	D	D	NR	D	D	D
Calhoun	R	D	D	D	D	D	D	NR	NR	D	D	D
Callahan	–	–	D	D	D	D	D	D	D	NR	D	D
Cameron	D	D	D	D	D	D	D	D	D	D	D	D
Camp	–	D	D	D	D	R	R	R	D	D	D	D

County	1872	1876	1880	1884	1888	1892	1896	1900	1904	1908	1912	1916
Carson	–	–	–	–	D	D	D	PO	D	NR	D	D
Cass	D	D	D	D	D	PO	R	R	D	D	D	D
Castro	–	–	–	–	–	D	D	D	D	D	D	D
Chambers	D	D	D	D	D	D	D	PO	D	D	D	D
Cherokee	D	D	D	D	D	D	D	D	D	D	D	D
Childress	–	–	–	–	D	D	D	D	D	D	D	D
Clay	–	D	D	D	D	D	D	D	D	D	D	D
Cochran	–	–	–	–	–	–	–	–	–	–	–	–
Coke	–	–	–	–	–	PO	D	NR	D	D	D	D
Coleman	D	D	D	D	D	D	D	D	D	D	D	D
Collin	D	D	D	D	D	D	D	D	D	D	D	D
Collingsworth	–	–	–	–	–	D	D	D	D	NR	D	D
Colorado	R	R	R	R	D	D	R	D	D	D	D	D
Comal	D	R	R	R	D	D	R	D	D	D	D	R
Comanche	D	D	D	D	D	PO	D	D	D	D	D	D
Concho	–	–	D	D	D	D	D	D	D	D	D	D
Cooke	D	D	D	D	D	D	D	D	D	D	D	D
Coryell	D	D	D	D	D	D	D	D	D	D	D	D
Cottle	–	–	–	–	–	D	D	D	D	D	D	D
Crane	–	–	–	–	–	–	–	–	–	–	–	–
Crockett	–	–	–	–	–	D	R	R	NR	D	D	D
Crosby	–	–	–	–	D	D	D	NR	D	D	D	D
Culberson	–	–	–	–	–	–	–	–	–	–	–	D
Dallam	–	–	–	–	–	D	D	D	D	D	D	D
Dallas	D	D	D	D	D	D	D	D	D	D	D	D
Dawson	–	–	–	–	–	–	–	–	–	–	D	D
Deaf Smith	–	–	–	–	–	D	D	D	NR	D	D	D
Delta	D	D	D	D	D	PO	D	D	D	D	D	D
Denton	D	D	D	D	D	D	D	D	D	D	D	D
De Witt	D	D	D	D	D	D	R	D	D	D	D	R
Dickens	–	–	–	–	–	D	D	D	D	D	D	D
Dimmit	–	–	D	D	D	PO	D	D	D	D	D	D
Donley	–	–	–	D	D	D	D	D	D	NR	D	D
Duval	–	–	D	D	D	D	R	R	NR	D	D	D
Eastland	–	D	D	D	D	D	D	NR	NR	D	D	D
Ector	–	–	–	–	–	D	D	NR	D	D	D	D
Edwards	–	–	–	D	D	D	D	D	D	R	D	D
Ellis	D	D	D	D	D	D	D	D	D	D	D	D
El Paso	D	D	D	D	D	D	D	D	R	D	D	D
Erath	D	D	D	D	D	D	D	D	NR	D	D	D
Falls	R	D	D	D	D	D	D	D	NR	D	D	D
Fannin	D	D	D	D	D	D	D	D	D	D	D	D
Fayette	D	D	R	D	D	D	R	D	D	D	D	D
Fisher	–	–	–	–	D	D	D	D	D	D	D	D
Floyd	–	–	–	–	–	D	D	D	D	D	D	D
Foard	–	–	–	–	–	D	D	D	D	NR	D	D
Fort Bend	R	D	D	D	D	D	R	R	R	D	D	D
Franklin	–	D	D	D	D	D	D	NR	D	D	D	D
Freestone	D	D	D	D	D	D	D	D	D	D	D	D

County	1872	1876	1880	1884	1888	1892	1896	1900	1904	1908	1912	1916
Frio	D	D	D	D	D	D	D	D	D	D	D	D
Gaines	–	–	–	–	–	–	–	–	–	D	D	D
Galveston	D	D	NR	D	D	D	R	D	D	D	D	D
Garza	–	–	–	–	–	–	–	–	–	D	D	D
Gillespie	D	D	R	R	D	D	R	R	R	R	P	R
Glasscock	–	–	–	–	–	–	R	D	NR	D	D	D
Goliad	D	D	D	D	D	D	R	D	D	R	D	D
Gonzales	D	D	D	D	D	PO	D	D	D	D	D	D
Gray	–	–	–	–	–	–	–	–	D	D	D	D
Grayson	D	D	D	D	D	D	D	D	D	D	D	D
Gregg	–	D	R	R	D	D	R	R	D	D	D	D
Grimes	R	R	R	R	R	D	R	D	D	D	D	D
Guadalupe	D	D	D	D	D	D	R	R	R	NR	D	R
Hale	–	–	–	–	D	D	D	D	D	D	D	D
Hall	–	–	–	–	–	–	D	D	D	D	D	D
Hamilton	–	D	D	D	D	D	D	D	D	D	D	D
Hansford	–	–	–	–	–	D	R	R	D	D	D	D
Hardeman	–	–	–	–	D	D	D	D	D	D	D	D
Hardin	D	D	D	D	D	D	D	D	NR	D	D	D
Harris	R	D	D	D	D	D	D	D	NR	D	D	D
Harrison	R	R	R	R	D	R	D	D	NR	D	D	D
Hartley	–	–	–	–	–	D	D	D	D	D	D	D
Haskell	–	–	–	–	D	D	D	D	D	D	D	D
Hayes	D	D	D	D	D	D	D	D	D	D	D	D
Hemphill	–	–	–	–	D	D	D	D	D	D	D	D
Henderson	D	D	D	D	D	D	D	D	NR	D	D	D
Hidalgo	D	D	D	D	D	D	D	D	D	D	D	D
Hill	D	D	D	D	D	D	D	D	D	D	D	D
Hockley	–	–	–	–	–	–	–	–	–	–	–	–
Hood	D	D	D	D	D	D	–	D	D	D	D	D
Hopkins	D	D	D	D	D	D	D	D	D	D	D	D
Houston	D	D	D	D	D	D	D	D	NR	R	D	D
Howard	–	–	–	D	D	D	D	D	D	D	D	D
Hudspeth	–	–	–	–	–	–	–	–	–	–	–	–
Hunt	D	D	D	D	D	D	D	D	D	D	D	D
Hutchinson	–	–	–	–	–	–	–	–	–	D	D	D
Irion	–	–	–	–	–	D	D	D	D	D	D	D
Jack	R	D	D	D	D	PO	D	NR	NR	D	D	D
Jackson	R	R	R	R	D	R	R	D	D	D	D	D
Jasper	D	D	D	D	D	D	D	R	D	D	D	D
Jeff Davis	–	–	–	–	R	R	R	R	D	D	D	D
Jefferson	D	D	D	D	D	D	D	NR	D	D	D	D
Jim Hogg	–	–	–	–	–	–	–	–	–	–	–	D
Jim Wells	–	–	–	–	–	–	–	–	–	–	D	D
Johnson	D	D	D	D	D	D	D	D	D	D	D	D
Jones	–	–	–	D	D	D	D	D	D	D	D	D
Karnes	D	D	D	D	D	D	D	D	D	D	D	D
Kaufman	D	D	D	D	D	D	D	NR	D	D	D	D
Kendall	R	R	R	R	R	R	R	R	R	D	D	R

County	1872	1876	1880	1884	1888	1892	1896	1900	1904	1908	1912	1916
Kenedy	–	–	–	–	–	–	–	–	–	–	–	–
Kent	–	–	–	–	–	–	D	D	D	D	D	D
Kerr	D	D	D	D	D	D	D	D	D	D	D	D
Kimble	–	D	D	D	D	D	D	D	D	D	D	D
King	–	–	–	–	–	D	D	D	D	D	D	D
Kinney	R	D	D	D	R	D	R	R	D	NR	R	D
Kleberg	–	–	–	–	–	–	–	–	–	–	–	D
Knox	–	–	–	–	D	D	D	D	D	D	D	D
Lamar	D	D	D	D	D	D	D	D	D	D	D	D
Lamb	–	–	–	–	–	–	–	–	–	D	D	D
Lampasas	D	D	D	D	D	D	D	D	D	D	D	D
La Salle	–	–	–	D	R	D	R	R	NR	D	D	D
Lavaca	D	D	D	D	D	D	D	D	NR	D	D	D
Lee	–	D	D	D	D	D	R	D	D	D	D	R
Leon	D	D	D	D	D	D	D	D	D	D	D	D
Liberty	R	D	D	D	D	D	D	D	D	R	D	D
Limestone	D	D	D	D	D	D	D	D	D	D	D	D
Lipscomb	–	–	–	–	D	D	D	D	D	D	D	D
Live Oak	D	D	D	D	D	D	D	D	D	NR	D	D
Llano	D	D	D	D	D	D	D	D	NR	D	D	D
Loving	–	–	–	–	–	–	–	–	–	D	NR	NR
Lubbock	–	–	–	–	–	D	D	D	D	D	D	D
Lynn	–	–	–	–	–	–	–	–	–	–	D	D
McCulloch	D	D	D	D	D	D	D	D	NR	D	D	D
McLennan	D	NR	NR	D	D	D	D	D	D	D	D	D
McMullen	D	D	D	D	D	D	D	D	D	D	D	D
Madison	D	D	D	D	D	D	D	D	D	D	D	D
Marion	R	R	R	R	R	R	R	R	R	D	D	D
Martin	–	–	–	–	D	D	D	D	D	D	D	D
Mason	D	D	D	D	D	D	D	D	NR	D	D	D
Matagorda	R	D	R	R	R	R	R	D	D	D	D	D
Maverick	D	D	D	R	R	D	D	R	D	R	D	R
Medina	R	D	R	D	D	D	D	D	D	R	D	D
Menard	D	NR	D	D	D	D	D	D	D	D	D	D
Midland	–	–	–	–	D	D	D	D	NR	NR	D	D
Milam	D	D	D	D	D	D	D	D	NR	D	D	D
Mills	–	–	–	–	D	PO	D	D	NR	D	D	D
Mitchell	–	–	–	D	D	D	D	D	D	D	D	D
Montague	D	D	D	D	D	D	D	D	NR	D	D	D
Montgomery	R	D	D	D	D	D	D	D	NR	D	D	D
Moore	–	–	–	–	–	D	D	D	D	D	D	D
Morris	–	D	D	D	D	D	–	–	–	D	D	D
Motley	–	–	–	–	–	D	D	D	D	NR	D	D
Nacogdoches	D	D	D	D	D	PO	D	D	D	D	D	D
Navarro	D	D	D	D	D	D	D	D	D	D	D	D
Newton	D	D	D	D	D	D	D	D	D	D	D	D
Nolan	–	–	–	D	D	D	D	D	D	D	D	D
Nueces	D	D	D	D	D	D	D	D	D	D	D	D
Ochiltree	–	–	–	–	–	D	D	D	D	NR	D	D

County	1872	1876	1880	1884	1888	1892	1896	1900	1904	1908	1912	1916
Oldham	–	–	–	D	D	D	D	D	D	D	D	D
Orange	D	D	D	D	NR	D	D	D	D	D	D	D
Palo Pinto	D	D	D	D	NR	D	D	D	D	D	D	D
Panola	D	D	D	D	D	D	D	D	D	D	D	D
Parker	D	D	D	D	D	D	D	D	D	NR	D	D
Parmer	–	–	–	–	–	–	–	–	–	D	D	D
Pecos	D	D	D	D	D	D	D	NR	D	NR	D	D
Polk	D	D	D	D	D	D	D	D	D	D	D	D
Potter	–	–	–	–	D	D	D	D	NR	D	D	D
Presidio	R	D	D	D	D	D	D	R	R	D	D	D
Rains	D	D	D	D	D	PO	D	D	D	D	D	D
Randall	–	–	–	–	–	D	D	D	D	D	D	D
Reagan	–	–	–	–	–	–	–	–	–	D	D	D
Real	–	–	–	–	–	–	–	–	–	–	–	D
Red River	R	D	D	D	D	D	D	D	D	D	D	D
Reeves	–	–	–	–	D	D	D	D	D	D	D	D
Refugio	D	D	D	D	D	D	D	D	D	R	D	D
Roberts	–	–	–	–	–	D	D	D	D	D	D	D
Robertson	D	R	R	R	R	R	R	D	D	D	D	D
Rockwall	–	D	D	D	D	D	D	D	D	NR	D	D
Runnels	–	–	D	D	D	D	D	D	NR	D	D	D
Rusk	D	D	D	D	D	D	D	D	NR	D	D	D
Sabine	D	D	D	D	D	PO	D	NR	D	D	D	D
San Augustine	R	R	D	D	D	PO	D	D	NR	D	D	D
San Jacinto	R	R	R	R	R	R	R	R	R	D	D	D
San Patricio	D	D	D	D	D	D	–	D	D	D	D	D
San Saba	D	D	D	D	D	D	D	D	D	D	D	D
Schleicher	–	–	–	–	–	–	–	–	D	D	D	D
Scurry	–	–	–	D	D	D	D	D	D	D	D	D
Shackelford	–	D	D	D	D	D	D	D	D	D	D	D
Shelby	D	D	D	D	D	D	D	NR	D	D	D	D
Sherman	–	–	–	–	–	D	R	D	NR	D	D	D
Smith	R	D	D	D	D	D	D	D	D	D	D	D
Somervell	–	D	D	D	D	PO	D	D	D	D	D	D
Starr	R	R	R	D	D	R	D	D	D	D	D	D
Stephens	–	R	D	D	D	D	D	D	D	D	D	D
Sterling	–	–	–	–	–	D	D	D	D	D	D	D
Stonewall	–	–	–	–	–	D	–	D	D	D	D	D
Sutton	–	–	–	–	–	D	R	D	D	D	D	D
Swisher	–	–	–	–	–	D	D	D	D	D	D	D
Tarrant	D	D	D	D	D	D	D	D	D	D	D	D
Taylor	–	–	D	D	D	D	D	D	D	NR	D	D
Terrell	–	–	–	–	–	–	–	–	–	D	D	D
Terry	–	–	–	–	–	–	–	–	D	PO	D	D
Throckmorton	–	–	D	D	D	D	–	D	D	D	D	D
Titus	D	D	D	D	D	D	D	D	D	D	D	D
Tom Green	–	–	D	D	D	NR	D	D	D	D	D	D
Travis	D	D	D	D	D	D	R	D	D	D	D	D
Trinity	D	D	D	D	D	D	D	D	NR	D	D	D

County	1872	1876	1880	1884	1888	1892	1896	1900	1904	1908	1912	1916
Tyler	D	D	D	D	D	D	D	D	D	D	D	D
Upshur	D	D	D	D	D	D	D	NR	NR	D	D	D
Upton	–	–	–	–	–	–	–	–	–	–	D	D
Uvalde	D	D	D	D	D	D	D	D	D	D	D	D
Val Verde	–	–	–	–	D	D	D	D	D	D	D	D
Van Zandt	D	D	D	D	D	D	D	D	D	D	D	D
Victoria	D	D	D	R	R	D	R	NR	D	D	D	D
Walker	R	D	G	R	UL	PO	D	D	D	D	D	D
Waller	–	R	R	R	R	R	R	D	D	D	D	D
Ward	–	–	–	–	–	D	D	NR	D	D	D	D
Washington	R	R	R	R	D	D	R	D	D	D	D	R
Webb	D	D	D	D	D	D	R	R	R	R	R	D
Wharton	R	R	R	R	R	R	R	D	D	D	D	D
Wheeler	–	–	D	D	D	D	D	NR	D	D	D	D
Wichita	–	–	–	D	D	D	D	D	D	D	D	D
Wilbarger	–	–	–	D	D	D	D	D	D	D	D	D
Willacy	–	–	–	–	–	–	–	–	–	–	D	D
Williamson	D	D	D	D	D	D	D	D	D	D	D	D
Wilson	D	D	D	D	D	PO	D	D	D	D	D	D
Winkler	–	–	–	–	–	–	–	–	–	D	D	D
Wise	D	D	D	D	D	D	D	D	D	NR	D	D
Wood	D	D	D	D	D	D	D	D	D	D	D	D
Yoakum	–	–	–	–	–	–	–	–	–	D	D	D
Young	–	D	D	D	D	D	D	D	D	D	D	D
Zapata	R	D	D	R	D	NR	R	R	R	NR	R	R
Zavala	–	–	–	D	D	D	D	D	D	D	D	D

County	1920	1924	1928	1932	1936	1940	1944	1948	1952	1956	1960	1964
Anderson	D	R	R	D	D	D	D	D	R	R	R	D
Andrews	D	D	R	D	D	D	D	D	D	R	D	D
Angelina	D	D	D	D	D	D	D	D	D	R	D	D
Aransas	D	D	R	D	D	D	D	D	R	R	D	D
Archer	D	D	D	D	D	D	D	D	D	D	D	D
Armstrong	D	D	D	D	D	D	D	D	R	D	R	D
Atascosa	D	D	R	D	D	D	D	D	R	R	D	D
Austin	O	D	D	D	D	D	D	R	R	R	R	D
Bailey	–	D	R	D	D	D	D	D	R	D	R	D
Bandera	D	R	R	D	D	D	R	R	R	R	R	D
Bastrop	D	D	D	D	D	D	D	D	D	D	D	D
Baylor	D	D	D	D	D	D	D	D	D	D	D	D
Bee	D	D	R	D	D	D	D	D	R	R	D	D
Bell	D	D	R	D	D	D	D	D	D	D	D	D
Bexar	R	D	D	D	D	D	D	D	R	R	D	D
Blanco	O	D	R	D	D	D	D	D	R	R	D	D
Borden	D	D	R	D	D	D	D	D	D	D	D	D
Bosque	D	D	R	D	D	D	D	D	R	D	D	D
Bowie	D	D	D	D	D	D	D	D	D	D	D	D
Brazoria	R	D	R	D	D	D	D	D	D	R	R	D
Brazos	D	D	D	D	D	D	D	D	R	R	D	D

County	1920	1924	1928	1932	1936	1940	1944	1948	1952	1956	1960	1964
Brewster	D	D	R	D	D	D	D	D	R	R	R	D
Briscoe	D	D	D	D	D	D	D	D	R	D	D	D
Brooks	D	D	D	D	D	D	D	D	D	D	D	D
Brown	D	D	R	D	D	D	D	D	R	R	D	D
Burleson	D	D	D	D	D	D	D	D	D	D	D	D
Burnet	D	D	R	D	D	D	D	D	D	D	D	D
Caldwell	D	D	D	D	D	D	D	D	D	D	D	D
Calhoun	D	D	D	D	D	D	D	D	R	R	D	D
Callahan	D	D	R	D	D	D	D	D	D	D	D	D
Cameron	D	D	R	D	D	D	D	D	R	R	D	D
Camp	D	D	D	D	D	D	D	D	D	D	D	D
Carson	D	D	R	D	D	D	D	D	R	R	R	D
Cass	D	D	D	D	D	D	D	D	D	R	D	D
Castro	D	D	D	D	D	D	D	D	R	D	D	D
Chambers	R	D	R	D	D	D	D	D	R	R	D	D
Cherokee	D	D	D	D	D	D	D	D	D	R	D	D
Childress	D	D	R	D	D	D	D	D	R	D	R	D
Clay	D	D	R	D	D	D	D	D	D	D	D	D
Cochran	–	D	R	D	D	D	D	D	D	D	D	D
Coke	D	D	R	D	D	D	D	D	D	D	D	D
Coleman	D	D	R	D	D	D	D	D	R	R	R	D
Collin	D	D	R	D	D	D	D	D	D	D	D	D
Collingsworth	D	D	R	D	D	D	D	D	R	D	R	D
Colorado	O	D	D	D	D	D	D	D	R	R	D	D
Comal	O	P	D	D	D	R	R	R	R	R	R	D
Comanche	D	R	R	D	D	D	D	D	R	D	D	D
Concho	D	D	R	D	D	D	D	D	R	R	D	D
Cooke	D	D	R	D	D	D	D	D	R	R	R	D
Coryell	D	D	D	D	D	D	D	D	D	D	D	D
Cottle	D	D	R	D	D	D	D	D	D	D	D	D
Crane	–	–	D	D	D	D	D	D	D	D	D	D
Crockett	D	R	R	D	D	D	D	D	R	R	R	D
Crosby	D	D	R	D	D	D	D	D	D	D	D	D
Culberson	D	D	D	D	D	D	D	D	R	R	D	D
Dallam	D	D	R	D	D	D	D	D	R	D	R	D
Dallas	D	D	R	D	D	D	D	D	R	R	R	D
Dawson	D	D	R	D	D	D	D	D	R	D	R	D
Deaf Smith	D	D	R	D	D	D	D	D	R	R	R	D
Delta	D	D	D	D	D	D	D	D	D	D	D	D
Denton	D	D	R	D	D	D	D	D	R	R	R	D
De Witt	R	D	D	D	D	D	D	D	R	R	R	D
Dickens	D	D	R	D	D	D	D	D	D	D	D	D
Dimmit	D	D	R	D	D	D	D	D	R	R	D	D
Donley	D	D	R	D	D	D	D	D	R	D	R	D
Duval	D	D	D	D	D	D	D	D	D	D	D	D
Eastland	D	D	R	D	D	D	D	D	R	R	R	D
Ector	D	D	R	D	D	D	D	D	R	R	R	R
Edwards	R	R	R	D	D	D	D	D	R	R	R	R
Ellis	D	D	D	D	D	D	D	D	D	D	D	D

County	1920	1924	1928	1932	1936	1940	1944	1948	1952	1956	1960	1964
El Paso	D	D	D	D	D	D	D	D	R	R	D	D
Erath	D	D	R	D	D	D	D	D	R	R	R	D
Falls	D	D	D	D	D	D	D	D	D	D	D	D
Fannin	D	D	D	D	D	D	D	D	D	D	D	D
Fayette	O	D	D	D	D	D	D	D	R	R	D	D
Fisher	D	D	R	D	D	D	D	D	D	D	D	D
Floyd	D	D	R	D	D	D	D	D	R	D	R	D
Foard	D	D	D	D	D	D	D	D	D	D	D	D
Fort Bend	D	D	D	D	D	D	D	D	R	R	D	D
Franklin	–	D	D	D	D	D	D	D	D	D	D	D
Freestone	D	D	D	D	D	D	D	D	D	D	D	D
Frio	D	D	R	D	D	D	D	D	R	D	D	D
Gaines	D	D	R	D	D	D	D	D	D	D	R	D
Galveston	D	D	D	D	D	D	D	D	D	R	D	D
Garza	R	R	R	D	D	D	D	D	D	D	D	D
Gillespie	R	P	R	D	R	R	R	R	R	R	R	D
Glasscock	D	D	R	D	D	D	D	D	R	R	D	R
Goliad	R	D	R	D	D	D	D	D	R	R	R	D
Gonzales	D	D	D	D	D	D	D	D	D	D	D	D
Gray	D	D	R	D	D	D	D	D	R	R	R	R
Grayson	D	D	R	D	D	D	D	D	D	D	D	D
Gregg	D	D	D	D	D	D	D	D	R	R	R	R
Grimes	D	D	D	D	D	D	D	D	R	R	D	D
Guadalupe	R	R	D	D	D	R	R	R	R	R	R	D
Hale	D	D	R	D	D	D	D	D	R	D	R	D
Hall	D	D	R	D	D	D	D	D	D	D	D	D
Hamilton	D	D	D	D	D	D	D	D	R	R	R	D
Hansford	D	D	R	D	D	D	D	D	R	R	R	R
Hardeman	D	D	R	D	D	D	D	D	R	D	R	D
Hardin	D	D	D	D	D	D	D	D	D	D	D	D
Harris	D	D	R	D	D	D	D	D	R	R	R	D
Harrison	D	D	D	D	D	D	D	D	R	R	D	D
Hartley	D	D	R	D	D	D	D	D	R	D	R	D
Haskell	D	D	D	D	D	D	D	D	D	D	D	D
Hayes	D	D	R	D	D	D	D	D	R	D	D	D
Hemphill	D	D	R	D	D	D	D	D	R	R	R	D
Henderson	D	D	D	D	D	D	D	D	D	D	D	D
Hidalgo	D	D	R	D	D	D	D	D	R	R	D	D
Hill	D	D	R	D	D	D	D	D	D	D	D	D
Hockley	–	D	R	D	D	D	D	D	D	D	D	D
Hood	D	D	R	D	D	D	D	D	D	D	D	D
Hopkins	D	D	D	D	D	D	D	D	D	D	D	D
Houston	D	D	D	D	D	D	D	D	D	D	D	D
Howard	D	D	R	D	D	D	D	D	D	D	D	D
Hudspeth	D	D	R	D	D	D	D	D	R	D	D	D
Hunt	D	D	D	D	D	D	D	D	R	R	D	D
Hutchinson	D	D	R	D	D	D	D	D	R	R	R	R
Irion	D	D	R	D	D	D	D	D	D	R	D	D
Jack	D	D	R	D	D	D	D	D	R	R	R	D

County	1920	1924	1928	1932	1936	1940	1944	1948	1952	1956	1960	1964
Jackson	D	D	R	D	D	D	D	D	R	R	D	D
Jasper	D	D	D	D	D	D	D	D	D	R	D	D
Jeff Davis	D	D	R	D	D	D	D	D	R	R	D	D
Jefferson	D	D	R	D	D	D	D	D	D	R	D	D
Jim Hogg	D	D	D	D	D	D	D	D	D	D	D	D
Jim Wells	D	D	D	D	D	D	D	D	D	R	D	D
Johnson	D	D	R	D	D	D	D	D	D	R	R	D
Jones	D	D	R	D	D	D	D	D	R	D	D	D
Karnes	D	D	D	D	D	D	D	D	R	R	D	D
Kaufman	D	D	D	D	D	D	D	D	D	D	D	D
Kendall	R	R	R	D	R	R	R	R	R	R	R	R
Kenedy	–	D	D	D	D	R	R	D	R	R	D	D
Kent	D	D	R	D	D	D	D	D	D	D	D	D
Kerr	D	R	R	D	D	D	D	R	R	R	R	D
Kimble	D	D	R	D	D	D	D	D	R	R	R	D
King	D	D	R	D	D	D	D	D	D	D	D	D
Kinney	R	R	D	D	D	D	D	D	R	R	D	D
Kleberg	D	D	R	D	D	D	D	D	D	D	D	D
Knox	D	D	R	D	D	D	D	D	D	D	D	D
Lamar	D	D	R	D	D	D	D	D	D	D	D	D
Lamb	D	D	R	D	D	D	D	D	R	D	D	D
Lampasas	D	D	R	D	D	D	D	D	R	R	D	D
La Salle	D	D	D	D	D	D	D	D	D	D	D	D
Lavaca	D	D	D	D	D	D	D	D	R	R	D	D
Lee	D	D	D	D	D	R	D	D	D	R	D	D
Leon	D	D	D	D	D	D	D	D	D	D	D	D
Liberty	–	D	R	D	D	D	D	D	R	R	D	D
Limestone	D	D	D	D	D	D	D	D	D	D	D	D
Lipscomb	R	D	R	D	D	D	D	D	R	R	R	R
Live Oak	D	D	R	D	D	D	D	D	R	R	R	D
Llano	D	D	D	D	D	D	D	D	D	D	D	D
Loving	–	D	D	D	D	D	D	D	R	R	D	D
Lubbock	D	D	R	D	D	D	D	D	R	R	R	D
Lynn	D	D	R	D	D	D	D	D	D	D	D	D
McCulloch	D	D	R	D	D	D	D	D	R	R	D	D
McLennan	D	D	R	D	D	D	D	D	D	D	D	D
McMullen	D	R	R	D	D	D	D	D	R	R	R	D
Madison	D	D	D	D	D	D	D	D	D	R	D	D
Marion	D	D	D	D	D	D	D	D	D	R	D	D
Martin	D	D	R	D	D	D	D	D	D	D	D	D
Mason	D	D	R	D	D	D	D	D	R	R	R	D
Matagorda	D	D	R	D	D	D	D	D	R	R	R	D
Maverick	R	R	R	D	D	D	D	D	D	D	D	D
Medina	R	D	D	D	D	D	R	D	R	R	D	D
Menard	R	D	R	D	D	D	D	D	R	R	R	D
Midland	D	D	D	D	D	D	D	D	R	R	R	R
Milam	D	D	D	D	D	D	D	D	D	D	D	D
Mills	D	D	R	D	D	D	D	D	R	R	R	D
Mitchell	D	D	R	D	D	D	D	D	D	D	D	D

County	1920	1924	1928	1932	1936	1940	1944	1948	1952	1956	1960	1964
Montague	D	D	R	D	D	D	D	D	D	D	D	D
Montgomery	D	D	D	D	D	D	D	D	D	R	D	D
Moore	D	D	D	D	D	D	D	D	D	D	R	D
Morris	D	D	D	D	D	D	D	D	D	D	D	D
Motley	D	D	R	D	D	D	D	D	R	D	R	D
Nacogdoches	D	D	D	D	D	D	D	D	D	R	D	D
Navarro	D	D	D	D	D	D	D	D	D	D	D	D
Newton	D	D	D	D	D	D	D	D	D	D	D	D
Nolan	D	D	R	D	D	D	D	D	D	D	D	D
Nueces	D	D	D	D	D	D	D	D	D	R	D	D
Ochiltree	D	D	R	D	D	D	D	D	R	R	R	R
Oldham	D	D	R	D	D	D	D	D	R	D	D	D
Orange	D	D	D	D	D	D	D	D	D	D	D	D
Palo Pinto	D	D	R	D	D	D	D	D	R	R	D	D
Panola	D	D	D	D	D	D	D	D	D	R	R	R
Parker	D	D	R	D	D	D	D	D	R	R	D	D
Parmer	D	D	R	D	D	D	D	D	R	D	R	D
Pecos	R	D	D	D	D	D	D	D	R	R	D	D
Polk	D	D	D	D	D	D	D	D	D	R	D	D
Potter	D	D	R	D	D	D	D	D	R	R	R	D
Presidio	D	D	D	D	D	D	D	D	R	D	D	D
Rains	D	D	D	D	D	D	D	D	D	D	D	D
Randall	D	D	R	D	D	D	D	D	R	R	R	R
Reagan	D	D	R	D	D	D	D	D	R	R	D	D
Real	D	R	R	D	D	D	D	D	R	R	R	D
Red River	D	D	D	D	D	D	D	D	D	D	D	D
Reeves	D	D	D	D	D	D	D	D	R	R	D	D
Refugio	R	D	D	D	D	D	D	D	R	R	D	D
Roberts	D	D	R	D	D	D	D	D	R	R	R	R
Robertson	D	D	D	D	D	D	D	D	D	D	D	D
Rockwall	D	D	D	D	D	D	D	D	D	D	D	D
Runnels	D	D	R	D	D	D	D	D	R	R	R	D
Rusk	D	D	D	D	D	D	D	D	D	R	R	D
Sabine	D	D	D	D	D	D	D	D	D	D	D	D
San Augustine	D	D	D	D	D	D	D	D	D	D	D	D
San Jacinto	D	D	D	D	D	D	D	D	D	D	D	D
San Patricio	D	D	R	D	D	D	D	D	D	D	D	D
San Saba	D	D	D	D	D	D	D	D	D	D	D	D
Schleicher	D	D	R	D	D	D	D	D	R	R	R	D
Scurry	D	D	R	D	D	D	D	D	R	D	D	D
Shackelford	D	D	R	D	D	D	D	D	R	R	D	D
Shelby	D	D	D	D	D	D	D	D	D	D	D	D
Sherman	D	D	R	D	D	D	D	D	R	R	R	R
Smith	D	D	R	D	D	D	D	D	R	R	R	R
Somervell	D	D	R	D	D	D	D	D	R	R	R	D
Starr	D	D	D	D	D	D	D	D	D	D	D	D
Stephens	D	D	R	D	D	D	D	D	R	R	R	D
Sterling	D	D	D	D	D	D	D	D	R	R	D	D
Stonewall	D	D	D	D	D	D	D	D	D	D	D	D

County	1920	1924	1928	1932	1936	1940	1944	1948	1952	1956	1960	1964
Sutton	D	D	R	D	D	D	D	D	R	R	D	D
Swisher	D	D	R	D	D	D	D	D	R	D	D	D
Tarrant	D	D	R	D	D	D	D	D	R	R	R	D
Taylor	D	D	R	D	D	D	D	D	R	R	R	D
Terrell	D	R	R	D	D	D	D	D	R	R	D	D
Terry	D	D	R	D	D	D	D	D	D	D	D	D
Throckmorton	D	D	R	D	D	D	D	D	D	D	D	D
Titus	D	D	D	D	D	D	D	D	D	D	D	D
Tom Green	D	D	R	D	D	D	D	D	R	R	R	D
Travis	D	D	R	D	D	D	D	D	R	R	D	D
Trinity	D	D	D	D	D	D	D	D	D	D	D	D
Tyler	D	D	D	D	D	D	D	D	R	R	R	D
Upshur	D	D	D	D	D	D	D	D	D	R	D	D
Upton	D	D	R	D	D	D	D	D	R	R	D	D
Uvalde	D	D	R	D	D	D	D	D	R	R	R	D
Val Verde	D	D	R	D	D	D	D	D	R	R	D	D
Van Zandt	D	D	D	D	D	D	D	D	D	D	D	D
Victoria	R	D	D	D	D	D	D	D	R	R	D	D
Walker	D	D	D	D	D	D	D	D	D	R	D	D
Waller	D	D	D	D	D	D	D	D	R	R	R	D
Ward	D	D	D	D	D	D	D	D	R	R	D	D
Washington	D	D	D	D	D	R	TR	R	R	R	R	D
Webb	D	D	D	D	D	D	D	D	D	D	D	D
Wharton	R	D	D	D	D	D	D	D	R	R	D	D
Wheeler	D	D	R	D	D	D	D	D	R	D	R	D
Wichita	D	D	R	D	D	D	D	D	D	D	D	D
Wilbarger	D	D	R	D	D	D	D	D	R	D	R	D
Willacy	D	D	D	D	D	D	D	D	R	R	D	D
Williamson	D	D	D	D	D	D	D	D	D	D	D	D
Wilson	R	D	D	D	D	D	D	D	D	D	D	D
Winkler	D	D	D	D	D	D	D	D	R	R	D	D
Wise	D	D	R	D	D	D	D	D	D	D	R	D
Wood	D	D	D	D	D	D	D	D	D	R	D	D
Yoakum	D	D	R	D	D	D	D	D	D	D	R	D
Young	D	D	R	D	D	D	D	D	R	R	D	D
Zapata	R	D	D	D	D	D	D	D	D	D	D	D
Zavala	D	D	R	D	D	D	D	D	R	R	R	D

County	1968	1972	1976	1980	1984	1988	1992	1996	2000	2004
Anderson	D	R	D	R	R	R	R	R	R	R
Andrews	R	R	R	R	R	R	R	R	R	R
Angelina	A	R	D	D	R	R	D	R	R	R
Aransas	D	R	D	R	R	R	R	R	R	R
Archer	D	R	D	R	R	R	R	R	R	R
Armstrong	R	R	D	R	R	R	R	R	R	R
Atascosa	D	R	D	R	R	R	R	D	R	R
Austin	R	R	R	R	R	R	R	R	R	R
Bailey	R	R	D	R	R	R	R	R	R	R
Bandera	R	R	R	R	R	R	R	R	R	R

County	1968	1972	1976	1980	1984	1988	1992	1996	2000	2004
Bastrop	D	R	D	D	R	D	D	D	R	R
Baylor	D	R	D	D	R	D	D	D	R	R
Bee	D	R	D	R	R	R	D	D	R	R
Bell	D	R	D	R	R	R	R	R	R	R
Bexar	D	R	D	R	R	R	D	D	R	R
Blanco	D	R	R	R	R	R	R	R	R	R
Borden	D	R	D	R	R	R	R	R	R	R
Bosque	D	R	D	R	R	R	R	R	R	R
Bowie	A	R	D	R	R	R	D	D	R	R
Brazoria	D	R	D	R	R	R	R	R	R	R
Brazos	R	R	R	R	R	R	R	R	R	R
Brewster	D	R	R	R	R	R	D	D	R	R
Briscoe	D	R	D	R	R	D	D	R	R	R
Brooks	D	D	D	D	D	D	D	D	D	D
Brown	D	R	D	R	R	R	R	R	R	R
Burleson	D	R	D	D	R	D	D	D	R	R
Burnet	D	R	D	R	R	R	R	R	R	R
Caldwell	D	R	D	D	R	D	D	D	R	R
Calhoun	D	R	D	R	R	D	R	R	R	R
Callahan	D	R	D	R	R	R	R	R	R	R
Cameron	D	R	D	D	R	D	D	D	D	R
Camp	D	R	D	D	R	D	D	D	R	R
Carson	R	R	D	R	R	R	R	R	R	R
Cass	A	R	D	D	R	D	D	D	R	R
Castro	D	R	D	R	R	R	R	R	R	R
Chambers	A	R	D	R	R	R	R	R	R	R
Cherokee	A	R	D	D	R	R	R	R	R	R
Childress	D	R	D	R	R	R	R	R	R	R
Clay	D	R	D	D	R	D	D	R	R	R
Cochran	D	R	D	R	R	R	R	R	R	R
Coke	D	R	D	D	R	R	R	R	R	R
Coleman	R	R	D	R	R	R	D	R	R	R
Collin	R	R	R	R	R	R	R	R	R	R
Collingsworth	D	R	D	R	R	R	R	R	R	R
Colorado	R	R	D	R	R	R	R	R	R	R
Comal	R	R	R	R	R	R	R	R	R	R
Comanche	D	R	D	D	R	D	D	D	R	R
Concho	D	R	D	D	R	D	D	R	R	R
Cooke	R	R	R	R	R	R	R	R	R	R
Coryell	D	R	D	R	R	R	R	R	R	R
Cottle	D	D	D	D	D	D	D	D	R	R
Crane	A	R	R	R	R	R	R	R	R	R
Crockett	D	R	D	R	R	R	D	R	R	R
Crosby	D	R	D	D	R	D	D	D	R	R
Culberson	D	R	D	R	R	D	D	D	D	R
Dallam	R	R	D	R	R	R	R	R	R	R
Dallas	R	R	R	R	R	R	R	R	R	R
Dawson	R	R	R	R	R	R	R	R	R	R
Deaf Smith	R	R	R	R	R	R	R	R	R	R

County	1968	1972	1976	1980	1984	1988	1992	1996	2000	2004
Delta	D	R	D	D	R	D	D	D	R	R
Denton	R	R	R	R	R	R	R	R	R	R
De Witt	R	R	R	R	R	R	R	R	R	R
Dickens	D	R	D	D	D	D	D	D	R	R
Dimmit	D	R	D	D	D	D	D	D	D	D
Donley	R	R	D	R	R	R	R	R	R	R
Duval	D	D	D	D	D	D	D	D	D	D
Eastland	D	R	D	R	R	R	R	R	R	R
Ector	R	R	R	R	R	R	R	R	R	R
Edwards	R	R	R	R	R	R	R	R	R	R
Ellis	D	R	D	R	R	R	R	R	R	R
El Paso	D	R	D	R	R	D	D	D	D	D
Erath	D	R	D	D	R	R	R	R	R	R
Falls	D	R	D	D	R	D	D	D	R	R
Fannin	D	R	D	D	R	D	D	D	R	R
Fayette	R	R	D	R	R	R	R	R	R	R
Fisher	D	R	D	D	D	D	D	D	R	R
Floyd	R	R	D	R	R	R	PE	R	R	R
Foard	D	R	D	D	R	D	D	D	R	R
Fort Bend	R	R	R	R	R	R	R	R	R	R
Franklin	D	R	D	D	R	D	D	R	R	R
Freestone	D	R	D	D	R	R	D	R	R	R
Frio	D	R	D	D	D	D	D	D	D	R
Gaines	R	R	D	R	R	R	R	R	R	R
Galveston	D	R	D	D	R	D	D	D	R	R
Garza	D	R	D	R	R	R	R	R	R	R
Gillespie	R	R	R	R	R	R	R	R	R	R
Glasscock	A	R	R	R	R	R	R	R	R	R
Goliad	R	R	D	R	R	R	R	R	R	R
Gonzales	D	R	D	R	R	R	R	R	R	R
Gray	R	R	R	R	R	R	R	R	R	R
Grayson	D	R	D	R	R	R	PE	R	R	R
Gregg	R	R	R	R	R	R	R	R	R	R
Grimes	D	R	D	D	R	R	D	D	R	R
Guadalupe	R	R	R	R	R	R	R	R	R	R
Hale	R	R	D	R	R	R	R	R	R	R
Hall	D	R	D	R	R	D	D	D	R	R
Hamilton	R	R	D	R	R	R	R	R	R	R
Hansford	R	R	R	R	R	R	R	R	R	R
Hardeman	D	R	D	D	R	D	D	D	R	R
Hardin	A	R	D	D	R	D	D	R	R	R
Harris	R	R	R	R	R	R	R	R	R	R
Harrison	A	R	D	R	R	R	D	D	R	R
Hartley	R	R	R	R	R	R	R	R	R	R
Haskell	D	R	D	D	R	D	D	D	R	R
Hayes	D	R	D	R	R	R	D	R	R	R
Hemphill	R	R	R	R	R	R	R	R	R	R
Henderson	D	R	D	D	R	R	D	R	R	R
Hidalgo	D	R	D	D	D	D	D	D	D	D

County	1968	1972	1976	1980	1984	1988	1992	1996	2000	2004
Hill	D	R	D	D	R	R	D	R	R	R
Hockley	D	R	D	R	R	R	R	R	R	R
Hood	D	R	D	R	R	R	R	R	R	R
Hopkins	D	R	D	D	R	R	D	D	R	R
Houston	D	R	D	D	R	R	D	R	R	R
Howard	D	R	D	R	R	R	R	R	R	R
Hudspeth	D	R	D	R	R	D	D	D	R	R
Hunt	D	R	D	R	R	R	R	R	R	R
Hutchinson	R	R	R	R	R	R	R	R	R	R
Irion	R	R	R	R	R	R	PE	R	R	R
Jack	D	R	D	R	R	R	D	R	R	R
Jackson	D	R	D	R	R	R	R	R	R	R
Jasper	A	R	D	D	R	D	D	D	R	R
Jeff Davis	D	R	D	R	R	R	R	R	R	R
Jefferson	D	R	D	D	D	D	D	D	D	D
Jim Hogg	D	D	D	D	D	D	D	D	D	D
Jim Wells	D	R	D	D	D	D	D	D	D	D
Johnson	D	R	D	R	R	R	R	R	R	R
Jones	D	R	D	D	R	R	D	D	R	R
Karnes	D	R	D	R	R	D	R	D	R	R
Kaufman	D	R	D	D	R	R	R	R	R	R
Kendall	R	R	R	R	R	R	R	R	R	R
Kenedy	D	R	D	D	D	D	D	D	D	D
Kent	D	R	D	D	R	D	D	D	R	R
Kerr	R	R	R	R	R	R	R	R	R	R
Kimble	R	R	R	R	R	R	R	R	R	R
King	D	R	D	R	R	R	R	R	R	R
Kinney	D	R	D	R	R	R	R	R	R	R
Kleberg	D	R	D	D	R	D	D	D	R	R
Knox	D	R	D	D	R	D	D	D	R	R
Lamar	D	R	D	D	R	R	D	R	R	R
Lamb	R	R	D	R	R	R	R	R	R	R
Lampasas	D	R	D	R	R	R	R	R	R	R
La Salle	D	R	D	D	D	D	D	D	D	D
Lavaca	D	R	D	R	R	R	R	R	R	R
Lee	D	R	D	R	R	D	R	R	R	R
Leon	D	R	D	D	R	R	R	R	R	R
Liberty	D	R	D	D	R	R	D	R	R	R
Limestone	D	R	D	D	R	D	D	D	R	R
Lipscomb	R	R	R	R	R	R	R	R	R	R
Live Oak	R	R	D	R	R	R	R	R	R	R
Llano	D	R	D	R	R	R	R	R	R	R
Loving	A	R	R	R	R	R	PE	R	R	R
Lubbock	R	R	R	R	R	R	R	R	R	R
Lynn	D	R	D	R	R	R	R	R	R	R
McCulloch	D	R	D	D	R	D	D	R	R	R
McLennan	D	R	D	R	R	R	R	R	R	R
McMullen	R	R	R	R	R	R	R	R	R	R
Madison	D	R	D	D	R	R	D	R	R	R

County	1968	1972	1976	1980	1984	1988	1992	1996	2000	2004
Marion	D	R	D	D	R	D	D	D	R	R
Martin	A	R	D	R	R	R	R	R	R	R
Mason	R	R	D	R	R	R	R	R	R	R
Matagorda	D	R	D	R	R	R	R	R	R	R
Maverick	D	D	D	D	D	D	D	D	D	D
Medina	D	R	D	R	R	R	R	R	R	R
Menard	R	R	D	R	R	D	D	D	R	R
Midland	R	R	R	R	R	R	R	R	R	R
Milam	D	R	D	D	R	D	D	D	R	R
Mills	D	R	D	D	R	R	D	R	R	R
Mitchell	D	R	D	R	R	D	D	D	R	R
Montague	D	R	D	D	R	D	D	R	R	R
Montgomery	A	R	R	R	R	R	R	R	R	R
Moore	R	R	D	R	R	R	R	R	R	R
Morris	D	R	D	D	D	D	D	D	D	R
Motley	R	R	D	R	R	R	R	R	R	R
Nacogdoches	D	R	R	R	R	R	R	R	R	R
Navarro	D	R	D	D	R	D	D	R	R	R
Newton	A	R	D	D	D	D	D	D	D	R
Nolan	D	R	D	D	R	D	D	D	R	R
Nueces	D	R	D	D	R	D	D	D	R	R
Ochiltree	R	R	R	R	R	R	R	R	R	R
Oldham	R	R	D	R	R	R	R	R	R	R
Orange	A	R	D	D	D	D	D	D	R	R
Palo Pinto	R	R	D	D	R	R	D	D	R	R
Panola	A	R	D	R	R	R	D	D	R	R
Parker	D	R	D	R	R	R	R	R	R	R
Parmer	R	R	D	R	R	R	R	R	R	R
Pecos	D	R	R	R	R	R	R	D	R	R
Polk	D	R	D	D	R	D	D	R	R	R
Potter	R	R	R	R	R	R	R	R	R	R
Presidio	D	R	D	D	D	D	D	D	D	D
Rains	D	R	D	D	R	D	D	D	R	R
Randall	R	R	R	R	R	R	R	R	R	R
Reagan	R	R	R	R	R	R	R	R	R	R
Real	R	R	D	R	R	R	R	R	R	R
Red River	D	R	D	D	R	D	D	D	R	R
Reeves	D	R	D	R	R	D	D	D	D	R
Refugio	D	R	D	D	R	R	D	D	R	R
Roberts	R	R	R	R	R	R	R	R	R	R
Robertson	D	R	D	D	D	D	D	D	D	R
Rockwall	D	R	R	R	R	R	R	R	R	R
Runnels	R	R	R	R	R	R	R	R	R	R
Rusk	A	R	R	R	R	R	R	R	R	R
Sabine	D	R	D	D	R	D	D	D	R	R
San Augustine	A	R	D	D	R	D	D	D	R	R
San Jacinto	D	R	D	D	R	D	D	R	R	R
San Patricio	D	R	D	D	R	D	D	D	R	R
San Saba	D	R	D	D	R	D	R	R	R	R

County	1968	1972	1976	1980	1984	1988	1992	1996	2000	2004
Schleicher	R	R	R	R	R	R	R	R	R	R
Scurry	D	R	R	R	R	R	R	R	R	R
Shackelford	D	R	D	R	R	R	R	R	R	R
Shelby	A	R	D	D	R	D	D	D	R	R
Sherman	R	R	D	R	R	R	R	R	R	R
Smith	R	R	R	R	R	R	R	R	R	R
Somervell	D	R	D	D	R	R	PE	R	R	R
Starr	D	D	D	D	D	D	D	D	D	D
Stephens	R	R	D	R	R	R	R	R	R	R
Sterling	R	R	R	R	R	R	R	R	R	R
Stonewall	D	R	D	D	D	D	D	D	R	R
Sutton	R	R	R	R	R	R	R	R	R	R
Swisher	D	R	D	D	D	D	D	D	R	R
Tarrant	R	R	R	R	R	R	R	R	R	R
Taylor	R	R	R	R	R	R	R	R	R	R
Terrell	R	R	D	R	R	D	D	D	R	R
Terry	R	R	D	R	R	R	R	R	R	R
Throckmorton	D	R	D	D	R	D	D	R	R	R
Titus	D	R	D	D	R	D	D	D	R	R
Tom Green	R	R	R	R	R	R	R	R	R	R
Travis	D	R	D	D	R	D	D	D	R	D
Trinity	D	R	D	D	R	D	D	D	R	R
Tyler	A	R	D	D	R	D	D	D	R	R
Upshur	A	R	D	D	R	R	D	R	R	R
Upton	R	R	R	R	R	R	R	R	R	R
Uvalde	R	R	R	R	R	R	R	R	R	R
Val Verde	D	R	D	R	R	R	D	D	R	R
Van Zandt	D	R	D	D	R	R	R	R	R	R
Victoria	R	R	R	R	R	R	R	R	R	R
Walker	D	R	D	R	R	R	R	R	R	R
Waller	D	R	D	D	R	D	D	D	R	R
Ward	R	R	R	R	R	R	R	D	R	R
Washington	R	R	R	R	R	R	R	R	R	R
Webb	D	D	D	D	D	D	D	D	D	D
Wharton	D	R	D	R	R	R	R	R	R	R
Wheeler	R	R	D	R	R	R	R	R	R	R
Wichita	D	R	D	R	R	R	R	R	R	R
Wilbarger	D	R	D	R	R	R	R	R	R	R
Willacy	D	R	D	D	D	D	D	D	D	D
Williamson	D	R	D	R	R	R	R	R	R	R
Wilson	D	R	D	R	R	R	R	R	R	R
Winkler	R	R	R	R	R	R	R	R	R	R
Wise	D	R	D	D	R	R	R	R	R	R
Wood	D	R	D	R	R	R	R	R	R	R
Yoakum	R	R	R	R	R	R	R	R	R	R
Young	D	R	D	R	R	R	R	R	R	R
Zapata	D	D	D	D	D	D	D	D	D	D
Zavala	D	R	D	D	D	D	D	D	D	D

Utah

County	1896	1900	1904	1908	1912	1916	1920	1924	1928	1932	1936	1940
Beaver	D	R	R	R	R	D	R	R	R	D	D	D
Box Elder	D	R	R	R	R	D	R	R	R	D	D	D
Cache	D	D	R	R	D	D	R	R	R	D	D	D
Carbon	D	R	R	R	R	D	R	R	D	D	D	D
Daggett	–	–	–	–	–	–	R	R	R	R	D	D
Davis	D	D	R	R	R	D	R	R	R	D	D	D
Duchesne	–	–	–	–	–	D	R	R	R	D	D	D
Emery	D	D	R	R	R	D	R	R	R	D	D	D
Garfield	D	R	R	R	R	D	R	R	R	R	D	R
Grand	D	D	R	R	D	D	R	R	R	D	D	D
Iron	D	D	R	R	R	D	R	R	R	R	D	R
Juab	D	D	R	R	R	D	R	R	D	D	D	D
Kane	R	R	R	R	R	D	R	R	R	R	R	R
Millard	D	R	R	R	R	D	R	R	R	R	D	D
Morgan	D	R	R	R	R	D	R	R	R	D	D	D
Piute	D	R	R	R	R	D	R	R	R	R	D	D
Rich	D	R	R	R	R	D	R	R	R	D	D	D
Salt Lake	D	R	R	R	R	D	R	R	R	D	D	D
San Juan	D	R	R	R	D	D	R	R	R	R	D	R
Sanpete	D	R	R	R	R	D	R	R	R	D	D	R
Sevier	D	R	R	R	R	D	R	R	R	D	D	R
Summit	D	D	R	R	R	D	R	R	R	D	D	D
Tooele	D	R	R	R	R	D	R	R	R	D	D	D
Uintah	D	D	R	R	P	D	R	R	R	D	D	D
Utah	D	R	R	R	D	D	R	R	R	D	D	D
Wasatch	D	D	R	R	R	D	R	R	R	D	D	D
Washington	D	D	D	D	D	D	R	R	R	D	D	D
Wayne	D	R	R	R	R	D	R	R	R	D	D	D
Weber	D	R	R	R	P	D	R	R	R	D	D	D

County	1944	1948	1952	1956	1960	1964	1968	1972	1976	1980	1984	1988
Beaver	D	D	R	R	D	D	R	R	R	R	R	R
Box Elder	D	R	R	R	R	R	R	R	R	R	R	R
Cache	D	R	R	R	R	R	R	R	R	R	R	R
Carbon	D	D	D	R	D	D	D	R	D	R	R	D
Daggett	D	D	R	R	D	D	R	R	R	R	R	R
Davis	D	D	R	R	R	R	R	R	R	R	R	R
Duchesne	D	D	R	R	R	D	R	R	R	R	R	R
Emery	D	D	R	R	R	D	R	R	D	R	R	R
Garfield	R	R	R	R	R	R	R	R	R	R	R	R
Grand	R	R	R	R	R	D	D	R	R	R	R	R
Iron	R	R	R	R	R	R	R	R	R	R	R	R
Juab	D	D	R	R	R	D	R	R	R	R	R	R
Kane	R	R	R	R	R	R	R	R	R	R	R	R
Millard	D	R	R	R	R	R	R	R	R	R	R	R

County	1944	1948	1952	1956	1960	1964	1968	1972	1976	1980	1984	1988
Morgan	D	D	R	R	R	D	R	R	R	R	R	R
Piute	R	R	R	R	R	R	R	R	R	R	R	R
Rich	D	R	R	R	R	R	R	R	R	R	R	R
Salt Lake	D	D	R	R	R	D	R	R	R	R	R	R
San Juan	R	R	R	R	R	R	R	R	R	R	R	R
Sanpete	R	R	R	R	R	R	R	R	R	R	R	R
Sevier	R	R	R	R	R	R	R	R	R	R	R	R
Summit	D	R	R	R	R	D	R	R	R	R	R	R
Tooele	D	D	D	R	D	D	D	R	R	R	R	R
Uintah	D	D	R	R	R	R	R	R	R	R	R	R
Utah	D	D	R	R	R	D	R	R	R	R	R	R
Wasatch	D	D	R	R	R	D	R	R	R	R	R	R
Washington	D	R	R	R	R	R	R	R	R	R	R	R
Wayne	D	D	R	R	R	D	R	R	R	R	R	R
Weber	D	D	R	R	D	D	R	R	R	R	R	R

County	1992	1996	2000	2004
Beaver	R	R	R	R
Box Elder	R	R	R	R
Cache	R	R	R	R
Carbon	D	D	R	R
Daggett	R	R	R	R
Davis	R	R	R	R
Duchesne	R	R	R	R
Emery	R	R	R	R
Garfield	R	R	R	R
Grand	D	R	R	R
Iron	R	R	R	R
Juab	R	R	R	R
Kane	R	R	R	R
Millard	R	R	R	R
Morgan	R	R	R	R

County	1992	1996	2000	2004
Piute	R	R	R	R
Rich	R	R	R	R
Salt Lake	R	R	R	R
San Juan	R	R	R	R
Sanpete	R	R	R	R
Sevier	R	R	R	R
Summit	R	D	R	R
Tooele	R	D	R	R
Uintah	R	R	R	R
Utah	R	R	R	R
Wasatch	R	R	R	R
Washington	R	R	R	R
Wayne	R	R	R	R
Weber	R	R	R	R

Vermont

County	1868	1872	1876	1880	1884	1888	1892	1896	1900	1904	1908	1912
Addison	R	R	R	R	R	R	R	R	R	R	R	R
Bennington	R	R	R	R	R	R	R	R	R	R	R	R
Caledonia	R	R	R	R	R	R	R	R	R	R	R	P
Chittenden	R	R	R	R	R	R	R	R	R	R	R	R
Essex	R	R	R	R	R	R	R	R	R	R	R	R
Franklin	R	R	R	R	R	R	R	R	R	R	R	P
Grand Isle	R	R	R	R	R	R	R	R	R	R	R	D
Lamoille	R	R	R	R	R	R	R	R	R	R	R	P

County	1868	1872	1876	1880	1884	1888	1892	1896	1900	1904	1908	1912
Orange	R	R	R	R	R	R	R	R	R	R	R	P
Orleans	R	R	R	R	R	R	R	R	R	R	R	P
Rutland	R	R	R	R	R	R	R	R	R	R	R	R
Washington	R	R	R	R	R	R	R	R	R	R	R	R
Windham	R	R	R	R	R	R	R	R	R	R	R	R
Windsor	R	R	R	R	R	R	R	R	R	R	R	P

County	1916	1920	1924	1928	1932	1936	1940	1944	1948	1952	1956	1960
Addison	R	R	R	R	R	R	R	R	R	R	R	R
Bennington	R	R	R	R	R	R	R	R	R	R	R	R
Caledonia	R	R	R	R	R	R	R	R	R	R	R	R
Chittenden	R	R	R	D	D	D	D	D	D	R	R	D
Essex	R	R	R	R	R	R	D	D	R	R	R	R
Franklin	R	R	R	R	D	D	D	D	D	R	R	D
Grand Isle	D	R	R	R	D	D	D	D	D	R	R	D
Lamoille	R	R	R	R	R	R	R	R	R	R	R	R
Orange	R	R	R	R	R	R	R	R	R	R	R	R
Orleans	R	R	R	R	R	R	R	R	R	R	R	R
Rutland	R	R	R	R	R	R	R	R	R	R	R	R
Washington	R	R	R	R	R	R	R	R	R	R	R	R
Windham	R	R	R	R	R	R	R	R	R	R	R	R
Windsor	R	R	R	R	R	R	R	R	R	R	R	R

County	1964	1968	1972	1976	1980	1984	1988	1992	1996	2000	2004
Addison	D	R	R	R	R	R	D	D	D	D	D
Bennington	D	R	R	R	R	R	R	D	D	D	D
Caledonia	D	R	R	R	R	R	R	D	D	R	D
Chittenden	D	D	R	R	D	D	D	D	D	D	D
Essex	D	R	R	R	R	R	R	D	D	R	R
Franklin	D	D	R	R	R	R	D	D	D	D	D
Grand Isle	D	R	R	R	D	R	D	D	D	D	D
Lamoille	D	R	R	R	R	R	R	D	D	D	D
Orange	D	R	R	R	R	R	R	D	D	R	D
Orleans	D	R	R	R	R	R	R	D	D	R	D
Rutland	D	R	R	R	R	R	R	D	D	D	D
Washington	D	R	R	R	R	R	R	D	D	D	D
Windham	D	R	R	R	R	R	D	D	D	D	D
Windsor	D	R	R	R	R	R	R	D	D	D	D

Virginia

County	1872	1876	1880	1884	1888	1892	1896	1900	1904	1908	1912	1916
Accomack	D	D	D	D	D	D	D	D	D	D	D	D
Albemarle	D	D	D	D	D	D	D	D	D	D	D	D

County	1872	1876	1880	1884	1888	1892	1896	1900	1904	1908	1912	1916
Alleghany	D	D	D	R	R	D	R	R	D	R	D	D
Amelia	R	R	R	R	R	R	R	R	D	D	D	D
Amherst	D	D	D	D	D	D	D	D	D	D	D	D
Appomattox	D	D	D	R	R	D	D	D	D	D	D	D
Arlington	–	–	–	–	–	–	–	–	–	–	–	–
Augusta	D	D	D	D	D	D	D	D	D	D	D	D
Bath	D	D	D	D	D	D	D	R	D	D	D	D
Bedford County	D	D	D	D	D	D	D	D	D	D	D	D
Bland	D	D	D	D	D	D	D	D	R	R	D	R
Botetourt	D	D	D	D	D	D	R	D	D	D	D	D
Brunswick	R	D	R	R	R	D	D	R	D	D	D	D
Buchanan	D	D	D	D	D	D	R	R	R	R	D	R
Buckingham	R	R	R	R	R	D	D	D	D	D	D	D
Campbell	D	D	D	D	D	D	D	D	D	D	D	D
Caroline	R	D	D	R	R	R	R	R	D	D	D	D
Carroll	D	D	D	D	D	D	R	R	R	R	R	R
Charles City	R	R	R	R	R	R	R	NR	D	D	D	D
Charlotte	R	R	R	D	D	D	D	D	D	D	D	D
Chesterfield	D	D	D	D	D	D	D	D	D	D	D	D
Clarke	D	D	D	D	D	D	D	D	D	D	D	D
Craig	D	D	D	D	D	D	D	D	D	D	D	D
Culpeper	T	D	D	D	D	D	D	D	D	D	D	D
Cumberland	R	R	R	R	R	R	R	D	D	D	D	D
Dickenson	–	–	D	D	D	D	D	D	R	R	D	R
Dinwiddie	R	R	R	R	R	R	D	D	D	D	D	D
Essex	R	R	R	R	R	R	D	D	R	D	D	D
Fairfax County	R	D	D	D	D	D	D	D	D	D	D	D
Fauquier	D	D	D	D	D	D	D	D	D	D	D	D
Floyd	R	D	D	R	R	R	R	R	R	R	P	R
Fluvanna	R	D	D	D	D	D	D	D	D	D	D	D
Franklin County	D	D	D	D	D	D	D	D	D	D	D	D
Frederick	D	D	D	D	D	D	D	D	D	D	D	D
Giles	D	D	D	D	D	D	D	D	D	D	D	D
Gloucester	R	D	R	R	R	R	D	D	D	D	D	D
Goochland	R	D	R	R	R	R	R	R	D	D	D	D
Grayson	D	D	D	D	D	D	R	R	R	R	D	R
Greene	D	D	D	D	D	D	R	D	R	R	D	R
Greensville	R	D	R	R	R	D	D	D	D	D	D	D
Halifax	R	R	R	D	D	D	D	D	D	D	D	D
Hanover	D	D	D	D	D	D	D	D	D	D	D	D
Henrico	R	R	R	R	R	D	D	D	D	D	D	D
Henry	R	D	R	R	R	R	R	R	D	D	D	D
Highland	D	D	D	D	D	D	D	R	R	R	D	D
Isle of Wight	D	D	D	R	D	D	D	D	D	D	D	D
James City	R	R	R	R	R	R	R	D	D	D	D	D
King and Queen	R	R	R	D	D	D	D	D	D	D	D	D

County	1872	1876	1880	1884	1888	1892	1896	1900	1904	1908	1912	1916
King George	R	D	R	R	R	R	R	R	D	D	D	D
King William	R	R	R	R	R	R	R	R	D	D	D	D
Lancaster	R	R	R	R	R	D	D	D	D	D	D	D
Lee	D	D	D	D	D	D	D	D	R	R	D	R
Loudoun	D	D	D	D	D	D	D	D	D	D	D	D
Louisa	R	R	R	R	R	R	R	R	D	D	D	D
Lunenburg	R	R	R	R	D	D	D	D	D	D	D	D
Madison	D	D	D	D	D	D	D	D	D	D	D	D
Mathews	D	D	D	D	D	D	D	D	D	D	D	D
Mecklenburg	R	R	R	R	R	R	R	R	D	D	D	D
Middlesex	R	R	R	R	R	R	D	D	D	D	D	D
Montgomery	R	D	D	D	R	D	R	R	R	R	D	R
Nelson	D	D	D	D	D	D	D	D	D	D	D	D
New Kent	R	R	R	R	R	R	R	R	D	D	D	D
Northampton	R	R	R	R	R	R	D	D	D	D	D	D
Northumber-land	R	D	D	D	R	D	D	D	D	D	D	D
Nottoway	R	D	R	R	R	D	D	D	D	D	D	D
Orange	D	D	D	D	R	D	D	D	D	D	D	D
Page	D	D	D	D	R	D	R	R	R	D	D	D
Patrick	R	D	D	D	D	D	R	R	D	R	D	D
Pittsylvania	R	D	D	D	D	D	D	D	D	D	D	D
Powhatan	R	R	R	R	R	R	R	R	D	D	D	D
Prince Edward	R	R	R	R	R	R	D	D	D	D	D	D
Prince George	R	R	R	R	R	R	D	D	D	D	D	D
Prince Wil-liam	D	D	D	D	D	D	D	D	D	D	D	D
Pulaski	D	D	D	D	D	D	R	R	R	R	D	D
Rappahannock	D	D	D	D	D	D	D	D	D	D	D	D
Richmond County	R	R	R	R	R	R	T	D	D	D	D	D
Roanoke County	D	D	D	R	R	D	R	R	D	D	D	D
Rockbridge	D	D	D	D	R	D	R	R	D	D	D	D
Rockingham	D	D	D	D	R	D	R	D	D	D	D	D
Russell	D	D	D	D	D	D	D	D	R	R	D	D
Scott	D	D	D	R	R	D	R	D	R	R	D	R
Shenandoah	D	D	D	D	D	D	R	D	R	R	D	R
Smyth	D	D	D	D	D	D	R	R	R	R	D	R
Southhampton	R	D	R	R	R	R	D	D	D	D	D	D
Spotsylvania	D	D	R	D	R	D	R	R	D	D	D	D
Stafford	D	D	D	R	R	D	R	R	R	R	D	D
Surry	R	D	R	R	R	D	D	D	D	D	D	D
Sussex	R	R	R	R	R	R	D	D	D	D	D	D
Tazewell	D	D	D	R	R	R	R	R	R	R	D	R
Warren	D	D	D	D	D	D	D	D	D	D	D	D
Washington	D	D	D	D	D	D	R	R	R	R	D	D
Westmoreland	R	R	R	R	R	R	R	D	D	D	D	D
Wise	D	D	D	D	R	D	R	R	R	R	D	R

County	1872	1876	1880	1884	1888	1892	1896	1900	1904	1908	1912	1916
Wythe	D	D	D	D	R	D	R	R	R	R	D	R
York	R	R	R	R	R	R	D	R	D	D	D	D

Independent City	1872	1876	1880	1884	1888	1892	1896	1900	1904	1908	1912	1916
Alexandria	T	D	D	D	D	D	D	D	D	D	D	D
Bedford City	–	–	–	–	–	–	–	–	–	–	–	–
Bristol	–	–	–	–	–	D	D	D	D	D	D	D
Buena Vista	–	–	–	–	–	D	D	D	D	D	D	D
Charlottesville	–	–	–	–	D	D	D	D	D	D	D	D
Chesapeake	–	–	–	–	–	–	–	–	–	–	–	–
Clifton Forge	–	–	–	–	–	–	–	–	–	D	D	D
Colonial Heights	–	–	–	–	–	–	–	–	–	–	–	–
Covington	–	–	–	–	–	–	–	–	–	–	–	–
Danville	R	R	D	D	D	D	D	D	D	D	D	D
Emporia	–	–	–	–	–	–	–	–	–	–	–	–
Fairfax City	–	–	–	–	–	–	–	–	–	–	–	–
Falls Church	–	–	–	–	–	–	–	–	–	–	–	–
Franklin City	–	–	–	–	–	–	–	–	–	–	–	–
Fredericksburg	D	D	D	D	D	D	D	D	D	D	D	D
Galax	–	–	–	–	–	–	–	–	–	–	–	–
Hampton	–	–	–	–	–	–	–	–	–	–	D	D
Harrisonburg	–	–	–	–	–	–	–	–	–	–	–	D
Hopewell	–	–	–	–	–	–	–	–	–	–	–	D
Lexington	–	–	–	–	–	–	D	D	D	D	D	D
Lynchburg	R	NR	D	D	D	D	–	–	–	–	–	–
Manassas	–	–	–	–	–	–	–	–	–	–	–	–
Manassas Park	–	–	–	–	–	–	–	–	–	–	–	–
Martinsville	–	–	–	–	–	–	–	–	–	–	–	–
Newport News	–	–	–	–	–	–	R	D	D	D	D	D
Norfolk	D	D	D	R	R	D	D	D	D	D	D	D
Norton	–	–	D	D	D	D	–	–	–	–	–	–
Petersburg	R	D	R	R	R	D	D	D	D	D	D	D
Poquoson	–	–	–	–	–	–	–	–	–	–	–	–
Portsmouth	R	D	D	R	D	D	D	D	D	D	D	D
Radford	–	–	–	–	–	D	D	D	D	D	D	D
Richmond City	R	D	D	D	D	D	D	D	D	D	D	D
Roanoke City	–	–	–	D	D	D	D	D	D	D	D	D
Salem	–	–	–	–	–	–	–	–	–	–	–	–
Staunton	D	D	D	D	D	D	D	D	D	D	D	D
Suffolk	–	–	–	–	–	–	–	–	–	–	D	D
Virginia Beach	–	–	–	–	–	–	–	–	–	–	–	–
Waynesboro	–	–	–	–	–	–	–	–	–	–	–	–
Williamsburg	R	R	R	R	R	D	D	D	D	D	D	D
Winchester	D	D	D	R	R	D	D	D	D	D	D	D

County	1920	1924	1928	1932	1936	1940	1944	1948	1952	1956	1960	1964
Accomack	D	D	D	D	D	D	D	D	R	R	D	D
Albemarle	D	D	D	D	D	D	D	D	R	R	R	R
Alleghany	R	R	R	D	D	D	D	D	R	R	D	D
Amelia	D	D	D	D	D	D	D	D	R	R	R	R
Amherst	D	D	D	D	D	D	D	D	D	D	D	D
Appomattox	D	D	D	D	D	D	D	D	D	D	D	R
Arlington	R	R	R	D	D	D	R	R	R	R	R	D
Augusta	D	D	R	D	D	D	D	R	R	R	R	R
Bath	R	R	R	D	D	D	D	R	R	R	R	D
Bedford County	D	D	D	D	D	D	D	D	R	R	D	D
Bland	R	R	R	D	D	D	D	R	R	R	R	D
Botetourt	D	D	R	D	D	D	D	R	R	R	R	D
Brunswick	D	D	D	D	D	D	D	D	D	D	D	R
Buchanan	R	R	D	D	D	D	D	D	D	D	D	D
Buckingham	D	D	D	D	D	D	D	D	D	R	D	R
Campbell	D	D	D	D	D	D	D	D	D	R	D	R
Caroline	D	D	D	D	D	D	D	D	D	R	D	D
Carroll	R	R	R	D	R	R	R	R	R	R	R	R
Charles City	D	D	R	D	D	D	D	D	D	R	D	D
Charlotte	D	D	D	D	D	D	D	D	D	D	D	R
Chesterfield	D	D	R	D	D	D	D	D	R	R	R	R
Clarke	D	D	D	D	D	D	D	D	R	R	D	D
Craig	D	D	D	D	D	D	D	D	D	D	D	D
Culpeper	D	D	D	D	D	D	D	D	R	R	R	D
Cumberland	D	D	D	D	D	D	D	D	R	R	R	R
Dickenson	R	D	D	D	D	D	D	D	D	D	D	D
Dinwiddie	D	D	D	D	D	D	D	D	D	D	D	D
Essex	D	D	D	D	D	D	D	D	R	R	R	R
Fairfax County	D	D	R	D	D	D	R	R	R	R	R	D
Fauquier	D	D	D	D	D	D	D	D	R	R	R	D
Floyd	R	R	R	R	R	R	R	R	R	R	R	R
Fluvanna	D	D	D	D	D	D	D	D	R	R	R	D
Franklin County	D	D	D	D	D	D	D	D	D	D	D	D
Frederick	D	D	D	D	D	D	D	D	R	R	R	D
Giles	D	D	R	D	D	D	D	D	R	R	D	D
Gloucester	D	D	R	D	D	D	D	D	R	R	R	D
Goochland	D	D	D	D	D	D	D	D	D	R	D	D
Grayson	R	D	R	D	R	R	R	R	R	R	R	D
Greene	R	D	R	D	D	D	R	R	R	R	R	R
Greensville	D	D	D	D	D	D	D	D	D	D	D	D
Halifax	D	D	D	D	D	D	D	SR	D	D	D	R
Hanover	D	D	D	D	D	D	D	D	R	R	R	R
Henrico	D	D	R	D	D	D	D	D	R	R	R	R
Henry	D	D	D	D	D	D	D	D	D	D	D	D
Highland	R	D	R	D	R	R	R	R	R	R	R	R
Isle of Wight	D	D	R	D	D	D	D	D	D	D	D	D
James City	D	D	R	D	D	D	D	D	R	R	R	D

County	1920	1924	1928	1932	1936	1940	1944	1948	1952	1956	1960	1964
King and Queen	D	D	R	D	D	D	D	D	R	R	D	D
King George	R	D	R	D	D	D	D	R	R	R	D	D
King William	D	D	D	D	D	D	D	D	R	R	R	R
Lancaster	D	D	R	D	D	D	D	D	R	R	R	R
Lee	R	R	R	D	D	D	D	R	R	R	D	D
Loudoun	D	D	D	D	D	D	D	D	R	R	R	D
Louisa	D	D	R	D	D	D	D	D	R	R	D	D
Lunenburg	D	D	D	D	D	D	D	D	D	D	D	R
Madison	D	D	R	D	D	D	R	R	R	R	R	R
Mathews	D	D	R	D	D	D	D	R	R	R	R	R
Mecklenburg	D	D	D	D	D	D	D	D	D	D	D	R
Middlesex	D	D	D	D	D	D	D	D	R	R	R	R
Montgomery	R	D	R	D	R	D	R	R	R	R	R	R
Nelson	D	D	D	D	D	D	D	D	D	D	D	D
New Kent	D	D	R	D	D	D	D	D	R	R	R	D
Northampton	D	D	D	D	D	D	D	D	R	R	D	R
Northumberland	D	D	R	D	D	D	D	R	R	R	R	R
Nottoway	D	D	D	D	D	D	D	D	R	D	D	R
Orange	D	D	D	D	D	D	D	D	R	R	R	R
Page	R	D	R	D	D	R	R	R	R	R	R	R
Patrick	D	D	R	D	D	D	D	D	D	D	D	D
Pittsylvania	D	D	R	D	D	D	D	D	D	D	D	R
Powhatan	D	D	D	D	D	D	D	D	R	R	R	R
Prince Edward	D	D	D	D	D	D	D	D	R	SR	R	R
Prince George	D	D	D	D	D	D	D	D	D	R	D	R
Prince William	D	D	D	D	D	D	D	D	D	R	D	D
Pulaski	D	D	R	D	D	D	D	R	R	R	R	D
Rappahannock	D	D	D	D	D	D	D	D	R	D	D	D
Richmond County	D	D	R	D	D	D	D	R	R	R	R	R
Roanoke County	D	D	R	D	D	D	D	R	R	R	R	R
Rockbridge	D	D	D	D	D	D	D	R	R	R	R	D
Rockingham	R	D	R	D	D	R	R	R	R	R	R	D
Russell	R	D	D	D	D	D	D	D	D	D	D	D
Scott	R	R	R	D	D	R	R	R	R	R	R	D
Shenandoah	R	R	R	D	R	R	R	R	R	R	R	R
Smyth	R	R	R	D	R	R	R	R	R	R	D	R
Southhampton	D	D	D	D	D	D	D	D	D	D	D	D
Spotsylvania	D	D	R	D	D	D	D	D	D	R	D	D
Stafford	R	D	R	D	D	D	R	R	R	R	D	D
Surry	D	D	D	D	D	D	D	D	D	D	D	D
Sussex	D	D	D	D	D	D	D	D	D	D	D	R
Tazewell	R	R	R	D	D	D	D	R	R	R	D	D
Warren	D	D	D	D	D	D	D	D	R	R	D	D
Washington	R	D	R	D	D	D	D	R	R	R	R	D
Westmoreland	D	D	R	D	D	D	D	R	R	R	R	D

County	1920	1924	1928	1932	1936	1940	1944	1948	1952	1956	1960	1964
Wise	R	D	D	D	D	D	D	D	D	D	D	D
Wythe	R	R	R	D	R	D	R	R	R	R	R	R
York	D	D	R	D	D	D	D	D	R	R	R	D

Independent City	1920	1924	1928	1932	1936	1940	1944	1948	1952	1956	1960	1964
Alexandria	D	D	R	D	D	D	D	D	R	R	D	D
Bedford City	–	–	–	–	–	–	–	–	–	–	–	–
Bristol	D	D	D	D	D	D	D	D	R	R	R	D
Buena Vista	D	D	R	D	D	D	D	D	R	R	R	D
Charlottesville	D	D	D	D	D	D	D	D	R	R	R	D
Chesapeake	–	–	–	–	–	–	–	–	–	–	–	D
Clifton Forge	D	D	R	D	D	D	D	D	R	R	R	D
Colonial Heights	–	–	–	–	–	–	–	–	R	R	R	R
Covington	–	–	–	–	–	–	–	–	–	R	D	D
Danville	D	D	R	D	D	D	D	D	R	R	R	R
Emporia	–	–	–	–	–	–	–	–	–	–	–	–
Fairfax City	–	–	–	–	–	–	–	–	–	–	–	D
Falls Church	–	–	–	–	–	–	–	–	R	R	D	D
Franklin City	–	–	–	–	–	–	–	–	–	–	–	D
Fredericksburg	D	D	R	D	D	D	D	D	R	R	R	D
Galax	–	–	–	–	–	–	–	–	–	R	R	D
Hampton	D	D	D	D	D	D	D	D	R	R	R	D
Harrisonburg	R	R	R	D	D	D	R	R	R	R	R	R
Hopewell	D	D	R	D	D	D	D	D	D	R	R	R
Lexington	–	–	–	–	–	–	–	–	–	–	–	–
Lynchburg	D	D	R	D	D	D	D	D	R	R	R	R
Manassas	–	–	–	–	–	–	–	–	–	–	–	–
Manassas Park	–	–	–	–	–	–	–	–	–	–	–	–
Martinsville	–	–	–	D	D	D	D	D	R	R	R	D
Newport News	D	D	R	D	D	D	D	D	D	R	R	D
Norfolk	D	D	R	D	D	D	D	D	R	R	D	D
Norton	–	–	–	–	–	–	–	–	–	R	R	D
Petersburg	D	D	D	D	D	D	D	D	R	R	D	D
Poquoson	–	–	–	–	–	–	–	–	–	–	–	–
Portsmouth	D	D	R	D	D	D	D	D	D	D	D	D
Radford	D	D	R	D	D	D	D	R	R	R	R	D
Richmond City	D	D	R	D	D	D	D	D	R	R	R	D
Roanoke City	D	D	R	D	D	D	D	R	R	R	R	D
Salem	–	–	–	–	–	–	–	–	–	–	–	–
Staunton	D	D	R	D	D	D	D	R	R	R	R	R
Suffolk	D	D	D	D	D	D	D	D	R	R	D	D
Virginia Beach	–	–	–	–	–	–	–	–	R	R	D	D
Waynesboro	–	–	–	–	–	–	–	D	R	R	R	D
Williamsburg	D	D	D	D	D	D	D	R	R	R	R	D
Winchester	D	D	R	D	D	D	R	R	R	R	R	D

County	1968	1972	1976	1980	1984	1988	1992	1996	2000	2004
Accomack	A	R	D	R	R	R	R	D	R	R
Albemarle	R	R	R	R	R	R	R	R	R	D
Alleghany	R	R	D	D	R	R	D	D	R	R
Amelia	R	R	D	R	R	R	R	R	R	R
Amherst	R	R	R	R	R	R	R	R	R	R
Appomattox	R	R	R	R	R	R	R	R	R	R
Arlington	R	R	D	R	D	D	D	D	D	D
Augusta	R	R	R	R	R	R	R	R	R	R
Bath	R	R	D	D	R	R	R	D	R	R
Bedford County	A	R	D	R	R	R	R	R	R	R
Bland	R	R	R	R	R	R	R	R	R	R
Botetourt	R	R	D	R	R	R	R	R	R	R
Brunswick	A	R	D	D	R	D	D	D	D	D
Buchanan	D	R	D	D	D	D	D	D	D	D
Buckingham	A	R	D	D	R	R	R	D	R	R
Campbell	R	R	R	R	R	R	R	R	R	R
Caroline	D	R	D	D	R	D	D	D	D	R
Carroll	R	R	R	R	R	R	R	R	R	R
Charles City	D	D	D	D	D	D	D	D	D	D
Charlotte	A	R	D	R	R	R	R	R	R	R
Chesterfield	R	R	R	R	R	R	R	R	R	R
Clarke	R	R	R	R	R	R	R	R	R	R
Craig	R	R	D	D	R	R	R	R	R	R
Culpeper	R	R	R	R	R	R	R	R	R	R
Cumberland	D	R	D	R	R	R	R	R	R	R
Dickenson	R	R	D	D	D	D	D	D	D	D
Dinwiddie	A	R	D	D	R	R	R	D	R	R
Essex	D	R	R	R	R	R	R	D	R	R
Fairfax County	R	R	R	R	R	R	R	R	R	D
Fauquier	R	R	R	R	R	R	R	R	R	R
Floyd	R	R	R	R	R	R	R	R	R	R
Fluvanna	R	R	D	R	R	R	R	R	R	R
Franklin County	A	R	D	D	R	R	R	R	R	R
Frederick	R	R	R	R	R	R	R	R	R	R
Giles	R	R	D	D	R	R	D	D	R	R
Gloucester	R	R	D	R	R	R	R	R	R	R
Goochland	D	R	D	R	R	R	R	R	R	R
Grayson	R	R	D	R	R	R	R	R	R	R
Greene	R	R	R	R	R	R	R	R	R	R
Greensville	D	R	D	D	R	D	D	D	D	D
Halifax	A	R	D	R	R	R	R	R	R	R
Hanover	R	R	R	R	R	R	R	R	R	R
Henrico	R	R	R	R	R	R	R	R	R	R
Henry	A	R	D	D	R	R	D	R	R	R
Highland	R	R	R	R	R	R	R	R	R	R
Isle of Wight	A	R	D	D	R	R	R	R	R	R
James City	D	R	R	R	R	R	R	R	R	R

County	1968	1972	1976	1980	1984	1988	1992	1996	2000	2004
King and Queen	D	R	D	D	R	R	D	D	R	R
King George	R	R	D	R	R	R	R	R	R	R
King William	R	R	R	R	R	R	R	R	R	R
Lancaster	R	R	R	R	R	R	R	R	R	R
Lee	R	R	D	D	R	D	D	D	R	R
Loudoun	R	R	R	R	R	R	R	R	R	R
Louisa	R	R	D	D	R	R	R	R	R	R
Lunenburg	A	R	R	R	R	R	R	R	R	R
Madison	R	R	R	R	R	R	R	R	R	R
Mathews	R	R	R	R	R	R	R	R	R	R
Mecklenburg	A	R	R	R	R	R	R	R	R	R
Middlesex	R	R	R	R	R	R	R	R	R	R
Montgomery	R	R	R	R	R	R	D	D	R	R
Nelson	A	R	D	D	R	R	D	D	R	R
New Kent	D	R	D	R	R	R	R	R	R	R
Northampton	D	R	D	D	R	R	D	D	D	D
Northumber- land	R	R	R	R	R	R	R	R	R	R
Nottoway	A	R	D	R	R	R	R	R	R	R
Orange	R	R	R	R	R	R	R	R	R	R
Page	R	R	R	R	R	R	R	R	R	R
Patrick	R	R	D	R	R	R	R	R	R	R
Pittsylvania	A	R	R	R	R	R	R	R	R	R
Powhatan	D	R	R	R	R	R	R	R	R	R
Prince Edward	R	R	R	R	R	R	R	D	R	D
Prince George	A	R	D	R	R	R	R	R	R	R
Prince William	R	R	R	R	R	R	R	R	R	R
Pulaski	R	R	D	D	R	R	R	R	R	R
Rappahannock	R	R	D	R	R	R	R	R	R	R
Richmond County	R	R	R	R	R	R	R	R	R	R
Roanoke County	R	R	R	R	R	R	R	R	R	R
Rockbridge	R	R	D	R	R	R	R	R	R	R
Rockingham	R	R	R	R	R	R	R	R	R	R
Russell	R	R	D	D	D	D	D	D	D	R
Scott	R	R	D	R	R	R	R	R	R	R
Shenandoah	R	R	R	R	R	R	R	R	R	R
Smyth	R	R	D	R	R	R	R	D	R	R
Southhampton	A	R	D	D	R	R	D	D	D	R
Spotsylvania	R	R	D	R	R	R	R	R	R	R
Stafford	R	R	D	R	R	R	R	R	R	R
Surry	D	R	D	D	D	D	D	D	D	D
Sussex	D	R	D	D	D	D	D	D	D	D
Tazewell	D	R	D	R	R	D	D	D	R	R
Warren	R	R	D	R	R	R	R	R	R	R
Washington	R	R	R	R	R	R	R	R	R	R
Westmoreland	R	R	D	R	R	R	D	D	R	R

County	1968	1972	1976	1980	1984	1988	1992	1996	2000	2004
Wise	D	R	D	D	R	D	D	D	R	R
Wythe	R	R	R	R	R	R	R	R	R	R
York	R	R	R	R	R	R	R	R	R	R

Independent City	1968	1972	1976	1980	1984	1988	1992	1996	2000	2004
Alexandria	D	R	D	R	D	D	D	D	D	D
Bedford City	R	R	D	D	R	R	R	D	R	R
Bristol	R	R	D	R	R	R	R	R	R	R
Buena Vista	R	R	D	D	R	R	D	D	R	R
Charlottesville	R	R	D	D	D	D	D	D	D	D
Chesapeake	A	R	D	R	R	R	R	R	R	R
Clifton Forge*	R	R	D	D	R	D	D	D	D	–
Colonial Heights	R	R	R	R	R	R	R	R	R	R
Covington	R	R	D	D	R	D	D	D	D	D
Danville	R	R	R	R	R	R	R	R	R	D
Emporia	R	R	R	R	R	R	R	D	D	D
Fairfax City	R	R	R	R	R	R	R	R	R	D
Falls Church	R	R	R	R	R	D	D	D	D	D
Franklin City	R	R	R	D	R	D	D	D	D	D
Fredericksburg	R	R	D	R	R	R	D	D	D	D
Galax	R	R	D	R	R	R	R	D	R	R
Hampton	D	R	D	D	R	R	D	D	D	D
Harrisonburg	R	R	R	R	R	R	R	R	R	R
Hopewell	R	R	R	R	R	R	R	R	R	R
Lexington	R	R	R	D	R	D	D	D	D	D
Lynchburg	R	R	R	R	R	R	R	R	R	R
Manassas	–	–	R	R	R	R	R	R	R	R
Manassas Park	–	–	D	R	R	R	R	R	R	R
Martinsville	D	R	D	R	R	R	D	D	D	D
Newport News	D	R	D	R	R	R	R	D	D	D
Norfolk	D	R	D	D	D	D	D	D	D	D
Norton	D	R	D	D	D	D	D	D	D	R
Petersburg	D	R	D	D	D	D	D	D	D	D
Poquoson	–	–	–	R	R	R	R	R	R	R
Portsmouth	D	R	D	D	D	D	D	D	D	D
Radford	R	R	D	D	R	R	D	D	R	R
Richmond City	D	R	D	D	D	D	D	D	D	D
Roanoke City	R	R	D	D	R	D	D	D	D	D
Salem	R	R	D	R	R	R	R	R	R	R
Staunton	R	R	R	R	R	R	R	R	R	R
Suffolk	R	R	D	D	R	R	D	D	D	R
Virginia Beach	R	R	R	R	R	R	R	R	R	R
Waynesboro	R	R	R	R	R	R	R	R	R	R
Williamsburg	R	R	R	R	R	R	D	D	R	D
Winchester	R	R	R	R	R	R	R	R	R	R

*Note: Clifton Forge is no longer an independent city and county equivalent as of 2004.

Washington

County	1892	1896	1900	1904	1908	1912	1916	1920	1924	1928	1932	1936
Adams	R	D	D	R	R	D	D	R	P	R	D	D
Asotin	R	D	R	R	R	R	D	R	R	R	D	D
Benton	–	–	–	–	R	P	R	R	R	R	D	D
Chelan	–	–	R	R	R	P	R	R	R	R	D	D
Clallam	R	D	R	R	R	R	R	R	R	R	D	D
Clark	R	T	R	R	R	D	R	R	R	R	D	D
Columbia	D	D	R	R	R	D	D	R	R	R	D	D
Cowlitz	R	R	R	R	R	R	R	R	R	R	D	D
Douglas	R	D	D	R	R	D	D	R	R	R	D	D
Ferry	–	–	D	R	R	D	D	R	P	D	D	D
Franklin	D	D	D	R	R	D	D	R	P	R	D	D
Garfield	R	D	R	R	R	P	R	R	R	R	D	D
Grant	–	–	–	–	–	P	D	R	P	R	D	D
Grays Harbor	–	D	R	R	R	R	R	R	R	R	D	D
Island	R	R	R	R	R	P	D	R	R	R	D	D
Jefferson	D	R	R	R	R	P	R	R	R	R	D	D
King	R	D	R	R	R	P	D	R	R	R	D	D
Kitsap	R	R	R	R	R	P	D	R	P	R	D	D
Kittitas	R	D	R	R	R	P	D	R	R	R	D	D
Klickitat	R	R	R	R	R	R	R	R	R	R	D	D
Lewis	R	R	R	R	R	R	R	R	R	R	D	D
Lincoln	R	D	D	R	R	P	D	R	R	R	D	D
Mason	D	D	R	R	R	D	D	R	R	R	D	D
Okanogan	R	D	D	R	R	D	D	R	R	R	D	D
Pacific	R	R	R	R	R	R	R	R	R	R	D	D
Pend Oreille	–	–	–	–	–	D	D	R	R	R	D	D
Pierce	R	D	R	R	R	P	D	R	R	R	D	D
San Juan	R	R	R	R	R	P	D	R	R	R	D	D
Skagit	R	D	R	R	R	P	D	R	R	R	D	D
Skamania	D	D	D	R	R	D	R	R	R	R	D	D
Snohomish	R	D	R	R	R	P	D	R	R	R	D	D
Spokane	R	D	R	R	R	P	D	R	R	R	D	D
Stevens	R	D	D	R	R	D	D	R	R	R	D	D
Thurston	R	D	R	R	R	R	R	R	R	R	D	D
Wahkiakum	R	D	R	R	R	P	R	R	R	R	D	D
Walla Walla	R	D	R	R	R	P	D	R	R	R	D	D
Whatcom	R	D	R	R	R	P	R	R	R	R	D	D
Whitman	R	D	D	R	R	D	D	R	R	R	D	D
Yakima	R	D	R	R	R	P	R	R	R	R	D	D

County	1940	1944	1948	1952	1956	1960	1964	1968	1972	1976	1980	1984
Adams	R	R	R	R	R	R	R	R	R	R	R	R
Asotin	D	D	D	R	R	D	D	D	R	D	R	R
Benton	R	D	D	R	R	R	D	R	R	R	R	R
Chelan	R	R	D	R	R	D	D	R	R	R	R	R

County	1940	1944	1948	1952	1956	1960	1964	1968	1972	1976	1980	1984
Clallam	D	D	D	R	R	R	D	D	R	R	R	R
Clark	D	D	D	R	D	D	D	D	R	D	R	R
Columbia	R	R	R	R	R	R	D	R	R	R	R	R
Cowlitz	D	D	D	R	D	R	D	D	R	D	R	D
Douglas	D	D	D	R	D	R	D	R	R	R	R	R
Ferry	D	D	D	D	D	D	D	R	R	D	R	R
Franklin	D	D	D	R	D	D	D	R	R	R	R	R
Garfield	R	R	R	R	R	R	D	R	R	R	R	R
Grant	D	D	D	R	D	R	D	R	R	R	R	R
Grays Harbor	D	D	D	D	D	D	D	D	D	D	D	D
Island	D	D	R	R	R	R	D	R	R	R	R	R
Jefferson	D	D	D	R	R	D	D	D	R	D	R	D
King	D	D	D	R	R	R	D	D	R	R	R	R
Kitsap	D	D	D	D	D	D	D	D	R	D	R	R
Kittitas	D	D	D	R	R	R	D	R	R	D	R	R
Klickitat	D	D	D	R	R	R	D	D	R	D	R	R
Lewis	D	R	R	R	R	R	D	R	R	R	R	R
Lincoln	D	R	D	R	R	R	R	R	R	R	R	R
Mason	D	D	D	D	R	D	D	D	R	D	R	R
Okanogan	D	D	D	R	R	D	D	R	R	D	R	R
Pacific	D	D	D	R	D	D	D	D	D	D	D	D
Pend Oreille	D	D	D	R	D	D	D	D	R	D	R	R
Pierce	D	D	D	R	D	D	D	D	R	D	R	R
San Juan	D	R	R	R	R	R	D	R	R	R	R	R
Skagit	D	D	D	R	R	R	D	D	R	R	R	R
Skamania	D	D	D	R	D	D	D	D	R	D	R	R
Snohomish	D	D	D	D	D	D	D	D	R	D	R	R
Spokane	D	D	D	R	R	R	D	R	R	R	R	R
Stevens	D	D	D	R	R	R	D	R	R	R	R	R
Thurston	D	D	D	R	R	R	D	D	R	D	R	R
Wahkiakum	D	D	D	D	D	D	D	D	R	D	R	D
Walla Walla	R	R	R	R	R	R	D	R	R	R	R	R
Whatcom	D	D	D	R	R	R	D	R	R	R	R	R
Whitman	R	R	R	R	R	R	R	R	R	R	R	R
Yakima	R	R	R	R	R	R	D	R	R	R	R	R

County	1988	1992	1996	2000	2004	County	1988	1992	1996	2000	2004
Adams	R	R	R	R	R	Garfield	R	R	R	R	R
Asotin	D	D	D	R	R	Grant	R	R	R	R	R
Benton	R	R	R	R	R	Grays					
Chelan	R	R	R	R	R	Harbor	D	D	D	D	D
Clallam	R	D	D	R	R	Island	R	D	R	R	R
Clark	D	D	D	R	R	Jefferson	D	D	D	D	D
Columbia	R	R	R	R	R	King	D	D	D	D	D
Cowlitz	D	D	D	D	D	Kitsap	R	D	D	D	D
Douglas	R	R	R	R	R	Kittitas	D	D	D	R	R
Ferry	T	D	D	R	R	Klickitat	D	D	D	R	R
Franklin	R	R	R	R	R	Lewis	R	R	R	R	R

County	1988	1992	1996	2000	2004	County	1988	1992	1996	2000	2004
Lincoln	R	R	R	R	R	Snohomish	R	D	D	D	D
Mason	D	D	D	D	D	Spokane	R	D	D	R	R
Okanogan	R	D	R	R	R	Stevens	R	R	R	R	R
Pacific	D	D	D	D	D	Thurston	D	D	D	D	D
Pend Oreille	D	D	D	R	R	Wahkiakum	D	D	D	R	R
Pierce	D	D	D	D	D	Walla Walla	R	R	R	R	R
San Juan	D	D	D	D	D	Whatcom	D	D	D	R	D
Skagit	R	D	D	R	R	Whitman	R	D	D	R	R
Skamania	D	D	D	R	R	Yakima	R	R	R	R	R

West Virginia

County	1868	1872	1876	1880	1884	1888	1892	1896	1900	1904	1908	1912
Barbour	R	R	D	D	D	D	D	D	R	R	R	D
Berkeley	R	R	D	D	D	R	R	R	R	R	R	D
Boone	R	D	D	D	D	D	D	D	D	D	D	D
Braxton	R	D	D	D	D	D	D	D	D	D	D	D
Brooke	D	R	R	R	R	R	R	R	R	R	R	R
Cabell	R	D	D	D	D	D	D	R	R	R	R	D
Calhoun	R	D	D	D	D	D	D	D	D	D	D	D
Clay	R	D	D	D	D	R	D	R	D	D	R	D
Doddridge	R	R	D	D	R	R	R	R	R	R	R	P
Fayette	R	D	D	D	R	R	R	R	R	R	R	D
Gilmer	R	D	D	D	D	D	D	D	D	D	D	D
Grant	R	R	R	R	R	R	R	R	R	R	R	P
Greenbrier	R	D	D	D	D	D	D	D	D	D	D	D
Hampshire	D	D	D	D	D	D	D	D	D	D	D	D
Hancock	R	R	R	R	R	R	R	R	R	R	R	R
Hardy	D	D	D	D	D	D	D	D	D	D	D	D
Harrison	R	R	D	D	R	R	R	R	R	R	R	D
Jackson	R	R	D	D	R	R	R	R	R	R	R	D
Jefferson	R	D	D	D	D	D	D	D	D	D	D	D
Kanawha	R	R	D	D	R	R	R	R	R	R	R	D
Lewis	D	R	D	D	D	D	D	R	R	R	R	D
Lincoln	D	D	D	D	D	D	D	D	R	R	R	D
Logan	D	D	D	D	D	D	D	D	D	D	D	D
McDowell	R	NR	D	D	D	R	R	R	R	R	R	R
Marion	R	R	D	D	R	D	D	R	R	R	R	D
Marshall	R	R	R	R	R	R	R	R	R	R	R	D
Mason	R	R	D	R	R	R	R	R	R	R	R	D
Mercer	D	D	D	D	D	R	D	R	R	R	R	D
Mineral	R	R	D	D	D	R	R	R	R	R	R	P
Mingo	–	–	–	–	–	–	–	D	D	D	R	D
Monongalia	R	R	R	R	R	R	R	R	R	R	R	P
Monroe	R	D	D	D	D	D	D	D	R	D	R	D
Morgan	R	R	R	R	R	R	R	R	R	R	R	R

County	1868	1872	1876	1880	1884	1888	1892	1896	1900	1904	1908	1912
Nicholas	R	D	D	D	D	D	D	D	D	R	R	D
Ohio	D	R	D	D	D	D	D	R	R	R	R	D
Pendleton	R	D	D	D	D	D	D	D	D	D	D	D
Pleasants	D	D	D	D	D	D	D	D	R	R	R	D
Pocahontas	R	D	D	D	D	D	D	D	D	R	R	D
Preston	R	R	R	R	R	R	R	R	R	R	R	P
Putnam	R	D	D	D	R	R	R	R	R	R	R	D
Raleigh	R	D	D	D	D	D	D	R	R	R	R	P
Randolph	R	D	D	D	D	D	D	D	D	D	D	D
Ritchie	R	R	R	R	R	R	R	R	R	R	R	D
Roane	R	D	D	D	D	D	D	D	R	R	R	D
Summers	–	D	D	D	D	D	D	D	D	D	D	D
Taylor	R	R	R	R	R	R	R	R	R	R	R	D
Tucker	D	D	D	D	D	D	D	R	R	R	R	P
Tyler	R	R	R	R	R	R	R	R	R	R	R	D
Upshur	R	R	R	R	R	R	R	R	R	R	R	P
Wayne	D	D	D	D	D	D	D	D	D	D	D	D
Webster	D	D	D	D	D	D	D	D	D	D	D	D
Wetzel	D	D	D	D	D	D	D	D	D	D	D	D
Wirt	R	R	D	D	D	D	D	D	R	R	D	D
Wood	R	R	D	R	R	R	R	R	R	R	R	D
Wyoming	R	R	R	D	D	R	R	R	R	R	R	D

County	1916	1920	1924	1928	1932	1936	1940	1944	1948	1952	1956	1960
Barbour	R	R	R	R	D	D	D	R	D	R	R	R
Berkeley	D	R	R	R	D	D	D	R	D	R	R	R
Boone	R	R	D	D	D	D	D	D	D	D	D	D
Braxton	D	R	D	D	D	D	D	D	D	D	D	D
Brooke	R	R	R	R	D	D	D	D	D	D	D	D
Cabell	D	R	D	R	D	D	D	D	D	R	R	R
Calhoun	D	D	D	D	D	D	D	D	D	D	R	D
Clay	D	R	D	R	D	D	D	D	D	D	R	D
Doddridge	R	R	R	R	R	R	R	R	R	R	R	R
Fayette	R	R	R	R	D	D	D	D	D	D	D	R
Gilmer	D	D	D	D	D	D	D	D	D	D	D	D
Grant	R	R	R	R	R	R	R	R	R	R	R	R
Greenbrier	D	D	D	R	D	D	D	D	D	D	R	D
Hampshire	D	D	D	D	D	D	D	D	D	D	R	D
Hancock	R	R	R	R	D	D	D	D	D	D	D	D
Hardy	D	D	D	D	D	D	D	D	D	D	D	D
Harrison	R	R	R	R	D	D	D	D	D	R	R	D
Jackson	R	R	R	R	D	R	R	R	R	R	R	R
Jefferson	D	D	D	D	D	D	D	D	D	D	R	D
Kanawha	D	R	R	R	D	D	D	D	D	R	R	R
Lewis	R	R	R	R	D	R	R	R	R	R	R	R
Lincoln	D	R	D	R	D	D	D	R	D	D	D	D
Logan	D	D	D	R	D	D	D	D	D	D	D	D
McDowell	R	R	R	R	R	D	D	D	D	D	D	D
Marion	D	R	R	R	D	D	D	D	D	D	D	D

County	1916	1920	1924	1928	1932	1936	1940	1944	1948	1952	1956	1960
Marshall	R	R	R	R	D	D	R	R	D	R	R	D
Mason	R	R	R	R	D	R	R	R	R	R	R	R
Mercer	D	R	D	R	D	D	D	D	D	D	R	D
Mineral	R	R	R	R	R	D	D	R	D	R	R	R
Mingo	D	D	D	R	D	D	D	D	D	D	D	D
Monongalia	R	R	R	R	D	D	D	D	D	D	R	D
Monroe	D	R	R	R	D	D	R	R	R	R	R	R
Morgan	R	R	R	R	R	R	R	R	R	R	R	R
Nicholas	D	R	D	R	D	D	D	D	D	D	R	D
Ohio	R	R	R	R	D	D	D	D	D	R	R	D
Pendleton	D	D	D	D	D	D	D	D	D	D	D	D
Pleasants	D	R	D	R	D	D	R	R	R	R	R	R
Pocahontas	D	R	R	R	D	D	D	D	D	R	R	D
Preston	R	R	R	R	R	R	R	R	R	R	R	R
Putnam	R	R	D	R	D	D	D	R	D	R	R	R
Raleigh	R	R	R	R	D	D	D	D	D	D	R	D
Randolph	D	D	D	D	D	D	D	D	D	D	D	D
Ritchie	R	R	R	R	R	R	R	R	R	R	R	R
Roane	R	R	R	R	D	R	R	R	R	R	R	R
Summers	D	R	D	R	D	D	D	D	D	D	D	D
Taylor	R	R	R	R	D	D	D	R	R	R	R	R
Tucker	R	R	R	R	D	D	D	D	D	D	R	D
Tyler	R	R	R	R	R	R	R	R	R	R	R	R
Upshur	R	R	R	R	R	R	R	R	R	R	R	R
Wayne	D	D	D	R	D	D	D	D	D	D	R	D
Webster	D	D	D	D	D	D	D	D	D	D	D	D
Wetzel	D	D	D	R	D	D	D	D	D	R	R	R
Wirt	D	R	D	R	D	D	R	R	R	R	R	R
Wood	D	R	R	R	D	D	D	R	D	R	R	R
Wyoming	R	R	R	R	D	D	D	D	D	D	D	D

County	1964	1968	1972	1976	1980	1984	1988	1992	1996	2000	2004
Barbour	D	D	R	D	D	R	D	D	D	R	R
Berkeley	D	R	R	R	R	R	R	R	R	R	R
Boone	D	D	R	D	D	D	D	D	D	D	D
Braxton	D	D	R	D	D	D	D	D	D	D	D
Brooke	D	D	R	D	D	D	D	D	D	D	D
Cabell	D	R	R	D	R	R	R	D	D	R	R
Calhoun	D	D	R	D	D	R	D	D	D	R	R
Clay	D	D	R	D	D	D	D	D	D	R	R
Doddridge	D	R	R	R	R	R	R	R	R	R	R
Fayette	D	D	R	D	D	D	D	D	D	D	D
Gilmer	D	D	R	D	D	R	D	D	D	R	R
Grant	R	R	R	R	R	R	R	R	R	R	R
Greenbrier	D	D	R	D	D	R	D	D	D	R	R
Hampshire	D	R	R	D	R	R	R	R	R	R	R
Hancock	D	D	R	D	D	D	D	D	D	R	R
Hardy	D	R	R	D	R	R	R	R	D	R	R
Harrison	D	D	R	D	D	R	D	D	D	D	R

County	1964	1968	1972	1976	1980	1984	1988	1992	1996	2000	2004
Jackson	D	R	R	R	R	R	R	D	D	R	R
Jefferson	D	D	R	D	D	R	R	D	D	R	R
Kanawha	D	D	R	D	D	R	D	D	D	D	R
Lewis	D	R	R	D	R	R	R	D	D	R	R
Lincoln	D	D	R	D	D	D	D	D	D	D	R
Logan	D	D	D	D	D	D	D	D	D	D	D
McDowell	D	D	R	D	D	D	D	D	D	D	D
Marion	D	D	R	D	D	D	D	D	D	D	D
Marshall	D	D	R	D	D	R	D	D	D	R	R
Mason	D	R	R	D	R	R	D	D	D	R	R
Mercer	D	D	R	D	R	R	R	D	D	R	R
Mineral	D	R	R	D	R	R	R	R	R	R	R
Mingo	D	D	R	D	D	D	D	D	D	D	D
Monongalia	D	D	R	D	D	R	D	D	D	R	R
Monroe	D	R	R	D	R	R	R	D	D	R	R
Morgan	R	R	R	R	R	R	R	R	R	R	R
Nicholas	D	D	R	D	D	R	D	D	D	R	R
Ohio	D	D	R	R	R	R	R	D	D	R	R
Pendleton	D	R	R	D	R	R	R	D	D	R	R
Pleasants	D	R	R	D	R	R	R	D	D	R	R
Pocahontas	D	R	R	D	D	R	D	D	D	R	R
Preston	D	R	R	R	R	R	R	R	R	R	R
Putnam	D	R	R	D	R	R	R	R	R	R	R
Raleigh	D	D	R	D	D	R	D	D	D	R	R
Randolph	D	D	R	D	D	R	D	D	D	R	R
Ritchie	R	R	R	R	R	R	R	R	R	R	R
Roane	D	R	R	D	R	R	R	D	D	R	R
Summers	D	D	R	D	D	R	D	D	D	R	R
Taylor	D	R	R	D	D	R	D	D	D	R	R
Tucker	D	D	R	D	D	R	D	D	D	R	R
Tyler	R	R	R	R	R	R	R	R	D	R	R
Upshur	D	R	R	R	R	R	R	R	R	R	R
Wayne	D	D	R	D	D	R	D	D	D	R	R
Webster	D	D	R	D	D	D	D	D	D	D	D
Wetzel	D	R	R	D	D	R	D	D	D	R	R
Wirt	D	R	R	D	R	R	R	D	R	R	R
Wood	D	R	R	R	R	R	R	R	R	R	R
Wyoming	D	D	R	D	D	D	D	D	D	D	R

Wisconsin

County	1868	1872	1876	1880	1884	1888	1892	1896	1900	1904	1908	1912
Adams	R	R	R	R	R	R	R	R	R	R	R	R
Ashland	D	R	D	D	R	R	D	R	R	R	R	D
Barron	–	R	R	R	R	R	R	R	R	R	R	R
Bayfield	D	R	R	D	R	R	R	R	R	R	R	P

County	1868	1872	1876	1880	1884	1888	1892	1896	1900	1904	1908	1912
Brown	D	R	D	D	D	D	D	R	R	R	R	D
Buffalo	R	D	R	R	R	R	R	R	R	R	R	R
Burnett	R	R	R	R	R	R	R	R	R	R	R	P
Calumet	D	D	D	D	D	D	D	D	D	R	D	D
Chippewa	D	R	D	D	R	R	D	R	R	R	R	D
Clark	R	R	R	R	R	R	R	R	R	R	R	R
Columbia	R	R	R	R	R	R	R	R	R	R	R	D
Crawford	D	R	D	D	D	R	R	R	R	R	R	D
Dane	R	R	D	R	D	R	D	R	R	R	R	D
Dodge	D	D	D	D	D	D	D	R	D	D	D	D
Door	R	R	R	R	R	R	R	R	R	R	R	R
Douglas	T	D	D	D	R	R	R	R	R	R	R	P
Dunn	R	R	R	R	R	R	R	R	R	R	R	R
Eau Claire	R	R	R	R	R	R	R	R	R	R	R	R
Florence	–	–	–	–	R	R	R	R	R	R	R	R
Fond Du Lac	R	D	D	D	D	D	D	R	R	R	R	D
Forest	–	–	–	–	–	R	D	R	R	R	R	D
Grant	R	R	R	R	R	R	R	R	R	R	R	D
Green	R	R	R	R	R	R	R	R	R	R	R	D
Green Lake	R	R	R	R	R	R	D	R	R	R	R	D
Iowa	R	R	R	R	R	R	D	R	R	R	R	D
Iron	–	–	–	–	–	–	–	R	R	R	R	R
Jackson	R	R	R	R	R	R	R	R	R	R	R	R
Jefferson	D	D	D	D	D	D	D	R	D	D	D	D
Juneau	R	R	R	R	R	R	D	R	R	R	R	R
Kenosha	R	R	R	R	R	R	D	R	R	R	R	D
Kewaunee	D	D	D	D	D	D	D	R	R	R	D	D
La Crosse	R	R	R	R	R	R	D	R	R	R	R	P
Lafayette	R	R	R	R	R	R	R	R	R	R	R	D
Langlade	–	–	–	–	D	D	D	R	R	R	R	D
Lincoln	–	–	D	R	R	R	D	D	R	R	R	D
Manitowoc	D	D	D	D	D	D	D	R	R	R	R	D
Marathon	D	D	D	D	D	D	D	R	R	R	R	D
Marinette	–	–	–	R	R	R	R	R	R	R	R	R
Marquette	D	D	D	D	D	R	D	R	R	R	R	D
Menominee*	–	–	–	–	–	–	–	–	–	–	–	–
Milwaukee	D	D	D	R	R	R	D	R	R	R	R	D
Monroe	R	R	R	R	R	R	R	R	R	R	R	D
Oconto	R	R	R	R	R	R	D	R	R	R	R	R
Oneida	–	–	–	–	–	D	D	R	R	R	R	R
Outagamie	D	D	D	D	D	D	D	R	R	R	R	D
Ozaukee	D	D	D	D	D	D	D	D	D	D	D	D
Pepin	R	R	R	R	R	R	R	R	R	R	R	R
Pierce	R	R	R	R	R	R	R	R	R	R	R	P
Polk	R	R	R	R	R	R	R	R	R	R	R	P
Portage	R	R	R	R	R	R	D	R	R	R	R	D
Price	–	–	–	D	R	R	R	R	R	R	R	R
Racine	R	R	R	R	R	R	R	R	R	R	R	D
Richland	R	R	R	R	R	R	R	R	R	R	R	R

County	1868	1872	1876	1880	1884	1888	1892	1896	1900	1904	1908	1912
Rock	R	R	R	R	R	R	R	R	R	R	R	R
Rusk	–	–	–	–	–	–	–	–	–	R	R	R
St. Croix	R	R	R	R	R	R	R	R	R	R	R	D
Sauk	R	R	R	R	R	R	R	R	R	R	R	D
Sawyer	–	–	–	–	R	R	R	R	R	R	R	D
Shawano	R	D	D	D	D	R	D	R	R	R	R	D
Sheboygan	R	D	D	R	D	D	D	R	R	R	R	D
Taylor	–	–	D	R	R	R	D	R	R	R	R	D
Trempealeau	R	R	R	R	R	R	R	R	R	R	R	R
Vernon	R	R	R	R	R	R	R	R	R	R	R	R
Vilas	–	–	–	–	–	–	–	R	R	R	R	D
Walworth	R	R	R	R	R	R	R	R	R	R	R	D
Washburn	–	–	–	–	R	R	R	R	R	R	R	P
Washington	D	D	D	D	D	D	D	R	R	R	D	D
Waukesha	D	D	D	R	D	R	D	R	R	R	R	D
Waupaca	R	R	R	R	R	R	R	R	R	R	R	R
Waushara	R	R	R	R	R	R	R	R	R	R	R	R
Winnebago	R	R	R	R	R	R	D	R	R	R	R	D
Wood	D	R	D	R	D	D	D	R	R	R	R	D

County	1916	1920	1924	1928	1932	1936	1940	1944	1948	1952	1956	1960
Adams	R	R	P	R	D	D	D	R	D	R	R	R
Ashland	R	R	P	R	D	D	D	D	D	R	R	D
Barron	R	R	P	R	D	D	R	R	D	R	R	R
Bayfield	R	R	P	R	D	D	D	D	D	R	R	D
Brown	D	R	P	D	D	D	D	R	D	R	R	D
Buffalo	R	R	P	R	D	D	R	R	D	R	R	R
Burnett	R	R	P	R	D	D	D	R	D	R	R	R
Calumet	R	R	P	D	D	D	R	R	R	R	R	R
Chippewa	R	R	P	R	D	D	R	R	D	R	R	D
Clark	R	R	P	R	D	D	R	R	R	R	R	R
Columbia	R	R	P	R	D	D	R	R	R	R	R	R
Crawford	R	R	P	R	D	D	R	R	D	R	R	R
Dane	D	R	P	R	D	D	D	D	D	R	R	D
Dodge	R	R	P	R	D	D	R	R	R	R	R	R
Door	R	R	P	R	D	D	R	R	R	R	R	R
Douglas	R	R	P	R	D	D	D	D	D	D	D	D
Dunn	R	R	P	R	D	D	R	R	D	R	R	R
Eau Claire	R	R	P	R	D	D	D	R	D	R	R	R
Florence	R	R	R	R	D	D	R	D	D	R	R	R
Fond Du Lac	R	R	P	R	D	D	R	R	R	R	R	R
Forest	R	R	P	R	D	D	D	D	D	R	R	D
Grant	R	R	P	R	D	D	R	R	R	R	R	R
Green	R	R	P	R	D	D	R	R	R	R	R	R
Green Lake	R	R	P	R	D	D	R	R	R	R	R	R
Iowa	R	R	P	R	D	D	R	R	D	R	R	R
Iron	R	R	P	D	D	D	D	D	D	D	D	D
Jackson	R	R	P	R	D	D	D	R	D	R	R	R
Jefferson	R	R	P	R	D	D	R	R	R	R	R	R

County	1916	1920	1924	1928	1932	1936	1940	1944	1948	1952	1956	1960
Juneau	R	R	P	R	D	D	R	R	R	R	R	R
Kenosha	R	R	R	R	D	D	D	D	D	D	R	D
Kewaunee	D	R	P	D	D	D	R	R	R	R	R	D
La Crosse	D	R	P	R	D	D	R	R	D	R	R	R
Lafayette	D	R	P	R	D	D	R	R	D	R	R	R
Langlade	D	R	P	D	D	D	D	D	D	R	R	R
Lincoln	R	R	P	R	D	D	R	R	R	R	R	R
Manitowoc	D	R	P	D	D	D	D	R	D	R	R	D
Marathon	R	R	P	D	D	D	R	R	D	R	R	R
Marinette	R	R	R	R	D	D	D	R	D	R	R	R
Marquette	R	R	P	R	D	R	R	R	R	R	R	R
Menominee*	–	–	–	–	–	–	–	–	–	–	–	–
Milwaukee	D	R	P	D	D	D	D	D	D	R	R	D
Monroe	R	R	P	R	D	D	R	R	R	R	R	R
Oconto	R	R	P	R	D	D	R	R	R	R	R	R
Oneida	R	R	P	R	D	D	D	D	D	R	R	R
Outagamie	R	R	P	D	D	D	R	R	R	R	R	R
Ozaukee	R	R	P	D	D	D	R	R	R	R	R	R
Pepin	R	R	R	R	D	D	R	R	D	R	R	D
Pierce	R	R	P	R	D	D	R	R	D	R	R	R
Polk	R	R	P	R	D	D	R	R	D	R	R	R
Portage	D	R	P	D	D	D	D	D	D	R	R	D
Price	R	R	P	R	D	D	D	D	D	R	R	R
Racine	R	R	R	R	D	D	D	D	D	R	R	D
Richland	R	R	R	R	D	R	R	R	R	R	R	R
Rock	R	R	R	R	R	D	R	R	R	R	R	R
Rusk	R	R	P	R	D	D	D	D	D	R	R	D
St. Croix	R	R	P	R	D	D	R	R	D	R	R	R
Sauk	R	R	P	R	D	D	R	R	R	R	R	R
Sawyer	D	R	P	R	D	D	R	R	R	R	R	R
Shawano	R	R	P	R	D	D	R	R	R	R	R	R
Sheboygan	R	R	P	R	D	D	D	R	D	R	R	R
Taylor	R	R	P	R	D	D	D	D	D	R	R	D
Trempealeau	R	R	P	R	D	D	R	R	D	R	R	R
Vernon	R	R	P	R	D	D	R	R	D	R	R	R
Vilas	R	R	P	R	D	D	D	D	R	R	R	R
Walworth	R	R	R	R	D	R	R	R	R	R	R	R
Washburn	R	R	P	R	D	D	D	R	D	R	R	R
Washington	R	R	P	D	D	D	R	R	R	R	R	R
Waukesha	D	R	R	R	D	D	R	R	R	R	R	R
Waupaca	R	R	P	R	D	D	R	R	R	R	R	R
Waushara	R	R	P	R	D	R	R	R	R	R	R	R
Winnebago	R	R	P	R	D	D	R	R	R	R	R	R
Wood	R	R	P	R	D	D	R	R	R	R	R	R

County	1964	1968	1972	1976	1980	1984	1988	1992	1996	2000	2004
Adams	D	R	R	D	R	R	D	D	D	D	D
Ashland	D	D	D	D	D	D	D	D	D	D	D
Barron	D	R	R	D	R	R	D	D	D	R	R

County	1964	1968	1972	1976	1980	1984	1988	1992	1996	2000	2004
Bayfield	D	D	R	D	D	D	D	D	D	D	D
Brown	D	R	R	R	R	R	R	R	D	R	R
Buffalo	D	R	R	D	R	R	D	D	D	D	D
Burnett	D	R	R	D	D	R	D	D	D	R	R
Calumet	D	R	R	R	R	R	R	R	R	R	R
Chippewa	D	R	R	D	R	R	D	D	D	R	R
Clark	D	R	R	D	R	R	D	D	D	R	R
Columbia	D	R	R	R	R	R	R	D	D	D	R
Crawford	D	R	R	D	R	R	D	D	D	D	D
Dane	D	D	D	D	D	D	D	D	D	D	D
Dodge	D	R	R	R	R	R	R	R	R	R	R
Door	D	R	R	R	R	R	R	R	D	R	R
Douglas	D	D	D	D	D	D	D	D	D	D	D
Dunn	D	R	R	D	D	R	D	D	D	D	D
Eau Claire	D	D	R	D	D	R	D	D	D	D	D
Florence	D	R	R	D	R	R	R	D	R	R	R
Fond Du Lac	D	R	R	R	R	R	R	R	R	R	R
Forest	D	D	D	D	D	D	D	D	D	R	R
Grant	D	R	R	R	R	R	R	D	D	D	D
Green	D	R	R	R	R	R	R	D	D	D	D
Green Lake	D	R	R	R	R	R	R	R	R	R	R
Iowa	D	R	R	D	D	R	D	D	D	D	D
Iron	D	D	R	D	D	D	D	D	D	R	D
Jackson	D	R	R	D	R	R	D	D	D	D	D
Jefferson	D	R	R	R	R	R	R	R	D	R	R
Juneau	D	R	R	D	R	R	R	D	D	R	R
Kenosha	D	D	R	D	D	D	D	D	D	D	D
Kewaunee	D	R	R	D	R	R	D	D	D	R	R
La Crosse	D	R	R	R	R	R	D	D	D	D	D
Lafayette	D	R	R	R	R	R	R	D	D	D	D
Langlade	D	R	R	R	R	R	R	R	D	R	R
Lincoln	D	R	R	D	R	R	D	D	D	R	R
Manitowoc	D	D	R	D	R	R	D	D	D	R	R
Marathon	D	D	R	D	R	R	D	D	D	R	R
Marinette	D	R	R	R	R	R	R	R	D	R	R
Marquette	D	R	R	R	R	R	R	D	D	R	R
Menominee*	D	D	D	D	D	D	D	D	D	D	D
Milwaukee	D	D	D	D	D	D	D	D	D	D	D
Monroe	D	R	R	R	R	R	R	D	D	R	R
Oconto	D	R	R	D	R	R	R	D	D	R	R
Oneida	D	R	R	R	R	R	R	D	D	R	R
Outagamie	D	R	R	R	R	R	R	R	D	R	R
Ozaukee	D	R	R	R	R	R	R	R	R	R	R
Pepin	D	R	R	D	D	D	D	D	D	D	D
Pierce	D	R	R	D	D	R	D	D	D	D	D
Polk	D	R	R	D	D	R	D	D	D	R	R
Portage	D	D	D	D	D	D	D	D	D	D	D
Price	D	R	R	D	R	R	D	D	D	R	D
Racine	D	R	R	R	R	R	D	D	D	R	R

County	1964	1968	1972	1976	1980	1984	1988	1992	1996	2000	2004
Richland	D	R	R	R	R	R	R	D	D	R	R
Rock	D	R	R	R	R	R	D	D	D	D	D
Rusk	D	R	D	D	R	R	D	D	D	R	R
St. Croix	D	D	R	D	D	R	D	D	D	R	R
Sauk	D	R	R	R	R	R	R	D	D	D	D
Sawyer	D	R	R	D	R	R	R	D	D	R	R
Shawano	D	R	R	R	R	R	R	R	D	R	R
Sheboygan	D	D	R	D	R	R	R	R	D	R	R
Taylor	D	R	R	D	R	R	R	R	D	R	R
Trempealeau	D	R	R	D	R	R	D	D	D	D	D
Vernon	D	R	R	R	R	R	D	D	D	D	D
Vilas	D	R	R	R	R	R	R	R	R	R	R
Walworth	R	R	R	R	R	R	R	R	R	R	R
Washburn	D	R	R	D	R	R	D	D	D	R	R
Washington	D	R	R	R	R	R	R	R	R	R	R
Waukesha	D	R	R	R	R	R	R	R	R	R	R
Waupaca	R	R	R	R	R	R	R	R	R	R	R
Waushara	R	R	R	R	R	R	R	R	D	R	R
Winnebago	D	R	R	R	R	R	R	R	D	R	R
Wood	D	R	R	R	R	R	R	R	D	R	R

*Menominee became a county in 1964.

Wyoming

County	1892	1896	1900	1904	1908	1912	1916	1920	1924	1928	1932	1936
Albany	R	R	R	R	R	D	D	R	R	R	D	D
Big Horn	–	R	R	R	R	R	D	R	R	R	R	D
Campbell	–	–	–	–	–	D	D	R	R	R	D	D
Carbon	R	R	R	R	R	R	D	R	R	R	D	D
Converse	R	R	R	R	R	R	D	R	R	R	D	D
Crook	PO	D	R	R	R	D	D	R	R	R	D	R
Fremont	R	R	R	R	R	D	D	R	R	R	D	D
Goshen	–	–	–	–	–	D	D	R	R	R	D	D
Hot Springs	–	–	–	–	–	D	D	R	R	R	D	D
Johnson	PO	D	R	R	R	D	R	R	R	R	D	R
Laramie	R	R	R	R	R	D	D	R	R	R	D	D
Lincoln	–	–	–	–	–	R	D	R	R	R	D	D
Natrona	R	R	R	R	R	R	D	R	R	R	D	D
Niobrara	–	–	–	–	–	R	D	R	R	R	D	D
Park	–	–	–	–	–	D	D	R	R	R	D	D
Platte	–	–	–	–	–	D	D	R	R	R	D	D
Sheridan	PO	D	R	R	R	D	D	R	R	R	D	D
Sublette	–	–	–	–	–	–	–	–	R	R	D	D
Sweetwater	PO	D	R	R	R	D	D	R	P	D	D	D
Teton	–	–	–	–	–	–	–	–	R	R	D	D

County	1892	1896	1900	1904	1908	1912	1916	1920	1924	1928	1932	1936
Uinta	PO	D	R	R	R	R	D	R	R	R	D	D
Washakie	–	–	–	–	–	R	D	R	R	R	D	D
Weston	R	R	R	R	R	D	R	R	R	R	D	D

County	1940	1944	1948	1952	1956	1960	1964	1968	1972	1976	1980	1984
Albany	D	D	D	R	R	R	D	R	R	R	R	R
Big Horn	R	R	R	R	R	R	D	R	R	R	R	R
Campbell	R	R	R	R	R	R	R	R	R	R	R	R
Carbon	D	D	D	R	R	D	D	D	R	R	R	R
Converse	R	R	R	R	R	R	R	R	R	R	R	R
Crook	R	R	R	R	R	R	R	R	R	R	R	R
Fremont	R	R	R	R	R	R	D	R	R	R	R	R
Goshen	R	R	R	R	R	R	D	R	R	R	R	R
Hot Springs	D	D	D	R	R	R	D	R	R	R	R	R
Johnson	R	R	R	R	R	R	R	R	R	R	R	R
Laramie	D	D	D	R	R	R	R	R	R	R	R	R
Lincoln	D	D	D	R	R	R	D	R	R	R	R	R
Natrona	D	R	D	R	R	R	D	R	R	R	R	R
Niobrara	R	R	R	R	R	R	R	R	R	R	R	R
Park	D	R	R	R	R	R	D	R	R	R	R	R
Platte	D	R	D	R	R	R	D	R	R	R	R	R
Sheridan	D	D	D	R	R	R	D	R	R	R	R	R
Sublette	R	R	R	R	R	R	R	R	R	R	R	R
Sweetwater	D	D	D	D	D	D	D	D	R	D	R	R
Teton	D	R	R	R	R	R	R	R	R	R	R	R
Uinta	D	D	D	R	R	R	D	R	R	R	R	R
Washakie	R	R	R	R	R	R	R	R	R	R	R	R
Weston	R	R	R	R	R	R	R	R	R	R	R	R

County	1988	1992	1996	2000	2004	County	1988	1992	1996	2000	2004
Albany	R	D	D	R	R	Natrona	R	D	R	R	R
Big Horn	R	R	R	R	R	Niobrara	R	R	R	R	R
Campbell	R	R	R	R	R	Park	R	R	R	R	R
Carbon	R	D	R	R	R	Platte	R	R	R	R	R
Converse	R	R	R	R	R	Sheridan	R	R	R	R	R
Crook	R	R	R	R	R	Sublette	R	R	R	R	R
Fremont	R	R	R	R	R	Sweetwater	R	D	D	R	R
Goshen	R	R	R	R	R	Teton	R	D	D	R	D
Hot Springs	R	R	R	R	R	Uinta	R	R	R	R	R
Johnson	R	R	R	R	R	Washakie	R	R	R	R	R
Laramie	R	R	R	R	R	Weston	R	R	R	R	R
Lincoln	R	R	R	R	R						

Bibliographic Essay

There has never been a definitive national popular-vote count since the tabulation of election returns has always been handled on a county and state basis. So there has rarely been agreement when different sources were responsible for compiling the returns.

I have used a number of different sources in order to confirm outcomes. *Presidential Elections Since 1789*, published by Congressional Quarterly, Inc., in Washington, D.C., and presently available in its fifth edition, is a reliable guide. So is *America at the Polls: A Handbook of Presidential Election Statistics 1920–1964*, compiled and edited by Richard M. Scammon (University of Pittsburgh Press, 1965), and its companion volume, *America at the Polls 2: The Vote for President 1968–1984*, compiled and edited by Richard M. Scammon and Alice V. McGillivray (Congressional Quarterly, 1988).

From 1988 to 2000, see *America Votes 18: A Handbook of Contemporary American Election Statistics*, edited by Richard M. Scammon and Alice V. McGillivray (Congressional Quarterly, 1989); *America Votes 20* (Congressional Quarterly, 1993); *America Votes 22* (Congressional Quarterly, 1997); and *America Votes 24* (Congressional Quarterly, 2001). Volumes 22 and 24 were edited and compiled by Rhodes Cook.

George Gallup's *The Political Almanac 1952* (New York: B.C. Forbes & Sons Publishing), is an excellent source for the 1948 election.

Before Congressional Quarterly and the Elections Research Center began to produce their election volumes, the best source was *The World Almanac and Book of Facts* (New York: World Almanac Books), published annually. It is still the best source for the 1892, 1912, 1924, 1948 and 1980 elections.

I have also used the following: Svend Petersen's *A Statistical History of the American Presidential Elections with Supplemental Tables Covering 1968–1980* (Westport, Connecticut: Greenwood Press, 1981); Walter Dean Burnham, *Presidential Ballots 1836–1892* (Baltimore: Johns Hopkins University Press, 1955); and Edgar Eugene Robinson, *The Presidential Vote 1896–1932* (Palo Alto, California: Stanford University Press, 1935).

Many states publish detailed election data, which are especially helpful for precinct, township and borough returns. The *Pennsylvania Manual* and the Wisconsin *Blue Book* are outstanding for their depth of coverage and continuity. Other useful volumes include *Minnesota Votes 1857–1977*, compiled by Bruce M. White, et al. (St. Paul: Minnesota Historical Society, 1977), and *Presidential Elections in Maryland* by John T. Willis (Mount Airy, Maryland: Lomond Publications, 1984).

Numerous volumes have appeared in the category of presidential election history. One of the most admirable is the 5-volume *History of U.S. Political Parties*, edited by

Arthur M. Schlesinger, Jr. (Philadelphia: Chatham House Publishers, 2002). My essay, "The Reform Party, 1992–2001" appears in volume 5, pages 4405–4445. A good general history is Eugene H. Roseboom, *A History of Presidential Elections* (New York: Macmillan, 1979). The most recent is Evan Cornog and Richard Whelan, *Hats in the Ring* (New York: Random House, 2000).

Politics during the Roosevelt years is the focus of Edgar Eugene Robinson, *They Voted for Roosevelt* (Stanford, California: Stanford University Press, 1947). Also useful is Kirk H. Porter and Donald Bruce Johnson, eds., *National Party Platforms 1840–1968* (Urbana: University of Illinois Press, 1972).

Two recent histories of our major parties are Lewis L. Gould, *Grand Old Party: A History of the Republicans* (New York: Random House, 2003), and Jules Witcover, *Party of the People: A History of the Democrats* (New York: Random House, 2003).

A number of presidential elections have captivated the interest of historians, political scientists and journalists, who devoted full book-length studies to them. Here are some recommended titles.

1876: Roy Morris, Jr., *Fraud of the Century: Rutherford B. Hayes, Samuel Tilden and the Stolen Election of 1876* (New York: Simon & Schuster, 2003).

1880: Kenneth D. Ackerman, *Dark Horse: The Surprise Election and Political Murder of President James A. Garfield* (New York: Carroll & Graf, 2003); Herbert J. Clancy, *The Presidential Election of 1880* (Chicago, Illinois: Loyola University Press, 1958).

1884: Mark Wahlgren Summers, *Rum, Romanism and Rebellion: The Making of a President, 1884* (Chapel Hill: The University of North Carolina Press, 2002).

1892: George H. Knoles, *The Presidential Campaign and Election of 1892* (Stanford, California: Stanford University Press, 1942).

1896: Paul W. Glad, *McKinley, Bryan and the People* (Philadelphia: Lippincott, 1964); Stanley L. Jones, *The Presidential Election of 1896* (Madison: University of Wisconsin Press, 1964); Kevin Phillips, *William McKinley* (New York: Times Books, 2003), especially chapter 3, "McKinley and the Realignment of 1896."

1912: James Chace, *1912: Wilson, Roosevelt, Taft and Debs—The Election That Changed the Country* (New York: Simon & Schuster, 2004).

1920: Wesley M. Bagby, *The Road to Normalcy: The Presidential Campaign and Election of 1920* (Baltimore: Johns Hopkins University Press, 1962).

1928: David Burner, *The Politics of Provincialism: The Democratic Party in Transition 1918–1932* (New York: Alfred A. Knopf, 1968), which also covers the 1924 election; Allen J. Lichtman, *Prejudice and the Old Politics: The Presidential Election of 1928* (Chapel Hill: The University of North Carolina Press, 1979); Edmund A. Moore, *A Catholic Runs for President: The Campaign of 1928* (New York: Ronald Press, 1956); Roy Victor Peel and Thomas C. Donnelly, *The 1928 Campaign: An Analysis* (New York: R. R. Smith, 1931).

1932: Samuel Gammon, *The Presidential Campaign of 1932* (Westport, Connecticut: Greenwood Press, 1971) and Steve Neal, *Happy Days Are Here Again* (New York: Morrow, 2004).

1940: Herbert S. Parmet and Marie B. Hecht, *Never Again: A President Runs for a Third Term* (New York: Macmillan, 1968).

1948: Jules Abels, *Out of the Jaws of Victory* (New York: Henry Holt and Company, 1959); Gary A. Donaldson, *Truman Defeats Dewey* (Lexington, Kentucky: University Press of Kentucky, 1999); Harold I. Gullan, *The Upset That Wasn't* (Chicago: Ivan R. Dee, 1998); Zachary Karabell, *The Last Campaign: How Harry Truman Won the 1948 Election* (New York: Alfred A. Knopf, 2000); Irwin Ross, *The Loneliest Campaign: The Truman Victory of 1948* (New York: New American Library, 1968).

1952: Louis Harris, *Is There a Republican Majority?* (New York: Harper, 1954).

1956: Charles A. H. Thomson and Francis M. Shattuck, *The 1956 Presidential Campaign* (Washington, D.C.: The Brookings Institution, 1960).

1960: Patricia Barrett, *Religious Liberty and the American Presidency* (New York: Herder and Herder, 1963); James A. Michener, *Report of the County Chairman* (New York: Random House, 1961) — both Barrett and Michener concentrate on the religious issue in the 1960 campaign; Paul T. David, ed., *The Presidential Election and Transition 1960–1961* (Washington: D.C.: The Brookings Institution, 1961); Lucy S. Dawidowicz and Leon J. Goldstein, *Politics in a Pluralist Democracy: Studies of Voting in the 1960 Election* (New York: Institute of Human Relations Press, 1963); Theodore H. White, *The Making of the President, 1960* (New York: Atheneum, 1961) — this was the first of a superb series of political reportage and in many respects is still the best.

1964: Bernard Cosman, *Five States for Goldwater* (Tuscaloosa: University of Alabama Press, 1966); Milton C. Cummings, Jr., ed., *The National Election of 1964* (Washington, D.C.: The Brookings Institution, 1966); George F. Gilder and Bruce K. Chapman, *The Party That Lost Its Head* (New York: Alfred A. Knopf, 1966); John H. Kessel, *The Goldwater Coalition* (Indianapolis, Indiana: Bobbs-Merrill, 1968); Robert D. Novak, *The Agony of the GOP, 1964* (New York: Macmillan, 1965); Richard H. Rovere, *The Goldwater Caper* (New York: Harcourt, Brace & World, 1965).

1968: Lewis L. Gould, *1968: The Election That Changed America* (Chicago: Ivan Dee, 1993); Kevin P. Phillips, *The Emerging Republican Majority* (New Rochelle, New York: Arlington House, 1969); The Ripon Society, *The Lessons of Victory* (New York: The Dial Press, 1969); Richard Scammon and Ben Wattenberg, *The Real Majority* (New York: Coward-McCann, 1970).

1972: Everett Carl Ladd, Jr., and Seymour Martin Lipset, *Academics, Politics and the 1972 Election* (Washington, D.C.: American Enterprise Institute, 1973); Samuel Lubell, *The Future While It Happened* (New York: W. W. Norton, 1973).

1976: Gerald Pomper et al., *The Election of 1976* (New York: David McKay, 1977).

1980: Paul R. Abraham, John H. Aldrich and David W. Rohde, *Change and Continuity in the 1980 Elections* (Washington, D.C.: Congressional Quarterly Press, 1982); Paul T. David and David H. Everson, eds., *The Presidential Election and Transition 1980–1981* (Carbondale: Southern Illinois University Press, 1983); Austin Ranney, ed., *The American Elections of 1980* (Washington, D.C.: The American Enterprise Institute, 1981); Ellis Sandoz and Cecil V. Craft, Jr., eds., *A Tide of Discontent: The 1980 Elections and Their Meaning* (Washington, D.C.: Congressional Quarterly Press, 1981).

1984: Michael Nelson, ed., *The Election of 1984* (Washington, D.C.: Congressional Quarterly Press, 1985); Marlene M. Pomper, ed., *The Election of 1984* (Chatham, New Jersey: Chatham House Publishers, 1985); Robert P. Steed, et al., *The 1984 Presidential Election in the South* (New York: Praeger, 1986).

1988: James L. Guth and John C. Green, eds., *The Bible and the Ballot Box: Religion and Politics in the 1988 Election* (Boulder, Colorado: Westview Press, 1991).

1992: James Ceaser and Andrew Bush, *Upside Down and Inside Out: The 1992 Elections and American Politics* (Lanham, Maryland: Littlefield Adams, 1993); Stanley B. Greenberg, *Middle Class Dreams* (New York: Times Books, 1996); Albert J. Menendez, *The Perot Voters and the Future of American Politics* (Amherst, New York: Prometheus Books, 1996).

1996: Laurence W. Moreland and Robert P. Steed, eds., *The 1996 Presidential Elec-*

tion in the South (New York: Praeger, 1997); Gerald M. Pomper, et al., *The Election of 1996* (Chatham, New Jersey: Chatham House Publishers, 1997).

2000: Gerald M. Pomper et al., *The Election of 2000* (New York: Chatham House Publishers, 2001); Mark Silk, ed., *Religion and American Politics: The 2000 Election in Context* (Hartford, Connecticut: Center for the Study of Religion in Public Life, 2003).

The following books provide important background to presidential election history: James Paul Allen, *We the People: An Atlas of America's Ethnic Diversity* (New York: Macmillan, 1988); Louis H. Bean, *Ballot Behavior: A Study of Presidential Elections* (Washington, D.C.: Public Affairs Press, 1940); Robert Bendiner, *White House Fever* (New York: Harcourt Brace, 1960); Paul F. Boller, Jr., *Presidential Campaigns* (New York: Oxford University Press, 1984); Walter Dean Burnham, *Critical Elections and the Mainsprings of American Politics* (New York: W. W. Norton, 1970); Roger Doyle, *Atlas of Contemporary America* (New York: Facts on File, 1994); Raymond D Gastil, *Cultural Regions of the United States* (Seattle: University of Washington Press, 1975); Merrill Jensen, *Regionalism in America* (Madison: University of Wisconsin Press, 1951); John B. Judis and Ruy Teixeira, *The Emerging Democratic Majority* (New York: Scribner, 2002); Everett Carl Ladd, Jr., and Charles D. Hadley, *Transformations of the American Party System* (New York: W. W. Norton, 1978); Alexander P. Lamis, ed., *Southern Politics in the 1990s* (Baton Rouge: Louisiana State University Press, 1999); Mark Levy and Michael Kramer, *The Ethnic Factor* (New York: Simon & Schuster, 1973); Seymour Martin Lipset, ed., *Party Coalitions in the 1980s* (San Francisco: Institute for Contemporary Studies, 1981); Samuel Lubell, *The Hidden Crisis in American Politics* (New York: W. W. Norton, 1970); Samuel Lubell, *The Future of American Pol-*

itics (Garden City, New York: Doubleday, 1956); Samuel Lubell, *Revolt of the Moderates* (New York: Harper & Brothers, 1956); Albert J. Menendez, *Religion at the Polls* (Philadelphia: Westminster Press, 1977); Albert J. Menendez, *Evangelicals at the Ballot Box* (Amherst, New York: Prometheus Books, 1996); Norman H. Nie et al., *The Changing American Voter* (Cambridge, Massachusetts: Harvard University Press, 1979); Eileen Shields-West, *The World Almanac of Presidential Campaigns* (New York: World Almanac, 1992); Irving Stone, *They Also Ran* (New York: Doubleday & Company, 1966); James L. Sundquist, *Dynamics of the Party System* (Washington, D.C.: The Brookings Institution, 1983); Ruy Teixeira, *The Disappearing American Voter* (Washington, D.C.: The Brookings Institution, 1992); G. Scott Thomas, *The Pursuit of the White House: A Handbook of Presidential Election Statistics and History* (Westport, Connecticut: Greenwood Press, 1987); Michael J. Weiss, *The Clustering of America* (New York: Harper & Row, 1988); Michael J. Weiss, *Latitudes and Attitudes* (Boston: Little, Brown and Company, 1994).

Several books probe the changing presidential politics in two regions of the nation — the South and the North — that are moving in opposite directions. Among the best are Earl and Merle Black, *The Vital South* (Cambridge, Massachusetts: Harvard University Press, 1992); Earl and Merle Black, *The Rise of Southern Republicans* (Cambridge, Massachusetts: The Belknap Press of Harvard University Press, 2002); an old reliable classic, V. O. Key, Jr.'s *Southern Politics* (New York: Alfred A. Knopf, 1949); Alexander P. Lamis, *The Two-Party South* (New York: Oxford University Press, 1984); Robert W. Speel, *Changing Patterns of Voting in the Northern United States: Electoral Realignment, 1952–1996* (University Park: The Pennsylvania State University Press, 1998).

Index